Frank Bertangue Green

The history of Rockland County

Frank Bertangue Green

The history of Rockland County

ISBN/EAN: 9783743330511

Manufactured in Europe, USA, Canada, Australia, Japa

Cover: Foto ©ninafisch / pixelio.de

Manufactured and distributed by brebook publishing software (www.brebook.com)

This facsimile edition
has been made available through the efforts
of the Rockland County (New York) Public Librarians Association

974. Green, Frank Bertangue
728   The history of Rockland County, by Frank
          Bertangue Green, M. D. New York, A. S. Barnes,
          1886.
          444p.

          1. Rockland County, New York - History

THE

HISTORY

OF

ROCKLAND COUNTY

BY

FRANK BERTANGUE GREEN, M. D.

A. S. BARNES & CO., NEW YORK.
1886.

Entered according to Act of Congress in the year 1886,
BY FRANK BERTANGUE GREEN, M. D.
In the Office of the Librarian of Congress, at Washington, D. C.

TABLE OF CONTENTS.

CHAPTER I.

The Indian tribes of Rockland County. Their dress, personal habits, weapons and utensils. Religious condition. De Vries Colony. Sketch of De Vries. Wars with the Indians. Destruction of Vriesendael. Treaties with the Indians. Disappearance of aborigines.

CHAPER II.

Van Werckhoven applies for a patent at Tappan. Claes Jansen's patent. Paulsen and Dowse Harmanse patents. De Harte patent. Orangetown patent. Welch and Marshall or Quaspeck patent. Honan and Hawden or Kakiat patent. Evan's patent. Wawayanda patent. Cheesecocks patent. Lancaster Symes patent. Stony Point patent. Ellison and Roome patent. Kempe, Lamb and Crom patent. Patents for lands in Ramapo. Lockhart patent.

CHAPTER III.

Early real estate speculation. Transfers of the De Harte patent. Survey of the boundaries between the De Harte and Cheesecocks patent. Sales from the Quaspeck patent. Settlement of division line between the Quaspeck and Kakiat patents. Division of the Kakiat patent. Sales from the Kakiat patent. Settlement of division line between the Kakiat and Cheesecocks patent. Sales of land from the Cheesecocks patent. Sales of land from the Stony Point patents. Transfers of land in Ramapo. The settlement of the Orangetown patent. The different systems of patronymics used by the Dutch and the origin of Dutch family names.

CHAPTER IV.

Organization of Orange County including the present Rockland. Physical condition of the County at the time of erection. Fraudulent election returns from it. First officers. Establishment of a court. Early census returns. Organization of the first church society. Early supervisors' records. Building of the first church edifices at Tappan, Clarkstown and Kakiat. Punishments inflicted on malefactors. Establishment of church societies north of the mountains. Opening of highways. Erection of County buildings north of the mountains. The establishment of inns. The beginning of the controversy with Great Britain.

CHAPTER V.

THE CIVIL HISTORY OF THE REVOLUTION.

A brief review of the ideas which led the colonists to revolt. A General Congress called for. It convenes. Election of Delegates from this State. Organization of the Sons of Liberty in New York. Organization of the Committee of Correspondence and Safety in Orange County. Its duties during the Revolution. Election of Delegates to a Provincial Congress. Organization of the State Government and Adoption of the Constitution. Synopsis of the first Constitution. First Election of State Officers. Recapitulation of the Revolution in Civil Government. Civil List of our County till the formation of a Federation.

iv.

CHAPTER VI.

THE WAR OF THE REVOLUTION.

The Militia Force of our County at the outbreak of the War. Organization of Troops. Insubordination among them. Building Fort Clinton. The Water Front Visited by a Hostile Fleet. Retreat of the Continental Army through the County. The Forays of the Enemy in our County, and the patriotic struggles to defend it. Washington encamps at Ramapo. From thence marches toward Philadelphia. The Battle of Fort Clinton. The construction of the West Point Chain. Massacre at Old Tappan. Capture of Stony Point by the British. Its re-capture by General Wayne. The Continental Army Encamps at Tappan. The treason of Arnold. Trial and Execution of Andre. March of the Continental Army through the County to beseige Yorktown.

CHAPTER VII.

THE WAR OF THE REVOLUTION.

Events at Tappan and Sneden's Landing. Conflicts between the British and Shore Guard at Piermont and Haverstraw. Naval fight in Tappan Zee. Conflicts at Nyack. The depredations committed by Cow-boys in the County. Forays at Slaughter's Landing. Joshua Hett Smith. Invasions of the Southern part of our County by the Enemy. Acts of individual bravery and suffering. Account of Claudius Smith. Confiscation of property at the close of the War. Roll of the names of men who served in the armies of the Revolution.

CHAPTER VIII.

Dreadful financial condition of the County at the close of the Revolution. Energy of the people to re-establish business. The first houses of the settlers. Later architecture. Domestic life among the Dutch: Their occupation and manner of work. The modes of travel in early days. The style of dress. Amusements. Causes of veneration for the clergy. Church attendance. Funerals. Forms of old wills.

CHAPTER IX.

The causes which led to the creation of a Federation. Their slight influence on this section. The feeling among the people regarding it and the reason for that feeling. The vote of the delegates at the Convention. Reasons why Rockland County was erected. Its boundaries. Its townships. Its first officers.

CHAPTER X.

EARLY INDUSTRIES OF ROCKLAND COUNTY.

The Hassenclever Iron Mine and Rockland Nickel Company Mine. Conglomerate sandstone and freestone quarries. Dater's Works. Works at Sloatsburgh. Ramapo Works. Brick Manufacture. Knickerbocker Ice Company.

CHAPTER XI.

The early militia of Rockland County. War of 1812. The militia of the County called upon for service. The companies of Captains Blauvelt and Snedeker leave for Harlem. The Light Horse ordered to report for duty. Organization of a batallion of artillery. Desertions. Organization of the National Guard. Muster roll of the militia of 1812.

v.

CHAPTER XII.

Proposition for a turnpike from Nyack to Suffern: Bitter opposition. The bill as passed. Renewals of the charter. An act incorporating the New Antrim and Waynesburgh Company, passed. The beginning of steamboat communication with New York. Later steamboats. Charters for ferry-boats. Chronological list of steamboats. Opening of the Erie and other railroads.

CHAPTER XIII.

History of the Reformed Church at Tappan, at Clarkstown. Of the "Brick" or Reformed Church at West New Hempstead. Of the Reformed Church at Nyack, at Piermont, at Spring Valley. History of the "English" or Presbyterian Church at Hempstead. Of the Presbyterian Church at Haverstraw, at Ramapo, at Greenbush, at Nyack, at Waldberg, at Stony Point, at Palisades, and of the Central and Mountville Presbyterian Churches. History of the Baptist Church at Nanuet, at Haverstraw, at Viola, at Piermont, at Nyack, at Spring Valley.

CHAPTER XIV.

History of the Methodist Episcopal Church in Rockland County. History of the Methodist Protestant Church at Haverstraw and Tomkins Cove. History of the Roman Catholic Church in Rockland County. History of the Protestant Episcopal Church in Rockland County. History of the Universalist Church at Nyack and Orangeville; of the Quaker Church at Ladentown; of the True Reformed Church at Monsey, at Nanuet and at Tappan. History of the Congregational Church at Monsey and Tallmans. Of the M. E. Zion at Nyack and at Haverstraw. History of the Union "Stone Church," or Upper Nyack, Wayside Chapel, Lake Avenue Baptist, West Nyack Chapel and Steven's Sunday Schools. History of the Rockland County Sabbath School Association.

CHAPTER XV.

Slavery in Rockland County. The "Underground Railroad." The County Buildings. The Rockland County Bible Society. The Rockland County Medical Society. Agricultural Society. Rockland County Teachers' Association. The Rockland County Historical Society. Civil List of the County.

CHAPTER XVI.

PERIOD OF CIVIL WAR

The political feeling in Rockland County and Election of 1860. Effect of the shot on Sumter. Split of the Democratic Party into Peace and War factions. Early volunteering and organization of companies. Movement among the Union Men to render aid to volunteers and their families. The early conception and growth of the Rockland County branches of the U. S. Sanitary Commission. Outburst of anger among the disloyal at the order for a draft. Organization of secret societies among the loyal. History of the drafts. Election of 1864. Joy over the news of the end of the conflict. The Census of Rockland County's contributions to the War.

CHAPTER XVII.

ORANGETOWN.

Erection of the Town: Area: Origin of Name: Census: First Town Meeting. Histories of Tappan, Greenbush, Middletown, Nyack, Piermont, Palisades, Orangeville, Orangeburgh, Pearl River. Railroad from Sparkill to Nyack. Highland and Midland Avenues. Town Officers.

vi.

CHAPTER XVIII.

HAVERSTRAW.

Origin of Name: Erection into a Township: Area: Census. Histories of Haverstraw Village, Thiell's Corners, Gurnee's Corners or Mount Ivy, Garnerville, Samsondale, Johnsontown, West Haverstraw, Monroe and Haverstraw Turnpike, Haverstraw Community, Town Officers.

CHAPTER XIX.

RAMAPO.

Date of Erection: Area; Origin of Name: First Town Meeting: Census. Histories of Sufferns, Sloatsburgh, Dater's or Pleasant Valley, Sterlington, Ramapo, Hilburn, Kakiat or New Hempstead, Sherwoodville, Ladentown, Mechanicsville or Viola, Cassady's Corners, Spring Valley, Monsey, Tallman's, Scotland, Pomona. History of the Old Taverns. New Jersey and New York Railroad Stations. The Orange Turnpike. Stages. Town Officers.

CHAPTER XX.

CLARKSTOWN.

Origin of Name: Erection of the Town: Area: First Town Meeting: Census. History of Clarkesville, New City, Rockland Lake, Nanuet, Dutch Factory, Mackie's and Stagg's Corners, Waldberg, Snedeker's or Waldberg Landing, Strawtown, Bardon's Station. Peat Beds. Silver Spoon Factory. The Brewery. Town Officers.

CHAPTER XXI.

STONY POINT.

Erection of the Town: Origin of Name: Area: First Town Meeting: Census. History of Grassy Point, Stony Point, Tomkin's Cove, Caldwell's Landing, Doodletown, Iona Island, Stony Point Promontory, Bear Hill, Pingyp' Hill. The House of the Good Shepherd. Historical Trees. Town Officers.

ERRATUM.

Chapter III, page 36, line 6. For "Abraham Lydecker—step-son of Elizabeth, &c.," read: step-son of *Sarah*.

HISTORY OF ROCKLAND COUNTY

CHAPTER I.

INDIAN HISTORY.

THE INDIAN TRIBES OF ROCKLAND COUNTY—THEIR DRESS, PERSONAL HABITS, WEAPONS AND UTENSILS—RELIGION—DE VRIES' COLONY—SKETCH OF DE VRIES—WARS WITH THE INDIANS—DESTRUCTION OF VRIESENDALE—TREATIES WITH THE INDIANS—DISAPPEARANCE OF THE ABORIGINES.

Hudson, sailing in search of a northwest passage that would bring to his patrons the wealth of the Indies by a shorter route than that about the capes, anchored inside of Sandy Hook on September 3, 1609. He had discovered not the strait he sought, but a New Amsterdam, that, under a different name, was to excel the old Amsterdam in metropolitan grandeur.

He found his discovery to be a land " as pleasant with grass and flowers, and goodly trees as ever he had seen," and peopled by a race whose birthright those that followed Hudson were soon to obtain by crushing that race from existence.

The " olive colored, well-built, naked savages," who inhabited this County, belonged to the Algonquin family, and were divided into the Tappan, Rewechnougs, Rechgawawancks, Rumachenanks, or Haverstraw, and doubtless, where tribal affiliation was so close, the Hackinsack tribes. Throughout this section game was abundant, and from it, and the fish that could be obtained in the many rivers and lakes that water the County, the Indian not only obtained food, the deer skin or woven turkey-feather mantle, " a fathom square," that fell from his shoulders, and his moccasins, but also from the bears, wolves, deer, foxes, beavers and otters, acquired the skins so much valued by the Dutch, and with which he started a thriving trade.

His life was simple. Like all people who depend for food upon the results of fishing and the chase, he was improvident to the last degree. Taciturn and brave, he spoke little of his deeds of prowess, and considered those, who were loquacious, as idle boasters. Unforgiving and vindictive, he waited for the object of his anger with quiet pertinacity, concealing his passion with great subtlety till the hour for its consummation, and then wreaking his vengeance unforgivingly. If he met his enemy on an equal footing he would fight fairly, but regarded it as no shame to fall upon him from ambush and slay him without warning, for treachery was a marked attribute of his nature. If the result of the attack was in favor of his enemy, he met the expected death without emotion, and tortures, so horrible as to exceed our conception, were borne by him with stolid composure and without the utterance of a groan.

In his personal habits he was exceedingly vain and very uncleanly. Water, as a means of ablution, was not necessary to his existence, and to the ever accumulating coat of dirt and grease with which his body was covered, he added another coating of paint, applied with some rude attempt at artistic effect, which, from the yellow pigment used when the Dutch first arrived, was changed to red when the material for that color could be obtained from the whites. In his domestic life the Indian was a monogamist, unless he held the position of chief, when polygamy was common; but he was deficient in the emotion of affection, and for the slightest cause or whim left one wife and took another. Unchastity, on the part of either man or woman, was not regarded as a sin, and but little notice was taken of it. No form of marriage service is recorded as existing. The duty of an Indian woman was to plant and tend to the cultivation of the maize, the only cereal these savages seem to have grown, and to perform such other manual labor as the simplicity of the life required. The chief of a tribe possessed but slight authority. At the feasts, dances and other ceremonies that were performed he presided, and in the inter-tribal treaties and those made with the Dutch he acted as spokesman for his tribe, but at the council fire, when questions of peace and war were discussed, his influence was no greater than that of any warrior present. Elevated to his position by the voice of his brethren, his tenure depended on their pleasure, and at their wish he surrendered his power.

The weapons of the hunt and war, possessed by these savages on the arrival of the whites, consisted of axes and arrows and spear heads made of flint or the bones of fishes or birds, and to a passing glance rudely fashioned ; if the observer will stop to think however of the means at the command of the artisan, he will find cause for wonder at the perfection reached. Other relics of their existence in this section are awls, with which they punctured the skins that they intended to sew together ; tables, on which and pestles with which they ground their corn, and bowls or basins for holding liquid. Of religious rites and ceremonies there is no mention.

It is claimed by some writers that these savages recognized a Supreme power in a vague manner, but of this I find no proof, and equally indefinite is all evidence of their belief in immortality. Their dead were buried in a sitting posture, facing the east ; but nothing yet found, warrants the belief that the red man of this section, regarded that interment like his Western and Southern brother, as but a period of waiting before a resurrection.

Such were the characteristics of the Indians when the settlement of Manhattan was begun. Upon the Dutch colonists—Swannekins, as he called them—the aborigine at first looked with the respect of awe. He saw these pale faces labor with tools made of shining metal, and huge forest trees fell at their blows. He saw those forest trees used in the construction of houses for shelter and a fort for refuge. He watched in bewilderment as these new people ploughed up the earth, and in a brief period saw more soil broken and prepared for sowing than he had beheld in his lifetime. With fear and amaze he observed, that when this strange race wanted food, they obtained it, by pointing toward the chase a long tube from which issued the lightning and thunder in a cloud of smoke, and the hunted animal fell dead at the sound. Truly, beings who thus used the elements for their purposes must be more than human, and the ignorant native gave to the new comers all the reverence that superstition commands from her votaries.

Twenty years passed, after the Dutch had landed in this colony, before a white man attempted to settle in our County. Then, in 1640, Captain De Vries, sailing up the Hudson in search of a location for a colony, "arrived about even at Tappaen." Here he found, in the meadows south of the present Piermont, "an extensive valley containing upwards of 200 or 300 morgens of clay land, which is three or four feet above the water mark. A creek coming from the highlands runs through it containing good mill seats." This land De Vries purchased from the Indians, gave it the name of Vriesendale, and began the formation of an establishment for trade with the savages.

David Pietersen De Vries " was a bronzed, weather-beaten sailor of the old school, without family ties, who had seen the world from many points of observation, and had been on terms of intimacy with the most cultivated men and the rudest barbarians. He was tall, muscular and hard visaged, but soft voiced as a woman, except when aroused by passion. He was quick of perception, with great power of will, and rarely ever erred in judgment." When, in 1629, the Dutch West India Companies' College of Nineteen, issued the charter by which it was intended to revive on this western continent the medieval condition of feudality, that even then was receiving its death blow in the old world; De Vries associated himself with Godyn, de Laet, Blommaert and Van Rensselaer, and acquired the proprietorship of a large tract of land upon the Horekill in the present State of Delaware. Early in 1631 he sent out thirty emigrants, who founded the colony of Swaanendael—the Valley of Swans. This settlement had but a brief existence, for, owing to a misunderstanding with an Indian, the savages fell upon and utterly destroyed it.

In 1639, De Vries bought property on Staten Island, and accompanying a party of immigrants, founded a new settlement nearer New Amsterdam. A year later, as we have seen, he began the formation of the establishment at Vriesendael. In his dealings with the savages, De Vries was ever honest and kind, and the natives grew to look upon him with veneration and to refer to him as arbiter in their controversies with the white race. More than once, the Dutch were warned of an intended Indian outbreak through his influence, and for a brief space in the horror of an Indian war, his property was spared, because he was pointed out as the good "Swannekin Chief" by a savage, whose life he had saved on the night of the massacre at Pavonia; but even his repute could not long save Vriesendael, and, at the close of the Indian war of 1643, he sailed for Europe ruined and disgusted, bidding the author of his troubles, Kieft, farewell with the bitter words: "Vengeance for innocent blood will sooner or later fall on your head."

The two decades from 1620 to 1640 were pregnant with momentous events for the New Netherlands. Those amicable relations, that existed between the Indians and Dutch on their arrival, had been strained to their utmost tension by causes almost entirely due to the lax rule of the Governors. The privilege of free trade in the colony, granted by the West India Company in 1638, had been eagerly grasped and used with avidity. Every individual might, and most of them did, deal with the aborigines on his own account; and to win his way into their good graces more deeply than his neighbor, each trader resorted to methods, which, however customary among civilized people, produced the most direful results in the case of these barbarians. The dusky warrior was invited into his house, was bidden to the table, was given the best of his viands and liquors and was greeted on terms of equality. These concessions, which were granted in all the settlements of the colony, were exceeded by the traders of Fort Orange. Soon they learned, that the Indians' desire for guns and ammunition was greater than for any other object; and unprincipled at the best, with little care for the future, and no wish, save that of accumulating wealth in a short time, these traders in the north bartered freely and for excellent prices with these weapons.

While these conditions were accruing throughout the province, other events took place which hastened the inevitable result. Long immunity from attack had rendered the colonists overbold, and they bought land, built homes, and began the cultivation of the soil further and further from the protecting guns of the fort on Manhattan Island. Their cattle, unguarded by a herdsman, too often entered the Indians' maize fields, which were unfenced, and utterly destroyed them. And, as if to tempt fate to its utmost, they employed the red men as domestics, associated with them in close relationship and betrayed to them, in the familiarity of social intercourse, their weakness and their fears.

The result was what might have been anticipated. Attentions, shown to the savage in the interests of trade, he grew to expect and was provoked when they were not forthcoming. The trespass upon and damage to his corn fields by the white man's cattle angered him, and he revenged himself by killing the domestic animals, whenever he had an opportunity, with an indiscrimination that belonged to his nature. As servants, the Indians were not only useless because of their resistance to all restraint, but also because their cupidity being aroused by the sight of objects they valued, they unhesitatingly stole them and fled away to their native wilds. To these petty causes of irritation between the two races, were added others of graver import. The Mohawks, now well armed and supplied with ammunition, not only ceased to be tributary vassals to the tribes living along the lower reaches of the river, but, by reason of their superior armament, compelled those tribes to contribute to them ; and, when these lower river Indians sought to obtain equal weapons of defence against their now powerful neighbors, and were refused by the settlers, who were controlled by a law of New Amsterdam, which made the trading of guns within its jurisdiction a capital offence ; they regarded the refusal as born of cowardice. A relationship so filled with mutual distrust and dislike could not long exist without open rupture, and this rupture was precipitated by an attempt on the part of the Director of the colony—William Kieft—to impose a tribute of maize, wampum and furs upon the tribes residing near New Amsterdam.

The first outbreak of open war occurred with the wily Raritans, who had been exasperated by an expedition of the Dutch sent against them in 1640. Early in the spring of 1641, these savages fell upon De Vries' Staten Island settlement and destroyed it. Later in the season a Westchester Indian murdered a settler, and though, under the terror of punishment his tribe promised to yield him to justice, it was not done. Shortly after a Hackinsack murdered an innocent man who was thatching a house, and his tribe, while offering to indemnify the Director with wampum, steadfastly refused to surrender the murderer.

While matters were in this condition, the Mohawks suddenly fell upon the lower river tribes, slew many of them, took more captive, and drove the remainder to seek protection from the Dutch. For a fortnight these fugitives were cared for by the colonists; then, regaining courage, they returned to their desolated villages. But the relief was only temporary and in a short time, being seized with a fresh panic, whole tribes deserted their homes and fled to Pavonia, to New Amsterdam, to Vriesendael. In this exodus were the Haverstraw, Tappan, and Hackinsack, together with the tribes of Westchester.

About Vriesendael the refugees collected in such numbers, that De Vries became alarmed for the safety of his goods, and, entering a canoe, he paddled down to New Amsterdam to ask that a guard might be sent to his settlement from the fort. His arrival was opportune. Then for the first time he learned that the Director had determined to attack the trusting red men, who had sought the protection and hospitality of the Dutch. In vain De Vries pleaded for a calmer consideration of the idea; in vain he pointed out the frightful horrors of an Indian war; in vain, as President of the Directors' Council, he insisted that the great majority of both council and people were opposed to the proposed attack. Kieft answered that he had determined "to make these savages wipe their chops," and that he would not be deterred from his purpose. On the night of February 27, 1643, the soldiers fell upon the unsuspecting Indians camped at Pavonia and Corlaer's Hook, and at the former place eighty, and at the latter forty of the savages were killed before the murder ended. "And this was the feat worthy of the heroes of old Rome!" cried De Vries in the awful bitterness of his contempt, "to massacre a parcel of Indians in their sleep, to take the children from the breasts of their mothers, and to butcher them in the presence of their parents, and throw their mangled limbs into the fire or water! Some were thrown into the river, and when the parents rushed in to save them, the soldiers prevented their landing and let the parents and children drown." In the morning, the valiant warriors came back to the fort wearied by their labor of murder, and were hailed as heroes by Kieft in his rapture. In the morning, after the enemy had left, the terrified Indians who had escaped, stole cautiously forth from their place of hiding; viewed the charred, distorted, mangled córpses of their tribes; and swore revenge.

The wind had been sown, it remained for the colonists to reap and the fruit of the harvest was a whirlwind. For a few days the stupefied savages believed they had been attacked by their old enemy, the Mohawks, then a knowledge of their foe came to them and the duplicity of the "Swannekins" was made plain.

The effect was immediate. Eleven heretofore peaceful tribes rose to a man, fell upon the frightened colonists, and showed to them the mercy they had meted out. For a brief space, two months later, the slaughter was stayed through the exertions of De Vries. The tribes near Vriesendael, the Tappaens, the Haverstraws and the Hackinsacks, through Oratamin the chief of the latter tribe, agreed to a treaty of peace with Director Kieft on April 22, 1643, and exchanged the customary presents of such occasions. But this treaty was only a hollow truce that gave the Indians time and opportunity to attend to their harvest. In August the Wappingers seized several traders' boats and killed the crews, and by September the war again raged with violence. On all sides arose the smoke of burning buildings. With a dreadful vengeance crops and stocks were destroyed, and the few worn and haggard fugitives that reached the fort, brought tidings of an indiscriminate but very thorough massacre.

Within that fort were confusion, terror and insubordination. Kieft, now that the result of his blunder was seen, cowered beneath the invective heaped upon him and fain would place the blame upon his Council. The Council gave him the lie; he blamed the settlers, and they, through their dominie, Bogartus, who had opposed the attack, answered by sardonic taunts; he accused the men who had advised him, and the servants of one of them attempted his assassination.

While chaos reigned within the last refuge of the Dutch, the foe having made a clean sweep of the surrounding country, now stood without the fort and menaced any one of the garrison who dared to appear. Truly the words of Kieft had been fulfilled, the savages "wiped their chops," but not till they had been filled to repletion on the product of the settlers' labors.

At length those within the fort ceased their internecine strife and combined in thought and action for their salvation. Successful expeditions against some Long Island and Connecticut tribes broke the spirit of all but the river Indians. The arrival of the vessel, Blue Cock, from Curacoa with one and thirty soldiers, still further encouraged the settlers; and the building of a wall across Manhattan Island at the present Wall Street, permitted the safe cultivation of a little soil. The following year, 1645, saw a more universal desire for peace among the Indians; one after another the tribes concluded treaties with the whites, and finally on August 30, 1645, the pipe of peace was smoked and quiet reigned. Sixteen hundred savages had been killed and the power of the Algonquin race forever broken; but there was not a settlement in all New Netherlands, except Rensselaerswyck and the military post on the Delaware River, that had not been attacked and generally destroyed. Vriesendael, as we have seen, had been saved from spoliation once through the efforts of a friendly Indian, but the passions of anger had been too excited to permit of long continued mercy, and before the close of the war, the establishment of the first settler in this County had perished from the face of the earth.

Among the chiefs from those savage tribes that were represented at Fort Amsterdam on that August day, and who, in the presence of the whole community and the Mohawk ambassadors, entered into an agreement of peace, were: Oratamin, sachem of the Hackinsacks; Willem and Sesekemu, chiefs of the Tappaens and Haverstraws; Maganwetinnemin, who answered for the tribe of Marechkawiecks. of Brooklyn, Nyacks, of Long Island, and their neighbors; and a Mohegan chief, Aepjen, for the Wappings and the Wiquaeskecks, Sintsings and Kichtawanghs, of Westchester. The treaty contained clauses, pledging both Dutch and Indians not to enter upon a war for real or fancied wrongs, without first mutually consulting the Governor of the colony and the Sachems of the tribes; and if any one of either race should be murdered, the slayer should be promptly delivered to justice; the Indians were not to come among the Dutch on Manhattan bearing arms, nor were the whites to go to them with guns, unless having previously warned them of their intention.

The destruction of Vriesendael ended all attempts to colonize this County for a period of six and forty years. Twice had De Vries seen his settlements swept away at their very outset and now—he was ruined. If he, who had always been friendly with the Indians, did not care to take further risk; it is certain that the miserable remnant of the colony would hesitate long before trusting again to the amity of the red men. That remnant remained close to the fort, and a section so wild and forbidding as our County, was left to the prowling of wild beasts or the stealthy tread of the scarcely less wild aborigine.

At different times during those three decades, the Sachems of the tribes inhabiting this territory appeared in New Amsterdam, and either rendered complaints of trespass by the white men upon their rights, or excused the trespass of their followers, confirmed the existing treaty, or acted as mediators for other tribes. Once more, in 1655, while Governor Stuyvesant was away on an expedition against the Swedes on the Delaware and New Amsterdam was left defenceless, the Indians became restive and desirous of war. In this movement the Tappaens joined, in spite of the wiser councils of their old men, and took part in the brief struggle of that year. Little harm, when compared with other settlements, was done in New Amsterdam; for one day the savages spread terror through the town, and were only expelled after several of them had been killed; but those outlying boweries, that the long period of quiet had led the more courageous colonists to start on Long and Staten Islands and the Jersey shore, were devastated and many of their occupants killed. The return of Stuyvesant, however, checked and awed the savages, and a peace was made, which ever after protected the inhabitants of New Amsterdam from Indian invasion.

In the wars with the Esopas tribes from 1660 to 1664, the chieftains of the tribes residing in this County and northern New Jersey, acted as negotiators between the beligerents, and succeeded in obtaining treaties time after time. Oratamin, Sachem of the Hackinsacks, always appears as the principal Indian figure in these numerous conferences, and was evidently regarded by his race as possessing more than ordinary ability. Indeed, if we judge from the trust that the Dutch imposed in him, he was a superior man. It was by his efforts, on more than one occasion, that war was prevented; and it was due to his influence, when the Esopas savages had dug up the hatchet, that the tribes of Westchester, Rockland and Bergen counties remained neutral; and, when at length the treaty of May 15, 1664, was made with the Esopas people, a resolution was drawn up and signed by Oratamin and Matteno, in which they pledged themselves as security for the keeping of the covenant, agreeing that they would lead their tribes against whichever party first violated its provisions.

One source of irritation between the white and red men, was the sale of brandy to the Indians. In spite of restricting laws forbidding such barter and the offer of generous rewards for the arrest of the offenders; in spite of reiterated permission and requests to the Sachems for the seizure of all dealing in this traffic; and in spite of the severe punishment —banishment from the colony with confiscation of property—meted out to those who were captured, the sale of liquor still continued. In exchange for it the savage gave whatever was demanded, and in a short time found himself stripped and hungry. To such alarming proportions did this nefarious trade grow, that whole tribes were impoverished by the crafty trader, who took their wampum, their guns and the skins they had brought to barter, and left them nothing save a remorseful awakening. Liquor at all times aroused the fiercest passions of these wild natures; but when the savage woke robbed as well as suffering, his vindictive disposition led him to brood over his injuries till a desire for revenge became dominant, and then, when again mad with drink, to glut his vengeance on the first white he met. In this manner occurred most of the outrages that terminated in the conflicts between the races.

After the experience of two wars, the Dutch were more careful about permitting the Indians to approach the settlements. Hence, when the chief of a Westchester tribe asked permission for his people to fish near Harlem, the request was granted on the condition that the savages should be unarmed ; and, for their protection from the Dutch, as well as the settlers' assurance that the fishing party were not Esopas Indians, the chief was given cards with a stamp of the Dutch seal upon them, which were to be shown to the whites whenever demanded. Four of these cards were for the use of the Haverstraw tribe.

At what period the sale of guns to the lower river tribes began is unknown. So many had been captured in the wars of 1643 and 1655, that there was probably no attempt made to longer continue the restriction. By 1663, the use of firearms among the tribes of this County was general, and no effort was made to conceal them. In one of their conferences with the Dutch, the Indians asked that their muskets might be repaired ; and shortly after, Unsicken, a Tappaen warrior, lost his gun, having pawned it to gratify his fondness for brandy, and then entered a complaint at New Amsterdam against Van Cowenhoven for cheating him.

The disappearance of the native from our soil was gradual and the exact date of his departure, from the land of his fathers from time unknown, is not certain. The last recorded conference between the Tappaen Indians and the authorities of New York, was on September 13, 1673, and took place to confirm and continue the existing treaty. In 1666 Balthazar De Harte purchased land at Haverstraw from the Indians ; in 1671, Claes Jansen purchased a tract of land at Nyack from the Indians; in 1686, the Orangetown patent was purchased from the Tappaen tribe, and in 1694, the Quaspeck, two years later, the Kakiat, and in 1703 the Wawayanda patents were obtained from the savages.

So far can we trace the existence of the aboriginal owners of the soil in Rockland County by documentary evidence, and then the record abruptly ceases. "There were traditions among the early farmers, of localities where the remnants of the once powerful tribes lingered, subsisting on what game and fish they could find in the woods and streams they had sold. One of these spots is situated north of Nanuet, and another is in a large tract of swampy, untillable land about two miles west of Tappan. This is described as 'a vast and almost unknown region, patches of forest;

exist in almost their primeval condition ; huge trees, brought to the earth by the unrelenting and resistless hand of time, lie decayed to a shapeless and pulpy mass. Near the center of this tract, in what is called the Green Woods, and on the shore of what was once an immense beaver pond or lake, is a sandy knoll which is called, in the dialect of the early settlers, the *Wilder mons kerk-hoff*—the wild man's burying place. It is said that the last remnants of the Tappaens sought this wild, untillable region for a home, and remained for a long time living in the same state as they were accustomed to, and raising corn on patches of land yet pointed out as the *Wilder mons Maize Lout.*' "

But for more than a century, the Indian has been foreign to our boundaries and but little trace remains to show that he has been. An occasional locality, which tradition has marked as his last dwelling place. A few arrow, spear and axe heads; remains of old fire places, and here and there a lonely grave, are the only visible evidences of his existence. Strange mystery of history ; whence the native came, whither he has gone. Standing very low in the intellectual growth of the human family, contact with civilization did not elevate, it exterminated him. No evidence is found to show that religion or culture made the least impression on his life. With little or no belief in a controlling spirit, he was found and he disappeared, making no sign that that belief had become less shadowy.

The construction of his weapons and utensils of stone, which he had roughly chipped into form, was the highest advance he ever reached. From his white neighbor, he learned of and obtained the weapons of civilization and by that act forever lost his inventive faculty.

The improvidence and personal uncleanliness of the savage rendered him peculiarly susceptible to the ravages of disease, and his mode of life tended to spread contagion. The deadly plague of small pox found him awaiting its ravages and decimated his people. Never rallying from the staggering blow dealt him in the wars with the whites ; he was still more rapidly exterminated by epidemics, and in the ceaseless struggle for existence dropped from the race.

For many years after the natives had disappeared from the County, our shores were visited by 'up-river Indians on their journeys to the aborigines living on Long Island. The last visit from them was in comparatively recent years—after 1817. On this occasion six canoe loads camped for a time under the old willow still standing on Mr. Harmon Snedeker's place at Upper Nyack, and on their return home the same party remained for a week on the point north of the Bight in South Nyack, occupying their time in making and selling baskets.

Authorities referred to:—Documents relating to the Colonial History, S. N. Y., vols. I, II, XIII, XIV. Documentary History S. N. Y. N. Y. Historical Society Collections, vol. 1 new series, III second series. Byrant's History U. S. History of New York, by Martha J. Lamb. History of New England, by J. G. Palfrey. I have been much pleased and instructed by the papers of R. H. Fenton, published in the City and Country.

Relics of Indian life are not rare in this County, and many are still found by skillful searchers. The finest collections I have seen are in the possession of Mrs. Harmon Snedeker, Mrs. Nellie Hart, and the heirs of Mr. E. L. Gedney, of Nyack. With scarcely an exception these relics are of a flinty stone not found in this section of the country, and this has given rise to much speculation as to how the Indians obtained the enormous quantities necessary for a hunter's use. We must not forget that other materials were used by the savages. Arrow and spear heads were often made of bones or with the claws of birds of the larger species, while fish hooks were fashioned of sharpened fish bones. As these would decay in the course of time, little or no trace of them would come to us.

I am aware that my statement regarding the absolute absence of religious ideas among the Indians at the first arrival of white men, is contrary to generally accepted belief, and have thought it necessary to give my reasons for the statement. The first Dutch visitors among the savages were traders, who themselves were not overburdened by religious convictions, but who were keen observers of savage nature. If these men had seen any indication of a religion among the aborigines, they would have been the first to abuse it for their gain, and in a short time the fact would have been known at New Amsterdam. Absolutely no mention of religious belief is made in a journal of New Netherlands and its inhabitants, written in 1641, 1642, 1643, 1644, 1645 and 1646, but to the contrary, it is stated, that there was none. New York Colonial Ms., vol. I, p. 179. From the narrative of the captivity of Father Isaac Jaques among the Mohawks in 1642, '43, we learn of the same lack of spiritual faith. Vide op. cit. vol. XIII, Appendix A." "They are a people without any religion, or knowledge of any God," wrote Edward Winslow, and the truth of this statement is borne out by both the early French and English explorers. If we look at the question in another way: Cotton, when preaching to the savages in their own language, could find nothing that would indicate a Supreme Being in that language, and had to use the English word God, and Eliot, in his translation of the Bible into the Indian tongue, was driven to a similar expedient. If we view the subject from still another standpoint, there was found no place for worship, no form of service, no priestly order; in fact no, if I may use the expression, machinery of religion. With peculiar inconsistency the white race has passed two centuries in exterminating the Indians because they were barbarous savages, and in weaving around their memories a romance that it will now take years to clear away. The American savage was about as low as regards habits in the social scale as any people yet discovered, and so little removed from the higher creation of beasts in intellect, that it is difficult to separate him from the brute existence.

CHAPTER II.

PATENTS.

VAN WERCKHOVEN APPLIES FOR A PATENT AT TAPPAN—CLAES JANSEN PATENT—PAULSEN AND DOWSE HARMANSE PATENTS—DE HARTE PATENT—ORANGETOWN PATENT—WELCH AND MARSHALL, OR QUASPECK PATENT—HONAN AND HAWDON, OR KAKIAT PATENT—EVANS PATENT—WAWAYANDA PATENT—CHEESECOCKS PATENT—LANCASTER SYMES PATENT—STONY POINT PATENT—ELLISON AND ROOME PATENT—KEMPE, LAMB AND CROM PATENT—PATENTS FOR LANDS IN RAMAPO—LOCKHART PATENT.

The establishment of feudalities by the Dutch West India Company, in 1629, almost immediately caused trouble. A few of the College of Nineteen were prepared for the passage of that act, and at once acquired enormous tracts of the most valuable land in the colony. Van Rensselaer located his purchase at the head of navigation on the Hudson. Michael Pauw purchased the present Hoboken, Pavonia and Staten Island, while others made haste to obtain vast landed property on the South, now Delaware River. These acquirements led less grasping members of the company to object strenuously, and their complaints, combined with the fact that colonization under the proprietorship of the Patroons was not as rapid as expected; influenced the College, in 1640, to so modify their act in regard to grants, as to permit future purchasers only one mile frontage along a river, with a depth of two miles, while no two tracts of land could be taken on both sides of a navigable stream opposite each other.

From the destruction of Vriesendael, in 1643, no attempt to purchase land in this County was made till 1651. Then Cornelis Van Werckhoven, an ex-Schepen of Utrecht, applied for two pieces of land, one at Nevesinck, the other at Tappan, stretching northward through the Highlands. Difficulty in regard to the first of these grants occurring with Baron Van der Capellen, who had purchased part of the Nevesinck land just previous to Van Werckhoven, and Governor Stuyvesant having entered a protest against the loose wording of the Tappan grant, which gave an unlimited stretch of boundary to the petitioner; the Directors of the West India Company called attention to the rule in regard to land grants in the following words addressed to Stuyvesant. "Your Honor has misunderstood our intention in regard to the colonies of the Honorable Van Werckhoven, whose two grants for colonies your Honor supposes to extend twenty miles in a straight line, or your Honor has not read the exemptions carefully, for all colonists are not to receive more than four miles on one side of a navigable river, or two miles on each side." The difficulty in this case was settled by Van Werckhoven declining to occupy either of these grants. Instead, he took up land at Nyack on Long Island, situated near the present village of Fort Hamilton on Gravesend Bay.

In April, 1659, there sailed from Holland in the ship Beaver, a wheelwright, Claes Jansen from Purmerend, with his wife, servant and child. For a time he lived below the present Jersey City, but in 1671, April 16, he obtained from the Duke of York, to whom Charles II had given the proprietorship of this with other provinces, a tract of land "lying on the Hudson River at the north end of Tappan, at a brook, thence northeasterly along the river 40 chains, thence northwesterly 60 chains to the foot of the mountains, thence south, southwest above the mountains 40 chains, thence south, southeast to the river at the point of the beginning, containing 240 acres. Also another tract lying on the north side of the above, running northerly along the river 80 chains, then west, northwest 50 chains to the top of the mountains, thence south, southwest over the mountains 80 chains, thence south, southeast to the river 50 chains, to the place of beginning." This property, covering largely what is now the corporate limits of South Nyack from the Bight to near De Pew's brook, was the first settled tract of land in Rockland County after the departure of De Vries.

Between this date, 1671, and October 20, 1678, two other purchasers, Tunis Paulsen and Harmanus Dows, who had sailed from Friesland with his wife and four children in 1658, by the ship Brownfish, had bought land in the present village of Nyack. The latter owned what is now the business portion of the village, while the former extended from his north line to Verdrietige Hook. In 1687, Harmanus Dows, or as he was originally called, Dowse Harmanse, added to his property by purchasing 250 acres west of the Nyack hills, bounded as follows: on the east by the land of Claes Jansen and Dowse Harmanse, south by the land of Daniel Clarke & Co., west by the middle of the Hackinsack River, and north by the top of a certain hill called Essawetene. And in 1694, Cornelius Clasen, son of Claes Jansen, makes record: that he had bought from Tunis Paulsen a portion of land in the present Upper Nyack, extending to the top of Verdrietige Hook, and had inherited from his father the land obtained by the patent of 1671.

On April 10, 1671, Philip Carteret granted to Balthazar De Harte, a tract of land and meadow in Averstraw, bounded on the west by a creek called Menisakeungue—Minisceongo—on the east and north by Hudson River, on the south by the mountains, estimated to contain about four hundred acres. It is claimed that De Harte purchased this tract from the Indians previous to 1666. On December 19, 1685, this patent was confirmed to Jacobus De Harte, brother of Balthazar, by Governor Thomas Dongan.

Of this first patentee in the present village and township of Haverstraw, Valentine's History of New York gives the following account: "Balthazar De Harte was a wealthy merchant who commenced trade here about 1658. * * * * he was a bachelor but left at his death several illegitimate children in this city for whom he provided liberally out of his large estate. Among other extensive tracts owned by this gentleman was the land called Haverstraw on the Hudson River which he purchased originally from the Indians. He died in 1672. He had three brothers who left numerous descendants."

In 1686, the following patent situated partly in this State and partly in New Jersey, was purchased by a party of sixteen individuals. "Thomas Dongan, Capt, Generall Governor in Cheife, and Vice Admirall in and over the Province of New York and territorys. Depending thereon in America under his most sacred Majesty, James the Second, by the Grace of God, King of England, Scottland, ffrance and Ireland, Defender of the faith, &c., To all whom these Presents shall come, Sendeth Greeting, Whereas it appears to mee that * * * * have Lawfully Purchased from the Native Indian Proprietors a certain Tract of Land lying on the west side of Hudsons River in the County of Orange on the north side of Tappan Creek, Bounded as hereafter is Exprest (viz.) beginning at the mouth of Tappan Creek where it falls into the Meadow, and runing from thence along the North side of the said Creek to a Creeple bush, and falls into Hackensack River Northerly to a place called the Green bush, and from thence along said Green bush Easterly to the Land of Claes Janse and Dowe Harmanse, and from thence Southerly along said Land upon the Top of the Hills to aforemenconed mouth of Tappan Creek, where it falls into the meadow aforesaid. And Whereas the said * * * * have made Applycacon unto me that I would Grant and Confirme the said Tract of Land unto them, their Heirs and Successors, and Erect the same into one Township by Pattent under my Hand & the Seale of the Province. Now Know Ye that I, the said Thomas Dongan, by Virtue of the Power & Authority Derived unto me from his Most Sacred Majesty, and in Pursuance of the Same in Consideracon of the Quitt Rent hereinafter Reserved to his Most Sacred Majesty aforesd, his Heirs, Successors and Divers of a Good and Lawfull Consideracons me thereunto moveing, have Given, Granted, Rattified, Released

& Confirmed, & by these Presents Doe Give, Grant, Rattific, Release & Confirme unto the said * * * * the aforesaid Purchasers, their Heires, Successors & Assignes, all the before recited Tract or Parcell of Land with Limitts and Bounds aforesaid, together with all & singular the Messuages, Buildings, Tenements, Houses, Barns, Stables, Orchards, Gardens, Pastures, fences, Meadows, Marshes, Timber Trees, Woods, Underwoods, Mills, Mill dams, Rivers, Rivletts, Streams, Quarryes, ffishing, ffoulcing, Hawking, Hunting, Mines, Minerals (Royall mines Excepted), and all the Rights, Members, Libertys, Privillidges, Jurisdiccons, Royaltyes, Hereditaments, Proffits, advantages & appurtenances whatsoever to the said Tract or Parcell of land belonging or in anywise appertaineing or excepted, Reputed or knowne or occupied as Parte, Parcell or Member thereof, to have & to hold all the said Tract or Parcell of Land & Premisses with all & every of the appurtenances unto the said * * * * their Heires, Successors and Assigns to the Proper use, beneffitt & behoofe of the aforesaid Purchasers, their Heires, Successors & assigns forever without any manner of Lett, Hindrance or Molestacon, to have or reserved pretence of Joynt Tenancy or survivorship anything contained herein to the Contrary in anywise notwithstanding and moreover by virtue of the Power & authority to me the said Thomas Dongan Given and in me Residing as aforesaid, and for the Reasons & Consideracons above recited I have and by these Presents Doe make, Erect and Constitute all the said Tract or Parcell of Land within the Limitts and Bounds aforemenconed, together with all and every the above Granted Premissess with the appurtenances into one Township to all intents and purposes whatsoever, and the same from henceforth shall be called the Towne of Orange, and I, the said Thomas Dongan, have also Given my hand, Granted & by these Presents Doe Give & Grant unto * * * * the Purchasers of the said Towne of Orange, their Heires, Successors and assignes forever all the Privilidges, benefitts, customes, Practices, Preheminces and Immunityes that are used or Exercised, Practiced or belonging unto any Towne within the Goverm't to be used, exercised, Imitated, Practiced & executed by the said Purchasers, their Heirs, Successors and assignes, forever to be holden of his most Sacred Ma'tie, his Heires and Successors in ffee and Comon Soccage according to the Tenure of East Greenwich in the County of Kent in his Majestyes' Realm of England, Yielding, Rendring and Paying therefor Yearly & every Yeare on every five and twentyth Day of March forever in Lieu of all services and Demands whatsoever as an acknowledgm't or Quitt Rent to his said Ma'tie, his Heirs and Success-

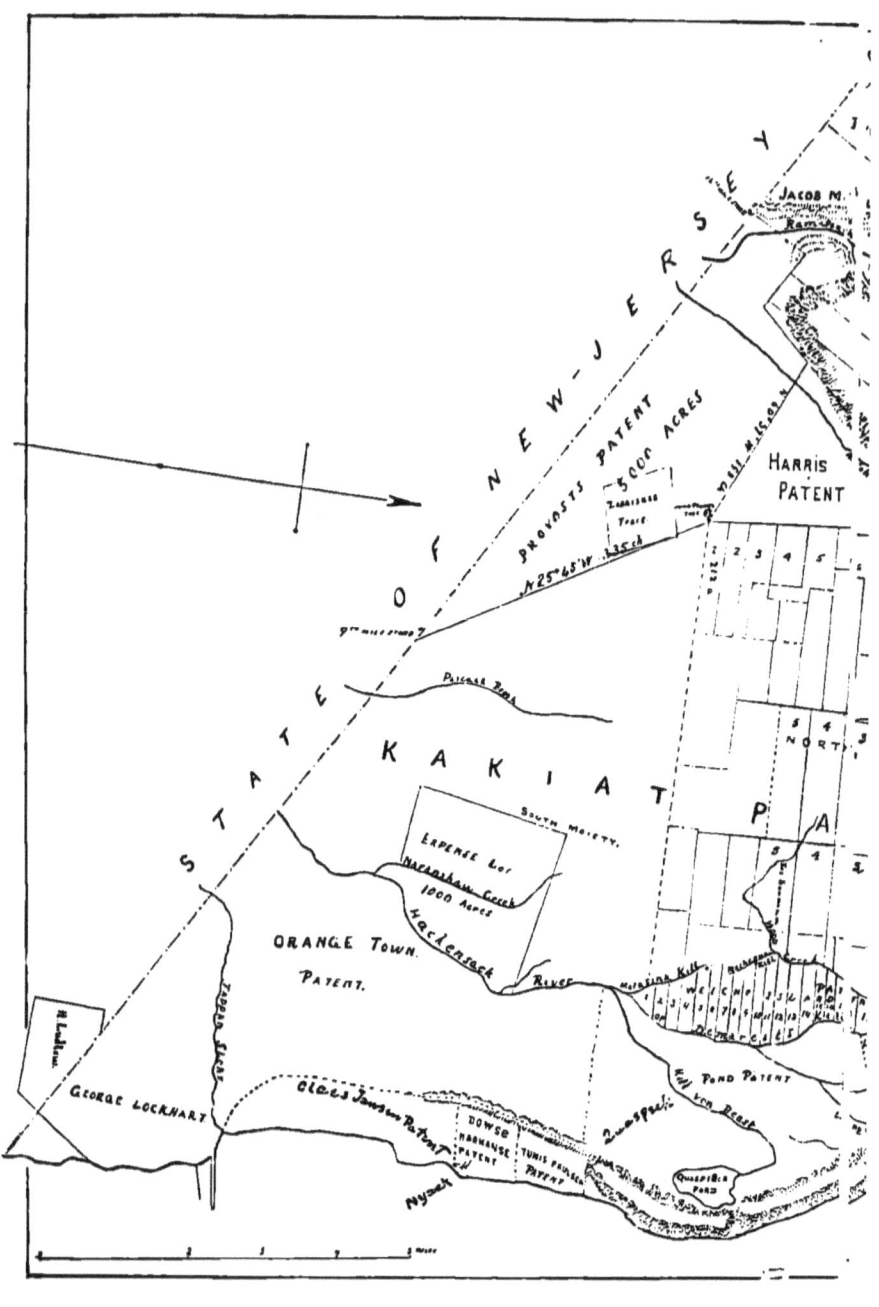

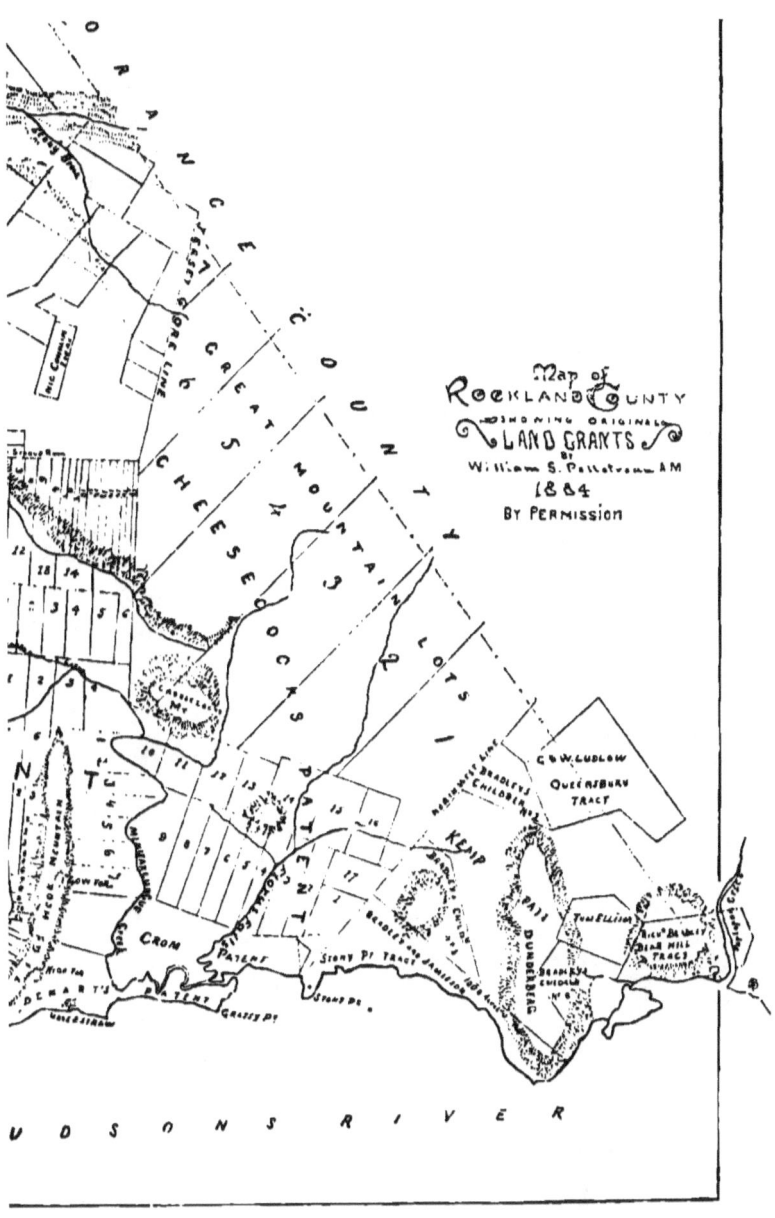

ors, or to such officer or officers as shall bee from time to time appointed to receive the same sixteen bushells of Good Winter Merchantable wheat att the Citty of New York, in Testimony whereof I have caused these Presents to be Recorded in the Secretarye's office and the Seals of the Province to be hereunto affixed this fouer & twentyth Day of March in the third year of his Majestye's Reign, and in the year of our Lord God, 1686, By Comand of his Excell'y. Tho. Dongan."

The names of the above patentees were: Cornelius Cooper, Daniel De Clarke, Peter Hearing, Gosin Hearing, Gerrit Stemmit, John De Vries, Sr., John De Vries, Jr., Claus Mande, Jan Straatmaker, Staats De Groot, Arean Lammuas, Lammuan Arens, Hybert Gerrits, Johannes Gerrits, Eide Van Voorst and Cornelius Lammerts.

On May 30, 1694, William Welch and Jarvis Marshall bought from seven Indians, only one of whose names—Copphichonock—I can decipher, five thousand acres of land at a place called Quaspeck, and on September 27th of that year the purchase was confirmed by patent from William and Mary through Benjamin Fletcher, then Governor of the Province. This purchase was bounded on the west by De Maries Kill, on the north by the land of Johannes Meille—Minne is meant—on the east by the Hudson River, and on the south by the lands of Cornelius Clausen and Thunis Dowen. It included the property extending from the top of the Hook mountain, north to the foot of the Long Clove in Haverstraw, and from the Hudson back to the Hackensack River, and its quit rent was one pepper corn a year for five years, and then twenty shillings annually, payable on the first day of each year O. S.

On September 8, 1694, William Welch and Apollonia, his wife, obtained a grant of five hundred acres beginning on the north side of the mouth of Mattasinck Kill and running thence along the north side of said kill west to a certain swamp at the head thereof; thence on the south side of the swamp to Mahequa Run; then by the said run to De Maries Kill, and along the kill to the place of beginning. This tract is between the Hackensack River and New City, and the place known as Strawtown is about in its center.

Two years later, June 25, 1696, Daniel Honan and Michael Hawdon purchased from the Indians, and had confirmed by patent from King William through Governor Fletcher, an enormous tract of land known as Hackyackawek or Kakiat patent. This was bounded on the east by the Christians patented land, on the west by a creek called Heamaweck or Peasqua, which runs under a great hill, from whence it continued in a direct west course until the west southwest side of a barren plain called

Wescyrorap bears south, thence to the west southwest side of the plain, from thence south southeast until the line comes to a creek that runs into David De Maries Creek to the southward of the land called Narranshaw, and thence down the said creek to the Christians patented lands; for a yearly rental of one beaver skin, payable on the first day of each year O. S. The Christians patented lands were those of Welch and Marshall, De Harte, Dowen or now Tallman, Clausen and the Orangetown grant.

The Directors of the Dutch West India Company had learned in a short time, that it was folly to grant unlimited tracts of land to an individual. After the cession of this territory to England, however, no limit was placed upon the size of the grants at the start, and the many changes of dynasty at home kept the government too much occupied with domestic affairs to give heed to wrongs that were being perpetrated in the colonies. Hence each patentee increased his demand for land till finally one was granted, just preceding 1698, to Captain John Evans, Commander of H. M. S. Richmond, that would have made even Van Renssylaer pause in wonder. This patent was for land on the west side of the Hudson, and covered a space forty miles in length and twenty in breadth. It extended from the south line of the present town of New Paltz west to the Shawangunk Mountains, thence south to the southwest angle of the present town of Calhoun in Orange Courty, thence easterly to the easter most angle of that town and then southeast to the Hudson River at Stony Point, and included the south tier of towns in Ulster, two-thirds of Orange, and all of Stony Point townships in Rockland County. The annual quit rent was to be twenty shillings.

Such a gigantic swindle could not escape notice, and the governor who permitted it—Fletcher—being superseded by the Earl of Bellomont, the new ruler called the attention of the home authorities to this flagrant wrong, and Captain Evans' patent was annulled.

Scarcely less outrageous was the Wawayanda patent, granted March 5, 1703, to John Bridges, LL.D., Hendrick Ten Eyck, Derick Vandeburgh, John Cholwell, Christopher Denn, Lancaster Symes, Daniel Honan, Philip Rokeby, John Meredith, Benjamin Aske, Peter Matthews, and Christopher Christianse by Lord Cornbury, Governor of the Province, and confirmed by Queen Anne. It was stated to contain 60,000, and did contain 150,000 acres, and was bounded on the east by the Highlands of the Hudson, north by the division line of the counties of Orange and Ulster, west by the high hill to the eastward of the Minnisink, and south by the division line between New York and New Jersey.

On March 25, 1707, Anne Bridges, Hendrick M. Ten Eyck, Dirck

Vanderburgh, John Cholwell, Christopher Denn, Lancaster Symes, and John Merritt obtained the Cheesecocks patent. This was the large tract of land west of Haverstraw, and was bounded as follows: " North by the patented lands of Captain John Evans and the Wawayanda patent, west by the Wawayanda and the Highlands, south by the Kakiat patent, and east by the Christian patented lands of Haverstraw and by the Hudson River." For this property an annual rental of twenty shillings was to be paid.

"To the north of the Pond patent was a tract, granted to Lancaster Symes and others April 23, 1708. The Snedekers always claimed nearly if not quite to the Short Clove, and the only known deed which refers to the Symes grant, is one from William Lupton to Claas R. Van Houten, dated 1760. This conveys 102 acres bounded west by Demarest's Kill, north by the land of John De Noyelles, east and south by the road to New City. This is now the farm of Barne Van Houten. A map of the farm, made in 1813 by David Pye, bears the following note: 'A map of the farm sold by William Lupton to Claas R. Van Houten, in patent of Lancaster Symes and others, one-half at least of this patent is in the patent to Marshall and Welch. Calculation to be made on this 100 acres, as if the remainder was only 600 acres.'"

It seems wise, before turning to the difficulties that surround the grants of land in Ramapo, to finish the eastern part of the County, and I therefore take up Stony Point without regard to chronological order.

On May 17, 1719, Richard Bradley and William Jamison obtained a patent from George II. for 1,000 acres, which was called the Stony Point tract. South of this, in 1743, Richard Bradley obtained from the same king 106 acres lying south of the Bradley-Jamison tract; and a further grant of 800 acres, known as the Bear Hill tract. On October 30, 1749, George II. patented to Sarah, Catharine, George, Elizabeth, and Mary Bradley, son and four daughters of Richard Bradley, the following pieces of land: A tract containing 370 acres, beginning at the most southerly corner of the tract of 1,400 acres granted to Gabriel and William Ludlow, and running thence southwest 38 chains to the northwest line, then along the line southeast 65 chains, then north 25 degs., east 113 chains to the tract granted to Gabriel and William Ludlow, and then along the line thereof to the place of division.

Another tract, beginning on the northwest line at the west corner of a tract of 1,000 acres granted to Richard Bradley and William Jamison, running thence along the said line northwest 87 chains, then northeast 40 chains, then north 79 degs., east 152 chains to the line of the Bradley and Jamison tract, and then along the line to the place of beginning, containing 840 acres.

Another tract, beginning at the southeast corner of the Bear Hill tract, and on the west side of a small creek, which runs on the west side of a meadow called Salisbury's meadow, and runs thence along the line of the Bear Hill tract north 62 degs., west 16 chains, then south 25 degs., west 79 chains, then south 50 degs., east 43 chains, then north 62 degs., east 86 chains to Hudson's River, and along the river to the meadow aforesaid, and then by the bounds thereof to the place of beginning, containing 500 acres.

On November 12, 1750, among six tracts of land granted to Thomas Ellison and Lawrence Roome by George II. was one in the present Rockland County, bounded as follows: Beginning at the northwest corner of a tract of 500 acres granted to Sarah, Catharine, George, Elizabeth, and Mary Bradley, running thence along this line south 25 degs., west 81 chains, then north 65 degs., west 52 chains, then north 50 chains, then north 49 degs., east 44 chains, and then south 62 degs., east 56 chains along the line of the tract granted to Richard Bradley to the place of beginning.

By patent bearing date March 18, 1769, George III. conveyed to William Kempe, James Lamb, and John Crum a large tract of land surrounded on all sides, except the southwest, where it lies upon the northwest line, and for a short distance on the east, on the river, by tracts previously patented. This grant contained 3,000 acres.

The northwest line runs northwest from the south side of Stony Point on the Hudson to the Delaware River. It was the south line of the grant to Captain John Evans. After that grant was revoked the present township of Stony Point was, as we have seen, divided into a number of small patents, and the northwest line became the boundary between those Stony Point grants and the great Cheesecocks patent.

In taking up the grants of land in Ramapo, I shall quote from the very excellent history of that town, written by the Rev. Eben B. Cobb of the Presbyterian Church at the Ramapo Works. In order to a clear understanding of the tenure of lands in Ramapo we must remember the following facts:

(1). That the land originally was claimed by two States, New York and New Jersey; and by three different patents in New York—the Kakiat, Wawayanda, and the Cheesecocks.

(2). That the controversy between Kakiat and Cheesecocks was settled in 1771, and that by this settlement, a line drawn from a heap of stones in the north bounds of the town of Ramapo, south 3 degs., 30m. east, to John Wood's tree, and thence south 25 degs., 40m. east, to the Pascack River, and crossing the New Jersey line a little to the east of the ninth mile stone, was made to separate the two.

(3). That the line between New York and New Jersey was settled October 7, 1769, when the Commissioners appointed by the Crown rendered the following decision : " The agents on the part of both colonies having offered to the court all that they thought necessary or proper in support of their respective claims, and the court having considered the same, do find—

That King Charles II. by his letters patent, bearing date the twelfth day of March, 1664, did grant and convey to his brother, the Duke of York, all that tract of country and territory now called the Colonies of New York and New Jersey, and that the said Duke of York afterwards by his deed of lease and release, bearing date the 23d and 24th days of June, 1664, did grant and convey to Lord Berkely, of Stratton, and Sir George Carteret that part of the aforesaid tract of land called New Jersey, the northern bounds of which in said deed are described to be, to the northward as far as the northernmost branch of the said Bay or River of Delaware, which is in 41 degs. 40m. of latitude, and crosseth thence in a straight line to Hudson's River in 41 degs. of latitude.

Among the many exhibits a certain map compiled by Nicholas John Vischer, and published not long before the aforesaid grant from the Duke of York, which we have reason to believe was esteemed the most correct map of that country at the time of the said grant, on which map is laid down a fork or branching of the river, then called Zuydt River or South River, now Delaware River, in the latitude of 41 degs. and 40m., which branch we cannot doubt was the branch in the deed from the Duke of York called the northernmost branch of the said river, and which in the deed is said to lye in the latitude of 41 degs. and 40m. And from a careful comparison of the several parts and places laid down on the said map, some of which, more especially toward the sea coast and on the Hudson's River, we have reason to believe were at the time well known. The distance of the said branch from the seashore on the South, and the relative situation of the same with regard to other places and the lines of latitude as they appear to be laid down on the said map at that and other places in the inland country.

We are of opinion that the said branch so laid down on the said map is the fork or branch formed by the junction of the stream or water called the Mahackamack, with the river called Delaware or Fishkill, and that the same is the branch intended and referred to in the before mentioned deed from the Duke of York as the Northern Station at the River Delaware, which fork or branch we find by an observation taken by the surveyors appointed by the Court to be in the latitude 41 degs., 21m. and 37 sec.

We are further of opinion that the Northern Station at Hudson's River, being by the words of the said deed from the Duke of York expressly limited to the latitude of 41 degs., should be fixed in that latitude, which latitude we have caused to be taken in the best manner by the surveyors appointed by the Court, and which falls at a rock on the west side of Hudson's River marked by the said surveyors, being seventy-nine chains and twenty-seven links to the southward on a meridian from Sneydon's house, formerly Corbet's.

It is therefore the final determination of the Court that the boundary or partition line between the said Colonies of New York and New Jersey be a direct and straight line from the said fork at the mouth of the River Mahackamack, in the latitude of 41 degs, 20m. and 37 sec. to Hudson's River at the said rock, in the latitude of 41 degs. as above described."

"Signed   CHAS. STEWART.
           ANDREW ELLIOT.
           ANDREW OLIVER.
           JARED INGERSOLL."

This decision was of great value to the town of Ramapo. Had the line run from 41 degs. on the Hudson to 41 degs. 40m. on the Delaware, which last point had been located by the joint surveyors of New York and New Jersey in 1719, it would have caused one-half of the town to lie in New Jersey. While the people of neither State was satisfied with the boundary thus chosen yet, it, probably being regarded by both as the best arrangement that could be made, was ratified by each and the task of running the line was completed in November, 1774. The division line between the States was resurveyed and marked in 1874.

(4). Having established the boundaries between the Kakiat and Cheesecocks patents, and the boundary between New York and New Jersey; the claims of the two remaining patents, Cheesecocks swooping down on the land from the north, and Wawayanda from the west, had also to be settled. This was done by drawing a line from the northwest corner of the Kakiat patent, which corner was located in the north boundary of the town, in a direct course to the thirty-first mile stone on the New Jersey line.

This line, which was run by Charles Clinton, Jr., son of General James Clinton, in 1786, was called the "Gore Line," and the land in Rockland and Orange counties bounded by it, the New Jersey line, and the line established as the west bounds of Kakiat, was familiarly known as the "Jersey Gore." By this gore line the patents, both of Cheesecocks and Wawayanda, were excluded from the town.

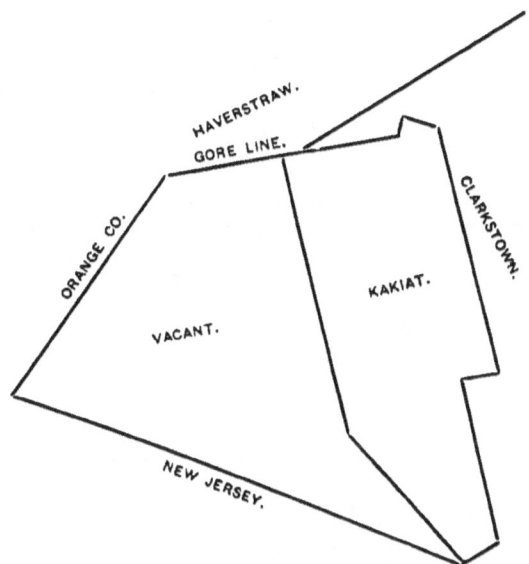

Diagram from Rev. E. B. Cobb's History of Ramapo.

The history of the "Jersey Gore," for which Mr. Cobb refers to Mr. B. Fernow, of the Department of Historical Records, Albany, is thus given: Blandina Bayard bought, August 10, 1700, five tracts of land from the Indians, called Ramapough, Jaapough, Jandekagh, Aringee, and Camguee, three Dutch miles wide and four long, covering most of the land in the triangle of which the "Gore line" is the northwest side. She improved and settled this land, and upon her death left it to her children, Petrus and Sarah. Petrus, and later his widow, lived on the land and continued the improvements. When the widow removed she left a certain Lucas Kiersted as superintendent. This Kiersted was corrupted by Peter Sonmans, one of the proprietors of East New Jersey, and induced to take out Jersey patents for these lands, which had hitherto not been patented by New York although Blandina Bayard had been promised a patent, and the proprietors of Cheesecocks and Wawayanda both claimed them. About 1786 it became necessary to settle the southern boundary of Cheesecocks, at which time Charles Clinton, Jr. made, in 1788, the maps on which probably for the first and only time, the term "Jersey Gore" was used. It was never so called officially, for the Surveyor-General, in a report to the Legislature on this tract, made March 12, 1801, calls it "Vacant lands between the lately established boundary line of the patent of Cheesecocks and the State of New Jersey."

It will be seen by consulting the diagram, that when the boundary line between New York and New Jersey was established, which put an end to the claims of New Jersey from the south, and the "Gore Line" was run, which silenced similar claims on the part of the proprietors of both Cheesecocks and Wawayanda from the north and west, that the town of Ramapo virtually became divided into two sections, one occupied by the Kakiat patent, and the other substantially vacant. Leaving the Kakiat divisions for later notice, we must turn our attention to the vacant lands.

In the large part of the town marked on the diagram as vacant, there were on January 1, 1775, but three persons who had titles to their property recognized by the Crown—John Sobrisco, who owned 630 acres near Tallman's; Coenard Wannamaker, who owned 105 acres near the fifteenth mile stone on the Jersey line; and Jacobus Van Buskirk, who owned a mill-right of one acre on the Mahwah near the point where that stream is now crossed by the Nyack Turnpike. In a foot-note Mr. Cobb says: "There were many inhabitants in this (Ramapo Pass) part of the town at that time, and some held recorded Indian deeds; nevertheless, the above statement is true. The only possible qualification may be in reference to the Sterling Company, who may have had a valid title to a few acres in the extreme west of the town."

To obtain an insight into how these three persons obtained their property will require a brief review of the early history of New Jersey.

On March 12, 1664, Charles II. granted to his brother, the Duke of York, the entire region between the Connecticut and Delaware Rivers. This grant was confirmed July 29, 1674. On June 24, 1664, the Duke of York sold, what is now New Jersey, to Lord Berkeley and Sir George Carteret, confirming his sale as above July 29, 1674. These two purchasers divided New Jersey into two divisions—called East and West New Jersey—by a line drawn from " Little Egg Harbor to a point on the Delaware in latitude 41 degs., 40 m.," Lord Berkeley having West New Jersey and Sir George Carteret East. With the further management of the first-named tract we have nothing to do.

On January 13, 1680, Sir George Carteret died, directing in his will that East New Jersey should be sold to pay his debts. According to this instruction the tract was sold February 2, 1682, to William Penn and eleven associates called the "Twelve Proprietors." Soon after, these "Twelve" each took a partner, making "The Twenty-four Proprietors of East New Jersey." On March 14, 1702, the Duke of York made a fresh grant of East New Jersey to the "Twenty-four Proprietors." One month later, April 15, 1702, the "Proprietors" surrendered "their right to govern" to Queen Anne, reserving their title to the lands, and on December 10, 1709, Peter Sonmans, representing himself as "Sole Agent, Superintendent, General Attorney and Receiver General of the rest of the Proprietors," but really only a single proprietor inheriting his property from his father, Aarent, conveyed to John Auboineau, E. Boudinot, Peter Fauconier, L. Kiersted, John Barbarie, Thomas Barjaux, Andrew Fresneau and Peter Bard, 42,500 acres in Northern New Jersey, lying between the Ramapo and Saddle Rivers, and called the "Romopock Tract."

The bounds of this tract may be described as: on the north by a line from the mountains to Saddle River, which line would pass a little to the north of Tallman's Station; on the east by Saddle River; on the south by a line from the Saddle River at the mouth of Hohokus Creek to Pompton; and on the west by the Ramapo Mountains, the northwest boundary being a line drawn across the entire Ramapo Pass, just northwest of the railroad bridge near Ramapo Works.

On November 6, 1724, Peter Fauconier, John Barbarie & Co., sold to John Sobrisco 630 acres of land near the present Tallman's Station.

After several years' contest, part of the time in the courts, the "Proprietors" finally offered to compromise with bona fide purchasers for £20 per hundred acres. On February 4, 1744, Peter Fauconier conveyed all his remaining interest in the Ramapo tract to Theodore Valleau and David Stout, and on August 10, 1752, they conveyed the same to Magdalene Valleau, daughter of William Fauconier. The following year, March 29, 1753, the proprietors of East New Jersey granted 900 acres to Magdalene Valleau on condition that she release her claim to the remainder of the tract, and on May 23, 1753, she conveyed to Coenard Wannamaker, 105 of the 900 acres, just granted her. In 1762, February 12th, David Ackerman, who in some unknown way had obtained the same from the proprietors of East New Jersey, sold a mill-right of about one acre to Jacobus Van Buskirk. When at length, in 1774, the line between New York and New Jersey was finally established, these three purchasers from New Jersey were confirmed in their title by the government of New York.

Leaving these first divisions of the Ramapo vacant lands in the present town, divisions which for the sake of lucidity I have thought it wisest to follow in Mr. Cobb's order; let us turn to the remainder of that vacant tract. On January 18, 1775, George III granted through Lieutenant Governor Cadwallader Colden, four patents to four reduced officers of the British Army.

The Provost patent, granted to James Marcus Provost, began in the division line between the Provinces of New York and New Jersey, as the same is run and marked by Commissioners as appointed by a law of this Province, 7 chains and 43 links eastward from the ninth mile stone in the said line, and running thence along a line marked for the western bounds of a tract of land formerly granted—the Kakiat patent—north 25 degs. 40m., west 335 chains and 30 links to John Wood's tree, thence north 60 degs. 37m., west 198 chains; thence south 45 degs., west 66 chains and 60 links; thence north 54 degs. 10m., west 77 chains; thence south 35 degs. 50m., west 73 chains to the said line run and marked by the Commissioners, and then along that line south 54 degs. 10m., east 579 chains to the place of beginning; excepting the tracts previously confirmed to John Sobrisco, Coenard Wannamaker and Jacobus Van Buskirk, containing 5,000 acres of land.

The Harris patent was granted to "Robert Harris, late Mate of His Majesty's Hospital," and contained the land within the following lines: Beginning at John Wood's tree, and running thence along the western line of the Kakiat patent, north 40 degs., west 247 chains 60 links; thence south 68 degs., west 11 chains; thence south 45 degs., west 205 chains to the north bounds of Provost's land; and thence along the same to the place of beginning, containing 2,000 acres.

The Muller patent, granted to Jacob Muller, began in the division line between the Provinces of New York and New Jersey, at the most westerly corner of Provost's patent, and followed the line of that grant north 35 degs. 50m., east 73 chains, south 54 degs. 10m., east 23 chains; thence north 36 degs., east 160 chains; thence north 54 degs. 10m., west 142 chains and 40 links; thence south 36 degs., west 233 chains to the division line aforesaid; thence along the same south 54 degs. 10m., east 119 chains and 60 links to the place of beginning, containing 3,000 acres of land.

The Spence patent, began in the division line between the provinces at the most westerly corner of the Muller grant, and ran along the western line of that tract to its northwest termination; from thence north 54 degs. 10m., west 59 chains 60 links; thence south 50 degs., west 185 chains; thence south 12 degs., east 40 chains to Potake Pond; thence along the same pond south 35 degs., west 27 chains to the aforesaid division line; and thence along the line south 54 degs. 10m., east 74 chains 33 links to the place of beginning, containing 1,820 acres of land.

Each of these patentees was to pay the yearly rental of 2s. 6d. for each and every acre of his patent. After this property had passed from the jurisdiction of the King of Great Britain to that of this State, the rent clause of the above patents was used as the basis of the quit-rents demanded from this property by the State; these rents were finally commuted by the payment of fourteen shillings for every shilling of rent.

On February 20, 1685, George Lockhart obtained by patent from James II. 3,410 acres of land bounded on the west by the Tappan grant, and extending from Piermont to Closter, N. J. This tract lay between the present Sparkill and the Hudson.

Authorities referred to: —I have personally consulted the Jansen, Quaspeck, and Kakiat patents—not copies, and have had the use of many of the first deeds for property in the County. Rev. Dr. A. S. Freeman's History of Haverstraw, Rev. E. Gay, Jr., History of Stony Point, Eager's History of Orange County, Doc. Relating to the Colonial History, S. N. Y., Documentary History S. N. Y., and in regard to Ramapo have followed the Rev. E. B. Cobb so closely that I have thought quotation marks superfluous.

CHAPTER III.

EARLY REAL ESTATE SPECULATION—TRANSFERS OF THE DE HART PATENT—SURVEY OF THE BOUNDARIES BETWEEN THE DE HART AND CHEESECOCKS PATENT—SALES FROM THE QUASPECK PATENT—SETTLEMENT OF DIVISION LINE BETWEEN THE QUASPECK AND KAKIAT PATENTS—DIVISION OF THE KAKIAT PATENT—SALES FROM THE KAKIAT PATENT—SETTLEMENT OF THE DIVISION LINE BETWEEN THE KAKIAT AND CHEESECOCKS PATENTS—SALES OF LAND FROM THE CHEESECOCKS PATENT—SALES OF LAND FROM THE STONY POINT PATENTS—TRANSFERS OF LAND IN RAMAPO—THE SETTLEMENT OF THE ORANGETOWN PATENT—THE DIFFERENT SYSTEMS OF PATRONYMICS USED BY THE DUTCH AND THE ORIGIN OF DUTCH FAMILY NAMES.

With the exception of a few isolated grants throughout the County and the Orangetown patent, the early purchases of property were made by speculators, who entertained no thought of personal settlement. The period was auspicious for real estate speculation. Whatever doubt existed prior to 1680, regarding the permanent success of the Colony, had passed away; the rapid growth of New York as a commercial port, the safety from further Indian depredation of adjacent land, gave every inducement to the colonists to obtain grants, and, when the fortunate patentees could secure several thousand acres of soil for an annual quit rent of a few pelts, a modicum of grain, or a sum of money less than five dollars of our time, the loss to be incurred, even if sales did not take place, was not great.

Hence, many of the first purchasers were never associated with our County, and probably never in it, except perchance to look at their temporary possessions. As soon as possible they resold the land, and the new buyer resold, till the era of speculation ceased and permanent settlers arrived. We are now to briefly review these transfers till we reach the location within our boundaries of the progenitors of families still resident.

Leaving the Orangetown patent for later consideration, the first transfers to note are those of the De Harte patent. This, as we have seen, was granted to Balthazar De Harte April 10, 1666. In 1685, December 19, it was confirmed to Jacobus De Harte, brother of the above. In 1694 Jacobus De Harte sold all, save ten acres, to Johannes Minne. The ten acres thus retained was woodland lying "between the creek commonly known by the name of Verdreitig Hook and the common great kill and cuts himself off from the aforesaid land with a small kill or creek which runs into Hudson River." Johannes Minne sold one-quarter of the tract to Albert Minnie in 1694, and dying in 1710, left the remainder to his only child Reynie, who married Lodowick Post. They sold 250 acres to Cornelius Kuyper and Albert Minnie, and in 1714 the remainder, about 43 acres, to Thomas Husk. Husk and Eleanor, his wife, sold this property to Charles Mott in 1715. He sold it to James Osborn in 1719, and he in turn sold to John Allison May 14, 1729.

Albert Minnie, by deeds bearing date May 15 and October 30, 1729, sold his quarter of the patent bought of Johannes Minnie and the lands bought of Lodowick Post, to John Allison for £270.

The ten acres of woodland reserved by Jacobus De Harte, was sold by his son, Balthazar, in 1719 to Cornelius Kuyper. Kuyper died in 1731 and left the property to his son Nicholas, who, dying about 1760, left it to his eight children, and they by 1767, had sold it to John De Noyelles.

In the boundaries of the Quaspeck patent, I find the northern line to read "by ye land of Johannes Meille." In a map of the patent made by Augustine Graham in 1700, the name is given as Johannes Melle, in deeds and papers that I have looked over, it is spelled Miller and Millie. I have followed Dr. Freeman and given it as Minnie.

The original patent of Balthazar De Harte covered, not only the land south of the Minisceongo, but also the low land to the north. He sold his interest in the tract north of the creek to Nicholas De Puy and Peter Marius. De Puy sold his half to Florus Williamse Crom in 1685, and the share of Marius having passed into the hands of Hendrick Van Bomell (or Hendrick V. Bomel), his widow, Rachel, sold it to Hendrick Ryker in 1685.

On December 13, 1685, Crom and Ryker obtained a patent from James II. through Governor Thomas Dongan for their land. Of the changes in ownership that took place between the date of the patent and to-day, I do not regard it necessary to speak in detail. For years one or more tracts of the patent remained in possession of some of the Crom family. The farm now owned by Adam Lilburn was the property, during the Revolution, of Captain James Lamb, of whom mention will later be made, and much of the Crom patent is now covered with brick yards.

Running through the centre of the Crom patent is a brook or creek called Florus Falls, after the Christian name of the patentee. In the grant of 1685, Hendrick Ryker, in his half, became the owner of the property north of the brook and between it and Stony Point. On June 15, 1716, Lewis Rynderson Van Ditmarson, Johannes Van Ditmarson and Grietie Van Ditmarson, spinster, who had in some way come in possession of Ryker's patent, sold it to Thomas Husk, of New York, for £159. In the deed of this sale the land north of Florus Falls is called Ahequerenoy.

Ahequerenoy, after passing through various hands, at length, in April, 1751, was sold in portions. That next north of Florus Falls, containing 135 acres, was bought by Resolvert Waldron; and that next north of Waldron, was bought in 1790 by Samuel Brewster.

In June, 1790, the boundary line between the Crom and Cheesecocks patents, which had long been in dispute, was settled by a survey made by General James Clinton as follows: " Beginning at a large oak sapling and a small birch one marked with three notches on three sides near three chestnut saplings, standing on the bank of Minnesecongo creek, and runs thence north 16 degs., east along the side of said creek 12 chains to the top of a bank, at 15 chains 26 links the top of a high stone or rock " (this is still standing in the old burying ground by the calico factory with a fence on the original line crossing it) "from which place the northwest corner of the meeting house now building (1790), bears south 21, east 47 links distant; at 16 chains, 80 links, the corner of Lots Nos. 8 and 9 Cheesecocks patent; at 30 chains, 75 links, touched the southeast corner of William Smith's house ; at 38 chains crossed a large stone or rock ; at 39 crossed another in William Smith's field; at 50 chains the southeast corner of Thomas Smith's house (The Treason House) bears north 82 degs., west 2 chains, 94 links distant ; at 55 chains the main road ; at 65 chains, 20 links, the southwest corner of John Crom's house bears south 80, east 74 links distant ; at 81 chains the northwest corner of Robert Henry's house bears south 76, east 45 links distant; at 90 chains the main road again ; at 107 chains and 70 links allowance for a steep bank, marked a small birch tree with three notches on four sides leaning over Florus Falls Creek, and trimmed some hemlocks near it; then south 54, east down said creek, 2 chains to a large buttonwood on the north side; at 4 chains, 80 links, to a stake by a fence on the north side of the road, 1 chain north of said creek and 1 chain west of a bridge, being the place of beginning of the second Haverstraw patent; then north 3 degs., west at 7 chains. 45 links, a bunch of pear trees, on the west side of the line ; at 17 chains, 25 links, set a stake on the south side of a steep hill; at 22 chains the road to Jacob Waldron's house " (the road leading east from the village of Stony Point) ; " at 30 chains, 35 links, marked a black oak tree in the line with three notches on two sides ; at 34 chains, 20 links crossed a spring brook."

" At 44 chains, 25 links, the southwest corner of John Waldron's barn bears south 10, east 92 links distant; at 64 chains, 75 links, set a red cedar stake with a heap of stones around it on the east side of the main road" (this angle is where the house of Frederick Tomkins stands); "then north 35, east at 9 chains, 40 links, made a heap of stones, on a large flat stone or rock; at 15 chains the said road west of a spring running from under a rock; at 21 chains the stump formerly marked for the said Brewster's corner bears south 69, east 19 links distant; at 26 chains, 30 links, set a stake on an island formed by Rasende water brook, 4 chains east of Jacob Roosa's house; then south 62, east 31 chains to a crooked white oak stump, near a black oak stump where there stands two white oak saplings marked with three notches on four sides on a point of upland joining a marsh on the west bank of Hudson's River."

In general terms it may be said the Crom, and Riker's patents covered all the land in Haverstraw, bounded south by Minisceongo creek, west by the hills, east by the river, and extending north almost to Stony Point.

Turning to the Quaspeck patent we find, that but little over a year had passed from the issuance of the grant before Jarvis Marshall assigned his share in it to Thomas Burroughs, a merchant of New York. A year later, December 18, 1696, William Welch transferred his, the original remaining half, to John Hutchins, of New York. A few days before this, December 4, Hutchins had bought one-half of Burroughs' interest for £100, and the property was now owned, three-quarters by Hutchins, and the remaining quarter by Burroughs. Two years later Hutchins transferred to John Sands, of Queens County, one-quarter of his right in the whole patent, it being still undivided. By October 15, 1700, the property had been surveyed and divided, and Burroughs had sold his interest to Captain Whitehead and William Huddleston. The property as then apportioned stood: the northernmost part, lying on the south line of De Harte's patent, containing 1,400 acres, belonged to John Sands; next south, running from the present Hackensack to the west shore of Rockland Lake was William Huddleston's land, consisting of 550 acres; next south of that was Captain Whitehead's tract similar in limit and number of acres to Huddleston's; and southernmost of all, bounded by Clausen's land on the top of Verdreitige Hoeck and Dowen's land west to the Hackensack, were Hutchins' 2,500 acres. At this time, 1700, the owners of the property agreed that a roadway should be laid out through the Clove to the Hudson River for the advantage of all resident on the property. This is the origin of the road to Rockland Lake landing. We have seen that Harmanus Dows, or Dows Harmanse, bought property extending from the Nyack hills to the Hackensack; Dows had a son named Tunis, and it was the property belonging to Tunis Dows that is mentioned in the boundaries of the Quaspeck patent as that of Tunis Dowen. This family name, as we shall see later, eventually became Tallman.

On February 7, 1716, John Sands, of Block Island in the Colony of Rhode Island, in the Providence Plantation, gave a quit claim deed of his Quaspeck land to his brother, Edward Sands, of Cow's Neck, in Queens County. March 5, 1729, Edward Sands, then residing in the County, sold his portion of the Quaspeck property, 1,300 acres, to Tunis Snedeker, of Hempstead, L. I., for £110. He had previously sold 30 acres to Nathaniel Youmans. From that period the transfers of the Snedeker farm were many up to 1840, when Hon. Abraham B. Conger became the possessor of almost all the original purchase.

Dispute arose between the owners of the Quaspeck and Kakiat patents regarding the division line, and before 1767 John De Noyelles, under the claim of the latter, and Garret Snedeker, on the part of the former, became involved in litigation. For years the question of this boundary was before the courts. At length a party line was agreed to, but before the necessary papers were signed, John De Noyelles died and the subject was left unsettled. Not long after, Garret Snedeker followed De Noyelles to the grave, leaving the question so long at issue between them for their heirs to agree upon. The subject continued one of vexation between the families till 1795, when a division line was at last agreed to by John Robert, John and Peter De Noyelles on the part of the Kakiat land, and Abraham Thew, Garret and Theodorus Snedeker on the part of the Quaspeck grant.

This line began " at the southwest corner of De Harte's patent, near the head of the Short Clove, in Haverstraw, in Orange County, and State of New York; and from thence runs south 7 degs. west, or thereabouts, to the Buttonwood tree (now a stump) standing by a small run of water on the northwest side of the road near the house of the late Richard Springsteel, deceased, and from the stump of the said Buttonwood tree southeasterly along the said run of water to a certain swamp called 'Old Woman's Hole;' thence along the easterly side of the upland to a small brook, then up the said brook to the before mentioned road, then southerly and westerly along the road to the bridge below the late Roelof Van Houten's mill a small distance west of the north bounds of Welches Island patent."

Of the transfers of the land of William Huddleston I can learn nothing. In 1737 it was owned wholly or in part by Jacob Polhemus. Huddleston was County Clerk of Orange County in 1702.

Whitehead seems to have resold his tract to Thomas Burroughs, for he, by will bearing date August 18, 1703, left it to his youngest son Joel and his daughter Mary Sylvester. A line from Quaspeck Pond to De Maries Kill divided this property into two sections, of which Joel took the northern. November 6, 1728, he sold this section to George Remsen.

On December 23, 1701, John Hutchins sold 825 acres of his half of the Quaspeck patent to William Smith of New York for £270. This lay next south of Whitehead's tract, and extended from Quaspeck Pond to the present Hackensack River. On May 22, 1711, Hutchins sold 200 acres east of Rockland lake to John Slaughter of Long Island. Slaughter had disposed of this property before Sand's deed to Snedeker in 1729. Later a company of German settlers bought a part or all of the remainder of Hutchins' tract. Among these was Peter Geslar, who sold to John Ryder June 8, 1753, "all that tract of land near the pond, in that (tract) the Germans have bought there of some gentlemen. This is a lot that did fall to the share of Peter Geslar, and is bounded by the lands of William Felta, Abrm. Paulding, Hendrick Snyder, John Ryder, and Yoris Remsen, containing 225 acres; but if there shall be more than 225 acres, then John Ryder must pay 40s. an acre." Valley Cottage Station on the West Shore Railroad stands on this tract, and a portion is still in possession of the Ryder family.

A tract on the east side of the Quaspeck Pond, extending to the river, was bought by John Earl and Stephen Bourdet. This is described as extending "from the south bounds of Tunis Snedeker to a straight line running along the northwest bounds of Hermanus Hoffman." It was divided between the purchasers in 1746 by a line "from the east side of the pond eight rods north of the corner tree of Hermanus Hoffman, and to run to the point of rocks called Stony Point, and to continue in a straight line to Hudson's River." It was agreed that "the place on the river under the mountain, called Kalk Hook, shall remain in common." Kalk Hook is now called Calico Hook.

The outlet of Rockland Lake was named Kill von Beast on the map made by Augustine Graham in 1700. This, on its way to the Hackensack, ran through the lands of George Remsen, who had a mill on it as early as 1750. George Remsen left his property to be divided among his children, and one of these, Artie, marrying an Onderdonk, part of the Remsen tract came into the possession of that family.

Michael Hawdon, one of the two patentees of the Kakiat grant, died about 1712, and John Johnston, Johannes Jansen, John Cook, and Nathaniel Marston, who were the executors of his estate, sold his half of the patent to Captain Cornelius Kuyper, Charles Mott, Timothy Halstead, Sr., Timothy Halstead, Jr., Johnathan Seaman, Thomas Barker, Caleb Halstead, James Searing, Jonah Halstead, Isaac Seaman, Abraham Denton, William Osborn, Nathaniel Osborne, John Searing, Thomas Williams, John Wood, and Samuel Denton. With the exception of Kuyper, all of these came from Long Island, and most of them from Hempstead township.

Before proceeding further in the sales from this patent, we must stop and look at its division. On November 5, 1713, Albert Minnie, John Pew, and Abraham Hearing, who were appointed to divide the property, began this work. They first laid out a tract of 1,000 acres to be sold to defray the expense of the survey. This tract, beginning "at Naranshaw Creek, at a black oak marked, thence ran north 80 degs., west 96 chains; thence to a beech tree marked, standing on Naranshaw Creek 98 chains; thence north 80 degs., east to a black oak tree by a small brook, 93 chains; then by said brook and David Demarest's Creek to Naranshaw Brook, and by the brook to the place of beginning."

On March 6, 1713-14, O. S., this tract was sold to Cornelius Kuyper and Johnathan Seaman for £104 4s., Kuyper owning two-thirds and Seaman one-third. Johnathan Seaman sold his share of the tract, except the third of the expense lot, to his son Joseph, May 1, 1715.

Having laid out the expense lot, the commissioners then proceeded to divide the property into two lots by a line, running from a white oak tree marked W on the W. S. W. side of the Wesegrorap Plain to a certain beech tree standing on the south end of Welch's Island. These divisions were called the north and south moieties. The north moiety becoming the property of Kuyper, Mott & Co., and the south falling to Daniel Honan.

The north moiety was surveyed and divided into lots in 1724 by Cornelius Low. If a full description of these was possible with our present knowledge, I much question whether it is necessary. Most of these lots are the property of descendants of early purchasers. For the purpose of location, it may be said, that two tiers of lots were formed, one called the East and the other the West Division, the line between the townships of Clarke's and Ramapo being the line of demarkation. For each of the original purchasers of Hawdon's half of the Kakiat grant, who owned a full share, a homestead of 400 acres was laid out. The "English Church" is on lot 4 of the west tier of the 400 acre lots, and the Court House, at New City, is at the east end of lot No. 5 in the East Division. On the west line of the patent was a tier of 14 lots called the "West Range." Lot 14, the last of this "Range," is just south of the Methodist Church at Ladentown.

On March 12, 1716, Daniel Honan sold his half of the Kakiat patent to John McEvers, a merchant of New York city, and the next year, 1717, McEvers sold half of his purchase to Lancaster Symes of New York. In 1728, McEvers, and Symes' heirs—his widow, Catharine, and his son, John Hendrick—sold their interest in the Kakiat land to a party of five men: Daniel De Clarke, Peter Hearing, Cosyn Hearing, Johannes Blauvelt, Sr., and Lambert Smet, the first three of whom had previously belonged to the party who purchased the Orangetown grant. Under their management the south moiety was surveyed and divided into lots.

Of the transfers that took place in the 1,000 acre or expense lot, I can learn but little. On December 3, 1716, Cornelius Kuyper conveyed to Hendrick Kuyper, of Bergen County, Province of New Jersey, "all that equal full third part of one thousand acres of land bounded as follows: Beginning at Narranshaw creek at a certain black oak tree marked on both branches on all four sides; thence running north 80 degs., west 96 chains; thence to a beach tree marked on all four sides standing on Narranshaw creek 98 chains; thence north 80 degs., east to a black oak tree standing by a small brook 93 chains; thence by said brook and David Maries Kill to Narranshaw brook aforesaid; and thence by the said brook to the place where it began," for £34, 15s.

Hendrick Kuyper, by will bearing date September 16, 1754, gave to his daughter Marretie, wife of Roelef Vanderlind, 100 acres on the north side of the track.

On July 16, 1764, Teunis De Clarke of "Clarkestown" in the County of Orange, &c; sold to "James Palden of the City of New York—Cordwainer" 25½ acres of land being "all that certain parcel of ground situate lying and being in Clarke's Town in the County of Orange and Province of New York: Beginning at a white oak marked on two sides on the west side of Hackensack Creek and so bounded on the east by said creek to the south line of Lot No. 14, in the southern division of Cackiate Patent, and bounded on the north by the said line, being John Vanderbilts land and bounded west by the road called the new road on the south west by the lots of John Anderson, Edw. Earle, James Campbell and John Jones and south by the Niack road and Casparies Mabies' meadow"; for £254.

This is the first mention I have found of Clarke's Town; the first time I have found De Maries or Demarest creek called the Hackensack, and the first list of names belonging to those Scotch settlers who gave the name to Scotland Hill.

Between 1764 and 1793, the Sickles family, from whom Sickletown takes its name, had purchased land in the 1,000 acre patent, for, on June 1, 1793, Elizabeth Sickles conveyed a lot to Robert Sickles and a year later, June 13, 1794, Major Cornelius J. Blauvelt and Robert Sickles, agreed to a party line between their lands in Kakiat.

In 1799, Sarah Lydecker, born Sarah Sickles, who had been the second wife of Albert Lydecker of English Neighborhood; bought, with her son Cornelius, 51 acres of Wm. Sickles for $1,250. At the same time Abraham Lydecker—step son of Elizabeth and half brother to Cornelius—bought a tract of 89 acres in Nyack for $4,000.

As in the Quaspeck, Ramapo, and Crom patents so in the case of the Kakiat, controversy arose as to its boundaries. We have followed the settlement with the Quaspeck owners, it remains now to trace the line between the Kakiat and Cheesecocks patents. By an act of the Colonial Legislature, passed May 29th, 1769, a commission composed of George Duncan Ludlow, William Nicolls, Benjamin Kissam, Samuel Jones, and Thomas Hicks, was chosen by a committee from each patent to settle the controversy, and they determined; "that the boundaries between the two patents should begin at the middle of a stream of water, commonly called Minnies Falls, from the easternmost extent of the two patents, and running up the stream to where two streams are coming along, one along the north and the other along the south side of Cheesecocks, commonly called Cheesecocks mountain, unite and form the stream called Minnies Falls. And from there along the middle of the stream, which comes along the south side of the mountain, till a line north 3 deg. 30 min. W. strikes a certain white wood tree, on the northwest side of the stream near the south east part of the mountain and on the north side, and at the edge of a large rock, partly in the stream and partly on the north bank, and from this tree a line S. 86 degs. 30 min. W. to a certain heap of stones erected by us for the northwest corner of Kakiat patent, and from the heap of stones a line S. 3 degs. 30 min east, to a certain white oak tree with a heap of stones now commonly called John Wood's tree, which line runs over a mountain called the Round Hill and crosses a large rock called the Horse Stable Rock, lying on the mountain on the south side thereof, and from John Wood's tree a line run by John Alsop, in the year 1723, S. S. E. to a certain stream called Pascack."

The Cheesecocks patent was surveyed and laid out in lots by Charles Clinton in 1738-39. A tier of nine lots, butting on the west line of the Crom patent and Bradley 106 acres grant, was first laid out. No. 1, being furthest to the north. West of these another tier of eight lots was surveyed, No. 10 being the southernmost and No. 17 touching on the North West Line. The remainder of the track was laid out into seven vast mountain lots, No. 1, being bounded on the east by the North West Line.

On Lot 9, of the first tier, the Rockland Print Works now stand. On Lot 7, is the "Treason House." Of the great mountain lots, Lord Sterling owned 14,000 acres, in Lots 1 and 2 which he mortgaged to William Livingston in 1767, and in 1789, they were assigned to Samuel Brewster.

Brewster sold 967 acres to Christopher Ming in 1793, who established the Cedar Pond Iron Works. Ming sold the land, forges and iron works to Halstead Coe in 1793; and he sold them to John De La Montagne in 1796.

The Stony Point tract, patented by William Jamison and Richard Bradley, was transferred as follows: Jamison transferred his share to Bradley, and Bradley, in 1742, sold 300 acres at the north end of the tract to Abraham Betts, and the remainder, supposed to be 750 acres, to Harrick Lent. Lent died, leaving his share to his son Hercules, who dying, bequeathed it to his daughters, Rachel, wife of James Lamb, and Catherine, wife of Hendrick De Ronde. On the death of De Ronde and wife the property was left to their seven children, and much of it still remains in the possession of their descendants.

Rachel Lamb, *nee* Lent, left her share of the original Stony Point tract to her children—Rachel, wife of John Crom; Elizabeth, wife of John Waldron; Catharine, wife of Jacob Waldron, and Hannah, wife of John Armstrong. The tract thus inherited by the daughters of Rachel Lamb was divided—except Stony Point proper—and after many transfers at length came into the possession of the present owners: the House of the Good Shepherd, Calvin Tomkins, and the Tomkins Cove Lime Company. Stony Point proper, after remaining undivided for a long time, was at last purchased by the Brewsters. The United States Government bought part of it in 1826, and the remainder was later purchased by Daniel Tomkins.

Of the tracts lying in Rockland County that were patented to Bradley's children, that directly west of the Stony Point grant was sold to James Johnson, by him to Theodorus Snedeker, and, after other transfers, it was divided into two parts, the western becoming the property of Noah Mott, and the eastern of the Tomkins. In this tract is the Back-berg, called by the Indians, Skoonnenoghky. The second tract was also sold to James Johnson, who sold it to Theodorus Snedeker. Snedeker's property was confiscated during the Revolution, as we will see more fully later, and this tract was sold by Simeon De Witt, Surveyor General, to Samuel Brewster in 1790.

Turning to the Ramapo patents, I find that in 1775 Provost sold his entire patent to Robert Morris, John De Lancey, and John Zabriskie for £200; and that in 1776 John Zabriskie sold his third part to Morris and

De Lancey for £200. In like manner the patents of Harris, Muller, and Spence came into the hands of these two men, from whom, therefore, all valid titles of land covered by the patents just described arise. By far the largest purchaser of lands from this company was John Suffern.

"It will be seen," says Mr. Cobb in his History of Ramapo, "that there still remains a portion of this so-called vacant section of our town, whose history has not yet been given. The tract of which we speak lies in the extreme west and northwest of the town For its history we recite a portion of an act passed by the Legislature of New York, March 28, 1800.

'Whereas, John Hathorn, Peter Townsend, Wm. Hause, Hezekiah Mead, Saml. Drew, Ezra Sanford, Jas. McCann, Wm. Booth, Daniel Benedict, Abner Patterson, Wm. Ellis, David Sanford, Thos. Sanford, David Hawkins, Samuel Ketchum, Henry Wisner, Henry Bush, Saml. Bush, Abraham Smith, Jno. Smith, Adolphus Shuart, Nicolas Conklin, Jno. Becraft and Jno. Jenkins, by their petition presented to the Legislature, have stated that they are settled on and have improved in Orange county (which at the time the petition was made included Rockland) under the Proprietors of the Patent of Waywayanda, which lands have been adjudged to be unpatented and to belong to the people of the State, and are included with other lands not settled on or improved as aforesaid, within the following boundaries, to wit:

'Southwesterly by the State of N. J.; northerly by a line (the Gore Line) running from the 31st mile stone in the line of division between this State and the State of N. J., to a monument erected by Commissioners at the N. W. Corner of a Tract of land granted to Daniel Honon and Michael Hawdon, called Kakiate, and easterly and southerly by patented lands. And by their said petition have prayed that they may be quieted in their said possessions, and to purchase in addition thereto such other quantity of vacant land within the boundaries aforesaid, and on such terms as the Legislature shall direct.

Therefore be it enacted by the people of the State of New York, Represented in Senate and Assembly, that it shall and may be lawful for the Surveyor General to grant to each of the Petitioners above named all the estate, right, title and interest of the people of this State of, in and to the lands improved by them respectively, with such other vacant lands within the said boundaries of not less than 100 acres and not more than 400 including their respective improvements, they paying therefore not less than the sum of 25c. per acre.'

From this it will appear that the first title of lands located in the northwest and extreme west of the town came from grants from the State to different individuals, which grants were made in the first years of the present century."

In 1724, John Van Blarcum purchased 400 acres of the Indians, in Ramapo Clove. This later passed into the hands of Isaac Van Duser, and he sold it to Samuel Sidman. At the death of Sidman, the west portion of the Van Blarcum tract came into the possession of his son-in-law John Smith; and the east, into that of John and Joseph Brown. Both of these tracts were bought by John Suffern in 1789, who completed his title by obtaining new deeds from Robert Morris and John De Lancey, into whose hands the property had come through their purchase of the Muller and Spence patents.

The Orangetown was one of the very few patents, within the limits of our present County, which was bought with the idea of a permanent settlement, and most, if not all of the purchasers, moved onto their new possessions and begun the founding of homes. Never, perhaps, did enterprise start with more enthusiasm and terminate with less result. It was the plan of those, who obtained that grant, to build a city which should eclipse all rivals in the Colony save its neighbor, New York. Nor, if we take the same view as did those settlers, will this project seem absurd. The wonderful agricultural resources of the Hudson Valley and the rapidity with which they were to be developed, were not foreseen at that time; what was realized was, the enormous profit to be obtained from trade with the Indians in furs, and surely no better location could be chosen for that purpose than Tappan.

From it to the north, west and south, stretched a country still filled with game. It was convenient to the local Indians, and what would be more natural than that its fame as a trading post should spread to the more remote tribes in the western mountains, and draw to it their dusky hunters laden with the spoils of the chase. As an outlet, it had the slote or creek, now known as Sparkill, which, after many a sinuous turn through the scene of De Vries' failure, at length emptied into the broad Hudson, at the mouth of which lay New York; and the flat-bottomed, broad bowed vessels of that day could navigate that creek well into the Orangetown grant.

Following out their idea, the settlers had a part of their patent mapped out and divided into small lots. Each holder of property in the patent was expected to buy and improve one or more of these, and the project started with great promise. Further than a start it never advanced, and to this day there is not, on all the original Orangetown grant, a place of sufficient size to amount to more than a country hamlet.

But, while the project fell short of the intention of its originators, partly because of the rapid settlement of the Hudson and Mohawk Valleys, partly because of the difficulty regarding the boundary line between New Jersey and New York, it was by no means in vain. From it sprung the settlement of a vast section, the present Orange and Rockland counties, now containing over a hundred and sixteen thousand people (116,245, census 1880), which in manufacturing, agricultural and mineral wealth is exceeded by no other provincial section of the State. From it, when these counties were divided, the southernmost and most populous township of our County took its name; and from its settlers arose many of those family names still the oldest and most respected in our midst.

I have thought that it might be a matter of great interest to speak of the origin of Dutch family names, a subject which has always filled the historian with dread and caused genealogists awful confusion. On this topic I shall quote extracts from a letter on the subject written by Hon. Henry C. Murphy while U. S. Minister at the Hague.

The first system of bestowing names adopted in Holland, " was the patronymic, as it is called, by which a child took, besides his own baptismal name, that of his father, with the addition of *zoon* or *sen*, meaning son. To illustrate this: if a child were baptized Hendrick and the baptismal name of his father were Jan, the child would be called Hendrick Jansen. His son, if baptized Tunis, would be called Tunis Hendricksen; the son of the latter might be William, and would have the name of William Tunissen. And so we might have the succeeding generations called successively Garret Williamsen, Marten Garretsen, and so on, through the whole of the calendar of Christian names, or, as more frequently happened, there be repetition in the second, third, or fourth generation, of the name of the first; and thus, as these names were common to the whole people, there were in every community different lineages of identically the same name. This custom, which had prevailed in Holland for centuries, was in full vogue at the time of the settlement of New Netherland. In writing the termination *sen* it was frequently contracted into *se* or *z*, or *s*.

The inconvenience of this practice, the confusion to which it gave rise, and the difficulty of tracing families, led ultimately to its abandonment both in Holland and in our own country. In doing so the patronymic which the person originating the name bore was adopted as the surname. Most of the family names thus formed and existing amongst us may be said to be of American origin, as they were first fixed in America, though the same names were adopted by others in Holland. Hence we have the names of such families of Dutch descent amongst us as Jansen (anglice,

Johnson) Cornelisen, Williamsen or Williamson, Clasen, Simonsen or Simonson, Tysen (son of Mathias) Lambertsen or Lambertson, Paulisen, Remsen (son of Rembrandt, which was shortened into Rem), Ryersen, Martense and others." "Another mode of nomenclature, intended to obviate the difficulty of an identity of names for the time being, but which rendered the confusion worse confounded for the future genealogist, was to add to the patronymic name the occupation or some other personal characteristic of the individual. But the same addition was not transmitted to the son; and thus the son of Hendrick Jansen Coster (sexton) might be called Tunis Hendrickson Browwer (brewer), and his grandson might be William Tunissen Bleecker (bleacher). Upon the abandonment of the old system of names, this practice went with it; but it often happened that while one brother took the father's patronymic as a family name, another took that of his occupation or personal designation. Thus originated such families as Bleecker, Schoonmaker, Snediker (which should be Snediger), Hegeman, Hofman, Bleekman, and Tieman."

Applying the observations of Mr. Murphy to our County, we find the first purchaser of land in Nyack, Claus Jansen (Nicholas Johnson) had a son Cornelius, who took the name of Cornelius Clausen, and his two sons, John and Henry, took their surnames from their business, that of coopers, and became John and Henry Cuyper, Kuyper, or Cooper. In regard to a surname being obtained by some personal characteristic, we have Harmanus Dows, not infrequently called Dowse Harmanse, whose son became Tunis Dows, and his son, the grandson of Harmanus Dows, from his great stature, was known as Tunis Dows Tallman, and thus created that family name. The Blauvelt family on entering the County bore the different names of Abram Gerritse, Johannes Gerritse, Harman Hendricksen, Gerret Huybertsen, and Joseph Hendricksen Blauvelt; a most excellent illustration of the confusion of this means of nomenclature.

"A third practice," continues Mr. Murphy, "evidently designed like that referred to, to obviate the confusions of the first, was to append the name of the place where the person resided—not often of a large city, but of a particular, limited locality, and frequently of a particular farm or natural object. This custom is denoted in all family names which have the prefix of *Van, Vander, Ver* (which is the contraction of Vander), and *Ten*, meaning respectively *of, of the,* and *at the*. From towns in Holland we have the families of Van Cleef, Van Wyck, Van Schaack; from Utrecht, Van Winkel; from Zeeland, Van Duyne. Sometimes the Van has been dropped, as in the name of Westervelt, of Drenthe and Wessels, in Guelderland. The prefixes of *Vander* or *Ver* and Ten were adopted when the name was derived from a particular spot; thus: Vanderveer (of the ferry), Vanderbilt (of the bilt—*i. e.*, certain elevations of ground in Guelderland and New Utrecht); Verhultz (of the holly), Ten Eyck (at the oak), Tenbrock (at the marsh). There are a few names derived from relative situations to a place; thus, Voorhees is simply *before* or in front of *Hess*, a town in Guelderland, and Onderdonk is *below Donk*, which is in Brabant. There are a few names more arbitrary—Bogaert (or hard), Blauvelt (blue field), Hooghland (highland), Dorland (arid land), Hasbrook (hare's marsh). Some names are disguised in a Latin dress. The practice prevailed, at the time of the immigration to our country, of changing the names of those who had gone through the university and received a degree, from plain Dutch to sonorous Roman. The names of all our earliest ministers are thus attired. Evert Willemse Bogaert became Everardus Bogardus, and that of Jan Doris Polheem became Johannes Theodorus Polhemius."

Of the older families in the County, the De Clarkes, Blauvelts, Smiths, Harings and De Groots, date back to the purchasers of the Orangetown patent in 1686. The Onderdonks first settled on Long Island, and descendants from that family bought 320 acres of land in 1736 on the present shore road from Piermont to Nyack for £350; other descendants from the same family settled at the present Spring Valley. The Snedeker family came into the County by the purchase by Tunis Snedeker, of Hempstead, L. I., of part of the Quaspeck Patent in 1729. The Cole family in this section was originated by Jacob Kool, who settled near Tappan about 1695. The Suffern family originated from John Suffern, who emigrated from Antrim, Ireland, and settled in the village that bears his family name in 1763. This family is noted for the number of offices which members of it have held. John Suffern was County Judge of Orange Co., from 1789 till 1792, and first County Judge of Rockland Co., from 1798 till 1806. His son, Edward Suffern, after being District Attorney from 1818 till 1820, was raised to the Bench and held the office of County Judge from 1820 till 1847. Andrew E. Suffern, grandson of the first and son of the second Judge of that name, was District Attorney from 1853 till 1859, and County Judge from 1859 till his death in 1880. Other members of the family held the following offices: Edward Suffern, Assemblyman in 1826 and 1835, John I. Suffern, Assemblyman in 1854 and James Suffern in 1867, and 1869. Edward Suffern was School Commissioner from 1859 to 1862 and Thomas W. Suffern from 1880 to the present time.

Other families whose progenitors settled in the County previous to the opening of this century, and who still bear the first settler's names, are the Allison's, of Haverstraw, who purchased the De Harte patent, the De Noyelles, who date from the same period, the Croms, whose ancestor took out a patent for Haverstraw, north of the creek, in 1685. The Thiells, Ver Valens, De Bauns, Secors, the Brewsters, the Waldrons, who by purchase and marriage obtained large possessions in Stony Point; the Youmans, Polhemus, Remsens, Ryders, Hoffmans, whose ancesters settled on the Quaspeck tract; the De Rondes, whose progenitor became interested in the County through marriage; the Swartwouts, who purchased property that had been sequestrated from Tories; the Conklins, De Bauns, Sickles, Campbells, Lydeckers, who purchased in the Kakiat patent, and the Snedens, Nagels, Lawrances, Gesners, Perrys and Mabies, of Rockland and Tappan; the Sarvents, Palmers, Williamsons, Cornelisons, De Pews and Greens, of Nyack; the Barmores, Storms, Demarests, Van Houtens, Smiths, Bogarts, Eckersons, Felters, of the Hackensack Valley; the Woods, Weiants, Roses, of Stony Point and Haverstraw; and the Sloats, Springsteels, Piersons, Van Blarcoms, Gurnees, Snyders, Johnstons, Tenures, Martines, Bensons, Wannamakers, Stephens, Posts, Forshees, Pyes, Van Ostrand and House families.

Authorities referred to. The Histories of the towns of Ramapo, E. B. Cobb, Haverstraw, A. S. Freeman, Stony Point, E. Gay, Jr. Deeds, wills and other old papers; Session Laws, S. N. Y. Stiles' History of Kings County. I am indebted to E. E. Conklin, for papers and maps relating to Rockland Lake.

CHAPTER IV.

ORGANIZATION OF ORANGE COUNTY INCLUDING THE PRESENT ROCKLAND —PHYSICAL CONDITION OF THE COUNTY AT THE TIME OF ERECTION— FRAUDULENT ELECTION RETURNS FROM IT.—THE FIRST COUNTY OFFICERS—ESTABLISHMENT OF COURTS—EARLY CENSUS RETURNS— ORGANIZATION OF THE FIRST CHURCH SOCIETY—EARLY SUPERVISORS RECORDS—BUILDING OF THE FIRST CHURCH EDIFICES AT TAPPAN— CLARKSTOWN AND KAKIAT—PUNISHMENTS INFLICTED ON MALEFACTORS - ESTABLISHMENT OF CHURCH SOCIETIES NORTH OF THE MOUNTAINS—OPENING OF HIGHWAYS—ERECTION OF COUNTY BUILDINGS NORTH OF THE MOUNTAINS—THE ESTABLISHMENT OF INNS—THE BEGINNING OF THE CONTROVERSY WITH GREAT BRITAIN.

On November 1st, 1683, under the administration of Thomas Dongan, the Province of New York was divided into counties for reasons best set forth in the following preamble and act: "Having taken into consideracon the necessity of divideing the Province into respective Countyes for the better governing and setling Courts in the same, Bee It Enacted by the Governour Councell and Representatives and by the authority of the same That the said Province bee divided into twelve Countyes." After naming and defining the bounds of these in their order, the act continues: "the County of Orange to begin from the Limitts or bounds of East and West Jersey on the West Side of Hudson's River along the said River to the Murderers Creeke or bounds of the County of Ulster and Westward into the Woods as farr as Delaware River."

Each of the counties thus created was given the name either of a home shire, title, or member of the royal family that then occupied the English throne, and the loyal government of the Province, little foreseeing the events of the next five years, gave to this section the hereditary title of James the Seconds Son-in-law.

The County at the time of its erection was a howling wilderness with scarcely a single settler located within its territory. Nor, as we have already seen when speaking of the patentees, was its early growth rapid. By 1693 the total population amounted to about twenty families and it was a ward of the Province. In the Militia returns for that year it was annexed to the city and county of New York, and held no civil existence for a brief period. Yet in that brief period the county was used as a means of fraud.

The Governor wished an Assembly devoted to his purposes and to obtain a majority of the members friendly toward him; the Sheriff of New York returned four members as elected by the popular franchise of Orange and New York Counties without an inhabitant of the former county having had a vote. Later the new Governor—Bellomont—deposed the Sheriff from office for this and similar acts.

Only a short time elapsed however when Lord Bellomont, having formed a new Council and appointed new Sheriffs ordered the election of another Assembly, and for the first time, in 1702, a representative—Peter Hearing, was elected in Orange as her peoples' choice. The Sheriff at that time was Tunis Tallman, who, a year later, incurred the anger of Lord Cornbury, on account of his ignorance, and drew from that Governor a long letter to the Lords of Trade in which, speaking of his inability to obtain a census from the sheriffs, he says: "and when they come to sign their letters it is said 'the mark of Theunis Talmane Esquire High Sheriff of the County of Orange.'" Cornbury removed Tallman from office and appointed John Perry in his stead.

In the same year in which the induction of Perry to the Shrievalty—took place, 1702, there was enacted on March 8th, an ordinance creating a Court of Sessions and Pleas for Orange County and on April 5, 1703, this act was signed by Queen Anne. The first Judges, appointed by Lord Cornbury and his Council, March 8, 1702, were William and John Merrit and they held the office till 1727. At the same time, March 8, 1702, Derick Storm and William Huddleston were appointed County Clerks, an office they held till 1721.

We have already seen that the settlement of Orange County began within the boundaries of the present Rockland. To the north of the Orangetown patent stretched the primeval wilderness. The few inhabitants on the patent clustered about the embryo city of Tappan and at Tappan the first county buildings were erected, the first sessions of the court held, and from its residents the first county officers selected.

It was not over a large population that the jurisdiction of the court or the authority of its officers extended. From the twenty familes of 1693, the increase had been slow. In 1698, there was a total of 119 people, composed of 29 men, 31 women, 40 children and 19 negroes. By 1702, the population had increased to 268 souls; and by 1710 to 439 people.

A litigious spirit was never a marked attribute in the Dutch character, and in the loneliness and need of mutual aid caused by their isolation in their new home the settlers grew into a close communism. One of their first acts on entering the land had been to form a church organization, which they accomplished in October 1694, and religion as well as friendship prevented many appeals to the law. Yet, while agreeing among themselves, these Dutchmen did not always extend their charity toward immigrants of a different nationality and language, and mutual jealousies produced by these factors oftentimes caused friction. Remembering this will explain the following entry in the Court Records of Orange County bearing date October 29, 1705, 8th Session of the Court: "Upon ye presentment of Coonradt Hansen, that George Jewell kept a dog which was injurious to many of the neighbors, it was ordered that the said Jewell should hang the said dog." This is the first record of capital punishment in the County.

On March 29th, 1723, occur the first records kept by the Supervisors. From them we learn that the average expense of the whole district was but £50 per year, and the greater part of this sum was expended in premiums for wolf heads. In 1724 the following motion was passed: "Att a meeting of ye Supervisors at Orangetown the thirtieth day of October, In ye Eleventh year of the Reigne of King George: Anno Domini 1724. Voted that John Meyer Do produce his book wherein he has Entered the paying and receiving money of the said County of Orange, and other proceedings and Minutes therein entered and contained, Immediately to us the Supervisors aforesaid, and that Gerhardus Clowes whom we have appointed Clerk for us Do enter and Translate the said Treasurer's book into English for our better understanding, and Satisfaction of the said County."

At a later period, in 1730, Cornelius Smith for the precinct of Tappan, Cornelius Kuyper for the precinct of Haverstraw, and John Gale for the precinct of Goshen, Supervisors—we find that the Board had difficulty in compelling the collectors to pay their receipts into the hands of the treasurer. For this reason it empowered Cornelius Cooper, Jr., to employ a lawyer and have writs issued for every collector that shall neglect, refuse or delay in the payment of his collections. At the same meeting it was ordered that the assessors for each precinct should appraise every negro at £5, every wagon load of produce at 10 shillings, every horse, mare or cow at 10 shillings, and every will at £5. Then the Board adjourned to meet Oct. 6th, 1731, at the house of William Ellison in Haverstraw.

Faithful guardians of the public trust were these County officials. In 1738 Cornelius Kuyper rendered his bill for service as a Member of Assembly, fixing his time at 118 days. In auditing this bill the Board held that: "It appearing to us that he (Kuyper) was absent from the house 24 days of the 118 days, and thinking it unreasonable to pay him for Sundays, have also deducted 13 Sundays, so remains due to him 85 days with an allowance of four days for travelling, being for two meetings at 6 shillings per day." With equal care did they watch each other, as the following entry will show: "To Gabriel Ludlow for two certificates, and he not being at home, he could not produce them, but thinks they contain about 35 days; the Supervisors think proper to allow him 25 days, till the certificates appear to us."

Yet, while careful of the public purse, the Supervisors seem not to have deprived themselves of the good things of life. Among the items for 1729 is one, "To Gabriel Ludlow for one gallon rum and a pound of sugar for ye Supervisors, 4 sh." And in 1730 another, "To Gabriel Ludlow for vittling and drink for the Supervisors, 18 shillings and 3 pence."

In 1727, the population of the County having reached over twelve hundred, more demand was made on the public buildings and an Assembly act was passed "to repair the County House and amend and enlarge the jail and prison." Before this period—in 1716—the congregation of the first church had grown strong enough to build a house for worship. This stood on the site of the present church edifice in Tappan and on the present common in front of the sacred building were the county buildings. Surely the rash infractor of law must have been conscience hardened to brave both the power of Heaven and earth. From his place of imprisonment, while awaiting trial, the malefactor could hear his eternal fate decreed from the pulpit, where the Reverend Frederic Muzelius in terse Dutch sentences pointed out the wrath to come; and in a short time Jeremiah Carriff, the trusty Sheriff of the county since 1706, would lead him for human judgment before Judge Cornelius Haring or John McEvers who had just been appointed to the Bench.

The punishments inflicted in those days read strangely now. In 1736 we find in the records of the Supervisors these items: "To Adrian Strought for whipping a man and conveying him away £2." "To Adolph Lent for conveying a Negro Wench out of the County by order of the justices, 7 shillings." In 1741 the records contain the following: "To Dolph Lent for transporting of vagabonds, £1-9-6." "To George Coleman for transporting of a vagabond man and watching him one night, and making a coat for said man by order of ye Justices, £1-19; also for transporting a vagabond woman and six other vagabonds, 7 shillings." "To Jas. Fleet for warning out two vagabonds by order of ye justices, 2 shillings." In 1755 are the following items: "For transporting one vagabond woman and three children, £2-7; Jacob Woodendyke to transporting a vagrant man six miles over the North River, 11 shillings 9 pence," and, ominous entry, "To Thomas Maybe to erecting and building of the stocks for Orangetown, £1." In 1768 the records show the following: "To

John Stevens for his transporting a poor person out of the County, £1." "To Henry Wesner, Wm. Thompson and Richard Edsell for whipping and transporting John Alexander, £1-2, and for whipping and transporting James Williams, £1-2." Among the charges for 1774 are several for whipping and transporting different persons. Finally we read among those old yellow leaves these charges against Haverstraw in 1785: "To Samuel Hutchkins for transporting three vagrant persons to New Jersey, £2-12-6; for transporting Richard Davis, his wife and four children, £1-16; and for transporting Hannah Stanton and four children, 15 shillings."

Steadily the increase of population in this territory continued and the soil was slowly cleared and cultivated on both sides of the ridge of mountains that divided the County into two sections. By 1737, the churches of Magaghamack, Minnisink, Walpeck, and Smithfield were organized and were all under the ministration of the Reverend Johannes Casparus Fryenmoet, a God serving, holy man; but the greater part of the increase was still in the section south of the mountains and the county buildings remained in Orangetown. In 1736 an Assembly act was passed, authorizing the building of a new jail at Tappan. Between that date and 1740 the court house was destroyed by fire, and a census, taken in the last mentioned year, showed a population for Orange County of some three thousand people, more equally distributed on both sides of the mountain than they had yet been.

The formation of Church organizations and the erection of public buildings would indicate an advancing spread of civilization, yet he would be deluded who regarded that struggling advance in the amenities of life as in any respect approaching the refinement of to-day.

The Dutch colonists had left a home where religion and law were dominant powers. Upon their clergy they looked with an awe of his sacerdotal office, with respect for his intellectual powers; and they obeyed him as a temporal as well as spiritual adviser. Almost their first proceeding, therefore, was to build a house dedicated to that Divine Power, whose Name they had been taught to lisp on the sea-washed shores of their old home thousands of miles away, and in whose care they now, in their loneliness and danger, more than ever felt themselves; where at stated intervals His messenger could meet them and strengthen their faith and revive their failing courage.

The creation of counties was before their settlement, and was accomplished by the Provincial Government at New York. The establishment of the machinery of the law, and the erection of buildings for the exercise of that machinery, were acquiesced in by the first settlers; not because they were rendered imperative by the quarrelsomeness of the inhabitants, but because they were a part of a civilization Dutchmen had long been accustomed to.

But between the hamlets where the houses of Eternal and earthly justice stood, and the settlers' rude homes, there was nothing pointing toward a reclamation of the savage wilderness, save here and there a clearing filled with stumps and unfenced, which rather tended to depress the mind by showing the magnitude of the work to be done, than to encourage it. Through the almost unbroken forests roamed savage beasts, which ceased their pursuit of wild prey when they could with greater ease feast on the settlers' domestic animals, and which filled the nights with their savage barkings or long, mournful cries. The mountains contained bears, which, oftentimes starved into boldness, would invade the colonists' cattle sheds and drag off a calf or colt; while wolves were so numerous and destructive that a bounty of 10 shillings was paid for every wolf's head, and the expense for their slaughter alone, in 1730, amounted to almost £15. Among the records of the Supervisors in those early days is one awarding a bounty of £2 to Joseph Manning for killing one full-grown panther. Nor was it from these wild animals alone that danger came, for where fear of wild beasts was least, as in the more compact settlements at Tappan and Goshen, the unfenced farms permitted invasions of herds of swine, which were turned out in the spring of the year to find their own support till autumn, and which too often ceased their roamings after the acorns and nuts of the forest, to trespass and feed upon the growing corn in the clearings.

The first vehicles, which passed through this trackless wilderness bearing the settler's goods, were driven through any opening which appeared in the direction toward which the immigrant was trending. The little travel which that immigrant had to perform, for the first few years after locating, was made on horseback or on foot. As the settlements grew more numerous and stronger, and as the land was cultivated further and further from the navigable waters and nearest hamlets, the demands of social or business life called for better paths. Passage ways from settlements to the nearest church, to the nearest mill, to the most convenient outlets on the river; were made by each body of settlers for their own ease. Sometimes a deer path through the woods became the line of a new road; sometimes the trail which the Indian had made from his village to that of his neighbors in days gone bye; and not infrequently those domestic animals—the cows—laid out a future highway by their daily journeys to and from the nearest good pasturing place.

Among the lines of travel thus laid out were some destined to become of great importance. From Paulus' Hook, through the English Neighborhood came a road, that pursued a tortuous course, always avoiding difficulties of construction and lying between the uplands of the Palisades and the marshy ground bordering on the Hackensack. It entered this County at Tappan, passed through the present Orangeburgh as the Clausland Road, swept along the western base of the Nyack hills, over Casper Hill by the old hotel at one time kept by John Storms, entered the present road from Nyack to Haverstraw near Valley Cottage, continued to and through Haverstraw, turned back through Doodletown, and at last passed from the present County, close to Forts Clinton and Montgomery, to continue its course through West Point, Newburgh, Esopus, Catskill, on to Albany. Later this route became and is still known as the Kings Highway.

In the early days of the County, this was the only line of travel used by the settlers in their land journeys to the city and to the county seat at Tappan. As the settlements along the Delaware grew, however, a nearer way had to be found. Those very settlements hastened the departure of savage man and savage beast from the Ramapo Clove, and soon these western residents were making their journeys to Tappan through this ever beautiful mountain gorge. The necessities of travel in the course of time demanded a better highway than the foretime narrow horse path, and a road was at length cut through which afterward became and still is known as the Orange Turnpike.

For the improvement of these first roads, Legislative acts were passed as early as 1730, and from that time till our own day, at nearly every session, some bill relating to public travel by highway has been enacted.

It has been said that by 1740, the population of Orange County had reached three thousand, pretty evenly distributed north and south of the mountains; this increase in the northern section led to reiterated complaints by those there resident, at the long and difficult journey they were compelled to make when attending court. It was because of these just complaints that in 1738, the Provincial Assembly passed an act "to enable the Justices of the Peace in that part of Orange County being to the northward of the Highlands to build a court house and goal for the said County at Goshen," and that in 1740 Lieutenant Governor George Clarke recommended and the Assembly passed another act "for raising in the south part of Orange County a sum not exceeding one hundred pounds for finishing and completing the court house and gaol in Orange Town."

"This," wrote Governor Clarke to the Lords of Trade, "is very necessary this county having a ridge of mountains running through the middle of it made it very inconvenient for those who live on one side of the hills to travel constantly on the other side, the courts being formerly held only in one place, but now there is a court house on each side and the courts are held alternately at them."

At this period a third was added to the County Judiciary and the list now contained the names of Abraham Harring, Cornelius Cuyper and Thomas Gaster. Theodorus Snedeker, who had been appointed in 1739, was Sheriff, and Vincent Matthews was County Clerk, an office he held from 1726 to 1763.

Orange County was unique in having double court houses, jails and sessions. The cause we have seen to be the physical conformation of its territory and the effect we shall yet see was to divide the section south of the mountains into a separate county.

In the previous chapter we have noted how this County grew in population by the purchase of lands, after the speculative era had ceased, by permanent settlers. Those who bought from the north moiety of the Kakiat patent formed a little hamlet, which they named after the Long Island town they had left, New Hempstead, a name which was later applied to the present township of Ramapo. In Haverstraw, settlers were erecting homes along the river front from the Long Clove to Donderberg. Just north of the little stream that runs down by the Short Clove, on the property now owned by Felix McCabe, Major E. W. Kiers had bought an acre of ground and built a dock in that village. This dock became the means of outlet for the produce from New Hempstead or Kakiat, and a road was cut through from that community to Haverstraw, entering the latter place by the Long Clove. Mills, both grist and saw, had been built where the water power and public demand warranted them, at Haverstraw, Nyack, Tappan Slote, Greenbush, and in Clarkstown; and roadways, that had been cut from the nearest highway to these mills, were sometimes further extended till they joined another highway.

The organization of the Tappan Church had been followed, in 1750, by the building of one in Clarkstown for the benefit of dwellers at Haverstraw and on the Quaspeck and Kakiat grants, and this, four years later, was followed by the organization of the English Church at Kakiat or Hempstead, for the benefit of the residents in that section, as well as the Scots then settling near Scotland Hill, who wished to hear religious service in the English tongue.

The introduction of saw-mills permitted a change in the construction of houses, and allowed the settler, now that the experiment of colonization was a success, to replace his foretime thatch-roofed log house by a structure of shingle or board sides, or a solid edifice of stone, stayed with firm timbers and covered with shingles.

On the long line of the Kings Highway, numerous inns were opened for the accommodation of travellers who journeyed by it. Of those in this County, one, still standing as the "'76 House," was at Tappan; one at the top of Casper Hill, now owned by John Storms, was kept by a Mr. Tenure, and one kept by John Coe was at Kakiat, on the road which had been cut through from Kings Ferry to the highway through Sidman's or the Ramapo Pass. Besides these hostelries, there were taverns or ferry houses at Sneden's Landing for Dobbs Ferry, kept by Captain Corbet, and at Stony Point for Kings Ferry.

The inn at Tappantown deserves more than a passing notice because of its use as a prison for Major John Andre during his last days. It was the first tavern in the territory of the present Orange and Rockland counties south of Newburgh, and is standing on a lot of the Van Vorst share of the original patent. In 1753 it was purchased by Casparus Mabie from Cornelius Meyers, and was kept by him for many years. In the New York Gazette for Feb. 26, 1776, it is advertised as follows: "To be sold at private sale, that noted house and lot where Casparus Mabie formerly lived, at Tappan, two miles from the North River and twenty-four from Hobuck Ferry. It is a convenient stone building, four rooms on a floor. There is likewise, on said place, a good barn, garden and sundry other conveniences. Whoever inclines to purchase may apply to Mrs. Elizabeth Herring on the premises, Mr. Cornelius C. Roosevelt at New York, or to Dr. G. Stowe in Morris County." Mabie sold the "'76 House" to Frederick Blauvelt and he to Philip Dubey in 1800, who still kept it as late as 1818. After Dubey's death the house was kept by Henry Gesner, Henry Storms, Thomas Wandle, Lawrence T. Sneden and Henry Ryerson. In 1857 it was purchased by Dr. J. T. Stephens.

It was an era of peace and plenty. The French war, that for a time had drawn New England into action, was too remote for the residents of this section to be involved. For the prosecution of that war New York, as well as the other Provinces, had been taxed, and some of the participants in it were sons of Orange who held commissions in the English army; but the interest in the conflict was transient among the Dutchmen, who were so numerous in the County. Not so was it in the polemical discussion that had been raging for some time in their church and had caused grave difficulties between pastor and people and between foretime friends.

The business of life was checked, social amenities were suspended, and brotherly love was replaced by anger and hatred in the quarrel. At last, after years of turmoil, the long controversy was ended, and the people prepared to resume their foretime quiet. Then, suddenly and mysteriously, there began to spread abroad whispers of a change in the actions of the home government toward her American colonies.

Just how or when these rumors started, no one knew. Perhaps some farmer returning from "York" had stopped at Mabie's tavern to rest and refresh himself and horse, and, while waiting, had told the host and few guests that were there of the excitement in the city, concerning the new acts being passed in England for the purpose of increasing her income from the Colonies. Perhaps some peripatetic "Yankee" trader or peddler, on his way from the East to the Indian stations on the Delaware and Susquehanna, had spoken of the matter at the Kings Ferry landing, as he paused for a drink of peach brandy or Metheglin—liquors not obtainable in his native colony—and becoming excited by the subject, as these nervous descendants of the Puritans were wont to do, had lashed himself into a fury and astonished his Dutch listeners by the violence of his emotion.

If the manner of the rumor's start was unknown, the substance spread. At the different inns, at the few blacksmith shops, at the mills, the settlers paused for a moment after the completion of their business to talk on the topic, and from these different foci the news was carried home to be discussed at the fireside. The Dutch mind was slow to act, and, having reached a conclusion, slow to change. Long and earnest were the arguments during the winter evenings of 1773-74, as to the right of Great Britain to impose a tax on the colonists without their representation or consent. At first the subject was one of talk only. The new impost, being in the form of customs duties, produced little immediate effect in an agricultural county whose people had few outside wants. If there was trouble in the Eastern colonies, doubtless it was due to the unrestful spirit of that people, who were always in a ferment and not content unless turning things upside down; and in "York City" there were now, as there ever had been, certain persons who delighted in confusion and combat.

Thus the sturdy farmers of this section reasoned and would fain banish the matter from their minds. But it could not thus be banished.

The rumors, indefinite and few at first, increased in number and took form. Boston was in an uproar; New York held the Sons of Liberty; Virginia contained a government and—a people. Thick grew the murk of the approaching struggle and its gloom, o'ershadowing this County, added bewilderment to the nascent thought of rebellion. The settlers in

Orange had slowly grasped the idea that England was attempting to perpetrate a wrong. Puzzled by the swift changing phases of the subject, their conservative dispositions led them to avoid either faction, to withdraw from active participation in open revolt and to follow out the subject only so far as they comprehended it. This plan caused them to enter a protest to the home government at a meeting held in Yoast Mabie's house on July 4th, 1774, which read as follows:

"1st. That we are and ever wish to be, true and loyal subjects to His Majesty, George the Third, King of Great Britain.

2nd. That we are most cordially disposed to support His Majesty and defend his crown and dignity in every constitutional measure, as far as lies in our power.

3rd. That however well disposed we are toward His Majesty, we cannot see the late Acts of Parliament, imposing duties upon us and the Act for shutting up the Port of Boston, without declaring our abhorence of measures so unconstitutional and big with destruction.

4th. That we are in duty bound to use every just and lawful measure to obtain a repeal of acts not only destructive to us, but which, of course, must distress thousands in the mother country.

5th. That it is our unanimous opinion that the stopping of all exportation and importation to and from Great Britain and the West Indies would be the most effectual methods to obtain a speedy repeal.

6th. That it is our most ardent wish to see concord and harmony restored to England and her Colonies.

7th. That the following gentlemen, to wit: Colonel Abraham Lent, John Haring, Esq., Mr. Thomas Outwater, Mr. Gardner Jones, and Peter T. Haring be a committee from this town to correspond with the city of New York, and to conclude and agree upon such measures as they shall judge necessary in order to obtain a repeal of said acts."

Two months later, when, in September 1774, delegates were to be elected to a Continental Congress, the people of this County had so little determined on their next step, had so little decided how to instruct a representative, that not over two score votes were cast.

But it was already too late for resolutions to check the progress of events. Before another year had passed Virginia's people were forever separated from the old government; New York was under the control of Sears and his fellow patriots; and from Massachusetts, as if borne by the blast, had come the news of Lexington. It was no longer a matter for waiting, the hour for action was come.

Awakened to the importance of the issue at last, the inhabitants of the

County met on the 17th of April, 1775, at Mabie's, to take into consideration the subject of their representation at the Provincial Convention, which was to meet in New York three days later, for the purpose of sending delegates to the Continental Congress. At this meeting John Haring was chosen from Orangetown and Col. A. Hawkes Hay from Haverstraw.

Three months passed, when, on July 17th, 1775, another meeting took place in this County for action on the "General Association adopted by freemen, freeholders and inhabitants of the city and county of New York on April 29th, 1775, and transmitted for signing to all the counties of the Province."

Petitions are permissible even in despotisms. Calm, firm remonstrances can never be construed into anarchy. A demand for the right to be heard is not revolt. Believing that they had been wronged most unjustly, our people had resorted to petition—to remonstrance, and had demanded the right to a hearing, and their efforts were vain. So far could they go with impunity. But the junction of two future courses was reached. By one road they threw themselves upon the mercy and clemency of a master; they renounced the right of individualism, of independence; they became, clothe it with whatever sophistries you please, call it by any name you like, cover it with all the paraphernalia and glittering generalities of diplomatic art—they became slaves.

By the other road, they entered upon revolt against a government, which regarded "rebellion as treason and rebellion persisted in as death." The confiscation of property, the ravages of a merciless conqueror, the horrors of incarceration and the dangers of exasperated military courts, stood along this route. There was no middle course. The end which was attained by our ancestors was not aimed for till long after the wave of war had swept back and forth across the Colonies. The hope of wresting national autonomy from Great Britain, when the people of Orange County were called upon to accept or reject the test of the General Association, had not been conceived, much less born. Let us, then, in reading the oath, remember these facts and judge fairly, and, with a knowledge of the end, let me premise sufficiently to state that some who signed the test proved traitors, that some who refused to sign it were patriots, and that both parties who adhered to their actions were influenced by an idea.

"Persuaded that the salvation of the rights and liberties of America depends, under God, on the firm union of its inhabitants in a vigorous prosecution of the measures necessary for its safety, and convinced of the necessity of preventing the anarchy and confusion which attend the dissolution of the powers of the government, we, the freemen, freeholders, and inhabitants of Orangetown, being greatly alarmed at the avowed design of the Ministry to raise a revenue in America, and shocked by the bloody scenes now acting in the Massachusetts Bay, do, in the most solemn manner, resolve never to become slaves; and do associate under all the ties of religion, honor, and love to our country, to adopt and endeavor to carry into execution whatever measures may be recommended by the Continental Congress, or resolved upon by our Provincial Convention, for the purpose of preserving our Constitution, and opposing the execution of the several arbitrary and oppressive acts of the British Parliament until a reconciliation between Great Britain and America, on constitutional principles (which we most ardently desire), can be obtained; and that we will in all things follow the advice of our general committee respecting the purposes aforesaid, the preservation of peace and good order, and the safety of individuals and private property."

Daniel Lawrence,	Spedwell Jacklin,	Abraham Tallman, Jr.
David Aljea,	Nathaniel Lawrence,	Peter Ketan,
Albert Aljea,	Abraham Post,	Daniel Onderdonk,
David Lawrence,	Conrad Gravenstine,	Jacob Conklin,
Edward Briggs,	Abraham Mabie, Jr.	John Westervelt,
Garret Blauvelt,	Jacob Wilfer,	William Bell, Jr.,
Kasparius Conklin,	Michael Cornelison,	John Vanhouten,
Adrean Onderdonk,	Jacobus De Clark,	Abraham Mabie,
John Rycher,,	William Martin,	Harman Tallman,
Avery Campbell,	Daniel Voorhees,	Garret Ackerson,
Ram Boll,	Abraham Onderdonk,	Jacob Ackerson,
Abraham Conklin,	Jonas Torrell,	Harman Tallman, Jr.
James Jacklin,	John Gissnar, Jr.	

Another party, while refusing to sign the pledge given above, did sign the following: "That we would not countenance rebellion, nor have any hand in a riot, but stand for King, Country and liberty, agreeable to the charter, but at the same time disallowing taxation in any wise contrary to the charter, and shall never consent to taxation without being fully represented with our consent."

Isaac Sherwood,	Derick Straws,	Anthony Crouter,
Cornelius De Gray,	Guysbert F. Camp,	Jacob Waldron,
Alberd Smith,	John Smith,	Thunis Crom,
Cornelius Smith,	John Darlington,	Peter Bush,
Garit Smith,	Johannes Bell,	Arthur Johnston,
Daniel Gerow,	John Van Horn,	David D. Ackerman,
Cornelius Benson,	R. Quackenboss,	Benjamin Secor,
John Palmer,	Auri Blauvelt,	Cornelius Smith,
John Cox,	John Rureback,	Johannes Forshee,
Harmanus Kiselar,	Abraham De Baum,	Reynard House, Jr.
Peter Forshee,	Thunis Emmut,	

In Haverstraw Precinct the test of the Association was signed as follows:

Robert Burns,	Henry Brower,	James Lanu,
Joseph Knapp,	Thomas Eckerson,	Samuel Knapp,
David Pye,	Adrian Onderdonk,	John Suffern,
John Coleman,	John Smith,	Abraham Reynolds,
John Coe,	Harmanus Blauvelt,	Abr'm Stephensen,
Robert Johnson,	John Ackerson,	John Springsteel,
Auri Smith,	Alexander Mannell,	Joseph Jones, Jr.,

Walter Smith,
John Lent,
Jacob Polhemus,
Cornelius Paulding,
Abraham Ackerson,
Thunis Snedeker,
Dowe Tallman.
John Wallace,
Nathaniel Barmore,
Thomas Morall,
David Hoofman,
Garret Cole,
Nathaniel Towenson,
Thomas Allison,
Henry Hallsted,
Harmanus Hoofman,
Harmanus Felter,
Johannes Demarest,
James Hannan,
Thomas Dolphen,
William Bell,
Abraham Polhemus,
Peter Snyder,
Abraham Blauvelt,
Edward Cane,
Rem Remsen,
Matthew Coe,
Peter Salter,
Stephen Stephenson,
Thunis Tallman,
Andrew Onderdonk,
William Stringham,
Garret Paulding,
Thunis Remsen,
James Thene,
Jacob Archer,
Joseph Seamonds,
John Toten,
John Toten, Jr.
Robert Ackerly,
Richard Osborn,
Thomas Dickings,
William Deronde,
John Dunscombe,
Abel Knapp,
Jerod Knapp,
Jobair Knapp,
Alexander Gilfon,
Thomas Gilfon,
Thomas Kingen,
Andrew Onderdonk,
Johannes J. Blauvelt,
Johannes Vanderbilt,

Rulef Stephenson,
John Van Dolsen,
Andrew Van Orden,
Derick Van Houten
Edward Ackerman,
Carpenter Kelly,
Jacob Jirekie,
John Martine,
Thomas Kelly,
Garret Onderdonk,
Rulef Onderdonk,
James Onderdonk,
Jacob Onderdonk,
Albard Onderdonk,
Henry Onderdonk,
Abraham Onderdonk,
Mauhel Tenure,
Johannes Defrees,
Jeremiah Martine,
Powlas Seamonds,
John Voorhis,
Jost Voorhis,
Stephen Voorhis,
Edward Jones,
Johannes Cole,
Jacob Coles,
E. W. Kesse,
Jacob Kenifen,
John Hill,
Amos Hutchins,
Peter Kiselar,
Patten Jackson,
Joseph Allison,
Benjamin Allison.
John Allison,
Peter Allison,
Robert Allison,
Adam Brady,
John Johnson,
William Concklin,
Joseph Concklin,
Michael Concklin,
Abraham Concklin,
Abraham Garrison,
Claus Van Houten,
Chas. R. Van Houten,
Garrit Van Houten,
Roosevelt Van Houten,
P. Van Houten, Sr.
Peter Van Houten,
Thunis Van Houten,
Rulef Van Houten,
Harmanus Trumper,

Powlas Vandervoort,
Nathaniel Odle, Jr.
John Graham,
John Jersey,
Siba Banta.
John Noblet,
Abraham De Puy,
John Thew,
A. Hawkes Hay
Daniel Morall,
Gilbard Crumm,
Peter Crum,
William Crum,
John Parker,
Robert Wood,
William Wood.
Henry Wood,
James Carmelt,
Moses C. Charter,
Benjamin Knapp,
John Ackerman,
Jacob Derunde,
Abraham Derunde,
Gilbart Hunt,
Joseph Hunt,
Reuben Hunt,
John De Grote,
Thomas Goldtrap,
John Cummings,
Benjamin Holstead,
John Stogg,
"Mud Hole" Tenure,
John Slott,
William Trunoper,
Johannes De Gray,
John Mead,
John Vandervoort,
John Hetcock,
Henry Mackrel,
Jonnas Dele,
Aurt Remsen,
Theodorus Polhemus,
Johannes Polhemus,
Jobais Derunde,
Timothy Halstead,
Daniel Parker,
James Shirley,
Abraham Mayers,
John Mayers,
Jacobus Mayers,
Johannes Meyer,
James Wilson,
Simond Trump,

Thomas Blauvelt,
Isaac Blauvelt,
Andrew Cole,
Isaac Manuel,
John Clark,
Johannes Blauvelt,
Johnathan Lounsberry,
Powlas Hopper,
Peter Salter,
Joseph Wood, Jr.
Harmanus Tallman,
James Paul,
Jeremiah Williamson,
Jacob Meyers,
Thunis Remsen,
Derick Vanderbilt,
Isaac Dutcher,
John Felter,
William Felter,
Johannes Remsen,
Theunis Tallman,
Abraham Tallman,
Ebenezer Wood,
John Ferrand,
Garret Meyers,
Abraham Thew,
James Sharp,
Theodorus Snedeker,
James Kelly,
John Brush,
Garret Van Cleft,
Aurt Polhemus,
Jacobus De Clark,
George Remsen,
Luke Stephenson,
Jobair Lauery,
Cobar DeClark,
Daniel DeClark,
Johannes Jenwie,
Samuel Wilson,
Henry Tenure, Sr.
Jacob Tenure,
Leonard Bayle,
Thomas Jacks,
Thomas Wilson,
Gilbert Fowler,
Peter Easterly,
Abraham Stag, Jr.
Jacob Seacor,
Isaac Seacor,
Jonah Wood,
Aurt Amorman,
Thomas Osborn,

Garit Snedeker,
Johnas Snedeker,
Daniel Cocklate,
Stephen Beane,
William Slatt,
Elis Secor,
James Secor,
David Secor,
John Secor,
Peter De Pue,
William Dozenberry,
Jonah Halstead,
John Halstead,
Johnathan Taylor,
Benjamin Jones,
Peter Reed,
James Stewart,
Thunis De Clark,
Joseph De Clark,
James Smith,
Stephen Smith,
William Smith,
Cornelius Smith,
Lambert Smith,
Peter Smith,
Daniel Smith,
John Smith,
Auri Smith,
Daniel Ward,
Jacob Jones,
Theunis Cuyper,
Gilbard Cuyper,
Cornelius Cooper,
Wilvart-Cooper,
Albard Cooper,
Jacob Cooper,
John Cuyper,
John Cuiper, Jr.
John W. Cogg,
Gabriel Fargyson,
Benjamin Coe,
John J. Coe,
Daniel Coe,
Daniel Coe, Jr.,
Samuel Coe,
Powlas Vandervoort,
Samuel Sidman,
Joseph Jones, Jr.,
Joseph Jones,
John Harper,
Garrit Ackerson,
Gilbert Wilson,
Samuel Youmans,

James Christe,
James Stagg,
Abraham Springsteel,
Francis Cline,
Joseph Palmer,
Henry Houser,
Fred. Uric,
Patrick Gurnee,
Stephen Girnee,
Francis Gurnee,
Francis Girnee, Jr.,
Isaac Girnee,
Isaac Girnee, Jr.,
Francis Girnee,
Paul Ruttan,
Harmanus Snyder,
Abraham Snyder,
Henry Snyder, Sr.,
Henry Snyder, Jr.,
Grasham Huff,
William Crum,
Edward Holstead,
Jacob Jones,
William Hause,
Hendrick Polhemus,
Thunis H. Tallema,
John D. Tallman,
David Sherwood,
Samuel Hunt,
John Jeffries,
Thomas Dinard,
John Burges,
John Hogencamp,
Richard Springsteel,
Hendrick Stephens,
William Stephens,
Benjamin Benson,
John Persall, Jr.,
Paul Persall,
James Rumsey,
Salvanus Mott,
Charles Mott,
Markel Mott,
Thomas Tillt,
H. Trumper, Jr.,
Joseph Johnston,
William Rider,
Jacob Mall,
Andrew Abrames,
M. Vandervoort,
David Babcock,
William Snyder,
Reynan Gerow,

Isaac Cole,
Reynard Hopper,
Abraham Brower,
Abraham Koll,
Daniel Van Sickels,
Albard Stephenson,
Petris Blauvelt,
Jacobus Van Orden,
Daniel Martine,

William Youman, Jr.,
Ezekiel Youmans,
Benjamin Furman,
John Parker, Jr.,
Jacob Parker,
Isaac Parker,
Paul Vandervoort,
John Gardner,
George Johnston,

John Lorillard,
John G. Lorald,
Jacob Bartholomew,
David Halstead,
Ezekiel Ward,
William Kempe,
Rev. Robert Burns,
Philip Sarvent,
Adrian Sarvent,

The following is the list of those in Orangetown who refused to sign the General Association:

Matthew Steel,
Jacob C. Ackerson,
Johannes Perry,
Dennis Sneeding,

Robert Sneeding,
Jessy Sneeding,
George Man,
Rahl Bogard,

Isaac G. Blauvelt,
Gesebert R. Bogardt,
Jacob Gessenar,

And in the Precinct of Haverstraw:

Roger Osburn,
Benjamin Osburn,
Richard Osburn,
James R. Osburn,
John R. Osburn,
Nathaniel Osburn,
James Babcock,
William Babcock,
Abraham Babcock,
Nathaniel Oddle,
Tompkins Oddle,
Gilbert Johnston,
Guyshert Johnston,
John G. Johnston,
Abraham Johnston,
Lawrence Johnston,
Lodowick Shumaker,
William Winter,
Andris Pallass,
Jonas Loderick,
Ezekiel Ferguson,
Raynard House, Sr.
William Dobbs,
A. Montgomery,
Matthew Ellison,
John Pollan,
John Johnston,
William Babcock,
Abraham Babcock,
John Springsteel,
Thomas Ackerman,
Benjamin Ackerson,
Jacob Ackerson,
Derick Ackerson,
Thomas Ackerson,

David Ackerson,
Abraham Concklin,
Lewis Concklin,
Lewis Concklin, Jr.
John Concklin,
Joseph Concklin,
Ezekiel Conkling,
S. Heyman,
Frederick Post,
Isaac Post,
Abraham Post,
John Post,
Joseph Heston,
Joseph Knapp,
Henry Holsted,
Henry Holsted, Sr.
Thomas Smith,
Isaac Conklin,
William Concklin,
Nicholas Concklin,
L. Van Buskirk,
Jacobus Van Buskirk,
Henry Wanamaker,
Peter Wanamaker,
Peter Frederick,
Samuel Banta,
Johannes Rush,
Haulberg Bucker,
John George,
Samuel Matthews,
Jost Short,
John Weaver,
Coon Fridrick,
Andrew Haldrom,
Peter Jersey,

Moses Van Nostrant,
G. Van Nostrant,
Daniel D. Clark,
John Rider,
Joseph Rider,
John Town,
John Armstrong,
Henry Warden,
John Secor, Jr.
John Secor,
Samuel Secor.
Isaac J. Secor,
Peter Stephens,
Henry Arsler,
Claus Corlosh,
Adam Deter,
John Dobbs,
Peter Vandervoort,
Jacob Sarvant,
Henry Sarvent,
Philip Sarvent,
John Sarvent,
Isaac Berea,
Jacob Tenick,
Henry Tenyck,
Henry Tenyck, Jr.
Samuel Bird,
James Lamb, Sr.
Cornelius Crum,
John Crum,
Jost Buskirk,
Jacob Waldron,
Edward Waldron,
Andrie Bellis.

The reader will remember that the Haverstraw Precinct embraced the present towns of Ramapo, Clarkstown, Stony Point and Haverstraw in 1775.

"Do, in the most solemn manner, resolve never to become slaves; and do associate under all the ties of religion, honor, and love to our country." Thus reads a section of the oath of patriotism.

The inhabitants of America in those days were eminently religious. No business however slight, no decision however trivial, no act however small its import, was undertaken without a consultation with Divine Power. Mad as the acts of the Sons of Liberty appear on superficial examination, a closer observation will find in them neither the fierce fanaticism of the Roundheads nor the thirst for blood of the French Revolutionists.

The leaders, in the commencing struggle for our freedom, were strong men; the actors were clear headed even in the excitement of contest. All were God-fearing. That there was thoughtlessness in speech it would be absurd to deny—profane ejaculations, dreadful threats—that there was thoughtlessness in deed is untrue.

Remembering this, the import of the clause above repeated from the test oath becomes clear. It was composed in solemn thought, with solemn prayer, and sent forth from the Provincial Committee for signature with a perfect knowledge that each signer would think earnestly of its meaning ere affixing his name. The members of the Provincial Committee knew the character of their constituents and the influence of the clergy in each district. Had the members of the English Cabinet been equally well informed, they would have made pause ere too late.

At a later period I am to speak fully of the influence that the early Dutch dominies exerted in this Colony, and of the reasons for that influence; it is but necessary to say that the trust their parishioners felt in them in all matters is beyond our comprehension. The intellectual advance of the past century has, in great measure, destroyed that authority and has raised nothing in its place.

Samuel Ver Bryck, ordained to the charge in 1750, was the dominie of the greater part of Rockland's people in the trying days that led up to the Revolution and the more trying days during its existence. He realized the trust imposed upon him and watchfully did he observe the discussion, earnestly did he gather from every source full information on the subject, that he might truly and fully carry out that trust.

At the different churches under his charge; at those half social, half religious gatherings in the houses of his prominent church members; in his ministerial visits to his congregation, we can conceive of his clear exposition of the controversy in its stage at the time of his speaking. We can almost hear his earnest exhortation to those true-hearted Dutchmen to be firm in their trust of liberty—an exhortation so potent in its effect as to draw from the British commander this, for him despairing, for us glorious, cry: "I can do nothing with this Dutch population, I can neither buy them with money, nor conquer them with force"—and feel his fervent prayers to the Almighty, that the cup of the horror of war might pass from their lips.

Events hastened toward the end. The conflict by speech passed to violence in acts and the blood shed at Lexington, proclaimed the wager of battle. Then followed the seige and evacuation of Boston, the defeat at Long Island, the battles preceding, and retreat to New Jersey; and this County was in the midst of the strife.

True to the cause he had adopted, true to his charge, the good dominie preached now in favor of a war that could no longer be avoided by true men, and urged his congregation on to battle. Still earnestly went up his prayers but now for victory to the cause of the colonists and safety for their lives.

Ah, Dominie Ver Bryck, the end is not yet! You shall preach sermons against English oppression, emphasized by the presence of some of your flock, killed on the field of battle. You shall yet be called upon to offer up prayers over soldier's graves and to comfort stricken households. The tramp of armed men, the roar of conflict, shall sound loud and horribly clear through the quiet valleys where so often you have ridden on your ministerial calls, meditating only of battle with the spiritual enemy. At the very door of your church, in the ruins of the old court house, the man of war shall build his cantonment, while the house of God itself shall be used as a prison and a court room and the decision there rendered shall make house and hamlet known while time shall be. Yet you shall live to encourage, to comfort, to condole through all these coming weary years, and, when peace has been won, to close your eyes on earthly strife, hailing within a few months your victory over tyrany and over death.

Authorities referred to. Documents relating to the Colonial History S. N. Y. Eager's History of Orange County. Magazine American History. History of Ramapo, by Rev. E. B. Cobb. History of Haverstraw, by Rev. Dr. A. S. Freeman. Papers in City and County by R. H. Fenton. Archives of Rockland County Historical Society. The New York Civil List.

CHAPTER V.

THE REVOLUTION OF CIVIL GOVERNMENT.

SYNOPSIS OF THE IDEAS WHICH LED THE COLONISTS TO REVOLT—A GENERAL CONGRESS CALLED FOR—IT CONVENES—ELECTION OF DELEGATES FROM THIS STATE—ORGANIZATION OF THE SONS OF LIBERTY IN NEW YORK—ORGANIZATION OF THE COMMITTEE OF CORRESPONDENCE AND SAFETY IN ORANGE COUNTY—ITS DUTIES DURING THE REVOLUTION—ELECTION OF DELEGATES TO A PROVINCIAL CONGRESS—ORGANIZATION OF THE STATE GOVERNMENT AND ADOPTION OF THE CONSTITUTION—SYNOPSIS OF THE FIRST CONSTITUTION—FIRST ELECTION OF STATE OFFICERS—RECAPITULATION OF THE REVOLUTION IN CIVIL GOVERNMENT—CIVIL LIST OF OUR COUNTY TILL THE FORMATION OF A FEDERATION.

Force may destroy a government, mind is necessary for its creation. A combination of force and mind had been the result of every social upheaval, which preceded our Revolution; and that combination had ever ended in a more despotic rule than that which the revolting peoples had thrown off. Was history to repeat itself on this western continent?

Nearly a century and a quarter had passed since the struggle of the Roundheads had ended in the destruction of royal power and the creation of a commonwealth. Yet the tests of government by popular assembly in 1651 and 1653, had been found a failure; Parliament had been prorogued at the point of the bayonet; and Oliver Cromwell, supported and sustained by his iron batalion, ruled as absolute under the title of Protector as any of his predecessors had under the title of King. Surely precedent was not encouraging to the American Colonists.

Nor had government by the people in any sense advanced since Richard Cromwell, weakly sinking into Lethe, rendered the Restoration possible. A so called popular House of Commons even at the time of which we are speaking existed, and its members, influenced by the tie of party; the ability of Burke, Fox and Pitt; or the bribes so lavishly bestowed by the Ministry; cast their votes for one or another measure. But he has illy read history, who would pretend for a moment, that those members were dependent for nomination or election on the free franchise of a free people, or that they were held responsible by their constituents as the members of Parliament are at the present day.

Fifteen years after the American Colonists had spontaneously formed a plan of self-government, which has waxed and developed into our Constitution of to-day. Six years after the Treaty of Paris gave this people a separate autonomy; an attempt at self-government was made by the French people. It is unnecessary to dwell on the result. The mad carnival of blood; the demoniac shouts for freedom by a people who had become a populace; the frenzied rule of anarchy were a startling exhibition of liberty passing on to license. Between the attempt at self-government of Cromwell's time and the attempt at self-government in 1789. A people on this continent accomplished self-government.

There is something very solemn in the death of a system of polity. There is something very wonderful in the birth of a new form of authority. All the experience, often gained at great expense; all the veneration developed through centuries of familiarity; all the respect, caused at first by force and fear, and afterward continued toward hoary decrepitude, is abruptly broken away from, and the enthusiasm and push of vigorous youth takes its place. Events, which in an old government were acted upon with ponderous deliberation and only after an exhausting search for precedents, are treated by the young power with startling abruptness. It creates precedents. It makes history. And yet it must ever be a sad contemplation to see the enthusiasm of a young government lead it into errors and blunders which more cool and careful deliberation would shun, and which the maturer judgment of age would avoid. The homely adage that "old heads cannot be put upon young shoulders" is as true of nations as of the children of men.

Yet while the English revolution had seemingly ended in complete failure, such was in fact not the case. The effect produced on the people of Great Britain was to teach them the fallibility of kings, their own power. The reaction which followed their momentary grasp of power left them for a time bewildered, and in the return of monarchy, they viewed the past upheaval as a hideous dream, as unreal as dreams ever are.

Not so, however, was the feeling in these colonies. In the midst of danger, privation, and suffering, the settlers had landed on these bleak, forbidding shores. Unaided, they had wrested homes from the gloomy wilderness, and had defended those homes against savage beasts and savage men. Without the help of royal favor, they had cleared farms, cultivated the soil, and raised crops for their sustenance. Without the assistance of skilled diplomats, they had formed treaties of peace and leagues with their Indian neighbors, or entered into unions with each other for mutual commercial advantage or for protection. Though acknowledging their dependence on the mother country by supporting her representatives, the different governors, these colonists gradually came to form their own town and county governments, and place their own representatives in authority; and, for their safety from absolute dominion, as well as a public means of intercourse between themselves and their governors, they selected the deputies that formed the colonial assemblies.

While this growth of government was a slow process in each colony, dependent for every fresh step on the increase of settlers and the wants of the communities, the spirit of independence had been strong from the first. The execution of Charles had caused no perturbation in the colonies. The accession of Cromwell to more than regal power produced no uneasiness. The Restoration created no commotion. While so little of the old belief in the divinity of kings remained in the northern colonies that the regicides were received and safely harbored. And why should these disturbances of royalty, three thousand miles away, cause excitement here? Had the king made it so pleasant for the Puritans at home that they should now grieve over the falling fortunes of his house? Men, who have pleasant surroundings, seldom leave them for the discomforts of a wilderness. Had the government afforded them such protection and safety for life and property in hours of trial and danger that they should revere that government? Men, who are carefully defended in their rights and possessions rarely go forth to battle with the vicissitudes and trials of a new settlement. No! From the beginning, persecution, bad faith and mismanagement had attended every interference of king or government with the affairs of the colonists, and they, now that the experiment was ended and their venture was assured of success, felt that the success had been attained not by the power of the throne, but by their efforts, their individual struggles, often despite regal intervention. The lesson which required a second revolution to teach to the inhabitants of the old world, was learned by personal experience in the new.

In this condition of strength and self-support were the inhabitants of the American Colonies when George, Lord Grenville, conceived the brilliant idea of imposing on these inhabitants a tax, expecting therewith to assist in paying the national debt.

Then began a turmoil such as the Colonists had never before witnessed, and such as would have made a minister with ordinary wit take pause. It was not the amount of the tax that stirred men's souls. What did the successful farmer of Orange County care for a penny or so of stamp duty. What impression would such a demand make on the wealth of a prosperous merchant in New York. It was the principle on which that tax was based. Humanity is so constituted, that it fails to recognize the advance of age. Till the physical infirmities of senility fall sorely upon men, they cannot realize that their work is ending and that another, younger, generation is pressing into their paths. But yesterday that young man, now so strong and self-confident was a boy to whom we never turned for advice, whom we put off with the idle fables and treated with the fondling tenderness which we use toward children. Now he refuses to be so set aside and demands the rights of his manhood respectfully but firmly. Astounded and with a mighty sense of outraged dignity we turn from the encounter, believing that an exhibition of our displeasure will be amply sufficient to cause at first meditation and then humble apology. But the next meeting only finds the young man firmer in his idea and more determined to explain his action. From this point men differ. Some gracefully submit and later fully acquiesce in the inevitable. Others attempt coercion and sooner or later come off worsted.

The Colonists protested against the imposition of a tax unless granted by their own consent through their own representatives. They attempted to explain to the parent country, the ground on which they based their actions; to show her how little she had done for them, how much they had done for her as well as themselves and thus to demonstrate the injustice of the Stamp Act.

Wise men in his own council chambers showed to the King the unrighteous nature of the proposition. Charles Townshend said of the Colonies that they were " children planted by our care, and nourished by our indulgence." " They planted by your care!"—exclaimed Barre— "No! your oppressions planted them in America; they fled from your tyranny to a then uncultivated wilderness, exposed to all the hardships to which human nature is liable! They nourished by your indulgence! —No! they grew by your neglect; your *care* of them was displayed in sending persons to govern them who were the deputies of deputies of ministers—men whose behavior, on many occasions, has caused the blood of those SONS OF LIBERTY to recoil within them; men who have been promoted to the highest seats of justice in a foreign country, in order to escape being brought to the bar of a court of justice in their own."

Yet, the respectful appeal for a hearing, was treated with scorn by a king, who expected the colonists to grovel at his feet, humbly suing for royal clemency; and the advice of his counselors fell on unheeding ears. The Stamp Act was repealed, but the right to impose taxation on the colonies was adhered to; and two years after the tax on stamps was removed, in 1767, a duty was placed on glass, paper, lead and painters' colors, not so much for the purpose of raising revenues as to express the right to lay impost.

I have said that the plan of self-government adopted by the colonists was of spontaneous growth. In hours of danger theretofore, representatives from each of the colonies had met together for consultation. By 1774, the need of concerted action seems to have been universally felt. On May 17th a general congress was recommended at a town meeting in Providence, R. I. May 21st a town meeting in Philadelphia, and on May 23d one in New York advised a consultation of delegates from each colony. May 27th the House of Burgesses in Williamsburgh, Va., and on May 31st a county meeting at Baltimore called for a general assembly and these were followed in the demand for a council of representatives, by a town meeting in Norwich, Conn., June 6th; a county meeting at Newark, N. J., on the same date; the Massachusetts Assembly and a town meeting in Boston on June 17th; a county meeting at Newcastle, Del., on June 29th; the Committee of Correspondence of Portsmouth, N. H., on July 6th; the General Province meeting at Charlestown, S. C., on July 8th, and a district meeting at Wilmington, N. C., on July 21st.

Pursuant to these demands, the delegates from the different colonies met and organized the Continental Congress, which began its sessions on September 5, 1774. In this Province all the active patriots combined in sending deputies to a Provincial Convention, which concurred in the nomination and election of Philip Livingston, John Jay, James Duane, John Alsop, Isaac Low, Henry Wisner of Orange County, and William Floyd of Suffolk. We have already seen that the people of this County were as yet so uncertain of their wishes, that but twenty votes were cast at the election; while the Colonial Assembly, either through loyalty or timidity, refrained from any action.

A wise man, a Talleyrand, would have hesitated at this juncture, would have temporized and conciliated, and would have withdrawn from the contest with credit to himself and honor to his nation. A weak man, a Bute, would have shrunk aghast from the storm he had raised, and resigned the reins of government. Lord North was neither wiser than Bute nor weaker than Grenville; he faced the impending conflict with the stubborn obstinacy of ignorance, and was sustained by a purblind king, who determined to coerce the young colonies into that respect for his royal functions which he regarded as due them.

"SONS OF LIBERTY," Barre had called those colonists who opposed the Stamp Act, and when his speech was read in America, those organizations which had grown out of the many conferences of the citizens on the questions at issue, adopted the name of Sons of Liberty as their designation. The residents of this County have often met together in the past, and may again assemble in the future, for the discussion of matters involving their welfare. In those conventions of the past, as in collections of people at present, the first proceeding of the gathering was to organize by the selection of a leader and assistants. This was all that occurred when the colonists denied and defied the authority of Great Britain, and dashed away the monarchial government.

The Sons of Liberty in New York city, taking the lead in the Revolution, advised the people of each county to meet and form committees of safety. Pursuant to that advice, the citizens of this County met, and after passing the resolutions given in the preceding chapter, selected Abraham Lent, John Haring, Thomas Outwater, Gardner Jones, and Peter T. Haring as a Committee of Correspondence and Safety. On the adoption by the Continental Congress of the articles of the American Association, the patriots in New York chose a Committee of Sixty to enforce the provisions of that act, and to exercise leadership in all political matters. At the recommendation of this Committee, the people of the various counties elected delegates for a Provincial Congress, which was to meet in New York on May 22d, 1775. The election in this County took place on April 17th, and resulted in the choice of:

John Coe,	Benjamin Tusteen,	Abraham Lent,	Israel Seely,
David Pye,	Peter Clowes,	John Haring,	Jesse Woodhull,
Michael Jackson,	William Allison,	Jeremiah Clarke.	

This Congress was in session from May 22nd, till July 8th; from July 26th, to September 2nd; and from October 4th, to November 4th, 1775. Meantime, the General Assembly of the Colony still held a nominal existence, but its last session was held on April 3rd, 1775, when it was adjourned to May 3rd, of the same year, from which time it was prorogued again and again till February 1st, 1776, when it passed from existence.

The members of the Committee of Safety in the present Rockland County at different periods during the war for Independence were:

John Coe,	John Coleman,	Johannes Vanderbilt,	James Kant,
John Smith,	Derck Vanderbilt,	Theodorus Polhemus,	David Pye,
		Johannes I. Blauvelt.	

The duties of these men were multifarious. The selection of officers for the local militia; the oversight of the election of delegates to the Provincial Congress; the general care of property and persons in their precincts; the prevention of treasonable correspondence with the enemy, and the preservation of the law. In the execution of these duties, the committee in this County was in constant communication, at first with the committee in New York City and later with the Provincial Congress. In no instance was complaint made against the justice of its acts by unbiased parties, and it stands in history as the connecting link between the royal government of the past and the constitutional government of the present.

On July 31, 1775, David Pye, notified the Provincial Congress, that Captain Robert Johnson had completed the enlistment of a company for the Continental Army and was ready for arms.

On Nov. 17th, 1775, the Orangetown Committee of Safety met at the house of John Van Dolsa, Jr., in Haverstraw Precinct, to join with the committee from Haverstraw in the selection of field officers. Disappointed by the non-appearance of the Haverstraw Committee, the deputation proceeded to select officers for their own township.

Local jealousy, the curse of every military and civil movement from the creation of the Continental Congress till the adoption of the Federal Constitution, obtained in this section in the early days of the Revolution, and at length grew so strong as to draw letters of complaint from David Pye and Major E. W. Kiers as early as Feb. 24, 1776.

In the second and third Provincial Congresses, from Nov. 14th, 1775, till June 30th, 1776, John Haring of this County was President *pro tem ;* A. Hawks Hay was appointed chairman of the committee for the apportionment of the different quotas of men and officers in the Colony ; Messrs. Allison and Pye were created a committee to inquire into the reasons why Capt. Blauvelt's company had not drafted its quota of men to reinforce the Continental Army ;* and John Haring was appointed a member of the committee to consider the resolutions passed by the Continental Congress.

The 4th Provincial Congress was to meet in New York City on July 8th, 1776, but before that date a British fleet appeared in the lower bay, and instead of New York, the Congress met at White Plains. The delegates from this, Orange County, elected to that Congress were:

| William Allison, | David Pye, | Isaac Sherwood, | Archibald Little, |
| John Haring, | Thomas Outwater, | Joshua H. Smith, | Jeremiah Clarke, |

At the moment the Congress met, it received intelligence of the adoption of the Declaration of Independence by the Continental Congress, a measure it approved by unanimous vote. On the second day of the session, July 10th, the name of the Assembly was changed from the " Provincial Congress of the Colony" to that of the " Convention of the Representatives of the State of New York," and its first act was to appoint a committee for the purpose of drafting a State Constitution. Thirteen members were placed on this committee, among whom was Henry Wisner of Orange County.

*See Page 78.

The changing scenes of war compelled the convention to migrate from place to place, and it held brief sessions at Harlem, King's Bridge, Yonkers, White Plains, Fishkill, and finally Kingston, where it continued in session from March 6th, till May 13th, 1777. At Kingston, the committee on the Constitution pursued its labors in peace and at last on March 12, 1777, reported the result of its work. The committee's draft was under consideration for more than a month, and was finally adopted April 20th. The first Constitution was printed at Fishkill, by Samuel Loudon, on the only patriot press in the State, and was the first book ever printed in the Commonwealth. Leaving the Constitution for a moment, let us look at local events.

While these greater deeds of statesmanship were being enacted by the Provincial Assembly, the Committee of Safety in this County was by no means idle. Busied at first in enlisting troops and selecting officers, it soon found occasion for active duty in watching the enemy and protecting the property of patriots from the depredations of the Tories. On July 29th, 1776, an order was issued from Clarkstown, notifying Dennis Snyden, Jesse Snyden, William Snyden and Samuel Snyden, not to run, nor employ any one to run, nor even to keep a boat as a ferry, and all people were warned to hold no communication with them as they were notoriously disloyal. At the same time the printer was directed to correct an error by which the name of John Snyder, a firm patriot, was given instead of that of Robert Snyden, as a pilot of the British ships in their voyages up the river.

Early in the struggle, Col. Allison had been ordered by the Provincial Congress to obtain all the saltpetre possible and have it manufactured into gunpowder, and later, Col. Benjamin Tusteen and Theunis Cuyper were directed to buy all the woolen cloth, linsey woolsey, blankets, woolen hose, mittens, coarse linen, felt hats and shoes obtainable, and to have the linen made up into sheets. For the perfection of this object the Assembly advanced £100 to each of the committee.

On November 9th, 1776, Joshua Hett Smith made a motion in the Convention that Thomas Outwater and others attend to their duties as deputies, or show cause on pain of punishment for contempt. Evidently this motion was adopted and a committee appointed to call the attention of the delinquents to its force, for on December 11th, Henry Wisner informed the Convention, that Messrs. Outwater and Sherwood declined to act as members of their body.

When the first Provincial Congress adjourned on July 8th, 1775, it left a Committee of Safety, composed of members from its body, to exercise the executive duties of the Colony. The existence of this committee ceased at Kingston, March 5, 1777. On May 3d, of the same year, a Council of Safety, composed of thirteen members, was appointed to administer the government of the State till a Governor could be elected and the Legislature meet. This committee exercised the power of government till September 10th, 1777, and again from October 8th, of that year, till January 7th, 1778, when it was superceded by a Legislative Convention, that was in session from that date till the assembling of the Legislature on January 28th, 1778.

It is now necessary to view briefly the State Constitution. According to its provisions, the elective franchise for Governor, Lieutenant Governor and Senators was granted to resident freeholders possessed of real estate of the value of £100 over and above all debts charged thereon. All male inhabitants, who had resided in the County for six months preceding the election and who owned real estate in the County valued at £20, or paid a yearly rent of forty shillings, and actually paid taxes, were entitled to vote for Members of Assembly. No discrimination was made against race or color, except that negroes were required to produce authenticated certificates of freemen. Elective officers were limited to the Governor, Lieutenant Governor, Senators, Assemblymen, Town Clerks, Supervisors, Assessors, Constables and Collectors. Loan officers, County Treasurers, and Clerks of Boards of Supervisors were to be appointed by the direction of the Legislature. One clause of this Constitution shows more clearly than anything ever written or spoken, the ignorance of the people concerning the completeness of the revolution they had accomplished. So long had they been accustomed to an executive who was irresponsible to them, who was an appointee of the crown, that they failed to realize that the ruler they had created was as much a creature of their making as the Assembly; that the executive as well as the legislative power was granted by their franchise.

Thus failing in the power of conception, the people confined the power of the Governor to the smallest possible limit, and extended the power of the Assembly. The Governor could not make an appointment, nor had he the sole power of nomination for appointment. This function was performed by a Council of Appointment chosen from the Senate, and in that Council the Governor was to have "a casting voice, but no other vote."

The new Constitution was immediately enforced and the election of officers under it begun. The result of that election was the choice of George Clinton for Governor. He took the oath of office at Kingston on

July 30th, 1777, but being in active command of the militia at the time, did not assume its duties till after the surrender of Burgoyne on October 17th; and Pierre Van Cortlandt for Lieutenant Governor. From the Middle Senatorial District, composed of Dutchess, Orange and Ulster Counties, six Senators were chosen, among whom was Henry Wisner of this County; and from Orange County four members of Assembly were elected, among whom were Theunis Cuyper and Roeloff Van Houten.

Among the officers appointed were County Judges John Haring, Thomas Cuyper, Elihu Marvin and John Wheeler; Isaac Nicoll was made Sheriff; Benjamin Tusteen, Jr., Surrogate, and Thomas Moffat, County Clerk.

Let me now briefly recapitulate the various steps in the progress of the revolution in the civil government in this State. By a spontaneous call from twelve of the colonies, a Continental Congress was determined on in 1774. For the nomination and election of deputies to that Congress, the Sons of Liberty in New York recommended the several counties in the Province to elect delegates to a Provincial Convention, to be held in New York city on April 20th, 1775. To this recommendation nine of the sixteen counties responded. The next step was the choosing by the patriots in New York city of a Committee of One Hundred as a Committee of Resistance, or a War Committee, and from the members composing it a Committee of Sixty was created for greater activity. At the suggestion of this Committee, each county elected a local Committee of Safety, to preserve law and order. At the further request of the Committee of One Hundred, each county proceeded to elect delegates to a Provincial Congress, which met first on May 22d, 1775—a little over a month before the General Assembly of the Colony adjourned never to meet again. The Provincial Congress selected a Committee of Safety from its body, to exercise the executive duties of the Province when the Congress was not in session, which remained in existence from July 8th, 1775, till March 6th, 1777. On the 3d of May, 1777, a Council of Safety was formed, from the members of the Congress, to exercise authority till a Governor was elected and the Legislature could meet, and existed till September 10th, 1777; and on the adjournment of the Legislature in October, a second Council of Safety was appointed, with the same powers as the first, which remained in control till the State Government was fully organized in January, 1778. Meantime, at the recommendation of the Continental Congress, the Provincial Congress had appointed a committee to draft a State Constitution in 1776, a work which was successfully completed and the result adopted on April 20th, 1777.

I have been thus prolix on the civil history of the Revolution, because it is by far the most important of the events of that or any subsequent time. The battle of Lexington and the siege of Boston were a resistance to a government. The battles preceding the adoption of State Constitutions were for the overthrow of a government. But governments had been overturned before and have been overturned since, only to eventually re-obtain power. The colonists' task was not only to demolish a form of government, but to erect a new form and a better one in its stead.

Carefully, thoughtfully, they set to the self-appointed task; maintained order in the midst of the license of war; continued steadfastly at the work, though often compelled to rapidly change the place of their sittings by reason of the proximity of the enemy, and at length produced a form of rule in which the people were absolute, in which self-government was the only power that could control the State. And at the very time of its adoption, the myrmidons of the government they had thrown off were preparing to invade this State in overwhelming numbers.

That in many respects that first Constitution, judged by the light of the experience we stand in, was crude and incorrect, cannot be gainsaid; and, doubtless, were its framers with us to-day, they would see the defects and vote for their change as readily as we. But the advance from king rule to self-rule was as absolute, as in the untried experiment, men could see.

As a vital factor in the demolition of the old, and the creation and erection of the new form of government, this County stands well to the fore. She was one of the nine that responded to the call for a Provincial Convention and a deputy from her was sent to the Continental Congress. She sent her delegates to every Provincial Congress that met; and from those delegates one was chosen a member of the committee that framed the new rules of government. We are to turn now and view her actions in another sphere—the struggle to render the new rules of government possible.

The members from Orange County to the General Assembly of the Colony, beginning with the Eighth Assembly in 1701, were:

EIGHTH ASSEMBLY.
August 19th, 1701, to May 3d, 1702.
Peter Haring.

NINTH AND TENTH ASSEMBLIES.
From October 20th, 1702, till May 5th, 1707.
Floris Crom.

ELEVENTH ASSEMBLY.
From August 18th, 1708, till January 5th, 1709.
Michael Hawdon.

TWELFTH ASSEMBLY.
From April 6th till November 12th, 1709.
Peter Haring.

THIRTEENTH AND FOURTEENTH ASSEMBLIES.
From September 1st, 1710, till March 3d, 1713.
Hendrick Ten Eyck.

FIFTEENTH AND SIXTEENTH ASSEMBLIES.
From May 27th, 1713, till August 11th, 1715.
Cornelius Haring.

SEVENTEENTH ASSEMBLY.
From June 5th, 1716, till August 10th, 1726.
Peter Haring. Cornelius Cuyper.

EIGHTEENTH AND NINETEENTH ASSEMBLIES.
From September 27th, 1726, till November 25th, 1727.
Lancaster Symes. Cornelius Haring.

TWENTIETH ASSEMBLY.
From July 23d, 1728, till May 3d, 1737.
Lancaster Symes. Cornelius Haring. Vincent Matthews.

TWENTY-FIRST ASSEMBLY.
From June 15th, 1737, till October 20th, 1738.
Vincent Matthews. Cornelius Cuyper.

TWENTY-SECOND AND TWENTY-THIRD ASSEMBLIES.
From March 27th, 1739, till May 14th, 1745.
Gabriel Ludlow. Thomas Gale.

TWENTY-FOURTH ASSEMBLY.
From June 25th, 1745, till November 25th, 1747.
Thomas Gale. Abraham Haring.

TWENTY-FIFTH ASSEMBLY.
From February 12th, 1748, till July 21st, 1750.
Thomas Gale. Theodorus Snedeker.

TWENTY-SIXTH AND TWENTY-SEVENTH ASSEMBLIES.
From July 24th, 1750, till December 17th, 1758.
Theodorus Snedeker. Samuel Gale, who died in 1757, then Vincent Matthews.

TWENTY-EIGHTH AND TWENTY-NINTH ASSEMBLIES.
From January 31st, 1759, till February 6th, 1768.
Abraham Haring. Henry Wisner.

THIRTIETH ASSEMBLY.
From October 27th, 1768, till January 2d, 1769.
Henry Wisner. Selah Strong.

Thirty-first Assembly.

From April 4th, 1769, till April 3d, 1775, and forever.

Samuel Gale.   John De Noyelles, who died and was succeeded by John Coe.

DEPUTIES TO PROVINCIAL CONGRESS.

First Congress.

From May 22d, 1775, till November 4th, 1775.

John Coe,	Peter Clowes,	Jeremiah Clarke,
David Pye,	William Allison,	Israel Seely,
Michael Jackson,	Abraham Lent,	Jesse Woodhull,
Benjamin Tusteen,	John Haring.	

Second Congress.

From November 14th, 1775, till May 13th, 1776.

John Haring, President *pro tem.*

Peter Clowes,	Jeremiah Clarke,	John Haring,
William Allison,	Theunis Cuyper,	A. Hawks Hay,

Third Congress.

From May 14th, till June 30th, 1776.

John Haring, President *pro tem.*

Henry Wisner,	Joshua H. Smith,	Peter Clowes,	David Pye,
William Allison,	Thomas Outwater,	Roeloff Van Houten,	John Haring.
Archibald Little,	Isaac Sherwood,		

Fourth Congress.

From July 9th, 1776, till May 13th, 1777.

William Allison,	David Pye,	Isaac Sherwood,	Archibald Little,
John Haring,	Thomas Outwater,	Joshua H. Smith,	Jeremiah Clarke.

STATE LEGISLATURE.

Council of Appointment.

John Haring, appointed July 22d, 1782.

First Session.

Senate.

Henry Wisner.

Assembly.

Jeremiah Clarke,	Theunis Cuyper,
John Hathorn,	Roeloff Van Houten.

Second Session.

Senate.

Henry Wisner.

Assembly.

Jeremiah Clarke,	John Coe,	Roeloff Van Houten,
Benjamin Coe,	Peter Ogilvie.	

Third Session.

Senate.

Henry Wisner.

ASSEMBLY.

John Coe,
John Hathorn,
Thomas Moffat,
Bezaleel Seely, Jr.

FOURTH SESSION.
SENATE.
Henry Wisner.

ASSEMBLY.
Jeremiah Clarke,
David Pye,
Bezaleel Seely, Jr.
John Stagg.

FIFTH SESSION.
SENATE.
John Haring, Henry Wisner.

ASSEMBLY.
Jeremiah Clarke, John Stagg,
John Hathorn, John Suffern.

SIXTH SESSION.
Ending March 23d, 1783.

SENATE.
William Allison, John Haring.

ASSEMBLY.
Jeremiah Clarke, John Hathorn,
Gilbert Cooper, John Stagg.

DELEGATES TO THE CONTINENTAL CONGRESS

September, 1774.
John Haring, Henry Wisner.

April 20th, 1775.
Henry Wisner.

March 19th, 1785.
John Haring.

March 29th, 1785.
John Haring.

February 27th, 1786.
John Haring.

January 26th, 1787.
John Haring.

Authorities referred to. "Field Book of the Revolution," Vols. II., B. J. Lossing. "Bryant's History United States," Vols. IV., S. H. Gay. "Force Papers." "The New York Civil List." "History of Orange County," S. W. Eager.

CHAPTER VI.

THE WAR OF THE REVOLUTION.

THE MILITIAMEN OF OUR COUNTY AT THE OUTBREAK OF THE WAR—INSUBORDINATION AMONG THEM—THE BUILDING OF FORT CLINTON—THE WATER FRONT VISITED BY THE ENEMY'S FLEET—RETREAT OF THE CONTINENTAL ARMY THROUGH THE COUNTY—THE FORAGES OF THE ENEMY IN OUR COUNTY AND THE PATRIOTIC STRUGGLE TO DEFEND IT—WASHINGTON ENCAMPS AT RAMAPO—FROM THENCE MARCHES TOWARD PHILADELPHIA—THE BATTLE OF FORT CLINTON—THE CONSTRUCTION OF THE WEST POINT CHAIN—MASSACRE AT OLD TAPPAN—CAPTURE OF STONY POINT BY THE BRITISH—ITS RECAPTURE BY GENERAL WAYNE—THE CONTINENTAL ARMY ENCAMPS AT TAPPAN—THE TREASON OF ARNOLD—TRIAL AND EXECUTION OF ANDRE—MARCH OF THE CONTINENTAL ARMY THROUGH THE COUNTY TO BESIEGE YORKTOWN.

Civil war tests men. In it there can be no wavering, no middle course, for wavering is equivalent to treason, and a refusal to assume the responsibility of supporting one or the other side betrays mental weakness or personal selfishness. Ideas, the grandest attributes of humanity, obtain full sway, and, supported by an idea, the partisan of one or the other faction will abandon all save the principle he seeks to make dominant. For a time passion eclipses reason and destroys all ties of love or friendship. Neighbors are separated by their differing views of a momentous subject of statesmanship, and family relations are abruptly severed. Humanity is so constituted, that when a discussion of national polity passes into a conflict for the supremacy of one or the other views, it makes a personal of a political matter, and, foretime friends becoming enemies, each contestant recalls the many kindnesses and favors he has rendered to his opponent, and grows to look upon that opponent not only as a traitor, who seeks the ruin of their common country, but also as an ungrateful wretch who has no thankfulness for past benefits. Hence, while combatants in battle may listen to appeals for mercy from an alien foe, and render the horrors of war as merciful as possible by sparing property and life, they regard with dulled ears the plea for quarter of their foretime neighbors, and witness the destruction of their possessions without pity.

Yet in every rebellion there will be found, within the revolting section, three classes of people, who, either from love of the existing form of government, motives of interest, or fear of war, oppose and harass in every possible manner the revolutionary armies. Our war for independence was no exception to this rule. Many people in these provinces loved and revered the government of Great Britain, regarded the uprising of the colonists against her as unfilial and outrageous, and either gave to the British their open aid by enlisting in the ranks, or more secretly by conveying to them information of the strength and resources of the Continental troops. This class found it advisable at the close of the war to follow their allies from our shores, and many, abandoning their worldly possessions, found new homes in England or her colonies.

Another class, uncertain as to which side would bear off the palm of victory, remained non-partisan, hoping by the assumption of neutrality to escape a confiscation of their property no matter what the result. The third class was composed of a mixed assembly of deserters and cowards, who abandoned their homes from fear of being pressed into service, and who, skulking along the outskirts of the armies, enriched themselves by the robbery of private property, the rifling of the dead upon the field of battle, or the betrayal alike of friend or foe for a few pieces of gold. Rockland County contained representatives from all these classes, and the history of that period is replete with accounts of the collisions and forays which occurred between them and the many patriots.

The militia of this, as of the other counties of the State, had long been organized under the command of the English Governor. At the last official inspection under the old *regime*, June 2, 1773, two regiments, three battalions, twenty-three companies composed the force of Orange County and this force was officered by two Colonels, three Lieut-Colonels, three Majors, twenty-three Captains, forty-six Lieutenants, and twenty-three Ensigns.

By no means did this force represent the patriot feeling in the County. Before the close of 1776, the Chairman of the Committee of Safety for the County—Daniel Coe—estimated the total strength of the militia as 280 men, most of them unarmed, one-third of whom were disloyal. The first duty of the Committee of Safety, as we have seen, was to organize a military force, for the purpose of guarding the County, on which they could depend. In Orangetown, Colonel Lent, long a commissioned officer in the militia, was given command of the troops, and in Haverstraw Colonel A. Hawks Hay organized a regiment. Lent's command was brief. On Dec. 22, 1775, he obtained his commission from the Provincial Congress, and on March 26, 1776, he resigned. This act was caused by the jealousy and insubordination of the rank and file under his command, a condition largely produced, doubtless, by the ignorance among the troops, not only of the discipline needed but even of the language in which the orders were given. The insubordination among the Orangetown troops at last reached so alarming a state, that Colonel Hays was ordered to place seven of the ringleaders of Captain Blauvelt's company under arrest and send them to the city of New York.*

The resignation of Lent resulted in the breaking up of the Orangetown regiment into separate companies of Minute men, who, under the lead of local officers, did good duty in defending our shores.

All the militia of both Ulster and Orange Counties were formed into a brigade commanded by General George Clinton. As Minute men, they were to assemble at the firing of two guns from Fort Montgomery, and two from Fort Lee, and these were to be answered by two at New Windsor. The capture and destruction of Forts Lee and Montgomery ended this signal, and the Minute men then depended on the beacon fires that blazed on the mountain tops. These beacons came into universal use through all the Colonies and flashed the news of the enemy's movement from peak to peak, rendering such helpful service to the sore-pressed patriots, that it seems a not inapt conceit to say, the American Colonists, like the sore tried people of Israel, were led out of bondage by a pillar of fire by night and a pillar of a cloud by day.

So far, the worthy settlers in this County had but heard rumors concerning the hostile movements in the east. The battles of Lexington and Bunker Hill had been fought, and Boston was under siege when, in the autumn of 1775, the construction of the first fortification on the present soil of Rockland County, Fort Clinton, was begun. This work, situated on the south bank of Peploaps † Kill, about one hundred and twenty feet above the river, was built of stones and earth and could contain a garrison of four hundred men. It was designed and commenced by Bernard Romans, and completed by Captain Thomas Machin. Immediately to the west and but a few paces from the fort, was Lake Sinipink, now known as Highland Lake, and from the lake to the steep river bluff, across the narrow road which led to the fort, were placed strong abatis. At the same period, the fort on Stony Point was determined on for the purpose, not only of supporting the forts higher up, but also, in conjunction with a proposed fort on Verplancks Point, to protect the ferry.

Ere these works were finished, Boston had been evacuated, and the scene of action was changed to New York. On June 29th, 1776, General Howe arrived at Sandy Hook with his troops and a large fleet; and on

* See Page 68.
† See note at end of Chapter.

July 12th, the ships of war Phœnix, 44 guns, and Rose, 21 guns, with four cutters, all protected by sand bags, sailed up the river past the American batteries, and came to anchor in the Tappan Zee.

This was the first time the residents of the County had looked upon a hostile armament, and, though unaccustomed to war, they opposed their enemy so firmly and with such vigilance as to frustrate his attempts to obtain fresh provisions and water or to convey arms to the Tories.

On August 27th, the battle of Long Island was fought, and, two days later, the long retreat of Washington began. New York was evacuated, Harlem was evacuated, and the Continental Army, pressed back step by step, at last occupied a line from the Hudson at Tarrytown to the Heights at Northcastle. At this time, November 8th, 1776, Washington determined to retreat into New Jersey with all his army, save the New England troops, and the movement was speedily begun. Part of the army crossed from Tarrytown to Sneden's Landing, where General Greene covered their debarkation with 500 men and one gun; part crossed from Croton Point to Piermont, then Tappan Slote, and on November 9th, Lord Sterling, with 1,200 men, crossed at Kings Ferry and seized the pass at Long Clove, followed next day by Col. Hand with 1,000 troops and General Bell with 1,700, belonging to Putnam's Division.

Washington, after inspecting the works at Peekskill and vicinity, crossed on the 13th, and joined his army, making his headquarters at Hackensack. On November 18th, General Howe crossed the river in pursuit of the Americans, and landed at Closter with 6,000 troops. With the retreat through New Jersey, it is not my province to deal. The effect of that retreat and the presence of the enemy, roused every Tory in northern New Jersey and southern New York, and Loyalists not only openly joined the British and obtained arms from them, but they joined with the foe in overrunning the southeastern part of the county, till Orangetown was well nigh wrested from the patriots.

To resist this elated enemy was a militia, half-armed, half-clothed, half-starved, and wholly insubordinate. Both officers and men were new to military duty. The opportunities granted to raw recruits in other countries and in the French wars in this country, the drills and encampments that gave them confidence in themselves and in their officers, had been prevented by the startling rapidity with which events had transpired, and our militiamen were now called on for action and answered that call, fearful of each other, distrusting their commanders, and in terror of the enemy. Their families had been left in many cases without meal, wood, or fodder for their cattle; never wealthy, their poverty now rendered their condition more pitiable, and the sight of their Tory neighbors, well dressed and enriched by the money of the King, while it did not touch their honor did cause them to grow mutinous. So widespread had this feeling become that on November 5th, 1766, General Greene, then at Kings Ferry, threatened to place Colonel Hays' regiment under guard and send it to Fort Lee for duty if the men did not change their conduct.

To protect the patriots, as well as to hold so important a communication, Col. Huntington was sent to the Ramapo Pass—then called Sidman's Pass—shortly after the army crossed the river, and began the building of barracks and the erection of earthworks. But his presence, instead of overawing the Loyalists, encouraged them to devise a plan for capturing his forces. In this condition of affairs, Col. Hays appealed to Gen. Heath, who was in command at Peekskill, to send him aid for the protection of the military stores at Haverstraw. In response to this urgent request, Brigadier-Gen. Scott was ordered to cross to Haverstraw with his brigade and assist in guarding the country. Scott's troops crossed on November 26th, 1776.

Finding themselves in greater strength, the Americans now assumed the offensive. Col. Tyler's regiment was dispatched from Ramapo to Tappan, while Col. Malcom, with one hundred men and several volunteer commissioned and non-commissioned officers, was sent to Nyack, opposite which lay the enemy's fleet. On December 3d, 1776, Malcom wrote Gen. Heath that he had stationed two guards a mile apart to prevent the British from landing; that the fleet consisted of 2 ships, 2 galleys, 1 schooner, a transport brig and sloop; and that the previous week parties from the vessels had landed twice, and besides looting a house, had carried off some cattle.

On the arrival of Malcom at Nyack, Tyler withdrew to Ramapo, which he reached on December 4th with six companies of his regiment, having left two at Haverstraw. Whether Tyler's withdrawal encouraged the enemy, or whether they had been exasperated by his sharp actions with them, does not appear; but whatever the reason, they organized a raid which filled the people south of the mountains with terror and drew down upon themselves sharp retaliation. On December 7th the combined force of Tories and cowboys entered Tappan, and, after maltreating such patriots as they could find, and destroying and stealing whatever of value they could reach, they finally withdrew, after cutting down the liberty pole, taking with them the father of an officer in Malcom's regiment as a prisoner, and driving off a horse and a yoke of oxen.

Malcom, believing he was to be attacked, took post in the mountain gorge at the Slote, and, stationing his guns in the road, deployed his men on both sides of the pass. The next day, he marched down into Bergen County and carried consternation into the Tory lines, driving them in headlong speed from their homes and capturing one of their number.

This foray of the enemy called from the County Committee of Safety an urgent request to General Clinton for aid, and the same day that their petition was forwarded, Dec. 9th, Clinton was ordered to march to New City with 1,500 men.

On Dec. 11th, 1776, Colonel Malcom sent word to General Heath that he was as completely isolated in Clarkstown as he would be in an enemy's country; that he could obtain no news of the movements of his foe save through his own scouts; that the Tories were recruiting and obtaining arms; and that with the force at his command, it was unsafe to attempt to protect Tappan. Upon the receipt of this information, Heath immediately left Peekskill and marched with 2,000 men to Tappan, which he reached on Dec. 12th. Remaining there two days, he then advanced to Hackensack, effectually crushing the Tory spirit by his presence. As soon as General Heath left Tappan, Colonel Allison was ordered to move into Orangetown with his regiment, while Colonel Hasbrouck was to remain at Haverstraw to afford support if needed.

The year 1777 opened in gloom for the American cause, Washington's army, encamped near Morristown, was an army that had steadily witnessed defeat, while Howe, who had returned with his troops to New York, was flushed with victory. Anxiously Washington awaited the English commander's next move. Already, in the previous year, a plan had been agreed upon, whereby Carleton was to force his way from Canada to the Hudson, and be met by Howe on that river, thus dividing New England from the Southern States. It was partly in pursuance of this movement that the ships of war had passed up to Haverstraw bay. Failure had greeted the attempt, but the project was only postponed, and this year saw the beginning of a new campaign, in which Burgoyne instead of Carleton commanded the Northern army. Whether Howe would attempt to force his way through the Hudson Highlands to meet Burgoyne, or sail for Philadelphia, was the perplexing question.

To be prepared for either movement, Washington marched his army northward, and on July 15th had it encamped in Ramapo valley. On the 23d of the same month he established his headquarters at Ramapo, and, from the summit of the Torne, often anxiously scanned the distant ocean and bay near Sandy Hook, to learn if possible the movements of the

British fleet. At length, receiving positive information that the fleet had passed out to sea, and feeling assured that Philadelphia was its destination, Washington broke camp and marched with his army to that city.

A legend, founded on one of these visits of the Commander to the Torne, remains to this day. While on its summit, on one occasion, Washington was winding his watch when it accidentally slipped from his hands, leaving the key in his grasp, and fell into a deep crevice. The fall, instead of stopping the timepiece, seemed to confer upon it perpetual motion, and the visitor to the Torne can hear its ticking even at this time.

Two months after the departure of the main army for Philadelphia, Aaron Burr, then ranking as Lieutenant-Colonel, was at Sufferns in command of Malcom's regiment—September, 1777.

The Ramapo valley, or Sidman's Pass, was the great pathway from West Point and New Windsor to the country south of the Highlands, and was in almost constant use by some portions of the army from 1776 till the close of the war. Through its narrow defile Burgoyne's army passed as prisoners, on their long march from New England to Virginia in the autumn of 1778. In June, 1779, it was again the camping place of the Continental Army, and was strongly intrenched at that time. The remains of the intrenchments are still visible, and relics of its military occupation are not few.

After the capture of Stony Point by "Mad Anthony" Wayne, on July 16th, 1779, a detachment of British prisoners were placed in a barn belonging to Abram De Baun, standing one-eighth of a mile east of Erastus Johnson's, and one-eighth of a mile north of the highway in Ramapo. One of the prisoners in his dreams cried "Fire!" and the guard, mistaking the source of the order, did fire on the prisoners, killing three and wounding eighteen.

Throughout the whole struggle, Sidman's Pass was the resort of cowboys, who issued forth upon their raids either into New Jersey, that portion of Orange County north of the mountains, or the fertile country east of Sufferns; and the name of Claudius Smith and his band of cut-throats still carries recollections of many a midnight horror to the descendants of the old settlers near the clove. At the time of the Revolution this whole section was known as West New-Hempstead.

On one of the occasions when the Continental army was encamped in Ramapo Clove an attempt to force it was contemplated by the British, which was only frustrated by a happy ruse. A notorious spy, whose information was regarded as reliable by the foe, was captured in the American camp. He was at once tried by drumhead court martial, found guilty, and sentenced to be executed on the following morning.

Before the hour appointed for punishment arrived, the father, mother and brother of the condemned man entered camp and entreated permission to visit the prisoner. This was granted under necessary restrictions. During the interview the commanding officer—said to have been General Greene—happened to pass the room where the spy was confined, and, hearing the lamentations, went in. The mother of the prisoner fell at Greene's feet and entreated him to spare her son, but was greeted with the stern response that that son must die in an hour. After leaving the room Greene paced thoughtfully to and fro for a few moments and then returned to the spy's chamber. Again the mother begged for her boy's life and Greene finally acquiesced on condition that the spy should immediately repair to the enemy's camp and report that the American army, six thousand strong, had begun to advance and would fall upon the British within an hour.

The prisoner at once consented to this plan. Greene was evidently cautious, for he further stipulated, that the prisoner's brother should take his place, and that, if the foe did not begin a retreat upon hearing the spy's report, the brother should be hung. At first that proposed hostage demurred to the arrangement, but the entreaties of his parents caused him at length to reluctantly yield.

In a short time all but the two brothers withdrew from the room. Then an officer appeared and removed the irons from the spy to his brother. Shortly after an old woman brought a knapsack and placed it beside the door of the prison room. Presently the spy came out, shouldered the knapsack, stole from the building, and, after dodging from an outhouse to the barn, skulked to the woods which were near by.

General Greene was so confident of the success of his artifice that the next morning he moved, with a strong detachment, upon the enemy's line. On arriving at their encampment a curious spectacle was presented.

The artillery and baggage was found scattered in the utmost confusion, not a tent was struck, and the fires were actually still smoking under the camp kettles. The foe had not been gone for over an hour when the Americans arrived, and Greene's troops halted to make a hasty meal on the viands that the frightened enemy had left.

The particulars of the retreat were afterwards learned from the spy. On his arrival in the British camp he at once repaired to the commandant's tent, with his hat and coat pierced with bullet holes. In that tent he found a large party of officers assembled, before whom he related a wonderful tale of Greene's advance and tremendous force, stating that he had inadvertently ran into the advance skirmish line and only escaped after the bullets had cut his clothing and grazed his flesh.

The British officers were seized with a panic, and, at a council of war which was hurriedly summoned, it was decided to begin an immediate retreat. While this council was being held the spy passed from camp-fire to camp-fire, spreading his direful news with additional lies until the troops were in a fit condition for flight. When the orders came for withdrawal from the camp they were obeyed with alacrity.

While Howe successfully prosecuted his Philadelphia campaign, Burgoyne had advanced into the Upper Hudson valley as far as Saratoga. Almost all the way, he had met with earnest opposition, and at last in dire distress sent word to Clinton, who commanded at New York in Howe's absence, to come up the river to his relief. As soon as a reinforcement arrived from England, Clinton started up the Hudson, with five thousand men in flatboats and transports, on Saturday evening, October 4th, 1777, and made a brief land at Tarrytown to draw General Putnam's attention from the main point of his attack. On the following day, the British transports proceeded to Verplanck's Point and three thousand troops debarked.

When Washington started to oppose Howe at Philadelphia, he left a quantity of stores at Peekskill under the guard of General Putnam and a large body of troops. In the course of the campaign about Philadelphia, Putnam had been called on for detachments from these troops till, at the time of General Clinton's movement, his whole force amounted to only about fifteen hundred militia. Believing, when Clinton landed at Verplank's Point, that the destruction of the stores at Peekskill was his object, Putnam fell back to high ground in the rear of that place, and sent for aid to the Generals commanding Forts Clinton and Montgomery.

The strategem of Sir Henry Clinton was successful in drawing attention from his design on the Highland forts, and on the following morning, October 6th, 1777, under the cover of a heavy fog, he crossed two thousand troops to Stony Point, ten miles below Fort Clinton. The transports were anchored near Stony Point; a corps of Royalists remained at Verplanck's Point; and the frigates Tartar, Preston, and Mercury, proceeded up the river to the southern entrance of the "Race"

Leaving a detachment near the present school house above Resolvert Waldron's to keep communication open, the troops, consisting of Emerick's corps of Chasseurs, a corps of loyalists and New York Volunteers, the Fifty-second and Fifty-seventh British Regiments, under the command of Colonel Campbell, one troop of the 17th Light Dragoons dismounted, and a large body of Hessians, guided by a Tory named Peter Keesler, crossed the Donderberg in single column, and at Doodletown separated into two divisions; one, under Lieut.-Col. Campbell, marching around the base of Bear Hill to attack Fort Montgomery, the other, under the command of Sir Henry Clinton was to storm Fort Clinton; each detachment consisted of about nine hundred men.

The forts were commanded by the brothers James and George Clinton, and garrisoned by not more than six hundred militia from Dutchess, Ulster, and Orange counties. On Sunday night, Governor Clinton obtained the information that the British were off Tarrytown, and on Monday morning had dispatched a scouting party of one hundred men, under Major Logan, to the Donderberg, to watch the enemy's movements. This party soon returned with the news that about forty boats filled with troops had landed at Stony Point. Dispatching a messenger named Waterbury to General Putnam for reinforcements, Governor Clinton ordered a small detachment of thirty men to scout down the old king's highway. At Doodletown, two and a half miles below the fort, this party met the advance guard of the approaching British army, and, greeting the demand for their surrender with a spirited volley, they retreated to the fort without loss.

Confining our attention to the fortification within the present Rockland County, Sir Henry Clinton, after a sufficient delay to permit of the left wings reaching the rear of Fort Montgomery, pressed forward with the right wing to the attack of Fort Clinton. After a severe fight at the abatis, the English troops finally forced their way to the fort, and both were invested about four o'clock in the afternoon. A flag, with a summons for the garrisons to surrender as prisoners of war within five minutes or be put to the sword, was received by Lieutenant-Colonel Livingston on the part of the Americans, who replied that it had been determined to defend the forts to the last extremity.

The battle was at once re-begun with great vigor. Commodore Hotham brought his frigates within cannon shot and opened a desultory fire, while the enemy pressed onward, gaining inch by inch. Twilight ended the conflict and in the friendly darkness of a cloudy evening many of the fugitive patriots escaped. General James Clinton, though severely wounded, as well as his brother, the Governor, escaped; the latter by swimming across the river with Surgeon Peter Vander Lynn. Lieutenant-Colonels Livingston, Bruyn, and Claghery; and Majors Hamilton and Logan were captured. The loss of the Americans in killed, wounded and prisoners was about three hundred, while that of the British was one hundred and forty in killed and wounded, among whom were Colonel Campbell and Count Grabowski. Putnam did not send reinforcements because he did not learn of the danger until too late, the messenger, Waterbury, having treacherously delayed his journey. The following day Waterbury joined the enemy.

In the confusion that followed the battle, and the short time allowed for the destruction of the works and re-embarkation of the troops, little heed was given to the burial of the slain; the bodies of friend and foe were alike tossed into Lake Sinipink, now Highland Lake, which was called from that occurrence, "Bloody Pond," or "Hessian Pond," and under these names is mentioned by Dr. Timothy Dwight—some time President of Yale College—in the following letter:

"Early in May [1778], I went down the river in company with several officers to examine the Forts Montgomery and Clinton, built on a point, six or eight miles below West Point, for the defence of the river. The first object which met our eyes, after we had left our barge and ascended the bank, was the remains of a fire kindled by the cottagers of this solitude, for the purpose of consuming the bones of some of the Americans who had fallen at this place and had been left unburied. Some of the bones were lying, partially consumed, round the spot where the fire had been kindled, and some had evidently been converted into ashes. As we went onward we were distressed by the fœtor of the decayed human bodies. * * * As we were attempting to discover the source from which it proceeded, we found, at a small distance from Montgomery, a pond of moderate size, in which we saw the bodies of several men who had been killed in the assault on the fort. They were thrown into this pond the preceding autumn by the British, when probably the water was sufficiently deep to cover them. Some of them were covered at this time, but at a depth so small as to leave them distinctly visible. Others had an arm, a leg, and a part of the body above the surface. The clothes which they wore when they were killed were still on them, and proved that they were militia, being the ordinary dress of farmers. Their faces were bloated and monstrous, and their postures were uncouth, distorted, and in the highest degree afflictive. My companions had been accustomed to the horrors of war, and sustained the prospect with some degree of firmness. To me, a novice in scenes of this nature, it was overwhelming. * * * From this combination of painful objects we proceeded to Fort Clinton, built on a rising ground at a small distance further down the river. The ruins of this fortress were a mere counterpart to those of Fort Montgomery. Everything combustible in both had been burned, and what was not was extensively thrown down. Everything which remained was a melancholy picture of destruction."

Among the many munitions of war captured or destroyed, at the loss of Forts Clinton and Montgomery, was the chain that had been stretched across the river, and an unobstructed passage was now open to the enemy's ships.

Congress at once determined to more strongly fortify the Hudson, and in the early spring of 1778 work was begun at West Point. To add to the forts a new chain was determined on, and Colonel Timothy Pickering, Secretary of War, was ordered to consult Mr. Peter Townshend, of Chester, Orange County, in relation to its construction. Late on a Saturday night, in March, 1778, Colonel Pickering, accompanied by Captain Thomas Machin, the engineer in charge at West Point, arrived at Mr. Townshend's house. That gentleman immediately consented to undertake the task, and the party started that same night in a blinding snow storm for the Sterling Iron Works. At daylight Sunday morning the forges were at work, and for the six weeks following the fires were not extinguished. By the middle of April the last link was finished, and on the 1st of May, 1778, the chain was stretched across the Hudson. The iron used in its construction was of equal parts of Long and Sterling Mine ore, each link was two and a half inches square, about two feet long, and weighed about one hundred and forty pounds; ten links were fastened in the usual manner, the eleventh was left open like an ox bow with bolt holes in the end for the purpose of connecting the clevice with another section; the total weight of the chain was one hundred and eighty tons, and it was conveyed to West Point by New England teamsters as rapidly as each section was finished.

In September, 1778, a horrible massacre occurred at Old Tappan. Lord Cornwallis at that time held possession of the eastern portion of New Jersey, and his foraging and scouting parties passed in all directions through this section. At the same time General Knyphausen, with a large force, was stationed at Dobb's Ferry on the east side of the river, and Washington suspected that an expedition up the river was intended. To watch the movements of the British, as well as to intercept their scouts and foragers, the Third Regiment of Virginia Light Dragoons, under the command of Lieutenant Colonel Baylor, was dispatched to this section and made their quarters at Old Tappan. Here they lay in such an unsoldierly manner that Cornwallis determined to suprise and cut them to pieces together with a body of militia under Wayne that was encamped a little north of the present Orangeburg.

Baylor's troops were scattered in the houses and barns of the Blauvelts, Demarests, Holdrums, Harings, and Bogarts, who resided in the neighborhood, while he and his staff were at the house of Cornelius Haring. General Grey, who, from his practice of ordering his men to remove the flints from their muskets that they might be confined to the use of the bayonet, had acquired the name of "No Flint General," or "No Flint Grey," was sent out on the night of September 27th to approach Baylor's detachment from the west, while a corps from Knyphausen's force crossed the river to Sneden's and advanced upon the unsuspecting troops from the east. Some deserters gave Wayne and his militia warning in time to permit their escape, but Baylor's dragoons were left ignorant of their danger.

At midnight, Grey cut off a sergeant's patrol of eleven men—one having made his escape attempted to arouse Baylor but was too late—and in an instant more was upon the main body. The surprise was complete, and the unarmed and scarcely awakened troopers could but beg for quarter. Their plea for mercy was vain. Grey, like Tryon, was merciless in his forays, and on this occasion he had given special orders that no quarter should be granted. In cold blood the helpless cavalrymen were bayoneted or beaten to death, till out of the troop of one hundred and sixteen twenty-eight were killed or mortally wounded, among whom was Major Alexander Clough, and thirty-nine prisoners were taken—eight of whom were severely wounded—among whom were Colonel Baylor and Surgeon Thomas Evans. The prisoners were taken to Tappan and confined in the old Dutch Church. Seventy horses and considerable booty was also obtained by the enemy. Among the few who escaped was Major William Washington, who later, in the stirring campaign of the South, fully avenged his comrades' slaughter. On Dec. 29th, 1778, a division under General Putnam crossed the river at Kings Ferry in batteaux and marched twelve miles in a storm of snow and sleet, camping at Kakiat.

With the exception of raids by cowboys and the constantly recurring conflicts between the patriots and Tories, nothing of import transpired in this County till the end of May, 1779. The enemy had transferred the scene of battle to the South and was overrunning Georgia and the Carolinas. To prevent the concentration of American troops before their armies and to destroy the stores that had been collected, an expedition under Admiral Collier and General Matthews had sailed early in May for Virginia. At the close of that month this expedition returned and was immediately used by Sir Henry Clinton in the attack on the forts at Verplanck's and Stony Points.

These works, included in the general plan of fortification agreed upon in 1775, had been neglected till after the capture of Forts Montgomery and Clinton in 1777. Then two small forts had been built at these points. To obtain possession of these works was Sir Henry Clinton's object, and in its furtherance he sailed from New York on May 30th, 1779, accompanied by General Vaughan, of Esopus fame, and Admiral Collier, who commanded the fleet.

On the morning of May 31st, the division intended for the capture of Stony Point, under the command of General Patterson, accompanied by Sir Henry Clinton, landed at Grassy Point, and began their march toward the fort. The garrison of that fort, consisting of only forty men, abandoned the Point and withdrew to the Highlands, upon the approach of the enemy, and the works fell into the hands of the British without resistance. On the following morning, June 1st, 1779, the guns of the captured fort reinforced by some cannon and mortars dragged up during the night, opened a heavy fire against Fort Fayette, on Verplanck's Point, and on the following day that fortress was surrendered.

Meantime Washington was encamped at Middlebrook, in New Jersey, awaiting the enemy's movements. As soon as he learned that an expedition had started up the Hudson, he put his army in motion toward the Highlands, and by rapid marches, reached Sidman's Pass on June 7th, 1779, with five brigades and two Carolina regiments, and so disposed his troops as to be able to reinforce a threatened point at once. At this time the fortifications and earthworks erected in the Pass were greatly strengthened.

Meantime Clinton had ordered the enlarging and strengthening of the captured forts, and supplied them with strong garrisons and necessary stores. The force at Stony Point, under command of Lieutenant-Colonel Johnson, consisted of the 17th Regiment of foot, the grenadier companies of the 71st Regiment, and some artillery, in all amounting to a little over six hundred men. As a further support, the British had several small war vessels at anchor in the river within cannon shot of the forts.

Among the dispositions of his army, Washington had stationed Wayne with the Light Infantry at a point not far from the Forest of Dean Mine, now in Orange County, but little north of the old Haverstraw and Monroe Turnpike, a position he occupied on July 1st.

From the results of his own and the observations of Major Lee, of the Light Dragoons, Washington determined upon expeditions to surprise and recapture both Stony Point and Fort Fayette. July 15th was fixed upon as the day for the assault, and the hour of midnight as the time. Wayne was appointed to the command of the detachment that was to storm the Point, while that against Fayette was commanded by General

Howe. It is only necessary here to say that, through the error of a messenger, the attack on Fort Fayette miscarried. On the morning of July 15th, all the troops under Wayne's command, consisting of Massachusetts men, were ordered to divest themselves of unnecessary accoutrements and prepare for their march of twelve or fourteen miles. So necessary was absolute secrecy and so numerous the watchful Tories, that it was deemed unwise to send Wayne reinforcements. A brigade of troops intended as a cover for the attacking force, should any accident befall it, was started for the scene early in the morning, and at noon the march of the main body began.

The day was intensely sultry, and the route of the troops through the mountain defiles was such as to prevent the light air that was stirring from reaching them. Without complaint they continued their march through that long, hot afternoon, now scrambling over broken rocks, anon threading their way single file across a morass, until at 8 o'clock in the evening they had arrived at Springsteen's, a mile and a half from the fort. Here a halt was called to allow a reconnoiter and rest the men. Each soldier had a piece of white paper fastened to his hat to distinguish him in the darkness, and the watchword of the night, that of the enemy: "The fort's our own," was passed along the line. The muskets of all were unloaded so as to compel the use of the bayonet only. To still further secure silence, all the dogs in the neighborhood had been killed lest their barking might alarm the enemy, and a negro guide named Pompey, the slave of James Lamb, was obtained to lead the troops.

As strengthened by the British, several breastworks and strong batteries were advanced in front of the fort, and about half way down the hill were two rows of abattis; the guns were ranged so as to command the beach and the only crossing place in the marsh that connects the Point with the main land, and to infilade an advancing column.

Wayne intended to attack the works on the right and left flanks at the same time, and made the following dispositions for that purpose: The regiments of Febiger and Meigs with a detachment under Major Hull formed the right; and Butler's regiment, with two companies under Major Murfree, formed the left column. One hundred and fifty volunteers under Lieutenant Colonel Fleury and Major Posey composed the van of the right; and one hundred volunteers under Major Stewart, the van of the left; while each column was preceded by a forlorn hope of twenty men, one under command of Lieutenent Gibbon, the other under that of Lieutenant Knox, whose duty it was to remove the abattis and other obstructions.

At half-past eleven the silent march was begun. The first sentinel on the high ground west of the morass, deceived by the negro whom he knew and who had the countersign, was seized and gagged without giving an alarm; the silence of the sentinel on the road across the morass was gained in the same way, and Wayne's party succeeded in crossing the marsh to the base of the rocks without discovery. General Muhlenburg with three hundred men was left as a reserve on the main land.

At twelve-twenty o'clock the assault was begun. In an instant more the advancing columns were discovered by the pickets, and, though the surprise was complete, a frightful fire was opened by the British upon the advancing troops. Undeterred, the Americans rushed on, passed the breastworks, cleared the *chevaux de frise* at the sally-ports, mounted the parapet, and entered the fort at the point of the bayonet, never ceasing in the headlong charge till the van of each column met at the centre of the works at the same instant. Colonel Fleury was the first to enter the fort and strike the British flag, while at the same instant Major Posey mounted the works, shouting the prophetic watchword: "The fort's our own." The garrison surrendered at discretion, and not a life was taken after the plea for quarter.

In this assault the Americans lost fifteen killed and eighty-three wounded, among whom were General Wayne, who was slightly injured, and Lieutenant-Colonel Hay. The forlorn hope of twenty men under Lieutenant Gibbon lost seventeen killed or wounded. The British loss was sixty-three killed, and Johnston, the commander, with five hundred and forty-three officers and men together with the stores and munitions of war, were captured. At two o'clock on the morning of July 16th, 1779, General Wayne sent to Washington the following dispatch:

"Dear Gen'l—The fort and garrison with Col. Johnston are ours. Our officers and men behaved like men who are determined to be free."

I have already said that the attempt on Verplanck's Point miscarried. But a short distance down the river lay the British vessels, that had slipped their cables and dropped out of gunshot during the attack on Stony Point. Sir Henry Clinton was already marching to the relief of Fort Fayette, with a large land force, and any attempt to capture it by siege would evidently fail. Under these circumstances, combined with a belief that a garrison of fully fifteen hundred men would be necessary to hold the place, Washington ordered the stores removed from Stony Point and the works destroyed. This was successfully accomplished, but in the moving a galley, loaded with the heavy ordnance, was struck by a shot from the British vessel Vulture and sunk off Caldwell's Point. On July 20th, 1779, the British repossessed themselves of Stony Point, but only held it till the middle of the following month, when Clinton ordered the evacuation of all posts along the Hudson and concentrated his forces at New York.

In recognition of the bravery displayed in this brilliant enterprise, Congress ordered a medal of gold struck and presented to Gen. Wayne, and, with the thanks of that body, presented silver medals to De Fleury and Stewart; while Lieutenants Gibbon and Knox were breveted captains. At the recommendation of Washington, Congress further resolved, "that the value of the military stores taken at Stony Point be ascertained and divided among the gallant troops, by whom it was reduced, in such manner and proportion as the Commander-in-Chief shall prescribe." That proportion was scaled as follows: To the first man who entered the fort, $500; to the second, $400; to the third, $300; to the fourth, $200, and to the fifth, $100. The total value of the munitions captured amounted to $158,640, which amount was to be divided among the troops.

The final abandonment of the river posts by the British, and the urgent necessity of sending re-enforcements to Lincoln in the South, led to the camp at Ramapo being broken up in the autumn of 1779. The main body of the army sought a winter cantonment about Morristown, strong detachments being stationed at various points in the Highlands.

The year 1780 was pregnant with stirring events for this County. Early in the season General Knyphausen crossed to New Jersey, led by the reports of disaffection among the American troops, and at Springfield sustained a battle which checked his further advance. But his continuation at that place led Washington to suspect some ulterior design, and, when information was conveyed to him that on June 18th Sir Henry Clinton had returned from the conquest of South Carolina, believing the fortifications in the Highlands to be his next object, Washington slowly marched his army to Tappan and encamped at that place. Learning, toward the close of July, that Clinton was about to attack the French allies ere they could land and fortify themselves at Newport, Washington hastily broke camp and, marching by the old Kings Highway through Haverstraw to Stony Point, crossed Kings Ferry with the intention of attacking New York. It was while waiting on this side of the ferry, on July 31st, 1780, that Benedict Arnold appeared and held the interview with the Commander-in-Chief that led to his assignment to the command of West Point.

The abandonment by Clinton of his design against Newport led to the American army retracing its steps. It again crossed at Kings Ferry and marched back to Tappan, where it went into camp for the next few weeks.

General Greene commanded the right and Lord Sterling the left wing, while six battalions of light infantry were stationed in advance of the main body under the command of La Fayette.

I am now to take up the treason of Arnold and the trial and execution of John Andre. So much has been said and written on the whole subject of that event that the story must be fresh in every mind, and my duty is to only touch on such portions of the transaction as relate to this County.

When Benedict Arnold took command at West Point he became intimate with Joshua Hett Smith.

Lot No. 7 of the Cheesecocks Patent, through sale, became the property of a William Smith, a lawyer and judge. At his death in 1769 he left six sons, William, Thomas, John W., James, Samuel, and Joshua Hett; and several daughters. Lot 7 was left to Thomas by his father and was occupied by his brother Joshua. The house on it, now known as the "Treason House," was built probably about 1770. After the death of Thomas Smith in 1795, this property came into the hands of his son Thomas, who died in 1815. His heirs sold the place, containing 90 acres, to William Nicolls for $5,500 on July 9th, 1832. Nicolls sold the place to William C. Houseman in 1836 for $8,600, and he sold it to James A. Houseman, of Alabama, in 1846. After Mr. Houseman's death the property was sold to David Munn in 1864, and he conveyed it to his son-in-law, Adam Lilburn, in 1871. It remained in Mr. Lilburn's possession till 1883, when he sold it to Brewster J. Allison, the present owner.

Of the Smith family—Thomas was a lawyer in New York; William became one of the Tory Justices of that city during the Revolution; and of Joshua Hett, we are to learn more fully in these pages.

Owners of large landed property in Haverstraw, the Smiths were landlords with many tenants, and were thoroughly disliked by those tenants for their proud carriage. In the exercise of the franchise it was a not uncommon thing to hear the holders of land under them say that they waited to see how the Smiths voted, and then they voted just the other way, and were then sure they were right.

With Joshua Hett Smith Arnold passed many hours during his command of West Point, either visiting at his house or receiving him as a guest at his headquarters in the Robinson House. In the cool calculation that Arnold was making, Smith was to play an important part, and the officer not only associated with the civilian because of social and intellectual affinity but also because of another affinity, in which he must gain or lose all. In another chapter we are to review Smith's actions in the attempted treason, and will then be better able to determine his guilt or innocence than now.

By Sept. 10th, 1780, Arnold had so far perfected his treasonable plans as to render a meeting with Andre necessary, and for this purpose he started to meet that officer by appointment at Dobbs Ferry. Passing the night of the 10th, at Smith's house, he left Haverstraw early the next morning for the rendezvous. It is a matter of history that that meeting was prevented. Seven days later, when Washington was on his way to Hartford, to confer with the French officers, Arnold met him with his barge and conveyed him across the river at Kings Ferry. On September 19th, Arnold visited Smith, and by various representations, obtained his consent to go off in a row boat to the sloop-of-war Vulture, and bring a man ashore whom Arnold wished to see on important public business. While at Smith's house, Arnold was joined by his wife and child, who had come on from Philadelphia, and returned with them in his barge to his headquarters. Among the other arrangements with Smith in regard to the proposed interview was one to the effect, that if their business could not be completed by dawn, the remainder of the interview, after that hour should occur in Smith's house, and to prepare for that event, Smith removed his family to Fishkill. On his return from this trip, he stopped at Arnold's quarters and obtained from that officer a pass for a flag of truce, and an order to Major Kiers, commanding at Stony Point, to supply Smith with a boat whenever he should want one. Arnold further directed Smith to visit the Vulture on the night of the 20th. Unable to obtain boatmen, Smith failed to obey his orders, and word having been sent to Arnold notifying him of the fact, that officer arrived at Smith's on the following day determined to see his wish obeyed. At his command a skiff was moored in Miniseeongo Creek, and under threat of punishment if they refused to acquiesce, he obtained the services of two brothers—Samuel and Joseph Colquhon, to man the oars. Close on the hour of midnight Smith and these two men set off for the Vulture, which was at anchor off Croton Point.

A short time elapsed, when the row boat again approached shore, and, landing under the mountain, at a place near the foot of the Long Clove road, John Andre stepped ashore and was conducted to the presence of Arnold, who was waiting near the spot. What transpired in that solemn night conference is only know to the Omniscient. Daylight found the business unfinished, and the warning voice of Smith bade the conspirators make haste. It was with reluctance that Andre consented to mount the spare horse Arnold's servant rode and accompany his new acquaintance to a more secluded spot, but there was still so much left unsettled and the bait was so alluring, that overcoming his scruples, Andre assented to visit Smith's house with Arnold. On their ride to that residence, the hail of a sentinel near Haverstraw warned Andre that he was within the American lines without flag or pass, but it was then too late to turn back, even if he had wished to.

At dawn Smith's house was reached, and the morning of September 22d, 1780, was passed by the two men in perfecting their plans. At length the conference was ended, and Arnold, after giving Andre a paper containing a full account of the fortifications and forces at West Point, and providing him with a pass, bade him adieu and departed in his barge up the river to his quarters.

The remainder of the day, after his departure, was passed by Andre alone. As the shades of evening began to fall, he applied to Smith to convey him back to the Vulture, which, having been fired upon from Croton Point in the early morning, had weighed anchor and dropped further down the stream; but this Smith positively refused to do, pleading an attack of ague and a fear of the night air on the water. At his earnest entreaty, and with no other means of return open to him, Andre at last consented to cross the river and ride down to New York by land. Following Arnold's advice, Andre changed his military coat for a civilian's dress, and a little before sunset on September 22d, accompanied by Smith and a negro servant, he rode down to Kings Ferry at Stony Point and embarked for the opposite shore.

Three nights later, an aid clattered through Haverstraw at his topmost speed, bound for Gen. Greene's quarters at Tappan. These he reached at midnight, with an order from Washington directing Greene to move the whole left wing of the army to Kings Ferry as speedily as possible. In the midst of the intense blackness and driving rain of a stormy night the movement was begun, and before dawn of September 26 the whole division was on its march up the King's highway. Little did Greene know, when he obeyed his commander's orders, that but a few miles away, across the river, Andre was also riding north through the storm, while Arnold had passed down the stream but a short distance from him to endless infamy.

The cause for the movement of Greene's division was the discovery by the Commander-in-Chief of Arnold's treason, and his uncertainty as to how far the disaffection had spread, or as to what the next move of the enemy would be. In this period of doubt he wished a large force to guard an important point under his immediate supervision. Whatever suspicions might have been in Washington's mind, of the fidelity of his other officers, they were speedily dispelled, and by September 28th Greene's forces were again in camp at Tappan.

During that date, September 28th, 1780, Andre, guarded by a strong force of cavalry commanded by Major Talmadge, once more passed through Haverstraw; passed Smith's house, where, but a short week before, his horoscope had seemed so bright; passed again near the spot where he and Arnold had met in the shadow of High Tor, to enter that other shadow of the Valley of Death.

Conveyed by water from West Point to Kings Ferry, the prisoner was then taken to Tappan and there confined in the inn, formerly kept by Casparus Mabie and still standing as the "'76 House." On the following day Washington arrived at Tappan, taking up his quarters in the De Windt House, and immediately ordered a Court of Inquiry composed of the following officers:

Major General Greene,	Major General La Fayette,
" " Sterling,	" " R. Howe,
" " St. Clair,	" " Baron Steuben,
Brigadier General Parsons,‡	Brigadier General Hand,
" " James Clinton,	" " Starke,
" " Knox,	" " Huntington,
" " Glover,	" " Patterson,

General Nathaniel Greene was President of this Board and John Laurence Judge Advocate General.

Before this court Andre appeared and told his story in a straightforward way. He was then remanded to his place of confinement, and, after a long consultation, the Court decided that he should be considered as a spy and, as such, suffer the penalty of war. On the following day, September 30th, Washington confirmed the finding of the Court and appointed the following day, October 1st, and the hour of five P. M., as the time for execution.

The sympathy of all the American officers was with Andre, and every effort conformable with the laws of war was made to save him. In pursuance of these endeavors both correspondence and an interview with officers from the enemy were used and the time of execution delayed. All conference proved futile, and at 12 M. on October 2d, 1780, in the presence of the troops, of all the officers stationed at Tappan, save the Commander-in-Chief and his personal staff, and of a vast concourse of people assembled from the surrounding country, John Andre was hanged, and by his death gained that immortal fame for which he had so earnestly toiled in life; for which he risked that life; for which he died.

‡ See note at end of chapter.

Dr. Thacher, a Surgeon in the Continental Army, who was present, thus speaks of the last hours: " Major Andre is no more among the living. I have just witnessed his exit. It was a tragical scene of the deepest interest. * * * The fatal hour having arrived, a large detachment of troops was paraded, and an immense concourse of people assembled. * * * Melancholy and gloom pervaded all ranks, and the scene was awfully affecting. I was so near, during the solemn march to the fatal spot, as to observe every movement, and to participate in every emotion the melancholy scene was calculated to produce. Major Andre walked from the stone house in which he had been confined between two of our subaltern officers, arm in arm. * * * He betrayed no want of fortitude, but retained a complacent smile on his countenance, and politely bowed to several gentlemen whom he knew, which was respectfully returned. * * * While waiting, and standing near the gallows, I observed some degree of trepidation—placing his foot on a stone and rolling it over, and choking in his throat as if attempting to swallow. So soon, however, as he perceived that things were in readiness, he stepped quickly into the wagon, and at this moment he appeared to shrink; but, instantly elevating his head with firmness, he said: 'It will be but a momentary pang;' and taking from his pocket two white handkerchiefs, the Provost Marshal, with one loosely pinioned his arms, and with the other the victim, after taking off his hat and stock, bandaged his own eyes with perfect firmness, which melted the hearts and moistened the cheeks not only of his servant, but of the throng of spectators.

The rope being appended to the gallows, he slipped the noose over his head, and adjusted it to his neck, without the assistance of the awkward executioner. Colonel Scammel now informed him that he had an opportunity to speak, if he desired it. He raised the handkerchief from his eyes, and said, 'I pray you to bear me witness that I meet my fate like a brave man.' The wagon being now removed from under him, he was suspended, and instantly expired."

I have had the good fortune to obtain the following account of another eye witness of Andre's execution, through the great kindness of William G. Haeselbarth. Mr. Haeselbarth obtained the data when he first entered our County in 1850 and used it in a series of lectures, which he later delivered, but this is the first time it has appeared in print. The story bears the stamp of truth, especially the error made by a camp attache in regard to the place of confinement. The Dutch Church building had been and at that time was used as a military prison, and Andre's trial had taken place in it. Nothing would be more natural then than for a private soldier, quartered perhaps at some distance from the spot, to suppose that Andre had been confined there.

"I was at that time," says the narrator, "an artificer in Colonel Jedathan Baldwin's regiment, a part of which was stationed within a short distance of the spot where Andre suffered. One of our men, whose name was Armstrong, being one of the oldest and best workmen at his trade in the regiment, was selected to make his coffin, which he performed and painted black, after the custom of those times. At this time Andre was confined in what was called the Dutch Church, a small stone building with only one door, and closely guarded by six sentinels. When the hour appointed for his execution arrived, a guard of three hundred men was paraded at the place of his confinement. A kind of procession was formed by placing the guard in single file on each side of the road. In front was a large number of American officers, of high rank, on horseback; these were followed by the wagon containing Andre's coffin, then a large number of officers on foot, with Andre in their midst. The procession moved slowly up a moderately rising hill, about a quarter of a mile to the west. On the top was a field without any enclosure. In this was a very high gallows, made by setting up two poles or crotches and laying a pole on top. The wagon that contained the coffin was drawn directly under the gallows. In a short time Andre stepped into the hind end of the wagon, then on his coffin, took off his hat and laid it down, then placed his hands upon his hips, and walked very uprightly back and forth as far as the length of his coffin would permit, at the same time casting his eyes upon the pole over his head and the whole scenery by which he was surrounded. He was dressed in a complete British uniform, the coat being of the brightest scarlet, faced or trimmed with the most beautiful green, his vest and breeches were bright buff.

He had a long and beautiful head of hair, which, agreeable to the fashion, was wound with a black ribbon and hung down his back.

Not many minutes after he took his stand upon the coffin, the executioner stepped into the wagon with a halter in his hands, on one end of which was what the soldiers called 'a hangman's knot,' which he attempted to put over the head and around the neck of Andre. By a sudden movement of his hand Andre prevented this. He then took off the handkerchief from his neck, unpinned his shirt collar, and, taking the end of the halter, put it over his head, placed the knot directly under his right ear, drawing it snugly to the neck.

Andre then took another handkerchief from his pocket and tied it over his eyes. At this time the officer who commanded spoke in rather a loud voice and said that his arms must be tied. Andre at once pulled down the handkerchief he had just tied over his eyes, drew from his pocket a second one, which he gave to the executioner, and then replaced his handkerchief. His arms were tied just above the elbows and behind his back. The rope was then made fast to the pole overhead.

The wagon was very suddenly withdrawn from under the gallows, which, together with the length of the rope, gave him a most tremendous swing back and forth, but in a few minutes he hung entirely still. During the whole transaction he appeared little daunted, but his face was pale. He remained hanging from twenty to thirty minutes, and, during that time, the chambers of death were never stiller than the multitude by which he was surrounded. At the expiration of that time orders were given to cut the rope and take down the body without letting it fall. This was done and the body carefully laid on the ground.

Shortly after the guard was withdrawn, and the bystanders were permitted to pass and view the corpse, but the crowd was so great that it was sometime before I could get an opportunity. When I reached the body, the coat, vest and breeches had been taken off, and the corpse lay in the coffin covered by some underclothes. The top of the coffin was not yet on and I viewed the corpse more carefully than I had ever done that of any human before. His head was very much on one side, in consequence of the manner in which the halter drew upon his neck. His face appeared to be greatly swollen and very black, much resembling a high degree of mortification; it was indeed a shocking sight to behold.

There were at this time standing at the foot of the coffin, two young men of uncommon short stature—not more than four feet high. Their dress was extremely gaudy. One of them had the clothes just taken from Andre hanging on his arm. I took particular pains to learn who they were and was informed, that they were his servants sent up from New York to take care of his clothes, but what other business I did not learn.

I now turned to take a view of the executioner, who was still standing by one of the posts of the gallows. I walked nigh enough to him to have laid my hand upon his shoulder, and looked him directly in his face. He appeared to be about twenty-five years of age. His face was covered with what appeared to me to be blacking taken from the outside of a greasy pot, while his beard was of two or three week's growth. A more frightful looking being I never beheld. His whole countenance bespoke him to be a fit instrument for the business he had been doing. Wishing to see the closing of the whole business, I remained upon the spot until scarce twenty persons were left, but the coffin was still beside the grave, which had previously been dug. I then returned to my tent with my mind deeply imbued with the shocking scene I had been called to witness."

At the time of the removal of Andre's remains, James Buchanan, under whose charge the disinterment took place, misled by one of the many errors in statement that Andre's execution gave rise to, became the unhappy means of spreading a rumor that the grave had been rifled by Americans, by the following statement: "After which I descended into the coffin, which was not more than three feet below the surface, and with my hands raked the dust together, to ascertain whether he had been buried in his regimentals or not, as it was rumored among the assemblage that he was stripped; for if buried in his regimentals I expected to find the buttons of his clothes, which would have disproved the rumor; but I did not find a single button or any article, save a string of leather that had tied his hair, in perfect preservation, coiled and tied as it had been on his hair at the time. I examined the dust of the coffin so minutely (as the quantity would not fill a quart) that no mistake could have arisen in the examination. Let no unworthy motive be attributed to me for recording this fact; I state it as one which I was anxious to ascertain for the reasons given. I do not pretend to know whether buttons would moulder into dust, while bones and strings would remain perfect and entire; but sure I am there was not a particle of metal in the coffin."

The gross injustice of embodying scandalous rumors against the American Army in an official report, when the basis for the rumors was ignorance, so exasperated Dr. Thacher, that he investigated the whole matter, publishing the result in the New England Magazine for May, 1834, under the caption. "Observations relative to the execution of Major John Andre, as a spy in 1780, correcting errors and refuting false imputations." From this article I can but quote extracts. From the Continental Journal and Weekly Advertiser, of October 26th, 1780, this sentence, taken from a letter dated Tappan, October 2d, 1780, is given. "He was dressed in full uniform, and after the execution, his servant demanded his clothing, which he received." A letter from Major Benjamin Russell, contains these words: "He was dressed in the rich uniform of a British Staff Officer, with the exception, of course, of sash, gorget, sword and spurs. * * * It was stated at the time in England, and, if I mistake not, in America, that he was buried in his regimentals. I can add my testimony, to that of others, that I saw the servant of Andre receive the military hat and stock of his master, immediately before the execution. I did not see the body placed in the coffin, but I did see, as I marched by the grave, that servant standing near it, and evidently overseeing the interment." It is but just to add that, when Mr. Buchanan's attention was called to his error, he at once apologized by a public letter in the New York Albion, on March 7th, 1834, and promised to forward the correction to the United Service Journal in London.

The body of Andre was interred at the foot of the gallows, and there remained till the year 1821, when it was exhumed, under the direction of James Buchanan, the British Consul at New York, and removed to England. The interest manifested in Andre at the time of the removal of the body, caused a Mr. Spafford, evidently an ardent American, to write to the *Gazeteer* in 1824:

"The memory of the spy and the traitor are, however, alike consigned to infamy. Snuff-boxes, royal dukes, poetry and sickly morality, fable, fiction, American clergymen, Westminster Abbey and the monument to the contrary notwithstanding."

The ravages of those who visited the grave, led the owner to remove the boulder which marked it, and which had been inscribed by the order of a New York merchant named Lee, from the spot and it was well nigh lost. Through the exertions of Henry Whittemore, three men, who had been present at the exhumation—John J. Griffiths, still living, David D. Brower, and John H. Outwater; located the place of the grave in 1878. Shortly after this event, the spot was visited by Cyrus W. Field and Arthur P. Stanley, Dean of Westminster, and these gentlemen agreed, one, Mr. Field, to erect a monument, the other to write an inscription. The monument was unveiled Oct. 2d, 1879. Three years later a member of the Order of Socialists in New York City, named Hendrix, evidently imbued with the ideas of Mr. Spafford, blew up the monument. As if to add to the tragedy of everything connected with the spot, Hendrix met a violent death at the Brooklyn side of Fulton Ferry in the spring of 1884.

Of those belonging to this County, who were connected with the attempted treason, Joshua Hett Smith, after leaving Andre, rode to Fishkill. At that place he was arrested on the night of Sept. 25th, by Colonel Gouvion, a member of Lafayette's suite and chief of artillery, and taken to Robinson's house, where he was examined by Washington, and remanded under guard to West Point. Three days later—Sept. 28th—he was conveyed to Stony Point and, under the same guard that held Andre, reached Tappan. Here he was confined in the old Dutch Church till called for trial before a court martial. That trial lasted four weeks and ended in his acquittal for want of evidence.

On Nov. 10th, he was removed to West Point and there detained till

Nov. 18th, when he was taken to Goshen and delivered into the hands of Sheriff Isaac Nicoll for civil trial, and by him placed in jail, a proceeding which, if the suspicion of the Marquis de Chastellux be correct, probably saved him from being lynched by his patriot neighbors. For a long time he remained in jail without indictment or trial, till, finally succeeding in making his escape, he made his way disguised as a woman to New York, where he remained till the surrender of that city, and then sailed for England with the British army. Some time previous to 1818, he returned to the United States and died in New York during that year.

The Colquhon brothers, who, at Arnold's command, conveyed Andre from the Vulture to shore, as well as Major Keirs, under whose supervision the boat was obtained, were justly exonerated from all suspicion. Strickland, the executioner of Andre, who was in confinement in the camp at Tappan as a dangerous Tory at the time of the trial, and was given his liberty for accepting the duty of hangman, returned to his home in the Ramapo Valley or Smith's Clove, and all further knowledge of him is lost.

Early in November, 1780, General Greene was detached from his command at Tappan and sent to take command of the Southern armies, and on November 27th, Washington issued orders from his headquarters at Preakness for the disposition of the troops in their winter cantonments.

But one of these encampments is of interest as regards this County, that of the New Jersey Brigade, which had its quarters from Pompton up to and in the Ramapo Pass. On January 20th, 1781, this brigade broke out in open mutiny. Hope of payment for their services had ceased; starved, naked, frozen, they thought of the members of Congress who, while feeding them on promises, lived on more substantial victuals; who, well protected from the inclemency of the weather, gave little heed to their pinched and chilled bodies; and the comparison of their wretchedness with the comfort of that imbecile debating society, which carefully avoided the exposure and danger of war, led them to forget their duty.

But three weeks had elapsed since the Pennsylvania troops had revolted, and, marching to Philadelphia, extorted from Congress a settlement of their demands. If the disaffection of the New Jersey soldiers was to end in a similar way, the *morale* of the army would be hopelessly ruined, and no one could predict the final issue. Reasoning thus, Washington ordered General R. Howe, with one thousand New England troops, to hurry down from the Highlands and nip this revolt in the bud. Howe speedily reached and surrounded the mutineers, and by the execution of two of the leaders reduced the remainder to order.

Among the minor military events in the County during 1781, were the entrance of three hundred troops by Kings Ferry at the close of January, and their march south to join the Pennsylvania regiments. During the following month, La Fayette with 1,200 New England troops passed through the Ramapo Valley, on his way to check Arnold's depredations in Virginia. In March, two hundred men with a gun marched from West Point and encamped at New City, while a militia camp was stationed at Tappan, and on June 22d, a portion of the army was encamped at the foot of the Long Clove in Haverstraw for some days.

Stony Point had been again occupied by the Americans after the withdrawal of the British, but not strongly fortified.' A messenger who passed there under the protection of a flag on April 21st, 1781, noted that some fifty flat bottomed boats lay at the Point, and that while he saw two field pieces, there were no works of any consequence; and later, on June 27th, Clinton was informed that thirty-five men, boys and blacks, with two pieces of cannon, were at Stony Point, and it was officered by a captain, lieutenant and ensign, while a lieutenant of artillery served both that and Verplanck's Point.

The last important move of troops through the County occurred on the occasion of the march to the seige of Yorktown. Ever since its evacuation by the American troops in 1776, Washington had aspired to recapture New York, and at this time, 1781, when that city was weakened by the campaign of Cornwallis in the South, while the Continental army was strengthened by the French allies, the project seemed feasible. To accomplish that recapture a junction had been effected between the allied armies in Westchester County, and for weeks the combined force lay with its right, composed of American troops, resting on Dobb's Ferry, while the French, who composed the left, stretched off toward the Bronx. Anxious as Washington was to expel the British from our metropolis, his wish was not to be immediately gratified, and New York was to be returned to the patriot army, not as the result of a bloody battle in her environs, but as a conquest of a glorious victory hundreds of miles away.

Strong reinforcements from across the sea reaching Clinton, and the disappointment of Washington by the French naval officers, led that Commander to suddenly change his plans and determine on the march to Virginia. Finding the plan possible, he at once set himself to the task of carrying it out successfully. To do this required the utmost secrecy, lest Clinton, learning of the movement, should detach strong reinforcements to Cornwallis.

Accordingly, the allied army was still handled as though New York was the determined object. Letters and dispatches, intended to mislead

Clinton, were intrusted to De La Montagne, who was ordered to take them to their destination by the way of Ramapo Pass. It is said that this gentleman, well aware that the Pass was infested by cowboys and Tories, demurred to the route, but the peremptory order of Washington led him to overcome his scruples. In the Pass De La Montagne was captured, as the Commander-in-Chief intended, and his messages being delivered to Clinton, completely deceived that officer as to the intention of the Americans.

On August 19th, Hazen's regiment and the New Jersey line were quietly crossed over to Sneden's Landing, and marched inland to Springfield. On the same day, the remainder of the force was slowly withdrawn up the country, and the crossing of the river at Kings Ferry begun. During this movement, portions of the army encamped on the line of march through the County and on one occasion a body of French troops was camped near the old Treason House. Finally, by August 26th, the last of the army was in motion on the west shore, and the long journey to Virginia begun.

In the march over our soil, the Americans passed over the old military road through Kakiat and Ramapo or Sidman's Pass; while the French, following the Kings Highway, advanced over the Long Clove; down through the Upper Hackensack Valley; skirted the western base of the Nyack hills; tarried for a brief space at Tappan; and then marched on south to again join the Americans and help them gain that victory, that gave this people peace, with a national existence, and greater political liberty than the world had yet seen.

---

† The name of this creek is spelled by different parties as follows: Benson J. Lossing. "Peploap's or Poplopen's;" Map of New York, in 1779. "Coplap's Kill;" Romans wrote it "Pooploop's;" when the boundaries of the County were defined in 1798, the Legislature called it "Poplopen's." In a plan of the attack on the forts drawn by a British officer and published in London, in 1784, it is given as "Peploaps."

‡ Samuel Holden Parsons, who was one of the eight brigade commanders on the Court of Inquiry that tried Andre, and unanimously found him guilty, was, within ten months after that trial, in correspondence with Sir Henry Clinton, and betrayed to him the position, strength, and intended movements of the Continental Army, so far as he was conversant with the facts. Magazine American History. Vol. XII. p. 166.

Authorities referred to: "Field Book of the Revolution," Lossing. Vols. II. "Life of Washington." John Marshall. Vol. I. "History of Orange County." S. W. Eager. "History of Ramapo." Rev. E. B. Cobb. "History of Haverstraw." Rev. Dr. A. S. Freeman. "History of Clarkstown." H. P. Fay. "History of Stony Point." Rev. E. Gay, Jr. Old Documents. "Force Papers." Magazine American History. Article by Dr. James Thacher, in the New England Magazine, May, 1834.

CHAPTER VII.

THE WAR OF THE REVOLUTION.

EVENTS AT TAPPAN AND SNEDEN'S LANDING—CONFLICT BETWEEN THE BRITISH AND SHORE GUARD AT PIERMONT AND HAVERSTRAW—NAVAL FIGHT IN TAPPAN ZEE—CONFLICTS AT NYACK—THE DEPREDATIONS COMMITTED BY COWBOYS IN THE COUNTY—FORAYS AT SLAUGHTER'S LANDING—JOSHUA HETT SMITH—INVASIONS OF THE SOUTHERN PART OF OUR COUNTY BY THE ENEMY—ACTS OF INDIVIDUAL BRAVERY AND SUFFERING—ACCOUNT OF CLAUDIUS SMITH—CONFISCATION OF PROPERTY AT THE CLOSE OF THE WAR—ROLL OF THE NAMES OF THE MEN WHO SERVED IN THE ARMIES OF THE REVOLUTION.

Far more interesting, than the march of armies or the fighting of battles, is the history of private deeds of men and women in trying hours of danger and death. By reason of its ease of access from the enemy's ships, its exposure to the raids of their foraging parties, and the number of the Tory marauders who lived near to or within its borders, Rockland County is rich in tales of the outrages produced by war. Patriot citizens assaulted and robbed, their buildings burned, their women violated, themselves not infrequently murdered. Parties of reprisal formed of these patriots, which gave but short shrift to the Tory when he was captured. Goodbyes exchanged between a brave wife, who though surrounded by every danger that chills a human heart, still loved the cause too dearly to shrink from risk; and husband, who, though leaving all which was of value to him on earth, hastening at the call of a duty, which might leave him unharmed, which might leave him sorely wounded, which might leave him lying asleep, after the turmoil of conflict was ended, with only a slight blue spot to show that that sleep was eternal, and with the "night dew and death dew mingling on his forehead;" or worse, far worse than wound or death, which might leave him a prisoner in British hands to suffer all that mind can dream or fear of hell on earth.

Yet, despite the interest that these acts of individuals and communities possess for us, it is with extreme difficulty that we can obtain accounts of them. The pioneers in the birth of this nation, the laborers in the foundation of this government, like their predecessors, the first settlers in the country, found other work to do besides noting their daily trials and deeds for the benefit of their descendants. They made history and left us in quieter times the peaceful task of recording it. Almost all of the local events and struggles of the Revolution in this County come to us by family tradition, and even the names of many who lived and participated in those events are lost. Perchance all would be gone but that here and there upon an old tomb stone can be found some record of patriotism.

As early as September 8th, 1776, Washington ordered the removal of his sick to the neighborhood of Tappan. Later, when General Scott encamped in Haverstraw to protect the stores which were there, he ordered ten tons of lead moved from Tappan to Major Smith's at Upper Nyack—the property now owned by Joseph Hilton. When Colonel Tyler had ceased to harry the Tories in Orangetown for a moment, and had withdrawn to Ramapo, Abraham Post, of Tappan, was ordered to remove eleven chests of armorer's tools, with bellows, anvils, &c., to the store of Abraham Mabie at the Slote. In 1780, General Greene had his headquarters in the stone house near the old road, which led from Sneden's Landing to Orangeburg, and which is now occupied by E. N. Taft and owned by Wm. Peet.

To protect the landing place at Sneden's the Americans erected a work, which was visited by a British spy on June 27th, 1781, and thus described: "It is a redoubt about a mile and half from the landing, on a very rough rocky height, picketted in all round with tops of trees and branches; no way to get in without climbing over; about four rods within this circle is a round breastwork running quite round the height, eight feet high, with a gate to pass in on the west side. Within that circle, about three rods, is another breastwork running round the top of the height, about the same height as the other, on which is wooden embrasures built, in which they have one piece of cannon on a travelling carriage. On the south side of the inward work a gate opens into the first breastwork. The rise of the height is so much as to cause the top of the first breastwork to be no higher than the bottom of the second. At this time it was commanded by a Lieutenant, two Sergeants, two Captains, and twenty-five men in the works."

At one time during the war Garret O'Blenis and a half-dozen comrades were watching a British vessel, which had anchored off Sneden's Landing —now Palisades. At last their watch was rewarded by seeing a barge filled with men start for the shore. Concealing themselves behind the rocks, the Americans permitted the barge to approach within a few yards of the landing, and then fired into her. After the first surprise the enemy endeavored to force a landing, assisted by the guns of the ship. For a few moments the conflict was severe, but, unaware of the numerical strength of the shore party, the foe at length withdrew. The only man seriously wounded among the patriots was Garret O'Blenis, who had a ball pass through his right arm and completely through his body, smashing two ribs and perforating the right lung in its course. His wound was regarded as mortal, but, after several months' illness, he entirely recovered.

The river shore from Taulman's Point at Piermont, north, was much exposed to the depredations of foraging forces from the enemy's ships, and the chief duty of Colonel Hay and the Minute Men was to guard this long and exposed line. On the first appearance of the British vessels, on July 12th, 1776, the enemy made two attempts to land at Nyack, but were repulsed through the watchfulness of Colonel Hay's men, who, by reason of their small number—only 400—and the distance to be patroled, were on duty day and night. On July 16th the fleet sailed up as far as Haverstraw and anchored off Kiers' landing, but here, too, their attempts to land were prevented. So deficient was the guard in the necessary munitions of war that Hays appealed for powder and ball to supply his men. Fortunately General George Clinton was able to reinforce him at the time, and shortly after he was sent twenty pounds of powder. For nine days the vessels remained off Haverstraw, but only once succeeded in obtaining provisions from the west shore. On that occasion they burned the house of a man named Halstead and took his pigs.

At last, on July 25th, the vessels sailed slowly down the river, anchoring for a time off Teller's, now Croton Point, to obtain some provisions from the Westchester shore. But their presence had roused the spirit of battle in the patriots, and on August 3d, 1776, the American galleys. Lady Washington, Spitfire, Whiting, and Crown, under Benjamin Tupper, attacked their vessels. Phenix, Captain Parker, and Rose, Captain Wallace, off Tarrytown and fought them for two hours.

Nyack, then but a hamlet of perhaps a dozen houses, became, before the end of the war, an object of the enemy's bitter aversion. This was partly due to those patriotic actions of its inhabitants, which ended in the repulsion more than once of their forces when they attempted to land for fresh provisions or water; partly because it was a rendezvous for the whale boat fleet, which patroled the river, and partly because of the residence at this place of Henry Palmer, who had rendered himself obnoxious to the British.

Captain Palmer had owned a vessel and been employed in the carrying trade for one of the largest firms in New York, before the Revolution. When the news of the battle of Bunker Hill reached that city, he was offered great financial advantages to serve the cause of the King but refused absolutely. Shortly after he conveyed two cargoes of arms and ammunition, which had been seized by the Sons of Liberty, from New York to the camp of the Continental Army. New York soon became uncomfortable for this patriot, and he removed with his family to a house, which formerly stood in Upper Nyack, on the east side of Broadway, opposite the old mountain road, by Garret E. Green's residence.

Owing to these causes, the British vessels, whenever they passed up the river, greeted the residents of the Nyack valley with a shotted salute from their guns. For their protection, those residents erected an earth work on the land east of the Methodist Church and just north of Depew Avenue, which covered the first dock in the village; while the section known as Upper Nyack, was defended by a swivel mounted on Major John L. Smith's place, and a company of Minute men under his and his brother —Captain Auri Smith's command.

As soon as hostilities had begun in this Colony the Shore Guard was placed on duty; this following order governing those stationed at Nyack.

"Haverstraw, October 16th, 1776. General orders for the commanding officers at the place called the Hook.

"Guards to mount daily at 4 or 5 o'clock in the afternoon, with sentries fixed as the commanding officer sees expedient. No soldier to fire a gun unless a sentry after hailing a craft or person three times, or at the enemy, or on an alarm. On every alarm, twenty hands to be sent to the commanding officer with intelligence. No person to pass without a permit from some commanding officer, or the committee from whence he came. No craft to be taken without liberty from the officer of the party of the place where said craft is. No liquor to be sold after 7 o'clock at night unless to a traveller, and none to be sold to any person in liquor. No sentry to leave his post until relieved. The commanding officer at the Hook to consult with the Major of the Riflemen, at New York, about the countersign. These orders to be read morning and evening to the guards until further orders."

"A HAWKINS HAY,
Commanding Officer."

In October 1776, the enemy attempted to land at Nyack, but were repulsed by the Shore Guard, not however till their cannon balls had marked Sarvent's house. In December of the same year, they effected a foot-hold and, besides looting a house, took off some cattle. In the summer of the following year—1777—two boats attempted to land at the present Piermont, at the point now known as the upper dock, at daybreak.

After a sharp conflict with the Shore Guard they were repulsed with three killed. Several of the Shore Guard were wounded, but none fatally.

Toward the close of July, 1777, the British sent a galley ashore to destroy a sloop which was moored to a dock at Abram Sarvent's place in Upper Nyack. To oppose this endeavor, Henry Palmer, Abram Sarvent, Cornelius Cuyper, Peter Freeland and Major Smith hastily collected, and concealed themselves in a quarry near the dock. Waiting till the enemy was within safe range, the patriots opened fire. The galley was at once put about and pulled out of gun shot for a time. A second attempt to force a landing, though assisted by the ship's guns, ended in failure. A third attempt was made, but the loss of the British was too great for further hope of success. The galley was then pulled up opposite Henry Palmer's house, and fire opened against that building from the bow carronade. So accurate was the aim of the gunners, that every shot struck the house or tore up the earth in the door yard. Mrs. Palmer, fearing each moment that a ball would pass through the building, took her infant in her arms and, creeping through the brambles and bushes along a water course, which passed alongside the house, till out of range, at length crossed the mountain and found a safe asylum at the house of a friend. In her flight, a ball struck the bank so close to the fugitive as to spatter dirt over herself and child.

The morning after the fight at Sarvent's Landing, the bodies of nine British sailors floated ashore and were buried by the Americans.

On another occasion Captain Palmer with a few comrades fired into a British vessel which was becalmed and floating with the tide. Thirty-six of the enemy were killed or wounded in this slaughter while of Palmer's force but one man was injured. He was wounded by a splinter from the rock behind which he was concealed.

Dreadful warfare did the patriots wage against the enemy's ships with the swivel, which was mounted east of Broadway, in Upper Nyack, opposite the residences of Joseph Hilton and S. C. Eaton, on property now belonging to Wilson Defendorf. At best this famous gun would barely carry a ball a half mile, and as the ships kept in the channel, some two and a half miles away, no very great injury was done by this long range shooting. Once however, during the war, two boats attempted to land at this shore for water and the Shore Guard opened so hot a fire with muskets and swivel, that one boat's crew surrendered at once while the other, braving the fire, pulled for the ships. The captured crew was sent to Tappan.

While the enemy did not, as a rule, invade the upper part of the valley, they did express their disapprobation of the swivel fire by returning its salute with great freedom.   One of their six pound balls was found some years ago on the property belonging to Harmon Snedeker some distance from the river.   In one of these artillery duels, a shot from the ships struck the stone fence on which the American gun rested, scattering stones in every direction, dispersing the Minute Men with startling rapidity, and knocking the swivel off its mount into the trench behind the earthwork.   On this occasion Cornelius Cuyper was standing on the fence when the ball struck it.   In the dust and excitement that followed he was heard to ejaculate: "H—ll, don't shoot my legs off!"

A messenger to Verplancks Point on June 27th, 1781, under a flag, reported on his return that he saw "opposite Tarrytown, on the west shore, six whale boats and about forty-two men in all. No appearance of any of them fitted for carrying swivels or wall pieces."

Recollections of cowboys and their deeds in Nyack is preserved, by a bullet hole in the wall of the house now occupied by John Salisbury, and the tradition, existing in the family, of the escape from their clutches of Michael Cornelison, Jr., who resided in the house during the Revolution, the capture of his father, and the looting of the place. The bullet was fired through the window, in the south-west corner of the house, at some American officers who were sitting in Mr. Cornelison's parlor.   It passed between them doing no injury.   Another attack by a party, supposed to have been from Westchester, who rowed across the river and landed at the "Bight," was made upon Mr. Cornelisons' one evening.

At the outbreak of hostilities Mr. Cornelison's house was unfinished, and, owing to the draft upon the people, it remained uncompleted till the close of the Revolution.   When it was evident that the struggle would be a protracted one, Cornelison, foreseeing the difficulty of obtaining provisions at a later period, laid in a store of tea, sugar, wines, crockery, &c., for the entertainment of travellers as well as for his own use. When the enemy, who were guided by a Tory neighbor of Cornelison, entered the house, Mrs. Cornelison had but time to throw a few silver dollars behind the back-log in the fire-place.   In their usual manner the foe proceeded to devastate the house.   The crate of crockery was opened and its contents broken, the tea was scattered all the way down the hill to the boat, while the pipe of wine was broached, and, after being used freely, it was turned upside down to empty it.

While this destruction was going on down stairs, the commanding officer, guided still by the Tory, passed up to the rooms above.   On a collar beam in those rooms lay Michael Cornelison, Jr., who had rushed to hide at the first alarm.   In his flight, his watch chain had caught on some projecting object and dragged the watch from its fob. As he lay upon the beam, scarcely daring to breath, the ticking of the dangling watch sounded like the roar of machinery, and doubtless, could he have but gotten his thumb on the works, it would have required more than mechanical ingenuity to repair the damage. He was espied by the Tory, but was saved by the fact that his discoverer was a brother Freemason.

After destroying everything they could lay their hands on, the marauders at length left, taking Michael Cornelison, Sr., with them. He was confined in the Sugar House for nine months and then released on parole. The morning following his capture, Mrs. Cornelison visited New York to secure his release. She, too, was detained within the enemy's lines, but was permitted to reside at the house of a friend named Walker, and to visit her husband daily, taking him food and luxuries. At length she made the acquaintance of a leman of one of the British officers, and, through her interposition, obtained greater freedom for the prisoner. After being detained some six months in the city, she was allowed to go home, followed, as we have seen, by her husband three months later. In 1840, when some needed repairs were being made to the old house, evidences of that night's visit of the enemy were found in abundance.

Adjoining the residence of John A. Hazzard at Rockland Lake is an old house, which seems to have acted the part of a target for the British gunners whenever they passed Slaughter's Landing. It has been marked over and over again with shot, and from its wall many old six pound balls have been taken.

On one of their many foraging expeditions, a boats' crew, which had landed at Rockland Lake and marched inland, came upon the house of a Mr. Ryder, which stood near the present Swartwout's pond. Mr. Ryder was from home at the time of this visit and his young wife was alone to meet the marauders. In compliance with their demands, she gave them all the food she had and waited on them during their meal. When they had finished eating, the invaders returned to the beach taking Mrs. Ryder with them. On reaching the shore these, worse than brutes, violated the poor woman and then left her, lying unconscious on the sand under Calico Hook, while they returned to their vessel. It was not till the following day that the poor creature could drag herself back to her home, and tell to her alarmed neighbors her horrible tale.

In more than one instance these predatory parties raided inland from Rockland Lake or Haverstraw after fresh provisions. Sometimes they would meet with success and get back to their boats without difficulty. Sometimes they would retire when they found they were discovered, and sometimes, they roused a hornets' nest of Minute Men about them and were glad to reach their boats without spoil. During an expedition of this nature in the neighborhood of Strawtown, Resolvert Stephens and a few others learned of the enemy's presence and attacked them. The British were in too great force, however, for this little band to do more than fire and run; but the patriots, at least, had the satisfaction of seeing one of the foe carried back to the shore by his comrades, and knew their volley had not been in vain.

On another occasion Major John Smith, having learned that a body of the enemy had landed at the present Rockland Lake, and proceeded inland, hastily gathered a party and rode up the Strawtown road. Ere the faintest suspicion was excited, the Major was in an ambush. His comrades wheeled and rode back as the enemy fired, but it was too late for the Major to turn and, finding himself surrounded, he spurred ahead, leaped his horse over a fence, and started across country for the Nyack and Haverstraw road. Believing that the enemy were below him, he turned toward the Long Clove, but when opposite the present Waldberg Church, he saw a group of invaders about a neighboring house. Again he was fired at and missed. Then two of the enemy, mounting in haste on two stolen horses, began pursuit. The race was kept up till Long Clove was reached, when the chase was abandoned, but not till one pursuer had been shot, and Major Smith's sword hand nearly amputated by a saber stroke. At a later period, this patriot was captured and confined in New York.

Toward the close of the war a boat load of marines landed at Rockland Lake, in the dusk of the evening, and under the guidance of neighboring Tories, started on a search for booty. On this errand bent, they marched around the lake and down the old lake road towards its junction with the Kings Highway. On the west side of the lake road and almost opposite the junction of the mountain road with it, lived Garret Meyers, a militia-man. All that day Mr. Meyers had been watching the British vessels, to alarm the country in case an attempt was made to land from them, and only at nightfall had returned to his home. Just before bed time, he heard the tramp of feet on the road, and surmising at once that the enemy had landed, he started out to light the beacon fire on Verdridica Hook, and thus warn the Minute Men. As he stepped from his door however, he saw that the enemy was between him and the mountain, and that it would be necessary for him to wait till the road was clear. Hastening to a pear tree, which stood near the house, he flattened himself against it, hoping to be unobserved in the darkness. But fate was against him.

In the yard was a pet white calf that Mr. Meyers had been accustomed to feed, and the animal had become so tame, that it would follow its master like a dog. Seeing him appear, the calf ran to the tree behind which he was standing, and stood beside it. Among the Tories, who accompanied the British, was a near neighbor of Meyers, who knew the habit of the calf, and when he saw it run to the pear tree he suspected the presence of his neighbor. He therefore told the commanding officer of the party that a rebel Whig was hidden at that spot, and the search that followed resulted in Meyer's capture. The party then visited his house, gutted it completely, knocked Mrs. Meyers senseless with a blow from the butt of a musket, which drove her teeth down her throat, and then took their departure for the landing with their prisoner. Mr. Meyers was confined in the Sugar House till the close of the war, and left it with his health forever broken. This unfortunate man always suspected a neighbor, who claimed to be a patriot, of having betrayed him, and, rendered frenzied by his sufferings while a prisoner, registered an oath to shoot the suspect on sight. Being informed one day, long after the war had ended, that this neighbor was coming down the road, the bed-ridden old man, toilsomely dragged himself to his loaded gun, but fell ere he could take aim, and the villain who caused his misery escaped the judgment of man.

Residing at the upper end of the Hackensack Valley, near the present Congers Station on the West Shore Railroad, during the Revolution, was Theodorus Snedeker, who, according to his statement, incurred the distrust and enmity of both parties and was relieved of his property by each. Early in the conflict, as Snedeker afterward stated, he furnished the Continental troops with provisions and forage, and, by so doing, attracted the watchful eyes of his Tory neighbors. When, in the changeful fortunes of war, the British vessels were at anchor off Snedeker's house, his aid to the Americans was remembered, and, guided by some Tories, the enemy visited his farm and looted it. Besides carrying off four horses, two yokes of oxen, fourteen cows and ten sheep, they took Snedeker into custody and only released him on his payment of a large ransom. Of his after difficulty with the Americans I will speak later.

Haverstraw, during the Revolution, like Nyack, was but a hamlet. Its proximity to the Kings Ferry at Stony Point, and its position on the Kings Highway, rendered it more than once, as we have already seen, the theater in which portions of the army encamped or through which they marched; while its connection with Arnold's treason gives it more than a passing fame. In this village, as elsewhere, the citizens were divided in their allegiance. Few were as deeply involved with the British as Joshua Hett

Smith, but all the loyalists wished success to the King, and in every way, commensurate with their safety, aided his troops. Of Smith's connection with Arnold and Andre, and of his final escape, I have briefly spoken in a preceding chapter. Of his actions at other periods of the war further mention may not be amiss.

Joshua Hett Smith was a man of more than ordinary ability, and was looked upon by his patriot neighbors as fitted to represent them in the Assembly then called "The Convention of the Representatives of the State of New York," of 1777. While serving in that body he voted for the State Constitution, which was adopted at Kingston, April 20th, 1777. For some unexplained reason his influence among the patriots seemed to wane from this time, and he was not taken into their full confidence when any enterprise was on foot. That this was because one of his brothers—William—was a noted Tory Justice in New York, would seem much more probable if another brother, Thomas, a firm patriot, had also lost the confidence of his Whig neighbors. Such was not the case, however. Thomas was not even suspected of treason after his brother's implication with Arnold. From the beginning, Colonel Lamb, whose wife was closely related to Smith's wife, suspected him of being a Tory and persistently refused to associate in any way with him. In regard to his being duped by Arnold. As before said, he was a man of intelligence. That his suspicions should not have been aroused by Arnold's previous career at Philadelphia, is entirely probable, but, that in conjunction with that career, the strange and earnestly pushed midnight visit to an enemy's ship; the conveyance from that ship to shore of a man in the uniform of the enemy, the secrecy of that nights' conference; that these things should not have excited the suspicion of a man with more than ordinary wit, seems improbable; and if, to still further clinch the evidence against Smith, we remember the removal of his family to Fishkill, that his house might be vacant in case the interview between Arnold and the stranger was prolonged; his anxiety, as the early hours of the morning passed on toward dawn, that the conspirators should seek a more concealed spot for further talk; his indifference to the presence of a stranger in his house during that September day, his refusal, point blank, to reconvey that stranger back to the British ship, while perfectly willing to ride anywhere with him, protected by Arnold's pass; his loan to that stranger of a coat to replace his military dress and thus disguise himself; these many things, while they *might not* have excited Smith's suspicions, would most certainly have excited the distrust of men far duller in mind than he.

In his defence, Arnold wrote Washington, that Smith was his dupe, and the Tory Justice wrote to the patriot Thomas, asserting that Joshua was Arnold's dupe because Arnold said so. The word of Benedict Arnold against the circumstantial evidence! We have seen that Smith was acquitted by a court martial and escaped from a civil trial by flight. That by that flight he escaped a fate he richly deserved was believed by his neighbors at the time, and the lapse of years has not cleared his reputation.

One incident connected with this period at Haverstraw has come to me. At that place was residing a wealthy widow named Robart, who had infatuated a Tory neighbor. When the section became unpleasantly patriotic for this class, and all could see that the Americans had won the long struggle, the loyalists made haste to embark on British vessels for Nova Scotia or New Brunswick. Mrs. Robart's lover had determined to move, but ere departing hastened to press his suit with the fair lady. That suit was rejected by the patriotic woman with scorn, and in revenge the suitor that night fired her buildings, which were totally destroyed, then fled for refuge to his British friends.

The furthest north that British troops passed by land in our County, was to a spot opposite the house formerly owned by James Lydecker, a few rods north of the turnpike at Clarksville. This invasion was made by a squadron of cavalry, doubtless acting as a scouting and foraging party. Major John Smith, commanding a small force of mounted men, met the enemy near Greenbush, but whether, believing discretion better than valor or being vastly outnumbered, certain it is that the meeting was not prolonged by the Americans, who hastened off at topmost speed.

While never advancing further up the Hackensack Valley than Clarksville, the enemy frequently overran the lower portions of the County. In 1777, a detachment of the foe marched into Orangetown in search of provisions. Avoiding the road along Snake Hill, this party followed the old Clausland road till about Greenbush, and then, finding no cattle, retraced their steps. Had this force advanced but a few rods further and ascended a small hill, they would have found a large number of cows and horses, which had been driven to this retired spot for safe keeping.

On the march north, the commanding officer halted at the residence of Mrs. Blauvelt, mother of Mrs. Elizabeth Haring, and asked her where her son was. He was told in the American army. He then stated that he was very dry, and asked for some liquor. This was produced. Raising the flask this officer said: "Here's health, safety and success to your son. May he always be a true soldier to his country and no harm befall him. I honor the man who is true to his country, but damn the one, who turns traitor." After a long drink he returned the flask, expressed his thanks, and promised that not a thing belonging to Mrs. Blauvelt should be molested by the troops.

When the order to counter-march was given, plunder began, and the residence of Mrs. Blauvelt was invaded by soldiers, bent on destruction. Looking-glasses were taken from the walls, laid on the floor, and jumped upon; crockery was smashed, furniture was broken, feather beds ripped open, and other acts common to a devastating army were carried on. When the uproar was at its height, the officer, who had stopped earlier in the day, appeared, ordered the destruction stayed and the soldiers to withdraw, and made every apology for his unavoidable detention. "Mammy," said he at parting, "don't blame my men for this, but blame the traitors among your own countrymen. They are the ones who lead the soldiers to plunder and tell them where to go, and, but for them, there would be no scenes like this."

Some two and a half miles west of Tappan, dwelt, in the early days of the Revolution, Minard Kissike, with his wife and a daughter about fourteen years of age. Kissike had accumulated a goodly property and was a patriot, either of which facts was sufficient inducement for the Tories, who infested the neighborhood of Tappan Town, to pay his place a visit. A raid by the cow boys was soon planned. Captain Outwater, of Tappan, had organized a company of Minute Men for the purpose of guarding the property of the patriots, and, learning of the contemplated attack on Kissike's house, gathered his men, silently marched to a wooded hill some yards west of the house, and prepared to receive the enemy.

The night passed without trouble, and the Minute Men, suspecting the Tories had gotten wind of their preparation, were about to retire when a large force of marauders appeared, and entered the house. The inmates had just sat down to their breakfast, when the foe entered, and were absolutely unwarned. Before anything had been accomplished, Outwater's men surrounded the house and demanded the Tories' surrender. But they had miscalculated the pluck of their opponents, and a conflict was at once begun. In the confusion that followed, Kissike pushed his wife and daughter through a rear door, and pointed toward the wooded hill the Americans had but just left. Before half the distance was covered, a bullet struck the daughter, and she fell to the earth. Only long enough did the mother pause to raise the wounded fugitive in her arms, and then continued her flight, bearing her precious burden, to the safe retreat afforded by the woods.

For a brief space the conflict between Outwater's band and the Tories continued, but the latter were protected by the house, and at length won the day. At their leisure they looted the place, and then took their departure after setting fire to the buildings.

In the evening, a few neighbors visited the spot, and found sitting near the ruins, and lighted by the fitful flashes of fire which still burned, a maniac, with the head of her dead child resting on her lap, and the charred body of her husband lying beside her. Were these the deeds of sons of men or the actions of demons direct from Hell?

Among the members of Captain Outwater's company was Samuel Garritson, third son of Dominie Ver Bryck. In one of the scouting expeditions of a detachment of his company, young Ver Bryck was captured by Van Buskirk's band of Tories, conveyed to New York, and lodged a prisoner in the Provost, under charge of the fiend, Cunningham. For a long time his rations consisted of old English peas, "hard enough," as Cunningham said, "to shoot the rebels with." These had to be parboiled in lye for four or five hours, and then pounded in a mortar before they could be boiled in clean water. In addition to this unpalatable food, each prisoner was allowed a quarter of a pound of rusty salt-pork weekly. If complaint was made about the food, the prisoner was beaten and might consider himself lucky, if Cunningham did not take the law in his own hands, and hang him ere midnight.

Unused to such treatment, and still a boy under twenty, Ver Bryck's health gave way and he rapidly failed. When almost beyond recovery he was visited by a Tory—then resident on Long Island—who had formerly been a communicant in his father's church, at Tappan. This man heard that his old dominie's and neighbor's son was a prisoner in the Provost, and visited it to ascertain the truth of the statement. Through his efforts, young Ver Bryck was bailed, and carried, for he could no longer walk, to the residence of a man named De Bevoise, on Long Island. Ten months had been passed in the Provost and nine and twenty months under bail at the house of De Bevoise, when Ver Bryck was paroled, through the intercession of an English officer, for whom he had performed some favor, and allowed to visit his house. Through the kindness of his English friend, he carried with him many luxuries to the parents he had not seen for over three years. Before his parole expired, Ver Bryck was exchanged. He immediately re-entered the patriot service and remained till the end of the war.

The Tory, who thus saved young Ver Bryck's life on one occasion, was on the verge of taking that of the Dominie on another. We have already said that this clergyman was, heart and soul, with the patriot cause, and that he never ceased his efforts for the success of liberty. Naturally his deeds and words drew upon him the wrath of his Tory neighbors, and he found it necessary to abandon the highway on his trips to and from the church, and follow a secret path through the woods. This path was discovered by the Tory above mentioned, and he laid in wait, with loaded musket, to kill his pastor. The Dominie appeared and the Tory took aim, but—was it the thought of the cup he had received from that venerable hand, of the mysterious symbol which represented the body of Him, before whom he must appear with his victim when the dead shall be raised, that stayed his purpose? He could not fire, and the aged disciple passed on his way unaware of how near the angel of death had passed him by. When young Ver Bryck was a prisoner, this Tory told him of this fact.

While in the Provost, Ver Bryck saw, among a number of newly arrived prisoners, a near neighbor, named John Frelin. According to the regulations of the British army, no one was allowed to purchase over a stated quantity of provisions at any one time, and the restriction on salt limited the amount to a half bushel. Frelin was in the habit of visiting New York at regular times and making such purchases as his neighbors might wish. On this occasion his commission embraced several half-bushels of salt. He had no sooner procured these, than he was placed under arrest, and taken to the Provost on a charge of violating military law. Explanations were useless, and Frelin was given his choice between joining Van Buskirk's band of Tories or being flogged. He chose the former with an idea of deserting at his earliest opportunity. The next morning he was taken to the yard of the Provost, stripped and lashed to a stake, and given one hundred lashes. For the first nine blows he bore his suffering unflinchingly. At the tenth he uttered a frightful yell, and, as blow followed blow, he gave shriek after shriek. Before the punishment was ended Frelin's cries had grown fainter and fainter, and at length ceased, and unconsciousness came to his relief. At last the stripes were ended and the victim, upon being unbound, fell to the earth a gory, mangled mass. Upon his recovery he was placed in Van Buskirk's band, and nearly four months elapsed before he effected his escape. From the hour of his freedom he devoted himself to revenge, and, only attending the demands of nature sufficiently to preserve life, he followed Van Buskirk's band to and fro, killing one or more at each and every opportunity till he actually destroyed more of that party than ever fell in any of their numerous combats.

In the autumn of 1780, a party of eight or ten patriots, living at Tappan or in its vicinity, learned that at the residence of one of their neighbors, strongly suspected of favoring the British, a large amount of provision, cattle and forage had been gathered; that a party of the enemy would make a pretended attack on this residence, and that, after a brief and bloodless resistance, the stores were to be carried off.

Quietly marching to the suspected point, these men found their story confirmed by the presence of a dozen British troopers, who were loading the provisions on wagons and preparing the cattle for removal. The Americans separated into two parties and attacked the foe on both sides. At the first volley four saddles were emptied, and the foe, unaware of the force which opposed them, thrown into confusion. The regulars fought well and, though defeated, only retired with Abraham Storms as a prisoner and after leaving most of the patriots severely and David Clarke fatally wounded.

Slowly the Americans retraced their steps toward home, taking with them the fruits of their capture, and tenderly bearing their wounded comrade, but the journey to Tappan was left uncompleted by Clarke, and by the roadside, where he was laid by grieving comrades, he uttered his last words, and started on the other journey which we all must take.

Abraham Storms, who was only three and twenty years of age and had but recently been married and settled near the Waldberg Church, was taken to New York and confined in the Sugar House. After a long imprisonment he was exchanged, and re-entering the American army, continued in the service till the close of the war.

On another occasion the patriots received word that a suspected Tory, living a short distance north of Tappan, was about to convey a heavily laden team to the British camp. A half dozen of them, determining to intercept this movement and take the goods for the American army, laid in wait for the Tory by the roadside. At length the rumbling of wheels was heard and the suspected man drove among them, but, owing to the intense darkness, he was unaware of their presence till ordered to halt. The night favored his escape, but the patriots seized the wagon and started toward home. As they proceeded, laughing and joking at the Tory's surprise, they were themselves surprised by marching directly into the midst of a foraging party of the enemy. Escape was their only thought and all were rapidly off in safety, except Abraham O'Blenis. This individual was snugly stowed away in the wagon. Upon discovery, he asserted himself to be a Loyalist and joined the troopers in a search for his comrades. In the course of the hunt he gradually drew further and further away from the main body until, with the exception of one trooper who accompanied him, he was alone. At the top of the declivity north of the

Tappan Church, which runs along the mill-dam, O'Blenis suddenly stopped as if listening. In an instant he called the trooper in a whisper and bade him look below. This the unsuspecting soldier did. With a lunge from his musket, which tumbled the Englishman into the dam, O'Blenis turned and fled, escaping before an alarm could be given.

During the period of hostilities the residence of Joost Mabie, at Tappan, was visited by the Tories, and the usual robbery and destruction took place. So unexpected was the attack, that Mabie's son, Peter C., had but time to hide behind an immense clothes-press which stood in one of the rooms. In the process of destruction this clothes-press was forced open and rifled, but not before the whole front was broken and battered by musket blows. Young Mabie escaped discovery, but his father was taken to New York and confined for some time in the old Provost. A few years ago the old press was in the possession of Peter R. Haring.

On one occasion, about 1778, Peter Van Orden, later a Division commander of militia in the war of 1812, and member of Assembly from our County, had been on a scouting expedition near the British camp. He was seen by the foe and chased till he found refuge in the swamp near the log tavern, which formerly stood on the property now owned by John A. Bogert. In this swamp the fugitive remained for a night.

About the same year, 1778, a man named Shuart, who had caused suspicion of his patriotism, was detected in the act of driving cattle, which he had stolen from about Kakiat, to the British camp. His pursuers overtook this cow-boy at a spot just west of the present school-house in Nanuet, near the house of the Rev. J. Cooper, and shot him dead.

Just north of the Ramapo valley, in the present village of Monroe, dwelt Claudius Smith, the most daring marauder, the most merciless cowboy, the most thorough scoundrel that ever met a just fate on the gallows. At the outbreak of hostilities in this region, Smith, with his three sons, William, Richard and James, collected about them a gang of desperadoes and began a warfare against mankind so lawless and violent as to terrorize this whole section, and call forth the offer of a large reward for their capture. A correct list of the names of those associated with Smith will probably never be obtained, nor is it needful, as most of them came from other parts of the country, attracted by the boldness of his crimes. Among the names preserved are those of Wm. Cole, John Babcock, Wm. Jones, Thomas Ward, John Everett, Jacob Ackner, Geo. Harding, James Twaddle, Martinus and Peter Dawson, John Mason, Henry McManus, Wm. Stagg, Geo. Bull, Jacob Low, James Terwilling and James Conners.

This band of banditti ravaged the southern section of the present

Orange county, raided down the Ramapo pass, and alternately visited the houses of patriots in the present township of Ramapo, or in the northern section of New Jersey. When they attacked a place it was not left till the process of looting was complete. Horses, harness, cattle, provisions were forcibly taken from the barns of the unfortunate recipients of their visits; everything of any value that could be carried was stolen from their houses, while the proprietor was either beaten or murdered, and his family outraged. Extending their sphere of operations as they grew stronger, this gang of cow-boys attacked government property as it passed through Ramapo pass, and among the spoils thus seized were several thousand muskets. On July 18th, 1777, Claudius Smith, then a prisoner at Goshen, and one of his band, named John Brown, were indicted for stealing a yoke of government oxen, but succeeded in escaping from custody.

Among the rocky fastnesses of the Ramapo mountains, this band found plenty of safe resorts. In one just east of the Augusta Iron Works, they frequently divided their spoils. In another, near Sherwoodville, at a spot called "Horse Stable Rock," on Round Mountain, they often rendezvoused, while among their neighbors were many who sympathized with them, and gave them shelter in time of need. Of these Tory participants in their hellish actions, were Benjamin Demarest, John Harring, John Johnson, Wm. Conkling, Peter Ackner, in Pascack, Arie Ackerman, of the same place, and one Isaac Mabie, at whose place these robbers had excavated a cave for a retreat. At length their deeds reached such an alarming state, that Governor Clinton, offered a reward of $500 for the arrest of Claudius Smith. This frightened that leader, and he hastened to place himself under British protection in New York, from whence, with the idea of reaching still greater safety, he crossed to Long Island. Through the instrumentality of Major John Brush, he was at length captured, conveyed to Goshen, and brought to trial January 11th, 1779. As already said, the result of that trial was his conviction and execution with two others of his band on January 22d, 1779. One of his last acts depicts his character. Always wicked, one of his early crimes had drawn from his mother the prophecy that he would "die like a trooper's horse with shoes on." The remembrance of this came to him at the last, and in presence of eternity, he kicked his shoes off to make his mother a liar.

After the death of Claudius Smith, his sons swore revenge and the excesses of the band were worse than before. On April 28th, 1779, a Goshen paper published the following: "We hear from Goshen that a horrible murder was committed near the Sterling Iron Works, on Saturday, March 26th, by a party of villians, several in number, the principal of whom was

Richard Smith, eldest surviving son of the late Claudius Smith, of infamous memory, his eldest son having been shot last fall at Smith's Clove, in company with several other villians, by one of our scouting parties sent out in search of them. These bloody miscreants it seems that night intended to murder two men who had shown some activity and resolution in apprehending these robbers, and murderers who infest this neighborhood. They first went to the house of John Clark, near the iron works, whom they dragged from the house and then shot him, and observing some remains of life in him shot him through the arm again and left him. He lived some hours after."

Among the homes visited by these British partisans was one, situated near the State line at Masonicus, occupied by a family named Lee. This home they devastated, killed young Lee, and violated the person of his sister Elizabeth. The sufferings she had witnessed and undergone, upset this poor girl's reason and from the time of the assault till her death, which occurred soon after from exposure in a bitter snow storm, Bessie Lee wandered through the present township of Ramapo, entreating by her appearance, far more potent than word of tongue, the revenge of her patriot neighbors.

In 1781, the British held several positions in New Jersey near the State line, and their presence gave rise to much uneasiness among the patriots in Ramapo township. On one occasion a Captain Babbitt, with a dozen horsemen, started on a reconnoissance, and at evening camped in a wood by the side of the road near the present village of Monsey. After breakfast, next morning, the troopers were lounging about, when a countryman was descried riding toward their place of concealment. After he passed he turned south on a narrow lane, which intersected the highway just beyond the Americans, and soon met a British troop of two score dragoons. With the commanding officer of this party he had a long conversation, frequently pointing toward the American's wood. Babbitt's band, concluding they were discovered, determined to charge.

With a whoop and cheer they broke cover and dashed at the startled foe. That foe had but just time to draw pistols and fire, but their aim was so hurried that not a patriot was injured. Before the dragoons could draw sabres the Americans were on them, overturning horses and riders, cutting them down with each sabre sweep, until, wild with terror, the British turned and fled through the narrow causeway. The pursuit was not abandoned by the patriots till the first picket line of the enemy was passed and one of the pickets made prisoner. Of the dragoon force, all were captured or cut down except one.

One other incident of a local nature in Ramapo township comes to my notice. An old gentleman in this section was, until the war begun, the happy owner of pictures of King George and Queen Charlotte. At the outbreak of hostilities this firm patriot, with grim determination, turned the pictures face to the wall. Long before the close of the struggle the old man was stricken with paralysis and bed-ridden. In one of the many alarms, when it seemed as though the enemy would overrun our County, the old gentleman was observed to be restless and uneasy, and, at length, when news was brought that the foe was approaching, he made the most violent gesticulations to have the faces of the pictures turned out again.

Sad had been the lot of the patriots during the long years of the war. From Tappan, whose residents had been harried by the incursions of British troops and Tory partisans, whose citizens had seen neighbor after neighbor robbed, beaten or slaughtered, to whom the awful realization of conflict had come in the execution of John Andre; to Peploaps kill, where the festering, bloated corpses of our yeomen poisoned the pure mountain air. From the shore of the Hudson, which had been the scene of many a sanguinary struggle; to the Ramapo Valley, where the patriots had been wasted by Claudius Smith and his band; there had arisen, time and again, the cry of agony: "How long; O Lord! how long!"

Now the war was ended, and, as the loyalists had acted toward the patriots in days gone by, they now, in their hour of triumph, took revenge seven-fold upon their foretime persecutors. Commissioners of Forfeiture, appointed by the State authorities, confiscated the property of such as had excited suspicion of their patriotism; and many of the old families of the County found it safer to abandon their homes and possessions, than to trust to the clemency of the victors. These people joined the refugees in New York, and sailed under British protection to other lands.

Among those who fell under the ban was Theodorus Snedeker. We have already seen that he claimed to have supplied the American army with food, and thus drawn upon himself the enemity of the British; that they had visited and robbed him. He then goes on to state that he visited New York to obtain redress for the robbery, and thus caused the distrust of his patriot neighbors while he was unsuccessful in his mission; and that, while he was absent, his furniture, stock and lands were sequestrated and sold. Snedeker's disloyalty to the patriot cause was too noted. His petition was rejected and his property was sold by Samuel Dodge and Daniel Graham, the Commissioners of Forfeiture, to Jacobus Swartwout, on Aug. 18th, 1782. Snedeker's house, still standing, is now owned by Hon. A. B. Conger.

Turn from this picture of human selfishness, greediness, cowardice, and treason, to that other picture, where, on Sept. 28th, 1779, wrapped in a few rags, in the midst of inconceivable filth and vermin, exhausted by privation and hunger, breathing the mephitic, noisome air of the old Sugar House; the son-in-law and nephew of Theodorus—Johannes Snedeker—lay dying; so crowded by fellow prisoners that his death struggles disturbed them, and hearing, with dulled ears, not the familiar voice of Dominie Ver Bryck in prayer, but the oaths and imprecations of men half frenzied with suffering.

Captain James Lamb, of Haverstraw, was another Tory whose property was confiscated. This land lay between Florus Falls and Stony Point. Owing to the patriotism of his sons-in-law Jacob and John Waldron, part of the property was saved and granted to Lamb's children.

Cornelius Mabie, of Tappan, had cast his lot with the British during the war. At its close, he sought a new home in Nova Scotia, while the Commissioners of Forfeiture disposed of his mill, farm and stock for the benefit of the State.

A. Hawks Hay, Colonel.		Gilbert Cooper, Lieutenaut-Colonel.
John Smith, Major.†		John L. Smith, Major.
John Ferrand, Surgeon.	James Clark, Adjutant.	Joseph Johnson, Quartermaster.
	Joseph Hunt, Quartermaster Sergeant.	
	James Onderdonk, Sergeant Major.	
	Jacob Onderdonk, Captain.	
Resolvert Van Houten, First Lieutenant,		Andries Onderdonk, Second Lieutenant.
	Resolveert Van Houten, Ensign.	
Rueloff Stephens, Sergeant.		Jacobus Blauvelt, Sergeant.
Claus Van Houten, Sergeant.		Abraham Blauvelt, Sergeant.
James Vanderbilt, Corporal.		Peter Stephens, Corporal.
Tunis Van Houten, Corporal.		Abraham Van Houten, Corporal
	Johannes Ackerman, Fifer.	
Blauvelt, John	Garrison, Abraham Jr.	Stagg, John
Blauvelt, Peter	Seaman, Joseph	Stephens, Albert
Copoelet, Daniel	Seaman, Towles	Stephens, Resolvert
Campbell, Luke	Secor, Isaac	Stephens, Stepen A.
Campbell, Stephen	Smith, Isaac	Stephens, Stephen H.
Campbell, William	Smith, John	Taylor, William
Cooper, Hendrick	Smith, Nathaniel	Van Houten, John
DePew, Peter	Smith, Stephen	Van Sickles, Daniel
Garrison, Abraham	Riker, Mathew	

Johannes Bell, Captain.	Joseph Crane, Captain.	John Fitcher, First Lieutenant.
William Graham, Second Lieutenant.		Daniel Onderdonk, Ensign.
Ackerson, Garrett	Gardener, John	Sickles, William
Blauvelt, Aurie	Hogenkamp, John A.	Smith, Aurie
Blauvelt, Johannes	Onderdonk, Jacob	Tourneurs, Henry

Captured at Fort Clinton and Fort Montgomery:

Conklin, John†	DeLa Montagne, James†	Lent, Jacob†
Crom, Herman†	Garrison, Samuel†	Sears, Francis†
	Storms, John†	

Colonel, Abraham Lent.
Lieutenant-Colonel, Johannes David Blauvelt.   Major, Johannes Joseph Blauvelt.
Adjutant, Jacobus De Clark.   Quartermaster, Isaac Perry.

Johannes Jacobus Blauvelt, Captain.
James Lent, First Lieut.   Hendrick V. Ver Bryck, Ensign.   James Smith, Second Lieut.

Isaac Smith, Captain.
Johannes Isaac Blauvelt, First Lieut.   Wm. Van Sickles, Second Lieut.
Lambert Smith, Ensign.

The appended list is of Rockland County people who served during the Revolution, but to what regiments or branch of the service they were attached, I do not know.

Ackerman, William	Freeland, Peter	Palmer, Henry, Captain.
Archer, Jacob*	Garrison, John	Paul, Arthur
Blanch, Thomas Colonel,	Jones, Jacob	Sarvent, Abram
Blauvelt, Abram	Lewis, James	Schucraft, James
Blauvelt, C. A.† Con., Army	Meyers, Gerrit†	Steel. John
Carson, James	O'Blenis, Abram	Storms, Abram†
Clarke, David*	O'Blenis, Gerrit	Suffern, John
Cuyper, Cornelius Lieut-Col.	Onderdonk, Andrew	Tallman, Harmanus†
Ellison, Robert	Onderdonk, Thomas	Taulman, Peter, Captain.
Trout, Adam	Weygint, Tobias	Dorey, James, Con. Army.
Trout, Michael	Wilson, James†	De Ronde, Abram*
Snedeker, Johannes‡	Gross, Peter	Cornelison, Michael,,Sr.†
Allison, Wm. Colonel.	Smith, Jacobus	Waldron, John
Tinkey, John	Waldron, Jacob	VerBryck, Sam'l Gerrit, Sr.†

Two companies from Haverstraw were in the Continental Army.
Benjamin Coe, Captain.
Abraham Onderdonk, First Lieut.   Paulus M. Vandervoort, Second Lieut.
Daniel Coe, Jr., Ensign.

---

*Killed †Captured ‡Died prisoners.

John Suffern was an officer in the Commissary Department, C. A. Blauvelt, of the Continental army, was captured, transported to England, and held there as a prisoner of war for nine months. James Wilson was confined in the Sugar House; after his release he lived to the age of 90 years. Peter Gross served in Colonel John Lamb's Regiment of N. Y. Artillery, and was present at the surrender of Yorktown. Abram De Ronde was captured by a party of Tories while conveying provisions to the American army at Stony Point. On the way to New York he and his captors were fired on by an American scouting party, and he was mortally wounded.

As an indication of the material condition of the County during those days, it may not be amiss to mention the following facts: General Heath, when on his march from Tappan to Hackensack to quell the turbulence of the Tories, sent to Col. Hays for flour, beef and pork. To his requisition Hays returned answer, that there was no pork, that while he could fill the order for flour there were neither horses nor wagons to transport it, and that plenty of beef was on the way.

At a later period, in 1777, the Legislature passed an act authorizing the Board of Supervisors for each county to meet and ascertain the real value of rye, oats, Indian corn, flour, beef and pork, in specie for the year 1777. The valuation in this County was fixed as follows: Wheat 8s. per bushel; rye and corn 5s. each per bushel; oats and buckwheat at 3s. per bushel; flour at 22s. per cwt.; beef, 40s. per cwt.; pork at 60s. per cwt. As may be imagined these prices fluctuated during the different quarters of the year, sometimes as much as 50 per cent.

We have seen that the old Tappan church was used both as a prison and court-room. The English church at Kakiat, if we may believe the tradition, was used as a stable, and from John Coe's hotel at that place, La Fayette dated, at least, one letter.

It is interesting to note that even the horrors of war could not entirely obliterate the gentler muse. Captain Johannes Jacobus Blauvelt appears to have had an ear for music, and the words of the following song, used by the Virginia troops, so attracted his fancy as to lead him to copy it in his Orderly Book.

"Com all you bref Virginiae man I have you all to know
It is to fight your enemy you must prepare to go
Our king he has fell out wyth us hes a mind to bindus slavs
Before we well put up wyth it will reither choose our graeves

We will put op with his Masety our anything
    that gust
And if he wont put op with et he may do his
    worste
Our king he has fell out with ous he is very
    angry now
I hope that brave America will conker general
    how
As for Lord north he es very proud and grand
He has no friend in America as we can under
    stand
Long thim has ben trying some quarrel to begin
That he might heuve a change the pretender to
    brign in
As for our gouvenor he acted very mene
He stole away our powder out of our magazine
He stole away our powder and likwist our led
And if hae dont return it he is surd to loose his
    head
This is one of the worst wars that ever was be-
    gun
It is lyke the father that wus against his sun
I never hard of such a war no not sens neohs
    flood
That any christian king crueves his subjects
    blood
Thir is manas a brave souldier must go and
    loose hys lyf
And menys louven husband must an leve his
    loven wif
But we will kill them my brave boys lik brim-
    ston kild the bes
Whear we cold find themse mongst the woods
    and thress
Dount you remember the issralits out of bond
    aege roodis be
And by the hand of moses end by the power of
    God
And by the hand of moses struck water with
    rod.

Johannes Blauvelt neeft gehut van Abraham ryker vooghi van die Staaet Van Kaspaarus Conklyn 4 Gin. mis."

Authorities referred to: "History of Haverstraw," by Rev. Dr. A. S. Freeman; "History Clarkstown," H. P. Fay; "History of Ramapo," E. B. Cobb; "History of Orange County," Eager; Papers in "City and County," R. H. Fenton. Magazine American History, Vols. III., V., IX., X., XI., XII. Old documents. "Lectures on Rockland County," by William G. Haeselbarth.

CHAPTER VIII.

OLD TIME CUSTOMS AND OCCUPATIONS.

DREADFUL FINANCIAL CONDITION OF THE COUNTY AT THE CLOSE OF THE REVOLUTION—ENERGY OF THE PEOPLE TO RE-ESTABLISH BUSINESS—THE FIRST HOUSES OF THE SETTLERS—LATER ARCHITECTURE—DOMESTIC LIFE AMONG THE DUTCH—THEIR OCCUPATIONS AND MANNER OF WORK—THE MODES OF TRAVEL IN EARLY DAYS—THE STYLE OF DRESS—AMUSEMENTS—CAUSES OF VENERATION FOR THE CLERGY—CHURCH ATTENDANCE—FUNERALS—FORMS OF OLD WILLS.

"Though one-third of the labor of the country at the close of the Revolution was probably devoted to the cutting of timber," says Greely, in his American Conflict, "the ax-helve was but a pudding stick; while the plough was a rude structure of wood, clumsily pointed and shielded with iron. A thousand bushels of corn (maize) are now grown on our western prairies, at a cost of fewer days' labor than were required for the production of a hundred in New York or New England eighty years ago." * * * * "Almost every farmer's house was a hive, wherein the 'great wheel' and the 'little wheel'—the former kept in motion by the hands and feet of all the daughters ten years old and upwards, the latter plied by their not less industrious mother—hummed and whirled from morning till night.

In the back room, or some convenient appendage, the loom responded day by day to the movements of the busy shuttle, whereby the fleeces of the farmer's flock and the flax of his field were slowly but steadily converted into substantial though homely cloth, sufficient for the annual wear of the family, and often with something over to exchange at the neighboring merchant's for his groceries and wares."

Peace found this County devastated and scathed. Where once had been great fields of waving grain or grass or tassled corn, now lay a waste rankly o'ergrown with weeds; where once capacious barns had stood, filled to bursting with the glad earth's produce and giving shelter to lowing kine, and bleating sheep, and well-fed swine; there now could be found a few charred, blackened fragments of the buildings, while the cattle had been long since taken by one or the other army; and, turning to the home, where once had been comfort and plenty, great chests and presses filled with home made cloth; cupboards stored with pewter, earthenware, and, perchance, china and silver table sets; garrets redolent with the odors of garden and orchard fruits; now stood open chest lids, cupboard doors ajar, exposing empty shelves, while the once filled garret was a home for bats and owls. Turn from this scene of sadness and look at the condition of New York City, the commercial depot for this County, and the spectacle is not more cheering. Two great fires had swept four hundred houses from existence, and in the ruins stood huts and dens built from rubbish and fragments of canvass; the long, cold winters fell chill upon the invaders, yet the dangers of attacks from the patriots, if they ventured far from their quarters, were such as to lead the enemy to cut down the trees in the city and the forest on the island for fuel, and now unsightly stumps and low underbrush stood in the streets and covered the adjacent country. Commerce was dead. The Continental money worthless. The States bankrupt.

This was the first fruits of the patriots' victory, death and ashes. From death and ashes in the physical world springs fresh life, and from the ashes of an old social life was to spring forth a new, a more thriving, a better social system. Brave men and women came from the crucible of suffering undismayed, and began once more the struggle for existence. The earth was theirs and on their industry depended the fulness thereof.

Where all alike were equally poor, each was dependent on his own labor, and at once, as if by magic, the Army of the Revolution melted into the busy citizens of the Republic, industriously reassuming the peaceful vocations they had abandoned at the call to arms. With wonderful rapidity, considering the exhausted condition of the people, houses and barns were rebuilt; the fallow land reploughed, and the deserted farm yards replenished with domestic animals. Soon again was heard from every house the hum of the " great wheel " and the " little wheel," and on countless looms was being woven the warp and woof of a new existence. Once more the many long untrammeled streams, were fretted into foam as the water came in great surges from the slow revolving mill wheels; and here and there, along the highways of the County, the ringing blows of hammer on anvil, the roar of the fire, and the scattering sparks, proclaimed that the brawny armed artisan within had only ceased to be a son of Mars to become a son of Vulcan.

The first houses of the settlers were of two descriptions, depending in great measure for the style on the location chosen. In one case an excavation in the side of a hill, lined with bark and faced with upright posts set in the earth, furnished with shelves and *slaap bancks*, was their home till better accommodation could be had. In the other case, a hut made of interwoven saplings, covered with bark, was used. These rude dwellings were only occupied till a log house could be erected. In the course of time the simple log houses were replaced by more pretentious and permanent buildings, and it is with these that we have to deal.

Before the introduction of saw-mills, frame buildings with shingled sides and thatched roofs were constructed. The shingles, made by hand from well seasoned cedar, were almost as durable as stone. Such houses, though expensive, were not as costly nor as difficult to build as those of stone. As their general arrangement was much the same as the latter, I need not give them a separate description. While a few of these shingle-built houses can still be found in the County, the great majority of those built before the close of the last century, which still stand, are of brown stone. These stone buildings were one story high, with an overshot roof, forming a portico, in some cases both in front and behind; in others the portico was only in front, while in the rear the roof, called a "lean-to," extended to within a few feet of the ground. Admission to the house was through half-doors, of which the upper half, containing usually four small panes of glass, could be opened for ventilation without disturbing the lower.

The entrance was into a broad hallway, through which a horse and carriage could be driven and then leave space between hubs and walls. Low and unceiled were hall and rooms. Overhead ran the heavy oak beams, which became a rich, dark color with age, and on these rested the garret floor. The lower half of the wall in many houses was wainscoted, the upper half plastered. The fire-places were enormous, generally extending to a width sufficient to accommodate the whole family with seats near the fire. The chimneys, which were capacious, were built outside of the house. They were generally kept clear by "burning out" during a wet day to prevent danger from fire.

In the more pretentious dwellings, the jambs of the fire-place were set round with glazed, blue, delft-ware tiles, imported from Holland, on which were depicted Scriptural scenes—these were a never-failing source of amusement and instruction to the children—and each had its huge andirons and heavy fire-shovel and tongs.

In the front of the house, on either side of the hall, were the parlor and kitchen, and in the rear, two bedrooms, which were lighted by a window in each end of the building. In many houses the parlor was never opened except for the purpose of a weekly cleaning, and as soon as that was finished it was closed again. This cleaning consisted of a thorough scrubbing, after which heaps of white sand were scattered on the floor, which, later, when the boards were dry, were swept into fanciful forms by the housewife's broom. In all houses, the parlor contained a high posted, corded, and unwieldly bedstead, which, with its hangings, formed the index of the social standing of its owner. Upon it, were two feather beds—one for the sleeper to lie upon, and another of a lighter weight, to be used as a covering. The pillow-cases were generally of check patterns, and the curtains and valance were of as expensive materials as could be afforded.

Not infrequently a round tea-table, with a leaf which could be dropped perpendicularly when not in use, also occupied the parlor and on this stood a family Dutch Bible with heavy wooden covers, bound and clasped with brass, which covers were seldom or never opened, except to record a marriage, a birth, or a death. Looking glasses, for common use, were small, with narrow black frames, but in the parlors of the wealthier families hung a large glass, framed with mahogany, trimmed with gilt, while from the top of the frame projected forward a gilded sheaf of wheat stalks or other like fanciful designs. Clocks were extremely rare—those great eight-day clocks, which are now so highly prized, being introduced into this country about 1720—and the early settlers marked the flight of time by an hour-glass and a sun dial.

The cellar, the entrance to which was always outside the house, was used as a storehouse for such farm products as needed an equal temperature in winter, and as the dairy all the year round.

The garret was the store house. Here were laid up the fruits of the harvest which needed to be kept dry. Along the collar beams hung strings of dried apples and ears of sweet corn; here in one corner stood the bin for rye, in another the bin for corn; along one side were piled bags of flour, along the other stood barrels of apples. Not infrequently boards were laid on the collar beams, and on this improvised floor the lighter farming utensils were placed side by side with the spinning wheel and loom.

What weird old places those garrets were. The one or two panes of glass placed in the gable served but to make the darkness more visible, and an air of ghosts always pervaded them. Tolerated they might be by the children during a stormy winter day when no other place could be found for play; but oh! what an agony of terror was produced by an order from the parent at night to go up there and bring down some needed article. How with quivering muscles and trembling limbs the messenger would start, trying to keep up an air of courage by whistling; how the whistle would die out at the head of the stairs; how each shadow thrown out by the candle light would assume grotesque, weird, and gigantic outlines; how the mind would rapidly fall into such a whirl that every action was performed automatically; and then, if a mouse disturbed by the unwonted light, should scamper across the floor, how, with bristling hair and starting eyeballs, the frightened messenger would fly to the stairs and get down any way, caring little whether it was head first or feet first, so long as he got down quickly, and without creating disturbance enough to be heard by his parents; for the terror of parental anger exceeded even the terror of ghosts, proving the power of the visible and tangible over the imperceptible and impalpable.

The kitchen in many houses was used alike as the cooking, eating and living room. On one side stood the vast open fire-place, with bright wood fire and shining andirons; across its top ran an iron bar upon which hung pot-hooks and trammels—the crane was as yet too expensive a luxury for common use. Along the walls hung racks for culinary utensils, and in one corner stood a three-cornered closet called a *pudabunk*, in which the plates, knives and forks were placed. The crockery was delft-ware, which came into use in this colony about the close of the seventeenth century; previous to the introduction of delft-ware, wooden and pewter dishes and vessels were used, and pewter continued the common table service in this County till the beginning of this century; the knives and forks were of steel. Among the very wealthy, blue and white china and porcelain, curiously ornamented with Chinese pictures, were kept for display, and used, perhaps, once in a lifetime. Some of these families decorated their parlor walls with China plates suspended by a strong ribbon passed through a hole drilled in their edges. Silver spoons, snuffers, candlesticks, tankards and punch-bowls were owned by such as had accumulated more money than they could otherwise use. With them the purchase of silverware was an investment for surplus funds, as the different interest-paying stocks and ventures which exist in our time were unknown in those days.

Further furniture consisted of high, straight-back chairs, sometimes covered with leather and studded with brass nails, but more frequently seated simply with matted rushes. The capacious chest, brought from Holland, occupied a prominent place in the house for several generations, and was ever kept filled to overflowing with clothing and cloth by the industrious good wife. Another useful article was the *kermis*, or trundle-bed, which was concealed under the large bed by day, and drawn out for the children's use at night.

Such was the general arrangement of double houses. In those of smaller size the interior was changed only by the hall occupying one side of the front, the other side being used as the parlor, after the manner of our city houses to-day, and opening into the sleeping rooms in the lean-to. In such houses the kitchen stood alongside the dwelling, generally communicating with it by a doorway. When the kitchen was thus detached from the house, its attic was used as the slaves' quarters, or, if there were many of these, for one family.

At a little distance from the dwelling stood a capacious barn with thatched roof, its mow floors being made of saplings laid loosely across the beams. Nearer the house was the well, with its long sweep heavily weighted at one end for greater ease in raising water; and not infrequently a building of logs, filled in with clay, was in close proximity, and was occupied by the slaves.

In such a community, everyone who was old enough to be of aid, worked. By nine or half-past, at night, the candle light was extinguished and the wearied men and women slept; at four o'clock in Summer and an hour and a half later in Winter, they arose. Before breakfast the male portion of the family had cleaned and watered the stock, the women had milked the cows, and, if it were Summer, the children had driven them to the pasture lot. After breakfast the men started forth to the fields, while the women, having attended to their household chores, began their apparently endless task of spinning and weaving, or else made up the linsey-woolsey garments, which were to clothe the family in the future.

The farm labor ran in regular and unvarying routine. In Spring came the ploughing, the planting of the maize and potatoes, and the sowing of the cereals and flax. In Summer the sheep were sheared, hay was gathered, grain was garnered by the men, while the women spun the wool. In Autumn the late fruits and cereals were harvested, the flax was broken, swingled and hatcheled, and everything prepared for the approaching cold season. In Winter the women tended to the manufacture of cloth, while the men threshed the grain and cut wood for the next year's supply.

Wonderful as is this picture of industry, it becomes more wonderful when we recall the implements of husbandry employed. The plough, clumsily shaped and light, was made of wood, and the share only was partially sheathed with iron. The motive power was a team of slow and patient oxen. As might be expected, the work was slow, but never monotonous, for the plough-boy was ever on the alert to keep the plough in the furrow; let it once get out and trouble began. Then came a tug to drag both plough and oxen back, and the ever obtuse beasts became more stupid whenever some intelligence was wanted. At first the sickle was the only implement used in gathering grain. Then came the tremendous invention of the cradle. Yet, if after using the cradle of to-day, one should grasp the implement that was first devised, he would lose all interest in agriculture. Pitchforks were made with wooden tines, and ax-handles were "pudding sticks," while the ax-head was poorly shaped and illy balanced.

Despite these difficulties, the settlers succeeded in supplying themselves with food and clothing, and soon acquired a surplus, which they exchanged with miller or storekeeper for money or commodities. Here and there throughout the County, as we have already seen, were mills—both grist and saw—and at convenient landing places along the river front were stores. In exchange for tea, coffee, tobacco and sugar; or crockery and silverware, the storekeeper received the surplus fruits of the farm or the cloth, butter and eggs of the housewife. Home-made cloth was of great value in those early days and the Dutch matrons took much pride in their packed clothes-presses. For his grain, the farmer obtained gold—Spanish Johannes or Joes ($16 pieces) or English guineas. In the eager search for this gold or plate, the British and Hessian soldiery ripped many a feather bed and sounded many a door yard and garden with their bayonets, during the Revolution. Beside the millers and storekeepers, the blacksmith took part of the surplusage of the harvest in payment for his labor, which he could exchange with miller or merchant for his necessities.

But while there were millers, merchants and smiths in the County, they by no means depended entirely on their calling for support. All owned and tilled land in conjunction with their other occupations. The first blacksmith that came into the Haverstraw precinct was led to do so by a grant of land.

"Know all men by these present, that we whose names are hereunto written, for and in consideration that Joseph Wood, of Hempstead, in Queens County, shall settle upon a certain tract of land hereinafter described, and then and there uphold the trade of a blacksmith, as long as he shall be able and capable of working at the said trade, and to work for the persons underwritten according to the custom of a Smith * * We do hereby grant and release unto him a certain tract of land at a place called Kakiat, bounded west by the rear of the first eastern division of lots, east by a creek or brook called Wood creek, containing 100 acres. July 15th, 1720."

"John Allison,   "Caleb Halstead,
James Searing,   William Hutchins,
Charles Mott,   Abm. Denton,
William Osborn,   Johnathan Rose,"
Johnathan Seaman."

When sufficient flour had been collected by the miller, and sufficient of the other products of agriculture by the merchant, they shipped the material to New York by sloop, and after exchanging for articles they needed, sold the balance.

We have already seen that the roads were few and far between. Once a year the King's Highway was worked and its bridges repaired, but the branch roads were never touched and bridges were unthought of. If necessity compelled the use of a vehicle, that vehicle was a springless lumber wagon, or, in winter, a sleigh running upon split sapplings, and was drawn at a uniform dog trot by pot-bellied nags. Before the Revolution the two wheeled one-horse chaise had been introduced into New York and its immediate vicinity, but I have yet to learn that the people of this County were guilty of any such foolish extravagance up to that period.

Travel was almost entirely carried on on horseback. If the heads of a family went out together, a pillion was used, the woman sitting on it and steadying herself by holding on to the man. This mode of journeying also extended to those who aspired to be heads of families, and courtship in those days was largely carried on in this manner. Trotting horses, under the saddle, were rare; a canter was the ordinary pace for the sturdy Dutchman; but these Dutchmen, like their descendants, were fond of their stock, and an attempt by any one to pass them, roused a spirit of emulation that took no heed of dignity or occasion. A race followed, even though the day was the Sabbath and the church doors were scarcely yet closed upon them. The Perrys of Rockland are said to have been hard riders and never missed an opportunity to race. If a neighbor did not come along frequently enough, these Jehus would run their own horses against each other.

The few trips, that the average resident made to New York in the course of his life, were generally made by the flat-bottomed, slow-sailing, side-board sloops of those days, and these trips were by no means free from danger. The sad experience of the past few years in Nyack and Haverstraw Bays, proves that with all the advance in boat-building, the Hudson can still be master; and whatever of danger renders the navigation of the noble river perilous at times even now, was ten times greater when the vessels were clumsy and difficult to manage. Solemn, indeed, is the inscription that meets the casual observer, who, in idle curiosity, perhaps, stops a moment in the Coe burying ground by the English Church: "Captain William Coe drowned in the North River with nine others, Nov. 25, 1774." If the observer makes inquiry regarding this catastrophy, he will be informed that it was occasioned by the capsizing of a sloop. Incredulous we may be, even if we allow the fullest sway to our imaginations in regard to sudden gust and howling gale, incredulous we may be, when told that the placid flowing Spar-kill has been the scene of drowning for three of these whilom passengers. Yet the statement is true.

Sometimes the trip to town was made on horseback or by wagon, and, not unfrequently, the traveler walked to New York and back. This has been done by more than one person whom I have known, and was not regarded by them as anything out of common.

In dress, the first comers were not particular. They wore what they had, and made it hold together as long as they could. As the success of their labors became assured, however, they adopted a garb which followed the fashion of their native land, being changed only by the necessities of their new home. Homespun coats, with great shirts, in which were capacious pockets, a loose-fitting, blouse-shaped, under-coat or waistcoat, knee-breeches, long blue worsted stockings and huge shoes, often home-made, with pewter, or in the very wealthy, silver buckles, formed their apparel; while the younger unmarried men wore short, square-frocked coats with rows of enormous brass buttons. The elderly dames attired themselves in close-crimped hats, long-waisted short-gowns, homespun petticoats, with scissors and pin-cushions, and gay calico pockets hanging on the outside; and their daughters only differed from them in attire by the use of a tastefully arranged bright ribbon or two, and a coquettish manner of wearing their clothing. If fortune had been unusually kind, silk dresses possessed by the matrons indicated their worldly success.

At a later period the garb of the men changed in style and gradually settled into the habit of to-day, with the exception that the top-coat was made with two or more capes, and contained the pockets that formerly belonged to the body coat. The hair of the men was allowed to grow long, and was generally dressed in a queue up to and during the Revolution. After that period this custom gradually ceased, until now it is an indication of affectation.

Industrious as were our ancestors they still found time for amusements, most of which were harmless, none absolutely brutal. Horse-racing had not degenerated into a gambler's occupation, but was a pure enjoyment into which horse and rider entered with equal zest. Two neighbors meeting upon the road would have a short brush, and each would feel convinced that his animal was the better horse. In a spirit of friendly rivalry they would agree to meet at a stated place, usually some long, level, green sward beside the highway, on the following Saturday afternoon and test the matter fairly; each would notify his friends of the coming match, and on the afternoon appointed a score or more of young men would be present to see the trial. Sometimes, in fact often, the spectators would feel satisfied that the animals they bestrode could defeat either of the contesting horses, or that of any one present; the result would be another and still another race, till the waning hours warned all present that their night work awaited them, then, with great good nature they would ride off home, determining to try again at the first opportunity.

But these were not the only contests of speed which the horses were put to. There were surreptitious night runnings, that the owners of the animals were not aware of. Emulation between the slaves of different families was as active as that between their owners, perhaps even more so, and when the rest of the household had settled down to sleep, these nocturnal contestants had many a struggle for first place. Sleepy, lazy, exhausted, they accounted next day for their weariness and the sweated condition of the horses by some convenient untruth. In later years, when Methodist itinerants travelled on horseback, the former night contests of the slaves were carried on by the worthy scions of those houses where the ministers tarried over night. They used and abused those ministers' horses to learn what stuff they had in them, and returned the wearied beasts to their stalls just in time to avoid detection. Bold, careful, and yet, withal, kind riders, the men of those days were gentle with their animals, and those animals responded with all the love of their natures to the caresses of their owners.

Other contests between the young men of those days grew out of faith in their personal strength. Matches between them in running, wrestling, and hurling heavy weights were common, and carried on in friendly rivalry. Occasionally, though justice demands that I should say only when braggadocio among them grew unbearable, the youthful owner of slaves pitted his negroes' butting powers against those of some neighbor's Cuffee, and then all the rising generation collected to see the battle. Backing off, till fifteen or twenty feet separated them, the black competitors would rush at each other and drive their heads together with a crash, that would break in the skull of an ordinary man, but which only resulted in the felling of one of them. In those rare instances, where one of these negroes had defeated all opponents in thickness of skull and strength of neck, small wagers would be made that he could not break in one of the heavy folding doors which led into the main floor of the barns; and then one of the conspirators would stand within and hold a heavy bar against that part of the door where he would strike. Defeat always greeted the black-a-moor's efforts in such cases, and drew forth from him many expressions of wonder at the stiffness of the particular door, but the fact that he had been deceived never seems to have entered his dull mind.

Hunting was so common as scarcely to deserve classification among the amusements. No one ever thought of going off to the woods or fields in pursuit of their daily toil without carrying their trusty gun. In the early days of settlement it would be rare if some of the family did not return at night bearing game which had been shot, and it was not infrequent even within the memory of men still living, for the laborer to cease from his toil, seize his gun and shoot a fox, that, hard chased by the dogs, entered the fields in his flight.

Among those enjoyments into which both sexes joined, were huskings and weddings. In both cases the merriment was carried on in the tremendous barns of those days. At the huskings, people were present from miles around. The great heaps of corn were piled up on the floor and the guests, selecting such places as were near their friends, sat round these heaps in circles. Gossip, flirtation, badinage, flew thick and fast, and one, who stood in the mows overhead, would have thought that Babel had been reproduced. Yet in all that tumult of laughter, and song, and jest, there was a ceaseless energy, which heaped high the baskets of yellow corn and ever diminished the piles before the busy talkers.

After the husking was ended all adjourned to the house for refreshment, and then, the barn floor having meantime been cleared by the slaves, once more visited it to end the day in jollity and mirth.

In some respects marriages were simpler in those days than in these. While due notice and invitation was given to every family within a radius of miles, for in those days, as has already been said, every one knew each other, the invitations were for what we would call the reception, never to witness the ceremony. Unostentatiously the wedding party drove to the parsonage accompanied only by their immediate relatives. There they were quietly married, and then started for home again, having added one to their number in the person of the good dominie.

At that home were collecting all the people from a wide area, coming on horseback, coming on foot, coming in wagons, and coming in the full spirit of innocent enjoyment. On the arrival of the wedding party came the wedding dinner. And what a dinner! none of the condiment soaked, highly-spiced foods; none of the knick-knacks, ycleped pates, and truffles and capons—products of disease, every one of them, which are chosen by the dyspeptic epicures of to-day; but the table groaned under the weight of solid, substantial victuals, which were eaten by men and women who ate to live—not lived to eat. Huge turkeys, long the pride of the farmyard; ducks and geese, swimming in their own gravy; chickens unnumbered, and at their head a famous chanticleer; great roasts of beef, and sides of bacon, the vegetables of the season—all these graced the board; and then for dessert came apple pies, and peach pies, and pumpkin pies, the tender olye kok, the crisp cruller, the famous Dutch doughnut—alas, that it is passing away! sweet cakes, short cakes and ginger cakes; preserved peaches, quinces, citrons; these and more tempted the appetites of the robust guests.

Nor was liquid refreshments lacking. Great tankards of New England rum, vessels of Holland schnapps, and bottles of rare old wine of Gaul stood waiting the beck of the harder-headed guests, while the women quaffed, with full knowledge of its potency, that delectable nectar, lost to us forever, Metheglin; or else sipped, with appreciative draughts of crusty wine from Oporto, or the wind-swept island of Maderia, while peach brandy, still rare, furnished the parting bowl.

After dinner came the dance. If it were warm enough, the barn was used as the dancing floor. At one end, on an improvised platform made by placing boards across barrels, sat two or more negro fiddlers with their battered but still musical violins. The bride and groom led off the first set. When all was ready, away they started, dance followed dance, more and more uproarious grew the fun, faster and faster the bow crossed the strings, brighter and brighter grew the eyes of the musicians as they entered fully into the spirit of the day; swiftly flew the hours, madly waxed the revel, until finally, wearied with excess of mirth and pleasure, the dancers ceased, the musicians obtained their needed rest and an allowance of rum, and about sunset the guests departed with a hearty good night, which meant from the visitors "God bless you," and from the host "God keep you."

In all the social gatherings of those times the dominie was present or the host was disappointed. The first Colonists, who settled in this State, were from the middle and lower class of Hollanders. All were compelled to labor for a living. The wealthy merchant or land owner saw no inducement to brave the perils of a long ocean passage, found no cause for leaving his comforts and enjoyments, to amass more wealth from the new world, when sufficient abundance was already in his possession. Among these industrious settlers, but little opportunity could be found for education, and with the exception of that shrewd common sense, which seemed an attribute of these Dutchmen, almost all were illiterate. For years after the settlement of our County, education among the people made but slight advance, and even up to the close of the last century, the great majority of residents were untaught.

While they were unlettered themselves, the settlers appreciated education, and gave to it that respect which it must ever command. The one, above all others, among them whom all knew to be studied was their dominie, and this was one of the reasons why that dominie was regarded with great esteem. But there was another and in those days a more important reason why the Dutch gave such veneration to their clergy. The fruits of the Reformation had not yet reached completion. For centuries the intellect of all Europe had been held subordinate to the will of Rome.

To be sure Lippershey, a Hollander, had discovered the telescope, but the fate of Bruno for theorizing, and the punishment of Galileo for stating as to what that telescope would and did reveal, was not encouraging to further investigation. To be sure, at the very moment of Dutch settlement on this Continent, Descartes was making Holland his home and was soon to issue a philosophy which would change the aspect of all civilization, but almost a century was to elapse ere his teachings became generally understood. To be sure two centuries had elapsed since Gutenberg had invented the printing press, but the Index Librorem Prohibitorem of the Church had checked free discussion long before. In reality the Pontifical authority still rested upon Europe. The habit of centuries is not changed in a day. From time beyond the conception of man's imagination, the clergy had been the greatest authority recognized by the common people. At their entrance into the world, a member of the sacerdotal order had baptized them in the name of Christ; such catechising as they had had was received from a servant of the Church of Rome; as the years advanced, they had learned to carry the burden of their earthly as well as spiritual sorrows to their parish priest, and in the privacy of the confessional had received wise worldly advice as well as spiritual comfort, and as the end of this life approached, and the mystery of the hereafter drew nearer; it was a clergyman who held the hand, stiffening in death, and pointed towards a glorious resurrection.

The Reformation had changed the form of worship. The Reformation unloosed the human intellect; but while the people now performed their devotions in greater simplicity and argued with their pastor concerning the meaning of Scripture, they still retained all the foretime affection and reverence for that pastor's holiness and wisdom. If this was true of the old world, far more true was it of the new, where dangers and sorrows, unknown in their native land, stood round the colonists on every side. In the full realization of the great responsibilities thrust upon them; in a clear comprehension of the many diversified duties they would be called on to perform; those pioneer ministers of God entered upon their missions, braved the perils of a stormy ocean, risked the unknown dangers of a new settlement, lent physical aid as well as administered religious consolation to the struggling pioneer, preached Christ crucified to the settlers in the midst of primeval forests, and by the uprightness of their lives and their Christian charity, extorted expressions of gratitude from even the taciturn Indians.

With their religious duties these dominies combined worldly knowledge. They kept posted on the important events of the day, and narrated and explained the tendency of these events to their congregations. Often they acted as arbitrators in neighborly disputes, and soothed down angry passions. Often their advice was sought in regard to proposed purchases or sales of land or stock, or new ventures in the business of life. Always welcomed at the plain but bounteous board, they visited much among their congregations, and entered into all their pleasures and sorrows as one of the family. Truly they followed the oft-repeated saying of one of the last of their number, Dominie Lansing: "I have never said to you, Do and Live, but Live and Do!"

As can be imagined, with such feelings toward the minister, all the residents of this County went to church. The first edifice erected for worship was, as we have already seen, that at Tappan, in 1716, and this was followed by the churches at Clarkesville and Kakiat, at which latter church the service was held in the English language. At the Tappan, and later at the Clarkesville church, for both churches were supplied by the same minister till 1830, the service was in Dutch, a language which held into and through the ministration of Dominie Nicholas Lansing, who alternated during the last years of his life, preaching one Sabbath in English and the next in Dutch.

At ten o'clock in the morning the first service was begun by the clerk, who also was chorister, reading the lesson and lining the psalms. Then the sermon would begin and last until noon, when the first service ended. But we must remember that many of the congregation had come a long distance, over wretched roads, which precluded all hope of their going home for dinner and returning in time for the afternoon service. These people brought their lunch with them, and while those, who resided near at hand, went home for their meals, the others ate either in the church or under the shade of the trees, and then had time, the men for a short smoke, the women for a brief gossip, ere the second service began. This was after an hour's intermission, and it lasted an hour and a half. Two services in a day were only held in the Summer and Autumn. Church edifices were unheated in those days, and while the fervor of religious zeal was strong, it was testing human endurance too far to sit more than two hours in an icy temperature. To alleviate, as much as possible, the suffering from cold, the elderly ladies carried quaintly designed foot stoves, some of which are still preserved in the older families, which they passed to others, who were unprovided, when their blue faces indicated actual distress; while the men resorted to the bar of Mabie's tavern, both before and after service, and fortified themselves against the cold or warmed their chilled blood by drinking hot gin. At a later period "box" stoves were introduced into the church, one of which stood on either side of the entrance doors. Even then it was not rare for some benumbed members of the congregation to rise, during the service, walk back and warm themselves at the stoves, and then return to their seats.

Not infrequently during the pleasant summer Sundays, several neighbors on the river bank at a distance from Tappan, or Clarkesville, would embark on sloop-board, and start for the church at *Slacperigh Hol* (Sleepy Hollow.) Sometimes they would get across the uncertain Tappan Zee without trouble and in plenty of time for service, but it often times happened, that when the sloop got well out from shore, the breeze would die out and then the vessel would drift idly about the bay till an afternoon wind sprang up and wafted the belated pilgrims back to shore.

The churches of those early days differed so radically from the buildings of our time that a brief notice of that at Tappan, may not be uninteresting. Opposite the entrance stood the wine glass shaped pulpit, fastened against the wall by its stem, and reached on either side by a flight of circular stairs. Surmounting it was a sounding board which was embellished by a sheaf of golden grain. Underneath and in front of the pulpit, was the clerk's desk. On each side of the church was a gallery which was reached by stairs built within the body of the church, that on the right being occupied by the young men of the congregation while the one on the left was used by the negro slaves. In keeping with the simplicity of the people and the universality of attendance at church, the quaint habit existed of making the doors of the sacred edifice a place of advertisement. Nailed to them might be seen, notices of strayed or impounded cattle, descriptions of lost property, or intelligence of an approaching vendue.

Other religious meetings were held at irregular intervals. Prayer meetings at the houses of the different church members, at which the Dominie would be present if it was possible; and every two or three weeks a lecture on Bible subjects would be given at the home of some deacon or elder. Saturday evening was the night always selected for these lectures, and as time and place were announced from the pulpit on the preceding Sabbath, the meeting was always well attended.

The healthful out-door life, the nature of their occupation, the plain but substantial articles which formed their food, the freedom from bad sanitation which exists in a sparsely settled country, and the homely common sense of our ancestors in this County; rendered them unusually free from disease and exceedingly long lived. Yet the custom of preparing for death was universal. From the hour of attaining his twenty-first year every man began to lay aside a sum in gold, which should be used to defray his funeral expenses, and under no circumstances was this ever touched except for that purpose. At the same time a linen shirt, handkerchief, etc., were laid away and were never allowed to be worn, but kept clean to be buried in. When sickness entered a household, domestic remedies were tried by housewives, who were by no means unskilled in the appearance or treatment of disease. If, to their keen sight, the symptoms were alarming, either Doctor Osborn, who had settled at Stony Point as early as 1730, and begun practice, or later his son, Doctor Richard Osborn, or Doctor Thomas Outwater, of Tappan, were sent for.

If the malady proved fatal, preparations were at once made for the final obsequies. The coffin, usually made from well seasoned, smooth, and beautifully grained boards, which had been selected many years before by the deceased and carefully kept for the occasion, was constructed by some neighbor skilled in carpenter craft, and covered with a black pall. In case a woman died in child-bed a white sheet, instead of the black pall, was spread over the coffin. In a community where all were neighbors and friends, but little call existed for funeral invitations, for, unless the illness had been unusually brief, the mortal sickness of one of their number was widely known among the residents; but, when such invitation was given, it was through the chorister of the church.

At the hour appointed for the last rites, the neighbors for miles around collected at the late home of the dead. In one corner of the parlor stood the coffin, resting on a table, near it was seated the dominie, while round the room were the mourners, for in those days all mourned as for one of their own. Just previous to the beginning of the service, the sexton entered, followed by a slave bearing a tray on which were glasses and decanters. These were passed to each guest and most of them poured out and drank a glass of wine or rum. Following this, the sexton again entered, bearing pipes and tobacco. Such of those present as smoked filled a pipe and puffed in silence; when the pipes were empty, the dominie rose to his feet and delivered his funeral remarks, ending the service by a short but fervent prayer.

The custom of using liquors and tobacco at funerals prevailed in this County as late as 1809. How much later it obtained here I do not know, but among the conservative Dutch families of Flatbush, in Kings County, on Long Island, it was still in vogue in 1819.

At the close of the house service, the coffin was carried to the vehicle by bearers, who were chosen from among the most intimate friends of the deceased, and then borne to the grave. The location of that grave depended altogether on the situation of the dead person's residence. If it was near the church the body was laid in the church-yard. At a distance too great to render this spot available, the corpse was either interred in some local spot of sepulture, chosen by the neighbors for that purpose, or the lumber wagon bearing the remains was driven to some place on the farm which the deceased or his ancestors had selected, and there consigned to the dust from which it came. Wills are still extant in which provision is made for the preservation of these family burying places through all time.

The last wills and testaments of those days are worded with remarkable clearness. The testator knew how he wished to dispose of his property, and, if he could write, placed his desires on paper, or, failing in penmanship, obtained the services of some educated and trusted neighbor to express his bequests for him. Competition for success was not as great in those days as at present because wealth was not regarded as so important a social factor; closer relationship existed between the different members of families, and fewer lawyers had to be supported; for these reasons wills were never contested in our County, and the importance of having them drawn up with a view to future attempts at breaking them, did not exist.

Before the adoption of the Constitutional form of Government, the law of primogeniture existed. To avoid its force, when desired, an opening clause devised a certain sum to the first-born male in lieu of legal privileges, thus: "Item, I do give, devise and bequeath to my eldest son, Gerret Lydecker, the sum of £5 current money of New York, which shall be in full of all demands or pretention he shall or may have to any part of my estate as heir-at-law." * * * After the disposal of this matter, the testator then proceeds with his bequests.

"These old Dutch wills seem not to trust a widow in a second marriage. The restraints placed upon re-marriages by wills were generally in favor of the children of the first marriage, and the widows thus restricted generally signed consents to accept the bequests in lieu of dower, for the good reason that propriety did not allow them to refuse so soon after the death of their first husband; and, because the devises and bequests in lieu of dower vested an estate for life, or three-thirds of the estate subject to a contingency in their own control, instead of one-third absolutely." Thus in the will already quoted from, which is that of Albert Lydecker, made in 1774 and is a type of others which I have read of that time. All the stock of furniture or its value, which he obtained with his wife at marriage, he bequeaths to her and directs his executors to deliver it in case she should marry again, and he again further directs his five sons to pay her a yearly sum, and gives her the use of a room in the home, so long as she remains his widow. Another will provides liberally for the widow of the testator during her widowhood. "But if she marry, then her husband must provide for her as I have done."

In reality, women, maids or widows, were not dealt by with what we should regard as a spirit of fairness. It was expected that they should marry and that their husbands should support them; and then, not in any sense regarding the fact that in the partnership of marriage the wife had done her share in accumulating the property devised, if she married a second time, she was disinherited by the will of her first husband.

The wills of those days entered most minutely into a list of behests; "cupboards," "pewter table sets," "silver plate," "beds and their furniture," "chairs," "tables," and so on; are devised piece by piece to the different heirs. Slaves were bequeathed, sometimes to one person in the total, and sometimes they were separated by the last earthly wish of a man, who shortly, before an inexorable Judge, to whom souls are alike whether in black skins or white, was to appear and answer for his life work.

In case disagreement followed the reading of the will; and in other cases where the testator thought it advisable; the executors were directed to sell everything at public vendue—spelled phonetically in those days, vandue—and divide the proceeds among the heirs according to the provisions of the will. Different terms of sale at those auctions were agreed to by the executors. Those of one held in 1773, I will quote.

"The articles of this Vandue held this 10th day of August, 1773, are that all Persons have their free Bid and be Entitled to such things as are struck off on their Bid, with giving good Shurety if regard (required) by the Collector, if such shurety be Refused, ye thing or things to be set up at a second Sale if sold for more than the first time the first Buyer to have no Profits, if sold for Less than the first time, the first Buyer to make good the Damage, the Buyer to have untill ye 10th day of February next, for time of Payment, if any money Remains unpaid after the time given, it is to draw Lawful Interest until paid. The Collector to have good Right to seize on the Buyer or goods any time before payment. And the Money to be paid to me.

GILBERT CUYPER, Collector."

Such were the customs, almost all now obsolete, of the people who dwelt in this region before the close of the eighteenth century. It has been said that they were bigoted in their religious opinions, crude and rough in their manners, and utterly without amusement. I have seen a lithograph, published many years ago, which was intended as a hit at the religious fanaticism of early days. It represents an inn, in front of which stands the inn-keeper, Bible in hand; around him are collected his family, all their faces wearing a cold, stern, rigidly just expression. Pendant from the branch of a neighboring tree hangs the body of the house cat, while a jolly-visaged guest standing by, explains the scene in these words:

> "To Banburry came I, O profane one,
> To see a Puritane one;
> A hanging of ye cat on a Monday,
> For ye killing of a mouse on a Sunday."

To the liberal ideas of the present time, the sectarian prejudices of olden days, must at a superficial glance seem bigoted; but when we remember that the spirit of their religion moved our ancestors to live honest, pure, and upright lives, trying as best they could to love their neighbors as themselves, to do unto others as they would be done by; when we remember that they paid their personal debts and kept the church as God's house and not as the property of some mortgage-holder; when we remember that they attended divine service to worship Him in whose care they committed their bodies and souls, and banished worldly thoughts and vanities at the church door, we may find cause to believe that with all our boasted liberality of views, our ancestors walked as near beatitude as we do.

True it is, that the culture and society polish of the present day were not known to that generation of men; but they reverenced their women next to their God and honored their old people as they themselves would wish in their age to be honored. True it is, that labor was severe and almost constant among the pioneers, and they had little of the amusement that we of to-day enjoy; but their labor founded a County, now rich and prospering, and kept poverty so far from the door that not a pauper was reported for over a century and a half—till 1845—in that section now known as Rockland County; and, as Greeley says, " a passionately earnest assertion, which many of us have heard from the lips of the old men of thirty to fifty years ago, that the days of their youth were sweeter and happier than those we have known, will doubtless justify us in believing that they were by no means intolerable."

Authorities referred to. "American conflict." Vols. II. Horace Greeley. "Field Book of the Revolution." Vols. II. B. J. Lossing. "History of Kings County." Vols. II. Stiles. "Sketch Book." Washington Irving. Archives of the Rockland County Historical Society. "History of Haverstraw." Rev. A. S. Freeman, D. D., and William S. Pelletreau.

CHAPTER IX.

THE CIVIL GOVERNMENT TILL THE ERECTION OF ROCKLAND COUNTY.

THE CAUSES WHICH LED TO THE CREATION OF A FEDERATION—THEIR SLIGHT INFLUENCE ON THIS SECTION—THE FEELING AMONG THE PEOPLE REGARDING IT AND THE REASONS FOR THAT FEELING—THE VOTE OF THE DELEGATES AT THE CONVENTION—REASONS WHY ROCKLAND COUNTY WAS ERECTED—ITS BOUNDARIES—ITS TOWNSHIPS—ITS FIRST OFFICERS.

The Confederation was a failure. Its Congress had been granted sole power to declare war, but it could neither compel the levying of troops, nor arm and support them should they be raised; it had been given sole power to fix the needed amount of revenue, but had no authority to enforce the collection of taxes; it had had conferred upon it sole power to decide disputes between the States, but had no means of enforcing its determination; it stood a political monstrosity, with just sufficient life to realize its own impotence, and just sufficient energy to feel that it was the laughing stock of the world.

Long before the close of our struggle for liberty, this weakling had demonstrated its inefficiency. The troops, naked and starving, had clamored without effect for their pay, and had, at length, broken out in mutiny, while Congress vainly sought financial assistance; its partisan bickerings and the intrigues caused by old local jealousies, which even the awful grandeur of its object could not lead it to lay aside, full often hampered the commanding officers in the field; and when, at length, the war was ended, and the terms of peace agreed upon, it was only by the most strenuous efforts and after repeated appeals that a quorum of its members could be obtained to sign the treaty.

A broken reed in the hour of danger, what hope could be entertained that in quieter times it would display more strength. Futile indeed were its efforts to meet the requirements of its position in peace. Many of the States neglected or openly refused to pay their allotted share of interest upon the public debt. The year after the evacuation of New York, bills of the Confederation for $600,000 were protested in Holland, and the annual requirement of the Treasury—$4,000,000—was universally felt to be a sum too large to demand, and which could not be collected. Nor did the following years bring relief to this helpless semblance of authority. Commercial and offensive and defensive treaties were formed between different States and between separate States and foreign nations. Matters rapidly advanced from bad to worse.

The value of the Continental money had ceased and further loans could not be effected because of the loss of credit. Commerce, ruined by the war, was prevented from reviving by two proclamations from Great Britain, one, that all importations of American products should either be carried by British vessels or by those belonging to the State from which the produce was shipped; the other, prohibiting American vessels or citizens from trading with British colonies. Our infant manufactures—abruptly checked by the war—were prevented from reviving by the influx of foreign goods, and a refusal by the States to permit Congress to impose a duty on imports, had caused those imports to exceed the exports by $20,000,000, and an incubus of debt amounting to $80,000,000 rested on this people.

Such were the conditions, which led Hamilton and his colleagues to commend and earnestly labor for a change in the form of authority, by which certain powers, then vested in each of the many separate States, should be granted to a central government, and from the many commonwealths a single nation exist. The result of a convention to decide on the necessities of the public weal, which met at Philadelphia, in 1787, was a recommendation for a federal form of government. This recommendation was transmitted to Congress with the suggestion that it be submitted to conventions in each State, chosen by the people thereof, called by the respective Legislatures. Congress, following the advice of the Philadelphia Convention, adopted a resolution on September 28th, 1787, referring the new Constitution to the various Legislatures for submission to the people of the respective States. In pursuance of the Congressional resolution, the Legislature of New York adopted a joint resolution, on January 31st, 1788, providing for a State Convention to meet at Poughkeepsie, June 17th, 1788. The delegates to that Convention, chosen by the people of Orange County, were: John Haring, Henry Wisner, John Wood, Jesse Woodhull.

We have already traced the growth of the spirit of liberty in the people of our County. We have already seen what they suffered to obtain their liberty. At the outset, they had found counties created which were subservient to the State; they had seen townships or precincts arise subject to the county; and they had learned to respect and revere their civil government from interest and association. The overthrow of royal power had been a sudden and tremendous revolution, and in the startling phases of the change, this people had failed to grasp the magnitude of the result.

Then, too, as we have seen, the disasters of war, which fell so heavily on manufacturing and mercantile counties and States, crushing their business and commerce from existence, touched lightly on Orange. She was a producer that supplied her own consumption and had surplusage. Liberty to her residents meant as little interference from outside sources as possible. It was with an unpleasant feeling that they submitted to a majority rule in the State government, when that rule did not benefit them, and they paid their ever increasing taxes for the benefit of sister counties, which were not yet self-supporting, with many a murmur. But those sections they thus aided indirectly were of their own State.

When now, therefore, the proposition to form a central government was heard, it was greeted by the residents of this County with vehement protest. Unable to grasp the fact, that if some of their liberty was not abnegated, they would lose all of it; unable to appreciate the ruin which was being accomplished, through lack of some central authority, in other States and even in parts of our own; the people of Orange felt that the proposed federation was only a name for another form of tyranny, and that under the simple title of President lurked the authority of King. Nor was the fact that all the branches of that government were to be under their control—the House of Representatives directly, the Senate and Executive indirectly—any relief to their feeling of concern. If they were annoyed at the power of majority vote in their own Legislature, among their own people, seven-fold more annoying would it be, when their States' Representatives in Congress were outnumbered and out-voted by the members of Congress from other, perhaps rival, and certainly far distant States, for whose welfare they cared nothing. Liberty to the different factors in this nascent State and Nation, while not yet reaching license, was trending toward it, and from the first had been a synonym for selfishness.

Perhaps no better illustration can be given of the feeling toward the Federation among our farmers, than to quote the language of a citizen from our neighbor State, New Jersey, concerning his sentiment toward the new form of government, and this ten years after the change was an accomplished fact.

"Timothy Meeker, at one time, while a portion of the standing army, under the administration of John Adams, was at Elizabethtown, visited General Dayton, in person to pay his direct tax for the support of the army. 'Of what use is your standing army?' asked Meeker. 'To support Congress;' replied Dayton, 'Ay, to support Congress indeed;' said the old man bitterly. 'To support Congress in taking away our liberties, and in altering the Constitution so as to place men in public office for life. I fought for freedom through the war for nothing (his Continental money was worthless), and now I want to pay for my land and be *independent* indeed, but tax upon tax keeps me poor. I could at any time raise one hundred men among my neighbors upon the Short Hills, say privately to your standing army, come and help us—and they would come, and we'd to Philadelphia and take your Congressmen from their seats. We will not have a standing army. Disband it.'

'Our standing army,' said Dayton, 'will intimidate the British.' 'Look ahere, General Dayton;' said Meeker, 'you are well acquainted in London. Write to your acquaintances there, and tell them that Timothy Meeker is dead, and that he has left seven sons, every one of whom is a stronger man than he. Tell them we are seven times stronger than before, and that will intimidate them more than all your standing armies, that suck the life blood from the people.'"

But there was another and perhaps even stronger reason for the bitter feeling against the proposed Federation among our County people. Her representative men were earnestly opposed to the change, and in their speeches to and conversations with the electors, denounced the step toward royalty in no measured terms. On the borders of a neighboring County—Ulster, in a section now belonging to Orange, Governor George Clinton was born and lived. In the early years of the War for Independence, he was in command of the militia of Orange and Ulster Counties, and with them had seen service in more than one well contested battle. The militiamen had grown to respect, admire and love their old commander, and had watched his elevation to and actions in the gubernatorial chair with pride. In the first election, Orange had given him the victory over Philip Schuyler, and at every following election, he had been returned by increasing majorities.

All history is filled with the records of successful generals raised to high command in the State, and generally, with the history of their advance, has been compelled to record their failure in civil office. But in the administration of George Clinton there were no grave political errors from his view of polity. He was a man who combined the power of winning men with great political astuteness, and his views were generally accepted by those who associated with him in affairs of State as exceedingly wise. To the student, who looks into Clinton's career, there can be no question, that in his opposition to the proposed federation, he was guided by strong conscientious principles. As a patriot, he had responded to the call for duty among the first, and had placed his property, his liberty and his life in jeopardy; and now he firmly believed that the proposed new form of government was but the beginning of another monarchy under a different name.

But with this conscientious objection to national power, there was another and a more avaricious scruple. Clinton was an ambitious man. He aspired to leadership among the people, and he had attained his ambition, only to see his power, in great measure, vanish by an unforseen proposition. In an instant his perspicacity had grasped the fact, that greater influence and fame belonged to the executive head of an independent commonwealth, than to the governor of a State, which with twelve others went to form a nation; and biased by personal as well as political reasons, he combatted the idea of centralization.

Among the electors of Orange and Ulster, as I have said, the word of Clinton was all-powerful. But to still further strengthen the Governor's stand, the leading statesmen of this section were his political allies. John Haring and Henry Wisner had both been fellow members with him in the Provincial Convention of 1775, and his vote had been cast for Wisner as a delegate to the Continental Congress. In the sessions of the Third and Fourth Provincial Congress, Haring, Clinton and Wisner, had again been fellow delegates. When Clinton was elected Governor, Wisner was sent to the Senate, and in this body, he was joined by Haring in 1781, both remaining till the period of which I am speaking—1788. To make the tie still closer if possible between the Governor and his allies, Haring was made one of the Council of Appointment in 1782, while in 1785-86-87 he was a member of the Continental Congress.

As may be imagined, these men now sided with their long time political companion and pointed out every weak place in the proposed new Constitution, magnified every clause which leaned toward centralization and roused every passion of fear, jealousy and anger against nationality, which still smouldered from the late war. By a tremendous vote, they with the two others before named, were sent to the Convention with instructions to cast their suffrage against the proposed Federation. This three of them did, but as we know, without success. Jesse Woodhull, alone, among the delegates from Orange, voted for the Federal form of government. His object in so doing, is not apparent. In 1772, he was appointed Sheriff of Orange, and served. Re-appointed in May, 1777, he obtained no commission, but held over till the first State Legislature met in September of that year, and then was succeeded by Isaac Nicoll. From September 9th, 1777, to July 1st, 1781, he was a member of the State

Senate. That his vote was contrary to the wishes of his constituents would appear from the fact that he never again held public office.

I have dwelt at length on the topic of the feeling in this section toward the National Constitution, because it explains Rockland's stand in politics. Two creeds are transmitted from parents to children through generations, that of their religion and that of their political faith, and it is seldom that either is changed. The question of Federation or not, found our County Anti-Federal. Incensed by defeat, the opposition to centralization grew, became stronger as the years passed, and at last, found its party affiliation and name in the rise of Democracy. The spirit of County love, the intermarriages between members of long resident families, have kept an unusually large proportion of natives in the County, and those old families still retain their reverence for the political faith of their fathers.

Another political change, altogether local, was beginning to agitate our people. From a howling wilderness, inhabited only by savages and wild beasts, the section of Orange County north of the mountain had slowly become populated and cultivated by the ever advancing pioneer. The population of twenty families for the whole County, in 1693, had gradually increased, till at the time of the adoption of the Federal Constitution 14,062 occupied this territory, and in 1790, 18,492, and the increase north of the mountains, though slow during the intervening years, had at length reached and excelled that in our southern section, till the census now gave 12,491 above and 6,001 below the natural division line.

In 1723, only three Supervisors met at Tappan for the whole County. This continued to be the place for meeting till 1764, when the following act was passed by the General Assembly:

"WHEREAS, The Court House at Orangetown, being the place appointed for the annual meeting of the Supervisors of the County of Orange, in October, is found by experience to be very inconvenient on account of its situation. For remedy, whereof: 1. Be it enacted by his Honor, the Lieutenant-Governor, the Commissioners and General Assembly, and it is hereby enacted by the authority of the same, that it shall and may be lawful for the Supervisors of said County of Orange, and they are hereby directed to meet at the house of Daniel Coe, at Cakiate, in said County, on the first Tuesday of October next, and from there adjourn to any other place as near the centre of said County as shall seem most convenient to them for the good of the public service." ABRAHAM HARING and HENRY WISNER,
Members from Orange.

The events preceding and during the Revolution, led them to change their place of meeting to Goshen, where they continued till more peaceful times. From 1789 till 1797, the Board met at New City. But, instead of four, there were now eight townships, an equal number for each section.

During the war the brunt of the invasion in Orange had fallen on the southern towns, and to relieve the distress of the people in our section the Supervisors voted, at the annual meeting in 1779, that $14.730 be taken off the quotas of Orangetown and Haverstraw, and added, $8,552 to the quota of Goshen, and $6,177 to the quota of Cornwall, which left the quota of the four precincts:

Goshen,	$123,662
Cornwall,	58,637
Haverstraw,	55,000
Orangetown,	25,000

Again, on March 31st, 1780, it was ordered that $20,000 be taken off the quotas of the lower towns and added to the upper precincts, leaving the quotas:

Goshen,	$161,049	Haverstraw,	$92,437
Cornwall,	73,578	Orangetown,	34,573

These considerations led to a desire, on the part of the people on both sides of the mountain, to form separate counties. Those in the northern towns pointed out that their population was now greater than that of the lower towns, and was increasing more rapidly, yet their Supervisors had to make a long trip to meet those of the southern section, and that, instead of being met half way, these lower town officers fell back on the situation of their county seat, and could be gotten to advance no further. To be sure, the journey was not like that of 1723, when it took their delegate to the Board, James Osborn, four days to get from Goshen to Tappan and back, but still it was very long and unpleasant. Then they failed to see why they should be called on to support two sets of County Courts. They could not and did not blame the people in the lower towns for wanting court buildings on their side of the mountains, but when they had paid for their own at Goshen, they did not feel called on to be taxed for others. Becoming more annoyed, they passed from complaint to unpleasant hints, that the lower towns were either extremely selfish or else little better than ungrateful paupers. Had they not suffered as much in the Revolution as their brothers in the south. Had not Brant and his Tory allies fallen upon their western borders and, besides killing many of their people, wiped hamlets and whole villages out of existence. Yet they had not only borne this loss without murmur, but had given aid to the people below the mountain, by assuming great part of their tax, as well.

To these complaints the residents of Orangetown, Clarkestown, Ramapo and Haverstraw made answer in kind. You complain, they said, about your Supervisors coming south to meet ours. Why, before you had even a log hut for the Board to assemble in we gave your delegate comfortable quarters, and the bill for the entertainment of the Board, 19s. 7½d, was largely incurred for his board and lodging. For years afterward we outnumbered you three to one, paid taxes to aid you in clearing away the wilderness and exterminating predatory beasts, and now, forsooth, when through our endeavors your success is rendered possible, you at once demand that we, the parent settlement, shall send our delegates over the mountain to save you the trouble of coming here.

You pay taxes for our County buildings! Has it slipped your memory that when the first court-house and jail were built in this County, we were scarcely aware of your existence so small was your number. Is it willful mendacity or madness that leads you to forget that this section has been taxed for its own court-house, as you have for yours, and that with you we have been equally assessed for court officers. As to not blaming us for wanting something which we pay for and which ante-dated your court buildings by more than a decade, consider us as truly thankful for your tender thoughtfulness. You regard us as ungrateful paupers. You feel that your sufferings were greater than ours. To answer the second complaint first: Did you, during those dark days of horror, when anarchy and rapine had full sway within our towns, which served as a bulwark to your section, did you then feel that you were suffering greatly? Orangetown was for periods in the hands of the enemy, her patriots in flight or seized, her autonomy destroyed. Haverstraw had sent her sons to battle the oppressor, little hesitating, in the call to arms, whether as militiamen they fought in the defence of their homes or as soldiers, in the Continental army, for the defence of the Confederation. We bore the brunt of the battle, the heat and burden of a long weary day to protect, to save you; and now you reward us in this way. Is not the evidence in your hands convincing? So overrun were these townships that the Supervisors dare not meet here, and adjourned to Goshen, and yet you essay to enter this plaint against us.

Your frontier hamlets suffered from Brant's incursion. Have you visited our towns to see how the violence of war has devastated them, how our brothers have been swept away until there is scarcely a patriot home unbroken. Come, and we will take you to many a dwelling which was visited by Claudius Smith and his followers, who made their home in your territory, and when you have hearkened to tales of agony that would make demons shudder, perhaps you may realize that even the dread Brant was more merciful than the band you harbored.

You have exercised charity toward us! You have exercised *charity* toward us! A set of roaring swash-bucklers, who had no existence yesterday and may have none to-morrow, whose soil belongs to us—referring to the fact that, owing to the great influx of poor immigrants to the northern towns in the years after the war, the people north of the mountain had borrowed largely of those south, to start new forms of business, and those individual loans were so great as to virtually make our people the owners of that land—whose very existence is in our hands, you complain of the fact that in laboring to save you and others we were so crushed as not to be able to meet, for a moment only, our financial obligation. Let us remind you of the conduct of the evil spirits that your dominies have told you of that came, reinforced, to rend and destroy.

You feel that you alone have cause for complaint. Stop a moment and look at our view of your conduct. Since the formation of the State government, there have been one hundred and twenty-six Senators from the Middle Senatorial District of which you have had thirty-five and we but thirty-two. Seven and seventy members of Assembly have been elected of which you to the north of the mountain have had forty-six while we have only had thirty-one.

Or take our County officers. Eight men have held the Shrievalty since 1777, and all have been from your section; two County clerks have been appointed, both from the northern towns. And as if to make your selfishness more noticeable, the only Representative to Congress, since its organization under the new Constitution, from Orange County, John Hathorn, is a resident in your section.

Such, as I have been informed by old people, in both Orange and Rockland counties, whose fathers were active participants in the controversy which led to the erection of our County of Rockland, were the feelings of the people in the northern and southern towns toward each other, and such the causes for those feelings. The ridge of mountains which separated the sections was a natural division line that, while it might be overcome in the days of weakness in population, was sure to prove an insuperable obstacle to unity of interests, when the number of residents in the County had sufficiently increased. That period had now arrived, and the people on each side of the mountains were anxious for separate County existence. Accordingly, in 1798, the residents of the present Orange County appointed Captain John Luthill and Richard Goldsmith a committee to go to Captain Sloat's to consult with a County Committee from the present Rockland County regarding the terms of separation.

At length the Legislature, being influenced by the representations of the members from Orange County and the petitions of its residents, passed, on Feb. 23d, 1798, the following:

Be it enacted by the people of the State of New York, represented in Senate and Assembly. That all that tract of land in the County of Orange, lying northward of a line beginning at the mouth of Poplopens kill, on Hudson's River, and running from thence on a direct course to the southeasternmost corner of the farm of Stephen Sloat, and then along the said bounds of his farm, to the southwest corner thereof, and then on the same course to the bounds of the State of New Jersey, shall be and hereby is erected into a separate County and shall be called and known by the name of Orange.

And be it further enacted. That all that part of the said County of Orange, lying southward of the above described line, shall be erected into a separate County, and be called and known by the name of Rockland.

The County of Rockland to contain all that part of this south, bounded southerly and southwesterly by the line of the County west where the same crosses Hudson's River, and the division line between this State and New Jersey. Easterly by the middle of Hudson's River, and northerly and northwesterly by a line drawn from the middle of the said river, west to the mouth of Poplopens kill, and from thence on a direct course to the east end of the mill-dam now or late of Michael Weiman, across the Ramapough River, and from thence a direct course to the 20 mile stone standing in the said division line between this State and New Jersey.

All that part of the County of Rockland, bounded easterly by the middle of Hudson's River, southerly by New Jersey, and westerly and northerly by a line beginning on Hudson's River, at the northeast corner of the farm late belonging to Harman Tallman, deceased, and running from thence east to the middle of the said river, and westerly along the said farm to the tract of land formerly granted to T. D. Tallman, and then southerly and westerly along the bounds of the same tract to Demarie's kill, or Hackensack River, and then down the stream thereof to the northeast corner of a tract of 1,000 acres of land formerly sold for defraying the expenses of dividing the patent of Kakiat, and then westerly along the same to the northwest corner thereof, and then northerly and westerly and southerly along the land now or late belonging to J. J. Blauvelt, to the northeast corner of the land now or late belonging to John M. Hogencamp, and then westerly and southerly along the same to the northeast corner of the land now or late belonging to John P. Mabie, and then westerly along his land to New Jersey, shall be and continue a town by the name of Orangetown.

All that part of the said County of Rockland bounded westerly by a line beginning at the north-west corner of the land of John M. Hogencamp called his middletown lot, and running from thence north $3°$ west to the division line between the north and south moiety of the patent of Kakiat, and then along the same east to the line of division between the east and west 400 acre lots of the said north moiety, and then along the last mentioned division line, and continuing the same to the line of division between the mountain lots upon the top of the Verdrietege hook mountain, and northerly by the line running along the top of the said mountain between the said mountain lots to the east end thereof, and from thence to the head of the stream of water which runs from the Long Clove to Hudson's River easterly by the middle of Hudson's River, and southerly by Orangetown, shall be and continue a town by the name of Clarkstown.

All that part of the said County of Rockland bounded easterly by Clarkstown and Orangetown, southerly by Orangetown and New Jersey, westerly by New Jersey and Orange County, and northerly by a line running from the north-west corner of Clarkstown, along the south bounds of the lands now or late of Francis Gurnee and Benjamin Coe, and along the south bounds of the land now or late of Gabriel Conklin, and the same course continued to the bounds of Orange County, shall be and continue a town by the name of Hampstead.

All that part of the said County of Rockland, bounded southerly by Hampstead and Clarkstown and easterly, northerly, and westerly by the bounds of the County, shall be and continue a town by the name of Haverstraw."

John D. Coe was Senator and James Burt, Benjamin Coe and Moses Hatfield were Assemblymen from Orange County in the Legislature that erected Rockland County, both John D. and Benjamin Coe being from our territory.

The new County was placed in the Third Congressional District, composed of the 7th Ward of New York City and Westchester County. In the Middle Senatorial District of the State, and sent John Suffern as her first Senator. Allowed one member of Assembly, Hendrick Smith remained during 1798 and was succeeded by her first Assemblyman, Benjamin Coe. For County Officers, John Suffern was appointed County Judge; Peter Taulman, Surrogate; Jacob Wood, Sheriff; David Pye, County Clerk; and in the towns: Orangetown elected James Perry; Haverstraw, Benjamin Coe; Clarkstown, Claus R. Van Houten; and Ramapo, James Onderdonk, Supervisors. The last meeting of the old Orange County Board of Supervisors occurred at the residence of Stephen Sloat, in the Ramapo Valley, October 2d, 1798, and there were present: James Perry, Claus R. Van Houten, Benjamin Coe, James Onderdonk, of Rockland County.

For over a score of years after the erection of Rockland—till 1821—the Supervisors of the two counties, together with a Judge of the Court of Common Pleas of each county, met together at the house of Stephen Sloat annually, "for the purpose of inspecting and examining the mortgages, minutes and accounts of the loan officers appointed in the County of Orange, under the act for loaning monies belonging to the State." In 1853 a Legislative Act was passed, directing that copies of all deeds and wills that affected titles in Rockland County previous to the division, should be taken from the Orange County records and placed in the County Clerk's office of the first named county.

The census of electors in the new county, according to the property qualifications of the first Constitution was, in 1801 and till the Constitution was changed in 1821, as follows:

1801.	Electors worth £100 or over,	-	-	-	-	599
"	"	" between £20 and £100,	-	-	59
"	"	paying an annual rental of 40s.,	-	-	166
1807.	"	worth £100 or over,	-	-	-	-	766
"	"	" between £20 and £100,	-	-	65
"	"	paying an annual rental of 40s.,	-	-	153
1814.	"	worth £100 or over,	-	-	-	-	838

1814.	Electors worth between £20 and £100,	-	- 63
"	" paying an annual rental of 40s.,	-	- 245
1821.	" worth $250 or more, - -	-	- 817
"	" " between $50 and $250,	-	- 59
"	" who pay a rental of $5.00 or more,	-	- 298

The population of Rockland County in 1800 was 6,353, of which the towns had:

Orangetown, - - - - - - -	1,337
Haverstraw, - - - - - - -	1,229
Clarkstown, - - - - - - -	1,806
Hampstead, - - - - - - -	1,981

REPRESENTATIVES IN THE STATE LEGISLATURE.

SEVENTH SESSION.
SENATE.

William Allison,   John Haring,   Jacobus Swartwout,

ASSEMBLY.

Jeremiah Clarke,   John Hathorn,
Gilbert Cooper,   William Sickles,

EIGHTH SESSION.
SENATE.

William Allison,   John Haring,   Jacobus Swartwout.

ASSEMBLY.

Jeremiah Clarke,   John Hathorn,
Gilbert Cooper,   William Sickles.

NINTH SESSION.
SENATE.

William Allison,   John Haring,   Jacobus Swartwout.

ASSEMBLY.

John Bradner,   Nathaniel Satterly,
Gilbert Cooper,   Henry Wisner, 3d.

TENTH SESSION.
SENATE.

John Haring,   Jacobus Swartwout,

ASSEMBLY.

Robert Armstrong,   Gilbert Cooper,
Jeremiah Clark,   Peter Taulman,

ELEVENTH SESSION.
SENATE.

John Haring,   Jacobus Swartwout.

ASSEMBLY.

Jeremiah Clark, William Thompson,
Peter Taulman, Henry Wisner, Jr.

TWELFTH SESSION.
SENATE.

John Haring, Jacobus Swartwout,

ASSEMBLY.

John Carpenter, Jeremiah Clark, Henry Wisner. Jr.

THIRTEENTH SESSION.
SENATE.

Jacobus Swartwout.

ASSEMBLY.

John Carpenter, Seth Marvin,
John D. Coe, William Sickles.

FOURTEENTH SESSION.
SENATE.

David Pye, Jacobus Swartwout,

ASSEMBLY.

John Carpenter, Seth Marvin,
John D. Coe, John Smith.

FIFTEENTH SESSION.
SENATE.

David Pye, Jacobus Swartwout.

ASSEMBLY.

John D. Coe, Seth Marvin, John Smith.

SIXTEENTH SESSION.
SENATE.

David Pye, Jacobus Swartwout,

ASSEMBLY.

Reuben Hopkins, John Smith, Daniel Thew.

SEVENTEENTH SESSION.
SENATE.

David Pye, Jacobus Swartwout.

ASSEMBLY.

John D. Coe, Seth Marvin, John Wheeler.

EIGHTEENTH SESSION.
SENATE.

John D. Coe, Jacobus Swartwout.

ASSEMBLY.

William Allison, John Hathorn, David Pye.

NINETEENTH SESSION.
SENATE.

John D. Coe.
ASSEMBLY.

Seth Marvin,   David Pye,   James W. Wilkin.

TWENTIETH SESSION.
SENATE.
John D. Coe.
ASSEMBLY.

Isaac Blanch,   Jonathan Cooley,   Seth Marvin.

TWENTY-FIRST SESSION.
SENATE.
John D. Coe.
ASSEMBLY.

James Burt,   Benjamin Coe,   Moses Hatfield.

TWENTY-SECOND SESSION.
SENATE.
None.
ASSEMBLY.

John Blake, Jr.   Moses Philips,
James Burt,   Hendrick Smith.
David W. Westcott.

Adjourned *sine die* April 3d, 1799.

REPRESENTATIVES IN CONGRESS.

FIRST CONGRESS.
John Hathorn,
FOURTH CONGRESS.
John Hathorn.

Authorities referred to: "Field Book of the Revolution," Vols. II., B. J. Lossing. "New York Civil List," "History of Orange County," S. W. Eager. "Documents Relating to the Colonial History, S. N. Y.," Vols. XIV. "Session Laws."

CHAPTER X.

EARLY INDUSTRIES OF ROCKLAND COUNTY.
THE HASSENCLEVER IRON MINE AND ROCKLAND NICKEL COMPANY MINE—CONGLOMERATE SANDSTONE AND FREESTONE QUARRIES—DATER'S WORKS—WORKS AT SLOATSBURG—RAMAPO WORKS—BRICK MANUFACTURE—KNICKERBOCKER ICE COMPANY.

In the middle of the 18th century, between 1730-50, a company of German miners, under the direction of Peter Hassenclever, visited this Colony and explored the mountains of Orange County for ore. Either with this exploring party or shortly afterward, Hassenclever came to America and at once set to work to organize capital for the development of the great iron veins in the colonies. In a short time he became the proprietor of mines in this Colony and that of New Jersey, and, with a partner named Seton, started several foundries. Before 1768, Hassenclever sailed for England and was given a letter of introduction to the Lords of Trade by Governor Moore, who stated that his wide range of knowledge, concerning the affairs of the Colony, would make his visit one of value to that body. In a short time he returned to this Continent, and in 1769, with sixteen others, obtained a patent for 18,000 acres of land situated in the present Herkimer county.

Among the mines which Peter Hassenclever developed was that which bears his name, situated on lot No. 3 of the Cheesecocks patent. The exact date of opening of the Hassenclever Mine has escaped my most earnest search, but the following data may lead to an approximation. The mine was first worked by the London Mining and Improvement Company. On March 12th, 1768, the Earl of Hillsborough wrote to Sir Henry Moore, Governor of this Colony : " I am desired by Major-General Greene and other gentlemen concerned in carrying on iron works in New York, under the direction of Mr. Hassenclever, to inform you that that gentleman misbehaves towards them and refuses to come to account, for which reason it is their intention to supercede him, and to appoint another Person in his place, and as these Works are represented to me to be of great Publick Utility, I think it my duty to recommend to you to give all the support and protection you can to the Person they mean to appoint, and to give any assistance in your Power towards bringing Mr. Hassenclever to a due performance of his Engagements." I believe this letter to refer to the Hassenclever Mine, and judge from it that work was begun there as early as 1766. In conjunction with the mine a furnace, situated on Cedar Pond Brook, and called Cedar Pond Furnace, was worked. The second owner of the mine was Captain Samuel Brewster, who worked it during the Revolution, and from it iron for the chain that crossed the Hudson at Fort Montgomery is said to have been taken.

On the death of Captain Samuel Brewster, in 1821, the Hassenclever Mine passed into the hands of his son James, and was conducted by him till his death. After him the mine was bought by Bradley, who, after working it a short time, failed, making an assignment of the property to Blackstick. The assignee sold the mine to Wm. Knight, who sold it to a company, organized about 1844, and known as the Haverstraw Iron & Mining Company.

Under this Company considerable change was made. Besides the old works, they bought eleven acres of the lowlands above the bridge, which had formerly been connected with the mine, and erected on it a large brick building near the site of the old furnace. The company intended this building as a place where the ore was to be converted into the iron of commerce without the intermediate process of puddling. The works were not a success; the company failed, and the building was torn down. The mine then passed into the hands of Colfax & Co., who still hold it. The works erected because of this mine, consisted of a furnace a short distance above the present lowland bridge; a foundry on Florus Falls Creek, a half mile further west; a forge or bloomery on the property now owned by Henry Goetschius; a bloomery a short distance from the old Slutton House, and still another bloomery and furnace just below the outlet of Cedar Pond.

In 1871, a Nickle mine was opened on the iron ridge in lot No. 2, of the Cheesecocks patent by John Sneviley, of New York City. Sneviley worked this mine till 1875, when he sold it to the Rockland Nickel Company by whom it is still conducted.

It was soon found that the gray and red conglomerate sandstone, of which large quantities exist in our County, formed the best hearth stones that could be obtained for iron furnaces, and quarries were speedily opened. The first worked was situated one and a quarter miles north of New City. This quarry was begun in 1788, and continued for twenty years. From 1808 to 1838, it was not used, but in the latter year work was again begun in it by Joseph Bird, who paid the owner—Isaac Van Houten—$10 for every set of furnace hearths quarried. About a half mile north of Van Houten's was the quarry of Cornelius De Pew, which supplied the hearths of the Greenwood, Woodbury and Cold Spring furnaces. Blauvelt's quarry, three miles northwest of New City, was worked in 1838 by Isaac Springsteen. Three miles north of New City, Richard Coe, had a quarry. One quarter of a mile west of this was one belonging to Levi Smith; while others were opened along the south base of the mountain by John Smith, Jacob Green and Jonas Conklin.

A common furnace hearth from these quarries, required 14 blocks of stone, 10 of which contained each about 20 cubic feet, and 4 contained each about 10 cubic feet, or in the whole 240 cubic feet. Bird, who leased the Van Houten quarry, estimated the value of a set of hearth stones, delivered at the landing, at $100 and the income from this business was about $6,000 a year.

Early in the history of the settlement of the County, freestone quarries were opened and worked sufficiently to supply the buildings of the settlers; but it was not till the close of the War for Independence that these quarries were developed as a business speculation. About 1785, quarries were opened south of Nyack by Garret Onderdonk, and at Upper Nyack by John L. and Auri Smith. The demand for stone from Nyack steadily, though slowly, increased till 1804, when the business obtained a solid footing, and another form of quarrying, that of trap-rock for dock-stone, was begun. In working a freestone quarry the workmen came first upon a facing of callus, which was perfectly useless, and had to be removed. Then came the material of commerce, which consisted of building stone, "principal" stone and "flagging." The "principal" stone was a better grade of building stone. It was compact, grainless, capable of being cut, but incapable of being split, and was used for finishing purposes, door and window sills, cornices and door-steps. The "flagging" was the most compact of the varieties of freestone; it contained a perfectly straight grain, could be split to almost any thickness, and was capable of a very good polish. From the "flagging" mantles were made.

For many years the freestone from the Nyack quarries was used for buildings in New York and neighboring cities. As the city increased, new quarries were opened along the shore from the present Grand View Station to the mountain at Upper Nyack. The exciting complications of our nation with foreign powers, during the early years of the century, gave a fresh impetus to the business, and from Nyack stone were built Fort Diamond on Hendrick's reef, later and now known as Fort Lafayette, before 1824. Castle Williams, on Governors Island, finished in 1811, and the Red Fort, which used to stand at or near the corner of Desbrosses and West streets in New York city. In filling the contracts for these works, the quarrymen were in no wise particular about the quality of the stone, and as a result the fort walls soon began to crumble. The labor of replacing the poor stone was not complete at the time of the destruction of Fort Lafayette by fire, Dec. 1st, 1868, and that work had cost the government, till that catastrophe, $350,000.

Never was the freestone business so good as during the decade between 1820 and 1830. In that period over two hundred outside laborers were drawn to the County, and it was common to see from ten to twelve vessels, loaded with stone leave the docks each day, while as many more were drawn in to take their places. Wages were high. The quarrying of building stone would pay from $3 to $5 a day, while, if a vein of "flagging" was struck, it was not uncommon to make from $10 to $15 a day.

In 1830, the quarries at Beleville, N. J., were opened, and the stone found to be of a better grade than that from our County. Quarrying here began to decline and never recovered its prestige. In 1838, the leading quarries at Nyack were those of Westervelt's at Upper Nyack, on the property belonging to George Green. Here the "flagging" was a foot and a half wide and from two to three inches thick; Clark's, two miles from Nyack; Wilkin's, one mile south of Nyack, from which 5,000 or 6,000 feet of slabs were annually shipped; Daniel Onderdonk and brother, who shipped from their two works 2,500 flags; Richard Clark's, near the Onderdonk's,; and Gesner's. In all, in 1838, there were thirty-one quarries at Nyack, sixteen being below and fifteen above the village, and from them were shipped during that year:

62,000 feet of slabs, valued at	$9,300 00
15,500 cart loads of rubble	9,687 00

Giving an annual income from the business of - .- $18,987 00

In the report of the State Geologist for the year can be read: "That the annual amount of sales a few years ago was near twenty times greater than this."

While these quarries at Nyack were being worked to an extent now unthought of, one was opened just south of the Long Clove road, at the present Conger's quarry by John Blackhurst. At the same time James Thom, a native of Scotland, purchased Richard Coe's quarry north of New City, and Blackhurst hired that of Cornelius De Pew, at Stagg's Corners, together with others.

The business relationship existing between Thom and Blackhurst is unknown, but they evidently worked together, and stone was taken from these quarries to build the Church of the Holy Trinity in Brooklyn, begun in 1844, and in part to build Trinity in New York. Besides these, many private buildings in New York were trimmed with stone taken from this County, and finished by Thom. After a short ownership, the quarry above New City was sold by Thom to John A. McPherson, of Paterson, N. J., but he still continued to get stone from it.

An anecdote of this sculptor may, perhaps, not be out of place. While resident in our County he was seized with a serious illness, which at one time threatened to terminate fatally. Many of his employees were Scots, and they loved the "Boss," as they affectionately termed Mr. Thom. During the hours of his illness, they had held many consultations regarding his condition, and at last determined that some one should pray with and for him. But who would be the petitioner? One after the other declined or excused himself till only the final member of the party remained unheard from, and he was deputed to perform the labor of love. At the hour appointed, the employees filed into the invalid's room and bent their knees while the prayer began. "O Lord bless Bossie Thom, an' if ye dinna ken who Bossie Thom is Lord; He's the mon that cut Tam O'Shanter."

While Tam O'Shanter was doubtless his greatest, it was by no means Thom's only work. "Old Mortality," "Touter Johnnie," and the "Statue of Washington," which many of the older inhabitants remember as standing in the door yard at the corner of the Nyack Turnpike and Erie Railroad, near Nanuet, were fashioned by his hand. The vine which twines over Trinity church entrance was hewn from insensate stone by his chisel, and much of the scroll work of old time houses in New York gives evidence of his masterly skill.

At length, in 1842, the work which had been growing less and less, practically ceased in the Nyack quarries. Since that time but little stone has been taken out and that almost entirely for local structures. For a short time longer the quarries, managed in Thom's interest were kept employed. Then Thom died, and these, too, were abandoned. That known as Conger's, on the river front south of Haverstraw, was worked to obtain material for the new bridge across the Minisceongo in 1883, and slightly to supply the West Shore Railroad, but to all practical purposes this industry has stopped.

Among the prominent buildings in this State, constructed in whole or part, from the freestone of this County, besides the forts already mentioned, is the old Capitol at Albany, built in 1807; the rear of the New York City Hall, built in 1806–10; and in New Jersey, the first building of Rutgers College erected in 1809.

I have already said that the dock stone business began to be active in

1804. Trap rock was the material used for this purpose, and, as the city of New York grew, fresh quarries were started from Fort Lee to Rockland Lake. From this material the first docks of New York, cribs of logs, were filled, foundations were occasionally built, and the sea wall at Governors Island constructed. Later the stone was tried as a pavement for the streets, but proved a failure owing to its certainty to split at the edges and become round. The ease with which gneiss could be obtained on the island, and the change from crib to spile piers in New York, led to the abandonment of this enterprise. In 1838, but three quarries of trap rock are mentioned in the County. Two of these belonged to Jacob Voorhis, and one, situated near by, to Peter White, and they were on the river front of the mountain north of Nyack. During the year, Mr. Voorhis shipped about 6,000 tons of stone, and Mr. White 1,200 tons. This was about one-fourth of the usual amount shipped annually. At the quarry the stone was valued at 1s. 3d. per ton, and sold in New York for 4s. per ton. The construction of the Hudson River Railroad in 1851, led to a temporary revival of trap-rock quarrying, and much of the sea wall of that road is built from this stone.

We must now turn back to the Ramapo Valley and observe the tremendous manufacturing interests which grew up there in the early days of our County. At the birth of the century, Abram Dater had established iron works at Pleasant Valley. In 1813, he had six forges at work and gave employment to about 140 people. These forges were located on both sides of the Ramapo, on the spot now occupied by the store of Geo. W. Dater.

In 1820, the firm controlling these works, was Dater & Ward. Thos. Ward being Mr. Dater's son-in-law. In 1831, upon the death of Abram Dater, the works were sold to the Sterling Company, and operated under this management for a short time. In 1849, they were managed by N. Potter Thomas, and later A. H. Dorr, ran them; after him, and till 1854, they were under charge of John Sarsen.

Besides these works, Mr. Dater also ran a grist mill, located on the west bank of the Ramapo, and a forge on Stony Brook, about three quarters of a mile from Sloatsburgh, at the present site of E. F. Allen's mill dam, known as the Split Rock Forge. At this spot about 1835, Thomas Ward, built a saw-mill, which, in 1847-49, was used by Adna Allen as a hoe factory. Later, as we shall see in the history of Ramapo township, it was used for other purposes.

A half mile south of Dater's were the Sloatsburgh Works. As early as 1792, a tannery was operated at this place by Isaac Sloat, but it was not till 1815, that the first mill for the manufacture of cotton cloth was built. This mill, still standing, was a frame building 20 by 60 feet, three stories in height, with two wings, one being a machine and smith shop where heavy mill screws and vices had previously been made. In this mill Jacob Sloat began the manufacture of cotton cloth in connection with stocks and dies, in which latter article he led the market of New York. Till 1836, the mill was continued with but little change. Then one of the wings was torn down and a new one—20 by 30 feet and three stories in height, was erected in its place; an addition was also built on the north side of the main structure.

In 1838, weaving was discontinued and the mill was run on fine and coarse wraps. In 1839, the firm of J. Sloat & Co., consisting of Stephen and Jacob Sloat, John Quackenbush, and John S. Westervelt—was established. New and improved machinery was added, and in addition to the old branches of business, the manufacture of cotton twine was begun.

In 1840 Jacob Sloat, patented a process for dressing cotton twine, and the demand for twine became so great, that all the spindles were turned upon its manufacture. This led to the building of the first brick mill in 1846, a structure, 152 by 34 feet, which increased the manufacturing capacity of the company from 2,500 lbs. per week to 6,000 lbs. In 1853, the company was incorporated under the name of the "Sloatsburgh Manufacturing Co." In 1857, 128 feet were added to the brick mill, connecting it with the original structure, and making a building 340 feet in length. This addition increased the capacity of the company to 8,000 lbs. per week. In 1858, Jacob Sloat, who had retired from the management of the business in 1851, died. The War of the Rebellion depressed this, as it did every business in which cotton entered as a factor, and the company finally ceased operations in August 1878.

Four men stand prominently forward, in the first half century of the County's history, as public benefactors. Other men have worked actively for the interests, the prosperity of this portion of the commonwealth; other and many other men have pushed forward a work, which was begun, to full completion, but to Jeremiah H. Pierson, who gave the present success to Ramapo township; to James Wood, who, by his discovery of the present plan of burning brick, rendered the enormous business, which is the source of vast wealth to Haverstraw and Stony Point townships, possible, to John Edward Green, through whose courage, energy and financial aid the first steamboat was built and successfully run, changing the career of Nyack; and which with the Erie Railroad, labored for and carried through by Eleazor Lord, LL. D., gave an entirely new character to the business interests of Orangetown, belongs, preeminently, the meed of praise.

Up to 1795, Sidman's Clove still retained its pre-revolutionary solitude, and the wonderful water power of the Ramapo flowed untramelled save by an occasional grist or saw mill, on to join the Pompton. The steam engine was in its infancy, and water power was of a value now little realized. The abundance and force of the river in Sidman's Pass, the vast quantities of wood, scarcely less necessary to the manufacturer than water, which lined the mountain sides, determined the Pierson Brothers in their selection of this site for the permanent home of their factories.

In 1795 Josiah G. Pierson was engaged in the manufacture of cut nails, by machinery of his invention, from iron imported from Russia, and rolled and cut at Wilmington, Del., the nearest rolling-mill to New York at that time. His factory was located on Whitehall street, where the Produce Exchange now stands.

The first purchase in the Pass was of 119 acres from John Suffern, and on this purchase preparations were at once begun, under the superintendence of J. H. Pierson, for the erection of the necessary dam and buildings. Mechanics and laborers soon raised factory walls in this primeval wilderness, and in 1798 the rolling-mill, slitting-mill, and nail factory were all in operation, under the firm of J. G. Pierson & Brothers. This firm consisted of Jeremiah H. and Isaac Pierson, Josiah G. having died Dec. 17th of the previous year, before the works he had planned were completed. From 1798 to 1812 the works were constantly employed. In 1807, the growth of whale fishery had so increased the demand for hoops for oil casks, that the rolling-mill was extended to meet it, and hoop-iron was added to the product of the Valley. In 1810 Pierson's works supported about 800 people.

In 1812, the buildings at the Ramapo Works were as follows: The river was spanned, as now, by a dam 120 feet long. On the north side, adjoining the dam, stood a blacksmith shop, rolling and slitting mills, and works for cutting and heading nails. On the south side of the river, adjoining the dam, was a saw-mill, next to this on the west was a "Straw House," a two-story building, in which was stored and cut by water-power, the straw for the numerous mules and oxen employed for the works. Still further west, up the stream, along the pond, stood the horse, ox, and four mule barns, all two stories in height.

On the south side of the river, also, a few rods east, and a little to the south of the saw mill, was a store, built in 1805, and now occupied by William Van Wagenen. A short distance to the east and north of this was the homestead of J. H. Pierson, built very soon after the works were established, rebuilt in 1805, and now occupied by F. Taylor. In the northwest corner of this homestead the first store was kept.

East by north from the homestead, and just west of the present depot, stood a grist mill, a four story building. Down the river, a few rods east of the grist mill, was a forge, and near by, to the south, a coal house. West by south from this last building, up the hill on the south side of the turnpike, stood the "Yellow store," built in 1810. In this was stored beef, pork and other provisions for winter use. East of this was a house built for John Colt, in 1808. It is now known as the "Prayer Rooms." The church, erected in 1810, still occupies its original site. The second school house, a yellow building in two parts, stood on the south side of the turnpike, nearly opposite the present "stone store." The first school house, built in 1798, was located on the north side of the pike just east of the present "prayer rooms." A gate, through which there was no admission except on business, filled the space between the store and the homestead, and through this gate the road, bending to the east, ran down the slope in front of the grist mill, and so across the river to the nail works and rolling mill, the present bridge being several rods east of the bridge of those days. Such, says the Rev. Eben B. Cobb, from whom I have drawn so largely in treating of the different works in the Ramapo Valley, that quotation marks would be superfluous, was the Ramapo of 1812. And, when we think of the multitudes of farmers' wagons bringing produce of all kinds to this, the market for the neighboring parts of Orange and Rockland counties—Mr. Cobb gives the names of sixty-one farmers who delivered their products at this mart—when we think of the four and six mule teams going and returning, with their heavy loads, to and from Haverstraw, Buskirk's Landing on the Hackensack, and Hoboken; when we read that in 1810 a million pounds of nails was the yearly output of the nail factory alone, I think that the placing of J. T. Pierson first in the list of the four leading men in the County, of that time, needs no further explanation.

But large as these works were, they were almost doubled by the erection of the cotton mill in 1814-15. This mill was built to spin yarn to send to Russia, in exchange for iron, three-fourths of that used in the Ramapo Works being Russian ore. It was a five story building with a dye house on the north end, and a machine shop—a four-story brick building with an attic; torn down in 1852, to give room for the double tracks of the Erie—on the south. On the Turnpike, too, the stone building, still standing, was erected, for the storing of cotton. From this building it was slid on a shoot to the mill below.

These mills, built at an expense of $155,848, were furnished with 7,500 spindles, capable of making 506,250 pounds of No. 13 yarn, per year, and 78 looms, capable of producing 486,720 yards of striped shirting, sheeting, and checks per year. In 1820, they furnished employment to 119 people. In 1822, the joint interest of the surviving brothers, J H. and Isaac Pierson, was incorporated under the name of the Ramapo Manufacturing Company. In 1830, the manufacture of blister steel and wood screws was commenced. In 1851, operations at Ramapo were virtually suspended and the works closed.

We may review the principal industries of this period from 1798 to 1851. Cut nails were manufactured from 1798 to about 1840; cotton yarn and cloth from 1816 to 1836; spring steel from 1810 to 1850; and blister steel and wood screws from 1830 to 1851.

To our County the Pierson brothers generally, but Jeremiah T. particularly, gave an impetus that has only been equalled by the discovery of James Wood. In the language of Mr. Cobb, "We see nothing of the traffic which 'strung along' them (the wagon roads) when teams were hauling grain and other produce for the sustenance of those who wrought, or of the droves of cattle which encumbered them when being driven hither to be slaughtered and packed away in huge cisterns or tanks. A record has been kept of this traffic, and we give a summary from it for the years 1820–21: 15,758 bushels of grain and 181,254 pounds of provisions (beef, pork, mutton, veal and butter) were brought to Ramapo in those years." It was owing to the existence of the Ramapo Works that the Nyack turnpike was cut through, in spite of opposition more violent and long-continued than ever greeted any other enterprise in this County, and the presence of the works and the opening of the Turnpike, rendered the building of the first steamboat feasible.

But it was not alone to the material prosperity of the village he founded, of the County where he became resident, that Mr. Pierson devoted himself. He looked beyond the temporal to futurity. In great measure the controller of his employees, lives, he so far respected the State as to foster and press forward educational facilities. Realizing the deleterious influence of liquor, he stopped the allowance of grog, which theretofore had been considered a necessity among employees, in 1828, and earlier, in conjunction with John Suffern, he had joined in buying out and tearing down a groggery kept by a widow named Jenkins. In 1810, he built the Presbyterian church, the first place for divine worship in Ramapo clove, and long bore the burden of its expense. For several years before his death, Mr. Pierson was afflicted with blindness; at length, on Dec. 12th, 1855, he found rest, in the 90th year of his age.

Preceding the Revolution some slight attempts at the manufacture of brick were tried where the clay was found, but, as in the case of the freestone, the little done in the business was only for local use. On the property of Mrs. Nellie Hart, in Upper Nyack, a yard existed before the beginning of this century, and some of the brick then made are now in the possession of Mrs. Hart; but so brief was the existence of the work, and so slight the impress which it made upon the minds of the residents in the neighborhood, that all data respecting it are lost. I have seen in the possession of Adam Lilburn a brick, which was taken from the chimney of the old Treason House, marked 1792, and made at Haverstraw.

The first kiln of bricks for a regular market ever prepared in this County, was baked about 1810, under the management of a company from Philadelphia, and the yard then opened was on the bank of the Miniseeongo, not far from where the present iron bridge crosses the stream. The enterprise ended in failure, and the work was abandoned. In that year the total number of bricks made in this country was only 94,371,646. Five years elapsed before a second attempt was made. Then, in 1815, James Wood, a native of England, who had learned the trade of a brickmaker in his native land, and who had been in the brickmaking business in Sing Sing and at Verplanck's Point, attracted to Haverstraw by the vast quantities of brick clay and the apparently unlimited supply of wood, leased from the De Noyelles a piece of land on the river shore, directly opposite their family burying ground, and started the first successful brickyard in the County.

When Wood opened that first yard in Haverstraw, the process of making brick was the same as that pursued by the Israelites while in their Egyptian bondage, over three thousand years before. True, it seems to be, that a few manufacturers in England had used coal dust in their brickclay, but so little was the advantage of this process known, that the cause of a long and bitter litigation was needed to demonstrate it. In the old primitive way the clay and a due proportion of sand were mixed, tempered by treading with the feet, and, when properly mingled, placed in the moulds by hand. These moulds—boxes without tops or bottoms, divided by partitions so as to hold the clay for three bricks placed lengthwise—were placed upon a table, the clay put in them and struck off and then the mould, drawn sideways to the edge of the table, was carefully tipped on its side, and thus carried to the drying ground. It does not require an inspection of that old process to become assured, that however much care might be used, the soft clay would settle out of shape and the bricks be distorted and rude.

Accident led to the two great discoveries in brick making. Through the mechanical genius of a belated boatman, whose vessel, fortunately for Haverstraw, had run aground on the flats before that place, James Wood was shown how to make a mould with a bottom and a vent. Soon after this, in 1828, happened the great discovery of his life. An English friend, with whom he had lived when he first arrived in this country, sent him a small quantity of anthracite coal, which was then being developed in Pennsylvania, as a curiosity. On burning it he found, that while the combustion gave forth intense heat, but little smoke was emitted.

At once the idea came to him that the coal could be used to burn brick, and he hastened to make the experiment. A piece of the coal was pulverized in a borrowed mortar and mixed with the clay for four bricks, which, after being marked, were placed in the kiln. The kiln was burned, the bricks examined, and the examination showed that the experiment was a success.

But the success in the case of four bricks only proved a part of the discovery. It remained to learn the proper proportion of coal dust to mix with the clay for a kiln. Mr. Wood obtained a load of anthracite coal and sent it over the mountain to Van Houtens' grist and plaster mill to be ground, and then mixed the dust with clay in nearly equal parts. That kiln burned to slag, and was ruined. At last the proportion arrived at was, according to the State Geologist's Report for 1838, 22½ tons of coal dust to a kiln of 450,000 bricks.

Further tests were tried. The coal dust was mixed with the bricks, which composed the upper layers of the kiln, with the result that they were burned as hard as those in the lower layers, a condition never before obtained. On still further trials it was demonstrated, that whereas up to that time it had been impossible to make bricks in a kiln of uniform quality, that of the three classes into which brick-makers divided a kiln— " Hard," " Salmon " and "Pale"—the latter were soft and perfectly useless, by this discovery they were all equally burned and all equally useful.

The discovery of James Wood revolutionized brick making. In a moment the custom of three and thirty centuries was changed. In a moment the vast growth of American cities was rendered possible because a quick, cheap and almost inexhaustible building material had been found. In a moment the brick yards, scattered along the Hudson, which had been dragging along with a slow and not over lucrative business, were turned into scenes of busy industry. In a moment the vast wealth of Haverstraw, her position as one of the three leading villages in the County, her present life itself, were rendered practicable.

And what have brick-makers done to reward James Wood? Ethically, they stole the benefit of his discovery, fought him year by year in the courts, and permitted him to die in comparative poverty, while they were amassing fortunes from the use of his experiments. It is vain to plead that the use of coal dust in brick clay had existed in England. It was not known here. It is vain to plead that his patent was defective, because he did not give the proper proportion of coal dust which should be mixed with different clays in different localities. He did give the proper proportion for the clay of Haverstraw and vicinity, and it is of Haverstraw and vicinity I am speaking. It is begging the question to point to the fact that he did not succeed in business when others did by following his discovery. Hundreds of men, who have benefitted the world, have been unsuccessful in business. · The fact remains, that on the brick-makers of this County rests a great crime, which may be boldly faced, but which can neither be argued away nor hidden.

In still another particular did Wood improve the means of making brick. He invented a machine, consisting of a wooden axle with spokes projecting from it, which, revolving in a central shaft, mixed the clay, coal dust, and sand more rapidly than before was possible. The time saved by these different discoveries was from seven to ten days on a kiln.

The next yard after Wood's was established by the Allison family, a short distance north of the foot of the present Main street, in Haverstraw, and in a brief time several yards were opened at Grassy Point, and below Caldwell's Landing. By 1834, these yards were dragging along in a precarious condition. In November of that year, David Munn, came to our County, bought land at Grassy Point, took hold of the brick business with a determination to make it pay, and succeeded. In 1838, the following yards were in operation with their annual production:

Hodges' yard at Grassy Point - - -	2,500,000.
Mackey's yard at Haverstraw - - -	2,500,000.
Wm. Holme's yard at Grassy Point - -	2,000,000.
Lent's yard, below Caldwell's - - -	500,000.
David Munn's yard at Grassy Point - -	3,500,000.
Churchill's yard below Caldwell's - -	1,000,000.

In the following years this industry advanced with rapidity, largely through the efforts and foresight of David Munn, who, taking instantaneous advantage of every improvement, demonstrated the lucrative value of the business.

"In 1852, a fresh impetus was added (to the brick making business) by the invention of the Automatic Brick Machine * * * of Richard A. Ver Valen. For some time previous, what was known as Hall's Improved Machine had been in use. * * * In the old machines the clay was pressed into the moulds by a lever worked by hand, and the moulds with the bricks were drawn out of the press by the man in charge. To do this with any degree of rapidity, required a combination of strength and quickness which few men possessed; and although higher wages were offered as an inducement, it was soon found that the labor was so exhausting that it could not be endured for more than a few days at a time. Another great disadvantage was the fact that to render it possible to press the clay in the moulds it must be in a condition so soft, that when placed on the drying ground, the bricks failed to retain their shape, if exposed to any pressure. * * * After long thought (Mr. Ver Valen) invented the machine now in use, which not only tempers the clay, but presses it into the moulds while sufficiently stiff to cause the bricks to retain their shape in the most perfect manner. A slight change in the motion shoves out the mould ready to be placed on the truck and carried to the drying field."

Litigation against Mr. Ver Valen and some of the brick makers who used his patent, was begun by the inventor of the Hall machine, and the matter dragged in the courts for some time, but was finally settled in Mr. Ver Valen's favor. This invention has not only increased the number of bricks manufactured, but it also gave to Haverstraw a new branch of business, of which we shall read under the history of the town.

In 1853, a brick maker's strike occurred on account of a reduction of wages. Hundreds of strikers marched from yard to yard, breathing threats of violence. At length the feeling of insecurity became so great that Sheriff Henry L. Sherwood, applied for troops, and Company R of the 17th Regiment—Rockland County Rangers, under the command of Major Isaac Pye, was ordered on duty.

In May 1877, another strike occurred. Again dissatisfaction arose among the laborers because of a reduction of wages, and they stopped work. The yard owners thereupon sent to Canada and obtained the services of a large number of French Canadians. As soon as the new laborers began work the strikers began to act violently, and Sheriff William Hutton called upon the Governor for aid. In response two companies of the 16th Battalion, N. Y. S. N. G., one from Nyack and one from Sing Sing, were sent to the scene of trouble, and in a week, quiet was restored.

Among the names of those who have been engaged in the brick business at Haverstraw, besides the few already mentioned, are:

Thomas Doyle,	Seamans,	John Campbell,
Isaiah Milburne,	Redner & Strang,	Briggs,
Wm. Call,	Close & Van Orden,	Rutherford & Marks,
O. C. Gerow,	Daniel Weed,	S. D. Gardner,
Cosgroves,	John Owen,	Geo. Oldfield,
Gardeners,	M. Nye,	W. Gordon.
	James Eckerson,	

The manufacturers in 1885 are:

B. J. Allison,	T. G. Peck & Co.,	James Morrissy,
Allison, Wood & Allison,	John Oldfield,	Malley & Goldrick,
Wood & Keenan,	Brockway & Smith,	Thos. Shankey & Co.,
Allison, Wood & Keenan,	Richard Crowley,	Gillies & Benjamin,
Diamond Brick Co.,	Snedeker Bros.,	Gillies & Frederick,
D. Fowler & Sons,	Sherwood & Baum,	T. McKearns,
John Derbyshire,	P. Buckley & Co.,	Archer Bros.,
Richard Murray,	John Dunn & Co.,	George Knapp,
U. F. Washburn & Co.,	Andrew Donelly,	G. G. Allison,
Carr & Smith,	McMahon & Co.,	Tomkins Bros.,
Felter Bros.,	Christie & McCabe,	Riley & Rose,
Josiah Felter,	Lynch & McCabe,	Riley & Clark,
	James De Groot.	

In 1883 there were forty-two brick yards in operation between Long Clove and Caldwell's Point, and the production was 302,647,000, the number of employees 2,400. In 1884 there were forty-three yards in operation between Long Clove and Tomkins Cove.

As now mixed, coal dust, in the proportion of one bushel to every thousand bricks, is used for the inside of the kiln, but for those that are nearest the shell double that quantity is necessary. The quantity of sand employed depends so largely on its quality that an absolute rule cannot be made. The size of the kiln varies, but few are as small as the old figure, 450,000. Double that number, a million, and even more are now burned at once. As regards the method of transportation, the sailing vessels of old have, in a measure, been supplanted by barges. In the former's favor was the fact that they carrried their own motive power, but as an offset to this the barges will carry four and five times larger cargoes. In regard to the leasing of brick property, there is, of course, variation, but the custom seems to be for the lessee to pay from twenty-five to fifty cents, and even $1, on every thousand bricks made.

Tradition has it that in 1826, C. Wortendyke, of New Jersey, came to and cut from Rockland Lake, then called "the Pond," two boat loads of ice, which he conveyed to the city in the sloop "Contractor," commanded by Captain John White.

The origin of the company with which I am to deal, however, the now famous Knickerbocker, dates from 1835, when John J. Felter, John G. Perry and Edward Felter cut a sloop load of ice from the Lake and sold it at an almost clear profit. In the following year, 1836, the following men joined together and formed an association for the purpose of supplying the city of New York with ice, under the name of Barmore, Felter & Co.:

Nathaniel Barmore,	Isaac Van Houten,	John J. Felter,
John De Baun,	Edward Green,	Edward Felter,
Thomas Wells,	Moses G. Leonard,	Ambrose Wells,
Benedict Wells,	Peter P. Gasque.	William Hutchison,
George Smith,	Alfred Wells,	John Smith,
William Smith,	Jacob Swartwout,	John G. Perry,
John Van Houten,	George Swartwout,	

Each member of the Association put $100 into the concern, forming a capital of $2,000. The articles of association for this company were drawn by Wm. F. Frazer, then District Attorney, later County Judge of the County.

With their capital the company built the dock at Slaughter's Landing and a small ice house, capable of holding two or three hundred tons of ice at the lake, and hired a cellar in Christopher street, near Greenwich avenue, and one in Amos street, to store the ice brought to the city. The hosts of the hotel that stood on the present site of Stewart's old store, corner of Chambers street and Broadway, and the hotel at number one Broadway, were seen and shown a specimen of the lake ice, which the canvasser, Hon. Moses G. Leonard, carried wrapped in a handkerchief.

Up to this time, 1837, the little ice used in the city was by butchers and the hotels. None was used in private houses, they being supplied with water from the wells and cisterns in the city. Ice was obtained from neighboring ponds, and was dirty and cut up. The purity of the Lake ice made it at once popular, and it was contracted for at $20 a ton. To the hotels already mentioned must be added the Astor House, which, though being built when the ice company started, was in readiness for their product the following year.

The encouragement thus given to the company led them to buy a periauger,—capable of carrying about thirty tons, and to instantly begin shipping their commodity. But so little was known of the business, so little calculation was made for the waste of melting, that even at the enormous price obtained there was but small profit and the supply of ice was exhausted by July. For the following year, 1838, still greater preparation was made; two small houses were built on the left hand side of the dock at Slaughter's Landing, capable of holding about 2,000 tons, which were filled by running the ice down a shute from the mountain top;— the first cake I have been told, came down with such velocity that it passed through the house and fell well out in the river beyond—ice was also stored in the cellar of the City Hotel and, as soon as the river was opened, ice was forwarded to the city by sloops and schooners,. In spite of the extra amount in storage the material was again exhausted in July.

By this time dissatisfaction, which had been growing for sometime in the company, became so marked that the future of the business appeared hopeless. The causes which led to that dissatisfaction seem to have been due largely to the ignorance of those who were interested, of the business they managed. The original capital was far from sufficient to start a new enterprise that was destined to gigantic growth, further assessment was not listened to by the members, the fact that the capital had been invested in implements and buildings necessary for success and that until success came the stock could not be held at par, seems not to have entered into their calculations; they only felt that the share for which they had paid $100 had apparently depreciated to almost nothing; they only wished to sell their certificates at any price that could be obtained.

For sometime Alfred Barmore, who was then engaged in the boot and shoe business, in Greenwich Street, New York, had been watching the efforts made by the company to start the new venture, and he had finally determined, that if properly looked after, there was money in the ice business, accordingly, when others were so anxious to sell, there was little difficulty for him to purchase, and, joining with Moses G. Leonard, the two bought up the stock of the old company and organized a new one under the name of Barmore, Leonard & Co., in 1840.

The entrance of Alfred Barmore into the ice business was the beginning of its success. Keen, far seeing, not so carried away by his belief as to be visionary, but willing to accept risk and bold to enter upon new fields, energetic, he brought all these qualifications into the new project; saw for it a wonderful future; labored to make that future as great as his prescience told him it would be, and had the great satisfaction of seeing the weakling he had nurtured in its darkest hours, developed into one of the strongest forms of business in a vast metropolis.

The advent of Mr. Barmore led to a radical change in the methods used in obtaining and disposing of the ice, and was the signal for opposition for over thirty years. It seems wise, then, to briefly review the process which had so far held in the business. From the first cargo of ice cut, till 1841, the sawing and cutting was done entirely by hand, part of the time with tools which were the invention of a Mr. Wright, and for which the users had to pay a royalty. The first workers in the material, under the impression that ice could not be preserved above ground, dug great pits, thirty feet deep and ten feet in diameter, into it, and stored the commodity, packed with straw, in these. When, under the management of the company of Barmore, Felter & Co., houses were built for storage, the ice was hoisted to the doors by means of a pair of ice tongs, a block and fall and horse power. Under this improved method one animal could house about 100 tons a day. The first carts used were mounted on wheels, made by sawing slices from the trunks of trees of requisite thickness, on the axles of this primitive vehicle, a roughly made box was placed and loaded and the cart driven down to the landing, there to be placed on board the steamboat Rockland, which ran from Haverstraw to New York every other day. On arriving at the city the ice was transferred to a cart which was driven to the place to be supplied.

The organization of the company of Barmore, Felter & Co., led, as we have seen, to the purchase of their own vessel and the hiring of cellars for storage in New York. But the carts still used bore no resemblance to the ice-wagon of to-day, and two or three were all that were required to meet the demands upon them. Somewhat of a small beginning this for a business that now requires sixty barges, with a capacity of 40,000 tons, and finds use for 1,000 horses and 500 wagons.

The first proceeding of Barmore, Leonard & Co., was to send to Boston for the purpose of inspecting the business there, and to obtain an insight into the improved methods and implements used for harvesting the ice. The person intrusted with this mission returned and started an opposition company, bringing to it the benefits of his observation. As if by magic competition grew. Cheeseman & Andros built a large house in 1841, at "Stony Point" on the east side of the lake, which was later bought by Ascough & Co., and finally destroyed by lightning about 1845. John D. Ascough, J. Kershaw, and Hutchison began cutting ice in 1841, and were followed by John Wright, who erected a small house, and later by C. R. Wortendyke. Besides beginning at the lake Wortendyke built at Hop-O-Nose, on the Catskill, and Cheeseman built at Flatbush, the first ice house on the Hudson, which later became the property of the Ulster County Ice Co.

A bitter contest for the control of the ice at Rockland Lake was now begun, for the understanding of which, a brief glance at its topography in 1840, must be taken. Then as now the road wound along close to the lake shore on the south and followed the same roadbed on the east, but then the road on the north lay so much further south that there was practically no property between it and the water. Opposite the road on the north side of the lake was the property of Thomas Wells. But one, the clove road exists or ever can exist from the lake to the river and that has been practically unchanged.

It was generally believed that the owners of property around the lake alone had the right to cut the ice from in front of it, and in pursuance of this belief, Barmore, Leonard & Co., bought or leased all the property adjoining the water on the east and north sides. Where the highway touched the water, the ice was regarded as public property. The south side of the lake is too far removed from the clove to make cutting there profitable, and leaving that to its own inaccessibility, Barmore, Leonard & Co., prepared to forestall all others by cutting at the point on the north where the road ran down to the water. But here they had calculated without taking Mr. Wells into consideration. Whether annoyed because he had sold his stock at a low price and now saw his error of judgment, or imbued with a conscientous belief that he was right in the matter; Mr. Wells, after cutting such ice as he needed for his own use, built a fence between the lake and the highway and demanded a royalty on every ton of ice collected. The first result was a physical struggle between the employees of the company and those of Wells in which the latter were worsted, and the matter was then carried into litigation. Shortly after, an appeal to the Commissioners of Highways led to the changing of the roadbed to its present position; the land between it and the water became the property of one of the firm, and Barmore, Leonard & Co. obtained virtual control of the ice business at the lake as they already controlled the landing on the Hudson.

Accepting the inevitable, the other companies eventually moved to Rondout Creek, where they combined and began the business under the name of the Ulster County Ice Co.

The introduction of Croton water to New York, on July 4th, 1842, gave a tremendous impetus to the ice business. With keen business foresight Alfred Barmore, hastened to test the temperature of the water which came from the pipes and the result of the test led to the exclamation, famous among the Knickerbocker people: "We must have more boats, more houses and more ice; for the demand is going to be greater than ever before." Up to this time, the company had sold about 30 tons of ice a day. During 1841, Barmore visited Baltimore, and started a branch of the business in that city.

In 1845, the legal contest with Thomas Wells was compromised without reaching a legal decision and the last barrier to the control of Rockland Lake removed. The following year, the company built two houses on the east side of the lake and bought a small steam engine, which had been used in a cotton press, to house the ice. In 1847, still further advances were made. A house was built in Cranberry Swamp, capable of holding 16,000 tons ; ground hired at the Red Fort, foot of Hubert street, in New York, and a house for storage purposes erected on it ; and, the uncertainty of sailing vessels having rendered them objectionable, two barges were built for the company at New Brunswick.

In the year 1853, E. E. Conklin, bought out Nathaniel Barmore's interest in the company and the firm became A. Barmore & Co. At this time all the ice business along the Hudson, was in the hands of three companies : John D. Ascough & Co., A. Barmore & Co., and the Ulster County Ice Co. It was determined to consolidate these companies under one management. Accordingly in the Legislative Session of 1854-55 Richard Compton, Moses G. Leonard and Ferdinand Nichols, visited Albany, to obtain an act of incorporation. Consultation with Ogden Hoffman, Attorney General, revealed the fact that unless the general law of corporation for mining, etc. was amended, their mission would be fruitless. An amendment was at once introduced, and after bitter opposition finally carried through. In pursuance with that act, the Knickerbocker Ice Company was incorporated in 1855, with a capital of $900,000, all paid up and clear of debt.

      Richard P. Compton, *President.*
      Jefferson Wilcox, *Secretary.*

DIRECTORS.

Anthony Compton.	Joseph Britton.
Alfred Barmore.	C. R. Wortendyke.
Moses G. Leonard.	Horace Demett.
Leonard F. Fitch.	

In the year 1858 the gravity railroad was built from the lake to the landing. The names of Quaspeck Pond and Slaughter's Landing had been changed to Rockland Lake in 1835. Difficulty having arisen between some of the members, E. E. Conklin, left the Knickerbocker Company in 1855, and, joining with Charles Scholey and J. Schineller under the name of E. E. Conklin & Co., built the first ice houses at Staatsburgh and Evesport. In 1856, J. L. Cheeseman, built a large ice house at Athens, and three barges, and incorporated the New York & Brooklyn Ice Company, with a capital of $500,000. In 1866, E. E. Conklin & Co. and the New York and Brooklyn Ice Company, united and bought out Nelson

Fuller, who had recently built a house at Marlborough. These transactions increased the capital of the New York and Brooklyn Company to $750,000. In 1868 the Knickerbocker and New York Companies joined their capital and property, $900,000 and $750,000, and added $1,350,000 in cash, making an aggregate capital of $2,000,000.

After the sailing vessels had been replaced by barges in the ice business, these latter vessels were towed to and from the city by boats belonging to the Cornell Towing Line.

For various reasons this arrangement became unsatisfactory, and the Knickerbocker Company finally determined, in 1867, to do its own towing. Accordingly, two heavy tugs were purchased and placed at work. As may be imagined, Cornell did not accept this act kindly, and to oppose the Knickerbocker Company he bought up the ice interests of R. Parker, Bonesteel & Van Etten, Manhattan Ice Company, and Stone & Bleecker, which had been started about the time the Knickerbocker Company was incorporated, and with them formed the Washington Ice Company. In retaliation the Knickerbocker Company extended its towing business so as to compete with Cornell's line.

For a short time violent opposition continued. Then the Knickerbocker Company discovered that it possessed in its charter no power to run tow-boats; Cornell found that he was managing the ice business at a loss, and the two rivals entered into an amicable agreement, in 1869, by which the Hudson River Towing Company was formed, and Moses G. Leonard took charge of the Washington Ice Company. Under his management its debts were paid, a dividend declared, and a house, with storage capacity of 80,000 tons, built. In 1873 the Knickerbocker bought the Washington Ice Company for $1,100,000.

In 1835 William Lyons began cutting ice on Lake Sinipink, then known, among those residing near by, as the "Bloody" or "Hessian Pond," now called Highland Lake. In a short time Lyons was succeeded by the Brown Brothers, and later, Dennett having joined the firm, it took the name of Brown, Dennett & Brown. For several years this firm continued the ice business at this place; then J. D. Ascough & Co. obtained control of the ice interest at Highland Lake, retaining possession till 1855. In that year the Knickerbocker leased the place, enlarged the storage capacity of the ice house and improved the methods of getting the ice to the landing on the river.

This company maintained control at the lake till 1861, and were followed by a company composed of Jefferson Wilcox, Hiscock, Coles and A. C. Cheney, who remained in possession till 1881, when the firm was changed to A. C. Cheney, George Robinson and Bigelow.

Under the new management an ice house, with storage capacity for 40,000 tons, has been erected and the gravity road by which the ice is gotten to the river landing improved.

The present officers of the Knickerbocker Ice Company are:

Robert Maclay, *President.* L. O. Reaves, *Secretary.*
E. A. Smith, *Treasurer.* E. E. Conklin, *Superintendent.*

Until 1856 the manufacturing and repair shops of the company remained at Rockland Lake. Then they were transferred to the foot of West Twentieth street, New York city. The present Knickerbocker manufacturing and repair shop covers 13,000 square feet. D. E. Felter has a wheelwright and blacksmith shop at Rockland Lake, at which the repair of ice wagons and ice tools is still carried on, but most of the business is done in New York. The company has storage capacity along the Hudson and its lakes and ponds for 3,500,000 tons of ice; it owns sixty barges, with a capacity of 40,000 tons; 1,000 horses, 500 wagons, and a ship yard and harness shop. The number of people steadily employed in the business is 1,200.

NOTE.—The separation of this Chapter on the industries of the County from the Chapters devoted to the histories of the towns is, in a measure, arbitrary. I have thought that it might give the reader a clearer idea of the causes which developed the County, in the early days of its erection, by placing them apart from the other data which must necessarily be touched on in the histories of the towns, and by grouping them together; and in the case of the stone quarry and ice business more than one town was interested. The other manufacturing interests will be found in the Chapters devoted to the towns.

Authorities referred to: "Documents relating to the Colonial History, S. N. Y.," Vols. VII., VIII. "Natural History, S. N. Y." Part III. "Mineralogy," by Lewis C. Beck, Part IV. "Geology," by Wm. W. Mather. "History of American Manufactures," 3 Vols., by Bishop. "History of Dutchess County, 1609 to 1876," by Philip H. Smith. "History of Herkimer County," by Nathaniel S. Benton. "N. Y. S. Geological Reports," Vol. I. "The Hudson from its Source to the Sea," B. J. Lossing. "History of Ramapo," by Rev. E. B. Cobb. "Catskill Recorder," January, 1877, article by E. E. Conklin. Archives of the Rockland County Historical Society.

CHAPTER XI.

THE EARLY MILITIA OF ROCKLAND COUNTY—WAR OF 1812—THE MILITIA OF THE COUNTY CALLED UPON FOR SERVICE—THE COMPANIES OF CAPTAIN'S BLAUVELT AND SNEDEKER LEAVE FOR HARLEM—THE LIGHT HORSE ORDERED TO REPORT FOR DUTY—ORGANIZATION OF A BATTALION OF ARTILLERY—DESERTIONS—ORGANIZATION OF THE NATIONAL GUARD—MUSTER ROLL OF THE MILITIA OF 1812—MUSTER ROLL OF THE BATTALION OF ARTILLERY.

The treaty concluded between the United States and Great Britain, at Paris, on September 3d, 1783, was but a hollow truce. Neither people were satisfied with the result, and the English Government, not realizing that the separation was final, was not active in complying with certain terms of the agreement. Clashing interests on commercial matters only aggravated the ill temper of both nations, an aggravation, which was increased by the evident sympathy of this people with France, in her conflict with England, and the retaliating acts of embargo and confiscation with which Great Britain hampered our merchant marine. One act of violence followed another, each side being mutually aggressive, till at length on June 18th, 1812, war was formally declared between this Government and Great Britain, because of the latter countries' acts, in laying blockades on American Ports; in insisting on the right to search American vessels for deserters; in refusing to comply with the treaty obligations of 1783. These, though the nominal reasons given for the war, were but the outcome of a far deeper feeling of jealousy and anger that existed between the two peoples.

With the acts of that war we have nothing to do save as it affected our County. We have already seen in a preceding chapter, that the attainment by this people of autonomy found them in a crude mental condition as regards the idea they had won, and that the process of education in their new relationship to government was attended by some friction and the organization of partisan ideas. On some points of policy however, nearly every citizen agreed and notably on that which opposed a standing army. In vain military men pleaded for this weapon of offense or defense; in vain the Chief-magistrates recommended an increase in this powerful auxilliary to government. Plea and recommendation were alike futile, with a people who had had too much regular army before and during the Revolution, and had suffered too greatly from it in days past to risk placing themselves again within the power of armed force. So that army, which had come forth from the War for Independence, with all the perfection of veterans, had been permitted to disintegrate until a mere handful of men remained.

At different times in the years that had passed, the regular force, of which a nucleus was always preserved, had been increased or diminished as the exigencies of the Nation demanded ; but as a general thing, the standing army did not exceed 1,500 men, a force only used then as now, to police the frontiers. While the people were thus niggardly in regard to a standing force, they were correspondingly generous in the laws enacted for the maintenance of the militia. With pride they boasted, that it was a volunteer army of citizens, which had accomplished at Louisburg, what men educated in the arts of war were afraid to attempt ; with pride they pointed out that it was citizen soldiers who had beaten the well trained troops of Great Britain, and her Hessian mercenaries in the Revolution, and with the same pride they proclaimed, that in any future contest the militia would be the saviors of liberty. It behooved the people then to combine with the quiet occupations of peace the sterner arts of war, and to carry out this plan every white citizen between the ages of eighteen and forty-five years, with a few exceptions, such as government officers, members of Congress, etc., was expected to provide himself with the accoutrements of war and appear, at least once a year, for inspection and drill.

Even in the first years of peace when, above all other times, the enthusiasm of victory and the stern pride of power would be most apt to lead to the observance of this law; men found this self imposed duty irksome. Peace by no means brought ease. The country was wretchedly poor, and hard, earnest work was necessary to maintain an existence. The devotion of a day to drill was felt to be an idle waste of precious time and it was given grudgingly. Time, instead of improving these musters, made them worse, and a general muster day became a period of riot and drunkenness. Straggling groups of men, clad in various forms of dress—here one, arrayed in a Continental uniform which had graced some Revolutionary hero and which had been inherited or bought by the present wearer without regard to the accuracy of the fit ; there another, clothed in home made stuff that had been grown and woven in the County, anon a third, who being more gifted with this world's goods than his neighbors, evinced the fact by appearing at muster in broadcloth and strutting before the gaping yokels who did not know him ; marched to and fro, armed with every imaginable object that could be used as weapons of offense or defense, while the shrill scream of fife and the rattle of drums attracted the attention of the women and children to this truly motly gathering.

Excellent material for an army was in this militia, doubtless, if it had been disciplined and properly officered, but as it was managed, rather fitted to be the admiration of slaves and school children than to strike terror to an enemy's heart. One branch, and one branch only, of the service made any pretention to uniformity in dress—the cavalry. Composed, as a rule, of a wealthier class than the foot soldier, the light horsemen did take some pride in their appearance and presented, on muster days, a fair semblance of force; but when the call to "boots and saddles" sounded, or when, at the order of "Return sabres" the swords clanked against their scabbards, then came a scene which baffles description. The horses, either taken from the plough or only half-broken colts, frightened by the unwonted excitement and noise, plunged, rolled, kicked or, gaining the mastery, ran away, while riders clung fast to saddle and mane, or rolled helplessly in the dust.

The congregation of such a numerous body of men, led to a liberal demand on the hospitality of the neighboring hostelries, and peach brandy, rum and apple whiskey were consumed to an alarming amount. Drinking, which began in a friendly way as acquaintances met, soon produced the effects of alcoholic stimulation on the different dispositions of the users, and maudlin greetings, bacchanal shouts of laughter and sullen threatenings resounded through the air. Boastfulness grew rampant. The different sections of the County were represented by bullies, each more abusive than the other, and at length from words the disputants passed to blows, and a general free fight ended up the day. From what I have said, it may be inferred that discipline and subordination were unknown. Such inference is correct. The officers were neighbors of the privates and met them in daily intercourse; their social standing and business relationship were too close all the year for familiarity not to breed contempt; and while the soldier might deign, out of respect to the day, to address his commanding officer by his military title instead of his Christian name and, in a good-natured way, obey his orders up to a certain limit; he most certainly would permit no autocratic commands of that officer to change his preconceived plans and intentions. To obtain that respect and obedience, to which his rank entitled him; the officer needed to be physically able to enforce his demands.

With firm dependence on an army, composed mainly of such material, this Nation declared war against Great Britain. Can we wonder, under the circumstances, that our land forces made such a poor showing in that war? Can we wonder that a force of only 3,500 men could march to and burn the Capital of a government whose population was 8,000,000?

As in the Revolution, English strategy again consisted in attempting to separate the New England from the other States by seizing the valleys of Lake Champlain and the Hudson; and while Sir George Prevost, with 11,000 men, invaded New York at the north, a British fleet blockaded the harbor, and transports with English troops were expected to land at its southern boundaries. Alarmed for the safety of New York city, the Government hastened the building of defences. A small fortification already occupied the site of the present Fort Hamilton, and Castle William, on Governors Island, which had been begun in 1807, was standing. To these were added the erection of Fort Diamond—now known as Fort Lafayette—on Hendrick's Reef, and the red fort, which used to stand at or near the corner of the present Desbrosses and West streets. At the same time the militia of the State, not previously called out, was ordered on duty.

One of the absurdities of the militia law now became plainly apparent. Every able bodied man in the State belonged to the militia, and the requisition for troops, in the midst of the harvest season, was equivalent to letting the harvest rot in the fields from lack of means to gather it. Government seemed to grasp this idea, and, to rectify the evil, granted permission to the commanding officers of the different counties to draft only such proportion of their command for service as could be spared from the necessary labors of life. Other commanders at once took advantage of this grant. But the officer in charge of the militia in this County—General Peter Van Orden—with more zeal than discretion, determined that the full force under his command should serve. He, accordingly, issued orders for the militia of the County to assemble on September 3d, 1814. This was not the last occasion in his life in which General Van Orden's ardor excelled his judgment, but it was one of the most unfortunate ones for the reputation of our County.

On September 3d, seventy-one, out of a company of seventy-seven men belonging to the 83d Regiment, N. Y. S. Militia, Lieutenant-Colonel Benjamin Gurnee commanding, assembled at John G. Blauvelt's, in Greenbush, under the immediate command of Captain Jacob I. Blauvelt, and, after a brief inspection, started for the front. Marching down to Tappan Landing, this force was there conveyed on board of a sloop by small boats and sailed for New York. It was a cloudless, hot day, such as often occurs in early Autumn, and the long march through the dust had made the men hot and thirsty. For some unexplained reason, no provision had been made on the sloop to supply the troops with water, and, as they idly drifted down the river, parched and choked, these worthy soldiers obtained their first lesson of the deprivations of war. By the time Phillipse—Yonkers—was reached their agony was unbearable, and the vessel was compelled to land and allow the troops to slake their thirst. Again they started for the city, which they reached at three A. M., September 4th. But their experience of the difference between playing at soldier and being in actual service was but begun. The relief, which had been given their thirst, had passed, and, aggravated by recollections of the freedom with which they had always heretofore obtained water, the warriors muttered curses, both loud and deep, at their present restraint. It was not till ten o'clock that they were landed and marched to the Battery where they obtained water. Re-embarking at the Battery, Captain Blauvelt's company proceeded up the East River to encamp on Ward's Island. But their trip was further prolonged by the error of a drunken pilot, who ran the vessel aground off Bellevue at sundown, and they passed another night on the water. Finally they reached their camping grounds on September 5th, and were quartered in a five story factory. For three weeks the company remained on Ward's Island. At the end of this time they were moved to Harlem Heights, where they were inspected on October 8th, 1814. At Harlem Heights they remained till November 29th, 1814, when, as their services were not longer required, they were permitted to return home.

When Captain Blauvelt's command started from Greenbush, the company of Captain John Snedeker set sail from Haverstraw and joined the other companies of the 83d Regiment of New York State Militia at Harlem Heights.

The exposure, the change in the manner of living and that disease so common to army encampments—measles—made sad havoc in the ranks of Captain Blauvelt's company. No less than one-third, among whom were the Lieutenant and Ensign, were on a sick furlough at one time or another; and of these the greatest number were suffering from measles, which became epidemic in camp about November 15th. Besides drilling and laboring on the fortifications either in the quarries or trenches, there was little to disturb the monotony of camp life except desertions. This offence was wonderfully common. The militiaman, who probably had never been away from his home for a week at a time before, grew dreadfully homesick in his strange surroundings and walked off from camp. When he felt so inclined, he returned to his comrades, not before; and when he had returned no punishment save that of confinement or extra labor awaited him. To shoot a militia deserter was unthought of, for, while a Congressional act had been passed at the outbreak of the war, placing the militia in the service under the same rules and regulations as the regular army, court-martials for the trial of a militiaman could only be composed of militia officers, and we can readily see that a board so composed would hesitate long before passing the death sentence. So, without terror of death to prevent, individuals or squads were constantly missing, and the evil became so widespread, that on November 16th, the 83d Regiment camp was suddenly called to arms at 9 o'clock in the evening, under the impression that some neighboring troops were about to desert.

If desertion was thus prevalent among the militia of other counties, some excuse can be found for it among the troops under command of General Van Orden. Not alone did they suffer from the same homesickness common to all, but a further and tremendous inducement to abandon camp was found in the complaints which reached them of the impossibility of those remaining at home, to gather the fall crops and prepare for the winter. Reiterated requests for furloughs met with constant refusal. So the men took the matter in their own hands and came home. By November 21st, forty of Captain Blauvelt's company had been returned for court-martial on account of being absent without leave; at one time no less than sixteen men were absent from duty; and during a period of twenty consecutive days the morning report shows never less than three and usually from twelve to thirteen, privates and non-commissioned officers recorded as deserters. Sometimes one would start alone or with a single companion but more commonly squads of five or six would go off together, followed next day by a similar number. The punishment meted out to these military sinners was the marching and counter-marching them up and down the roads from breakfast time till nightfall without rest. This means may have been chosen on the principle, that the men would be so tired out by evening as to be content to remain quiet and not walk off home again, but from the expressions of one of those, who was punished, I judge the plan was not effectual.

In the Light Horse, the cavalry branch of the militia, a draft of seven men was made in the County. Five immediately disqualified, and only Isaac S. Lydecker and James De Clark responded. These gentlemen started for the rendezvous, Montgomery in Orange County, on a bright Sunday afternoon, and were accompanied as far as Sufferns by a cavalcade of neighbors. On reaching Montgomery, they, with some seventy or eighty others of the force, who had assembled, were inspected and were then dismissed to their homes subject to instant recall in case of need. The call never came.

In the year 1814 a battalion of artillery was organized in the Middle Senatorial District composed of Rockland, Orange, Duchess and Ulster Counties. This battalion was at first under the command of Major Harmon Tallman, of Nyack. The uniform was composed of white pants and vest, dark blue coat, turned and faced with red, and fur caps with red plume. The armament consisted of brass field pieces. The battalion entered camp at Harlem Heights. Almost immediately trouble arose between the rank and file, and Major Tallman was relieved of the command, which was given to Major Tyler Dibble. During part of its period of service, this battalion remained at Harlem Heights, and for a portion of the time at Greenwich, Connecticut. Captain Jonathan Reynolds' company remained in service the longest period, entering August 18th and being mustered out November 18th, 1814. The other companies remained on duty from August 18th to September 30th, when they were discharged.

In proportion to her population Rockland County turned out more men in the War of 1812 than in our late Civil War, but not one of those men ever saw more of war than is comprised in a fortified camp, except the few who enlisted in the United States Army. Doubtless, if placed in action, the militia of this County would have acquitted itself in as worthy a manner as raw troops ever do. There would have been the usual amount of malingering; the usual number of desertions ; and the usual stampede that follows a break in the line when green soldiers are in battle. The militia system in the Revolution, in the War of 1812, and up to the organization of the National Guard, was the most illusive system that ever deceived a people; and though that delusion must have been apparent to the dullest intellect, the citizens of this country did not wish their favorite hobby disturbed, but hugged it the closer to them, and were lulled by it into fancied safety. Fortunate for us was it, that, when the crucial test of war came upon this Nation in 1861, the opposing army was as new to conflict as we, and that each side became skilled in battle in the same proportion as the other.

At the close of the War of 1812, the militia resumed its former apathetic indifference to discipline, and the annual muster gradually became more and more of a useless farce. Occasionally some enterprising Legislator would stir up the topic of the State's military force, and then a new law or two would be passed to add to the many already on the Statute books, nugatory because of their non-enforcement; and if enthusiasm enough could be roused, the whole service would be reconstructed. By 1848, the companies in this County had become a part of the 17th Regiment, N. Y. S. Militia, Colonel William W. Scrugham, commanding, and the regiment was attached to the 7th Brigade under the charge of General Aaron Ward. A momentary interest in the service had been caused by the Mexican War, but recently ended, and during its excitement, a cavalry company of about fifty men was organized and mustered into service in 1848, bearing the title of "Rockland County Rangers." The officers of this company at its organization were: Captain, Isaac Pye; First Lieutenant, Charles McOblenis; Second Lieutenant, Edward Pye.

The "Rangers" were ordered on duty during the Haverstraw riot of 1853. Sheriff Henry L. Sherwood, finding himself unable to cope with the rioters by the civil powers, and remained on duty two days and a night before quiet was restored. In 1855, General Ward resigned his commission on account of age, and W. W. Scrugham, was promoted to the command of the brigade, while Edward Pye, became Colonel, and Isaac Pye, Major of the 17th Regiment, and Charles McOblenis, Captain of the "Rangers." Thus officered the regiment remained till the Civil War. At the call by the National Government for protection to the Capital; the 17th Regiment was ordered to proceed to Washington, by Governor Seymour. Ere the hour for departure, however, the immediate danger to the Capital had passed, and the 17th Regiment remained on waiting orders for the next three or four weeks; at the end of which time it was relieved from duty. By the departure of members either as volunteers or conscripts, the organization was practically abandoned, the small remnant remaining, being used for home duty, and, without its members being mustered out, the company of "Rangers" ceased to exist for want of men. Once more it was ordered out, as we shall see in the chapter on the Civil War, and performed duty at the front in the year 1863.

The accoutrements of a "Ranger" consisted of horse, saddle, bridle, saddle-cloth, knapsack, holster, pistol, belt, saber, and spurs; while dark blue coat, trimmed with red, blue pants with red stripe, and bear skin cap with long black feather tipped with red formed his uniform.

Early in the Civil War the whole subject of the State troops was taken up by the Legislature, and on April 23d, 1863, the result of the deliberations of that body took form in the organization of our present National Guard. On June 19th, of that year, Adjutant-General Sprague issued the necessary orders for the formation of a regiment or battalion in each Assembly district, and under those orders the Fifty-seventh Regiment, N. G. S. N. Y., was organized, with General James Ryder, of the Seventh Brigade, brigade commander; James S. Haring, Colonel, and John H. Stephens, Lieutenant-Colonel. This regiment, composed entirely of Rockland County men, contained seven companies.

By 1870 the Fifty-seventh had followed in the footsteps of its military predecessors, and become a skeleton regiment, and, by the expiration of the seven years' term of service, in the following year it passed from existence.

A year or two now elapsed with virtually no militia organization in our County. Then a company, lettered B, was raised and joined to the Sixteenth Battalion, Seventh Brigade, Fifth Division. The commissioned officers of this company were: Henry E. Smith, Captain; William Salters, First Lieutenant; Eugene Gardner, Second Lieutenant. The armory of Company B was in Nyack, and the great majority of its members resided there. During the brick-makers' strike in Haverstraw, in 1877, Company B was ordered to that village, and remained on duty from May 24th to May 30th, ere quiet was restored, being quartered in the United States Hotel. Again, during the railroad strikes and riots of 1877, this organization was ordered on duty in the armory, and remained under orders from July 24th to August 2d.

The same difficulty, that has always met every County movement, met this. Distance between the villages prevented citizens of one from attending regular meetings in another, and neither Nyack nor any other village in the County had population enough to keep a military organization full. The change from a seven to a five year term of service brought the end of military duty for two sets of men at the same time. There was no recruiting to meet the vacancies thus caused, and the company at once fell below its legal number. Then came the legislative act, under which the National Guard was reorganized and consolidated, and all skeleton organizations disbanded, and, as Company B came under the list of skeletons, it was wiped from existence on December 17th, 1881. Since that time no effort has been made to raise a militia organization in Rockland County.

A list of the dates of the commissions of the officers in the Regiment of Militia commanded by Lieutenant-Colonel Cornelius A. Blauvelt, in the County of Rockland, November 28th, 1812.

Nicholas Gesner	Lieutenant's Commission,		May 12th, 1798.
	Captain's	"	April 25th, 1806.
	First Major's	"	June 26th, 1811.
Michael Salyers	Lieutenant's	"	April 25th, 1806.
	Captain's	"	April 2d, 1811.
	Second Major's	"	March 7th, 1812.
Thomas T. Eckerson	Ensign's	"	April 25th, 1806.
	Lieutenant's	"	April 24th, 1807.
	Captain's	"	June 26th, 1811.
Frederick Barbarow	Ensign's	"	April 25th, 1806.
	Lieutenanant's	"	April 24th, 1807.
	Captain's	"	June 26th, 1811.

Jacob D. Onderdonk	Ensign's Commission,		June 15th, 1808.
	Captain's	"	June 20th, 1811.
Cornelius Sickles	Ensign's	"	April 25th, 1806.
	Lieutenant's	"	April 2d, 1811.
	Captain's	"	March 7th, 1812.
Jacob I. Blauvelt	Captain's	"	June 26th, 1811.
Samuel S. Ver Bryck	Captain's	"	June 20th, 1811.
Erastus Colt	Lieutenant's	"	June 26th, 1811.
	Captain's	"	March 7th, 1812.
William Herbert Gesner	Ensign's	"	June 20th, 1811.
	Adjutant's	"	March 7th, 1812.
Daniel A. Blauvelt	Paymaster's	"	March 7th, 1812.
Daniel Tallman	Quartermaster's	"	June 3d, 1812.
Ralph Bush	Surgeon's	"	June 3d, 1812.
Daniel Ackerman	Ensign's	"	April 24th, 1807.
	Lieutenant's	"	June 26th, 1811.
John Van Orden	Ensign's	"	June 15th, 1808.
	Lieutenant's	"	June 26th, 1811.
Samuel Sidman	Ensign's	"	June 26th, 1811.
	Lieutenant's	"	March 7th, 1812.
John T. Eckerson	Lieutenant's	"	June 26th, 1811.
George Washington Sneden	Lieutenant's	"	June 20th, 1811.
James Hudson	Lieutenant's	"	March 7th, 1812.
Henry Gesner	Ensign's	"	June 20th, 1811.
John Mackie	Ensign's	"	June 20th, 1811.
John T. Yeury	Ensign's	"	June 26th, 1811.
Alpheus S. Colton	Ensign's	"	March 7th, 1812.
Mathias A. Concklin	Ensign's	"	March 7th, 1812.
Stephen Hennion	Ensign's	"	June 26th, 1811.

Captain, John Snedeker.

Abraham Storms, First Lieutenant.   Dowah A. Blauvelt, Second Lieutenant.

Ensign, James Swartwout.

Adrian Onderdonk, First Sergeant.   Garret G. Snedeker, Third Sergeant.
John Stevens, Second Sergeant.   Abraham Snedeker, Fourth Sergeant.
Charles Ferlwood, First Corporal.   George Smith, Fourth Corporal.
Shobal Hall, Second Corporal.   William Gilchrist, Fifth Corporal.
Samuel Lawrence, Third Corporal.   Garret F. Snedeker, Sixth Corporal.
Thomas Gilchrist, Fifer.   Harmon Tremper, Drummer.

Abbott, C.	Hoffman, John	Richards, Lawrence
Allison, Daniel	Harrison, Matthew	Rogers, Jesse
Baker, Thomas	James, Paul	Rose, James
Brady, David	Jaycocks, Timothy	Ryder, Hercules
Brewer, Paul	Johnson, Samuel G.	Short, William
Barmore, Nathaniel	Knapp, David	Slott, Lewis
Brinkerhoff, Christian	Knapp, Jacob	Smith, Richard
Bennet, John	Lum, John	Smith, William
Baker, Joseph	Lydecker, John Jr.	Snedeker, Tunis
Carsick, Alexander	Minford, Robert	Snyder, Hendrick
Corby, Isaac	Meyers, Stephen	Springsteen, Garret
De Baun, Christian	Meyers, Abraham	Storms, John
Felter, Harman	Mullen, Marcus	Tallman, A. A.
Felter, Edward	Onderdonk, Garret	Tallman, J. D. D.
Felter, David	Paul, Arthur	Tallman, Harman

Felter, John	Paul, Uriah	Vanderbilt, Jacob
Felter, John P.	Perry, John	Van Orden, Jacob
Felter, Jacob	Tremper, John F.	Williams, Elias
Felter, George	Pierson, Silas	Van Houten, Jacob
Felter, Benjamin	Polhemus, Theodorus	Van Orden, John
Thew, William	Remsen, John	Williamson, Jeremiah
Finch, Henry	Remsen, Theodorus	Van Houten, John, Jr.
Gilchrist, Budd	Short, William	Wiley, William
Gerow, Isaac		

Attached to 83d Regiment N. Y. S. Militia, Lieutenant-Colonel Benjamin F. Gurnee.

Captain, Jacob I. Blauvelt.
First Lieutenant, John Eckerson.   Second Lieutenant, George Wiants.
Ensign, John Mackie.

John Taulman, First Sergeant.   Abram A. Johnson, Third Sergeant.
William Hutton, Second Sergeant.   John I. Johnson, Fourth Sergeant.
Henry Oblenis, First Corporal.   James D. Clark, Third Corporal.
Derick Van Houten, Second Corporal.   John Duryea, Fourth Corporal.
John Wooder, Fifth Corporal.
Peter Cole, Fifer.   Abraham D. Blauvelt, Drummer.

Ackerman, Cornelius	Eckerson, Lucas	Smith, John
Ackerman, Abraham	Eckerson, Thos. T.	Smith, Garret A.
Blauvelt, John C.	Eckerson, Abr'm	Smith, Garret I.
Bulwer, Henry	Eckerson, Derick	Smith, Garret S.
Blanch, Thomas	Eckerson, Jacob T.	Serven, John G.
Baker, George	Fox, Stephen	Sudderland, John
Barbarow, John N.	Hopper, Garret A.	Smith, Aury
Blauvelt, C. J.	House, John, Jr.	Serven, Aury
Brewer, Abr'm	House, Henry	Taylor, John
Cole, Isaac	Hopper, John	Taylor, William
Carlow, James	Johnson, Peter	Taylor, Johnathan
Carlow, George	Johnson, Abr'm I.	Taylor, Edward
Demarest, Jacob P.	Lydecker, Albert	Taylor, Isaac
Demarest, David	Mackie, James	Tinkey, George
De Clark, James C.	May, Coonrod	Van Buskirk, Andrew
De Clark, Peter	Norwood, Cornelius	Van Ostrand, Jacob
Demarest, James	Osborn, Nathaniel	Van Ostrand, Moses
De Baun, Abr'm	Peterson, Abr'm	Van Houten, Joseph
Demarest, Peter M.	Remson, A.	Van Wort, John
De Clark, Moses	Ronseau, John P.	Van Orden, David
Wanamaker, Cornelius	Wilson, Caleb	

Attached to the 83d Regiment, N. Y. S. Militia.

Abraham Ackerman, George Carlow and Nathaniel Osborn; never reported for duty and James Carlow, furnished a substitute named Jacob Miller.

Roll of the field and staff officers of a battalion of New York Detached artillery at first commanded by Major Harman Tallman, later by Major Tyler Dibble, in the service of the United States, in 1814.

Major, Tyler Dibble.

Clermont Livingston, Adjutant.
William L. Cande, Surgeon.
Henry Van Nostrand, Sergeant Major.
William S. Wilkin, Paymaster.
Joseph Ellicott, Quartermaster.
M. B. Gager, Quartermaster Sergeant.

COMPANY.

Alanson Austin, Captain.†
Purdy Fowler, First Lieutenant.
Edward L. Welling, Second Lieutenant.
John Hathorn, Jr. First Sergeant.
William Robison, Second Sergeant.
Joseph Roe,† First Corporal.
William Munger,† Third Corporal.
James W. Finch, Fifth Corporal.
John Welling, Drummer,

Henry Butterworth, Captain.‡
Francis Armstrong, First Lieutenant.‡
Garret Henion, Second Lieutenant.
Nathaniel R. Denton, Third Sergeant.
Henry W. Houston, Fourth Sergeant.§
John Welling,§ Second Corporal.
George Wandel, Fourth Corporal.
Henry Feagles,§ Fifer.

Armstrong, Daniel§
Armstrong, George
Applebee, Elnathan
Baird, Nath. W.§
Broad, James B.‡
Bloomer, Thos. B.
Bazly, Loal
Blair, Barnard
Byram, Cantwell‡
Beedle, Peter**
Conkling, Joseph
Cornelison, John
Crostgrove, Chris.‡
Dusenbery, Dan'l C.†
Dekay, Sam'l L.
Dolsen, John§
Finn, Daniel
Felter, Jeremiah P.
Griggs, Daniel

Gourdinier, Barney
Hartwick, John**
Harris, Robert§
Hedges, John
Gilbert, Elnathan B.
Johnson, John
King, John
Lawrence, Nathaniel§
Ludlow, Daniel
Lydecker, Albert A.
Matthews, Samuel
Minthorn, James
Mapes, Lewis
Murray, John
McDowell, Robert††
Onderdonk, Ruliff§
Onderdonk, Garrett†
Orvins, Benjamin

Pickins, Edward§
Polhemus, Daniel
Quimby, John H.††
Roe, John S.
Roads, Matthew
Strong, John§
Sterns, Elisha
Tice, Jubal
Tice, Lee
Tallman, John
Taller, James T.
Vanorsdol, Cornelius
Welling, Thos. H.
Welling, Hezekiah D.
Wheeler, James††
Hunter John
Stevens, Abr. S. S.
Lyon, Jabez

The waiters attached to this company were: John Carter, James Demarlo, Henry Scott, and John Call.

COMPANY.

Jonathan Reynolds, Captain.
Leonard Thompson, First Lieutenant.
William Kalstine,† First Sergeant.
Derrick Husted,† Third Sergeant.
Milo Winchester,† First Corporal.
Samuel Garlick, Third Corporal.
Charles Perry, Fifer.

Tunis Tallman,‡ Captain.
Ezra L. Barrett,† Second Lieutenant.
John Jenks,† Second Sergeant.
James G. Husted, Fourth Sergeant.
George Reynolds,† Second Corporal.
Isaac Latimer, Fourth Corporal.
Morse Couch, Drummer.

Allison, Abraham
Alexander, Andres §
Anson, William

Holmes, Morgan L.
Huysrodt, William,
Husted, Walter

Reynolds, Ambrose
Reed, Morris
Record, William

Anson, Robert	Hamblin, George	Smith, James S.
Armstrong, John W.†	Hamblin, Hiram	Springsteel, Benj.
Baker, William	Hicks, Stephen†	Story, William§
Buel, Charles	Knickerbocker, Peter H.	Velie, C. I.
Castle, Moses†	Knickerbocker, Cornelius	Wheeler, Isaac
Card, Elijah B.	Knickerbocker, Andrew	Winans, Gerhardus
Conklin, Wm. II.	Knapp, Nicholas§	Wood, Sirren
Conklin, Burnett	Miller, Lewis	Wood, John
Colepoughs, John‡‡	Martin, William	Jacocks, Lawrence§
Drake, Samuel	Noble, Nathaniel	Jarvis, Henry†
Davis, Samuel D.	Polhemus, Theodorus*	Bird, Milo
Furman, William §	Platt, Jonas D.	WAITERS.
Dodge, Samuel K.	Pulves, John P.	Williams, John
Flinn, Rufus	Reynolds, Jno. P.†	Wilkins, Wm.
Gritman, B. D.	Reynolds, Nathaniel	Perry, Jno.

James S. Smith, Benjamin Springsteel and John Wood were detached, September 15th, to work in the stone quarries getting out material for the forts.

COMPANY.

Philip P. Schuyler, Captain.
Stiles R. Fox, First Lieutenant.
O'Farra D. T. Fox, First Sergeant.
Peter Stoutenbergh,† Third Sergeant.
William King, First Corporal.
Joseph Dill, Jr., Third Corporal.
Jacob Ludlum, Fifer.

William Mulner,‡ Captain.
Joseph F. Dill, Second Lieutenant.
James Smilie, Second Sergeant.
Moses Comfort, Fourth Sergeant.
John Bart, Second Corporal.
Isaac Bishop, Fourth Corporal.
Henry R. Bush, Drummer.

Arnet, John	Doty, Joseph I.†	Pottenbergh, John
Ames, Elisha W.	Doty, Calium	Pye, William‡
McBride, James	Frederick, John	Redfield, William
Buchanan, John	Falls, George	Redfield, Henry,
Buckstaver, Moses	Fundy, Isaac	Sherman, Jacob,
Brockway, Amos	Felter, Peter W.†	Strachan, Charles C.
Baker, Daniel S.	Grivens, Samuel†	Sneden, Robert †
Buskirk, David‡‡ Substituted for him	Gregor, John	Simpson, William
	Hunt, Levi‡‡	Stewart, Samuel‡‡
Bates, Isaac	Hazelton, Chas. A.	Sherman, Jacob, Jr.
Brown, Nathaniel A.	Johnson, Richard	Voorhouse, William‡‡
Badgly, William	Knapp, Daniel	Wakerman, Elisha
Curtis, William	Van Keuren, Tobias§	Winans, Jonathan
Catlin, Hamlin	Keeler, Daniel B.	Wright, Joseph
Canfield, Samuel	McKenzie, John††	Wigham, Robert, Jr.
Carr, John, Jr.	Lent, Henry§	John Tentt, Ward Master.
Cromwell, Smith	Lawrence, Peter	
Case, Gabriel	Morris, States†	WAITERS.
Campbell, John‡‡	Mann, Isaac	Brown, James
Coe, Samuel I.	Miller, Thomas‡‡	Jackson, Harry
Davis, John I.	Macinus, John	Freeman, Henry
Davis, John C.	Meyers, William	McRea, Abraham
Davis, Samuel	Oliver, James,	

COMPANY.

John J. Woolley,† Captain.
Alonzo De La Vergne, First Lieutenant.
Simon Williamson, First Sergeant.
Joshua Flagler, Third Sergeant.
Jeremiah Duel, First Corporal.
Edward W. Briggs, Third Corporal.
Smith Steward, Fifer.

William Smith,†† Captain.
Cornelius J. Swarthout, Second Lieutenant.
James A. Stoutenburgh, Second Sergeant.
Joshua Cheeseman, Fourth Sergeant.
Gilbert Southard, Second Corporal.
Durias J. Covel, Fourth Corporal.

Abiah Bishop and Stephen Tompkins, Drummers.

Aspel, Thomas†	Luckky, George, Jr.	Tilbets, Lyman
Barrum, Nathaniel†	Jacob, Israel	Tompkins, William‡‡
Burch, Charles§	Maccord, Wm. W.	Totten, John H.
Bradner, John	McFarlin, Abr.	Taylor, William‡
Bodel, Isaac,	Martin, John‡‡	Van Tassel, Tryon††
Bigger, George	Maden, Edw. S.†	Williams, Henry
Benedict, Henry T.	Mills, James	Wesley, Franklin
Coe, Daniel	Ocoy, Patrick§	Wilsey, George
Dusenberry, Stephen	Olivet, William	Wilcox, Simeon‡‡
Ferris, John D.	Owen, Increase§	Whitney, John
Graham, Richard	Oakly, Jeremiah	Wheeler, Joel, Jr.†
Grinder, John††	Purdy, David	Williams, Isaac
Halley, Eleazar P.‡‡	Poppano, William	Winslow, Joseph††
Hulright, Wm. A.	Scryver, William	Thompson, Henry
Johnson, Andrew	Sims, David‡	Peters, Hulet§
Jones, Stephen S.	Savage, Rowland,	Hall, Ira S.‡‡
Lake, Ebenezer	Spooner, Nathan‡	Wilcox, Benajah
Lake, Crapo	Smith, Acon‡‡	Brinkerhoff, Abr. L.
Lake, Stephen	Seaman, Peter	Gipson, Solomon
Luckky, William‡‡	Tripp, Samuel	Gage, M. B., Promoted Quartermaster Sergeant.

The last parade, review and inspection of the old 17th Regiment, in which Rockland County was represented, occurred at Verplanck's Point on October 21, 1862. This regiment belonged to the 7th Brigade, General S. C. Parmenter, of Newburgh, commanding, and to the 5th Division, Major-General S. S. Burnside, of Oneonta, commanding. In the Adjutant General's report for that year the roll of officers was as follows:

Isaac Pye, Major.

James Creney, Jr., Haverstraw, Regimental Engineer. W. Govan, M. D., Stony Point, Surgeon. Ferdinand L. Nichols, Nyack, Quartermaster.

WAYNE GUARDS.

Co. B. Dominick Kennedy, Captain. Thos. Murphy, First Lieutenant. John Bannon, Second Lieutenant. All of Haverstraw.

Co. C. John V. B. Johnson, Captain. Richard Wandell, First Lieutenant. J. D. Blauvelt, Second Lieutenant. All of Piermont.

STONY POINT GUARDS.

Co. D. Edw. W. Christie, Captain. Abr. S. Greene, First Lieutenant. M. B. Marks, Second Lieutenant. All of Haverstraw.

---

*Died. †Furloughed. ‡Discharged. §Sick. **Extra Duty. ††Enlisted in the U. S. Army. ‡‡Deserted.

INGOLD GUARDS.

Co. F.   C. P. Hoffman, Captain.   S. W. Allen, First Lieutenant.   I. De Baun, Second Lieutenant.   All of Haverstraw.

Co. I.   W. D. Furman, Captain, of Monsey.   Reuben Riggs, First Lieutenant, of Monsey.   Augustus Coe, Second Lieutenant, of Suffern.

"ROCKLAND COUNTY RANGERS."

Co. R.   Charles M. O'Blenis, Captain, of Clarksville.   John A. Campbell, First Lieutenant, ot Nyack Turnpike.   Henry Palmer, Second Lieutenant, of Nyack.

Authorities referred to: "Federal Government," by Alden Bradford; "Morning Report" of Captain Jacob I. Blauvelt's Company; Diary of Captain Jacob I. Blauvelt; Muster Roll of Battalion of Artillery from United States Records; Reports of the Adjutant-General S. N. Y.; Archives of the Rockland County Historical Society.

CHAPTER XII.

PROPOSITION FOR A TURNPIKE FROM NYACK TO SUFFERN—BITTER OPPOSITION—THE BILL AS PASSED—RENEWALS OF THE CHARTER—AN ACT INCORPORATING THE NEW ANTRIM AND WAYNESBURGH TURNPIKE COMPANY PASSED—THE BEGINNING OF STEAMBOAT COMMUNICATION WITH NEW YORK—LATER STEAMBOATS—CHARTERS FOR FERRYBOATS—CHRONOLOGICAL LIST OF STEAMBOATS—OPENING OF THE ERIE RAILRAOD AND OF OTHER RAILOADS.

We have already seen that Tappan Landing was the original port of entry for the County, and that for years its store and its market sloop were amply sufficient to carry on the outside business of the southern part of her territory. When Kakiat was settled by the Hempstead people, an outlet for their produce was afforded by a dock at the foot of the Long Clove road, the existence of which would have remained unknown but for the discovery of Prof. Lavalette Wilson, of Haverstraw, who found in it the spot where Andre landed. Later, Major Kiers, built a dock further north to meet the wants of shippers. Nyack in 1804, began communication with New York through the market sloop of the Tallman's, DePew and Meyers. The development of manufacturing interests at Ramapo, created a demand for better means of transportion.

An examination of the map of Rockland County, will show it to be an almost perfect triangle, its base extending along the Hudson, its apex, stretching away into the Ramapo Mountains. Almost in the centre of this apex were the works of J. G. Pierson, and Brothers; the Dater Works, and but two or three miles away was the woolen factory of John Suffern. As the roads then ran, it was both a shorter and easier route from Ramapo to Haverstraw, than to any other village on the Hudson, and the tide of travel naturally set in that direction. But at best this was a round-a-bout way to get to the Metropolis, the roads, compared with to-day, were horrible, the grades heavy, and when at last the river was reached, the means of communication, dependent on tide and wind, very uncertain. A study of this subject soon convinced Mr. Pierson, that either easier and surer modes of travel must be found, or the magnificent water power of the Ramapo could not be utilized to its full capacity. While he was thinking out the problem in the western part of the County, keen, far-seeing men were moving in the same matter at the east. Nyack was waking from a lethargy. A young and pushing generation was coming to the fore, and its members saw at once, that while the water power for manufacturing purposes was wanting, and space for an extensive pursuit of agriculture did not exist, there was a chance to infuse life into the hamlet by making it the port of shipment for the County. Conference between Mr. Pierson and the active men in Nyack, resulted in a determination to improve communication in the County, by obtaining a legislative act creating a turnpike road, which should run as nearly as possible in a straight line from the Orange Turnpike at Sufferns, to the river at Nyack.

No one can justly accuse Haverstraw people of being thick-witted when their interests are at stake, and when this new project was broached, they saw as clearly as their Nyack neighbors, the drift of the enterprise. It meant a removal of business from their village with a gain of that business which they would lose for Nyack, it meant a strife for supremacy between the two places, and, if Haverstraw lost, she must not only go to the wall but indirectly be taxed to see her rival succeed; and the people of that village joined as one man in a long and bitter struggle against the proposed new road. For years the contest continued with unflagging vigor and exerted an influence on County politics never since seen. Every method was used, from the election of members of Assembly to the influencing of commissioners; from appeals to the courts to bitter personal conflicts; by one or the other sides and used freely. In vain, those favoring the proposed road, pointed out that it would be self-supporting by reason of its tolls and the issue of bonds would prevent it becoming a County burden; in vain they argued, that rather than continue thus hampered by bad means of communication, the mill owners of Ramapo would close their factories and thus settle the controversy; in vain they said that Nyack was chosen because of its not only being nearer to the city but also because the depth of water at its landing was greater than at Haverstraw, and heavily loaded vessels could get away without reference to the stage of the tide, and would not be so apt to be stopped by the ice in winter. Every argument was met and answered and the member of Assembly during the early years of the discussion—General Peter S. Van Orden—being opposed to the bill, it could not be passed. At length, after a hard political canvass, Van Orden, who had been the member from Rockland County, continuously from 1809 to 1816, was defeated, and in the latter year Cornelius A. Blauvelt was the Assemblyman. During his first term of office, on April 17, 1816, the bill was passed for a Turnpike to run from a point between the houses of Teunis and Peter Smith, "running thence westerly along the old road until in front of the said Peter Smith's dwelling house, and from thence, the most direct and convenient route to the Orange Turnpike Road and to pass in front of the dwelling house of John Suffern, in the Town of Hempstead, same (Rockland) County."

Those favoring the proposed road had won, so far as obtaining a legislative act could go, but the struggle was by no means ended. By one or another method the opponents of the bill fought its progress, till, in 1822, the Turnpike was no nearer existence than six years before. In 1823, John J. Suffern was member of Assembly, and through his efforts a new act was passed for the construction of the Turnpike, dated April 23d, by which Andrew Suffern, William Yeoury and Tunis Smith were appointed commissioners and ordered to begin their duties as such on or before June 1st. The year 1824 saw General Van Orden, the long opponent of the bill, again in the Assembly, and, the contest over the road now taking the form of objections, by those who combated it, to the route selected, a new act appointing two more Commissioners was passed February 28, 1824. The new members thus appointed were Roger Parmely and George Kyles. Two more years passed away, during which some progress was made in surveying the proposed route, and then, on April 17th, 1826, a fresh act was passed by the Legislature for the correction of the survey of the Turnpike. At last, on April 30, 1830, the final act, entitled, "An Act to Improve the State Road from the Orange Turnpike to Nyack in the County of Rockland," was passed by the Legislature, and settled the long controversy. George S. Allison was Member of Assembly from this County at the time of the passage of this act.

AN ACT to improve the State road from the Orange Turnpike to Nyack, in County of Rockland. Passed April 20, 1830.

The People of the State of New York, represented in Senate and Assembly, Do Enact as follows:

SEC. 1. Jeremiah H. Pierson and Edward Suffern, of the town of Ramapo; Lucas Ackerson and Isaac S. Lydecker, of Clarkstown, and John Green, Tunis Smith and Peter Smith, of the Town of Orange, in the County of Rockland, shall be and hereby are appointed Trustees to superintend the construction, repair and improvement of the State Road from the Orange turnpike to Nyack, in the County of Rockland, five of whom shall be a board for the transaction of business, and the acts of a majority of them shall be valid and binding, and the said Trustees are hereby empowered, from time to time, in the manner and upon the security hereinafter mentioned, to borrow such sum or sums of money as may be necessary to be expended in the further construction, repair and improvement of said road, which said sum or sums of money may be borrowed, as aforesaid, before any part of said road shall be constructed, repaired or improved, in the manner hereinafter directed, and that the said Trustees shall be further authorized to accept of donations to the said road, and contributions in labor to be performed on the same, and that the said Trustees shall commence and complete such section of the said road, not less than six miles in length, as persons who may or shall provide the funds, or contribute the labor for completing the same, shall designate and prefer, but the said Trustees shall, in no event, be liable or responsible for the repayment of the money borrowed or the labor performed, as aforesaid.

SEC. 2. As soon as said Trustees shall have completed, in the manner hereinafter directed, six miles of said road it shall be the duty of the said Trustees to give notice thereof to the person administering the Government of this State, for the time being, who shall thereupon forthwith nominate and appoint two discreet persons, not interested in the said road, residing in the County of Orange, to view the same and to report to him in writing whether such road is completed according to the true intent and meaning of this act, and if the report shall be in the affirmative then it shall be the duty of the person administering the Government of this State, and he is hereby required by license, under his hand and the privy seal of this State, to permit the said Trustees to make and erect gates across and upon the said road at such place or places, as they or a majority of them shall deem best, to collect the duties and tolls, hereinafter granted, from all persons travelling or using the same, so that no more than one full toll-gate or two half toll-gates shall be erected upon and across the same.

SEC. 3. The said Trustees, or a majority of them, may, and hereby are empowered, from time to time, and before or after the said road shall have been constructed, repaired or improved, as aforesaid, by any writing or writings, under their hands and seals, to assign over or mortgage the said tolls to be received at both or either of the said gates, in and by separate securities, or jointly to the individuals or companies who advance the funds or perform the labor for each, or all the sums of money advanced or the amount of a just compensation for the labor performed on the said road, the costs and charges of such assignments or mortgages to be borne and paid out of such tolls, so to be assigned or mortgaged, respectively, for any time or times during the continuance of this act, which said tolls, so to be respectively assigned or mortgaged, as aforesaid, shall be pledged and applied by the said Trustees: First, To the maintaining and keeping the said road in repair. Second, To the annual payment of the interest, not exceeding five per cent.—per annum—for such sum or sums of money borrowed or the amount of labor performed on said road (other than the annual statute labor hereinafter specified) and, lastly; if there shall be any surplus remaining in the hands of said Trustees, it shall be applied for the payment of the principle of the said sum or sums of money and amount of labor performed, as aforesaid, and that the said mortgages and assignments may be, from time to time, assigned over by such person or persons to whom the same shall be respectively made his, her and their executors, administrators and, assigns to any other person or persons whomsoever, and that copies of all the said assignments or mortgages shall be entered at length in a book to be kept for that purpose by the Clerk of said Trustees, which book or books shall and may be examined at all reasonable times without fee or reward.

SEC. 4. The said Trustees, or a majority of them, from time to time, by writing, under their hands and seals may appoint a clerk, toll-gatherers and such other sufficient officers as shall be necessary for putting in execution this act, and shall take such securities to the people of the State of New York for the faithful execution of their respective offices as the said Trustees or a majority of them shall approve of, and also that the said Trustees or a majority of them shall and may from time to time remove such clerk, toll-gatherers, and other officers, or any of them, as they shall deem proper, and appoint new ones in case of death or such removals, and the said Trustees or a majority of them shall and may out of the said tolls, or out of the money to be borrowed on the credit thereof, make such allowances to the said clerk, toll-gatherers, or other officers as the said Trustees, or a majority of them shall deem reasonable.

SEC. 5. If any Trustee shall die, remove out of the County, refuse to act, or otherwise become incompetent to discharge the duties of such Trustee, it shall and may be lawful to and for the surviving Trustees, or a majority of them, to elect and appoint a fit person, or persons, in the place of such Trustee or Trustees dying, moving out of the County, or refusing to act, or becoming incompetent, and such person or persons so elected or appointed shall be joined with the other Trustees in the execution of this act to all intents and purposes in as ample a manner as the Trustees hereby appointed are empowered to act and subject to the provisions of this act, and notice in writing of any vacancy occurring in the office of such Trustee shall be given to the remaining Trustees, and of the time and place of meeting for the election of such new Trustees shall be given by the clerk to the said Trustees at least ten days before such meeting, and that the said clerk shall enter such new appointment of Trustee or Trustees from time to time in the book kept by him.

SEC. 6. It shall, and may be, lawful to and for the said Trustees, or a majority of them, to improve the course of the said road, and to alter the same wherever they may deem the public good requires, particularly by straightening and avoiding the hills in the same wherever it can be conveniently done, and to order to be discontinued so much and such parts of the old route as in the opinion of the said Trustees have become unnecessary, whose decision in the premises shall be conclusive and final, which alteration, improvement and discontinuance shall also be recorded in the book of the said Trustees to be kept by their said Clerk, and a copy thereof shall be delivered to the Town Clerk in the Town where the said alteration or discontinuance shall take place, to be recorded by him in the Town records of Roads in said Town, and notice in writing of such alteration shall be given by the said Clerk to the owner or occupant of any enclosed or improved lands through which the said road shall be laid out or altered, but no road or alteration shall be laid out through any orchard, garden, or building contrary to the 57th Section of the 4th Article, first title, 16th Chapter of the 1st part of the Revised Statutes.

SEC. 7. If any owner or owners through whose improved or enclosed land the said road shall be laid out or altered shall refuse to have same opened or worked and improved without compensation for the damages thereof, it shall be the duty of such owner within twenty days after having received notice of such alteration to have his damages assessed, in the manner prescribed in Article 4th, Title 1st, Chapter 16th, of the 1st part of Revised Statutes; which damages, together with the expense of surveying, shall be levied and paid by the Town in which the alteration is made, in the same manner as other contingent charges of said Town are paid, and it shall be lawful for the said Trustees after the expiration of the time aforesaid, to enter uponthelandsandtoopen, or cause to be opened the said road, and to construct, make and improve the same.

SEC. 8. The first meeting of the said Trustees shall be on the first Tuesday in June, next, at house of Jno. I. Yourey, in the Town of Ramapo, and they, or a majority of them may from time to time thereafter meet at such place as a majority of them shall determine.

SEC. 9. It shall be duty of the said Trustees, previous to the erection of any gate, so to construct, repair and improve said road, that all standing timber shall be cut down to the width of said road twenty feet, of which exclusive of the ditches to be made on each side thereof; shall be cleared of all stumps, roots, stones or any other obstruction whatever; when practicable, and the soil of said road shall be well compacted together and faced with gravel, of a depth not less than six inches where required, so as to secure a firm and even surface, rising in the middle by a gradual arch.

SEC. 10. As soon as permission so as aforesaid shall be granted to erect a gate or gates, upon and across the said road, it shall and may be lawful for the Toll-gatherers to be appointed as aforesaid, to collect and receive of and from all and every person using the said road, at each of the said gates, for any number of miles not less than ten, and so in proportion for any greater or less distance, to wit: For every wagon drawn by two horses, mules or oxen 12½ cents; and 3 cents for every additional horse, mule or ox attached to such wagon. For every cart drawn by two horses, mules or oxen 12½ cents; and for every additional horse, mule or ox attached to such cart 3 cents. For every horse and rider 6 cents, for every horse led or driven 4 cents. For every sled or sleigh drawn by two horses, mules or oxen 6 cents; and so in proportion if drawn by a greater or less number of horses, mules or oxen. For every chair, chaise, sulky, pleasure wagon or carriage drawn by one horse 12½ cents. For every coach, coachee, chariot or phaeton or other four wheeled pleasure carriage 25 cents. For every score of hogs, sheep or calves 6 cents, and so in proportion for a greater or less number. For every score of horses or cattle 25 cents, and so in proportion for a greater or less number. It shall be lawful for the Trustees or a majority of them, to reduce the toll aforesaid whenever they shall deem it necessary to do so, and it shall and may be lawful for any Toll-gatherer to stop and detain, any person riding, leading or driving any horse or horses, cattle, sheep or hogs, sulky, chair or phaeton, chaise, wagon, sleigh or sled or other carriage of burden or pleasure, from passing through any of the said gates until they shall have respectively paid the tolls aforesaid. But no toll shall be exacted or demanded from any person or persons who are exempt from the payment of toll by the 36th Section of the 3d Article, 1st Title, 18th Chapter of the first part of the Revised Statutes; and no more toll than is specified in the 37th Section of the same Article, for wagons of the width of tire therein respectively mentioned, and the said Trustees shall cause to be affixed and kept up, at or over each gate, in a conspicious and convenient place to be read, a printed list of the rates of toll which may be lawfully demanded.

SEC. 11. Whenever complaint in writing shall be made to any of the Judges of the Court of Common Pleas of the County of Rockland, that the said road or any part thereof is out of repair, it shall be the duty of such Judge to whom such complaint is made to repair to such part of said road and to view the same, and if the same shall in the opinion of the said Judge be out of repair, then the said Judge shall give notice in writing of such defect to the Toll Gatherer or person attending the gate nearest to the place so out of repair, and shall also in his discretion in said notice, order such gate to be thrown open, and the gate so ordered to be thrown open shall immediately after the service of such notice aforesaid, be opened and shall remain open and no toll shall be demanded for passing the same until a certificate is received by the person keeping such gate, under the hand of two of the said Judges, that said road is in sufficient repair, and granting permission to shut such gate and receive toll.

SEC. 12. If any person shall willfully break or throw down any of the said gates, or shall obstruct, dig up or spoil any part of said road, or any bridge or acqueduct drain or anything thereunto belonging or shall forcibly pass either of the said gates, without having paid the legal tolls, such person or persons shall, for every such offence or injury forfeit and pay the sum of twenty-five dollars, to be recovered by and in the name of the clerk of said Trustees, in an action of debt before any Justice of Peace in the County, or where the offender can be found, which said sum when received by the said clerk, shall be paid over to said Trustees, and by them expended and laid out in the improvement and repair of the said road, and if any person or persons shall, with his team, carriage, or horse, turn out of said road or pass either of said gates, or ground adjacent thereto, and again enter on said road, having passed said gate or gates to avoid payment of the toll due by this Act, such person or persons shall forfeit and pay a fine not exceeding ten dollars, to be recovered in like manner, and for the same use, with the costs of suit.

SEC. 13. If any Toll Gatherer shall unreasonably delay or hinder any traveller or passenger at either of the said gates, or shall demand and receive more toll than by this Act, is established, he shall, for every such offence, forfeit and pay five dollars, to be recovered by the person so unreasonably detained, for his own, use with costs of suit in any court having cognizance thereof.

SEC. 14. The said Trustees shall keep a just and true account of all monies borrowed, received or to be received by the several Toll Gatherers, and of all monies expended, or to be expended, or labor performed, (other than the ordinary annual Statute labor hereinafter mentioned) by virtue of this Act, and shall, on or before the first day of January, in each year, transmit a copy of the said account to the Comptroller of this State, and file a copy with the Clerk of the Board of Supervisors, of the County of Rockland, which said accounts may be examined at all reasonable times without fee or reward.

SEC. 15. Each of the said Trustees to be appointed or elected as aforesaid, shall, before he enters upon the duties of his office, take and subscribe an oath or affirmation that he will faithfully discharge the duties of the office of Trustee according to the best of his ability, and each of the said Trustees shall execute to the people of this State a bond, with two or more sufficient securities, to be approved of by two of the Judges of the County of Rockland, which approbation shall be endorsed upon the said bond in the penal sum of two thousand dollars, conditioned for the true and faithful performance of the trust reposed in him by virtue of this Act, and for the due application of all monies which may come into his hands by virtue of this Act, to the improvement of the said road, which said oath or affirmation and bond shall be filed in the Clerk's Office of the County of Rockland.

SEC. 16. If any of the Trustees shall not faithfully perform the trust reposed in them by virtue of this Act, the Court of Common Pleas in the County of Rockland shall cause said bond to be prosecuted, and the amount that shall be recovered upon the said bond shall be paid over to the said Trustees, to be expended upon the improvement of said road.

SEC. 17. The Commissioners of Highways of the several Towns through which said road shall pass shall divide said road into as many road districts as they shall judge convenient, and shall cause the same to be worked by the inhabitants residing on and near said road, or attached to said districts in the same manner as other road districts in the said several Towns are worked and repaired, subject, however, to the direction of the said Trustees.

SEC. 18. The said Trustees may from time to time commute with any person who resides near said road, for Toll payable on the same for one year, and may renew the same annually at the expiration of each period.

SEC. 19. The several Toll-gatherers to be appointed by virtue of this Act, shall take and subscribe the oath of office required by the Constitution of this State, which said oath shall be filed with the Clerk of said Trustees, and said Trustees shall have power to construct or hire suitable houses for their Toll-gatherers, and procure suitable situations for the same upon such terms as they shall deem advisable.

SEC. 20. This Act shall continue in force for the term of 21 years, or until the monies which shall have been borrowed, or labor performed, (except as aforesaid), upon the credit of Tolls to be received at the said gates, as aforesaid, shall have been paid off and discharged together with the interest thereon, not exceeding 5 per cent. per annum, upon [which] the said gates shall be taken down, and said road shall thereafter be a free public highway, and the Toll-houses, if any erected, sold, and money paid to the Town Commissioners of Highways, to be applied on said road and bond of said Trustees, to be cancelled by direction of Comptroller by the Clerk of the County.

SEC. 21. The Legislature may by law remove any one or more of the said Trustees and appoint others in their stead, and the said Trustees shall annually account with the Board of Supervisors of the said County for all monies received and expended on said road, labor performed and expenses incurred by virtue of this Act, and shall be allowed such compensation for their services, under this Act, as the Board of Supervisors of the said County shall deem just and reasonable, to be paid out of the Tolls collected on said road.

SEC. 22. This Act shall be deemed and taken to be a Public Act, and the Legislature may at any time alter, amend, or repeal the same.

ALBANY, MAY 4, 1830.

The Turnpike from Nyack to Sufferns, while it shortened the distance between the two places some four or five miles by measurement, shortened it more in time and ease than can be calculated. The traveller between the two villages, before this new road was opened, would leave Nyack by a narrow unworked lane, following the course of the present Main street, until he reached a point east of the ice house. The lane then swept up to and along the northern base of the hill where John W. Towt, now resides, turning back to the present pike just east of the former location of the toll gate, from there it followed the course of the present pike closely till it reached the old Kings Highway, the first road running north and south, west of the Nyack hills. If the traveller's horse should arrive at the highway without being lamed by the roots and rocks he had stumbled over or being exhausted by wading through the mud if it was spring time, and if the traveller's courage still held out; he had the choice of two routes before him. One, following the highway north to Casper Hill, and then west, north of the Hackensack swamp; would bring him out at Clarksville or Mont Moor, by Isaac Pye's corner. Continuing on west, he would pass the old Dutch Church, and ride along from a half mile to a mile north of the Turnpike until he reached the vicinity of Spring Valley, when he would turn south toward the Dutch Factory. Not quite reaching it, the traveller would again turn, ride west and north, pass from a mile to a mile and a half north of Monsey Station, continue west about that distance from the Turnpike till he reached the old Kings road from Sufferns to Haverstraw, when his journey would be nearly ended.

If, on reaching the highway west of Nyack, the traveller decided on the southern route; he would ride down the highway till he reached the present Rockland Driving Park, and then turning west, would pass through Greenbush, Sickletown, and Scotland, reaching the present Turnpike just south of Spring Valley, and southwest of the Dutch Factory. Till nearly midway between Monsey and Taulmans, he would follow the course of the pike, then abruptly turning to the south and west, he would make a long detour through the present Masonicus, and from there pursue a comparatively direct course to Sufferns.

During the long controversy preceding the final building of the Nyack Turnpike, the opponents of the road sent several prominent citizens, of unimpeached veracity, to measure the depth of a swamp west of Spring Valley, through which the proposed road was to run. It was a most forbidding spot, from all accounts, covered with water and oozy mud. These prominent citizens later testified that they had endeavored to reach hard bottom, first with fence rails and then with poles, twenty or more feet in length; that their efforts had been in vain, and that they had discovered, at the depth of a few feet, the existence of a quick-sand so active as to draw the poles and rails from their hands into the gruesome depths below. In their estimation the "Bear's Nest Swamp," as it was called, was a bottomless morass, containing, at a slight depth, frightful quicksands, which, in case an attempt was made to build a road across it, would swallow road-bed and traveller, till the expense, thus produced, would bankrupt the County.

The Clarksville swamp was met and conquered, but when the Commissioners approached the "Bear's Nest," they were influenced by the reports concerning it, and laid out the Turnpike south of the spot. Ten years later, when the Erie Railroad was being built, it was run through the "Bear's Nest," and the somewhat curious facts were discovered, not only that the morass was but five or six feet deep, but that the bottom was hard clay on which the ties of the railroad rest. In 1871 the Alturas Company cut a road directly through the old swamp bed from Monsey to near the Dutch Factory, and thus did away with the long detour.

In 1853 the Turnpike charter was renewed, and again in 1873. In April, 1855, that clause of the original act, which prevented the collection of toll from people residing within a mile of the toll-gates, was rescinded and the collection of half tolls from such residents allowed. On April 3d, 1883, "An act, to amend Chapter 286, of the Laws of 1830," was passed by the Legislature.

SEC. 1. Section four of Chapter 286 of the laws of 1830, entitled "An Act to improve the State Road from the Orange Turnpike to Nyack, in county of Rockland: " * * * is hereby amended so as to read as follows :

4th. The said Trustees, or a majority of them, from time to time, by writing, under their hands and seals, may appoint from their number a Clerk and Treasurer, and shall further appoint Toll-gatherers and such other sufficient officers as shall be deemed necessary by said Trustees for the purpose of this act, and shall take such security or securities to the people from the Treasurer and Toll-gatherers for the faithful execution of their respective offices, as the said Trustees, or a majority of them, shall approve, and also that the said Trustees or a majority of them, shall and may, from time to time, remove such Clerk, Treasurer, Toll-gatherers, and other officers, or any of them whenever they shall deem proper, and appoint new ones in case of death or such removal; and the said Trustees, or a majority of them, shall and may out of the said tolls, make such allowance to the said Clerk, Treasurer, Toll-gatherers, or other officers as to the Trustees or a majority of them shall seem reasonable.

2d. Section Twelve of said act is hereby amended so as to read as follows :12. If any person shall willfully break or throw down any of the said gates, or shall obstruct dig up, or spoil any part of said road, or any bridge, or aqueduct, drain, or anything thereunto belonging, or shall forcibly pass either of the said gates without having paid the legal toll, such person or persons shall for every such offence or injury forfeit and pay the sum of twenty-five dollars, to be recovered by and in the name of the said Trustees in an action for debt before any justice of the Peace of the County, or where the offender can be found; which said sum, when received, shall be paid over to the Treasurer and shall be by said Trustees expended and laid out in the improvement and repair of the said road, and if any person or persons shall with his team, carriage or horse, turn out of said road or pass either of the said gates or ground adjacent thereunto, and again enter on said road, having passed the said gate, or gates, to avoid the payment of toll due by this act such person or persons shall for each such offence forfeit and pay a fine not exceeding ten dollars, to be recovered in like manner, and for the same use with costs of suit; and any tolls due from any person by reason of this act shall be recovered in like manner and for the same use.

Section fourteen of said Act is hereby amended so as to read as follows : 14. The Treasurer shall collect and receive from the Toll-gatherer or toll-gatherers from time to time as he shall deem expedient all tolls collected by them and all monies received, or to be received by them, and shall keep a just and true account of the same, and of all monies expended and to be expended and labor performed (other than the ordinary Statute labor hereinafter mentioned) and shall make report thereof to said Trustees whenever required so to do by virtue of this Act and all money expended or to be expended, shall be paid by said Treasurer upon the order of the said Trustees, or a majority of them, and said Treasurer shall on or before the first day of January in each year transmit a copy of the said account to the Comptroller of this State, and file a copy with the Clerk of the Board of Supervisors of the County of Rockland, which said accounts may be examined at all reasonable times without fee or reward.

Section Fifteen of said Act is hereby amended so as to read as follows: 15. Each of the said Trustees to be appointed or elected, shall, before he enters upon the duties of his office, take and subscribe an oath or affirmation that he will faithfully discharge the duties of the office of Trustee according to the best of his ability, which oath or affirmation shall be filed in the Clerk's Office of the County of Rockland.

The Trustees hereafter to be appointed by virtue of this Act shall be appointed for the terms of one, two, three, four and five years respectively, and at the expiration of the term of service of each Trustee respectively, the County Justices of the County of Rockland with the Supervisors of the towns of Clarkstown and Orange, shall appoint their successors each and every year for the term of five years during the term of this charter.

The Act incorporating the State road aforesaid is hereby renewed and extended for the further term of ten years from the expiration of the present charter.

Shares to the number of 700 at a par value of $25 were issued for the expense of constructing the road and no gate was to be placed upon it within a half mile of its junction with the Orange Turnpike.

When the project of building a Turnpike from Nyack to Sufferns was first broached, the people of Haverstraw made an effort to save the travel to their village by obtaining a turnpike charter for their advantage. With this object in view the New Antrim and Waynesburgh Turnpike Company was incorporated, by Act of Legislature on April 1st, 1814, to construct a road to " begin at the dwelling house of John Suffern, situated in the Town of New Hempstead, from thence in a direct course as nearly as may be, to such a point in the village of Waynesburgh, late Warren (now Haverstraw), as the Commissioners, Edward Suffern, John Knapp, John D. Coe, Josiah Conklin, Elias Gurnee and George Smith shall direct." The Trustees of this proposed road were: Halstead Coe, Edward Suffern, Josiah Conklin, John Knapp, John D. Coe, Elias Gurnee, Andrew Suffern, John Felter and Abram Dater. These Trustees were authorized to issue 640 shares of stock at $25 a share. Further than the obtaining of the charter, this work never progressed.

In the history of the Townships, it will be my duty to speak of the Orange, and Haverstraw and Monroe Turnpikes; and in that division of this work I shall also place the history of Highland and Midland Avenues, which have recently caused so much ill feeling and such a prolonged resort to law in the eastern section of our County.

Ere leaving the subject of the County's roads, it is but just to say; that in a matter, usually one of commotion and ill will, she has been singularly happy. As the exigencies of life made more demand for shorter means of communication, neighbors along the proposed routes have as a rule, willingly given the ground and aided in the construction of the road-bed, while the expense of new bridges has been borne without murmur. As a result of this friendly feeling, distance has been shortened by the simple act of straightening a winding road, or by the serious labor of breaking through there-to-fore primeval forests, or climbing along the edges of thereto-fore impregnable mountain sides ; until now almost every point in our County is easy of access.

While the subject of a Turnpike was disturbing the peace of the community, another and tremendous venture was being determined on at Nyack. With the same enterprise which led them to favor closer and better means of travel in the County, two men of that place decided to attempt to obtain surer and more rapid communication with New York, and the result of many long and anxious consultations ended in the building of the steamboat Orange.

Looked at from our point of vantage, it seems impossible that the projectors of this enterprise should have hesitated for a moment. The uncertainty of sailing vessels was such as to practically place the County, so far as getting produce to the market was concerned, further from New York, than Albany, with its steamboats was, and this cause in great measure prevented that development of her resources which later obtained. It is evident that any safe means of conveyance capable of overcoming the cause of obstruction to the County's development, would be a financial success. But John E. Green, and Tunis Smith, the movers in the building of the Orange, did not have our point of vantage. By hard labor and close economy they had accumulated a little money, and the investment of that money was a serious matter. Not yet had a score of years elapsed since the first steamboat, the Clermont, passed up the river ; and the idea of a little country village, with less than two hundred people, building a steam vessel seemed an extreme risk. Those who took a gloomy view of the project were many and they did not hesitate to express their idea of what they regarded as the height of folly. Had it not been for the belief, on the part of those active in this venture, that the Turnpike would succeed in getting through, the enterprise would not have been tried; but with firm faith that the road would be built, the Nyack people started their boat.

On July 12th, 1826, Henry Gesner, John Green, Benjamin Blacklidge, and others, issued the following prospectus :

" Whereas Henry Gesner, Benjamin Blacklidge and John E. Green, and all those that will associate with them and have subscribed their names hereto, have in contemplation to form themselves into a company for the purpose of building or otherwise obtaining and navigating a steamboat or vessel on the Hudson River, which will require a capital of about $10,000 which is to be divided into shares of $50 each, and each share to constitute one vote in the proceedings of said company, and no less than one share to be subscribed for; and as soon as the said capital is subscribed for, the subscribers will meet, according to notice to be given thereof, at any convenient place in the village of Nyack, there and then to make such rules and regulations as shall be required concerning the same; and for the above purpose we the undersigned do hereby promise to pay the several sums annexed to each of our respective names in such manner and proportion as may be required by said company or their representatives."

NAME.	NO. SHARES.	AM'T INVESTED.
John E. Green	100	$5,000
Tunis Smith	20	1,000
William Perry	20	1,000
Henry Gesner	20	1,000
Peter Smith	15	750
Benjamin Blacklidge	10	500
John G. Perry	10	500
Isaac P. Smith	10	500
C. T. Smith	6	300
William Shurt	5	250
John Shaw	1	50
	217	$10,850

On July 20, 1826, a meeting of the subscribers was held at the house of Peter Smith in Nyack. John E. Green was chosen Chairman, and Benjamin Blacklidge, Secretary, and the Nyack Steamboat Association was organized with John E. Green as President and Tunis Smith and William Perry Directors.

September 1, 1826, a contract was made with Henry Gesner to build a boat, seventy-five feet in length, twenty-two feet beam, inside the guards, and seven and a half feet depth of hold for $4,124, the vessel to be finished and ready for her engine by March 1, 1827. In November, 1826, a contract was made with William Kimble, agent of the West Point Foundry, for an engine with 26-inch cylinder and 4-foot stroke for $4,500; and on December 27, 1826, a contract was made with Elnathan Applebly to do the joiner work according to the following plans, for $230.

One after cabin, two lengths of berths and one under berth on each side, with a closet at the end of each length. A bulkhead between the after and main cabins, with double doors; and the after cabin to be finished in the way sloops' cabins generally are. Main cabin to be about fifteen feet long, with a row of lockers on each side for seats, and a covered stairway, the height of an ordinary man, with side windows in and closet under it to the deck; forecastle to be about twelve feet long, with two lengths of berths on each side and stairway to the deck, similar to that in the main cabin, a closet under the stairway and one in the bow; the cabins and forecastle to be lighted by ports. Main deck, wheel-houses with small rooms fore and aft of each, built flush with the top of the paddle boxes, in the top of which were to be scuttles; a desk for the captain, a table, and "spitting boxes." Of these rooms on deck, one was used for the office, one as a refectory and one as a freight office.

Little note is made during the progress of the work. Before its completion, William Shurt and Benjamin Blacklidge had sold out their stock at par, the former to William Perry, the latter to Garret Green.

While those who predicted failure for this steamboat enterprise had not had sufficient influence to stop it, their gloomy prognostications did affect the directors to such an extent that the boat was so modeled that, should she prove a failure under steam, her hull could, without difficulty, be turned into use as a coasting schooner. The Orange was not a handsome boat. While we may admire the courage of those who built her, while we may feel deep veneration for her as the pioneer of all the steam communication to this County that has followed, while, as lovers of this County, we may appreciate the material prosperity her construction gave rise to: it would be gross mendacity for us to pretend that the old Orange was a thing of beauty. Ycleped by some the "Pot-cheese," because of her shape, and by others called the "Flying Dutchman," a sarcastic allusion to her lack of speed, the first steamboat from Nyack bore testimony in her build and velocity to the sturdy determination and careful calculation of her sponsors. It may not be foreign to the subject to place the Orange in comparison with the first steamboat which ran upon the river and with the last steamboat built at Nyack, to ply between the County and New York.

Clermont—built 1806-7; builder, Charles Brown, N. Y. Length, 130 feet; beam, 18 feet; depth, 7 feet; cylinder, 24 inch, stroke, 4 feet.

Orange, built 1826-7; builder, Henry Gesner, Nyack; length, 75 feet; beam, 22 feet inside guards; depth, 7 feet, 6 inches; cylinder, 26 inch; stroke, 4 feet.

Chrystenah—built 1866; builder, William Dickey, Nyack. Length, 196 feet; beam, 32 feet; depth, 9 feet; cylinder, 50 inch; stroke, 11 feet.

At last, in March, 1828, the Orange had so nearly reached completion, that arrangements were made for her management. John White, Jr., was chosen captain, and paid $110 a month, with the income of the bar and dining-room, on condition that he was to supply and board all the help except the engineer. Harman Felter of Rockland Lake, was taken as pilot, and Isaac P. Smith became engineer. The regulations of the boat state, that she will leave Nyack every day at 4 P. M.; returning, leave the city at 11 A. M.; rate of fare, two shillings for adults, children, half price, and infants in arms, included in the mother's fare; baggage and freight at the same rates charged by sloops, and all freight not given in charge of the captain, carried at the owner's risk. The after cabin being for females, no smoking in it was allowed; no peddlers were permitted to sell such wares on board as were kept in the refectory; passengers were expected to behave in an orderly manner, and no disputing, quarreling or profanity was to be tolerated, and no games of chance of any kind could be played on the boat. An advertisement of the Nyack Steamboat Association, prepared for the Evening Post, in April 1828, read as follows:

"The Steamboat Orange, Captain John White, Jr., will commence running daily between Nyack and New York, on the 5th day of May next, and will leave Nyack every day of the week, Saturdays and Sundays excepted, at 4 P. M., New York, 11 A. M., Saturday, Sunday and Monday excepted. On Saturday, the boat will leave New York at the time appointed weekly by the captain, and will stop at State Prison, New York, and Closter as usual. Every exertion has been made to entertain boarders, and many houses are now in readiness for the accommodation of guests; carriages will be in waiting at Nyack on the arrival of the boat, to convey passengers to any part of the County. Military, or other organizations wishing an excursion into the country can be accommodated at any time, by giving the captain notice of their intention four days in advance."

The following were the freight and passenger rates of those days:

Passengers	$0 25	Flour per barrel	$0 12½
Children	12½	Paint per quarter keg	4
Horses and Cows	75	Crates	25
Calves	25	Boxes of soap or candles	6
Sheep	12½	Horse, gig and driver	1 50
Lambs	9	Turned stuff per bundle	37½
Hogs	25	Shingles per 1,000	1 00
Salt per load	50	" bundle	25
" bushel	3	Sealing lath per 1,000	18¼
Lime per load	50	Boards per 100	1 00
" bushel	4	Plank "	2 00
Coal per load	50	Timber per load	50
Hogsheads	75	Brick "	50
Tierces	37½	Sack of salt	12

Close indeed would communication with the city have been if the boat could have been kept up to her time-table. As a matter of fact, the trip to New York took place on one day, the trip home on another. It was not till 1847 that the Warren was advertised to make a trip each way in one day, and then only twice a week. In 1861 the Metamora made two trips each way between Haverstraw and New York daily.

From the outset the Orange proved a success. The tide of travel, which had been divided between Haverstraw, Nyack and Tappan landings, now centered on the points touched at by the steamboat, and the quantity of freight carried was enormous. From the landing at the foot of the present Main street, in Nyack, rows of wagons, waiting their turn to unload, would extend to Franklin street on steamboat days, and at Tappan and Closter landings the scene was but little different. From Ramapo, from Ladentown, even from Haverstraw, both passengers and freight came to the Nyack boat, and she was loaded till the water was within a few inches of her guards, and then was frequently compelled to take one or two sloops in tow to carry the surplus freight. Under such circumstances it was impossible to attempt speed, even if the boat had possessed it. A trip in three hours was a fast one, and double that length of time was not infrequent. Yet the passengers seem seldom to have complained of delay. Everyone for miles around knew each other, and a meeting on the steamboat gave an opportunity for a renewal of those social relations, which had been interrupted by the labors of life. While the men gathered on deck or in the main cabin, according to the season and weather, the women met in the after cabin and enjoyed their gossip. Each brought her knitting along, all talked in Dutch, and the click of the needles and hum of the gutterals kept not unmusical time. Who shall say what material prosperity was started with those busy needles—what plans were discussed in that gutteral patois, which should reach full completion long after the skillful hands that used the needles so deftly should be folded— long after the knitter had sailed down that other river which enters the shoreless ocean of eternity. In his recollections of Rockland County for thirty years, the Rev. Dr. A. S. Freeman states, that as late as 1846 this custom and language still existed among the travellers on the local steamboats.

The fuel used on the Orange was wood, and huge piles of cord-wood stood along the roadside, from the foot of Main street up to Piermont avenue. On the arrival and unloading of the boat, the next duty was to get fuel on for the following trip, and this labor kept the crew employed till far into the night. For a year or two the Orange ran without competition. Then trouble arose with the Tappan people, and, on April 16th, 1830, a Legislative Act was passed, incorporating John Blanch, Cornelius J. Blauvelt, Peter H. Taulman, and their associates, into "The Orangetown Point Steamboat Company." This company was allowed to issue $10,000 worth of stock—each share representing $100, with the privilege of increasing to $15,000, and was to build a "good, substantial steamboat" to perform regular trips on the water, between Orangetown Point, in the County of Rockland, and New York city. A vessel was built on the shore north of Taulman's Point, named the Rockland, and placed in opposition to the Orange. The new steamboat could beat the old one without difficulty, and the usefulness of the "Flying Dutchman" seemed about over.

Those who remember Captain Isaac P. Smith need not be told that he was not a man to accept defeat calmly, and under his representations the Directors of the Nyack boat resolved on adding a false bow to the Orange, on widening her guards and on altering her wheels; changes which proved successful, and placed the vessel ahead. Some of the stock of the Orangetown Point company having been bought by Haverstraw people, the route of the Rockland was extended to that village in 1831, and she touched on her trips at Upper Nyack.

After running a few years in this way, Edward De Noyelles, John S. Gurnee and Leonard Gurnee, of Haverstraw, and John Blanch and Peter H. Taulman of Piermont, with others, formed a stock company and had the steamboat Warren built at New York by Sneden and Lawrence. This boat plied between De Noyelles' dock at Haverstraw and Vesey Street, New York, leaving the former place every Monday, Wednesday and Friday at 11 A. M., and the latter every Tuesday, Thursday and Saturday at 2 P. M. She landed at Snedeker's—now Waldberg,—Slaughter's Landing, Nyack, Sneden's, Closter, Huyler's and Hammond St. each way.

In 1838, Capt. Isaac P., David D., Abram P., and Tunis Smith built the Arrow and ran from Haverstraw to New York. On the completion of the Arrow, the Orange was sold to Mr. Cox for five or six thousand dollars and run as an opposition boat from Peekskill to New York. On the first trip passengers were carried free, and the boat was so overcrowded, that her human freight was landed at Hastings to prevent her sinking. The next trip she did not carry a passenger. Later, the Orange was bought by the Rockland County Farmers' Association, and run as an opposition boat to Upper Nyack. The project did not pay, and the projectors lost heavily by their operation. I find no further mention of either the Orange or Rockland, and presume they were broken up.

In 1840, the Arrow was burned at the Nyack landing. At once rebuilt, she continued running till 1841, when she again caught fire at Nyack and burned. Rebuilt again, the boat was called the George Washington, and under that name continued running from Haverstraw to New York for a year or two. The boat was then sold, was enlarged, called the Broadway, and run to Albany as a day boat; still later she was run to Haverstraw, on the east shore route, by Radford and Cox. In 1865 the Smiths re-purchased the boat, keeping her on the same route and under the same name, till the law compelling vessels to take their original name came in force, when she again became the Arrow. In 1866 a flue burst on the boat, causing loss of life, and after this the vessel was condemned.

In 1850, the Smiths, of Nyack, bought the Warren, changed her name to Swallow, put her on the line with the Arrow, and with the two boats made trips from Haverstraw at 6 and 11 A. M. and 3 P. M. daily, returning from New York at 7 and 11 A. M. and 4 P. M.

I append copies of the time tables of the Arrow and Warren:

"NYACK,
N. Y. & ERIE RAILROAD
Fast Sailing Steamboat
'ARROW'

Will leave New York, the foot of Duane Street, every day (Sundays excepted) at 3 o'clock, landing at the New York and Erie Railroad; returning, leaving Nyack, every day (Sundays excepted) at 7 o'clock, and the railroad at the arrival of the cars from Goshen. The Arrow will leave Nyack every Monday, Tuesday, Thursday and Friday evening at 5½ o'clock. Freight taken as usual (excepting live stock).

Touching at the foot of Hammond Street each way.

N. B.—Freight taken only at the risk of its respective owners.
NEW YORK, May 10, 1842."

"On and after Monday, April 30, the steamboat Warren, Captain J. Mausell, will leave Haverstraw every morning at ¼ to 7 o'clock. Returning, will leave New York from the Steamboat Pier at the foot of Vesey Street every afternoon at 3 o'clock (Sundays excepted).

For Freight or Passage apply on board. No freight taken on board at Hammond Street Dock.

N. B.—All Freight, Baggage, &c., at the risk of its respective owners.
HAVERSTRAW, April 26, 1849."

The Warren—now Swallow—only ran a few days under the new management. On Saturday, June 22d, 1850, she left her pier in New York at 11 A. M. When off Fifty-fourth Street, she was found to be on fire, and headed for the shore. Becoming unmanageable, she struck the dock and sheered off into the middle of the river, where she burned to the waters' edge. The steamboats Ivanhoe and Pioneer immediately came to the aid of the imperiled passengers, and saved most of them from a horrible fate; but in the excitement and fright many jumped overboard and were drowned. The hull of the Swallow was, later, sold at the Warren Hotel in Haverstraw, exclusive of the engine and bell, for $25. All the hull, except that containing the engine, was cut away, and from that part a new boat, the Isaac P. Smith, was built. To supply the place of the Swallow, the Norwalk was put on the route, and continued till the Isaac P. Smith was ready.

Returning to Nyack, we find that in 1845, Abram P. Smith bought a steamboat named the Union, and ran it as a freight boat from Nyack, leaving every other day at noon. In 1848, he sold the Union and purchased a smaller boat named the Stranger, which left Nyack every afternoon at five o'clock. She was mostly used for freight, though passengers were carried. In 1850, the Thomas E. Hulse, Captain, E. Van Wart, Pilot, Alfred Conklin, was run as a morning boat from New York to Haverstraw. From this period till within a dozen years, there was a constant opposition to the Smith's steamboat line for the control of the freight and passenger traffic of this County, an opposition which was fought down, but carried the old line with it in the moment of victory. The extension of railroads, first to Piermont, then to Nyack, at length to Stony Point, and finally to Haverstraw, has furnished the County with travelling facilities more regular, more rapid, and far more frequent than anyone could ever hope to accomplish with steamboats, and has turned the tide of travel. At first, the slow-sailing, uncertain sloops, sufficed to accommodate the few who journeyed. The steamboat came as a revelation to the people, and was the miracle of its time; and ere people, who saw the launch of the old Orange, have passed away, a new means of locomotion has come and ceased to be a wonder.

The franchises granted to individuals to run ferries between the Rockland and Westchester shores are many. On March 19th, 1800, Joshua Colwil and Joseph Travis obtained a charter for a ferry between Caldwell's Point and Peekskill. On May 4th, 1835, an act was passed permitting S. W. Bard, of Haverstraw, and Ward Hunter, of Peekskill, to establish ferry communications between those places; and on May 11th, of the same year, John Haff, of Sing Sing, was given permission to run a ferry between that village and Slaughter's Landing. On April 1st, 1840, George W. B. Gedney was given the franchise for a ferry between Nyack and Tarrytown for fifteen years. March 25th 1837, Samson Marks of Haverstraw, obtained a franchise for a ferry from Call's Dock to Verplanck's Point. April 23d, 1844, George E. Stanton, Peter B. Lynch, William H. Peck, Robert Wiltse, Gaylord B. Hubbell, and A. P. Stephens obtained the passage of an act incorporating them into "The Sing Sing and Rockland Lake Ferry Company," and on March 2d, 1849, Benjamin L. James and James L. Shultz obtained a franchise for a ferry from Piermont to the opposite shore.

The first ferry at Caldwell's was carried on by means of a row boat and this supplied the wants of the people till about 1830. Then a horse-boat was put on this route and continued till the little steam ferry-boat Jack Downing came into use.

The next mention of a steam ferry-boat that I find in the County was the Vinton, plying between Haverstraw and Crugers in 1852. She was owned by Elisha Peck, and run by Samuel A. Vervalen to connect with the Hudson River Railroad, which was then being built, and in which Mr. Peck was financially interested. In 1852 Captain John Bard ran a small boat named the John T. Rodman, between Haverstraw, Peekskill and intermediate landings; later replacing her by a boat named the "Sarah." In 1853 Abram P. Smith bought a little side wheel steamer named the Daniel Drew, and started her as a ferry-boat between Nyack and Tarrytown. A year later, 1854, he bought the J. J. Herrick for a ferry-boat, and ran her until he sold the ferry to D. D. and T. Smith in 1862. The number of names which that boat sailed under was legion. In the patriotic fervor of the civil war, she was called the Union, and at another time the Nyack and Tarrytown; ere being broken up, she was given her old name, Bergen, and as such is remembered by the residents of Nyack. In 1874 the present ferry-boat, Tappan Zee, was built and has since continued on the route. Row boat ferries between Caldwell's and Peekskill and between Grassy Point and Crugers have intermitted with steam ferries for many years. During the early days of the Knickerbocker ice business, a row boat ferry plied between the present Rockland Lake and Sing Sing; and after the construction of the Erie Railroad, before the Hudson River Railroad was opened a row boat ferry ran between the present Irvington and Piermont Pier.

For forty years the steamboat interests of Nyack remained in the hands of the brothers, Isaac P., D. D., Tunis and Abram P. Smith, the latter retiring first in 1862, and Isaac P. dying a few years later. In the last few years of this long period a stock company was formed, but D. D., and T. Smith still controlled the business. The advent of the railroad to Nyack, following on years of strong opposition, proved too heavy a load for the management longer to carry, and the business crisis of 1878 crushed the company. For a short time the boats were in the hands of a receiver, and then were bought by A. M. C. Smith and continued on the old route. For a brief period an opposition was kept up by D. D. Smith, but a fatal accident on the boat he had chartered—The Magenta—caused the vessel to be withdrawn, and no further attempt was made to hold the route by the long time proprietors.

Chronological list of Steamboats to Nyack and Haverstraw.

1828. ORANGE. Captain John White, Jr., followed by Harman Felter and Isaac P. Smith.
1831. ORANGE. Since time of starting.
" ROCKLAND. Built Piermont. Captain David Clark, followed by Jacob Mausell. Opposition to Orange. Route from Upper Nyack. Later to Haverstraw.
1838. WARREN. Built in New York. Sold in 1850 and named Swallow. Burned in 1850 with loss of life.
" ARROW. Built at Nyack, and was the second steamboat built there. Burned twice at the Nyack landing. Rebuilt and named, at different times, George Washington, Broadway, Metropolitan, and Broadway again. Burst a flue in 1866, with loss of life, and condemned.
1845. WARREN. Captain Jake Mausell.
" ARROW.
" ORANGE. By Rockland County Farmers' Association to Upper Nyack.
" UNION. Freight boat from Nyack, owned by A. P. Smith.
1850. STRANGER. Freight boat in place of Union, owned by A. P. Smith.
" SWALLOW. Captain Mausell. Burned.
" ARROW. Captain S. A. Vervalen.
" NORWALK. To replace the burned Swallow.
1852. GEORGE WASHINGTON. Formerly Arrow.
" ISAAC P. SMITH. Built from wreck of the Warren-Swallow. Captain George McDonald.
" THOMAS E. HULSE. Morning boat. Captain E. Van Wart. Pilot, Alfred Conklin.
" VINTON. Ferryboat from Haverstraw to Crugers. Later a small boat named Three Bells.
1853. GEORGE WASHINGTON. Captain R. T. Blanch.
" JENNY LIND, for a short time. Morning boat. Also the John Farron, opposition to the Hulse.
" DANIEL DREW. Ferryboat from Nyack to Tarrytown, owned by A. P. Smith.
1854. ISAAC P. SMITH. Captain R. T. Blanch.
" GEORGE WASHINGTON. Captain A. A. Lydecker.
" THOMAS E. HULSE. Morning boat.
" SARAH. Ferryboat from Haverstraw to Peekskill.
" J. J. HERRICK. Ferryboat from Nyack to Tarrytown.
1856. ISAAC P. SMITH.
" METAMORA. Opposition boat on the West Shore. Captain William Perry.
" BROADWAY. Opposition boat on the East Shore. Captain House.
" GEORGE LAW. Opposition boat.
" THOMAS E. HULSE. Morning boat from New York.
1860. METAMORA. Captain R. T. Blanch. Ran from New York to Newburgh, stopping at Peck's Dock.
" BROADWAY. Captain F. Frost.
" ISAAC P. SMITH. Captain G. O. House.

1860. EDWIN. Freight and passenger boat from Nyack, of Smith's Line. Named later Champion.
" AURORA. Captain Anning Smith. Morning boat from New York. Became Norwalk in 1865.
" DANIEL DREW. Captain J. F. Tallman. Albany boat, stopping at Peck's Dock.
" ARMENIA. Captain Isaac P. Smith. Albany boat, stopping at Peck's Dock. This boat was built by Cox, Radford & Colyer, and ran opposition to the Smiths for part of a season, when they bought her and put her on the Albany route.
1861. METAMORA. Captain J. F. Tallman. Two trips a day from Haverstraw. 5.45 A. M. and 12.45 P. M.
" ISAAC P. SMITH.
" BROADWAY.
" AURORA.
" M. S. ALLISON. Captain Field. Ran from Sing Sing to Newburgh.
" AMERICA. This boat was obtained by Smith's Line in exchange for the Champion. She soon took her original name, Peter G. Coffin, and ran thus till 1871, when she was rebuilt and called the Alexis. At a later date this name was changed to Riverdale. Her boiler exploded off New York, in 1883, with loss of life.
1865. ISAAC P. SMITH.
" ARMENIA. On the East Shore for a time.
" J. B. SCHUYLER. Captain F. Frost. On the East Shore.
" NORWALK. Formerly Aurora.
" IDA PELL. Ferryboat at Haverstraw in 1864.
1870 CHRYSTENAH. Built entirely new at Nyack in 1867. Always run on West Shore. Pilot
and from the start, Alfred Conklin.
since. ADELPHI. Formerly the City of Albany. Rebuilt at Nyack in 1868, and run on the East Shore. Sold in 1879, and is again called City of Albany.
" ALEXIS. Formerly Peter G. Coffin, run as a freight and passenger boat till her explosion.
" RALEIGH. Freight boat.
" TAPPAN ZEE. Ferryboat at Nyack, built in 1874.
" SLEEPY HOLLOW and SUNNY SIDE. Built by a company of New York merchants, and run for two or three years as opposition boats on the East Shore. The former, now called the Long Branch, is used as an excursion boat. The latter was cut through by ice and sunk above Poughkeepsie with loss of life.
" GENERAL SEDGWICK. Opposition boat on the East Shore.
" THOS. COLYER. Opposition boat on the West Shore for a short time.
" SHADY SIDE. Opposition on the West Shore for a short time.
" BOARDMAN. Captain Chas. Stevens. Ran first between Nyack and Newburgh and later between Haverstraw and Newburgh Named now River Belle.
" G. T. OLYPHANT. Captain Chas. Stephens. Same route as Boardman for a time.
" EMELINE. Running from Haverstraw to Newburgh.

Among other boats in the local travel have been the Washington Irving, Telegraph, Antelope, Naushon, Erie, St. Nicholas, and Magenta. Freight boats—Marshall Nye, sunk off Hatteras during the war, Walter Brett, River Queen, Edith Peck, and Maid of Kent. Preceding the extension of the Rockland's trips to Haverstraw, the people of that village were dependent on steamboats from up the river stopping at Grassy Point. Among the boats landing there were the Kosciusko, Cinderella, Water Witch, and General Jackson. In the year 1831, a fierce rivalry existed between the owners of the last named boats, and the latter blew up while lying at the Point with the loss of life.

Four years passed away after the Orange made her first trip, when the initial movement of another advance was begun in this State. New York, ranking as the third city in the new Nation at the close of the Revolution, had been given an impetus by the far-seeing wisdom of De Witt Clinton, and was moving forward with giant strides toward her future material prosperity. Scarcely had the people of this State ceased to talk of the opening of the Erie Canal ; scarcely had the echoes of the cannon, which on that October day in 1825, thundered the news from Buffalo to New York in the unprecedented time of one hour and twenty minutes, that the first fleet of boats had started for tide water, ceased to reverberate along the Hudson Highlands ; when a train of cars on the Mohawk and Hudson Railway made its first trip from Albany to Schenectady. In April of that year, 1832, the Legislature granted a charter to the New York and Erie Railroad, and a year later, 1833, the company of that railroad was organized, with Eleazar Lord as President. With the long struggle of that corporation before the work of constructing the road in this County began, I am not to deal. In 1838, work was begun on the section between Piermont and Goshen, and by 1841, trains were running from the latter place. According to the original charter, the New York and Erie Railroad was forbidden to connect with any road which passed into Pennsylvania or New Jersey ; to reach New York, therefore, it was run to the Hudson, close to the New Jersey line, and at Piermont, where, owing to the shallowness of the water, an enormous pier, one mile in length had to be built, connected with the city by the strongly-built steamboats, New Haven and Iron Witch. By 1852, that clause which forbade connection with New Jersey had been repealed, and the Erie Railroad Company leased the Paterson and Ramapo, and the Paterson and Hudson Railways together with the Union railway .79 of a mile long that formed the connection between it and the Paterson and Ramapo road. When first built, the Erie was a single track, six foot gauge, road. In 1853 a double track was laid through the Ramapo Valley, but the section running to Piermont was not touched ; and in 1878, the standard gauge was obtained by the laying of a third rail.

The construction of the Erie Railroad was an invaluable aid to the growth of this County. From its necessities Piermont was born, and by the communication thus opened, the villages of Blauveltville, Nanuet, Spring Valley and Monsey were rendered possible. Not alone did it bring in ready money, by the erection of its car works and round house, and the residence of its employees at its eastern terminus, but it also left a more lasting impress in the permanent development of our agricultural and mineral resources.

Four years after the Erie road changed its route from Piermont to Jersey City, via Paterson, the Northern Railroad of New Jersey was begun, and opened for travel from Piermont in 1859. The line belonging to the Northern road only extends in this State from the line just below Tappan to the present Sparkill. From that station to Piermont the road, as we have seen, is the original Erie track. In 1869, the Nyack and Northern Railroad company was organized. As this lies entirely within the boundaries of Orangetown, full mention of it will be given in the history of that township.

The opening of these roads changed the course of travel in the County as radically as the building of the Orange did. While in summer the boats still carried their share of traffic; in winter, when the river was blocked with ice, Piermont Pier at first, and later, Piermont village, became the shipping port. From the building of the Erie up to the opening of the Hudson River railroad, and when the ice would not permit a crossing to Crugers, up to recent days, that road was the only winter outlet for Haverstraw. From that place to Piermont—an always rough, generally cold, and oftentimes bleak and stormy ride of fourteen miles—Charles P. Snedeker ran a stage for the accommodation of travellers. It was by this route that the Rev. Dr. Freeman introduced the first melodeon in Haverstraw, and probably the first one in Rockland County, in 1847.

For many years a railroad had been running from Jersey City to Hackensack ere the effort was made to extend it onward toward Albany. In 1869 the Hackensack and New York Extension Company was organized, and by 1870 had extended the road from Hackensack to Nanuet. In 1873 the New Jersey and New York Railroad Company was formed and under its management the road was extended through the County from Spring Valley on the Piermont and Sufferns Branch of the Erie, along the eastern line of Rámapo township and, winding around the western point of Verdrietige Hook Mountain, near Camp Hill, reached a hay-field near Stony Point, its terminus, after touching Garnerville in 1875. The pledge of the company to the people of Stony Point and Grassy Point villages, had been to extend the road into the latter by passing through the former. In this way financial aid was obtained from the inhabitants of these places. Then one of those peculiar business transactions known as "railroad financiering" took place. The road and its appurtenances passed into the hands of a receiver. Then it was bought in by a new company and the just claims of Stony and Grassy Points ignored. As now situated its northern terminus is a half-mile away from everything. From Nanuet a short road was built north to New City, under the name of the Nanuet and New City Railroad, and opened for travel early in May, 1875. This road, which gave the first rail communication with our most inconveniently situated County Seat, was bought by the New Jersey and New York Railroad Company.

The Jersey City and Albany Railroad was opened as far as Tappan about 1876. It is unnecessary that I should attempt to unravel the web of railroad swindling which this corporation represented, a task that would be thankless even if possible. Through misrepresentation and flagrant deceit, money and land were obtained sufficient to permit the extension of the road to Haverstraw. This village was entered by means of a switch-back down the mountain side, and the terminal station was about a quarter of a mile south of the present Main Street. This road was never intended to be a success and it never was. For two or three years the trains were kept running, and then, in 1883, the New York, Ontario and Western Railroad was built through the County.

The New York, West Shore and Buffalo Railroad bought the road bed of the New York, Ontario and Western Company in 1883. Early in 1880, the latter company had begun the construction of a road from Middletown to Cornwall, and then through the medium of a construction company extended their line to Weehawken, buying up the old road bed of the Jersey City and Albany.

Almost immediately this company sold the line from Cornwall south to the N. Y. W. S. and B. Railroad, and then leased back their sale. Of the management of these roads, of the scandalous way in which they have been used to perpetrate fraud, it is needless to speak. Built during the latter years of the railroad building mania, and with no particular demand for their existence, they fell into hopeless financial ruin, as soon as the bubble was pricked, and carried down in their fall many private fortunes.

Authorities referred to: Civil List S. N. Y.; Session Laws S. N. Y.; Minutes and Papers of the Nyack Steamboat Association; History of the Town of Haverstraw, and lectures entitled, "Thirty Years in Rockland County," and "Thirty Years in Haverstraw," by the Rev. A. S. Freeman, D. D.; History of the Town of Ramapo, by the Rev. Eben B. Cobb; Archives of the Rockland County Historical Society; Files of the Rockland County Messenger.

CHAPTER XIII.

HISTORY OF THE REFORMED CHURCH AT TAPPAN—OF THE REFORMED CHURCH AT CLARKSTOWN—OF THE "BRICK" OR REFORMED CHURCH AT WEST NEW HEMPSTEAD—OF THE REFORMED CHURCH AT NYACK OF THE REFORMED CHURCH AT PIERMONT—OF THE REFORMED CHURCH AT SPRING VALLEY—HISTORY OF THE "ENGLISH" OR PRESBYTERIAN CHURCH AT HEMPSTEAD—OF THE PRESBYTERIAN CHURCH AT HAVERSTRAW—OF THE PRESBYTERIAN CHURCH AT RAMAPO—OF THE PRESBYTERIAN CHURCH AT GREENBUSH—OF THE PRESBYTERIAN CHURCH AT NYACK—OF THE PRESBYTERIAN CHURCH AT WALDBERG—OF THE PRESBYTERIAN CHURCH AT STONY POINT—OF THE PRESBYTERIAN CHURCH AT PALISADES, AND OF THE CENTRAL AND MOUNTVILLE PRESBYTERIAN CHURCHES—HISTORY OF THE BAPTIST CHURCH AT NANUET—OF THE BAPTIST CHURCH AT HAVERSTRAW—OF THE BAPTIST CHURCH AT VIOLA—OF THE BAPTIST CHURCH AT PIERMONT—OF THE BAPTIST CHURCH AT NYACK—OF THE BAPTIST CHURCH AT SPRING VALLEY.

Eight years elapsed after the settlement of the Orangetown patent ere a church organization was formed in this new County. Then, on October 24, 1694, the little band of settlers formed themselves into a society under the name of the "Low Dutch Christian Reformed Church of Tappan."

For many years—twenty-two—this society had no church edifice, and thirty years passed ere it possessed sufficient strength to afford a settled pastor. The first ministrations to this body were given by Guilliam Bertholf, who was the settled pastor of the united churches of Hackensack and Acquackanonck but extended his ministrations, and during his term of ministry organized the Sleepy Hollow Church at Tarrytown, in 1697, and the church at Raritan in 1699.

Guilliam Bertholf was a native of Holland, and had immigrated to this new world in the capacity of school-master, catechiser and *voorleser*, this word signifying a leader in singing, prayer and reading of the scriptures. In 1693, the people of Hackensack and Acquackanonck sent him to Holland to be examined, licensed, and ordained to the ministry. He was the first regularly installed pastor in New Jersey, and for the first fifteen years of his ministry, the only Dutch preacher in that State. Dominie Bertholf had spiritual charge of all the Dutch people on the west side of the Hudson, south of Ulster County, and of those of Tarrytown and Staten Island. The salary of this pioneer in the ministry in our County reached £50 a year in 1717.

Not alone was Rev. Bertholf in this great work of Christianity. Wherever settlement was begun, before the wilderness had been cleared, ministers of God entered upon their mission of love. On Long Island, at Fort Orange, at Esopas, clergymen had preceded him, and in the section north of the mountain—the present Orange County—Johannes Casparus Fryenmoet followed his example, ministering in 1737 at the churches of Maghaghamack, Minnisink, Walpeck and Smithfield, and receiving from the four churches £70 in money, 25 schepels of oats from each church, and his firewood.

By 1716, during the pastorate of Rev. Mr. Bertholf, the Tappan congregation had attained sufficient strength to build a church, and erected a square stone edifice on their glebe, which contained fifty acres. This church building which stood upon the site of the present house, remained unchanged till after the Revolution. In it the military court which tried John Andre sat, and in it Joshua Hett Smith was confined.

In 1724 the congregation at Tappan called and settled its first pastor, Rev. Frederic Muzelius. During his occupation of the pulpit, which lasted for twenty-five years, occurred the controversy in the Dutch Reformed church in America over the question whether the American Church should continue in or should break from its ecclesiastical dependence upon the church in Holland. In the schism produced by the disputation, the advocates of an independent American classis organized themselves into a body called "The Coetus," while the party favoring a continuance of the relations with Holland, was known as "The Conferentie."

In this contest, which began in Dominie Muzelius' time and, after causing his removal from the pulpit, lasted far into his successor's period of ministration and ended in 1770, Rev. Mr. Muzelius favored the cause of "The Conferentie," while a majority of his congregation sided with "The Coetus." Ill-will and annoying acts were caused by this disagreement, and these, combined with growing physical ailments in Rev. Mr. Muzelius led to his being set aside in 1749, as pastor emeritus, and to the call to Rev. Samuel Verbryck.

In the dissolution of the pastoral relations between Muzelius and his congregation. It was agreed by the latter to furnish him with a house and pay a yearly sum of £20 for his support.

As has happened in every religious controversy, before and since this quarrel, the pastor had many adherents. To these he continued steadfast, and from them organized, in 1767, a separate congregation, which continued in existence till 1778, long after the cause of its creation had ceased to exist. Frederick Muzelius died at the age of 78 years in 1782.

By 1749, settlement had extended throughout the rest of the County so rapidly, that the residents further north demanded and formed a separate church organization under the name of the Low Dutch Christian Reformed Church of New Hempstead, and three years later a house for worship was erected at Clarkstown. In the "call" to Rev. Mr. Verbryck, given July 17th, 1750, both the Tappan and Clarkstown churches were placed under his care. At the former, he was to serve two-thirds of the time, at the latter, one-third. £80 a year was to be his salary so long as the emeritus pastor lived, and this was to be raised by each congregation in the same proportion as his time was devoted. With this salary, the people were to furnish him with a parsonage, barn, orchard and garden at Tappan, "also a well, and sufficient firewood, and to keep everything in good repair."

Samuel Verbryck entered upon his duties with a people irritated and divided by questions of church government. Ere this cause of trouble had ceased in 1770, the mutterings of the approaching civil revolution began, and in the intense excitement which followed, through years of war and months of reprisal, he passed away on January 31st, 1784, at the age of 84 years.

The next pastor at the Tappan and Clarkstown churches was Rev. Nicholas Lansing, who was "called" August 11th, 1784, at a salary of £170 a year. Dominic Lansing was the last of the old Dutch pastors, and the last minister who commanded that obedience and respect, which has long ceased. In regard to the former statement, he was the last pastor who preached in the Dutch language, at first altogether, toward the close of his long service of over a half century, when the English had become the language of the younger people, alternately in Dutch and English. In regard to the latter statement—entering upon his duties when the total population of the town did not reach nine hundred souls, and when no church save that of his denomination existed, he knew personally all of the residents and ministered to most of them. Ere his death, steam communication had brought the County closer to the outside world; the restless and ceaseless struggle for wealth had already begun; Orangetown had increased in population to more than two thousand people, and church organizations of three different denominations existed.

Till 1830, Rev. Nicholas Lansing remained in charge of the churches at Tappan and Clarkstown. At that time, owing to his great age and its attendant infirmities, he gave up the latter, which has since maintained a separate existence. From this time he devoted himself entirely to the church at Tappan till his death on September 26th, 1835, at the age of 87 years.

The fourth settled, and fifth pastor of this church was Rev. Isaac D. Cole, who was born at New City, Rockland County, January 25th, 1799. Upon entering the ministry, he was called in 1829 as assistant pastor to the Tappan church. During the year from December 16th, 1832, till December 16th, 1833, Rev. Mr. Cole was absent from the Tappan church; then he returned and remained with this congregation till February 9th, 1864. After his retirement from the church and ministry in that year, a retirement necessitated by failing health, Rev. Mr. Cole removed to Spring Valley, where he lived quietly till his death on August 30th, 1878, at the age of 79 years.

The next settled pastor at Tappan was Rev. George M. S. Blauvelt, who was called in 1864 and remained in charge of the church till 1882, and he was followed in the last named year by Rev. William H. Williamson, the present pastor. In its history of one hundred and ninety-two years, the church society at Tappan has had but seven pastors, and of these but six were settled. The lengths of pastorates have been respectively 30, 25, 34, 51, 30, 18, and 4 years.

The first church edifice remained unchanged till about 1784. Then the four-sided roof was removed, the house was lengthened, covered with a gambrel roof, and a spire was added in which was placed a bell. The interior was painted in imitation of mahogany, and the columns which supported the roof were done in imitation of marble.

Over half a century more elapsed before further change was made in the church edifice, then, during the early years of Rev. Mr. Cole's pastorate, and the closing years of Dominie Lansing's life—he died before it was completed—the present brick building was erected in 1835, at a cost of $11,000. Of the church lands, some has been sold, some devoted to the purpose of a cemetery, till at present only about fifteen acres remain with the parsonage. The present house of worship stands upon the site of the original church.

CLARKSTOWN CHURCH.

This society, as has been said, was organized in 1749, and the first house built was in 1752. This stood on the site of the old stone building on the New City road. Until 1830, the congregation was under the ministration of the Tappan pastor. At that time, Rev. Christopher Hunt was called to the church and remained till 1832, when he was followed by Rev. Alexander Warner in 1832, who occupied the pulpit till 1837. In 1837 Rev. Peter J. Quick began his pastorate at this church, and continued his ministrations till 1866. Dominie Quick was followed by Rev. Benjamin C. Lippincott, who was called in 1866 and remained till 1872. In 1872, Rev. Ferdinand Schenck settled at this church, and continued five years. In 1877, Rev. Samuel Streng was called and served several years, and in 1884 the present incumbent, Rev. D. M. Talmage entered upon the pastoral duties.

Until 1840 this church society was known as the First Reformed Protestant Dutch Church of New Hempstead. On May 6th, of that year, the Legislature passed an act changing the name of the corporation to the First Reformed Protestant Dutch Church of Clarkstown.

The original church edifice stood till 1825, when a new building was erected on the site of the first house, which is still standing. In 1871 the new church building was finished, and has since been occupied. Disagreements have been frequent in the Clarkstown Church Society since 1812, and from it have split the Methodist Church at Nyack, the Presbyterian Church at Blauveltville, the True Reformed Church at Nanuet, and the Waldberg Church. Serious trouble was threatened at the time that the new house of worship was built in 1871, but the annoyance was finally soothed peacefully.

THE REFORMED PROTESTANT DUTCH CHURCH OF WEST NEW HEMPSTEAD, OR "BRICK CHURCH."

On Wednesday, September 28th, 1774, a meeting of believers in the creed of the Dutch Reformed Church was held at the house of James Christie, in Kakiat, and a society of that denomination organized by the selection of Cornelius Smith, Abraham De Baun, Rynier A. Quackenbos, and Johannes Smith as elders; Jacob Servant, Petrus Demarest, Gerret Smith, and Abraham Onderdonk, deacons, and Garrett Van Houten and Johannes W. Cogg were chosen a committee to accomplish full ecclesiastical organization. On the Sunday following this meeting, October 2d, 1774, the congregation assembled at the house of James Christie, and John W. Cogg read a sermon to those present.

Garrett Van Houten being ill, his place on the committee was supplied by Cornelius Smith, and on October 8th, 1774, the committee called on Dominie Benjamin Van der Lind, pastor at Paramus, and, having obtained his approval, wrote to Rev. J. H. Goetschius, at Schraalenburg, requesting an extra session of Synod at Hackensack, on November 15th, 1774. The

Synod met and established the "Reformed Protestant Dutch Church in the upper part of Kakeath," and, on Sunday, December 4th, 1774, Dominie Van der Lind formally ordained the elders and deacons, previously elected, and ecclesiastically organized the church.

The first church edifice was erected in 1788 and remained till 1856, when the present house was built. Previous to 1824 the name of the society was changed from that of "Kakiat" to "West New Hempstead." Dissentions and schism entered the congregation, and as a result the True Reformed Church of Monsey was formed.

The pastors of the "Brick Church" have been: David Marinus, 1774 to 1778; Peter Leydt, 1789 to 1793; George G. Brinkerhoff, 1793 to 1806; James D. Demarest, 1808 to 1824; Jefferson Wynkoop, 1824 to 1836; Peter Allen, 1837 to 1862; John R. Brock, 1862 to 1865; George J. Van Nest, 1865 to 1869; Henry Mattice (supply), 1869 to 1871; Benjamin T. Statesir, 1872 to 1881.

The Sabbath-school belonging to this church was established during the pastorate of Rev. Jefferson Wynkoop. Its superintendents have been, beside the clergymen just mentioned: Rev. Peter Allen, Henry Seaman, C. E. Blauvelt, Rev. Henry Mattice, Rev. B. T. Statesir and C. E. Blauvelt.

THE REFORMED DUTCH CHURCH OF NYACK.

The long journey to and from the Clarkstown church had already caused one different denomination to succeed at Nyack, and in 1830, Nyack constantly increasing in population, the members of the Dutch Reformed belief living there began to grow clamorous for accommodation at home. In 1830, members of this church, resident in Nyack, began to hold meetings on Sunday afternoons; at first in the Presbyterian church, later at private residences, and very frequently in the parlors of the Mansion House. At length, in 1836, the church was completed, being dedicated in June of that year by the Rev. John Knox, D. D.

Until 1838, the pastor of the Clarkstown church supplied the pulpit at Nyack, preaching at the former place in the morning, at the latter in the afternoon; then, the congregation feeling sufficiently strong, Rev. Philip M. Brett was called to the pastorate. Mr. Brett remained in charge of the church till 1842, when failing health compelled his resignation. Since that time the pulpit has been supplied by: Rev. Charles S. Hageman, now D. D., from 1842 to 1852; Rev. Benjamin Van Zandt, 1853 to 1856; Rev. Daniel Lord, 1857 to 1860; Rev. Uriah Marvin, 1860 to 1870; Rev. Henry V. Voorhees, 1870 to 1878; Rev. W. A. McCorkle, 1878 to 1881; Rev. William H. Clark, D. D., 1881 to the present writing.

In 1850, the congregation had so largely increased in the Nyack Church that greater seating capacity became a necessity. Accordingly, the house was rebuilt, a new front being added, and the edifice enlarged laterally, affording two additional rows of pews. The new building was dedicated January 7th, 1851. In 1870, the church was again repaired and enlarged, by an addition of eighteen feet in the rear, the work being completed in 1871. A prosperous Sunday School is connected with the church.

REFORMED PROTESTANT DUTCH CHURCH OF PIERMONT.

The society of this church was organized January 27th, 1839, and, Rev. Cornelius C. Vermiule having accepted an invitation to supply the society, began his labors May 19th, 1839, and continued till September, 1842, when Rev. Cornelius E. Crispell was ordained and installed pastor of the church at a salary of $400 a year. Since that time, the church has had the following pastors: Daniel Lord, 1847 to 1850; J. Romeyn Berry, 1850; Jacob West, 1852; A. D. Laurence Jewett, 1855; Henry E. Decker, 1860: Augustus F. Todd, 1865; William C. Stitt, 1872 till the present time.

The first house of worship was erected in 1840, on the hill-side near the hill railroad station. In 1850, a new church edifice was built, on the site of the present structure, and remained unchanged till 1873, when it was greatly enlarged and improved. In 1879, the building was again enlarged by the addition of a lecture room in the rear. The first members of the Dutch Church at Piermont came by letter from the Tappan church. A prosperous Sabbath School exists.

THE REFORMED PROTESTANT DUTCH CHURCH OF SPRING VALLEY.

By 1850, a number of families, members of the "Brick Church," resident at Spring Valley, made efforts to have preaching held at that village. To accomplish this object, the necessary committees were appointed to obtain a site, raise the required funds, etc. At length in 1853, a building was erected on the spot occupied by the present church edifice, and at this place divine service was regularly held by the pastor of the "Brick Church" on Sunday afternoons.

In 1863, the first house of worship became too small for the increased membership, and preparation was made to erect a larger edifice. A building committee was appointed, and the old building was sold to Alfred Tallman for $400, and by him moved to a lot owned by himself. This building was afterward sold to the Baptist Society, as we shall see, and is now known as Van Houten Hall. On January 5th, 1865, the new church structure was completed, and, it having been amicably decided by the congregations of both churches that it was better to have separate organizations, on April 17th, 1865, the organization at Spring Valley was legally incorporated.

The pastors of the Spring Valley Church have been : Rev. John R. Brock, May 7th, 1865 to April 10th, 1869; Rev. Marshall B. Smith, July 7th, 1869 to November 1st, 1870; Rev. Richard De Witt, October 8th, 1871 to April 1st, 1876; Rev. Peter E. Kipp, (stated supply) July 1876 to April 1877 ; Rev. Daniel Van Pell, July 16th, 1877 to September 23d, 1878 ; Rev Cornelius E. Crispell, D. D., September 9th, 1879 to present time.

THE PRESBYTERIAN CHURCH IN ROCKLAND COUNTY—THE "ENGLISH CHURCH," OR PRESBYTERIAN CHURCH OF NEW HEMPSTEAD.

In the *Magazine of American History*, Vol. XIII., p. 39, in an article entitled "Puritanism in New York," an account of the early Presbyterian churches in New York State is given. As early as 1640 the first Presbyterian Society was formed on Long Island at Southold. 1641 saw one at Southampton; 1642, one at Mespat, and in 1644 Richard Denton, a pastor of the Presbyterian Church, formed a society at Hempstead, with which he remained till 1658. During Dutch rule this sect was left undisturbed, but, on the final surrender of New York to the English, a determined effort was made by the Governors, especially Lord Cornbury, to crush out Presbyterianism, and make the Church of England dominant. In this attempt, which continued till 1716, the Presbyterian Society in Hempstead came in for its full share of annoyance, and great bitterness of feeling was the result.

Persecution has ever ended in a more vigorous and rapid spread of the ideas attacked, and, in thus harassing the believers in Presbyterianism, the adherents of the Church of England not only failed, most signally, in the attempt to proselyte them, but also increased to greater fervor and zeal the believers in that creed. Fresh from the conflict of church doctrines, and filled with anger at the injustice of the English rulers, the Colonists in Kakiat, emigrants from Hempstead, Long Island, arrived in our County. But time enough to get settled and started elapsed, when these new comers organized a Presbyterian Church Society, and at their earliest convenience erected a house of worship.

Already had the English language become the common dialect on Long Island, east of Brooklyn, ere the immigration to Kakiat took place, and at, or shortly after, that time the Scots, who gave its name to Scotland, settled in the County. A heterogenous congregation, consisting of French Huguenots, of Englishmen, Scots and Dutchmen, would naturally agree upon a tongue common to a majority of the community, and that language was the English. While, therefore, the service of the first Presbyterian Church, and its records were at first in Dutch, the will of the majority at length obtained, and English was substituted; and, in a community already settled by Dutch and sustaining two churches in which the exercises were carried on in that speech, this innovation could but excite interest and lead the worthy Dutchmen to speak of the church as the English Church.

But little record of the early days of this church can be found. A deed dated December 12th, 1754, "Between Samuel Coe, of New Hempstead, of the precinct of Harvuerstraw in the County of orange and province of New York, yoemen of the one part, and Jacob Hallsted, Jonah Hallsted Guysbert Cuyper, Samuel Coe, John Coe, Alexander Mc(N)nought, (A) alexander (M) montgomery, Francis Garnee, John Secar and (W) william (C) coe, Elders and Deacons in the Presbyterian Church or Congregation of said New Hempstead on the other part, for and in consideration of twenty-six pounds, two shillings and six pence, Currant Lawfull money of New York," sets aside a portion of land to this church society for a parsonage farm, and speaks of: "Forty and eight square rods whereon the meeting house stands, which is my free gift to the Presbyterian Church and Congregation for their use and benefit forever."

The first building of this society, a frame edifice, stood a few feet north of the present structure, and remained in use till 1827. On the military road through the County during the period of the Revolution, it is reported to have been used for military purposes, and it is supposed that during that period its records were mislaid or destroyed. Be that as it may, it is now certain that the early records are wanting, and but fragmentary data touching its history can be given.

Rev. E. B. Cobb has found an account between the Board of Trustees of the church and the Rev. John Lindsley, the pastor, extending from November 25th, 1785, to September 23d, 1786, by which it appears that during that time the pastor received goods and money to the value of £43 19s, 3d. The date of Mr. Lindsley's departure is not known. In a call to Rev. John Townley, issued October 27th, 1788, is found the statement: "The said church and congregation having been long destitute of a Settled Gospel Ministry for Divine Worship and the regular Dispensation of Gospel Ordinances amongst them, etc." On April 24th, 1797, Rev Allen Blair was called to the pulpit of the English Church, it being his duty to preach alternately in the Presbyterian church at Haverstraw—now Garnerville—and New Hempstead. On the departure of Mr. Blair, evil days fell upon the "English Church" congregation. It is recorded that the rite of communion was administered December 4th, 1808, by Rev. Mr. Hillyer; in June, 1809, by Rev. Mr. Thompson, on November 19th, 1809, by Rev. Mr. King; on July 8th, 1810, by Rev. Mr. Riggs; and on December 22d 1811, by Rev. Mr. Williams.

From this time to December 26th, 1816, when Rev. Samuel Pelton was called to the pastoral care of the Society, occurs a hiatus in the work of the church. Rev. Samuel Pelton was installed pastor of the "English Church" February 20th, 1817, and began his labors with fifty-nine communicants. He prospered greatly in his efforts, and in 1821, one hundred and ten people united with the church at one time. In 1839, Mr. Pelton was stricken with apoplexy and left partly paralyzed, a condition which led him to resign his charge in 1840. He was followed by Rev. John N. Boyd, from November 11th, 1840 till 1852; Rev. Abijah Green, November 1st, 1852; Rev. Samuel Kellogg, December 18th, 1853, and Rev. Thomas Mack, July 26th, 1866, till the present time. The church was incorporated May 1st, 1792; but on May 13th, 1822, it was found necessary to re-incorporate it.

On May 31st, 1879, the church edifice was struck by lightning, and in the course of the electric fluid to the earth, part of an iron bracket fastened to the pillar in the back of the church, down which the lightning passed, was hurled across the entire length of building and buried several inches deep in the wall over the pulpit.

FIRST PRESBYTERIAN CHURCH OF HAVERSTRAW.

Previous to 1781, the few residents of the Haverstraw Valley attended either the Dutch Reformed church near Kakiat, or Clarksville, or the Presbyterian Church at Kakiat. In that year an effort was made to establish a church society at Haverstraw, and seventy-one residents subscribed toward paying a pastor's salary. On April 8th, 1789, the English Protestant Society of Haverstraw had been organized by the election of Jacob Waldron, Amos Hutchings and Peter Allison, Trustees. On August 17th, 1789, Thomas Smith sold to the Trustees of this first Presbyterian church in Haverstraw, for the sum of ten shillings, a lot of land situated on the northeast corner of the land at present belonging to the heirs of Elisha Peck, on the south side of the road to Thiells Corners, and next east of the Calico Factory. On this the congregation proceeded to erect a wooden building, about forty feet square, for a house of worship.

Until 1839, the pulpit of this church was supplied by the ministers from the " English Church " at Kakiat. Among others, the Rev. Robert Burns, a resident of Haverstraw, is mentioned as one of the pastors. In 1816, Rev. Samuel Pelton was called to the charge of this in conjunction with the " English Church," and continued at labor till failing health compelled his resignation in 1839. Since Mr. Pelton's time the pastors have been: Rev. James Hildreth, June 23d, 1839 till May 4th, 1848; Rev. Livingston Willard, 1849 to 1850; Rev James H. Trowbridge, till November, 1853; Rev. Peter J. H. Myers, from September 7th, 1854 to December 30th, 1859; Rev. Spencer Marsh, from November 26th, 1861 to 1868, and Rev. J. J. McMahon, who took charge as a stated supply in September, 1868, dividing his time between this church and the one at Stony Point till 1875, when he resigned the latter charge. He was installed pastor of the church at Haverstraw, May 9th, 1876, and remains in charge at the present time.

The last service held in the first church building was on Sunday, November 21st, 1847. The building was then sold to Elisha Peck, who moved it away and turned it into a barn, which was later destroyed by fire. The second edifice of the First Presbyterian Church Society, of Haverstraw, was built in 1848-49, and dedicated February 8th of the latter year. This structure was built of brick, and is still standing.

PRESBYTERIAN CHURCH, RAMAPO.

This church building was erected in 1810, by Jeremiah H. Pierson, for the accommodation of the employees at the Ramapo Works, there being, at that time, no church nearer than the " Island Church " at Mahwah, which was built in 1791. From the beginning, services were held in this church on alternate Sundays, the pulpit being supplied by pastors from other churches. One of the first to fill this pulpit, and the one whose visits were most frequent, till he assumed charge of the congregation in 1834, was Rev. Samuel Fisher, D. D. Beside him, between 1815 and and 1824, the pulpit was supplied by Rev. Messrs. Ford, Spaulding, Condet, Wilder, Mills, Gildersleeve, Armstrong, Crane, Babbitt, Chandler, Pollhman, Barton, Hendricks, Tuttle, Osborne, Harris, and Pierson; and between 1824 and 1834, by Stebbins, Chansen, Olds, Romeyn, Wynkoop, Judson, and Smith.

On May 1st, 1834, Dr. Samuel Fisher assumed charge of the Ramapo Church, and remained till 1840; he was followed by: Rev. J. C. Day, 1841 to 1844; Rev. S. J. Harker, 1845 to 1846; Rev. William A. Westcott, 1846 to 1848; Rev. William H. Kirk, 1848 to 1853; Rev. William

T. Van Doren, 1853 to 1857. At this time, owing to the decline of the industries at Ramapo, and the withdrawal from that village of employees, services in the church stopped. In September, 1867, the church was reorganized, and later, April 21st, 1868, was formally taken under the care of the Presbytery of Hudson. Since 1867, the pastors have been: Rev. Goodloe B. Bell, until May, 1871; Rev. Peres B. Bonney, November 1871 to November 1875; Rev. George A. Ford, April 16th, 1876 to April 29th, 1880; Rev. Eben B. Cobb, April 29th, 1880 till the present.

This church edifice is probably the oldest one which has been kept free from the touch of those iconoclasts, who desire to destroy everything old, and replace with modern improvements. A brief description of the interior, as furnished by a newspaper article published in 1878, and by the present pastor, Rev. E. B. Cobb, seems wise.

The box pulpit, pentagonal in shape and canopied, is raised some feet from the floor, and reached by a narrow stairway. Large enough to hold but one person, the occupant may still further shut himself from all worldly distractions by closing a door, which bars ingress to the pulpit. The box pews, entered through high doors swung upon wrought-iron hinges, still remain, the only change from their original construction being a slight slant of their backs. This innovation was accomplished when the church was reorganized in 1867, and perhaps better suits the easier methods of worship which obtain now, as compared with those of three-quarters of a century ago. About 1876 a grand pipe organ was introduced into the church, and added its sweet tones to the hosannas of the worshippers. But let no one think this was the first instrumental music in the old church. Early in its history, it is recorded that six and thirty people subscribed £11 for a bass viol.

At present, the church has three Sunday Schools under its charge.

GREENBUSH PRESBYTERIAN CHURCH.

In the autumn of 1812, application was made to the Presbytery of Hudson to organize a church at Greenbush, and on October 18th, 1812, Rev. Eliphalet Price, by appointment of the Presbytery, preached to the congregation at Greenbush, and gave notice that in the evening of the same day, he would proceed to the forming of a church society. In accordance with this request, ten people came together and formed an organization.

About the year 1813, (no record appears of the exact date) Rev. Andrew Thompson was installed pastor of the church, and continued in that position for about twenty years. For several years the Presbyterian

Church Society of Greenbush held their services in the upper room of the Greenbush Academy. The first church edifice, built of stone on the site of the present building, was erected in 1823, and dedicated January 14th, 1824. The lot for the structure was given by Abraham G. Blauvelt by deed bearing date May 21st, 1823.

The second pastor of this church was Rev. Jared Dewing, who held that position from April 24th, 1834, to October 8th, 1855. He was followed by Rev. Thomas Evans, called as a stated supply, November 12th, 1855, installed June 17th, 1856, resigned 1877; Rev. Henry E. Decker followed, remaining with the church till December 1883. Since December 2d, 1883, Rev. Charles H. Lester has been the stated supply.

On September 18th, 1835, the Presbyterian church building at Greenbush was destroyed by fire and the congregation left without a home. Preparations were made to rebuild it and the new edifice, which was erected in 1836, was dedicated April 5th, 1837. On October 24th, 1882, the second church building together with the parsonage was burned. This last fire was believed to be of incendiary origin, and charges against the suspected party were made before the Grand Jury. The evidence was insufficient, and that body failed to find an indictment. In 1883, the present structure was built and dedicated November 27th of that year.

THE PRESBYTERIAN CHURCH AT NYACK.

I have been credibly informed, by people conversant with the facts, that the split from the Dutch Church at Clarkstown, which gave origin to the Presbyterian congregation at Nyack, grew out of disputes regarding the location and construction of a proposed country road. A lawsuit between some of the church members was begun, and the bitter feeling engendered by this litigation prevented further peaceful communion in the same church organization.

By deed, bearing date, March 18th, 1816, Peter De Pew gave to the society the lot of land on which the present church stands, and on this the first church edifice, a sandstone building, was erected. The first pastor of the Nyack Church was the Rev. Andrew Thompson, of the Greenbush Church, who gave one-quarter of his time to Nyack. On March 27th, 1834, Rev. Jared Dewing was called to the pastorate of the two church societies, installed April 24th, and retained those relations till June 14th, 1841, when, the Nyack Church society, having been granted a separate autonomy by the Presbytery of New York on May 10th, 1841, his connections with that church were severed. Following Mr. Dewing, and the first pastor of the separate Nyack church, came Rev. Charles M. Oakley, from October 25th, 1841, to September 11, 1843; Rev. Joseph Penny, D. D., from November 30th, 1843, to April, 1847; Rev. J. S. Davison, from October 26th, 1847, to October 19th, 1852; Rev. Joseph Cory, from May 31st, 1853, to 1867; Rev. Francis L. Patton, from November 25th, 1867, to May 25th, 1871; Rev. A. McElroy Wylie, from May, 1872, to September 19th, 1876; Rev. George H. Wallace, from October 3d, 1877, to 1880; Rev. J. Elwy Lloyd, from June 14th, 1881, to the present time.

The first church edifice stood till 1839, when it was torn down and a wooden building erected in its place. This second church has since been enlarged and improved at different times until little vestige of the original frame building remains. Up to October 22d, 1834, the Nyack and Greenbush societies belonged to the Presbytery of Hudson, but at that time the ecclesiastical relation with Hudson was severed, at their request, and transferred to the Presbytery of New York. The causes that led to the creation of the Nyack Church, as a separate organization, grew out of financial difficulties regarding the rent of the parsonage and the pastor's salary.

THE "POND," "YELLOW" OR WALDBERG PRESBYTERIAN CHURCH.

This church society was formed by a split from the Clarkstown church, which occurred in 1830. As originally composed, the society was neutral, Presbyterians and members of the Dutch Reformed church being alike subscribers, and it was agreed that the ultimate connection of the church should be determined by a majority of those who supported, as well as contributed to the building of the edifice. The present structure was erected in 1831 and opened for service the same year.

Rockland Lake was still almost universally known by the residents as the "Pond," and this church took its name from the common appellation of the original patent on which it was built, an appellation which had become applied to the neighborhood. As the name of Rockland lake became localized by the growth of the present village, that of "Pond" in connection with this church became incongruous, and the edifice having been painted yellow, a striking color at all times, but probably more so among the dull brown stone houses and unpainted barns of those times than at present, the building naturally took the name of the "Yellow" church and retained it till 1860, when it received the present name of Waldberg from the name of the school district.

In the early years of its existence the pulpit of this church was supplied in connection with those of other churches, and service was held in the afternoon. When Hon. A. B. Conger built and moved into this neighborhood valuable assistance was given to the church, and stationed pastors were obtained, who took charge of the district for some years. At length, owing to the removal from the neighborhood of some of the richest members, the church society dwindled, and during recent years the edifice has been used by members of the Methodist faith.

THE PRESBYTERIAN CHURCH AT STONY POINT.

This church society was formed from the Haverstraw Presbyterian Church, organized in 1789. It is necessary to remember that until 1865, the present township of Stony Point was part of Haverstraw township, and that the first Presbyterian church edifice in Stony Point was erected upon land then belonging to Haverstraw. In 1844, the members of this church, resident in the present Stony Point, built a house of worship on land donated for that purpose by Richard Brewster.

Until 1855, this society was under the care of and supplied by the pastor of the Haverstraw church. Then the Stony Point church was organized as a separate body, under the care of the Presbytery of New York. In 1869, the church edifice was rebuilt and enlarged to its present size. The pastors of the church before its separation were: Rev. Mr. Burns, Rev. Samuel Pelton, from 1816 to 1839; Rev. James Hildreth, 1839 to 1848; Rev. Livingston Willard, 1849 to 1850; Rev. J. H. Trowbridge, to 1853; Rev. P. J. H. Meyers, from 1854 to 1855. Since its separate existence the pastors have been: Rev. Abijah Green, from 1855 to 1856; Rev. David Eagan, from 1856 to 1858; Rev. Frederick King, 1858 to 1866; Rev. J. J. McMahon, 1866 to 1876; Rev. R. B. Mattice, 1879 to 1880; Rev. T. C. Straus, 1881 to 1884; and the present pastor, Rev. John S. Gilmore, from 1885.

MOUNTVILLE CHURCH.

When John Beverige of Newburgh, determined on Iona Island as his place of residence, he bought property on the mainland at Doodletown, and erected at his own expense, in 1851, the building known as the Mountville Church. A strong Presbyterian in belief, Mr. Beverige started this church as a society of that denomination, and for a time had its pulpit supplied by a pastor from Newburgh. Earnest as were his efforts, they called forth little response from the mountain inhabitants of this section. After trying for some time to excite some interest among the people, Mr. Beverige at last gave up his idea, and donated the building to the people of Doodletown. It was at once turned into a Methodist mission, and has since been supplied by circuit preachers of that denomination.

THE CENTRAL PRESBYTERIAN CHURCH OF HAVERSTRAW.

This church society was organized by a committee of the Fourth Presbytery of New York, April 22d, 1846. The use of the building belonging to the Methodist Protestant Church was obtained for divine service, and the pulpit was supplied by different ministers till the last Sabbath in June, 1846, when the Rev. Amasa S. Freeman commenced his pastoral duties.

Ground was given for the church edifice by Hon. George S. Allison and Rev. Edward Hopper, and the erection of the building begun, the corner stone being laid August 21st, 1846. Two months later, when the walls were up and ready for the roof, a gale destroyed the uncompleted work. Until the inclemency of the weather prevented, divine service was held in a structure put up for the convenience of the workmen on the church lot and now used as a horse shed. February 7th, 1847, the basement of the church was used for the first time by the congregation, and, on the third Sunday in September, 1847, the audience room was completed and the building dedicated to the service of the Triune God.

On April 25th, 1849, Rev. A. S. Freeman was formally installed as pastor of this church and still occupies the pulpit. In 1860, the church was enlarged. In 1883, the thirty-seventh anniversary of the pastoral relation was commemorated by the congregation of this church by the erection of a tower, with a bell and clock.

I have steadily refrained in this work from panegyric or the laudation of living men, and, with the exception of the case of Rev. Amasa S. Freeman, D. D., shall continue so to refrain, believing that if any past or present resident of the County has done aught commendable, his name will appear in connection with the work, and readers are as well fitted to praise or blame as I am. But the work of Dr. Freeman has been so unostentatious, so like that of the good Master, his afflictions have been so sore, the mad passions which at times have raged in our midst have been so trying and yet have been met by this man and conquered; that a few words concerning him may not be a trespass.

"I came here to spend one Sabbath, and little anticipated that one Sabbath would be so long drawn out." In the morning of the long Sabbath, which Dr. Freeman began with us in 1846, all was peace and beauty. A church edifice was erected, a congregation of large size was built up, marriage gave him a partner and children blessed the union. Never did a day open more auspiciously. As the noon approached, symptoms of a coming storm appeared—"A little cloud out of the sea, like a man's hand."

The tempest of civil war burst upon us, and men's souls were sorely tried. Through the seething hate of that period Dr. Freeman passed unscathed. From the pulpit and rostrum, in the press and by deed, he upheld the Union, undeterred by menace, and in his church the first company of volunteers from Haverstraw said their good-byes, from his hand its Captain—Edward Pye—received the flag given by the loyal women of Haverstraw, by his efforts was money raised for the Sanitary Commission.

Then came a period of dishonor in our County's financial history, and the blow fell with peculiar force on Dr. Freeman's church. For a time it seemed as though the spirit of discord would win, as though the happy relationship, theretofore existing between pastor and people, would be dissolved. The crisis passed, and the strained feelings became again happily relaxed. The evils of intemperance have assumed greater import in Haverstraw than in any other place in our County, because of the unstable laboring population of that village. For thirty years the liquor interest has been one of controversy and conflict, and the subject has been carried into societies politic, social and religious. Never, in all the long years of contest, has Dr. Freeman been found wanting or doubtful. He has combatted the evil whenever opportunity arose.

Yet, in the inscrutable wisdom of God, these social trials were to pale before the domestic bereavements which fell with crushing force upon his household. Death entered his family circle and took from him the hopes of his declining years. Before the tragic awfulness of his affliction he bowed, murmuring only the words of resignation, and patiently yielding his loved ones to Him who gave them, continued his labors here, sanctified by suffering.

And so the long Sabbath is passing like a summer day, with peace and storm, and now the even-tide approaches, calm and fresh. For almost two score years has Dr. Freeman labored and suffered amongst us, and his name is now known and venerated throughout our County, and remembered by Rockland's sons wherever resident. But one has excelled him in the duration of pastoral relationship—Nicholas Lansing—who labored at Tappan for a year over a half century; but one nearly reached his term of pastorate—Joseph W. Griffith—who labored in one church for eight and thirty, and among the Baptists of our County for five and forty years; and but two others toiled in the Master's work in this County over a score of years—Rev. James D. Demarest, who preached from 1804 till November, 1855, and Samuel Pelton, who continued his pastorate in the "English Church" four and twenty years.

THE PALISADES PRESBYTERIAN CHURCH.

On April 23d, 1863, C. R. Agnew, M. D., Clinton Gilbert, W. S. Gilman, Jr., I. N. Sears and C. F. Park, met at the residence of one of the number in New York city and determined to erect a Presbyterian church at Palisades. At a later meeting, the above-named gentlemen engaged the services of Rev. Joseph Greenleaf, Jr., to December 1st, 1863. On May 15th, 1863, the first service of this church society was held in the first Methodist church building at Palisades. On June 1st, 1863, the foundations of the present Presbyterian church edifice were begun, and by the close of the year the building was completed, being opened for divine service January 3d, 1864.

This church society was formally organized by the Presbytery of New York Oct. 14th, 1863, and on October 21st of the same year, Rev. J. Greenleaf, Jr., was installed. Following this first pastor have been: Rev. John K. Demorest, from October 16th, 1866 to February 13th, 1870; Rev. Aaron H. Hand, D. D., from October 18th, 1870 to September, 1879; Rev. J. W. McIlvain, from December 26th, 1879 to September 30th, 1882; Rev. Newton L. Reed, from October, 1883, to the present time.

THE BAPTIST CHURCH IN ROCKLAND COUNTY.

About 1782, Elder Luke Reuland, of Long Island, came to Sneden's Landing on a visit. While in the County he preached in different houses, and under his teachings five persons were baptized. Subsequently Elder J. L. Thompson, of Orange county, and Elder Cox, of England, preached occasionally in the County. In 1796, Edward Salyer, then residing at Middletown, embraced the views of this church, and was baptised in New York in connection with the Second Baptist church of that city, and shortly after James Blauvelt, of Middletown, was baptised in the Hackensack by Rev. Dr. Foster of the First Baptist church of New York City.

In 1797, Elder Daniel Steers, who had immigrated from England and was then resident on Staten Island, preached on different occasions at Middletown, and under his ministrations a few were baptized. These, with others in this and the adjacent part of Bergen county in New Jersey, to the number of twelve, formed themselves into an independent Baptist church on October 18th, 1798, under the name of the *Rockland Baptist Church*.

THE ROCKLAND, MIDDLETOWN OR NANUET BAPTIST CHURCH.

At the organization of this, the first Baptist Society in our County, the sermon was preached by Elder Davis of New York, from the text: "In whom ye also trusted, after that ye heard the word of truth, the gospel of your salvation: in whom also, after that ye believed, ye were sealed, with that Holy Spirit of promise." The charge to the church was given by Elder Daniel Steers.

Early in 1800, this society invited Elder Steers to become its pastor, and, at a regular church meeting held May 3d, 1800, he was received by letter from the Baptist church at Staten Island. In January, 1802, the name of the church was changed to the *Middletown Baptist Church.*

For several years, the congregation of this church worshipped in a private house; then a small building was erected on the Middletown road, directly at the head of the road from Pascack. The date of erection of this first Baptist church seems in doubt. Elder J. W. Griffiths in his history of the Baptist church in Rockland County fixes it "about the year 1805," while the deed for the land on which the first church stood, bears date February 20th, 1810.

On June 14th, 1811, the members of this church residing at Masonicus, now Hempstead, asked for and obtained their dismissal, for the purpose of forming a separate church. The same year, Elder Steers, who had previously removed to Haverstraw, resigned his charge of the Middletown church. Until 1815, the society was without a settled pastor; then Elder Joseph W. Griffiths was called and entered upon his pastoral duties in June of that year. Besides preaching at Middletown, Elder Griffiths held service every alternate Sabbath at Haverstraw, during the first eighteen months of his pastorate, and subsequently held frequent service at Hackensack, Hempstead and Tappan Slote, when opportunity offered, until 1837. After this time, he devoted himself especially to the Middletown church till his resignation in 1853. Following Elder J. W. Griffiths have been: Elder J. L. Thompson, from 1853 to 1859; Rev. W. Pauline, from April 7th, 1859 to December 1859; Rev. J. C. Page, 1860; Rev. A B. McGowen, 1871; Rev. Frederick Greaves, 1873; Rev. Frank Fletcher, 1880; Rev, W. S. S. Warden, who is now supplying the pulpit.

During Elder Griffiths' pastorate, about the year 1820, a new church edifice 20 by 40 feet was built some half-mile south of the old one on the same road. In 1859 the church was moved within the Clarkstown limits, and the building, now occupied by the congregation, erected. In 1865, the name of the society was changed to the *Nanuet Baptist Church.*

In 1838, this church, in conjunction with that at Piermont, organized a Bible Society called the Middletown and Piermont Bible Society, which was auxiliary to the American and Foreign Bible Society.

THE HAVERSTRAW BAPTIST CHURCH.

In 1802, a number of the Baptist members, living at Haverstraw, were constituted as a branch of the Middletown Baptist Church, and Elder Daniel Steers held divine service on alternate Sundays at different private houses. By 1809, the edifice belonging to the Presbyterian Society at Haverstraw had become much dilapidated, and a union was entered into with the members of the Baptist faith, there resident, for the support and repair of the church. So utterly at variance are the statements of Elder Griffiths and the Presbyterians in this matter, that necessity compels me to be prolix on the subject. The deed for the lot on which the first Presbyterian church of Haverstraw was erected, was granted by Thomas Smith to the Trustees of the English Protestant Society at Haverstraw, and bears date August 17th, 1789. When the boundary line of the Cheesecocks Patent was being run in June 1790, the church is spoken of as "now building." Finally we have the following record: "The subscribers, members of the First Presbyterian church in the Town of Haverstraw and others attached by Education and principle to the Congregation, viewing with the utmost regret the present disgraceful state of repairs in which the House of God has for a long time continued, and considering the present smallness of the Congregation, and their inability to keep the House of God in tenantable Repair and support a pastor of their own. And having always considered the Baptist and Presbyterian churches as nearly and intimately allied, differing only in principle, and in fact Sister Churches, do therefore consent and agree that the Baptist congregation of Haverstraw, of the New York Association, shall and may be permitted to repair the said house of worship, and shall have the privilege of hereafter using the house equally with the Presbyterians, Sabbath for Sabbath alternately, and all other times when the same is not occupied by the Presbyterian Congregation. March 25th, 1809."

Such is the documentary evidence in the case, and at this day we are not able to go behind this evidence. That this matter was not so understood by the Baptists at Haverstraw, will be evinced by the following extract from Elder Griffith's history, taken, doubtless, from the accounts of the members of the Baptist faith in Haverstraw, and relating the story as they understood it.

"In 1807 a liberal minded and wealthy gentleman, named Smith,"—one of the sons of the Smith who had given a lot to the Presbyterian congregation—"donated the church at Haverstraw a fine lot of ground in the centre of the village, on condition that a house of worship was erected upon it. Within two years time, after the lot was presented, they (the Baptists) had the greater part of the materials purchased and some money collected. They then injudiciously entered into an arrangement with the Presbyterians of that village to make a joint interest of the same, each to furnish one-half of the materials and to pay one-half of the expense of repairing and fitting up the old meeting house, and, when the house was completed, each congregation was to occupy it on alternate Sabbaths. The house was finished, and peace and harmony prevailed for several years, Elder Steers preaching for them (the Baptists) regularly till 1811, when he changed his field of labors to Peekskill.

The removal of many of the members to Western New York, coupled with a mortgage which the Presbyterian clergyman held on the house to secure his salary, so discouraged and disheartened the remainder, that regular meetings were not held till about the year 1815."

This finished the first Baptist Church in Haverstraw; the society had the name and the Presbyterians the edifice. Until 1847 no further effort was made by this church to build a house of worship. During the years between 1815 and 1844, the few members of the society still clung together, and, whenever it was possible, Elder Griffiths visited and ministered to them. In the last named year a fresh impetus was given to the society by the advent of the employees of Higgins' carpet factory, and the scattered members were again collected. The first meeting of the reorganized church was held in the upper part of what is now the store of Isaac De Baun, on the south side of Main street.

Rev. William Pike, a native of England, had taken charge of the congregation, and under his efforts regular meetings were held each Sabbath at private residences, till the congregation had again obtained sufficient strength to build a church edifice. In 1847 a lot was bought from George S. Allison, and a house for worship was raised. In the efforts to obtain funds for this purpose, both the Presbyterians and Methodists of Haverstraw gave efficient aid, "and the large contributions on the day of dedication of the building were mainly attributable to the appeal of the Methodist clergyman, who was present and took part in the exercises." The edifice was dedicated by Rev. John Dowling, D. D.

Elder Pike remained with the congregation a few years and then removed to the West Baptist Church, Staten Island, from which he had received a call. In 1850, the carpet factory stopped and the employees moved away. Feeling now that their place of worship was too far away from Haverstraw village, the congregation sold it to the Roman Catholics —it is still standing and used as a school-house—and purchasing another lot on the west side of Rockland street, near Broad, erected another building. Experience had not taught this congregation wisdom. A loan of $700 was made to the church by parties in New York, and the deed of the property was given to them as security. In a short time the money was demanded, and as it could not be raised, the property was sold to the Episcopal church for $1,000. Since that time no further effort has been made to re-organize this church.

THE BAPTIST CHURCHES AT VIOLA.

The original Baptist church at Masonicus, later Hempstead, now in the township of Ramapo, west of Viola, was organized, as we have seen, from the Middletown Baptist church in 1811. For several years it had no settled pastor, but divine service was held by Elder Steers and Elder Griffiths, whenever possible. About 1815, the first house for worship was erected on the site now occupied by the "Old School" church building. In the years 1820–21, a great revival took place in this church, and for eleven consecutive Sabbaths Elder Griffiths administered the rite of baptism.

In 1823, Rev. Gilbert Beebe was ordained to the ministry, and assumed pastoral charge of the church. Until 1826, Elder Beebe remained in this field of labor and then removed to Middletown, to edit a church paper. He was succeeded by Elder Evan J. Williams, during whose pastorate the Society was split asunder by unfortunate controversies between the conservative and liberal members.

In the division which followed, each faction claimed the house of worship, and at last resorted to litigation to determine the question of ownership. Neither obtained the building, for, on the eve of the trial, in 1853, it was burned and the cause of dispute thus removed.

Ere this time, Elder Williams had resigned his charge of the church, and removed to Brooklyn. Not long after his resignation, Elder Edwin Westcott visited Hempstead, assumed the pastoral charge of the church, and collected once more a portion of the scattered flock. An interest was again awakened, and under his charge a house of worship, thirty-five by fifty feet was erected on the north side of the New City road, a half mile nearer Suffern, in 1853. This society is known as the Liberal Baptist Church of Viola. Upon the resignation of this charge by Elder Westcott, the care of the church was assumed by Edwin Browe, a licentiate of the Middletown church. He remained with the congregation for some time, but was finally obliged to resign.

When the liberal portion of the old congregation became reunited, that faction which adhered to the views of Rev. Gilbert Beebe, also formed an organization, and in 1857, erected a church building on the site of the burned edifice. This society is known as the "Old School" Baptist Church of Viola. Neither of these societies now have more than a nominal existence.

THE PIERMONT BAPTIST CHURCH.

In 1817, Elder Griffiths, who was then located at Middletown, made appointments to preach at Tappan Slote, and in the following year, he held services at Piermont every Sabbath, preaching one week at Middletown in the morning, and at the Slote in the afternoon, and the next week reversing the order. Under his ministrations a congregation was collected, which at first occupied the school house. Increasing numbers soon rendered this too small an accommodation, and a house for worship was built, which was dedicated on the second Sunday in November, 1819.

This church remained an auxiliary of the Middletown church till 1839, and during this period Elder Griffiths continued pastor of both congregations. On May 15th, 1839, the communicants at Piermont were constituted an independent Baptist church, under the name of the *First Baptist Church at Piermont.*

The next day, A. M. Torbet was ordained to the ministry and assumed the pastoral care of the church, which he held till November, 1842, Following him have been: Rev. David Logan, from 1843 to 1844; Rev. Andrew Hopper, 1844 to October 1847; Rev. Charles W. Waterhouse, August, 1847, to January, 1849; Rev. G. P. Martin, August, 1849, to December, 1851; Rev. B. Slaight, from June, 1851, to 1856; Rev. W. A. Bronson, May, 1855, till his death, May 14th, 1858; Rev. Alfred Earle, till February, 1860; Rev. Benjamin Wheeler, till 1863, Rev. Robert Fisher; Rev. J. W. Taylor, from March, 14th, 1866, to May, 1867; Rev. W. I. Loomis, till August, 1868; Rev. Joshua Wood; Rev. B. Lounsbury, from January 1870 to June, 1873; Rev. James S. Carr, to 1877. Since this time the church has had no stated pastor. In 1866, during the pastorate of Rev. J. W. Taylor, the church edifice was rebuilt and enlarged.

THE NYACK BAPTIST CHURCH.

With prophetic foresight, the Father of the Baptist Church in this County, Rev. Joseph W. Griffiths, wrote in 1855: "The last, and that which will become one of the strongest interests in Rockland County, is the Baptist church at Nyack." The worthy pastor never lived to see the fulfillment of his prophecy, as he died in 1860 at the age of three score and eight years. But if we may be permitted to believe that from a happier sphere those who have gone before are cognizant of our deeds, then we may feel that his "feet hath trod the battlements of heaven, his eye hath viewed the struggles of the children of men."

As early as 1806, Elder Daniel Steers, while pastor of the Middletown chruch, preached occasionally in the school house at Nyack. When the Presbyterian Society was established in the village and was presented with a lot of ground for a church building by Peter DePew; it was stipulated by the donor, that the Baptist congregation should occupy the house of worship alternately with it. This arrangement was carried into effect and continued till Elder Steers' illness and death. From that period till 1838, little effort was made to carry on the Baptist cause in the village. In the last named year, Elders Williams, of Hempstead, Torbet of Piermont, and Griffiths of Middletown, after consultations, decided to establish a Baptist interest at Nyack, each agreeing to take his turn in the work so that regular service should be held. A room, standing on the site now occupied by Union Hall, was hired, and a fair congregation collected. For two years the labor continued, and was then abandoned because of the apprehension of the members of the Piermont church, that a society at Nyack would impair the strength of their church. From this time till the Union Hall was built in 1853, the members of this faith had no regular preaching, but met occasionally at private houses. On the opening of the Union Hall it was hired by Elder Griffiths and five others, who became personally responsible for the rent of the room and who agreed to pay a supply till the church became strong enough to take care of itself, and on February 2d, 1854, the First Baptist Church of Nyack was duly constituted with thirteen members.

For three years, the Baptist members continued to meet in Union Hall under the pastoral care of Rev. G. P. Martin, whom they had called as their first minister, and who labored with this congregation as well as that at Piermont, till December 1854, when he resigned the latter charge. Then they determined to build a house for worship. This building was completed in 1857, and on the 19th of August in that year, it was dedicated with appropriate ceremonies. On August 23d, 1857, Rev. G. P. Martin resigned, and his place was occupied by Rev. T. T. De Van, who began his pastoral duties December 2d, 1857, and remained in charge of the church till June 1862. Following him in pastoral duties have been: Rev. B. H. Benton, from November, 1862 to May 1864; Rev. F. Greaves, March 1865 to April 1867; Rev. James W. Frazer, October 1867 to March 1868; Rev. R. T. Middleditch, August 1868 to July 1869; Rev. F. Greaves, October 1869 to April 1873; Rev. N. B. Thompson, May 1873 to June 1875; Rev. J. K. Wilson, June 1876 to February 1878; Rev. J. G. Shrive, April 1878 to April 1879; Rev. J. H. Gunning, M. D., October 1879 to February 1884; and Rev. J. L. Campbell, from March 1884 to the present time.

The career of the church for the first quarter of a century of its existence, was not uncheckered by financial troubles and exhaustion, and from 1875 till 1878, it appeared as though the struggle must be abandoned. But there were members of the society steadfast in faith and good works; others joined the society and gave aid and advice; under Rev. J. H. Gunning new life was given to the struggling sect, and at last, in 1881, so greatly had the church attendance increased that further accommodations became imperative. During the summer of that year, the congregation met for worship in Voorhis Hall while the edifice was being enlarged and renovated, and on Thursday, January 12th, 1882, the new building was opened for divine service. Truly the prophecy of Elder Griffiths, written seven and twenty years before, as he drew close " to the banks of asphodel that border the River of Life," had come true. During Rev. J. H. Gunning's pastorate, 161 people were added to the church by baptism, and 23 by letter, a result only approached during Rev F. Greaves' two terms, when 91 were added by baptism and 21 by letter. Since the organization of the church 303 members have been added by baptism and 87 by letter.

THE SPRING VALLEY BAPTIST CHURCH.

On February 19th, 1867, a church meeting was held by the Nanuet Baptist Church to consider the advisability of buying the old Dutch Church building, in Spring Valley, for an outpost of the Nanuet Church. After investigation, such action was decided on, the property bought and repaired, and the edifice dedicated September 19th, 1867. From this time till July, 1870, services were held in the Spring Valley Church every Sunday afternoon by the preacher holding service at Nanuet in the morning.

As early as 1869, the members of the Spring Valley Church agitated the subject of a separate existence, but it was not till November 9th, 1870, that the society was formally organized as a distinct church. On November 20th, 1870, Rev. Wm. H. Sherman assumed charge of the society, and, a year later, added to his labors by ministering to the church at

Viola. October 3d, 1871, the Spring Valley Church was received as a member of the Southern New York Baptist Association, to which body the church reported forty-five members and a Sunday school, organized in 1868, with Matthew Persons as superintendent, having 24 teachers, 218 scholars, an average attendance of 107, and a library of 300 volumes.

In February, 1872, Rev. Wm. H. Sherman resigned this charge, and in May, 1873, he was succeeded by Rev. F. Greaves. In June of the same year Mr. Greaves resigned, and the church was left without a pastor. From this time the pulpit was supplied by Mr. E. J. Hillman, a member of the congregation. From the time the building was repaired and opened a heavy mortgage rested on the Society, and in spite of noble efforts to meet it, now, in the financial panic following 1873, crushed it. On June 20th, 1875, the last sermon in this church was preached by Mr. Hillman, and the following day the building was sold at auction. For a brief period, the members of the society clung together and then the organization passed from existence.

Authorities referred to. History of the Reformed Church at Tappan, by Rev. David Cole, D. D. Translation of the Records of the Clarkstown Church, by I. C. Haring, M. D. History of the Town of Ramapo, by Rev. E. B. Cobb, translation by A. S. Zabriskie, M. D. Magazine of American History Vol. XIII, page 39. Greenbush Church Records. Microcosm by Hon. Seth B. Cole. History of Haverstraw by Rev. A. S. Freeman, D. D. Letters and papers from Wm. Govan, M. D. History of the Baptist Church in Rockland County, by Rev. Joseph W. Griffiths. History of the Nyack Baptist Church, by George F. Morse. Lecture "30 years in Haverstraw," by A. S. Freeman, D. D.

CHAPTER XIV.

HISTORY OF THE METHODIST EPISCOPAL CHURCH IN ROCKLAND COUNTY—HISTORY OF THE METHODIST PROTESTANT CHURCH AT HAVERSTRAW AND AT STONY POINT—HISTORY OF THE ROMAN CATHOLIC CHURCH IN ROCKLAND COUNTY—HISTORY OF THE PROTESTANT EPISCOPAL CHURCH IN ROCKLAND COUNTY—HISTORY OF THE UNIVERSALIST CHURCH AT ORANGEVILLE AND NYACK—HISTORY OF THE QUAKER CHURCH AT LADENTOWN—OF THE TRUE REFORMED CHURCH AT MONSEY, AT NANUET, AND AT TAPPAN—OF CHRIST EVANGELICAL LUTHERAN AT MASONICUS—OF THE GERMAN EVANGELICAL LUTHERAN AT HAVERSTRAW - OF THE GERMAN M. E. CHURCH AT TAPPAN—HISTORY OF THE CONGREGATIONAL CHURCH AT MONSEY, AND AT TALLMANS—OF THE M. E. ZION AT NYACK AND AT HAVERSTRAW—OF THE SYNAGOGUE AT NYACK - HISTORY OF THE UNION, STONE CHURCH OR UPPER NYACK, WAYSIDE CHAPEL, LAKE AVENUE BAPTIST, WEST NYACK CHAPEL, AND STEVENS SUNDAY SCHOOLS—HISTORY OF THE ROCKLAND COUNTY SABBATH SCHOOL ASSOCIATION.

And now there came into this County a new religious movement, which was destined to spread and grow in spite of hardship, and obloquy, and detraction, because of its enthusiasm and democratic teachings. Two score years had passed since John Wesley, rejecting that conception which regarded faith as the union of intellectual belief and of voluntary self-submission, a conception from which the element of the supernatural was wanting, as well as that of personal trust for salvation on the atonement of Jesus; had accepted the teachings of a "present, free and full salvation." But three decades had gone by since the followers of Wesley had erected their first house of worship in New York City; and but fourteen years had elapsed since the first Bishop of the Methodist Church in America—Rev. Francis Asbury, had been consecrated at Baltimore, when exhorters from that society entered our County.

With the causes which led to the formation of the sect, with the polemical discussions that it has given rise to, I am not to speak. With the reasons for its growth in this County, with the different church organizations which have sprung up in our villages and towns, it is alone my duty to deal.

Methodism is aggressive with an enthusiasm born of its youth and its teachings, that each individual is a personal and special factor in the care of divine providence. By psychologic change, which each convert claims to experience, the neophyte feels that he has entered a state of beatitude, that he has been, as expressed in the denomination, "born again." By the teaching that without constant religious struggle he will fall from grace, his religious life becomes a fervid effort to remain steadfast in the faith. By the government of his church, he is placed in contact with others as earnest as himself, and in the class meetings a form of open religious confessional, the prayer meeting, and the love feast, encouraged and strengthened by religious association, his enthusiasm grows more intense.

In this idea of a new birth, this psychologic and supernatural change, lies the strength of the Methodist church. The new convert, regenerated and sanctified, at once feels that his fellow man, unless a Methodist, has not experienced the transition, and he at once sets to work to bring him within the pale of the church. Each convert becomes a priest with a vital mission. A human being, whatever the race, sex or social standing, becomes a tremendous factor in such a creed—an immortal soul to be saved.

As can readily be seen, the teaching of this doctrine is essentially democratic. No matter what the social or intellectual status of an individual—the beggar in his squalor and rags; Lazarus in luxury and riches; the laborer living by the sweat of his brow, or the potentate wielding all but despotic power: all, all alike, must return to dust in the body, while before the inexorable Judge, their souls must answer at the day of judgment for deeds done here.

Members of this denomination came to Rockland County. It is not positive when or where they first began their labors, for at every hamlet they seemed to arise spontaneously. The first society of the sect was formed at Haverstraw before 1799, but already they had converts in this section. With customary enthusiasm they entered on their mission. The sturdy landholder, still bearing in his disposition the phlegm of his Dutch ancestry, was startled from his mental repose by the earnest exhortation of his whilom guest, and left sorely perplexed in mind at the utterances he had listened to. The laborer in the quarries was surprised at his noonday meal by the religious conversation of his fellow-toiler. In the workshops and factories at the Ramapo Clove, the creed advanced, and discussion led to curiosity, curiosity to observation, observation to conversion.

Nor did these all but fanatics confine their journeys to the haunts of civilization; they penetrated the mountain fastnesses and the grimy, unkempt charcoal burner was surprised by the appearance of a stranger at his fire-heap, who grasped his hand, who called him "brother," who entreated him to seek salvation; the long-neglected dweller among the inhospitable rocks was filled with wonderment at finding some one from the unknown, outside world in his presence, telling him, that in the ages gone by a fellow man had died for him and urging him to repent and be saved.

At first looked upon as fanatics and treated with contempt and ridicule, the very lives and deeds of the acceptors of the Methodist faith at last encouraged respect and then belief. The itinerant ministers who visited the County in early days, were seen riding through the blinding heat and dust of summer, the bitter blasts and snows of winter, or facing the driving rainstorm, often thinly clad and scarcely protected, to meet a scant gathering of believers at the end of their journey, without a murmur, and yet oftentimes, these journeys covered over a score of miles before morning service, and a score more before the evening sermon. The various meetings of the church, which perhaps had been visited by outsiders in a spirit of levity, produced a very different feeling, when some ignorant and illiterate convert, filled with holy zeal, told in uncouth language, mayhap, the story of his trials with tear-stained cheeks and a fervor born of inspiration. And when to these things, this despised sect added the spirit of their Master's teachings, visited the highways and the by-ways, extended a helping, strengthening hand to the outcasts and pariahs of society, made them self-respecting and respected citizens, and sent them forth with their new experience to add others to the fold; even the most skeptical mind drew back abashed and acknowledged the great benefit of the movement.

The first Methodist Church Society, as has been said, was organized in Haverstraw, in the closing years of the eighteenth century. In 1799, this Society contained eighty members and in 1800, their first house for worship was erected on land given by the same family (Smith) who had previously given to the Presbyterians and later gave to the Baptists, lots for their church buildings. The first religious services of the sect held here were conducted by Barney Matthias, an exhorter and local preacher, who was a ship carpenter by trade. I have been told by old people, who had heard Mr. Matthias exhort in the old school house at Nyack, that he was rarely gifted with vocal power and that, when he became intensely earnest, his voice could be heard a mile and a half away. This statement lacks authentic confirmation, and was made by people, not members of the Methodist Church, who I fear were prejudiced.

The first regular minister at this church was Rev. William Vreedenburgh, in 1805, and the first minister, who made his home in the village, was Rev. James MacLaurins in 1829. By 1840, the church edifice had become too small for the congregation, and a new building thirty by fifty-four feet was erected. This house was dedicated December 16th, 1840. The old church building was sold to Phineas Hedges, and is still standing, in use as a barn, on the north side of the road beyond Thiell's Corners.

By 1860, the new church was also found to be too small, and the building was enlarged. At this time an organ was introduced into the church, which so outraged the ideas of simplicity of a worthy member—Jonathan Wood—that he left the house in disgust. As the ameliorating influence of time was felt, Mr. Wood became reconciled to the innovation, and was at last, after a long life of good works, laid at rest, his grave being marked by a plain tombstone. This was broken by a team of runaway horses, and replaced by a new one. When the new organ was placed in the church, weights were needed for the bellows, and the two portions of Mr. Wood's broken tombstone were employed for the purpose. O! Si sic omnia.

In the history of this church occurred one of those odd events of which many belong to our County history. The doctrines of Methodism had spread rapidly and been accepted by the people with eagerness. Societies had been formed at Nyack, Sherwoodville, Palisades, Stony Point, and other places in the County, and the topic of the growth of the sect was uppermost among the residents. With any but a friendly eye had this development been viewed by the pastors of the older churches—one of these is said to have greeted its appearance by a sermon from the text: "These men, who have turned the world upside down, have come hither also," and none perhaps viewed it with more annoyance than Rev. Samuel Pelton, whose charge was the first invaded. At last, no other means of showing its supposed falsity appearing, Mr. Pelton challenged the minister of the faith at Haverstraw to a public debate. This was declined, but Rev. Lawrence Kean, of New York, happening to be at Haverstraw, accepted the wager of battle. The debate took place April 2d, 1821. Preparations were made by the erection of a platform before the Methodist house of worship, and the choice of three persons as moderators and of four to take notes.

A large number of people, many drawn by interest in one or the other parties, more by idle curiosity, attended, and at ten o'clock in the morning the debate began. From ten till twelve, and from two to four o'clock, these disputants met in polemic strife. At the close of the discussion neither was satisfied, and each thought of what he might have said. From speech, Rev. Samuel Pelton resorted to the pen, and published a work entitled *Absurdities of Methodism.* This was answered by Mr. Kean by a work called: *A Plain and Positive Refutation of the Rev. Samuel Pelton's Unjust and Unfounded Charges Entitled, " The Absurdities of Methodism." Containing, First: A Public Debate held at Haverstraw, Rockland County, N. Y.; Second: Remarks on the Several Articles Debated; Third: The Perfect Conformity of the Methodist Doctrine, and Discipline to Scripture, Reason and Common Sense.* J. & J. Harper, 1823.

In following the history of this church, I must be governed in chronology, not by the date of the Societies' organization, but by the date of the erection of their church edifice. Next in this arrangement comes the

METHODIST EPISCOPAL CHURCH AT NYACK.

As early as 1806, the teachings of the Methodist church were introduced into Nyack, and meetings alternating with those of the Baptists, were held in the school house, then just built, by Barney Matthias and Rev. George Banghart, who was called the "singing preacher." The organization of a church society, and the erection of a house of worship by that denomination however, did not occur till 1813, and was then brought about by the obtuseness of the classis of the Reformed Dutch Church. In 1812, members of the Clarkstown church presented a petition for the establishment of a branch of that church at Nyack, setting forth as their reasons: that Nyack was strong enough to support a church; that on account of the distance between the hamlets, many were unable to attend divine service; that if the opportunity was not seized, other sects would build at Nyack. The classis refused to grant the petition.

Immediately after this decision, a portion of the petitioners, William Palmer, Nicholas Williamson and John Green, met at the house of the last named gentleman, organized a meeting by the election of the proper officers, and passed resolutions to organize a Methodist Episcopal Church in Nyack, and to begin the erection of a house for worship on the following day.

In aid of the work, William Palmer gave the ground and stone from his quarries, and John Green and Nicholas Williamson gave money in the proportion of $1 of the former to $2 of the latter; Garret Onderdonk also gave financial aid. In 1813, the building begun with such laconic brevity was opened to the public as the First M. E. Church, of Nyack.

When first used, the pulpit, a high, square box, entered through a door, stood against the north wall of the church six steps high; the altar-rail was three feet high and rested on upright slats set close together. This gave it somewhat the appearance of a picket fence; the seats were straight-backed and hard, not furnished with doors. Across the south end of the church extended a heavy gallery. For heating purposes a cast iron stove was used. For light, dependence was placed on one copper oil lamp, suspended from the centre of the ceiling, and some half dozen quaintly-shaped tin candle-holders. The Bible was bought with money raised by subscription, and on the fly-leaf is the following: " This Bible was procured by Joseph Bennet for the use of the Nyack Meeting House of Methodist E. Church, A. D., 1814." Then follows the following names of contributors: Rev. J. Bennet, $3.00; Rev. Michael Swing, 25 cents; Rev. Benjamin Sherwood, 12 cents; Mr. Joart, N. Y., 25 cents; Mr. Peter Bourdett, N. Y., 25 cents; Mr. Barnas DeKline, 19 cents; Mrs. Hester Ackerman, 19 cents; Mrs. Abigal Gurnee, 25 cents; Rev. Abram Gurnee, 25 cents; Mr. James Cunningham, 50 cents; Mr. John Ten Eyck, 12 cents; Mr. Garret Onderdonk, 25 cents; Mr. Benjamin Bourdett, 25 cents. The Bible is still in use in the Sunday-school.

For many years the pulpit of this church was supplied either by local preachers or circuit riders. Then, under the preaching of Rev. Benjamin Day, a series of revival meetings were held in a building which stood on the site of the present Union Hall, and many were added to the faith. The old church building was now felt to be too far from the village, which had grown up since its erection, and an effort was made to sell it and build a new house more central. Through the efforts of Garret Williamson and Jacob Voorhis, this attempt was defeated by a majority of two votes. Once again, in 1877, when an attempt was made to erect a new church edifice in Nyack, the sale of the old stone church was discussed, but defenders of the land-mark still existed and the attempt was frustrated.

In 1870, the building was sadly out of repair. By the efforts of George Green sufficient money was raised to put on a new roof and place it in thorough order. Many changes were made in its interior, better fitting the present time. Sunday school and other religious services are regularly held in the building.

THE SECOND M. E. OR ST. PAUL'S CHURCH.

Though out of the proper order in date of erection, it seems wiser to mention this church in this place and thus avoid confusion.

Upon the defeat of the attempt to sell the old house of worship, the members at once began efforts to erect a new building. Ground was bought and a frame building put up in 1843.

In a few years the building was found too small for the increased attendance, and an addition was made upon the east end of it. No further change was attempted till 1877, when a lot was bought on Broadway, south of the Universalist Church, and the construction of a new building begun. Further than the foundation this never advanced. Financial troubles fell thick and fast on the church, and under the weight of calamities, the society was dissolved, their property foreclosed upon, and St. Paul's Society organized. As a business move this procedure relieved the Methodists from a judgment. As a movement of a religious society, its ethical advisability was doubtful. After this failure the frame building was repaired and renovated, and is still in use by the church.

WESLEY CHAPEL, SHERWOODVILLE.

The origin of the Methodist Society at this place dates back to 1805. Already I have gone into the subject of the spread of this sect, with sufficient fullness and further mention is unnecessary. One of the first meetings of the denomination was held in the old stone house, near the chapel, now owned by E. G. Sherwood. Later services were held at the houses of Stephen Gurnee, William Osborn and Benjamin Sherwood, till 1813, when Rev. James Sherwood and Abigal Gurnee, purchased the property, on which stands the stone house above mentioned, and after that, services were held there.

In the early days of the society, preaching took place every other week, during the afternoons in summer, and evenings in winter, till the chapel was built. During this period, it was not rare for the quarterly meetings, which were largely attended, to be held in an old Dutch barn, standing near the house, owing to the necessity for more room than the house afforded.

At length, through the efforts of James Sherwood, Garret Onderdonk, Benjamin Odell, Stephen B. Johnson, Mrs. Abigal Gurnee and her daughter; sufficient money was obtained to begin the building of a house for worship on land given by James Sherwood. He also, with others, furnished timber for the frame and Hon. J. H. Pierson, gave the nails. When the building was enclosed more money was needed, and Rev. James Sherwood, walked to New York, soliciting donations on the way to and in that city from all friends of the enterprise. Success greeted his endeavors, and in September 1829, this edifice was dedicated to the worship of God by Rev. George Banghart, Presiding Elder.

Until 1834 or '35, the primitive seats, made by taking poles, putting legs in them after the manner of a saw-horse, and laying loose planks across them, remained, then, through the efforts of the present Mrs. Hollis Holman and Mrs. H. A. Blauvelt, sufficient money was raised to seat their side of the house. Their example was shortly after followed by the men.

In 1856, a split occurred in the congregation of this church on the question of building a new house of worship nearer Mechanicsville, now Viola, and a portion of the congregation withdrew. Those that remained re-roofed and sided the building and painted it. In 1875, the interior of the church was improved by taking out the old gallery, putting in new seats and pulpit, frescoing the walls, carpeting the floor and making two aisles instead of one.

THE METHODIST CHURCH OF PALISADES.

Before 1810, the teachings of Methodism were introduced at Tappan Slote and services were held in the old schoolhouse. In the course of time, Moses Taylor established his residence at the present Palisades, and in 1820, a class was formed. As the society grew stronger, the project of building a house for worship was considered, and, largely through the efforts of Mr. Taylor and his wife, this project was accomplished, and the building dedicated in 1832.

By 1858, the need of a larger building became apparent, and the congregation set themselves to the work. In the summer of 1858, the corner stone of the new building was laid, and on May 15th, 1859, the new edifice was dedicated by Bishop James. The old church building is still standing. A flourishing Sabbath School in connection with the church exists.

THE METHODIST EPISCOPAL CHURCH AT STONY POINT.

Shortly after the Methodist sect became established in our County, preachers of the denomination visited Stony Point and in 1804, began to hold religious services in private houses. At length this congregation grew strong enough to erect a house for worship and, land having been given for the purpose by Matthew Gurnee and his wife, work was begun. By June 14th, 1834, the building was completed and dedicated. The first edifice stood on the site of the present church. In the course of time this first house became too small for the increasing congregation, and it became necessary to enlarge it. Finally, in 1882, the church was entirely rebuilt.

THE METHODIST CHURCH AT ROCKLAND LAKE.

Here, as elsewhere in the County, the Methodist circuit riders early started meetings of their society, holding services in the private houses of those who had accepted their views. In 1834, Benedict Wells and his wife Bridget, gave the society a plot of ground for a church building, and in the following year, 1835, the first edifice was erected. For some years, this building was sufficiently large for the congregation, but at last, the growth of the ice business so increased the population of Rockland Lake, and thus the church attendance, that further accommodation became necessary. Efforts were successfully put forth to obtain the needed money, and the present edifice was erected and dedicated.

THE SLOATSBURG METHODIST CHURCH.

Johnsontown was one of the first hamlets visited by the Methodist circuit preachers, and in their journeys to and from that place through the Ramapo Clove, they frequently held service in the old stone school house, which stood on the Orange Turnpike, in the village of Ramapo Works. These services began as early as 1802. At a later period, services were held in the Smith house, and still later, at the house of John Becraft.

In 1837, Jacob Sloat and his wife gave the property on which the church now stands to the society, and the erection of a house for worship was begun. By 1843, the building was finished, and in the same year it was dedicated. In 1860, this church, which had formerly, with the other churches of the same denomination in the town, belonged to the Newark Conference, became part of the New York Conference. A Sabbath school is connected with the church.

THE METHODIST CHURCH AT NEW CITY.

The early meetings of the Methodists at this place were held for a time in a wheelwright's shop, and later, at a private residence. By 1845, the congregation had grown sufficiently strong to erect a house for worship, and in March, 1846, the building was dedicated. A Sabbath school has been connected with the church since its organization, and at the present time has an average attendance of about five and twenty scholars.

THE PIERMONT M. E. CHURCH.

As seen when speaking of the Palisades M. E. Church, services at Tappan Slote were held by itinerant ministers of this denomination before 1810. The organization of the Society at the present Palisades, drew the members of the faith to that place, and it was not till 1854, that we find positive mention of a distinct Methodist society at Piermont. For some time this organization met for worship in Odd Fellows' Hall. At length the congregation grew strong enough to warrant the erection of a house of worship, and in 1856 the present edifice was built, being ready for use January 10, 1857. This society, as a rule, has been connected with a circuit in which were the church at Palisades and the society at Tappan.

It has met with the reverse of having its membership largely reduced by the removal of inhabitants from Piermont on the withdrawal of the railroad shops.

THE TAPPAN M. E. CHURCH.

It was not till 1854, that an attempt was made to build up a society of this church at Tappan. Then some of the members and the minister of the Piermont society visited the hamlet and held divine service on Sunday afternoons at the homes of different members of that faith. At length, in 1856, thinking the time opportune, this new-formed church society bought the edifice, which had been built in 1826, for the True Reformed Church Society. Until 1866, the congregation of this church was under the charge, first of the minister of the Piermont church, and later of Piermont and Palisades. Then the edifice was purchased by the congregation of the German M. E. Church Society.

THE GERMAN M. E. CHURCH AT TAPPAN.

This society was incorporated by Christian Kern on July 25th, 1866, and purchased the edifice then owned by the M. E. Church Society. Since that time the society has continued in existence, and has met with varying success, never being very strong.

THE METHODIST CHURCH AT VIOLA.

When speaking of the Wesley Chapel, it was mentioned that a split occurred in the congregation of that society, and that a portion, who favored the building of a new church withdrew to Mechanicsville and organized a separate society in 1856. Proceeding at once to carry out their idea, the construction of a church edifice was begun and the building was completed, and on December 25th, 1856, dedicated by Bishop Wiley. Since that time services have been regularly maintained.

THE SPRING VALLEY M. E. CHURCH.

The birth of this village is of such recent date as to preclude a long existence for any church organization. It was not till 1853, that a thorough effort was made to hold divine service at the nascent hamlet according to the doctrines of the M. E. Church. In the summer of that year Rev. George Jackson, then in charge of the New City Church, began holding church services in the Union Sunday School building, which had been erected in 1852.

On August 4th, 1859, a church society was organized, and at the same time the present site was bought from the Spring Valley Land Association. Work was at once begun upon a church building, and in the spring of 1860, the completed edifice was dedicated. At first this society was connected with that at Mechanicsville—now Viola—but in 1861, it began a separate existence, unbroken, save by an association of two years with the Middletown Church. A Sunday School early organized is now in a strong condition.

THE METHODIST CHURCH AT LADENTOWN.

At just what date ministers of the Methodist Church first began to hold religious services at Ladentown, has escaped my search, but by 1825, this locality was included in their circuits. It was many years ere a permanent society strong enough to erect a church building could be formed. At last however, in 1865, a house for worship was built on land given for the purpose by John J. Secor, and the church society incorporated. No idea can be formed of the great work this church has accomplished, by the size of the present membership. For years it has been laboring to spread religious teachings among the residents in the Ladentown Mountains with results both encouraging and gratifying. A Sunday School, now connected with the church, was organized in 1862.

THE METHODIST EPISCOPAL CHURCH AT MIDDLETOWN.

This church society was organized by the Rev. Nicholas Vansant, the then Presiding Elder of the district, June 25th, 1865. For the first year, after its organization, the services of the society were held in the building belonging to the Independent Baptist Church Society. In 1866, the congregation failed to obtain a renewal of their lease, and from May, till the middle of November, services were held in L. A. Leache's barn. In November the society leased the old Baptist church building, and in the following year, 1867, purchased it. Since that date, services have been regularly held in the church, and the society has slowly increased in numbers. A Sabbath School was organized in connection with the church in 1866.

THE SUFFERN M. E. CHURCH.

This church society was organized October 28th, 1867, through the efforts of Rev. A. H. Brown of the church at Viola. Services were at first held in the house of James Norris, which formed part of the store occupied by A. Traphagen, and later, in the school house of District No. 3. In 1868, a site for a building was obtained by purchase from William D. Maltbie and wife, and in July 1869, work upon the present edifice was begun. On September 11th, 1870, the completed building was dedicated and by January 1884, through the persistent efforts of Rev. A. J. Conklin, the church was cleared of debt.

At first this society was associated with the church at Viola in the support of a minister, later with the church at Monsey, and later still with Wesley Chapel and Ladentown. In 1884, however, it became a separate station. A Sunday School, organized in the early days of the church still exists.

THE METHODIST CHURCH AT MONSEY.

This society was organized in October 1871, by members from the Spring Valley and Viola Methodist Churches. Services were first held at the house of J. J. Hogan, and afterward, till the building of a house for worship, in the loft of a blacksmith shop. Work upon a church edifice was at once begun, a site having been donated by H. P. Dexter and wife, and in July 1873, the completed building was dedicated. This church is at present associated with those of Saddle River and Mount Vail. A Sunday School was organized shortly after the formation of the society. It is now a part of the union school held in the village.

THE M. E. CHURCH AT THIELL'S.

This society was formed and a house for worship erected before 1850. At first the pulpit was supplied in conjunction with that at Stony Point, which was then known as the North Haverstraw Church. In 1872, this union was dissolved and the church at Thiell's, which was then officially known as the West Haverstraw Church, was joined to that at Garnerville. In 1872, the parsonage at Thiell's was built.

THE M. E. CHURCH AT STAGG'S CORNERS.

This building was erected about 1865, and has since been regularly open for service. It is a circuit church. A strong Sabbath school has long been in existence in this neigborhood.

THE MOUNTVILLE M. E. CHURCH.

As we have seen when speaking of the Presbyterian Societies, John Beverige donated the edifice he had erected at this spot to the mountain residents, who used the building as a Methodist Church. Service is regularly held at this place on Sunday afternoons by the minister, who supplies the Johnsontown and Caldwell Point Societies.

THE M. E. CHURCH AT GARNERVILLE.

This society was organized at a meeting held in the school house at Mead's Corners, June 10th, 1872. The corner stone of the church edifice was laid September 8th, 1872, and the completed structure was dedicated June 27th, 1873. It is the only church building now standing in Garnerville, and is but a short distance from the site of the first church building north of the mountain.

THE M. E. CHURCH AT CALDWELL'S POINT.

This tiny chapel was erected by the Methodists of this neighborhood in 1883 It stands beside the Episcopal chapel, almost at the end of the Point, and under the very shadow of Donderberg. It is a circuit church, being supplied with Johnsontown and Doodletown.

THE METHODIST PROTESTANT CHURCH AT HAVERSTRAW.

As is too often the case in church as well as other societies, trouble arose between the members of the M. E. Society at Haverstraw and led to schism.

Under the circumstances, it was felt that the congregation of the church could no longer abide in harmony, and a portion of it seceded, formed a separate organization under the name of the Associated Methodist Church, on June 15th, 1831, and began efforts to obtain a house for worship.

A lot was purchased from Samson Marks and wife, and a church building erected in 1831. On September 20th in that year, this society was formally incorporated. The organization was never one of great strength, and when, under the soothing influence of time, the causes which had led to irritation and schism had been removed, the society gradually passed from existence, and on November 26th, 1867, the building and lot were sold to the German Evangelical Church.

THE METHODIST PROTESTANT CHURCH AT TOMKINS COVE.

For some years, preceding the stationing of the first clergyman of this branch of the Methodist church at Tomkins' Cove, this section of the County had been in a circuit, and preaching had been held at the Cove once in every month. In March, 1841, Rev. T. K. Witsel was stationed at Tomkins' Cove and services were held in a building furnished by the Lime Company. In 1853, a lot of land was given by Calvin Tomkins & Company as a site for the church buildings of the Methodist Protestant Society, and on this the erection of a house for worship was begun, at the instigation of Calvin Tomkins through whose aid it was finished, which was dedicated in 1854. This society has maintained a strong existence, and at the present time has a large membership.

THE ROMAN CATHOLIC CHURCH IN ROCKLAND COUNTY.

In 1832, John Dubois, Bishop of the French Roman Catholic Church in New York, bought of the heirs of William Perry, the property extending between the present south line of Joseph Hilton, the north line of Mrs. Nellie Hart, the Hudson River and the top of the mountain, and now owned by A. J. Smith, George Green, Rudolph Lexow, Owen and Draper and the heirs of Joshua Brush, containing in all 162 acres; for the purpose of erecting thereon a seminary building for the education of priests and a church for the propagation of his faith.

With the power of hind-sight, it is easy for us to see how ill-timed this movement was, nor would it have been difficult for the worthy Bishop to have discerned the feeling he would create, had he been at all conversant with our County's history. If that history shows any one thing more than another, it is, that up to within a few years our people have been unusually conservative. Children of neighbors have grown up, have intermarried, have settled down in business in the County, through generation after generation, till the genealogist will find almost all the old family names interwoven by ties of relationship. Our educational facilities, good or bad, have not been embraced as they should have been; opinion, formed on a narrow knowledge of the subject under question, has prevented research; tradition has been all prevalent as historical truth.

He who has read thus far will recall that the first settlers were Dutchmen, with whom were associated a few Huguenots, who, escaping the persecution which followed the revocation of the Edict of Nantes in 1685, by flight into Holland, had joined their protectors in the immigration to the new world. What the people of Holland had suffered, for the sake of their religious belief, is known to all readers. In the close communion of neighborhood and marriage in this new home, the experience that too many of the immigrants had passed through was still fresh in their minds. Tales of homes abandoned in the night. Of secret flight from the lands, long family possessions, to the charity of strangers. Of sudden change from affluence to poverty, from a position of hospitality to wandering vagrants. And these things, not because of civil or moral crime, but because of a demand to use that mind with which God had endowed them, as they saw fit.

Through generation after generation these family traditions had been transmitted until the descendants of the original sufferers grew to look upon the Roman Catholic Church as the abomination of abominations, the veritable Scarlet Woman ; upon the Pope as Anti-Christ. Nor was this all. In the center of the County dwelt the offspring of the English and Scotch settlers, who had founded the "English Church." Of the former, a majority were descendants of those stern Puritans, who had landed on the inhospitable shores of Massachusetts, whose children had migrated to Connecticut, and whose grand-children had crossed to Long Island, from whence, in due course of time, their progeny had come to our County. Of the latter, a majority were fresh from vivid tales of the multiple conflicts of sects, which so long agitated and annoyed their native land. Much as the stern Puritan and Scot might despise all religious beliefs, except his own, he could still tolerate their presence. But the Church of Rome he hated beyond conception, and, while that hatred may have grown less in his children, it was by no means banished. It was in such a field that Bishop Dubois, in 1832, began the endeavor to establish his church.

But this was not the only error in his judgment in this matter. He had based his idea of the need of a church in the County on the rapid development of the quarry business at Nyack and the consequent influx of laborers to the place. Here, also, he was at fault. The proprietors of the quarries were opposed to the Roman Catholic belief, and many of them were members of the Protestant societies then existing in the village. The majority of laborers were natives, who, if they belonged to no denomination, dreaded the entering church and sided against it. And, as if to make matters worse, the Methodist congregation had their place of worship but a short distance from the proposed new school.

Despite these conditions, the Bishop began his labor. In the fall of 1832 his purchase was completed and the following year ground was broken and work upon the seminary building begun, with a Mr. McCool as the master mason and Mr. Marsh the contracting carpenter. Both of these gentlemen were from Newburgh. At first the supervision of this work was in charge of Father McGeary, but ere the building was completed, he was superceded by Father Marshall.

From a map of the property drawn for "Milord, the Bishop of the Church French at New York, October, 1832," I learn that on the property now owned by George Green, in Upper Nyack, stood an old house with farm outbuildings, and in this house, which stood north of Green's present residence and nearer Broadway, was held the first church service of the Roman Catholic Society ever performed in our County. In this house, also, was opened a school under the auspices of the pastor in charge of the parish. That pastor was Hugh McCloskey; later, first Cardinal of the Church in America.

For five years, work on the seminary building was continued, and in 1838, there stood upon a site still marked by the ruins, midway between the present Midland Avenue and Broadway, just south of Lexow Avenue, on the property of George Green, a three-story brown stone structure, eighty feet long, and forty feet deep, composed of a central building and two wings, with vaulted slate roof. The stone for this structure had been obtained from a quarry on the property, the lumber bought from a firm of which the present owner of the property was a member. When the building had approached thus near completion, and it but remained to finish and fit the joinery, a fire broke out in the south wing, and the building was totally destroyed.

So bitter had been the feeling against this institution, and so apparent was the joy of the residents at this termination of the work—it is said that cheers were heard when the roof fell in—that every excuse can be found for the belief, which obtained at the time among the members of this church, that the fire was of incendiary origin. In 1878, I had occasion to thoroughly investigate the matter, and in the intervening years have consulted many people, both Protestants and Catholics, who were either engaged in the work, in one or other capacity, or present at the fire. The account I gave in 1878, has been thoroughly corroborated, and I repeat it verbatim. One day at noon, one of the mechanics had taken the inside box out of his glue pot and was boiling eggs for his dinner in the shell pot; he had started a fire in one of the rooms of the south wing; over the floor of this room was a litter of shavings from six inches to a foot in depth, and piled against the wall were a number of doors and window sashes; for some reason the mechanic left the room for a few moments; upon his return he found that the fire had spread and was rapidly running through the mass of dry shavings. Without calling for help he seized one of the doors lying on the pile and threw it on the fire, intending to smother it. As might be imagined, the effect was disasterous, for the current of air caused by the falling door scattered the burning shavings all over the room; in an instant more, the whole room was ablaze, and before help could arrive the building was doomed.

After the fire the walls of the building were found cracked and warped, and the expense of reconstruction, together with the bitter feeling against the sect, led Bishop Dubois to decline to rebuild. The walls were taken down and the stones removed to Brooklyn, but I cannot learn that they were ever used in any other church institution.

Thus ended all attempts to organize a society of the Roman Catholic Church in our County for a decade, and twenty-nine years passed before the service of that faith was again held in a church edifice at Nyack.

THE ROMAN CATHOLIC CHURCH AT HAVERSTRAW—ST. PETERS.

In 1843, an old stone house, standing on the road north of the first Presbyterian Church, and formerly belonging to Joseph Allison, was occupied by Patrick Riley, and in it was celebrated the first mass in Haverstraw. Father Volamus was the first priest who officiated. Until the opening of their own church for service on Sunday, November 14th, 1847, the Catholics at Haverstraw attended service at Verplanck's Point. At length, when strong enough, four lots situated on the west side of Ridge street, were purchased from George S. Allison, and the erection of a church building was begun. In 1849, the completed structure was dedicated by Bishop Hughes.

This first structure was used by its congregation till the increased demands made by the rapidly enlarging church attendance led to the erection of the present church edifice. The parish was at first under the charge of Father Hacket, who officiated at Verplanck's Point, and after him for a short time came Father Maguire. The first settled pastor was Rev. Francis McKeone, who was given spiritual charge of all the Catholics in the County in 1848, and remained pastor of this church till 1852. Following him have been: Rev. Terence Scullen; Rev. Patrick Mahony, who served a long pastorate of three or four and twenty years, and the present incumbent, Rev. Henry T. Baxter.

THE ROMAN CATHOLIC CHURCH AT PIERMONT—ST. JOHNS.

Through the efforts of Father McKeone, a congregation of this denomination was gathered at Piermont, which met at the present Odd Fellows' Hall. Attention was at once given to the erection of a church edifice, and land was obtained on the north side of the creek, nearly opposite the present church building of the Reformed (Dutch) Church Society. Work was begun on the structure in the summer of 1851, and on January 1st, 1852, the first mass was celebrated in the new building.

On July 1st, 1852, Rev. John Quinn was appointed pastor of Piermont, then created a separate parish, which included beside the Catholics of Piermont, those of the rest of the County, south of Haverstraw. For nine years, this church building proved sufficient to meet the wants of its congregation. But the distance from Nyack made it a labor for members of the congregation there resident, to attend service, and the increase of church members, brought about by the location of the Erie Railroad shops at this spot necessitated the erection of a larger building. Accordingly, with an eye to the needs of the members from Nyack as well as Piermont, the site of the present edifice was purchased, and the work of construction was begun in 1860. When the building was raised and ready for the roof, a terrific storm fell upon this section, and the walls of the structure were almost completely demolished.

In spite of this depressing blow, the courage of the congregation was not lost. Work was resumed upon the building, and on August 13th, 1861, mass was celebrated in the new house. In 1859, the present parochial school was built for the care of the children of the congregation. For twenty-three and a half years did Father Quinn labor among this people, and under his pastorate and through his efforts were the churches at Nyack, Suffern and Spring Valley organized and built, and that at Blauveltville aided. On December 24th, 1875, this worthy priest died. His successor was Rev. William L. Penny, who remained pastor of the church till 1885. Among the assistant priests of the parish have been: Rev. Christopher Farrell, Rev. John Fitzharris, Rev. Henry J. Gordon, and, at present, Rev. Patrick J. O'Meara.

CHURCH OF THE IMMACULATE CONCEPTION.

The rapid development of the brick industry along the river shore north to Caldwell's Point, drew to the present township of Stony Point many members of the Roman Catholic Church. For their accommodation a church edifice was determined on and that of the Immaculate Conception near Tompkins cove—at the former Blauvelt's Four Corners—was built in 1860 and consecrated two years later. Until June 1885, this church was under the pastoral charge of Rev. Henry Baxter, then it was made a separate parish under the care of Rev. Joseph Brennan.

About 1865, the Roman Catholics bought property for a church building at Rockland Lake. As yet this congregation has not grown strong enough to build. It is under the pastoral care of Rev. Henry Baxter, and the rites of the church are administered once a month at the residence of Timothy McClafferty.

THE ROMAN CATHOLIC CHURCH AT NYACK—ST. ANNS.

The long and often unpleasant trips which they had to make, if they wished to attend service, had led to many complaints by the Catholics at Nyack, and it was to relieve them, as we have seen, that the new church at Piermont was built so far north. But by 1867, when their number had increased, the Nyack congregation felt the necessity of a house for worship in their village.

For two years before the erection of a church building, this congregation met for worship in a building, which stood on the corner of Main and Orchard Streets. At length, the site of the present edifice on Jefferson street was purchased, and work upon the church was begun in 1869. The building was completed and opened the same year. Since its completion the church has had added to it, a gallery, a new vestry room, and a new altar. It is now a separate parish under the charge of Rev. William L. Penny.

THE ROMAN CATHOLIC CHURCH AT SUFFERN—ST. ROSE OF LIMA.

Previous to 1868, the Catholics of Suffern could only attend service by a long journey to either Paterson, N. J., Greenwood, in Orange County, or Piermont, save that occasionally Rev. John Quinn held service at the house of William Cannon. At length in 1868, a site for the present edifice was given by George W. Suffern and the church building erected. The first pastor of this church was Rev. John Brogan who was succeeded in 1870, by the present pastor, Rev. James Quinn.

THE ROMAN CATHOLIC CHURCH AT BLAUVELTVILLE—ST. CATHERINES

As early as 1853, a colony of Germans was established at Blauveltville to which, as the years passed, constant accessions were made. Most of these new comers were worshippers according to the Roman Catholic faith, and the distance from the church at Piermont together with their slight acquaintance with the English language, led them to determine first, on a church in their midst and next, on a church in which service should be held in their native tongue. By 1868, this society felt strong enough to begin the building of a house for worship. Four acres of land was donated for church purposes by George M. Lediger, and on January 17th, 1869, the completed edifice, a building thirty by sixty-five feet, was dedicated.

Until 1870, the pulpit of the church was supplied from St. Nicholas in New York, then Rev. Joseph Bruhy became pastor, and remained in charge of the congregation till his death, May 1st, 1874. From August 1874 to October 1876, Rev. Emil Stenzel was pastor. After his resignation, the congregation was cared for by Rev. W. L. Penny and Rev. P. J. O'Meara for some time. From February 1877 to March 1879, Rev. Nicholas Sorg was pastor, and he was succeeded by the present pastor, Rev M. Kuhnen. During the charge of Rev. Joseph Bruhy a parochial school was commenced under the supervision of A. Germersdorf. The pastoral residence was built in 1872.

THE ROMAN CATHOLIC CHURCH AT SPRING VALLEY—ST AGNES.

The foundation of this church edifice was laid by Rev. John Quinn in 1868. The congregation, however, was not a largeoneand means for the completion of the work not coming in, it was discontinued for a time. Little by little the building was advanced, and finally in 1880, the structure was completed. The congregation is under the parochial care of the pastor at Piermont.

THE PROTESTANT-EPISCOPAL CHURCH IN ROCKLAND COUNTY.

The first service of the Episcopal Church held in our County, was probably that conducted in the Methodist Church edifice at Haverstraw, in 1846, by Rev. W. F. Walker. In a short time a room over a dry-goods store on Main street was hired for the services of this society, and then the edifice belonging to the Protestant Methodist Society—now owned by the German Lutheran Society—was leased for three years. A vestry was soon organized, and in 1847, the church became a member of the P. E. Church in the diocese of New York.

After this beginning but little seems to have been done, and services were discontinued for a long time. In 1850, Rev. G. S. Hitchcock, who had assumed charge of the society at Piermont during the preceding year, occasionally held services, according to the forms of the P. E. Church, in Haverstraw as well as at other villages in this and adjoining counties. In 1854, Rev. J. B. Gibson took charge of the society at Haverstraw, and entered upon the task of building it up. He obtained the use of a building, then known as the "Yellow School House," which stood at the foot of the street opposite the station of the N. Y., West Shore and Buffalo Railroad, and there held his first service in Haverstraw, February 4th, 1854. Only for a short time did the congregation meet in this building. Then it removed to a room in the building nearly opposite the present Trinity Church, where it remained till the erection of a house for worship. On December 10th, 1856, this society was incorporated under the name of

TRINITY CHURCH.

The corner stone of this church building was laid in 1855, and on June 17th, 1856, the church was dedicated, according to the rites of the society, by Rev. Horatio Potter, D.D. LL.D. This is the oldest church building of the P. E. Society in Rockland County. The first confirmation was held in the First Presbyterian Church, August 27th, 1854. In 1861, Rev. J. B. Gibson resigned his charge and was succeeded by Rev. G. H. Hepburn, who assumed charge in February, 1861, and remained less than a year; Rev. E. Gay, Jr., from April, 1862, to August, 1869; Rev. Walter Delafield, from 1869 to 1873; Rev. D. G. Gunn, for six months; Rev. C. B. Coffin, from July, 1874, for ten months; Rev. G. W. West, from September, 1875 to 1878; Rev. A. T. Ashton, from November 3d, 1878, to the present time. About 1855 a Sabbath school was organized in connection with this church.

THE PROTESTANT EPISCOPAL CHURCH AT PIERMONT—CHRIST CHURCH.

In 1847, Rev. William Walker held the first service, according to the rites of the P. E. Church, in Dr. Lord's lime kiln building at Piermont. On March 1st, 1848, at a meeting of the congregation held at a private residence, the parish of Christ Church was organized, and on April 10th, 1848, the articles of incorporation were legally filed in the County Clerk's office. In the summer of 1848, Rev. William Walker resigned, and shortly after Rev. John Canfield Sterling was called to the rectorship. He remained till the fall of 1849, and was succeeded by Rev. Solomon G. Hitchcock.

In 1864, this society had grown sufficiently strong to begin the erection of a church building on land presented by Thomas E. Blanch, and on July 20th, 1865, the corner stone of the present stone building was laid. The building was consecrated September 7th, 1866. Rev. S. G. Hitchcock remained rector till his death on Sept 14th, 1877. He was succeeded by: Rev. Joseph M. Waite, from January 1st, 1878 till May 1st, 1883, and Rev. Theodore M. Peck, from June 1st, 1883, to the present time.

THE PROTESTANT EPISCOPAL CHURCH AT SUFFERNS—CHRIST CHURCH.

For some years prior to the organization of this society, services according to the rites of the P. E. Church, were held in different private dwellings, especially in that of George W. Suffern, by Rev. S. G. Hitchcock, and at this residence on August 25th, 1860, the present society was legally incorporated. Efforts were at once begun to build a house for worship. A site was obtained from W. B. Maltbie and wife, and the work of construction begun. On June 10th, 1864, the church was consecrated by Bishop Horatio Potter. Until 1874 the edifice stood without change. During a storm on November 23d of that year, however, the steeple was blown over. The present one was built shortly after this catastrophe.

The rectors of this parish have been: Revs. Eastburn Benjamin, F. W. Lusen, Henry R. Howard, John Steele, C. B. Coffin, Joseph F. Jowitt, Edwin J. Lessel, A. B. Leeson, G. E. Pumcker, F. T. H. Horsefield, and since April 7th, 1878, Rev. R. S. Mansfield. A flourishing parish school is connected with this church.

THE PROTESTANT EPISCOPAL CHURCH AT NYACK—GRACE CHURCH.

In his missionary labors among the people of the County, Nyack was not overlooked by Rev. S. G. Hitchcock, and services according to the forms of the P. E. Church were held in Union Hall as early as 1859. The establishment of this church society, however, depended on the efforts of Rev. Franklin Babbitt, who came to Nyack in 1861, and began holding regular services. The first meetings of the church were held in the school room of Christopher Rutherford's Military Academy, now Rockland College, beginning in October, 1861, and continuing until the chapel was ready for occupation in February, 1862. After seven years indefatigable work, the congregation had grown large and strong enough to erect a church edifice. Work was begun. The corner stone of the new structure was laid by Bishop Potter, August 25th, 1869, and the building consecrated by the same church dignitary, May 30th, 1882.

At the opening of the chapel Mr. Babbitt established a parochial day school, and, in the years which have elapsed, has given his time to an evening school as well, when circumstances warranted its existence. With the church society a prosperous Sabbath school is connected. At the beginning of Rev. Franklin Babbitt's rectorship, but a dozen communicants, according to this form of faith, existed in Nyack, and to his efforts under God, often against grievous obstacles, does the present large congregation owe its existence.

ST. JOHN'S P. E. CHURCH AT NEW CITY.

In 1866, Rev. E. Gay, Jr., began holding service in the Court House, and awakened interest among the people. A congregation was formed and in 1866, St. John's parish was organized. In 1867, the congregation felt themselves sufficiently strong and began the building of a church edifice on a site donated by Charles W. Root. The structure was consecrated at a later time. The rectors of this parish have been: Revs. Thomas Marsdon, R. S. Mansfield, Mr. Cruikshank, Mr. Capron, J. F. Esch, and, at present, Thomas Stephens. A Sabbath school was organized at the time the parish was established and is now in a prosperous condition.

THE P. E. CHURCH AT SPRING VALLEY—ST. PAUL'S.

On August 1st, 1868, this society was legally incorporated. For some time previous to this, the services of this church had been held by Rev. S. Hitchcock at different residences in the village until, in the early part of that year, 1868, Mr. A. B. Noyes fitted up one of his buildings, formerly used as a cider-mill, as a place for meeting. Services were then held in this building for several years. The corner-stone of the present church edifice was laid August 5th, 1872, by Bishop Potter, but the building, owing to the financial obligations resting upon it, has never been consecrated. The first rector of this parish was Rev. R. S. Mansfield, from August 11th, 1868, to April 7th, 1878. He was succeeded by Rev. Joseph Tragget, and he by the present laborer, Rev. Thomas Stevens.

THE PROTESTANT EPISCOPAL CHURCH AT STONY POINT—GRACE CHURCH.

The first services of the Protestant Episcopal Church in this township were held in 1869, by Rev. E. Gay Jr., who resigned his charge of Trinity parish in Haverstraw during that year. In the spring of 1871, services were begun at Tomkins Cove. In July, 1877, services were held, and a Sunday School was organized at Caldwell's Landing. On November 9th, 1881, the erection of a house for worship was begun on a site donated by Charles H. Jones, which was sufficiently advanced toward completion to permit of services being held in it during the Summer of 1882, and which was consecrated under the title of the *House of Prayer* March 29th, 1883. In April 1884, a parish was organized under the name of *Grace Church, Stony Point*, with Rev. E. Gay, rector.

ST. LUKE'S P. E. CHURCH—HAVERSTRAW.

Until September 19th, 1871, the congregation at Benson's Corners, and at Haverstraw were under the direction of one and the same vestry; at that time the latter congregation was incorporated under the name of *St. Luke's Church in the Village of Warren*. The further history of this society is that of Trinity Church and need not be repeated. Services are held on Sunday afternoons in the building formerly built by the Baptists. A parochial school and Sabbath School exist in connection with these societies. Of St. John's in the mountains, full mention will be made later.

THE UNIVERSALIST CHURCH AT ORANGEVILLE.

In 1853, a minister of the Universalist faith—Rev. Mr. Rainor—begun preaching in Rulef Van Houten's mills at this place, and so far succeeded in organizing a society that in 1856, a house for worship was erected on property donated by Tunis Cooper. In 1857, Mr. Rainor was succeeded by Rev. Henry Lyon, who preached at Orangeville on alternate Sabbaths till 1871. Upon his resignation, Rev. C. C. Gordon took charge of the church and continued in this field of labor for some time. Since his withdrawal the church has been without a pastor, though services are held occassionally.

A Sunday School in connection with this church was early organized, and is now in a flourishing condition under the superintendence of George R. Van Houten.

THE UNIVERSALIST CHURCH AT NYACK.

In 1859, Rev. Henry Lyon extended his field of labor in our County, and began preaching at Nyack on alternate Sunday afternoons. These services were held at first in the residences of members of the congregation, but in 1868, when the wigwam was opened, the congregation met there. In 1870, the congregation felt strong enough to erect a house for worship, and work was accordingly begun on a site purchased for, and presented to the society by Mrs. Mary Gunn Partridge. The first service was held in the basement of the new building in 1871, Rev. C. C. Gordon preaching the dedicatory sermon. Among the ministers not mentioned, who have officiated in this church are; Revs. Mr. Shepard, W. P. Payne, J. A. Seitz, J. C. Partridge, and F. Hitchcock, who continued holding service till his death in 1883. Since that time the church has been without a regular pastor.

TRUE REFORMED CHURCH.—MONSEY.

In speaking of the "Brick Church," it was stated that a split from the congregation occurred June 11th, 1824. The seceding party, with their pastor, Rev. James D. Demarest, withdrew from the Classis of Paramus, and connected itself with the True Reformed Synod of Hackensack. In the spring of 1825, this society was organized as the True Reformed Church at Monsey, and shortly after, work was begun upon a house for worship on land granted for the purpose by Judge Sarven. The site of this first building was about one-third of a mile north of Monsey, at the intersection of the Spring Valley road with that leading from Monsey to Viola. The spot is still marked by a burying ground.

In 1827, the edifice was opened for service, and continued to be used by this congregation till 1869, when it was sold to Samuel D. Haring. In 1868, the site of the present church was donated by Samuel D. Haring;

work was begun upon the new building, and on August 19th, 1869, it was dedicated to the worship of God. The ministers of this society have been: Revs. James D. Demarest, John Y. De Baun, Abram Van Houten, and since 1865, John R. Cooper. The congregation is now connected with that at Nanuet in support of a pastor.

TRUE REFORMED CHURCH.—NANUET.

In July, 1824, a portion of the congregation of the Reformed Protestant church at Clarksville seceded from that society, and on the thirteenth of that month presented a petition to the classis of Hackensack for union with that body. On August 25th, 1825, this society was duly incorporated as a distinct body. The first services of this church were held in a barn, which stood on property now belonging to W. Van Weelden, and later, until the house for worship was built, in an old stone house belonging to James De Clark. In 1826, the church edifice was built and occupied. The pastors of this church have been: Revs. V. S. Lansing, James D. Brinkerhoff, James D. Demarest, Abram Van Houten, and since November, 1865, John R. Cooper.

By 1825, the secession which had been going on for many years in the Dutch Reformed Church Society, reached the congregation at Tappan and led to a split in that church. On February 24th, 1826, the seceders organized a society under the name of the True Reformed Church, with Cornelius Blauvelt, Daniel C. Haring, John A. Ferdon and Daniel Auryansen as its first officers. A frame house for worship was erected, and the society continued in existence till 1856, when the building was sold to the Methodists.

CHRIST'S EVANGELICAL LUTHERAN CHURCH.—MASONICUS.

The early history of this congregation is connected with that of the church at Mahwah. In January, 1855, Rev. N. Wert, pastor of the church at Saddle River, began work among the Lutherans in our County, with the idea of building up a church at Ramapo. Until a house for worship was erected, services were held in the dwelling of Adolphus Shuart, or in A. M. Litchholt's barn. Ground for a building was first broken on Wannamaker's Corner, but the donation of the present site by Mrs. Margaret Straut led to the erection of the edifice at Masonicus. On October 11th, the completed church was dedicated by the Rev. N. Wert. The pastors of this church since the departure of Mr. Wert in 1856 have been: Rev. E. De Yoe, 1856 to 1874, and Rev. T. J. Yost, from 1875 to 1884. A Sabbath-school connected with this church is successfully conducted.

GERMAN PRESBYTERIAN CHURCH.

On May 29th, 1860, a party of the Germans, who have settled between Nanuet and New City, organized a church society, and were incorporated under the name of the *Dutch Evangelical Church*. Shortly after, the present edifice, standing just west of the road from Nanuet to New City, was built on land purchased by Henry Screver. Until 1879, this society retained its first name, but then that was changed to the German Presbyterian Church. The pastors of this church have been: Revs. Mr. Warrenberger, Bartholomaus Kruise, C. D. Rosenthal, George Loock, John U. Tschudi. A Sabbath-school, which was organized by Rev. C. D. Rosenthal, in connection with this church, is in existence and is well attended.

THE GERMAN EVANGELICAL LUTHERN CHURCH AT HAVERSTRAW.

The first services of the *German United Congregation* in Haverstraw were held in 1857. From that time till the organization of the *German United Societies*, which took place in the building of the Methodist Protestant Society, January 8th, 1861, mission services were held. Rev. Mr. Wahrenberger, who also preached at the Dutch Evangelical Church in Clarkstown—see above—was the first pastor, and was followed by Rev. Mr. Wirtz, who occupied the pulpit from January, 1866 to 1867, and Rev. Mr. Berger. Under this pastor a division occurred in the congregation and a portion of it withdrew with the pastor, organized the *German Lutheran Church*, and erected a house for worship on Division street. Rev. Mr. Berger, after remaining in charge of this new organization for some time was succeeded by Rev. Dr. Sommers.

After the separation, that portion of the congregation, which worshipped in the building of the Protestant Methodist Church, purchased, November 26th, 1867, and organized under the name of the *German Evangelical Church*. Among the pastors who supplied this pulpit was Rev. Mr. Weinacher, who died during his ministry in Haverstraw. The following ministers officiated in one or the other church. Revs. Strecker, C. A. Weisel, Winteieck, H. Schoppe, under whom the unhappy division was healed and the people united, P. Andrus and A. Tully.

In 1875, the two congregations united under the name of the German Evangelical Lutheran Church. Since that time the society has grown in membership, and has built a school and parsonage. A Sabbath school, which is connected with the church, has a large attendance.

CONGREGATIONAL CHURCH, MONSEY.

It has already been seen, that when the congregation of the True Reformed Church Society erected a new edifice in 1869, the old building was purchased by S. D. Haring. By him the structure was moved to its present site, and, after being thoroughly renovated, it was dedicated September 1st, 1869. Until November 1st, 1870, there was no change in the ownership of the building. Then it was sold, and in 1871 again sold, the last purchase being made by the Congregational Society, who have since worshipped in it. The ministers of this church have been: Revs. George Hicks, Lemuel Jones, and Ernest G. Wesley.

CONGREGATIONAL CHURCH—TALLMANS.

In the autumn of 1870, a Sabbath School was started in De Baun Hall by Henry Tallman and wife, Mrs. J. H. Goetchius and Francis Gurnee. From the interest manifested in this school arose the determination to build a church, a determination strongly encouraged by the pastor of the Lutheran church at Masonicus, Rev. E. De Voe. The first intention of the society was to erect a building, dedicated to the tenets of the Lutheran church, and the corner stone of the structure was laid by a Lutheran minister. Ere the edifice was completed, circumstances arose which led to a change in the first idea, and the building was completed and dedicated as a Congregational church in 1874. The pastors of the society have been: Rev. Samuel Switzer, Lemuel Jones, Ernest G. Wesley, Mr. Wrightmeyer. A Sabbath School is connected with the church.

THE QUAKER CHURCH AT LADENTOWN.

Long before the first group of immigrants, from Hempstead, Long Island, thought of the far distant wilderness in which they were eventually to found a *new* Hempstead, members of the Society of Friends, had found a refuge from persecution among them. When the emmigrants at length moved to our County, many of their Quaker neighbors joined with them, and settling back by the present Ladentown, began here the form of worship which seemed best to them. For many years their services were held in private residences, but at length, having gained sufficient strength, this Society erected a house for worship in 1816 on land given for the purpose by Benjamin Secor. The frame building of this society still stands, but the membership is small. From one or another cause the belief has lost ground among us, and few beside the decendants of the first Quaker settlers are now active members of the Society.

THE AFRICAN M. E. ZION.—NYACK.

In 1860, through the efforts of John W. Towt and George Green, a house for worship was built for this congregation on Burd street, and it was aided financially until it became able to sustain itself. In the years which have passed, the society has steadily increased in strength and now has a large membership with a flourishing Sabbath school.

THE AFRICAN M. E. CHURCH.—HAVERSTRAW.

This society was organized at the same time as the African church in Nyack, and in its early history was supplied by the same pastor. The church edifice which stands on Division street was built through the efforts of the friends of the church and the congregation.

In May, 1882, rooms were hired on Piermont Avenue at Nyack, for a Synagogue, and services according to the rites of the Jewish church have since been held regularly.

It may not be uninteresting to read the statement, that two score years ago—in 1845, there was not an Episcopal, Congregational, Roman Catholic, Jewish, Universalist or Unitarian church building in Rockland County.

Besides those Sabbath-schools which have been mentioned, there have been others established in the County at points, sometimes far distant from houses of worship, in which not only the children of tender years have been instructed in religious precepts during the Sabbath, but in which also " children of a larger growth " have been directed and strengthened, to better meet the never ceasing conflict of life, by the different forms of religious worship.

I have already made mention of the Sunday-school established in connection with the Middletown Baptist Church. The next Sabbath-school started in our County seems to have been that begun in 1828 by James Stevens. This school assembled on the property now owned by Samuel Coe, situated near the mountain in the northern part of Clarkstown. On the first Sunday that this school was opened, there were five and twenty scholars. The following summer saw this number increased to one hundred, and in the third year the attendance had reached two hundred. For many years this school continued in existence, but was finally discontinued because of the organization of church societies, and the erection of houses for worship in the neighborhood.

THE UNION SUNDAY-SCHOOL OF SPRING VALLEY.

This school was founded by Rev. Christopher Hunt, pastor of the Reformed church at Clarksville, in the Spring of 1830 with the idea of supplying the lack of means for worship existing in the section about the Dutch Factory. For some twenty-one years the school was continued in the district school building of the neighborhood, being often interrupted and discontinued by the vote of the majority at a district meeting. Finally, on June 29th, 1851, after a long discontinuance, the School was again reorganized with I. Remsen Blauvelt as Superintendent. Owing to the fact that permission to use the school house could not be obtained till the annual meeting in December, the Sunday school was re-begun in the carriage house of Stephen D. Herrick. There it continued for three months and then was moved to a small building near by, where it continued two months longer, and was then moved to the school house. In July, 1852, the last move was made to the Union Sunday School house, which had been erected for its special use. For about ten years longer the school was continued, and was at length disbanded because of the organization of church societies in the neighborhood.

THE UPPER NYACK OR "STONE CHURCH" SUNDAY SCHOOL.

A Sabbath school was organized in this building in 1835 with Robert D. Clement as Superintendent. After the building of the Methodist church at Nyack this school was abandoned. In 1859, it was reorganized through the efforts of George Green and William and Peter Voorhis. For many years it was supported almost entirely by George Green, and school was held only nine months in the year. For the past five years, school has been held throughout the year, and religious services during the week. Matthew Green is the present Superintendent. The school is non-sectarian.

THE SOUTH NYACK OR "WAYSIDE CHAPEL" SUNDAY SCHOOL.

On January 22d, 1860, a Sabbath-school was organized at the house of Mrs. Hester Onderdonk in South Nyack. By 1866, the school had grown strong enough to warrant the erection of a building, and on November 4th of that year a lot was purchased. On November 17th, 1867, the corner stone of the present chapel was laid, and on February 7th, 1869, the building was dedicated. Religious services are held in the chapel whenever practicable on Sabbath evenings. From the start, the general care of this school has been in the charge of John L. Salisbury.

THE LAKE AVENUE BAPTIST SUNDAY-SCHOOL.

This school was organized by A. P. Campbell in 1866, and sufficient funds having been obtained through his efforts together with those of J. Polhemus and A. Smith, the erection of a building was begun on land donated for the purpose by Mrs. Bridges. On October 10th, 1867, the Lake Avenue School-house was dedicated free of debt. A. P. Campbell was the first Superintendent. When the infirmities of age compelled Mr. Campbell to relinquish his charge of the school, it was carried on for some time by the neighbors. At length, however, the building was closed. In 1882, George F. Morse, assisted by George A. Ennis, re-opened the building and reorganized the school. Interest was again awakened. The edifice was repaired and renovated, and the organization is now in a prosperous condition. Religious services are held in this building during the week, whenever opportunity offers.

THE WEST NYACK CHAPEL SUNDAY-SCHOOL.

The first meeting of this school was held in the old building, across the road from the present edifice, on October 18th, 1874, D. D. Smith, J. C. Wool, George D. Cooke, James P. Cooke and William D. Felter being present and aiding in the work. On June 13th, 1877, the West Nyack S. S. Association was organized for the purpose of holding, besides Sabbath school, prayer meetings and other religious services. The first officers of the school, under the regular organization, were: Edwin Outwater, Superintendent; Victor S. H. Waldron, Secretary and Treasurer. In the same year, 1877, a lot of ground was given to the Association by William Stillwell, and a building erected which was completed early in 1878, and dedicated on June 2d of that year.

ROCKLAND COUNTY SABBATH SCHOOL ASSOCIATION.

This association was organized at a meeting held in the Reformed Church at Nyack, March 12th, 1867, for the purpose of more thoroughly systematizing Sunday school work, of obtaining more correct statistical returns, and of gathering into the schools all the children of the County. The first officers of the organization were: David D. Smith, President; Christopher Rutherford, G. O. House, J. Remsen, George Wright, D. D. S., and J. O. Blauvelt, Vice-Presidents; Rev. George J. Van Nest, Secretary and Treasurer; and J. G. Haring, M. D., W. A. Sherwood, William S. Gilman, Jr., Warren M. White, and G. S. Wood, Town Secretaries.

Following D. D. Smith, who served as President for ten years, have been: George S. Wood, of Stony Point, and H. B. McKenzie, of Haverstraw, who has held the office since 1877. Since its organization, annual and semi-annual meetings of the Association have been held at different places in the County. Recently town organizations, auxiliary to that of the County, have been formed for the better accomplishment of their good work.

Authorities referred to: History of Trinity and St. Lukes, by Rev. A. T. Ashton. History of St. Anns and St. Johns, by Rev. P. J. O'Meara. History of St. Catherines, by Rev. M. Kuhnen. History of the Stony Point M. E. Church, by Rev. W. R. Kiefer. History of Ramapo, by Rev. E. B. Cobb. History of Clarkstown, by H. P. Fay. Lecture, "30 Years in Haverstraw," by Rev. A. S. Freeman, D. D. History of the Union Sunday School, by I. R Blauvelt. History of the Nyack Baptist Church, by George F. Morse. County Records.

CHAPTER XV.

SLAVERY IN ROCKLAND COUNTY—THE "UNDERGROUND RAILROAD"—THE COUNTY BUILDINGS—THE ROCKLAND COUNTY BIBLE SOCIETY—THE ROCKLAND COUNTY MEDICAL SOCIETY—AGRICULTURAL SOCIETY—ROCKLAND COUNTY TEACHERS' ASSOCIATION—THE ROCKLAND COUNTY HISTORICAL SOCIETY—CIVIL LIST OF THE COUNTY.

Slavery was introduced into this Colony almost at its first settlement, and early became one of the staple articles of commerce. In 1644, negro slaves were imported from Brazil, and were entered as part of a general cargo of merchandise. Twenty years later the directors of the West India Company wrote the director at New Netherland that a contract had been entered into with one Symen Gilde, of the vessel *Gideon*, to transport a cargo of 300 slaves from Loango to New Netherland. These slaves, the letter states, were only to be used for agricultural labor in the New Netherlands, and under no circumstances taken out of the district. In 1676, the Governor of this Colony was instructed that there was no objection to the introduction of negro slaves into New York, provided, however, that those slaves should not be brought from Guinea and should only be sold in New York by the Royal Company or its agents. Two years later Governor Andros stated that "some few slaves are sometimes brought from Barbados, most for provisions, & Sould att abt £30 or £35, Country pay."

Like other articles of merchandise, these slaves early became subjected to the laws of the Colony governing imports and exports. A customs duty was fixed upon them, and was regulated by the demand for the commodity. In a certain sense realizing the wrong they were perpetrating in this traffic with human beings, the Dutch legislators of those early days endeavored to make amends for the wrong by manumitting the slaves after a certain length of service. They further passed laws making it a capital crime to wilfully kill a slave, and inflicted punishment upon such as should deliberately maim their bond people. Many laws were enacted for the baptising and educating of the negroes in the Christian religion. Our ancestors were consistent in the spread of religious light.

And yet, paradoxical as it may seem at first glance, slavery was unpopular among the people of this Colony from the beginning. As early as August 4th, 1628, Rev. Jonas Michaelius wrote, from New Amsterdam, to Rev. Adrianus Smoutius, in Old Amsterdam: "The Angora slaves are thievish, lazy and useless trash." People still living, who remember the slaves in our County of two centuries later, agree that the reverend gentleman's statement applied as perfectly to the bond-men of 1828 as to those of 1628.

While their useless expense was a serious objection to their possession at all times, a still more potent objection was found when, in 1712, the slaves in New York rose in insurrection and killed nine Christians. It is necessary to say but little regarding that uprising. Perhaps the thoughtful reader may see many more objections to the custom than I have space or desire to point out. The uprising occurred in the late evening and only lasted till the appearance of armed force. Then the slaves sought safety by hiding in the woods on New York Island. On the morning following the uprising, these slaves were hunted and captured, but not "till six had made away with themselves." In all, one and twenty were executed. Some were burned, some hanged, one broken on the wheel, and one hung alive in chains. The theory of Christianity without its practical workings does not seem to have been successful with these negroes. Doubtless this was, as we have been told, because they were not human; because the animal so largely predominated. We seldom hear of animals committing suicide, but the utter horror of that life of bondage, the dreadful misery of days of unrequited toil, in a strange land, among cruel taskmasters, led these negroes to revolt, and caused six of them to commit suicide rather than bear the weary burden longer.

Slavery was introduced in this County by the settlers on the Tappan patent. The slaves were never numerous, and the custom was never popular among our people. The different laws passed by the State Legislature, one during the Revolution, by which all slaves, who enlisted in the army with the consent of their owners, should be free; another, enacted in 1798, providing for their gradual emancipation, and finally that of March 31st, 1817, which decreed, that all slaves born after July 4th, 1799, should be free, males at the age of twenty-eight, females at the age of twenty-five, while all slaves born before 1799, should remain slaves for life—prepared the people for the abolition act of 1828, and that act was greeted by most of the people in our County with more joy than by the slaves themselves.

In 1698 the number of slaves in our County was	19.
In 1702 " " " " " "	33.
In 1723 " " " " " "	147.
In 1731 " " " " " "	184.
In 1737 " " " " " "	293.
In 1749 " " " " " "	360.
In 1800 " " " " " "	551.
In 1810 " " " " " "	316.
In 1820 " " " " " "	124.
In 1830 " " " " " "	None.

The forms of the bills of sale so closely resemble each other that a specimen will answer: "Know all men by these presents that I Isaac Onderdonk of the Town of Orange in Rockland County and State of New York for the sum of two-hundred and fifty dollars in hand paid or secured to be paid. Have bargained and sold and hereby do bargain and sell to 'John Roe' of the Town aforesaid his executors, administrators and assigns, one certain negro man named Jack aged nineteen years on the first day of May next or thereabout. To have and to hold to him, his executors, administrators and assigns for ever, which said negro man I deliver to him the said 'John Roe' at the sealing of these presents—and I the said Isaac Onderdonk for myself, my heirs, executors and administrators do warrant and defend the said 'John Roe' in peaceable possession of the said negro man against all persons whomsoever.

Witness my hand and seal the twenty-fifth day of March, one thousand eight hundred and nine."

ISAAC ONDERDONK." [SEAL.]

"Sealed and delivered in presence of us:
P. Taulman.
David Clark."

Like other forms of property, these slaves were also transferred by will. Thus in the last will of Abraham Snedeker in June, 1771, is a clause in which he leaves to Abram Thew his "Negro man Tune, my Negro woman Suke, their two youngest children Harry and Sara, and the young wench named Nan."

Yet, even in those days there were people not conscience-hardened, who realized that in this traffic with human beings they were dealing with that over which they had no control. And, to be consistent in their lives, these citizens freed their bond people. Among the bills of freedom thus given, I find the following: "To whom these presents shall come. Know ye that John Blauvelt, of the town of Hemstead, in the county of Rockland and State of New York is minded and by these Presents Does freely Manumite a Negro man named Will aged about twenty-one years ; and said Negro appearing to be a hail hearty well man, both in body and limbs and whereas John myer and Abram Onderdonk Poor-masters of the town of Hemsted abovesaid having Duly took the case into consideration ; and think the said Negro man of sufficient abilities to provide for himself, and Do by these presents allow his manumission."

Witness our hands the Seventh Day of april one thousand Eight hundred and four."

"JOHN MYER.
ABRAHAM ONDERDONK.
Overseers of the Poor."

"To all to whom this present writing shall come may in any way concern, Know ye that I, Abraham Van Houten, of Clarkstown, in the County of Rockland, and State of NewYork, have manumitted, and by these presents do manumit a negro woman by the name of Jane, to be forever hereafter Manumitted and Declared Free of and from me, the said Abraham Van Houten, my Heirs, Executors, Administrators and assigns, in Witness whereof I have hereunto set my hand and seal this Twenty-third day of April, one Thousand Eight Hundred and Eight."

"ABRAHAM VAN HOUTEN. [SEAL.]

"Witness Presents signed :
JOHN VAN HOUTEN.
JACOB WOOD."

"Entered by JOHN WOOD,
Town Clerk."

Once again, before the Civil War cast its gloom over the Nation, slavery became an important factor with a few people in this County. While in that mysterious and secret, but active and thorough movement for the escape of fugitive slaves known as the "Underground railroad," the west bank of the Hudson River was not on the direct line of travel, still it was used to an extent now unknown. The station next south of Nyack was at Jersey City, that next north, at Newburgh.

The station at Nyack was in charge of Edward Hesdra, who lived at that time on the south side of the turnpike, almost opposite the reservoir.

..., attention was not drawn to this matter till after Hesdra's demise, and that of the few who aided him. The almost absolute secrecy which was preserved by those interested in the matter, has prevented me from obtaining statistical data on the subject, and we can now but learn of the main features of the system as carried on here.

The plan of the "Underground railroad" was so arranged, that only a few leaders knew its complete workings. The agent at Jersey City knew of Hesdra's place, and Hesdra knew the agent at Newburgh. Any one of these three might or might not know the agent next south of his place. If so, that was as far as their knowledge extended. After nightfall, the escaping slave would start from Jersey City with full instructions how to travel, and a thorough description of Hesdra's house. Before daybreak, he would reach Nyack, see Hesdra, and then disappear. After he was rested, fed, and if necessary, clothed, he again started under the cover of darkness, and ere another day broke was safely hidden in Newburgh. So, station by station he advanced in his flight, till at length, crossing the Canadian border from this land of liberty, he breathed the air, a freeman.

It speaks well for the retentive memory of these fleeing negroes, that they so seldom made errors in regard to the places they were directed to. Travelling only at night, and in a strange country, in constant fear of capture, they could ask no directions, but must trust entirely to their perception and recollection. Looked at in this way, their success in escaping from the happy condition of their bondage, seems miraculous. In only one case have I heard of a run-a-way making an error in regard to his destination at Nyack. This fugitive passed Hesdra's in the darkness, and reached a vineyard on the property of George Green, at Upper Nyack. Fortunately he was discovered by the owner of the farm, and safely directed to his haven of refuge.

Another, and most active worker in the "Underground railroad" was John W. Towt. Most of his efforts for fugitive slaves were conducted in New York in conjunction with the leading Abolitionists, Arthur and Lewis Tappan, and with them he labored most earnestly in all abolition movements. Only once, after his coming to Nyack, was Mr. Towt called upon to lend personal assistance to a fugitive negro. On that occasion, he concealed the run-a-way in his house until he was able to travel further, and then saw him safely off on the way to freedom.

Doubtless this all seems strange to a younger generation now coming on the stage of life. The thought that a living being, guilty of no crime, should ever have had to pass through our soil in time of peace by skulking and hiding from human sight, appears well nigh impossible. Perhaps it is well so. Perhaps the part of wisdom is to conceal from the children the crimes of the parent, to hide from them the fact, that the South with slavery was a large purchaser, the North without slavery, a large seller; that for the sake of business the North endeavored in every way to overlook the damning wrong perpetrated by her no more guilty sister, and stooped to the lowest social position, that of slave-catcher, for a few dollars. The last act preceding the result, the "Fugitive Slave Law," was necessary before we could fully see how debased we had become. In a later chapter we shall find that punishment, that retribution only waited.

In Rockland County were many, who, for one reason or another, defended slavery. The passage of the "Fugitive Slave Law" found those citizens willing and anxious to execute its mandates, and because of the existence of this slave-hunting feeling, the almost absolute secrecy of the "Underground railroad" system became imperative. It was realized among the pro-slavery residents, that escaping negroes were being passed through this section, and dire were the threats made against Abolitionists if they were detected, but those engaged in the enterprise took good care not to be discovered.

In another chapter we have traced the County Buildings from their original erection at Tappan till their removal to New City. The first Court House after the separation and creation of our County was built in 1798-9, at New City. In 1802, this structure was injured by lightning. Until 1820, this building sufficed for the wants of our people, but it was too small and inconvenient for a growing section and a new one was determined on. It was one thing to decide on the necessity of new County buildings; when it came to deciding where they should be built, a very different problem was met. That New City was the most central part of the County could not be disputed, so far as the geographical center was concerned; but New City was by no means the spot most easy of access in our territory, and, like its predecessor, Tappan, instead of being built up by the presence of the public buildings, it seemed to sink into deeper lethargy. To the west of it was Ramapo, a thriving and populous village; to the Northeast, Haverstraw which was rapidly increasing in population. From those two villages came most of the law business of the County and from them the majority of the jurors were drawn. It was natural then, that each of these townships should insist that the new edifice must be built within its borders.

The controversy which followed was one that has had many repetitions in our history. Local interest and local jealousy were roused, and neither township would yield. As was usual in such contests, the whole subject was taken to the State Legislature, and, on April 19, 1823, an Act was passed authorizing the erection of a new court house and jail in the County and appointing D. M. Westcott, of the town of Goshen, in Orange County; Benjamin Barney and James Wood, Commissioners to locate the site.

This proceeding but complicated matters, and the wrangling factions of Haverstraw and Ramapo turned from each other to attack the Commissioners. To escape the conflict which appeared inevitable, those Commissioners at length proposed that Ramapo, Haverstraw and Orangetown each select a delegate to meet and confer, and that the opinion of a majority should be final. This was agreed to and Peter De Noyelles, of Haverstraw; William Yeury, of Ramapo, and John E. Green, of Orangetown were chosen delegates. So bitter was the feeling between the peoples of the two first-named townships that the delegate of each assured Green privately that, should he select Nyack as the site, each would vote with him to prevent his rival township from obtaining the prize.

The choice of Nyack as the County seat was about the last thing Green desired. With strict economic views, he regarded the enforced idleness of court week as subversive of all forms of commercial business, as tending to disorganize industry. The temptation which many, who were drawn to the court house while court was sitting, had to convivial greetings at the tavern bars, was conducive to disorder and confusion; and last, but by no means least, the presence of lawyers, who, for their own convenience, are apt to settle near the depository of a county's records, seemed likely, to him, to lead to a litigious spirit.

Influenced by these views, John E. Green decided to leave the site of the public buildings at New City, and in this decision the other delegates concurred. Accordingly, work upon the present Court House was begun in 1827, and the structure was completed during the following year. In 1873 a fire-proof addition was added to the Court House, at an expense of $23,000, for the purpose of affording greater safety to the records. In 1856 a new jail was erected at a cost of some $8,000.

Perhaps no decision was more unfortunate than that of the choice of New City as the site of the public buildings. Ere the structure was completed a steamboat was running from Nyack, and, within a few years, almost every village in the County had better communication with the other villages, and with the outside world, than the County seat. It was not till 1875, that a railroad spur was at last run to New City, and, even to this day, that hamlet is viewed by our own and the lawyers of other counties, who have to visit it on business, as the most out-of-the-world spot that could possibly have been chosen.

While many capital crimes have been committed in this County, capital punishment has been meted out to but one person, sentenced by a civil court. In 1793, Isaac Jones was hanged at New City for the crime of murder. My search for records in this case has been almost in vain, and, with the exception of the items, which I add, taken from the Supervisor's records, and the heresay remembrance of old people, I can learn nothing.

The stories of the crime, though differing as to the immediate cause of the act, all agree on the fact that the murderer and his victim were both intoxicated, and that, in a drunken brawl, Jones stabbed one of a number who beset him. I have heard it said that the evidence in the case, if given to-day, could not have resulted in conviction. Unable, on the few records left, to enter into speculation, enough to know that Isaac Jones was found guilty and sentenced to death. He was confined in the jail at New City till the day for execution and hanged just south of the present County buildings in that village. The Supervisor's records contain:

"To Daniel Coe; for making irons for Isaac Jones a criminal before execution. £ 0.8.0
"To Evert Hogenkamp for timber and making a gallows, coffin, etc., for Jones. - - - - - - - 1.4.0
"To John Wallace Jr., for guarding the Goal when Jones was under sentence of death. - - - - - - 5.19.6
"To William Bell and two others for the like service. - - 4.12.6
"Ebenezer Wood for John Cole, John Palmer and 30 others for the like service. - - - - - - - 17.12.6
"To John Cole for iron work done for Isaac Jones in Goal. - 9.0
"To Walter Smith for ammunition to the guard for the Goal when Jones was under sentence. - - - - - 14.6."

The Sheriff at the time of the execution was Thomas Waters.

Until 1837, no alms-house existed in the County. Perchance a reference to the Supervisor's record may explain the needlessness of a home for the poor in early days. It was a simple manner of settling the subject when, as has been shown in a previous chapter, the great class of mendicants could be classed as vagabonds and transported out of this into another county. In other cases, however, when circumstances forbade this summary way of avoiding charity, the applicants for alms were boarded at the residences of private individuals and the bills charged to the County; or, if only aid was needed, the Supervisors gave it and charged the

County. Thus in the records of 1755, we find an entry "John Kinner for 4 yards of cloth for the Widow Rude £1.18.0" "George Thompson for nursing and attending Susannah Smith in sickness, for 6 weeks £2.8.0." "Captain Thomas Smith for keeping Susannah Smith's child one week, £0.4.0."

Among the items for 1762, appear the following charges for charity:
"To Isaac Roades for a pair of half-worn shoes for Hendrick. - £0.4.0
"To the same for a pair of shoes and old trowsers. - - 12.6
"To William Oldfield for ½ gallon rum and digging Mary's grave. 8.6
"To 6 yds. tow cloth at 2s.6d for Cornelius Decker, a poor person. 15.0
"To 4½ pounds of soap for said Decker. - - - - 1.6
"To ½ hundred of flour and carting it for said Decker. - - 11.0."

At length this primitive method of disposing of paupers was rendered impracticable by the increasing population, and a County farm of 42 acres was purchased in July 1837, at Mechanicsville, now Viola, and an almshouse erected.

From the opening of this charitable institution until the present time, it has been used as a place of restraint for County people, who have been smitten by loss of reason, but not severely enough to require confinement in an asylum. In his report to the New York Medical Society in 1864, Dr. Sylvester D. Willard thus speaks of the alms house: "The whole population of the Rockland County poor house is 50. During the year there were 16 insane people among the number, but at present the number in confinement is 10. Of these 6 require occasional confinement: one has been in the poorhouse since 1841. Only one male is capable of labor. The remaining 9 invalids have neither amusement, occupation nor employment except reading and singing; the house has not a full supply of water, and no bath tubs. The building is of wood, two stories high, rooms, 6x10, ceilings, 9x8 feet. The bedsteads are of wood, and fastened to the floor. Sleeping rooms are not heated."

In 1870, the Supervisors determined on the erection of a building for the care of insane persons. In 1879, this structure was completed, was rejected as an asylum, and was turned into a home for male paupers.

THE ROCKLAND COUNTY BIBLE SOCIETY.

This society, the oldest continuous organization in our County, was organized on June 4th, 1816, with Joseph Dederer as President, Cornelius C. Blauvelt, Secretary, and John Cole, Treasurer. No records except the original constitution, with one or two amendments, existed till 1828. The society was designed for the purpose of supplying the poor with copies of the Bible, and, at a later period, added to this the education of the children of the poor.

In 1838, the society was reorganized as the *Young Men's Bible Society of Rockland County*, with Rev. Peter Quick, President, Revs. Peter Allen, Jared Dewing, Isaac D. Cole and Mr. I M. Dederer, Vice-Presidents, Cornelius Sickles, Secretary, and John Polhemus, M. D., Treasurer. In November, 1847, another reorganization took place, and the society became the *Rockland County Bible Society*. The officers of this new body were: Hon. Hugh Maxwell, President; Judges William Fraser, Edward Suffern, and James Garner, Vice-Presidents; Rev. A. M. Kettle, Secretary, and D. D. Smith, Treasurer. This society still exists a strong and active organization.

THE ROCKLAND COUNTY MEDICAL SOCIETY.

In 1730, Dr. Osborn came to Haverstraw, and from that time till his death attended to the maladies of such as called upon him. After this first physician came his son, Dr. Richard Osborn, who began practice in Haverstraw precinct before the Revolution. At this time also Dr. John Outwater was practicing in Tappan. At this early period there was but little demand for medical skill. The population was small; the manner of life among the people healthful; and such intercourse as was held with the outside world seems not to have introduced pestilence.

While the records of the large towns of those days show a plentiful number of impostors and quacks, this County seems to have been free from them, and the only record of layman treatment that I find was in 1755, when Adam Weisner was paid £4-19-5 "for keeping old Decker's daughter two months and twenty-six days and doctoring her."

Early in the Revolution, after the disastrous battle of Long Island, the army hospital was removed to Tappan. The medical staff at that time consisted of William Shippen, Chief Physician of the Flying Camp; Isaac Foster, Department Director General; Ammi R. Cutler, Physician General of the Hospital; Phillip Turner, Surgeon General of the Hospital; William Burrett, Physician and Surgeon General of the Army. Beside these, were Surgeon Van der Weyde, who, with George Clinton, escaped capture after the surrender of Fort Clinton, by swimming across the Hudson River; and Dr. James Thatcher, whose Military Diary has preserved many of the events of the War of Independence for us.

The first Medical Society in Rockland County was organized in 1829, with Dr. Abraham Cornelison, President. From the close of the Revolution till the organization of the County Society, the list of physicians seems to be unknown. Dr. Abraham Cornelison was located on the road from Clarksville to the brewery, and bills of his for 1813-14 and '15 exist, Dr. John Polhemus, by the old mill at Clarksville, and others, doubtless, in other sections of the County. In the Coe burying ground, near the English church, is a stone to the memory of Jesse Coe, M. D., who died in 1825, at the untimely age of thirty-five years, and in the same plot is a stone erected to the memory of Dr. William Duzenberry's wife, Margaret, who died August 3d, 1828.

The first society does not seem to have flourished. So onerous are the duties of a physician, so uncertain the time that he can call his own, that the time and labor of attending a meeting, even but once a year, was a burden. Then, too, the distance was great for most of the members, and the roads not over-excellent. These causes led to a gradual decay of interest, and the virtual death of the organization.

From the origin of the Society till its reorganization in 1850, many physicians practiced in the County, among whom were: Dr. Mark Pratt, who settled in Haverstraw in 1833, and remained there till his death in 1875, and Drs. Smith, Noble, Lee, Hegeman, Johnson, Lilienthal, Ropeke, McKnight, Reisberg, Slip, Talman, Chamber, Bogert, Staal, Springer, Tyler, Allen and Owen.

In 1850, the Medical Society was reorganized with Dr. John Demarest as President, the following physicians being present and becoming members.

M. C. Hasbrouck.	James A. Hopson.	Lucius Isham.
Chas. Whipple.	J. C. Haring.	John Purdue.
Daniel L. Reeves.	James J. Stephens.	Chas. Hasbrouck, of N. J.
S. S. Sloat.	Jacob S. Wigton.	

The Presidents of the Society following Dr. John Demarest have been:

Caleb H. Austin, 1854. Jacob S. Wigton, 1870–71.
John Purdue, 1855.   James J. Stephens, 1876.
J. C. Haring, 1856–57–58–59. James A. Hopson, 1877.
John Demarest, 1860–61. Edward H. Maynard 1878.
Moses Cantine Hasbrouck,
  1862–63–64–65.   C. H. Masten, 1880.
S. S. Sloat, 1866–67 and 1872. Gerrit F. Blauvelt, 1881.
Thomas Blanch Smith, 1868–69. A. O. Bogart, 1882.

Among the medical men who have joined the society since its reorganization are, besides those mentioned among the presidents: Daniel Lake and C. L. Humphrey, of Spring Valley; Bernard O'Blenis, J. C. Haring and J. Hengler of Clarksville; William Govan, of Stony Point; Benjamin O. Davidson, John O. Polhemus, Frank Hasbrouck, George A. Mursick, W. S. Stevenson, C. H. Teneyck and J. W. Swift, of Nyack; H. H. House, of Rockland Lake; Rykman D. Bogart of Pearl River; E. B. Laird, D. F. Wemple and Thomas C. Wood, of Haverstraw; N. R. Van Houten, of New City, and G. H. Hammond, Wm. S. House, Henry Reisberg, H. C. Near, John Sullivan, Isaac J. Wells and George A. Lockwood.

Many others doubtless have practiced the healing art in this County, but their names have passed away. They lived, they labored as no other men except physicians ever will labor, they died. Yet, though the names of these simple country physicians be forgotten, their work lives. It is through these earnest men that Medicine has advanced, has ceased to be a theory, has become a science. They have met pestilence and from their battle with it arose quarantine. They have seen the agony produced by the surgeon's knife, and to alleviate it discovered anæsthesia; the perils of travail have been overcome and its pains diminished; they have made the blind to see, the deaf to hear, the lame to walk; they have lived close to the example of the Good Physician, and died in the consciousness of work well done.

ROCKLAND COUNTY AGRICULTURAL SOCIETY.

In the Spring of 1844, B. P. Johnson, then Secretary of the State Agricultural Society, suggested to N. C. Blauvelt, of our County, the advisability of calling a meeting of the citizens, with a view to forming a society for the encouragement of agriculture. Accordingly, Mr. Blauvelt called such a meeting, and on June 29th, 1844, many of our farmers met at the Court House in New City and organized the County Agricultural Society, with Abraham Stephens, President, and N. C. Blauvelt, of Spring Valley, Secretary.

The first County Fair was held in 1844, and for several years afterward, on the common in front of the Court House. In those days more attention was given to agricultural products, and there was no horse racing. The *Rockland County Messenger* said, in regard to one of the features of a fair of those days: "Five teams of oxen entered the list for a ploughing match, and earned for themselves great credit as adepts in this *manly* art." At length some of the citizens, who kept fast horses and wished a place to try their speed, leased the common, laid out a half-mile track, fenced in their property, and permitted the Agricultural Society to use the grounds. Horse racing, after this, became part of the regular programme of the annual exhibitions.

In 1875, J. A. Van Riper opened a fair ground, with a half-mile race track, at Spring Valley; whereupon the Agricultural Society selected that place for their fairs, and erected buildings on the spot. These new grounds were objectionable to many, and from the feeling thus caused sprang a second agricultural society, which selected for its annual fairs the old grounds at New City. Forty-two exhibitions have been held by the Society since its organization.

ROCKLAND COUNTY TEACHERS' ASSOCIATION.

This organization was effected on October 29th, 1859, with S. D. Demarest, President; Ebenezer Lane, Vice-President; L. Wilson, Secretary, and T. H. Gimmel and H. D. Gesner, Executive Committee. The first name of the society was, "The Rockland County Educational Association," and its purpose was the advancement of education in our County. In 1860, it was thought that greater benefit could be obtained by joining with the teachers in Westchester county. Accordingly union was formed under the name of the Hudson River Educational Association.

This organization soon died and the teachers in this County again consulted among themselves. The society is now called the Teacher's Association of the County of Rockland. Within the past few years this body has increased its activity, and is now exerting a most excellent influence in our social life. It is a pleasing feature of later years that our citizens are taking greater interest in educational matters, and encourage, by that interest, the labors of our educators. It is a pleasing feature, that the too often over-worked and under-paid teacher is at last being appreciated as the only sure hope of a successful continuance of this republican form of government. It is a pleasing feature that both the number and the proportion of the illiterate in Rockland County is steadily decreasing and the number, who are obtaining a higher education, increasing.

ROCKLAND COUNTY HISTORICAL AND FORESTRY SOCIETY.

On February 22d, 1878, a meeting of people, who took an interest in the history of this County and desired to obtain the story of its origin, progress and vicissitudes ere that story should have become altogether legendary, was held at the Rockland Female Institute, now the Tappan Zee Hotel, for the purpose of organizing a county historical society, which should be the collector and custodian of historical records. On February 30th, of the same year the organization was completed and the society incorporated, under the name of the Rockland County Historical and Forestry Society, by Hon. John W. Ferdon and Charles W. Miller, of Piermont; Dr. C. R. Agnew and W. S. Gilman of Palisades; John L. Salisbury and Garret Van Nostrand, of Nyack; Henry Whittemore, of Tappan; and W. S. Searing, of Tomkin's Cove.

Like many exemplary movements, this one, after a brief period of activity, fell into a condition of lethargy. The distances between the larger villages were great, and it was difficult to obtain a well attended meeting. Then, too, the majority of the people did not altogether understand the purposes of the Society, and were loth to yield their documents and curios to its keeping. A few noble efforts were made to excite enthusiasm, efforts that, while they seemed to produce but little effect at the time, did really tend to educate the public for the future, and then the Society passed into a condition of dry rot and seemed in a fair way to pass from existence. Through the efforts of some of its former members it was rescued from this fate and has now become an active and growing organization, that already is accomplishing a task that generations to come will be thankful for, and that has a bright future before it.

We have given the list of the Representatives in Congress, and the State Legislature from this section till the organization of Rockland County. It is now my duty to add the names of our citizens, who have since been chosen to represent us in the councils of the Nation and State.

THIRTEENTH CONGRESS.

From May 24th, 1813, till March 3d, 1815. 3d District, comprising Rockland and Westchester.

Peter DeNoyelles.

SEVENTEENTH CONGRESS.

From December 3d, 1821, till March 3d, 1823. 3d District, comprising Rockland and Westchester.

Jeremiah H. Pierson.

TWENTY-THIRD CONGRESS.

From December 2d, 1833, till March 3d, 1835. 2d District, comprising Kings, Richmond and Rockland.

Isaac R. Van Houten.

TWENTY-SIXTH CONGRESS.

From December 2d, 1839, till March 3d, 1841. 2d District, comprising Kings, Richmond, and Rockland.

James B. L. Montanya.

THIRTY-SECOND CONGRESS.

From December 1st 1851, till March 2d, 1853. 7th District, comprising Rockland and Westchester.

Abraham P. Stephens.

FORTY SIXTH CONGRESS.

14th District, comprising Rockland, Orange and Sullivan.

John W. Ferdon.

STATE SENATE.

John Suffern, from Jan. 28th, 1800, till April 6th, 1803.
Benjamin Coe, from Jan. 27th, 1807, till June 19th, 1812.
Samuel G. Verbryck, from Jan. 25th, 1814, till April 14th, 1817.
Abraham B. Conger, from Jan. 6th, 1852, till July 21st, 1853.
John W. Ferdon, from January 1st, 1856, till April 18th, 1857.

STATE ASSEMBLY.

Benjamin Coe, 1798-9.
Sam'l G. Verbryck, 1800-1-4-7-9-20.
Peter De Noyelles, 1802-3.
John Coe, 1805.
John Haring, 1806.
Peter S. Van Orden, 1810-15-24.
Cornelius A. Blauvelt, 1816-17.
*Abr. Gurnee, 1818-19-21-25-26.
Cornelius Blauvelt, 1822.
John I. Suffern, 1823-1854.
*Edward Suffern, 1826-1835.
Levi Sherwood, 1827.28.
George S. Allison, 1829-30.
John J. Eckerson, 1831.
Isaac I. Blauvelt, 1832.
James D. L. Montanya, 1833.
Daniel Johnson, 1834-1836.

Abraham J. Demarest, 1837.
David Clark, 1838.
Benjamin Blackledge, 1839.
William F. Fraser, 1840.
Edward De Noyelles, 1841-2.
Cornelius M. Demarest, 1843.
John Haring, Jr., 1844.
Joseph P. Brower, 1845.
Samson Marks, 1846.
John A. Haring, 1847.
Lawrence J. Sneden, 1848.
Matthew D. Bogart, 1849.
Brewster J. Allison, 1850.
Jacob Sickles, 1851.
John Demarest, 1852.
Nicholas C. Blauvelt, 1853.
John W. Ferdon, 1855.
Edward Whitemore, 1856.
James Westervelt, 1857.

Wesley J. Weiant, 1858-9.
Peter S. Yeury, 1860.
William R. Knapp, 1861-1874.
James S. Haring, 1862-63-64.
Prince W. Nickerson, 1865-66.
James Suffern, 1867-69.
Thomas Lawrence, 1868.
James M. Nelson, 1870-71-78.
Daniel Tompkins, 1872.
William Voorhis, 1873.
James C. Brown, 1875.
George W. Weiant, 1876-7.
James W. Husted, 1879-80.
John Cleary, 1881-2.
William H. Thompson, 1883.
John W. Felter, 1884-5.
George Dickey, 1886.

* The election of 1826 was contested by Edward Suffern. Abraham Gurnee was unseated, and Edward Suffern declared elected.

Authorities referred to " Documents Relating to the Colonial History of the State of New York." County Records, " Transactions of the New York State Medical Society." " History of the Rockland County Medical Society," by William Govan, M. D. " The New York Civil List."

CHAPTER XVI.

PERIOD OF CIVIL WAR—THE POLITICAL FEELING IN ROCKLAND COUNTY AND THE ELECTION OF 1860.

THE EFFECT OF THE SHOT ON FORT SUMTER—SPLIT OF THE DEMOCRATIC PARTY INTO PEACE DEMOCRATS, AND WAR DEMOCRATS OR UNION MEN—EARLY VOLUNTEERING AND THE ORGANIZATION OF COMPANIES—THE MOVEMENT AMONG THE UNION MEN TO GIVE FINANCIAL AID TO VOLUNTEERS AND THEIR FAMILIES—THE EARLY CONCEPTION AND GROWTH OF THE ROCKLAND COUNTY BRANCHES OF THE U. S. SANITARY COMMISSION—THE OUTBURST OF ANGER AMONG THE DISLOYAL AT THE ORDER FOR A DRAFT—ORGANIZATION OF SECRET SOCIETIES AMONG THE LOYAL MEN OF THE COUNTY FOR SELF-PROTECTION—THE HISTORY OF THE DRAFTS—THE ELECTION OF 1864—THE DEMONSTRATIONS OF JOY OVER THE NEWS OF THE END OF THE CONFLICT—THE CENSUS OF ROCKLAND COUNTY'S CONTRIBUTIONS TO THE WAR.

In a previous chapter I made mention of the political feeling among a vast majority of the voters of our County, and gave, what appeared to me, the reasons for that feeling. Little change had occurred in the belief of the people during the three score and two years which had elapsed between the organization of the County and the election of 1860. Few immigrants had arrived within our boundaries, and few had gone forth. Dominant by such majorities as to be secure beyond peradventure, the Democratic party had indulged in bitter family fights for office and such spoils as existed, but its organization was so perfect that, on all important questions, the warring factions joined against their common enemy.

One after the other, in the years that had passed since the erection of the County, the Democrats of Rockland had seen the decay and death of the Federal and Whig parties, and had come to look upon the opponents of their principles as malcontents, as disgruntled office seekers, as, in fact, political anarchists, who, if they could not rule, would ruin the Nation rather than see it well administered by their political enemies.

With this feeling they viewed the organization of the Republican Party, seeing in it nothing more important than the old anti-Democratic movement, unless it was perhaps, that this new organization had allied itself with and adopted the principles of that band of fanatics known as Abolitionists. The election of 1856, dispelled in a measure this sense of security. The events, which followed each other with such startling rapidity between that election and the campaign of 1860, the uproars in the National Legislature, the insurrection of John Brown and the threats of resignation made by Representatives from the Southern States in case a Republican was elected to the presidency; had centered attention on this new party, and led the Democrats to unite in a solid front.

And yet neither party realized the meaning of the contest of 1860. The Democrats still felt that their opponents only sought office. That those opponents meant to carry out the idea of the abolition of slavery never seemed probable. Such a statement might be made to the masses, threats of the introduction of ex-slaves into competition with the laborers of the County were often indulged on the stump as were pleasantries regarding the Republican desire to have miscegenation made legal; but among the thinking Democrats the subject was not mentioned as a likely contingency. Nor were the Republicans less ignorant of the result of the campaign. Time after time compromise had followed compromise, and they viewed the threats of secession made by the Southern Democrats, as a bold attempt to retain power or the usual prelude to a demand for the extension of slavery. A majority and a vast majority of the Republican voters of 1860 in this County did not expect to see abolition successful. A still greater majority of the Democratic voters did not expect to see the doctrine of State Sovereignty carried into rebellion.

After an unusually active campaign, in which many of the leading statesmen of the time stumped the County, the election was held November 6th, 1860, and gave the following results:

United Candidates:	Orangetown.			Haverstraw.		
	1st. Dist.	2d. Dist.	3d. Dist.	1st. Dist.	2d. Dist.	
Breckenridge, ⎫ Douglass, ⎬ Bell, ⎭	422	288	79	419	250	
Lincoln,	174	155	59	378	122	
United Candidates:	Clarkstown.			Ramapo.		
	1st. Dist.	2d. Dist.	3d. Dist.	1st. Dist.	2d. Dist.	3d. Dist.
Breckenridge, ⎫ Douglass, ⎬ Bell, ⎭	230	121	216	124	75	145
Lincoln,	29	60	92	103	153	85
Total United Democrats:	2,369.					
Total Lincoln:	1,410.					
Democratic majority:	959.					

As all of my readers know, the result of the election was the choice of Abraham Lincoln as President of the United States by a popular majority greater than that of any one of his rivals, and by a majority of 57 votes in the Electoral College.

For a time the feeling in Rockland County was one of uncertainty

No one knew just what course to follow. The Democrats, beaten at last after years of authority, had to await the action of their national leaders before they could agree on a line of policy ; and the leaders, with the sole exception of those composing the Southern wing, who had a definite policy in view, had no plans. The Republicans, after the subsidence of their first enthusiasm over the victory, awaited anxiously the action of the South.

It is unnecessary to enter into the details of the events that occurred in the Nation at large, between Dec. 1, 1860 and April 14, 1861. These belong to the broader field of national history, and the reader must refer to works devoted to the subject for information. My duty is to confine myself as closely as possible to the effect produced upon the people of Rockland County by these events. In entering upon this work I fully realize the delicate nature of my task. Too young to take any active part in the contest, but old enough to distinctly recall the bitter feelings engendered by the fratricidal strife ; the severing of the friendships of years, the disruption of social ties, the hatred which arose between neighbors, the threats uttered against each other by active partisans of one or the other side, with all these recollections vividly awakened, it may seem unwise that I should more than touch upon this period. Still another objection may be urged—that by education and association during the war and by observation since, my political bias is Anti-Democratic.

Yet, in spite of these things, I prefer to dwell somewhat upon this time. Beyond the mad passions of the contest there appears a something grand, God-like. Men who took sides during the Civil War were driven to that course, not by military or civil authority, but by their views of what was right. They acted under the influence of an IDEA. The war is ended. The bitterness of the war is nearly, will soon be forgotten. What families in England are still estranged by recollections of their civil wars ? The idea for which the war was fought will live forever.

With abiding faith in the good of men, who follow an idea through persecution even unto death ; with confidence in the existence of this Government so long as her citizens shall be moved to act for what they think right, I now undertake the labor of telling the story of our County in the war, uninfluenced by party bias or personal hatred. From all sources, without regard to political taint, I have drawn my data, and will give it without fear and without favor.

The secession of one after another of the Southern States produced a peculiar political condition in our County. The Republican party still viewed the action as part and parcel of a more than usually determined effort to obtain fresh concessions, and was outspoken in its condemnation of the movement. The Democratic party began the division which afterward obtained. One wing adhered absolutely to the radical doctrine of State Sovereignty. It accepted as a right, the act of secession, sympathized in every movement of the revolting States, and denied with reiterated asseveration, the constitutional power of the National Government to coerce a State. The other wing, while willing to adhere to the principles of its party up to a certain point, stopped short as it faced the inevitable issue of those principles, and announced its faith in the inviolate nature of the Federal Union.

Even while events were in this strained though still non-belligerent condition, matters at Washington had grown so warlike, that the militia of the State was placed under marching orders. On January 5th, 1861, the 17th Regiment N. Y. S. M., Colonel Edward Pye, was ordered to be in readiness to move instantly. It was not called upon to advance further at this time, but at a later period, as we shall see, was sent to the front.

Finally, on Saturday, April 13th, 1861, the news reached our County that Fort Sumter had been fired upon, and on the following morning the daily papers brought an account of its surrender to the Confederate forces. Perhaps I may digress for a moment and endeavor to reproduce the scenes in Nyack during April 13th and 14th, 1861. On the former day the news was received with a dumb uncertainty: no one seemed to fully realize the awful tidings that war had begun. On the latter, which was Sunday, Spier street, leading to the old steamboat dock, was filled with people, while the dock was crowded, all awaiting the arrival of the steamboat Aurora with the morning papers. Long before the papers could be distributed, the news that Sumter had fallen spread to the outermost edge of the waiting crowds. Instantly men became frantic with rage and patriotism; the church congregations, which had begun service, were soon made aware of the news by the cheers and yells in the streets, and by eager couriers, who hastened to the sacred edifices bearing the news. From every pulpit in Nyack that day, arose fervent and patriotic prayers, and from every pulpit words were spoken that stirred men's souls.

On the receipt of the news in Rockland County, party ties were abruptly broken. The radical wing of the Democratic party assumed the stand-point of disunion under the name of "Peace Democrats," while the Union wing at once joined the movement to save the Nation, and became known as "War Democrats."

The first burst of patriotic enthusiasm in our County bore instant fruit. At the call of the President for volunteers to save the Union, recruiting was begun in Nyack, which led the County in this matter, and by May 1st, 1861, the following company, lettered G, was ready to take its place in the 17th Regiment, N. Y. S. Volunteers, called the "Westchester Chasseurs."

Captain, James H. Demarest.*

First Lieutenant, Luther Caldwell.		Second Lieutenant, James H. Christie.
Brevet Second Lieutenant, L. C. Mabie.		Orderly Sergeant, William Matthews.
Second Sergeant, Chas. H. Hawkins.		Third Sergeant, Jacob Baker.
Fourth Sergeant, Geo. E. Ingalls.		First Corporal, Anthony Lydecker.
Second Corporal, Towt J. Waldron.*		Third Corporal, Chas. H. Putnam.

Fourth Corporal, George Phillips.

Bolmer, Henry	Foley, T. V.	Rose, David
Bennet, J. H.	Garrabrant, Alfred	Salters, Dennis
Baker, David	Hawkins, George	Smith, I. D.
Blauvelt, Isaac*	Harrison, Bernard	See, Thomas
Bertenshaw, Philip	Hoffman, Joseph*	Tremper, George*
Curtis, Harvey	Ives, William*	Thompson, A. G.
Conover, J. H.	Knapp, James	Waldron, Edgar N.
Dailey, John	Lyng, George	Waldron, Wm. J.
Devoe, George	Meissner, Charles*	Waldron, Carrol S.
Decker, George	Mondawka, W.	White, Adam
Dutcher, David	Minerly, Joseph	White, Richard
Dutcher, Jacob	Neve, George	Wood, Henry
Dealing, Wm. H.	Neal, Walter B.	Wood, John N.*
Dines, James N.	Palmer, John H.	Wood, Daniel*
Driscoll, James	Parcells, John	Wotten, Daniel
Ennis, Wm.	Putney, Burril	Dean, Isaac
Foster, George	Ryder, Alexander	Dean, Daniel
Foster, Anthony	Ryder, John H.	Baker, Wm. H.

On the evening of May 8th, 1861, the farewell services of Company G. were held in the Dutch Reformed Church at Nyack. Long before the hour appointed for the exercises to begin, that edifice was crowded, and after the volunteers had entered, it was difficult to find standing room. The sermon was given by William G. Haeselbarth, from the text found, Isaiah XXVI: 12; an address was delivered by L. D. Mansfield, and a copy of the Bible was given to each volunteer by William Voorhis.

On the following morning, Thursday, May 9th, the company rendezvoused at Union Hall, and marched from there to the steamboat landing, foot of Smith Place, from whence it was transported to New York by the steamboat Isaac P. Smith.

It seems wise to follow the further course of this organization before continuing with the story of events in the County. On its arrival at the

*Died in service.

City, the company was quartered at the Park Barracks, where it remained till June 14th. Then it was moved to Staten Island. While at New York, Luther Caldwell was promoted to the position of Paymaster of the 17th Regiment, and L. C. Mabie became First Lieutenant of Company G. At Staten Island the men received their uniforms, consisting of light blue pantaloons, dark blue coat and cap, and light blue overcoat. On June 21st the start for Washington was begun. The subsequent history of this Nyack company is brief. During the autumn of 1861, dissention arose between the officers and men of the organization, and the company was disbanded, the men being billeted among the other companies of the 17th Regiment. Thenceforth the local identity of the original company was lost. That the services of the men who composed it were not lost, is only too grimly told by the asterisks which mark so many names.

To return to the County, and, for the sake of clearness, still continuing with Nyack; we find the feeling produced by the outbreak of the war not only dividing all social ties, but even extending so far as to affect the places chosen for public meetings. Union Hall, situated on the north side of Main street, a few steps west of Broadway, became the resort and head-quarters of all Union partisans, while only next in the frequency of its use was the chapel of the Rockland Female Institute, or, in warm weather, its grounds. The disunionists met at the York House, corner of Main street and Piermont avenue.

A public meeting was held in Union Hall, May 24th, 1861, to take some action in regard to assisting the families of volunteers until such time as should permit them to be beyond danger of want. At this meeting a relief organization was effected with the following officers:

President, D. D. Smith.

Vice Presidents.

Isaac S. Lydecker,	D. D. Demarest,	F. L. Nichols,
Aaron L. Christie,	John W. Towt,	Isaac Hart,
Tunis Smith,	Peter De Pew,	John V. Burr,
George Green,	D. J. Blauvelt,	Wm. B. Collins.

Secretaries.

William Voorhis,	Daniel Burr,	Col. Isaac Sloat.

The following committee was appointed to take charge of and supply the families in need of aid:

John W. Towt,	William Voorhis,	D. J. Blauvelt,
David D. Smith,	D. D. Demarest,	John W. Moison,
Tunis Smith,	John V. Burr,	R. P. Eells,
George Green,	Isaac Sloat,	S. G. V. Edwards.
	William B. Collins.	

D. D. Demarest was made the treasurer of this organization. During the meeting speeches were made by Wm. G. Haeselbarth, Isaac Sloat and others. John W. Moison made a forcible plea, that Blauveltville should be permitted to do her share in the work in hand, and a letter was read from L. D. & C. F. Mansfield pledging $100 toward the fund. I may be permitted to state here, that the people of Blauveltville had contributed $700 toward the purpose of this meeting by July 4th, 1861.

While Nyack was thus actively moving in the cause of the Union, other parts of the County were by no means idle. As early as April 22d a public meeting was held in the Wigwam at Haverstraw for the purpose of encouraging volunteering and raising funds to assist the families of recruits. The Wigwam had been erected on the common directly south of the Central Presbyterian church and was opened to the public July 27. 1860. This edifice was used by the Unionists during the war. The meeting was organized as follows:

> General George S. Allison, Chairman.
> John I. Cole, Secretary.

The following committee was appointed to receive and disburse contributions.

Henry M. Peck,	Alexander Davidson,	Gen'l G. S Allison,
Alexander Waldron,	Rev. Fred. L. King,	J. L. DeNoyelles,
Rev. Patrick Mahoney,	Rev. J. J. Smith,	William Call,
Rev. Dr. Crane,	Rev. A S. Freeman,	John W. Felter,

The following citizens at once subscribed to the fund:

George S. Allison,	$100	William Knight,	$100	John Biggs,	$ 25
William Call,	100	Samson Marks, Sr.,	100	Edwin Brockway,	25
H. M. Peck,	100	Isaiah Millburn,	100	T. J. Fredericks,	25
John M. Gardner,	100	George Benson,	100	R. A. VerValen,	25
John D. Gardner,	100	Levi D. West,	50	Sam'l A. VerValen,	25
Silas D. Gardner,	100	F. J. Wiles & Co.,	50	C. P. Hoffman,	25
A. Davidson,	100	Robert Smith,	15	Wm. J. Penny,	25
Calvin Tomkins,	100	Uriah Washburn,	50	A Friend,	25
Daniel Tomkins,	100	John I. Cole,	50	J. O. Schneder,	25
G. C. Vancleaf,	25	Thos. Shankey,	50	I. M. Gardner,	25
John Oldfield,	100	Geo. S. Wood,	50	G. G. Allison,	25
J. L. DeNoyelles,	100	J. H. Stephens,	50	Abram Felter,	25
Arnet Seaman,	100	Bradley Keesler,	50	James King,	10

By May 25th, 1861, the officers of this association were: George S. Allison, President; George S. Oldfield, Secretary; Edward Pye, Treasurer. In December of the same year the committee had fifty families to care for.

Enlistments in Haverstraw were early begun, and continued through the summer of 1861. By October, a company called the DeNoyelles Guards had been formed, consisting of the following men:

Captain Edward Pye *

Abbott, John	DeLaMontanya, J.	Odell, Abram
Ackerman, Wm. E. *	Dolson Chas.	Osborn, P. M.
Adams, F. C.	Frazer, Wm. M.	Palmer, John
Agnew, James	Fletcher, T. A.	Peck, Joseph *
Allison, Wm. J.*	Frederick, Levi	Phillips, John *
Babcock, S. W.	Gardner, Fenton	Rose, J. J.
Babcock, J. P.	Glassing, Adam	Ryan, Patrick
Barry, John	Gurnee, F. M.	Seely, R. J.
Blower, John	Hastings, Thos.	Snedeker, Abram
Brooks, Dan'l	Hedges, Ira M.	Smith, John H.
Broderick, P.	Hedges, Jesse B.	Sm h, Dick O.
Burke, Edw.	Herod, Wm.	Smith, Wm. G. *
Buno, B. B.*	Holden, Jas.	Slack, Wm. C.
Call, Nicholas	Hinman, W. C.*	Sherwood, Wm. L.
Conklin, W. S.	King, John. W.	Stammers Geo. *
Conklin, Lorenzo D.*	Knapp, Chas. E.	Stalter, John
Coleman, John	Knapp, J. N.	Scott, Wm.
Connolly, Mat.	Knapp, Daniel E.*	Titus, John J.
Cornelison, James	Jersey, Enos	Terry, Seth
Cornelison, Wm.	Jones, Elihu *	Turner, Chas. G.
Cosgrove, W. M.	Larkin, Jas.	Thompson, Edw.
Creney, Jas.	Luke Jas.	Traphagen. R. D.
DeBevoise, Pete.	Mackey, S. G.	Welch, Richard
Doyle, Hugh	McGuirk, John	Weiant, Edw.
DeNoyelles, P.	McDonald, John	Wright, Wm. H.
DeNoyelles, John. F.	Nye, M.	Phillips, Wm. H.
	Phillips, Edw.	

On October 13th, 1861, the DeNoyelles Guard attended the Central Presbyterian church for their farewell service. The exercises on this occasion were conducted by Revs. Mr. Marsh, Dr. Crane, Mr. Hepburn and A. S. Freeman. On the following day, October 14th, a flag, raised through the efforts of Misses L. Ver Valen and L. Demarest, was presented to the company by Rev. A. S. Freeman, the exercises being conducted in the lot east of the Wigwam. On Tuesday, October 15th, 1861, the company marched to the steamboat landing, through streets crowded with people, and took passage on the steamboat Isaac P. Smith for New York. On reaching the city, the men were transported to Harlem, and entered camp at the Red House with their regiment, the 95th New York Volunteers. Thenceforth the organization was known as company F.

Even while this company was being enlisted, recruits were received for

* Died in service.

another organization, and as soon as arrangements were completed, Colonel A. F. Ingold, A. S. Gurnee and L. B. Weaver moved to the Wigwam and set actively to work. By November 20th, 1861, the Stephens Guards were ready to leave Haverstraw for the camp at Harlem.

Captain, A. F. Ingold.   Lieutenant, A. S. Gurnee.   Lieutenant, J. H. Weaver.

Aiken, Isaac
Brewster, Morgan
Brewster, Dan. B.
Benson, William
Bostedo, Charles
Waldron, Charles
Fales, William
Hammond, Theo.
Hill, Jas. M.
Hudson, John

Knapp, Isaac
Knapp, George
Weiant, Wm.
Keesler, Bradley
Keesler, Daniel
Monroe, Jesse
McCormick, Jas.
Lent, James
Weiant, Alexander

Osborn, Chas. W.*
Thorn, William
Phillips, George
Phillips, Wm.
Stalter, Theodore
Stammers, Jos.*
Smith, Richard
Springted, Winfield
Seeley, John

On the morning of November 21st, 1861, this company started. Marching first to the quarters at Beebe's, the members had breakfast, and then went to Bogert's dock where they took the steamer Metamora for New York. On arriving at the city they were transported to Harlem and entered camp with the 95th Regiment New York Volunteers as Company B.

In October, Dominick Kenedy began recruiting at Haverstraw for the 95th Regiment. By December 5th, 1861, he had obtained twenty-seven members for a new company, and left Haverstraw with this nucleus for the camp at Red House. Beside these organized companies, volunteers were being recruited at Haverstraw for other regiments. As early as August 10th, 1861, ten recruits were obtained from Johnsontown and two from Haverstraw for the 5th Regiment New York Volunteers. In October of the same year, Captain James E. McGee was recruiting for Company F, of the Irish Brigade. A month later, Lieutenant Samuel W. Babcock was appointed to recruit for the 95th Regiment, and had his quarters at W. W. Oldfield's—the Washington Saloon. By December, Lieutenant J. H. Weaver was recruiting for the same regiment, having his quarters on Main street.

The 95th Regiment, N. Y. Volunteers, was largely made up of Rockland County men. It was at first called the "Warren Rifles," and its first Chaplain was Rev. A. S. Wolfe, of the M. E. Church at Mechanicsville, now Viola; its first Surgeon, Dr. S. S. Sloat, of Haverstraw. The regiment remained in camp at Harlem till February 20th, 1862. It was then moved to New Dorp, Staten Island, and lay there till March 8th, of the same year, when it started for Washington with 900 men. The first

* Died in service.

colonel of the regiment was George H. Biddle, who resigned, owing to bad health, in the fall of 1863. He was followed by Edward Pye, who died in June, 1864, from wounds received at the battle of Cold Harbor. From that time till the regiment was mustered out of service, on July 16th, 1865, it was under the command of Lieutenant-Colonel James Crency. During its service in the field this command had 1,900 men. It was mustered out with 255.

The loyal movement in the western part of the County was as spontaneous and active as that among the citizens of the east. At the news that Fort Sumter had fallen, that war had been begun, meetings for the raising of troops to support the Union were held at Ramapo Works and Sloatsburgh, and, on September 7th, 1861, a rousing Union meeting was held at Sufferns, with the following gentlemen as chairman and assistants:

Henry L. Pierson, President.

Vice-Presidents:

Charles D. Wood,	Isaiah Paterson,	A. C. Wannamaker,
John D. Christie,	Abraham Cornelius,	D. C. Cooper,
Charles T. Ford,	Henry Kelly,	John Crum,
	E. J. Straut.	

Speeches were made by H. S. Barnes, Abram S. Hewitt, Henry L. Pierson, Jr., W. B. McLauren and others. In November, 1861, Lieutenant-Colonel J. Fred Pierson opened a recruiting office at the Post office at Ramapo Works to obtain volunteers for the 1st Regiment, N. Y. Volunteers. Most of the volunteers from this section, however, enlisted in companies formed in Nyack and Haverstraw.

At Spring Valley, a meeting for the purpose of raising volunteers and obtaining funds to provide for their families, was held at the Union School house as early as April 30th, 1861. At this meeting Leonard Gurnee was chosen Chairman, and Henry E. Armstrong Secretary, while speeches were made by W. B. McLauren, Frank Charlton, Stephen D. Herrick, John Stillwell and others. A second meeting was held in the Spring Valley House, May 8th, 1861, under the following officers:

Andrew Hopper, Chairman.

Vice-Presidents,

Peter Yeury, William Van Wagenen, Henry Sherwood, Henry De Ronde.
Henry E. Armstrong, Secretary.

A collection was taken up at the meeting for the benefit of volunteers and their families, and the following committee appointed to solicit subscriptions for the fund:

Francis Charlton,	W. B. McLauren,	H. E. Armstrong,
William Van Wagenen,	E. E. Straut.	Andrew Smith,
	W. T. Hesketh.	

Recruiting was begun, not only in the companies at Nyack and Haverstraw, but also by Captain J. G. Wellington at Nanuet. By October 1861, the local company, known as the Nanuet Guards, was about half enlisted, and barracks had been erected for their accommodation a little east of the railroad station. At a later period, an attempt was made to merge this organization into some other company and the Guards at once disbanded.

Upon this termination of his efforts in Ramapo township, J. G. Wellington visited Nyack and opened a recruiting office for the purpose of enlisting a company of sharpshooters to be known as "Mad Anthony Wayne Scouts." In Nyack, since the departure of Company G., volunteering had been energetic, and the following members of Companies A. and B., 127th Regiment, New York Volunteers, had enlisted:

Ayres, Wm. H.*	Fields, James	Smith, Henry E.
Ackerman, Edw. H.	Gorry, Thomas	Smith, George
Ackerman, James	Henderson, John	Snedeker, Chas. H.
Benson, Wm. A.	Hoffman, George	Thompson, Alfred G.
Brewer, Isaac, Sr.	Hefferman, ——	Tompkins, Brundage
Christie, C. A.	Kelly, Richard	Tompkins, James
Christie, D. I.	Lowdie, Alfred *	Tucker, Edward
Cooper, George	Murray, James	Tallman, Peter
Conover, A. Jr.	Osborne, Jesse	Warner, Chas. H.
Creany, James	Rhodes, Josiah	Warner, T. V. W.
Conklin, Samuel	Rutherford, John	Ware, J. Bradley *
De Baun, Henry	Rodgers, Charles	Welsh, Thomas *
De Baun, John	Scott, Daniel	Wood, George W.
Forshay, Simeon	Seaman, Tunis D.	Ward, John
	Waldron, Albert.	

Among the other volunteer regiments, which contained men from our County, I may mention the the 65th N. Y. Vols. organized in July, 1861, as the 1st U. S. Chasseurs. This organization took from Rockland the following:

Brooks, Leonard	Rose, Albert	Whitaker Lewis
Felter, John	Lent, James	Hinman, W. C.*
Kirkpatrick, Hiram	Lawson, James	McKenzie, John
	Weinant, Edward	

The 6th N. Y. Heavy Artillery was organized and mustered into service at Yonkers, on Sept. 2d, 1862, as the 135th Regt., N. Y. Vols.

---
*Died in service.

On October 3d of the same year, the organization was changed from an infantry to an artillery regiment. The following are among the volunteers from Rockland:

Company K, 6th Artillery.
Captain, Wilson Defendorf.
First Lieutenant, Charles H. Leonard

Campbell, Wm.	Higgins, R. E.*	No. 2. Phillips, George
Cypher, Edwin	Hyer, George*	Sherman, Wm.
Conklin, Alfred	Haeselbarth, Frank	Smith, Daniel.
Dailey, John G.	Jordan, William J.	Tetnure, Irvin
Dean, Chas.	Murphy, Peter C.	Temper, Wm. N.
Dean, John	Meissner, Chas. Jr.	Waldron, Matthew
Dickey, Wm.*	Osborn, Cornelius	Wergen, Simon
Felter, Isaac	Phillips, Wm.*	Youmans, Timothy*
Hagerman, Chas.*	No. 1. Phillips, George	Youmans, Wm. H.
	Wotten, John H.	

Other company members from Rockland County.

Anderson, George	Foster, Henry	Nife, Geo.
Allison, Geo. G.	Hudson, Lemuel H.	Nife, Abram.
Babcock, E.	Higgins, Wm.	Neilor, And.
Babcock, Wm. H.	Ennis, Geo. A.	Phillips, Geo. H.
Babcock, H. H.	Ennis, Henry	Purdy, Edward
Basset, M. V.	Jones, Jno. H.	Parcells, Wm.*
Blanch, Isaac*	Jones, Geo. H.	Tallman, Chas. W.
Bolmer, Abr.	Henion, John	Sutherland, Geo. B.
Frisbie, Wm. A.	June, Baxter	Weyant, Wm.
Call, John	Gilman, Wallace	Rose, Jacob
Conklin, F. P.	Larkin, Jas.	Rose, James
Concklin, Francis	Goose, Wm.	Rose, Moses
Concklin, Geo. W.*	March, Isaac	Rose, John
Concklin, Wm. G.*	March, Wm.	Strickland, J. H.*
Conklin, Orville	Mann, D. L.	Strickland, Jno.*
Cosgrove, Henry	Hudson, Chas.	Strickland, J.
Davidson, John	Morgan, D.	Wood, Daniel R.
Fields, Valentine*	Miller, Jno. C.	Youmans, J. E.*
Dutcher, David	Moore, J. W.	Yerks, Wm. H.

The 6th Artillery, which was recruited in the 8th Senatorial District, comprising Westchester, Putnam and Rockland Counties, was mustered into service with 1,100 men. It was engaged in the following battles: Wapping Heights, July, 1863; Wilderness, May 6th and 7th, 1864; Laurel Hill, May 12th; Po River, May 15th; Ellison's Farm, May 19th; North Anna River, May 23d; Bethesda Church, May 30th; Mechanicsville Pike, June 2d and 3d; Front of Petersburg, June 18th and July 26th; Burnside's Mine Explosion, July 30th; Cedar Creek, October 19th, 1864; Bermuda Front, Jan. 22d and April 2d, 1865. The regiment reached

---
*Died in service.

New York to be mustered out July 2d, 1865, with 698 men. Of these about 250 were original volunteers, the balance being one year men, recruited while the regiment was in the field.

At the invasion of Pennsylvania by the Army of Northern Virginia, in 1863, the militia regiments of this and neighboring States were hurried to the front. Among those called upon for duty was the 17th Regiment, N. Y. S. M. This organization at once responded and left Yonkers, July 8th, 1863, nearly 400 strong. The companies from our County in this Regiment were "D," of Stony Point; "F," of Haverstraw, and "I," of Ramapo. The officers and men of these companies at the time of departure were as follows:

John P. Jenkins, White Plains, Lieutenant-Colonel Commanding.
Wm. Govan, M. D., Surgeon.   F. L. Nichols, Quartermaster.

COMPANY D, STONY POINT GUARDS.
Captain, E. W. Christie.

First Lieutenant, M. D. Marks.
First Sergeant, E. Rose.
Third Sergeant, D. D. Mackey.
First Corporal, P. G. Rose.
Third Corporal, John Loyd.

Second Lieutenant, Abr. S. Vanderbilt.
Second Sergeant, Robert Sims.
Fourth Sergeant, W. F. B. Gumer.
Second Corporal, J. H. Owens.
Fourth Corporal, T. W. Blauvelt.

Basley, Henry	Dykins, Abr.	Oldfield, W. W.
Bird, Geo. W.	Dykins, Thos.	Peterson, Benj.
Bradbury, Lewis	Fox, Henry	Peterson, David
Brewster, R.	Jones, Chas.	Phillips, R.
Brooks, N. B.	Jones, Samuel	Phillips, J.
Burras, W. H.	June, Peter	Rose, J.
Call, James	King, A. J.	Rose, Peter
Crum, George	Marks, S. J.	Smith, Geo. S.
Davidson, T.	Macauly, Wm.	Van Wart, C.
Decker, Wm	McElroy, Chas.	Van Wart, Jacob

Herman B. McKenzie, Wm. Percival, Drummers.

COMPANY F, INGOLD GUARDS.
Captain, C. P. Hoffman.

First Lieutenant, Stephen W. Allen.
First Sergeant, Geo. S. Oldfield.
Third Sergeant, J. M. Minnerley.
First Corporal, Dan. R. Lake.

Second Lieutenant, Isaac De Baun.
Second Sergeant, S. H. Davidson.
Fourth Sergeant, James Wood, Jr.
Second Corporal, Wm. Redner.

Third Corporal, Abr. P. Jersey.

Allison, E. T.	Fredericks, T. J.	Miller, B.
Anderson, Geo.	Felter, Edw.	Owens, R. H.
Babcock, John	Grimshaw, J.	Parson, O. W.
Babcock, Hiram	Gurney, M.	Phillips, Abr.
Babcock, William	Gurney, Wallace	Robinson, L. V. E.
Blauvelt, S. C.	Johnson, W. S.	Ritzgo, Henry
Buchanan, R.	Kingsland, Wm. H.	Ryan, Wm.

Bengkert, Wm.
Cranston, J.
Comerford, A.
Denike, C. A.
King, Joe
King, Stephen
Keesler, Wm. H.
Kirkpatrick, Hiram
Seaman, Wm. A.
Secor, Geo.
Stickinrider, Jno.
Waldron, Matthew

Alonzo Bedell, Walter Hicks, Drummers.

COMPANY I, RAMAPO GUARDS.
Captain, William D. Furman.

First Lieutenant, Reuben Riggs.
First Sergeant, C. A. Blauvelt.
Third Sergeant, Daniel Springsteen.
First Corporal, J. H. Goetschius.
Third Corporal, Jno. H. Crum.

Second Lieutenant, Augustus Coe.
Second Sergeant, J. J. Wannamaker.
Fourth Sergeant, D. Sherwood.
Second Corporal, Leonard Cooper.
Fourth Corporal, Alpheus J. Coe.

Ackerson, Geo. E.
Bertholf, Edw. O.
Blauvelt, S. P.
Bush, Harvey
Charlton, Francis
Coe, Larry, D. N.
Conklin, Nelson
Crum, Edw.
Dussenberry L.
Forshee, C.
Forshee, Hiram
Furman, Wm. H.
Gurnee, Wm. H.*
Hendricks, Wm.
Hoyt, Rufus

Hoyt, Harrison
Hoyt, Wm.
Johnson, A.
Johnson, Levi
Johnson, Robert
Johnson, Tunis
Johnson, Wm. D.*
Jones, B. J.
McElroy, C.
McElroy, J. M.
McMurty, A.
Murray, Wm.
Morris, T. J.
Osborn, A.
Osborn, Chas. H.

Perry, Wm.
Phillips, D.
Sherwood, J. B.
Slim, B. S.
Smith, Alfred
Springsteen, R.
Taylor, Edw. E.
Wallace, John
Walmsley, Edw.
Whaley, Ira
Youmans, C.
Young, Alfred
Young, Charles
Young, Judson

The 17th Regiment N. Y. S. M., which had been called upon for thirty days' service, was mustered into the United States service July 22d, 1863, though its time counted from July 8th. It was hurried to Baltimore and did garrison duty, first at Fort Independence, and later at Fort McHenry. On August 6th, 1861, the regiment returned to New York, and later to the County. The trip from New York to Yonkers was made by steamboat Metamora. At this town the regiment disembarked for a dress parade, and remained ashore longer than the steamboat captain liked. Accordingly, on the return of the Rockland County companies to the vessel, the captain refused to carry them further. The difficulty was at length compromised by his agreeing to transport them to Nyack, from whence they were taken to Haverstraw by the Nyack ferry-boat, reaching that village at 2 A. M.

Fortunate it was for this County, that her soil was not, in the Civil War, exposed to the march and battles of opposing armies, as in the War for Independence. In one sense our people did not realize what war was. The current of ordinary life, of ordinary business, flowed on, unbroken

---

* Died. Gurnee from typhoid fever contracted in camp. Johnson from sunstroke.

within our boundaries, and the carnage of battle, the exposure of camp life, the devastation that marks the track of marching forces, the sicknesses that beset military cantonments, were too distant to produce the effect which would have followed personal contact. But in another sense, the war did come home to us. Of a total population of military age amounting to 3,979, no less than 558 served in the armies, and of these, 89 died from camp exposure or wounds, or were killed in battle. Surely, any one who lived during those days of dread—dread, if a battle was not fought, that the South would be successful; dread, if a battle was fought, that the lives of loved ones might have gone out in the conflict, or that they might be lying sorely wounded—surely, any one who has passed through such heartache, in a measure understands what is meant by war.

It is with pleasure that, for a moment, I turn from the enlisting of men, who went forth to inflict wounds and death, to the noble efforts and work of the men and women who toiled to alleviate suffering and prevent death.

When Company G. was enlisted, its members were supplied by the Union women of Nyack with flannel underclothing, handkerchiefs, towels, socks, combs, brushes, needle-books and havelocks, and on July 9th, these Union women made up and sent a box of dainties and $25 to the Nyack Company. During the fall of the same year—1861—a number of the Union women of Nyack organized a branch of the United States Sanitary Commission, which magnificent and unique organization, after every discouragement from the Government authorities, had at length obtained recognition, June 9th, 1861. The first officers of the Nyack branch of the society were:

    Mrs. Mary Corey, President.
    Mrs. Mary Gunn, Vice-President.
    Miss R. Annie Green, Secretary.
    Mr. John Gunn, Corresponding Secretary.
    Mrs. Elizabeth Hasbrouck, Treasurer.

The names of the members of the Nyack Society, which have come to me, I give. I would that this list, as well as that of the volunteers from this County, was more perfect, and again urge upon the public the importance of getting this matter completed before it is too late.

Mrs. Caroline Dixon,	Mrs. John W. Towt,
Mrs. James Cooper,	Miss Louise Towt,
Mrs. George Green,	Mrs. Christopher Rutherford,
Mrs. George H. Livermore,	Miss Sarah M. Green,
Mrs. De Pew Tallman,	Mrs. Delos Mansfield,
Mrs. B. Davidson,	Miss Lizzie Towt,

    Mrs. Blauvelt, (Mrs. Cranston's Mother).

Previous to the organization of the Nyack Society, Mr. and Mrs. John Gunn, and Mrs. Hasbrouck had visited different sections of the County, asking donations of clothing, etc., and had obtained 106 articles, consisting of bed-clothing, under-clothes, etc. The first meeting of the Society was called by Mrs. Aaron Remsen, and met at Union Hall. After that, meetings were held every week, at first in the different churches, till the sexton of one of those edifices objected to heating the building for the use of "Black Republicans," then at the homes of the members, and finally at Union Hall.

In the winter of 1861, the Nyack branch of the Sanitary Commission sent to the Central Association, three boxes of delicacies and several boxes of clothing. In 1862, 1,500 articles, consisting of sheets, pillow-cases, bed-ticks, quilts, pillows, muslin and flannel shirts and drawers, and 50 pairs of woolen socks were sent. In 1863, 800 articles, similar to those of the preceding year, were forwarded, together with a large amount of lint and bandages. In 1864, up to November 12th, 534 articles were forwarded to the Central Association. On April 20th, 21st, and 22d of this year, a fair in aid of the Sanitary Commission was held in Union Hall, at Nyack.

One of the leading features of this fair was an old Dutch kitchen and dinner. Once again, and perhaps for the last time was seen the Dutch oven, the open fire-place, the crane, pot-hooks and trammels; once again did descendants of the Dutch settlers don short gown and petticoat, and busy themselves in cooking an old-fashioned Dutch dinner. When the feast was ready, the company sat around a table, then over two centuries old, loaded with savory viands, talked in the County Dutch patois and sang songs, long forgotten, in the same language.

Another feature of the fair was the presence of Captain Wilson Defendorf, with his Company from the 10th Regiment Veteran Reserve Corps, which was stationed at Tarrytown. Before leaving Nyack, this command marched up Broadway, to the residence of Jesse Blackfan, stepfather of the commanding officer, and later, counter-marched in the door-yard of George Green. The amount raised by the Nyack Sanitary Fair was $800. To this sum should be added the proceeds obtained from two fairs held by the pupils of the Rockland Female Institute, at which they obtained $40 and $12.

The last shipment of articles by the Nyack branch society was made June 28th, 1865, and was acknowledged as follows:

"U. S. SANITARY COMMISSION,
Woman's Central Association of Relief,
11 Cooper Union, Third Ave.,
N. Y., June, 30, 1865.

"Mrs. Gunn. Dear Madam:
I have the pleasure of acknowledging the receipt of one barrel and one bale of hospital supplies from the society at Nyack, according to your note of the 28th inst.

Nyack has worked very faithfully for the Sanitary Commission during the war, and we feel sincerely thankful. It seems impossible to realize that the work is indeed over. Our friends continue faithful to the end, as our 27 boxes received to-day show. Hoping that you and the other members of the Nyack Society will heartily enjoy your well-earned rest,
"I am, gratefully yours,
GERTRUDE STEVENS,
Committee of Supplies."

The last meeting of the Nyack branch of the Sanitary Commission was held July 4th, 1865.

On the organization of the military companies in Haverstraw in 1861, the Union women of that place formed a Sewing Circle, which met at the homes of its different members, most frequently at that of Mrs. J. L. De Noyelles.

Among those associated in the work were:

Mrs. A. S. Freeman,	Mrs. J. C. Coe,	Mrs. Mark Pratt,
Mrs. J. L. De Noyelles,	Mrs. J. S. Gurnee,	Mrs. A. B. Conger,
Mrs. Edw. Pye,	Mrs. Blanch,	Mrs. A. Wiles,
Mrs. Henry M. Peck,	Mrs. J. W. Crane,	Mrs. Cosgrove,
Mrs. George S. Wood,	Mrs. B. McKenzie,	Miss House,
Mrs. John H. Stephens,	Mrs. J. Gillem,	Mrs. Robert Smith,
Mrs. W. C. Hinman,	Mrs. Alfred Marks,	Mrs. Susan De Noyelles.
Mrs. A. E. Suffern,	Mrs. S. C. Blauvelt,	

The last named lady knit enough "nice yarn mittens" to allow of a pair being sent to every man in Company F.

"CAMP WARD, Dec. 9, 1861. Alexandria, Va.
"The undersigned, members of Company A. 31st Regt. N. Y. V. would most respectfully tender to Mrs. Henry M. Peck and the ladies associated with her, their warmest thanks, for the very generous present of India Rubber Blankets, Under clothing, Stockings and Mitts, they have forwarded by express to us."
"JOHN DAVIDSON, MADISON KING,
"THOMAS DAVIDSON, CHARLES HICKS,
"JAMES THOMPSON, CORP. WM. H. BAKER."

On Feb. 10th, 1864, Henry M. Peck stated that several boxes of goods had been sent to the soldiers by the ladies of Haverstraw, through his hands valued at $600. Beside this grand work of the women, aid was given to the U. S. Sanitary and Christian Commissions by church collections and from the proceeds of lectures. On Dec. 1st, 1863, Rev. James M. Freeman gave, as the result of a collection for the Christian Commission, $28.75. On April 13th, 1864, Rev. A. S. Freeman delivered a lecture, for the benefit of the Sanitary Commission, and raised $67.15. The result of a Thanksgiving collection in November of the same year, taken in Rev. A. S. Freeman's church, added $61.00 more to the result of the noble work carried on in Haverstraw. Among other organizations, beside those of Nyack and Haverstraw, which worked for the U. S. Sanitary Fund, must be mentioned the Piermont Knitting Society.

We must turn now and view an act of the National Legislature, which created greater excitement and bitterness in Rockland County than any person living had ever seen during her existence, which completed the disruption of social relations between Peace Democrats and Unionists; which at one time, for a brief instant, seemed likely to terminate in mob violence; which ended in the practical annihilation of the disunion influence, and left it stricken, pitiable in its impotence. I refer to the Act commonly called the "Conscription" or "Draft Act."

The first outburst of enthusiasm, which had led to volunteering on every side, was ended. Many had enlisted, regarding the war movement as a gigantic holiday excursion, expecting it to be terminated in a few months, and feeling that they could enjoy a good time at Government expense without inconvenience. The long campaigns in the West, during which the battle of Shiloh was fought, which ended in only forcing the enemy into a more compact and impregnable position; the dreadful Peninsula campaign which ended when McClellan and his army were hurled back on Washington, leaving every step of the retreat slippery with human blood; and which was followed by Lee's invasion of Maryland, dissipated all absurdity in regard to the strength of the contest. Men began to learn what war meant by 1863. Many had enlisted on account of the emolument, wages, board and clothing, because there was little employment at home. The departure of the volunteers, the necessities of the Government in every form, created a fresh impetus in business; employees were scarce, wages high. Financially, there was no longer any inducement to enlist.

By the close of 1862, volunteering had practically ceased, and the calls for 600,000 men, made by the President on July 2d, and August 4th, of that year, were unanswered, each State insisting that the other States should furnish proportional numbers of men for the army. It was at this stage of affairs that conscription was proposed. If, argued those who favored the prosecution of the war, we abandon the struggle now, we stand before the world, not a laughing-stock, for the lives already sacrificed forbid laughter, but a helpless semblance of authority. We must go forward, to do so, we must have troops; men claim the right to vote; if they have this power they should support that which confers the power. It was under such feelings that the Act for enrolling and calling out the National Forces was passed by both branches of the National Legislature; in the

Senate without the yeas and nays having been called; in the House by a vote of 115 to 49.

Not without reluctance was the power of conscription conceded. All men recognized the gigantic stride toward centralization, that it represented, and all feared the effect of such a precedent. Dire extremity alone made the motion popular, as dire extremity in 1814 had led the then Secretary of War, William Eustis, to propose a similar measure. The Conscription Act became a law, March 3d, 1863. By its provisions all able bodied male citizens, irrespective of color, including aliens who had declared their intention to become naturalized, between the ages of 18 and 45; were to be enrolled. Those between the ages of 20 and 35 were to constitute the 1st class, all others the 2d. "The President was authorized, on and after July 1st, 1863, to make drafts at his discretion of persons to serve in the national armies for not more than three years, any one drafted and not reporting to be considered as a deserter. Persons drafted might furnish an acceptable substitute, or pay $300, and be discharged from further liability under *that* draft."

In accordance with the Act the enrollment was begun, and in May a draft of 300,000 men was ordered.

To the disunionists of Rockland County the passage of this Act seemed too monstrous for belief. From the outbreak of hostilities they had persistently called for peace, insisting that the war was unconstitutional, that the Nation had no power to coerce a State, which wished to withdraw from the Union. With unfeigned horror they had seen coercion begun. At National victories they mourned; at National defeats rejoiced. Thoroughly consistent in following their ideas, except in the rather vital matter of voting in a government they disbelieved in, and drawing sustenance under its protection, while endeavoring in every way to injure it; these disunionists viewed the Emancipation Proclamation as an outrage, the suspension of habeas corpus as an unheard of desecration of the Constitution. But the slaves freed were the property of men hundreds of miles away, and so long had they been allowed to express their beliefs without annoyance, that the probability of the Government interfering with them at last seemed slight.

The Conscription Act was an entirely different matter. It struck close home. They with others would be enrolled; they with others must take their chance on the turn of a wheel: if drawn, they must either serve in the armies or pay toward the support of a cause they hated, and consternation and rage filled their minds.

Ever since the beginning of hostilities, the disunionists had drawn more and more apart from the Union men, and at length had come to form secret organizations for the better manipulation of their plans. In their wrath at the Conscription Act, these disunionists now turned on their patriot neighbors and threatened dire consequences if the draft proceeded. Among the threats was one to burn the residences of prominent Republicans throughout the County, another, to attack and loot the Provost Marshall's office at Tarrytown, and destroy the rolls.

Through the imprudent utterances of some of the less intelligent members of the disunion party, sufficient information of the incendiary plan was obtained to determine the Union men on action, and for their mutual protection and aid, the Rockland County branches of the Loyal National League were formed. These societies had pass-words, employed titles, and used the other belongings, that attach to secret societies. That at Nyack met weekly and oftener, if necessity demanded. Their mission was ended at the close of the war, and they passed from existence. The branch of the Loyal League at Haverstraw was organized May 9th, 1863, at a meeting at Benson's Hall, the following officers being chosen:

Alexander Davidson, President.

Vice-Presidents,

George Benson,	Peter Van Valer,
Levi Knapp,	Sylvester Knapp,
George S. Sherwood,	Richard Washburn,
John I Cole,	John Oldfield.

Spencer J. Weiant and Brewster J. Allison, Secretaries.

This society was joined by most of the Union men of Haverstraw township.

The organization at Nyack was completed about the same time as that at Haverstraw, and contained among its members the following persons:

Delos Mansfield,	Charles Mansfield,
John V. Burr,	Moses G. Leonard,
F. L. Nichols.	Edward Burr,
George Green,	E. B. Johnson,
Thomas Austin,	John W. Towt,
J. B. Pomeroy,	D. J. Blauvelt,
John Gunn,	Peter Voorhis,
Christopher Rutherford,	William G. Haeselbarth.

This Society contained most if not all of the Union men of Nyack in its membership.

For the purpose of enrollment and draft, a board was created in each Congressional District, consisting of the Provost Marshall, a Commissioner and a Surgeon. Rockland County was in the 10th Congressional District of New York, together with Putnam and Westchester Counties. In May, 1863, Hon. Moses G. Leonard of Rockland Lake was appointed Provost Marshall for this District, and established his office at Tarrytown.

It was evidently the part of the disunionists to throw every possible obstacle in the way of the Government in its efforts to carry out the Conscription Act, and their first move was to question the accuracy of the enrollment. A State law existed, requiring an enrolment of all persons liable to bear arms, but, owing to the neglect of the Legislature to appropriate money, no enrollment could be had until the means were provided on the personal responsibility of Governor Morgan. By this enrollment, as reported by Adjutant-General Hillhouse, Rockland County stood as follows:

Population,	22,462
Number of men enrolled,	3,979
Number of men exempt,	988
County's quota,	696
Volunteered since July 2d, 1862,	258
Deficiency,	438
Liable to draft,	2,991

This enrolment was regarded as too imperfect for the draft ordered by the President, and a new one was ordered under the supervision of each district Board of Enrollment. These local boards were under the command of the Provost Marshall Generals of each State, and these, in turn, were under the orders of James B. Fry, Provost Marshall General of the United States. New York State was divided in three divisions, and the State Provost Marshall General for the Southern division, which contained the Tenth Congressional District, was Colonel Robert Nugent, who was appointed April 25th, 1863.

Under the Board of Enrollment for our district, which comprised thirty-one townships, the enrolling officers for Rockland County were: John I. Cole, for Haverstraw; James H. Christie, for Orangetown; William D. Furman, for Ramapo, and A. Cornelison, for Clarkstown. These officers at once began work and soon completed their duties, the first to finish being A. Cornelison. The enrolment for the County together with an estimated quota of one-fifth, to which 50 per cent. is added for exemptions, was as follows:

Haverstraw,	{ White, 1270 = 1282 { Black, 12	{ 1st class, 879 { 2d class, 403	quota, 176×50 per cent.=264
Orangetown,	{ White, 721 = 774 { Black, 53	{ 1st class, 537 { 2d class, 237	quota, 107×50 per cent.=161
Ramapo,	{ White, 519 = 529 { Black, 10	{ 1st class, 353 { 2d class, 176	quota, 71×50 per cent.=106
Clarkstown,	{ White, 522 = 541 { Black, 19	{ 1st class, 351 { 2d class, 190	quota, 70×50 per cent.=105

As soon as the enrollment was completed, the slips and other necessaries were made out and Marshall Leonard prepared for the drawing, which was ordered to be begun at Tarrytown in the 10th District, July 20th, 1863. Meantime the disunionists had grown bolder in their threats to resist the draft, proclaiming, beside the usual formula about the unconstitutionality of the measure, that the enrolment was unjust and burdensome. In pursuance of their plan of action a mass meeting, to discuss the legality of the Conscription Act, was advertised to be held in Tarrytown, Monday, July 20th, 1863.

Through his deputy marshalls, the Union men in his District, Revs. John Quinn, of St. John's Church at Piermont, and Patrick Mahoney, of St. Peter's Church at Haverstraw, and Michael Murphy, his hired man, Marshall Leonard was informed, that a delegation from New York City was to be present at the proposed mass meeting, that incendiary speeches were to be made, and that, in all probability, a riot would follow, in which the Marshall's office was to be destroyed, with the books, slips, enrolment lists and other contents. On the morning of July 17th, when the Provost Marshall reached Tarrytown, he learned that a mob from the lower Westchester towns was on its march to Tarrytown. What preparation had been made by the disunionists of that place to aid them, no one knew. The Provost Marshall's office was defenceless—it will be remembered that the 17th Regt. N. Y. S. M., had started from Yonkers for the front July 8th—and if the outbreak had been advanced three days, as appeared probable, little resistance seemed possible.

With all haste the books and papers of the office were packed in the carriage of James A. Hamilton, of Irvington, who happened to be in the village, and by him were driven out of town and safely concealed. The next step was to obtain the muskets from the Tarrytown Military Academy, and with these, and the shot-guns, that could be secured in the village, as many as could be supplied were armed. This armed guard was stationed in and around the Provost Marshall's office. From two to three score Union men had by this time collected, armed with every conceivable weapon, and at once organized for duty. The mob, delayed by its fondness for liquor, at last reached Irvington, where it was met by word from Tarrytown, that as it was ahead of time and unexpected, no aid could be given it, while the Marshall had made thorough preparation for determined resistance. At this point it disintegrated, and the members returned to their homes. At the first alarm word had been sent to the Union men in the District, and by afternoon aid came from every quarter. A company, which was to remain on duty till military help could be obtained, was formed among the citizens, and in the care of this guard everything was left for the night.

Among the incidents of that day should be mentioned an act of Michael Murphy. Learning that there was trouble in Tarrytown, he started from Mr. Leonard's home at Rockland Lake, to meet him at the ferry landing, earlier than usual, and, before proceeding to the dock, drove up to Mr. Rutherford's Military Academy in Nyack, from which he obtained the muskets. On reaching the river he found that the last boat for Tarrytown had gone. On Marshall Leonard's arrival at Nyack, the muskets, which Murphy had loaded in a row boat to take across the river, were replaced in the wagon and driven to the residence of William Voorhis, in Upper Nyack—the house next north of the old stone church—where they were concealed in the cellar.

The next day Marshall Leonard and a number of the Union men of the District visited New York to obtain military aid. At first they were disappointed, the Military Commander General John A. Dix, referring them to Governor Seymour and he hesitating to render assistance. In this plight, Mr. Rhind, one of the party who had a brother in the navy, suggested a visit to the Brooklyn Navy Yard. It was made. The Commandant, Rear-Admiral Hiram Paulding, listened to their story, and promised them all possible help. On their return to New York, the committee called upon the Police Commissioners and stated their fears, receiving promise of aid from them likewise.

At 4:30 o'clock, on the morning of July 19th, a strong police force under the command of Captain Dickson and Sergeants McCleary and Barnett, left New York to patrol the lower Westchester towns; and a few hours later an U. S. gunboat sailed up the river and anchored off Tarrytown.

The presence of this gunboat, which patrolled the river from Tarrytown to Haverstraw, was a revelation to both Union and disunion men. It represented a mighty government, which, however much disturbed by distant foes, could still watch and care for its interests every where and punish without fail those who injured them. It brought fresh courage to the loyal people of Rockland County. It cast so great a fear upon the disunion men, that from the peaceful Sunday, when it was first seen at anchor, till the close of the war, no further open threats of violence were heard, and no acts of violence committed.

The draft riots in New York were at length ended by sharp measures. Veteran troops were forwarded to that city to prevent further outbursts. The militia was returning from the front. People at last realized the fact that the Government at Washington was in earnest, and meant to carry out the draft. Instantly, pleas for more time to meet the emergency came from the townships in the 10th District.

At a special town meeting held in Orangetown, it was voted to borrow $30,000 on the credit of the town, to cover the exemption fee of $300 of every one who should be drafted. In Clarkstown and Ramapo, it was resolved at special town meetings, that each person residing in those townships, liable to the draft, should pay $25 to the committee-man of his school district on or before September 12, 1863, which should go into a general fund, to be used to pay exemptions; those who did not pay were not to enjoy the benefits of this sum. It was further resolved in each township, that the Supervisor should petition the Legislature to permit the raising of a sufficient sum by a tax upon taxable property, to pay the exemptions of such as might be drafted over the amount raised by the $25 payments.

In Haverstraw township, which, the reader will remember, at that time embraced the present township of Stony Point, a call for a special meeting to raise money for the purpose of paying exemptions, was signed by sixteen of her leading citizens on September 10th. Pursuant to that call, a special town meeting was held at Benson's Corners on September 17th, and organized with Prince W. Nickerson as Chairman, and S. C. Blauvelt Secretary. At that meeting the following resolution was adopted:

"WHEREAS: The President of the United States, in his superior wisdom, by a Proclamation dated September 16th, 1863, has suspended the writ of Habeas Corpus, and whereas it is apparent that the suspension of said writ has reference to the pending draft, and the electors of the town of Haverstraw may unconsciously place themselves in antagonism to the ' powers that be,' and subject themselves to severe penalties by reason of any action that they may take;

Resolved : That the electors of said town suspend all action in reference to procuring exemption from the operation of the Conscription Act."

The firemen of Warren, however, raised a fund, to exempt any of their number who might be drawn, by the contribution of $50 per man, and petitioned the people of the village to aid them. This, the citizens decided to do, at a special election, and voted to raise $900, or as much of it as was needed, by a general tax upon the taxable property in Warren village.

Perhaps a word in regard to Haverstraw in the draft matter is necessary. From the beginning, her people proclaimed that the enrolment in her case was incorrect, that it was taken when the laborers in the brickyards and the employees in the rolling-mills, print works and other factories were at their busiest season. Many of these men were non-residents, and at the end of their season, before the drawing occurred, had gone from Haverstraw, leaving her citizens with a disproportionate quota. This complaint is certainly worthy of attention. But the drawing as originally ordered, was to have been held on July 20th, when this floating population was still in Haverstraw. It was not held at that time, because the violent feeling of the disunionists led them to threaten opposition to the draft instead of preparing to meet it. When it was discovered that the National Government was not in sport but thorough earnest, a plea for more time was made from all the townships, and through the clemency of that Government, which many of the residents had threatened to resist, in Haverstraw so openly that the gunboat had to patrol the river as far as that village, the extension of time was granted. This delay in time permitted the departure of the artisans and laborers.

On September 5th, 1863, Provost Marshall Leonard reported to Colonel Robert Nugent, Acting Assistant Provost Marshall General, that he was ready to begin the drawing, and suggested to him the advisability of having a military force at Tarrytown during the days of the draft. The draft began Wednesday, September 23d, 1863. On Tuesday, September 22d, three companies of the 26th Michigan Volunteers and one battalion of the 2d Connecticut Flying Artillery with two guns, arrived at Tarrytown and went into camp. On the following morning a detachment of 60 men of the Metropolitan Police, under Inspector Dilks, reported to Marshall Leonard for duty. The drawing proceeded in the most peaceful manner. Rockland County was drawn during the third day.

The number of men from this County held for service by this draft was 204. Of the conscripts, an even half dozen served in person, namely: Odell Gardner, of Haverstraw; Richard Williams, Isaac Osborne, John Van Zile, Lewis Matthews, of Ramapo, and Wm. Brown, á Negro, of Clarkstown.

On October 17th, 1863, the President called for 300,000 volunteers, and ordered a draft to fill all deficiencies which might exist, Jan. 5th, 1864. Under this call the quota for Rockland County was 221 men divided among the towns thus:

Haverstraw - - - 91	Clarkstown - - - 38
Orangetown - - - 55	Ramapo - - - 37

In order to facilitate recruiting, a recruiting agent was appointed for each town in the 10th District, by the Board of Enrolment, by Dec. 1st, 1863. Those appointed in our County were: Lieut. James H. Christie, for Orangetown; Capt. William D. Furman, for Ramapo; William Snyder, for Clarkstown, and Frederick Tomkins, for Haverstraw.

A special town meeting was held at the Town House, in Orangetown, on Dec. 21st, 1863, at which it was resolved that every person liable to the draft should pay $25 before Jan. 4th, 1864; that the town should offer a bounty of $350 cash for volunteers to the number of 72; that $28,000 or as much of it as was needed, should be raised for those bounties by the issue of town bonds of the value of $100 or upward; that a committee of seven should be appointed by Town Clerk, Henry Blauvelt, to obtain volunteers. The following were appointed:

I. P. Smith,	David I. Tallman,	Richard De Cantillon.
John H. Westervelt,	Lawrence Mann,	C. Van Antwerp,
	Tunis J. Blauvelt.	

On Dec. 28th, a special town meeting in Clarkstown resulted in a resolve to give a bounty of $380 for volunteers, and that the sum of $19,000 be raised by tax to meet this appropriation. On Dec. 31st, the people of Ramapo decided, at a special town meeting, to pay $375 bounty for volunteers, and to raise $18,000 by tax for this purpose.

On Jan. 11th, 1864, a special town meeting was held at Benson's Corners. It was then decided, by a vote of 186 to 108, that the town of Haverstraw should raise 75 men, or as many of that number as possible, by a bounty of $350 each; that the Supervisor should raise $27,000 on the town's credit, this latter to be met by a general town tax, for the purpose of paying these bounties; that each person liable to be drawn should pay $25, the money from this fund to be used, first to pay bounties and then to pay exemptions for such as join the fund; that John I. Cole, Prince W. Nickerson, James Eckerson, Denton Fowler and Richard Washburn should be the committee to receive the $25 payments, and that the committee should have the power to reduce or remit this sum in the cases of people too poor to pay, they to have the same benefit as the payers.

On January 18th, 1864, another special town meeting was held in Haverstraw, in pursuance of a call issued January 13th, to reconsider the resolutions passed January 11th. At this meeting those resolutions were rescinded by a majority of 137, and the following carried by a vote of 134:

That volunteers and substitutes be furnished for all persons who pay $25 and are drawn. That the Supervisor of the town should borrow on its credit a sufficient sum to pay each volunteer or substitute not more than $400. If a sufficient number of volunteers or substitutes could not be obtained, then the exemption fee of each man, who had joined the fund, should be paid. By February 18th, the Supervisor reported that 312 people had paid $25. Of these, 144 at a later period withdrew their money.

By March 10th, 1864, volunteering to fill the quotas had been carried on in the district to the following extent: Veteran re-enlistments, 358; volunteers, 613; Invalid Corps, 4. The number above or under the quota for each township in our County then stood as follows:

  Orangetown, over quota, 44 Ramapo, over quota,   40
  Clarkstown, " " 14 Haverstraw, under quota, 133

A special town meeting was again held at Benson's Corners on March 30th, 1864, at which the Supervisor of the town of Haverstraw was empowered to raise $36,000 for bounty purposes on the town's credit, no single bounty to exceed $300, and further, "to raise 120 men to fill the quota of said town, or so many thereof as in the opinion of the Town Board of said town it may be just right for the said town to furnish as her proper quota, under the late calls of the President for men." All former resolutions passed at any special town meeting since the beginning of the year, were rescinded. On April 21st, 1864, the *Rockland County Messenger* contained the following editorial:

"OUR QUOTA."

<blockquote>"Our four towns present quite a contrast with reference to the draft, or rather, we should say, Haverstraw is quite in contrast with the other three towns. Including all calls for troops, Ramapo has not only filled her quota, but has ten surplus. Orangetown will have a deficiency of *one*; Clarkstown of *seventeen*, and Haverstraw of *two hundred and twelve*."</blockquote>

Previous to the second draft, on March 1st, 1864, Hon. Moses G. Leonard resigned from the position of Provost Marshall and W. W. Pierson, of Westchester County, was appointed in his stead. The second draft began on May 9th, 1864. Three hundred and eleven were drawn from Haverstraw and sixteen from Clarkstown. The other townships had filled their quotas. On the same day that the draft occurred, "the Supervisor of Clarkstown presented sixteen volunteer enlistments, effected previous to the draft and the notices (to drafted men in that township) were not served."

In the second draft the names were taken from the same enrolment as that used at first, and, for reasons of which I have spoken, Haverstraw had 126 names drawn of persons who did not report. In this draft her people determined, if possible, to put in men, instead of paying exemptions, and for this purpose offered the sum of $300 to each drafted man, who would furnish a substitute, he to furnish the difference between this amount and the bounty paid. By June 9th, 1864, only 17 volunteers had been obtained by the payment of bounties ranging from $500 to $600. Under these circumstances a further draft became necessary to meet the deficiency, and the drawing of 213 names was held on June 15th. This drew a protest from the people of Haverstraw. For various reasons a new enrollment had been ordered for Rockland County, and Silas G. Mackey appointed enrolling officer for Haverstraw.

On June 23d, at a special town meeting held at Benson's Corners, resolutions were passed that the Board of Town Auditors should raise a sum, not exceeding $75,000, or so much thereof as might be necessary, for the purpose of paying bounties to volunteers for the army or navy during the continuance of the war. It was then voted that all previous resolutions made since January 1st, 1864, should be rescinded.

The third call for men, made by the President, was issued July 18th, 1864, and gave 500,000 as the number needed. Quotas for this call were based on the revised enrolment.

To meet this demand, the people of Orangetown, at a special meeting held during the first week in December, voted to raise the bounty to $800 per volunteer. The draft to fill the quotas took place at Tarrytown, September 23d, 1864. Orange and Clarkstown, having filled their quotas, were not drawn upon; but 194 names were called from Haverstraw, and 112 from Ramapo.

The annual meeting of the Board of Supervisors in our County was held October 4th, 1864. At this the following resolution, introduced by William Dickey, Supervisor for Orangetown, was unanimously adopted: "That the resolutions passed by this Board at their special meetings, held June 14th, June 23d and September 2d, 1864, empowering the several towns to raise the sums therein named severally, are hereby reaffirmed; and that, in addition, and for the same purpose, and in the same manner, the town of Orangetown be empowered to raise a further sum of $25,000; the town of Clarkstown, $8,000; the town of Haverstraw, $75,000, and the town of Ramapo, $25,000." Early in December, 1864, the President called for 300,000 more men, and gave till February 15th, 1865 to raise this number, fixing that date for a draft to fill all deficiencies. The quotas for Rockland were:

Haverstraw,	-	-	136	Ramapo,	- -	81
Orangetown,	-		107	Clarkstown,	- -	82

Before the close of the year, the people, at special town meetings in Orangetown, Ramapo and Clarkstown, had determined on raising volunteers by the payment of bounties, the funds for which should be obtained by a tax on taxable property. In Haverstraw a special meeting was held January 5th, 1865. At this it was determined, that each person in the town liable to be drawn should pay $25 into a fund to be used, either for the purpose of paying exemptions or bounties, on or before January 20th. Any drafted person who had not paid this sum would have to pay $100 to obtain the benefits of the fund. It was further decided, that sufficient money be raised by a tax on taxable property, to meet any deficiency. This Special meeting was followed by another at Benson's Corners on February 3d, at which it was resolved to test the legality of the resolutions held on January 5th, because, among other things, it fixed no sum for bounties. At this meeting it was further resolved to pay $300 for each substitute.

A drawing took place in Tarrytown on February 21st, 1865, at which 112 names were taken from Haverstraw. The other townships in our County having filled their quotas were not called upon.

Still another special meeting was held at Benson's Corners on February 27th, at which the resolutions passed at the meeting of January 5th were re-affirmed as according to an act of the Legislature, passed February 10th, 1865. It was then resolved that a further sum of $10,000 be raised if necessary, and that the bounties offered should be: $300 for one year men; $400 for two year men; $600 for three year men, and $100 hand money in addition thereto. Before any further calls were made, General R. E. Lee had surrendered, closely followed by Gen'l Johnson, and the long war was over.

In summing up the results of the draft, the Rockland County Journal for August 4th, 1865, makes the following statement: " Each of our towns has met in full all the calls upon it with the single exception of Haverstraw, which is indeed the only town in the entire district which had not a surplus at the time of the order to stop recruiting.

The vast expenses of the war, the appreciation in values, the tremendous issue of promises to pay, called greenbacks; led to recklessness in the handling of money, led to dishonest practices. One very common method in connection with the draft was for the Supervisors of the towns to pocket the difference between what the towns offered for bounties and the bounty paid. Thus if the bounty offered was $300, and the Supervisor obtained a substitute for $200, in too many cases the $100 difference was not turned back to the town's credit. It is with pleasure that I here record the action of John E. Hogencamp, Supervisor for Clarkstown from 1862 to 1867. With every temptation which beset others, and with too common usage as an example, this public officer remained true to his constituents and his manhood, and every dollar that he could save for his electors was turned into the town funds. The amount expended by Clarkstown, in filling the different calls made for men, was $115,891.25.

In regard to the debt incurred for war purposes, known as the War Debt, Rockland County was one of the first in the State to pay it in full and her financial record on this momentous matter stands among the highest in the State.

It is necessary now to review the political actions of our citizens during the period of Civil War. I have already said that the Democratic Party was abruptly split into two wings by the opening of hostilities, a schism which constantly widened, until by the autumn of 1861, each faction had adopted principles which prevented any possible re-union. The Peace or disunion, I would here state that I use the name disunion in its correct sense and not as a title of reproach, party named its adversary "Black Republican," a name intended to express obloquy and given because of the abolition principles held by its members. The Republicans retaliated by calling their opponents "Copper-heads," a term of opprobrium taken from a venomous and sluggish snake common to the Northern States, which bites without the warning given by the rattlesnake. Each side gloried in its appellation, members of one wearing pins made from the Indian heads cut from the copper coin then in circulation.

Shortly after President Lincoln's inauguration he called an extra session of Congress to meet July 4th, 1861. To this the Peace Democrats sent a petition from our County, addressed to "The Honorable, the Senate and House of Representatives in Congress assembled," which was signed by the names that follow it, most of the signatures being in the original handwriting of the signers.

"The undersigned citizens of the State of New York beg leave to present to your honorable body most respectfully the following petition, to wit:

While they hold themselves ready to maintain and uphold their government in the constitutional exercise of all its powers, yet they would respectfully pray, for the purpose of preventing the horrors of civil war, and for securing the perpetuity of our Union, that you will adopt the policy of an immediate General Convention of all the States as suggested in the Inaugural of the President, or any other compromise by which these ends may be obtained. Earnestly deploring civil war as the greatest calamity that can befall a nation, WE PRAY YOU MAY ADOPT ANY COURSE that may bring peace to our distracted country.

John M. Baker,
David I. Tallman,
M. M. Dickinson,
Henry Palmer,
P. A. Harring,
John Wm. Voris,
Martin Knapp,
John Stephens,
John Storms,
Cornelius Seaman,
George Stephens,
Jacob Mackie,
H. L. Sherwood,
A. T. Seaman,
Claus Meyer,
Isaac L. Sherwood,
John H. Ryder,
William L. Richards,
Peter Stephens,
James C. Wool,
A. B. Cornelison,
John C. Polhemus,
James F. McKenzie,
Thos. Van Orden,
George Derondi,
D. D. Ackerman,
H. T. Blauvelt,
H. B. Fenton,
Jacob Horn,
John W. Stephens,
John Tallman, Jr.,
Samuel Helms,
Abr. Iserman,
John Iserman,
A. G. Polhemus,
James P. Woertendy,
John A. Bogert,
John T. Blanch,

D. Van Houten,
Jacob H. Derondi,
Spencer Youmans,
Henry House,
John S. House,
William Palmer,
Joseph Wool,
I. F. Hawpton,
Abr. F. Laloe,
John Vanhouten,
Nelson Gurnee,
Joseph Baker,
Spencer Gurnee,
A. J. Smith,
J. A. Vanderbilt,
Wm. R. Knapp,
John Blauvelt,
Chauncey Brady,
Aaron Ryder,
George Knapp,
Joseph Blauvelt,
Isaac Blanch,
Christine Huber,
Jacob Blanch,
Christian Popp,
Isaac Tallman,
Nelson Stephens,
P. Wm. Nickerson,
Garret Stockum,
John J. Post,
Wm. Bleecker,
Tunis Blauvelt,
Jeremiah Knapp,
P. D. W. Smith,
S. D. Demarest,
Leonard A. Gurnee,
Daniel M. Clark,
C. C. Burr,
A. H. Tyson,

J. F. Hogencamp,
A. A. Demarest,
Wm. D. Youmans,
Isaac Vervalen,
T. A. Demarest,
Peter Van Houten,
Wm. Coates,
Wm. Knapp,
J. C. Haring,
Peter A. Smith,
Samson Marks, Jr.
John Garrabrant,
Wm. Garrabrant,
H. Hoffman,
John Morphed,
C. H. Demarest,
R. H. Cooke,
G. A. Demarest,
Chas. E. Smith,
Aaron T. Remsen.
Edwin P. Palmer,
A. Van Tassel,
M. Green,
G. W. Chamberlain,
J. W. Bates,
Thos. Burd,
Ed. McGowan,
Rich. Grandwell,
John W. Felter,
A. Blakeslee,
John Palmer,
Peter Conklin,
James Allen,
Peter De Pew,
David O. Storms,
Peter T. Stephens,
William Dickey,
Richard Gilhuly,

Shortly after this petition had been forwarded the following call was issued:

"PEACE! COMPROMISE!! UNION!!!

"All persons that are in favor of preserving the Union of States, by a peaceful settlement of our present difficulties, and opposed to the SHEDDING OF BLOOD UNNECESSARILY, all who are in favor of freedom of Speech, and the Press, and the right of Petition, all who are opposed to an ENORMOUS NATIONAL DEBT, and DIRECT TAXATION, are invited to attend a public meeting to be held at the York House, in the village of Nyack, on Monday evening, July 15th (1861), at 7½ o'clock, for the purpose of giving a calm and decided public expression of their views and sentiments."

Peter De Pew,	John G. Perry,	Garret Sarvent,
Thomas Lawrence,	Henry E. Storms,	Henry Palmer,
Daniel M. Clark,	Wm. Dickey,	James C. Wool,
Wm. Palmer,	George W. Towner,	R. De Cantillon,
	Peter Stephens,	

The meeting was called to order by Peter De Pew, who nominated John Nafie as Chairman. William Dickey then nominated the following Vice-Presidents:

William R. Knapp,	A. A. Demarest,	J. J. Ackerson,
P. W. Nickerson,	Thomas Ackerson,	J. D. Swartwout,
John B. Gurnee,	John Storms, Sr.,	Marcus Hoffman,
John A. Johnson,	Jabez Wood,	Azariah Ross,
Joseph Wool,	P. D. W. Smith,	Henry House.

M. M. Dickinson and George P. Stephens were made Secretaries of the meeting. Among the resolutions adopted were the following, introduced by Thomas Lawrence:

> *Resolved:* That while we yield to none in love for the Union of our States, in respect and attachment to our glorious flag, and in fealty and willing obedience to the Constitution and laws of the United States, we nevertheless protest against the attempt to subjugate the people of any State, to bayonet them into a love for our Union, or sabre them into brotherhood.
>
> *Resolved:* That every Government having a written Constitution for its guide, should strictly adhere to its very letter, and no emergency can justify its violation. That the frequent violation of the Constitution of the United States by the present Executive, and by those under his authority, deserves, and should receive the unqualified condemnation of every American citizen.
>
> *Resolved:* That we earnestly entreat our fellow citizens throughout the length and breadth of our land without distinction of party, to meet together and place the seal of popular condemnation upon the acts of violence and aggression which are dividing our beloved Union; inviting foreign interference; subverting Constitutional and State rights; educating a republican people to favor a dictatorship destructive to the dearest rights of freemen, and tending to the wildest anarchy and despotism."

The next call for a Peace Meeting was as follows:

PEACE! PEACE!! PEACE!!!
PATRIOTS AROUSE!

> "All persons in favor of Peace, and the preservation of the Union, all who are opposed to the destruction of our glorious country by the PRESENT FRATRICIDAL WAR, all who are opposed to an ENORMOUS NATIONAL AND STATE TAX, and in favor of FREEDOM OF SPEECH, and the RIGHT OF PETITION, are invited to attend a mass meeting, to be held at the Court House, at New City, on Saturday, the 20th day of July, inst., at 12 o'clock, noon, for the purpose of adopting such measures as will tend to a peaceful settlement of our present National difficulties, and permanently restoring our beloved country to its once happy and prosperous condition."

Wm. R. Knapp,	John Nafie,	Peter Stevens,
J. B. Gurnee,	J. T. Ackerson,	J. G. Perry,
Joseph Wool,	Thos. Howell,	R. De Cantillon,
T. Ackerson,	J. M. Baker,	Garret Sarvent,
Jabez Wood,	Richard Gilhuley,	W. Palmer,
J. J. Ackerson.	R. H. Cook,	Isaac Hart,

M. Hoffman,	A. Haring,	James Wool,
D. D. Demarest,	A. J. Storms,	Joe. Blauvelt,
H. House,	E. P. Rose,	George Dickey, Sr.
M. M. Dickinson,	I. A. Lydecker,	G. A. Demarest,
Peter De Pew,	Thos. Lawrence,	John L. De Noyelles,
Henry Palmer,	P. W. Nickerson,	F. Van Orden,
H. E. Storms,	J. A. Johnson,	A. Smith,
D. M. Clark,	A. A. Demarest,	I. W. Canfield,
Wm. Dickey,	John Storms, Sr.	Levi Gurnee,
W. Willett,	M. D. Bogert,	G. A. Harring,
J. L. Conklin,	J. D. Swartwout,	Jim Coates,
W. Perry,	J. S. Haring,	Wm. Skelly,
G. C. Stephens,	D. I. Tallman,	J. T. Blanch,
David Munn,	A. Ross,	Sylvester Gesner.

The meeting was organized with John A. Johnson, as Chairman.

Secretaries.

Abr. D. Blauvelt, Abr. A. Demarest,
M. M. Dickinson, Jacob Horn,
John A. Bogert, Thos. Howell,
Garret A. Blauvelt, John H. Stephens,

Among the resolutions passed at this meeting was the following:

"*Resolved*, That we witness with dismay the Constitution violated in many of its plainest provisions; the military power over riding the civil; the liberty of speech and of the press, the writ of habeas corpus, that venerable and almost sacred safeguard of the citizen—all, all swept away, or ruthlessly trampled upon by those in power, under the specious plea of a military necessity."

The "War Democrats" through James Smith Haring, Chairman, and Wm. Govan, M. D., Secretary of the Democratic Central Committee for Rockland County; called a meeting at New City, for October 5th, 1861. At this meeting Hon. Wm. F. Fraser, was chosen to the chair, and Nicholas C. Blauvelt, J. S. Haring, Joseph Cosgrove and Austin L. Fitch, were elected Vice Presidents, while M. M. Dickinson, J. L. De Noyelles and William W. Gurnee, were chosen Secretaries. Speeches favoring the Union over party and expressing a determination to sustain the Government, were made by Hons. A. E. Suffern, Moses G. Leonard, A. B. Conger and others.*

The following resolutions were then passed unanimously:

"*Resolved*, That we acknowledge our allegiance to the general government, and recognize in the present unhappy crisis of the public affairs, our duty as loyal and patriotic citizens to sustain the government in restoring its authority throughout the Republic.

"*Resolved*, That the rebellion which has been inaugurated and is being carried on in certain of these States against the authority of the United States, and the enforcement of the laws therein,

---

*See note at end of chapter.

has for its unholy object the disseverance of these States, the overthrow of the Constitution, the subversion of the laws, and the dissolution of the Federal Union.

"*Resolved*, That we believe the rebellion against the government by the so-called Confederate States is without just cause, palliation or excuse, and that it deserves, as it received, the abhorrence and detestation of every good citizen and loyal subject, and that it may be effectually and forever suppressed and destroyed, we hereby tender to the government our undivided support in its loyal and praiseworthy efforts to meet it force by force.

"*Resolved*, That the government should, by all the power of its arms, and every requisite expenditure of its treasure, prosecute this war for the maintenance of its jurisdiction, the supremacy of its authority, obedience to its laws, and for the protection and vindication of every guaranteed right—National, State and individual—until the Constitution be acknowledged and re-established, the Union restored, the flag of the Republic, the symbol of nationality and union, with not a star obscured, not a stripe erased, float proudly from every eminence throughout the land, and our common country march on her future course in all the majesty of peace, justice and freedom."

From this time till the close of the war, many of the "War Democrats" acted and voted with the Republicans under the name of the Union Party, and received from the other wing all the hatred and vituperation with which they treated the Republicans. Political feeling was carried into the churches, and dissolved the ties of Christian brotherhood, and between pastors and peoples; it entered the family circle and estranged blood relations.

Such was the political animosity which existed at the opening of the campaign of 1864. For that contest the Republican party had renominated Abraham Lincoln, while the Democrats had selected George B. McClellan. As weapons of offence the latter party openly denounced the prolongation of the war, while privately they condemned the Emancipation Proclamation, the draft and the suspension of habeas corpus. Once again, and for the last time, a Peace meeting was held at New City, on August 5th, 1864. It was organized by the selection of the following:

Marcus Hoffman, Chairman,

Vice-Presidents.

John Nafie,   Luke Van Orden,   Jacob Horn,   Daniel Lake.

Secretaries.

M. M. Dickinson,   H. Fenton,   Henry Palmer.

A series of peace resolutions were read by Thomas Lawrence and adopted. A letter was read from Hon. Gideon J. Tucker, expressing sincere sympathy with the meeting, and regret that he could not be present, as he was in 1861; and a speech was made by C. Chauncey Burr, of Bergen County, N. J., from which I quote an opening extract; "About three years since, I had the honor to address the people of Rockland County, and I then denounced the present war as a crime against humanity and the

Constitution. That sentiment was then applauded to the echo by the listeners."

The election took place on November 8th, 1864. In the campaign of 1860, 3,779 votes were cast in our County, and the Democratic majority was 959.

	Haverstraw.			Orangetown.		
	1st Dist.	2d Dist.	3d Dist.	1st Dist.	2d Dist.	3d Dist.
Lincoln	152	121	126	171	188	90
McClellan	126	275	286	253	242	79
	Clarkstown.			Ramapo.		
	1st Dist.	2d Dist.	3d Dist.	1st Dist.	2d Dist.	3d Dist.
Lincoln	92	153	116	36	59	134
McClellan	128	129	189	248	106	224

For Governor.

	Haverstraw.			Orangetown.		
	1st Dist.	2d Dist.	3d Dist.	1st Dist.	2d Dist.	3d Dist.
Seymour	126	280	286	258	242	79
Fenton	153	116	125	171	188	90
	Clarkstown.			Ramapo.		
	1st Dist.	2d Dist.	3d Dist.	1st Dist.	2d Dist.	3d Dist.
Seymour	127	128	189	247	106	225
Fenton	93	153	112	36	59	132

For Assembly.

	Haverstraw.			Orangetown.		
	1st Dist.	2d Dist.	3d Dist.	1st Dist.	2d Dist.	3d Dist.
Nickerson	128	277	286	254	244	80
Fenton	151	107	120	165	180	87
	Clarkstown.			Ramapo.		
	1st Dist.	2d Dist.	3d Dist.	1st Dist.	2d Dist.	3d Dist.
Nickerson	126	122	190	246	106	220
Fenton	89	150	109	34	59	128

The total vote cast for Presidential Electors was 3,723. Democratic majority, 847.

And now events hastened to the inevitable issue. The awful hammering process, which Grant had been pursuing upon the Army of Northern Virginia, the march of Sherman, the annihilation of Hood's army, all bespoke the approach of the end. The political hope of the South died on Lincoln's re-election.

It is not uninteresting to look over the files of our County papers during the period of the war. At first they are filled with military ardor and military news, to the exclusion of other data; later, the military news is condensed, while the usual County news becomes more prominent; toward the last they settle down to a few brief items concerning the operations of the armies, while the greater part of the papers is filled with information regarding burglaries, church sociables and donations, the annual fair, reviews of concerts and other matters of local import. There had been occasions during the later years, when some of the papers dwelt more fully on military events. 'Tis not difficult to recall an old and sorely stricken man, bowed and broken, writing the obituary of a son, killed at Gettysburg. 'Tis not likely that those who lived in those times will forget the sorrow which filled them when they saw the local papers in mourning for Colonel Pye. As a rule, however, military information had become so much a part of the daily events that slight attention was paid to it by the County sheets. Oh, the long, long, weary war!

Early on Monday, April 10th, 1865, the residents of the County along the river bank heard the firing of guns across the river, and, suspecting from the character of the news during the last few days what it indicated, anxiously awaited the arrival of the morning papers. Those papers told of the surrender of General Robert E. Lee and his army. Immediately began a scene of rejoicing. The private schools in Nyack were closed, bunting was displayed from every Union house, and enthusiastic congratulations were exchanged between the loyal people. At Haverstraw all the schools were closed and the children marched through the streets two abreast, singing patriotic songs; guns were fired; flags unfurled, and the church bells were rung during the remainder of the day and night. On board the steamboat Isaac P. Smith an impromptu meeting was organized by Hon. Moses G. Leonard, and speeches were made and songs sung during the continuance of the trip.

Ere a week elapsed, the flags, which had been thrown to the breeze at Lee's surrender, were dropped to half-mast at Lincoln's assassination. The last act in the drama of rebellion was a cruel murder. A description of the long funeral procession, which escorted the martyr to his grave, is not appropriate in this work, and I can only mention the part our people took in the matter. Grief among the Union people was universal, and emblems of mourning were profuse. In the calamity, even a majority of the disunionists seemed sobered and saddened, though a few of the most outspoken expressed gratification and rejoicing till advised to be quiet. The funeral train journeyed north on the Hudson River Railroad. On the day it passed through Tarrytown, the ferry-boat between Nyack and that place transported such crowds of people as she never carried before and never did again, to see the train.

As rapidly as possible, after the surrender of Johnson's army, the Union armies were disbanded and the men returned to their homes. Those from

Nyack arrived on the steamboat early in the summer, and were received at Nyack by the citizens, and a procession composed of the fire department, students of Rutherford's Academy, and civic societies, and escorted to Union Hall. In front of that building speeches were made by representatives of both parties, a most unwise proceeding, which led this last, and what should have been happiest action in connection with the struggle, to end in bitterness.

According to the State Census Report, taken in 1865, Rockland County furnished 558 men to the Civil War, of whom 89 were killed in battle, or died from wounds or sickness in camp. The statistics (for the correctness of which I will not vouch), stand as follows: Clarkstown furnished 74 men, of whom the greatest number enlisted in any single organization was in the 6th New York Heavy Artillery. Haverstraw furnished 198 men, of whom many enlisted in the 95th Regiment New York Volunteers, and many in the 6th New York Heavy Artillery. Orangetown furnished 123. Many in the 17th Regiment New York Volunteers, the 127th Regiment New York Volunteers, and the 6th New York Heavy Artillery. Ramapo furnished 163: many in the 95th Regiment Volunteers; the 124th Regiment Volunteers; the 6th New York Heavy Artillery, and the 17th Regiment N. Y. S. M. Of these troops, 127 were discharged at the end of their term of service; 126 resigned or otherwise left the service. At the time of taking the census, the condition of health in 195 was good; in 37 permanently impaired. Of the deaths:

Killed in Battle, - - 25	Died of Wounds, - - 13
Killed by Accident, - 1	Died of sickness acquired 37
Died of sickness not acquired in service, - - 1	Unknown, - - - 12

The months and years of enlistment are given as follows:

1861.

Apr.	May.	June.	July.	Aug.	Sept.	Oct.	Nov.	Dec.
16	21	6	8	26	14	40	21	10

1862.

Jan.	Feb.	Mar.	Apr.	May.	June.	July.	Aug.	Sept.	Oct.	Nov.	Dec.
4	2	4	3	3		4	64	33	8	6	2

1863.

Jan.	Feb.	Mar.	Apr.	May.	June.	July.	Aug.	Sept.	Oct.	Nov.	Dec.
6		3	1	1	3	48	4	4	5	1	6

1864.

Jan.	Feb.	Mar.	Apr.	May.	June.	July.	Aug.	Sept.	Oct.	Nov.	Dec.
18	5	1	6		2	4	11	29	12	2	6

1865.

Jan.	Feb.	Mar.	Apr.	May.
1	7	12	4	1

Unknown, 60

See Appendix—A.

NOTE.

While obtaining material for this chapter, I was told by a member of the War Committee that there was treason in that committee; that certain members of it would hasten from the meetings and give information of the proceedings to the leaders of the disunionists. Inquiry among other members of the Committee confirmed this statement, and I was given the names of men who were said to be guilty. I have been unable to find any written or printed proof of this statement, and have therefore refrained from giving it as fact. In the case of the meetings of the Peace and War Democrats, however, I have taken the names from hand-bills, newspaper files, and the reports of the proceedings. The reader who sees these names attached to resolutions condemning the Government; then to resolutions sustaining the Government; and then to resolutions decrying it again, can judge of the fine sense of honor and patriotism, which must have been inherent in these men, as well as I. That they were regarded as intelligent, is evinced by the fact that they were selected to fi.l the offices which are necessary in any organization.

Authorities referred to: "American Politics," Johnson; "The Civil War in America," Draper; "Notes on Nyack;" "A Retrospect," from the *Rockland County Journal;* "New York and the Conscription of 1863," James B. Fry; "Adjutant-General's Report for the State of New York." *Evening Journal* and *Herald* Almanacs. Files of the *New York Herald*; *Rockland County Messenger; Rockland County Journal.* "The American Conflict," Greely; "New York State Census Report." Copy-Book of the Provost-Marshall's Office, (through the kindness of Wm. G. Haeselbarth). Letters and Minutes of the Nyack branch of the Sanitary Commission. Hand-bills, Advertisements, &c., &c.

CHAPTER XVII.

ORANGETOWN.

ERECTION OF THE TOWN—AREA—ORIGIN OF NAME—CENSUS—FIRST TOWN MEETING — HISTORIES OF TAPPAN — GREENBUSH—MIDDLETOWN—NYACK—PIERMONT—PALISADES—ORANGEVILLE—PEARL RIVER—RAILROAD FROM SPARKILL TO NYACK—HIGHLAND AND MIDLAND AVENUES—TOWN OFFICERS.

As we have already seen in the chapter relating to patents, a tract of land about eight miles long, by from three to five miles wide, was granted to sixteen men on March 24th, 1686, and named in the grant the town of Orange. We have also read that at the time of this grant, the division line in this colony and East Jersey was not understood, and that the grant extended into the latter province. When the division line between the two States was finally agreed upon, part of the grant of 1686 belonged to Bergen County, and the area of Orangetown was reduced to 16.023 acres. Still further have we learned, that when this section was set off as a County, in 1683, it was named by the courtiers, whose only desire was to please their royal patron, after the son-in-law of that patron. It was a foregone conclusion therefore, that the first town erected in that County should be given the County's name. But, besides the cognomen accorded it by the grant, it was often called by the early settlers and their descendants other names. That of the Indians—Navvasunk Lands—was used frequently till the middle of the Eighteenth Century; and that of the tribe from which it was purchased—the Tappæns—which was given to their first settlement by the early colonists, was often extended to a broader use, and the whole patent called Tappan Town. Up to a very recent date I have heard the last written name and doubt not, that among the older families in the County, it is often used to designate the village o Tappan.

It has been already stated that the census returns of Orangetown, during its early history, were returns for the whole County, and that any attempt to separate the population according to towns, appears futile. Not till 1738, do I find any mention of such division, when Eager, in his History of Orange County gives the population of each of the four towns. A hiatus again occurs till 1790, after which the census returns are returned without intermission.

In 1738, Orangetown had	830 inhabitants.			In 1835, Orangetown had 2079 inhabitants.			
In 1790,	"	"	1175	"	In 1845,	" " 3227	"
In 1800,	"	"	1337	"	In 1855,	" " 5838	"
In 1810,	"	"	1583	"	In 1865,	" " 6166	"
In 1820,	"	"	2257	"	In 1870, U. S. Census,	6810	"
In 1825, State Census,		1536	"	In 1880,	" 8266	"

The truthfulness of census reports is always open to suspicion, and reference to the returns of 1820, in the above table, will only confirm doubt.

The earliest record of the town is of an election April, 1744. At this were chosen: "Henry Ludlow, Town Clark and Supervisor; John Cornelius Haring and John Ackerson, overseers of the fence; Dolph Lent, constable; John Ferdon, John Nagle, John Perry, Commissioners of the highways; Overseers of the high road: Robert Holly, for the Greenbush; J. Bartus Blaufilt, for the wagon road; Daniel Vervelia, for Closter; Thomas Van Houtten, for Skeairecloy; Daniel Blaufilt, for John Clows Land (Clausland); Johannies Bogart, for the mill road; Johannies Meyer, pound master; Renier Wortendyke, Dirck and Tisa Borgard, Assessors; John ———, Peter Dau, to record the quit rent; Daniel Skureman and Cornelius Tallman, overseers of the poor; Abraham Smith, collector."

The early records of the County, as set forth in the Documents relating to the Colonial History of the State, give constant legislative acts intended to prevent the tresspass of swine. In keeping with those acts is the following resolution, agreed upon by the inhabitants of Orangetown, in April, 1783:

"That No Swine, having their noses well ringed and yoked with yokes the length of the pieces running up and down, being below the Lower Cross piece at Least five inches and above the Upper Cross piece at least six inches, Shall be liable to be impounded. Swine not so ringed and yoked, Who shall get into any person's inclosure, may be impounded, and, unless the owner Redems them in four days after notice Shall be given by advertisement, be put up at the Church Dore of Such impounding by paying the damages and costs and three shillings for each Swine So impounded, then the Swine so impounded to be Sold at publick Vendue, and the residue of the money arising by such sale, after Such damages, Cost and pounding Shall be paid to be delivered to the overseers of the poor.

Recorded by me,

M. HOGENKAMP, Town Clerk,"

TAPPAN.

Whenever, in entering upon local history, we come upon unlimited and unbounded sections of land under a local name, it is safe to feel that we are treading on soil granted to first settlers. Their scope was wide and they took full advantage of it. In the neighboring State of New Jersey, we have Paramus, which formerly was the name of all the country from Sneden's Landing, to the Ramapo; Pasacack or more commonly, Pascack; a like unlimited tract. In our own County was Kakiat, later Hempstead, which covered all the present Ramapo Township, and extended east to the Hackensack: and Tappan, which was only confined by the boundaries of the Orangetown patent, and the smaller neighborhood of Greenbush.

Tappan Landing was the present Piermont. Tappan Slote, the present Sparkill. The village proper of Tappan, was as we have seen, the first organized hamlet in the whole section from Newburgh to the Jersey line. Here were built the first houses; here were organized the first church society and school; here were erected the first house for divine worship the first court house and jail; and then—Tappan Village stopped.

Eradicating those villages which have since taken other names from her history, and placing the history of her church under the chapter devoted to that subject; we find but little left to say. In 1694, a school was organized in the village under the charge of Hermanus Van Huysen. For many years this place was the County Seat, the county buildings were located here and here the Board of Supervisors met. In May 1832, the Rev. Jacob Cole, opened a boarding school in the village which was continued for about a year. The building of the Erie Railroad left the village to the south and the opening of the Northern Railroad in 1857-59 passed by it to the east. Recently, the New York, West Shore & Buffalo Railroad, has passed through the hamlet, and it may be that this enterprise will bring to Tappan more life.

Similar to that of Tappan is the history of Greenbush. This place, now known as Blauveltville, obtained its name from some object of physical nature. In the original patent for Orangetown, we find the name as the Greenbush. At this place, near the present graveyard, settled one of the original patentees of the Orangetown grant, Lammert Ariansen, and built a storehouse. In the case of this man, as in that of others in those days when patronymics were changed to suit the necessity or fancy of the time, his trade became at length his surname and from Lammert Ariansen the Smith we find Lammert Smidt or Smith. Three sons were left by this settler. Garrett, who was the great grandfather of the late Cornelius T. Smith and Rachel Lydecker, settled south of the Greenbush Swamp. Abraham remained on his father's place, and Cornelius built on what was then called the ridge, west of the present Erie Railroad.

BLAUVELTVILLE.

Till the construction of the Erie road, this place bore the name of Greenbush; then, in honor of Judge Cornelius J. Blauvelt, it was given its present name. Like Tappan, it is a small agricultural hamlet with one store, a blacksmith shop, and a few houses. The first storekeeper remembered was John Blauvelt, who was succeeded by Judge Blauvelt, he by Isaac Dederer, and he by Smith Demarest. John Raab then took the store and conducted it till 1882. In 1867, a store was built and opened by the firm of Edebohls & Lediger. Mr. Edebohls died in 1871, and Mr. Lediger has since continued the business.

The post office was first started here on October 14, 1828, with Cornelius J. Blauvelt as postmaster. On April 9, 1834, this office was discontinued, but was re-established June 25th of the same year, with Cornelius J. Blauvelt in charge. In 1840, Michael Klain became postmaster, and held the position till April 12th, 1844, when he was succeeded by Isaac M. Dederer. On March 31st, 1854,, Simon D. Demarest became postmaster. He was followed by John Raab, Feb. 3d, 1864, Henry Edebohls, Jan. 6th, 1868, and George M. Lediger, Feb. 24th, 1871.

On May 15th, 1809, John I. Blauvelt gave a lot of ground for the erection of a school. Shortly after, a building was erected, which was called the Greenbush Academy. This edifice was of stone and two stories in height, the first floor being used for the teachers' residence and a school-room, while the second floor was turned into a public hall. About 1850, this building was torn down, and the present structure was erected.

The Roman Catholic Juvenile Asylum property at Blauveltville, was purchased in December, 1878, by the Sisters of the order of St. Dominic. Its design is the education of indigent female children.

MIDDLETOWN.

The name Middletown was given to a section of Orangetown situated about a mile west of the Orangeville mills. It was so called because, in the days of early settlement in the then Orange County, the tavern that stood here was midway between the pioneers on the Kakiat patent and those at Tappan. As early as 1720, a log house and tavern owned by a man named Ackerman, was built in this section on the farm now owned and occupied by John A. Bogert. Some of the foundation of this old tavern can still be seen. In 1780, this log house was torn down by David Bogert, who then owned the property, and a stone house erected further north. Shortly after the completion of this structure, an earthquake occurred, which cracked the walls from the roof almost to the foundation.

Perhaps it may not be amiss to mention in this connection the legend told of Marias' Rock, a boulder situated on the property of Lansing Blauvelt about a mile south of Nanuet on the Middletown road. Tradition has it that in 1730, a little girl some ten years old, was lost from the Tappan Settlement and never after heard from. A few years later, the skeleton of a child was found lying on the rock, which now bears the lost girl's name, and this was supposed, doubtless correctly, to be the remains of the wanderer.

What a vivid picture this gives of the Wilderness our forefathers settled, of the frightful solitude they entered. Barely a few years over a century and a half have passed since a ten year old child, wandering into the woods after berries or wild-flowers, became lost in a section, where now it would be impossible to get beyond the sound of a gun from a human habitation and walked on and on, screaming for help, till exhausted and famished, she fell asleep on the hard stone. Years passed before her skeleton was found.

NYACK.

On the southwest shore of Long Island, between the present villages of Bay Ridge and New Utrecht, formerly lived an Indian tribe named Nayack, Nayeeck, Neyick, or Nyack. At this place, as we have read in the chapter on patents, Van Cowenhoven bought land after his disappointment in regard to the Staten Island grant. The present Gravesend Bay, was then called Nyack Bay, and in it the English fleet anchored previous to their capture of New Amsterdam in 1663. Suddenly the name of Nyack, as applied to that section ceases, and I next find it, applied to the present village of that name on the Hudson, in an old deed bearing date, 1764, under the spelling Niack. There can be no doubt, that during the intervening years, some former resident from the original Nyack on Long Island, moved to the newer Nyack, and finding it nameless gave it baptism.

In the chapter relating to patents, I have already mentioned the earliest patentees of this village, as Claes Jansen in 1671, and Harmanus Dows—now Tallman—and Tunis Paulson previous to 1678.

The growth of the village was slow. In 1799, so little value was attached to its future, that the property lying between the present 1st avenue on the north, and De Pew avenue on the south, and extending from the river to Highland avenue, was purchased by Abraham Lydecker for $4,000. In a previous chapter I have spoken of the lane that led from Nyack to the King's highway. Besides this, a road, if the reader cares to consider a lane as a road, passed up the present Hudson street, and at Franklin street branched, one lane being continued down Franklin street to Hillside avenue, then down the present Smith avenue to Piermont avenue, and followed the course of that road to the present Piermont. On the present Broadway, north of Main street, there were gates at the end of every farm—one stood at the corner of the present 1st avenue as late as 1810, and the last, at Mr. Pollock's place, was removed within a score of years. On the mountain road at Upper Nyack, just east of Highland avenue, is a deep hollow—still known by the older residents of the vicinity as "Spook's Hollow." From this, north, ran a lane that continued to the property now belonging to Joseph Hilton, where it turned east and north, and finally reached the mountain near the terminus of Broadway.

While Nyack had but this small communication inland, the valley itself was very productive, and in addition to the agricultural products, a good business as we have seen had already grown up from the quarries. To meet the wants of the growing hamlet, Abraham and Harman Tallman, Peter De Pew and Captain Stephen Meyers, built the first market sloop—the Aurora—in Nyack, in 1804. This vessel landed at the first dock in Nyack, the remains of which can be seen between De Pew avenue and the flock factory dock. In the same year Abram Tallman opened the first store in the village on the site of the present Smithsonian Hotel. This store was later sold to the firm of Austin & Edgar, who eventually failed. The next store was opened by Tunis Smith, grandson of Lammert Ariansen Smidt, in the building standing on Main street, at the head of Court street, in 1810, and this was followed by one opened by Peter Smith, on Main street, at the head of Cedar street.

A few years later John Green, started the first lumber yard just north of the dock at the foot of Main street, and followed by opening a store in 1819, on Main street, at the foot of Canfield street. Later this store came under the firm of Green & Gurnee, and after the latter's death Green & Goetchius. Next, Benjamin Blackledge, opened a store on the site of the present York House—corner of Main and Court streets. Coming down to more recent days, we find D. D. Demarest, opening a store and lumber yard at the present steamboat dock, foot of Smith Place, in 1833. In 1839, we find the Smith's buying Demarest's store, Azariah Ross building the large brick store, on the corner of Court and Main streets, opposite the York House, and D. D. Demarest opening the store, corner of Broadway and Burd street, now occupied by R. Gedney.

Meanwhile Upper Nyack had awakened to activity, pushed by the same cause that was aiding Nyack, the quarry business. In 1824, the first store was opened by John Van Houten, on the property now owned by J. P. Voris. This was afterward occupied by T. Smith Tallman, and was then used by Richard Gilhuly, as a restaurant from 1861 till 1864. Elijah Appleby, opened a store in 1833, on Broadway opposite the new school. In 1840, Daniel Clark took this store afterward moving up to the property now owned by J. W. Schuler on the corner of Broadway and Tallman street, and later when Tallman street was opened to the river by T. S. Tallman, in 1850, he moved to the spot now occupied by George Stephens.

The first drug store opened in Nyack was by James Clark, on the corner of Broadway and Burd street, in 1843. This store afterward passed into the hands of Johnson, Townsend & Pomeroy, then to Erastus Van Houten, afterward to Wolheim, to Corner, and finally to Philip Moeller. Next came Mrs. Blauvelt's drug store, still occupied by her, in 1858, and De Graff & Ross in 1872. The population of the village in 1860 was 2,016; in 1865, 2,400.

It is now necessary to look at another business started by the quarry growth, that of boat building. The early vessels that sailed on the river were known as "keel boats" and "board boats." The first, built with a deep keel, had far greater carrying capacity than "board boats," because their holds, as well as decks, could be used for storage. But it was only when deep water ran close to the shore that these boats could be landed, and for Tappan Landing and Haverstraw, they were practically useless. For shallow water, the flat bottomed vessel with lee-boards was used.

The first centre-board boat of any size built in this County, if not in the world, was constructed at Nyack, in 1815, by Henry Gesner, for Jeremiah Williamson, and named the "Advance." On one of his trips to Pavonia with stone, Williamson had seen a Staten Island skiff with a centre-board, and the ease with which she was handled, and the closeness with which she sailed to the wind, determined him to try the centre-board in a larger vessel. In the "Advance" the board was set through the keel, which was built of two pieces, with a space for the board, bolted together, instead of, as at present, alongside. As may be imagined, there were many detractors of the new idea, who said that it would be impossible for the weakened keel to be as strong as an unbroken stick of timber, and that wood and iron could never be put together strongly enough to stand the wrenching of the heavy board amidships. In spite of their gloomy view the "Advance" did succeed. Like wine, she improved with age, and in later years made the remarkable record of six trips, between New York and Nyack in six days, starting on her first trip with a load of stone early Monday morning and returning from her sixth trip Saturday evening.

In 1825, the centre-board sloop, "Parthenia" was built at Nyack, for use on Long Island Sound. In this case the board was placed alongside the keel, and secured by the bed piece as at present. Again opponents to the idea felt positive, that, while a centre-board might work in the comparatively smooth water of the river, it would fail in the rougher water of the Sound. The "Parthenia" disappointed these disparagers and proved very successful. From this time, centre-board boats were almost universally built for inland navigation.

Up to 1830, when a marine railway was built at Staten Island, it had been customary for the purpose of cleaning a boat, to run her ashore on a sandy beach at high water, and on the ebb tide to scrub her bottom, and apply a coat of tar below the water line. But the beginning of railways at Staten Island, compelled Nyack builders to advance still further, and add this improvement to their yards. The first marine railway in Rockland County was built by John Van Houten at Upper Nyack, on the property now owned by J. P. Voris, in 1834. Next, John Felter built a railway just south of Van Houten's in 1839. In later years Felter's yard came into the hands of William H. Dixon. In 1874, Voris owned it, and built two large coasting schooners there. Since that time it has been dismantled.

Shortly after this beginning, the Smiths built two railways at Nyack, in or near the ferry slip. Mr. Ross followed in 1845, by building a ways where those by the foundry now stand. Perry put down the next ways at the dock below the gas-house; and in 1853, Isaac Canfield built two railways in the yard since 1867 belonging to Edward Smith. Nurtured by the demands of the quarry men, boat building at Nyack grew with rapidity, The most busy season in the yards was in 1835-6, when there were sixteen new vessels on the stocks at one time.

An attempt to name the different vessels built at Nyack would be out of place even if the task were possible, and I may but make brief mention of those that were out of the ordinary run. In 1863, Wm. Dickey built two steamboats for the Camden & Amboy R. R. Co. on the property now, belonging to Wilson Defendorf, and in 1865-6, he built the "Chrystenah" in front of the foundry at Nyack. I would state here that the "Chrystenah" was a new boat, and not, as so many think, built from or on any part of an old hulk. In later years yacht building has grown to large dimensions here. At Nyack, too, were built the "Duck," a steamboat experiment for canal towing, and the catamaran "Henry W. Longfellow," designed by Wm. Voorhis and launched in 1880. This vessel as built consisted of two segar-shaped hulls 200 feet long, $5\frac{1}{2}$ feet diameter at the largest part and 9 feet apart. The hulls were made of boiler iron $\frac{3}{16}$ inch in thickness at the centre, thinning toward the ends. On the hulls rested a single deck 125 feet long, 25 feet breadth of beam, on which was built the saloons. The original motive power was a Well's balance engine of 476 horse power, and a six-blade propeller of 8 feet diameter.

In 1882, the domed vessel "Meteor" was built at Edward Smith's yard. This vessel, built as an experiment, was mastless and covered with a "turtle back" dome, or oval roof, from stem to stern. The "Meteor" was 156 feet long over all, 21 feet $8\frac{1}{2}$ inches extreme beam, and, as originally built, had a doubled balanced engine, capable of 400 revolutions per minute. She was built for the American Quick Transit Co. of Boston and was intended to demonstrate that a vessel of this construction was more rapid and less liable to injury from the sea than those with masts and undomed. In lieu of spars, the large vessels are to have auxiliary screws, that can be used in case of accident to the main engine.

On May 15th, 1883, there was launched from the yard of J. P. Voris at Upper Nyack, the steamboat. "Wilbur A. Heisley," built for the Long Branch & Seabright Steamboat Co. This boat was 155 feet length of keel ; 33 feet beam ; 7 feet depth of hold, and 3 feet draught loaded. She was moved by a Ward's tubular boiler and a large stern paddle wheel.

We must now turn to the manufacturing interests of Nyack. July 12th, 1826, Wm. Perry started a shop for the manufacture of shoes in Upper Nyack. In 1828, he removed to Main Street just west of Broadway, and, his business steadily increasing, by 1832, he found it necessary to employ a dozen men.

Following Perry, we find Daniel Burr starting a factory, and shortly after forming a partnership with Nathaniel and Edward Burr, under the firm name of Burr & Co. A year later Nathaniel left the firm and started alone and the firm name was changed to Daniel & Edward Burr, and still later, the members of this firm separated, each going in business alone. In 1855, Edward Burr sold his business to T. Austin and John Burr, who, under the firm name of Austin & Burr, opened in Union Hall. Later Frederick Dezendorf, joined this firm, the name becoming Austin, Burr &

Co., and bought out the business of Daniel Burr. In a short time, the firm name again changed, Dezendorf starting alone.

In 1857, the firm of Ketchel, Caywood & Burr, was organized, changing two years later into Ketchel & Caywood, John Burr having started alone. About the same time, the firm of Smith & Baker started in the shop of Wm. Perry. About 1864, Dezendorf gave up the business at Nyack, and was succeeded by Mr. Cooke. Later, Edward Burr returned to Nyack and began business continuing for three or four years.

Daniel Burr was the first to introduce the sewing machine into the Nyack business. Previous to the general introduction of the machine, very much of the sewing on shoes was done at the employee's home, and it was a common sight to meet people from Rockland Lake, from the mountains at Lyons Hill, now called Mountain View avenue, from Clarksville and from Piermont; walking to Nyack with a great bundle of finished shoes. In 1866-67, Ketchel & Caywood built the factory on the corner of Railroad and Depew avenues, and introduced the steam sewing machine. They were the pioneers in steam power in Nyack. Later the firm changed, by reason of the withdrawal of Caywood and the entrance of Purdy, into Ketchel & Purdy. Later this firm failed and for some time the factory stood vacant.

In 1876, the shoe business which had fallen into a torpid condition, was again revived. The year previous—1875—C. B. Kenedy had begun the manufacture of this commodity on Broadway, but now the business was given greater impetus by the opening of the factory at Railroad and De Pew avenues, by G. T. & C. Morrow; by P. Morrell's and A. H. Jackman's entrance into the business at Nyack; and by the opening of a factory by Wm. E. Tuttle. In 1878, Conrad Doersch began the manufacture of shoes, followed in 1879 by Charles Theis on the corner of Main and Franklin streets, and Jacob Siebert, who started in a 40x80 feet frame building on Main street.

In 1879, G. T. Morrow built a brick factory, three stories and basement 40x125 feet, on the corner of Railroad and Cedar Hill avenues. On his removal to this building, the old factory was occupied; the 1st floor by C. B. Kenedy, and the 2d by Conrad Doersch, the 3d by P. Morrell. In 1884, G. W. Tremper & Sons began manufacturing on Main street. Jackman's present factory is a brick building, three stories in height and 40 feet wide by 180 feet deep. Besides the manufacturers mentioned, the shoe business has been carried on in Nyack by Mr. Gardner, by Mr. Gedney, and by Glenn & Hadley. The total product of the different manufacturers for 1884 was 688,424 pairs of shoes. The pay roll of the employees was estimated to be $5,000 per week.

In 1832, John Tallman, later Tallman & Randall, began the making of pianos in a small shop on Burd street. Later they moved up to Fifth avenue, and erecting a large building, carried on the business for a number of years. After the retirement of Tallman & Randall from the business, Mr. Thompson, formerly an apprentice with them, started in a small shop on Piermont avenue. In 1850, Mr. Ross joined Thompson and they built the factory corner of Broadway and Third avenue. In 1853, Thompson died and the business stopped. Four years elapsed before the factory was again opened and the business recommenced by Sumner Sturtevant in 1857. In recent years additions have been added until the building is now 40x60 feet.

The manufacture of carriages and sleighs was begun in Nyack by Aaron L. Christie in 1835, when he opened a shop on Main street near Broadway, moving to the present site in 1851, and carried on by him till 1871, when the business came into the hands of A. E. & J. H. Christie. Following Christie, E. L. Wright began the wheelwright business in 1843, and still later, Taylor opened a shop on Main street.

In 1840, Henry and Abram L. Storms began the manufacture of wooden ware in a factory, still standing as the large frame building corner of Burd and Cedar streets. In 1850, the business was moved to De Pew's old grist mill, at the place now occupied by Grant's Flock Mill, and when steam power was used, a brick engine house was added. In 1856, the factory caught fire and the old mill burned down, the brick engine house only being saved. After the fire, the present factory was built. For many years the wooden ware business was very heavy, branch factories existing in several places.

Previous to 1850, the manufacture of sulphur matches was carried on in De Pew's mill for a number of years by a Frenchman, named George Dimfelt, who employed about a dozen children in the business. But little can be learned of this industry.

The first stone yard at Nyack was started by Tunis Smith at his place at the head of Court street, and, later, his son C. T. Smith, engaged in the business. In later years, Blakie started a stone and marble yard on Main street, east of Franklin. In 1854, Blakie having left the business, George Towner started a marble yard on Main street.

In 1850, Wm. Crumbie & Sons opened the Nyack foundery, being later joined by Captain Isaac P. Smith. Under their management many engines were built and "set up," and the works obtained a wide-spread reputation. Thomas Magee bought the foundery in 1863, and has since carried on business at it. Under Magee's management many boilers have been made, but he has had little to do with the manufacture of engines.

In 1879, George W. Griffen began business in Smithsonian Hall, and his enterprise, the Rockland Car Head Lining and Decorated Ceiling Works is still in operation. In 1881 Coplestone began the manufacture of hats in a brick factory, 32 by 96 feet, situated at the foot of Smith Place. Two years before, 1879, the factory of the Rockland County Straw Works had been built by Nelson Puff at the Bight.

In 1881, the wooden-ware factory, which had remained closed for several years, was again opened by D. A. Grant as a Flock Mill, and the business has been continued. The material made at this mill is used in the manufacture of woolen goods and wall paper.

In 1883, the Lockwood Manufacturing Company was incorporated for the purpose of manufacturing wrought iron railings. The first officers were W. F. Storms, President ; E. B. Sipple, Secretary and Treasurer.

Nyack has been used as a summer resort for many years. The first hotel in the village, the Mansion House, was built by C. T. Smith in 1827, and stood on Main street, just east of the Voorhis building, to make room for which, it was torn down in 1878. It was a large, shingle-sided building, with two stories and an attic, facing Main street. During the first epidemic of Asiatic cholera in 1832, this house had eighty guests, and Mr. Smith was compelled to hire other houses to accommodate his boarders. In 1829, Peter Smith opened his house on Main, at the head of Cedar street for boarders, and was followed in a short time by Robert Hart. The building of the Orange led largely to the growth of this business and, as we have seen in the chapter relating to her, special note was made of the accommodation for boarders in the advertisement of the boat.

In 1849, the Pavilion was built, and opened by Abram P. Smith. It has since been added to as occasion required, until it has now attained large dimensions. In later years, the increased demand has led to the opening of other houses, and the building of the Palmer, now Prospect, House. Among the buildings thus employed is the Tappan Zee House, which was formerly the Rockland Female Institute, and was first opened for summer boarders by the Mansfields in 1859 ; the Smithsonian Hotel, formerly the residence of D. D. Smith, the Clarendon and others.

In 1835, the first post-office was opened in John Van Houten's store at the landing in Upper Nyack, and Van Houten was post-master. The mails were carried by the steamboat, and that for Nyack was kept in a segar box. In those days of primitive honesty, the inquirer for letters was handed the box and allowed to sort his own material out. Following Van Houten in 1836, Samuel Canfield received the appointment as post-master and the office was moved to his place of business, the Dry Dock

Hotel, corner of Main and Canfield streets. In 1844, Charles Humphrey was post-master, and the office was taken to his residence, corner of Broadway and Main streets, now occupied by Lydecker & Wool. Under the administration of Taylor and Fillmore from 1849 to 1853, William B. Collins was post-master, and had the office on Main near Cedar street. From 1853 to 1861, D. D. Demarest was post-master, and the office was kept in his store, corner of Broadway and Burd street, now occupied by R. Gedney.

In 1861, Aaron L. Christie was appointed post-master by Lincoln, and held the office continuously till his death in July, 1880. His daughter, Sarah L. Christie, was then appointed, and held the office till July, 1885, when Orlando Humphrey was appointed. During the period while Mr. Christie was post-master, the office was moved several times. It was first opened on Broadway, on the spot where Hinton's stationery store now stands.

In 1869, a law rating offices according to their mail distribution was passed, the classes running from 1 to 4; Nyack was classed as third. In 1878, the Nyack office was the largest in the County. Two southern mails were made up daily, and in summer, a northern mail was added, by tapping the Hudson River Railroad at Tarrytown. Besides these, a daily mail was made up for Piermont, Sparkill and stations up the " branch " of the Northern Railroad, and for Clarksville, New City, Haverstraw and Rockland Lake. The opening of the New York, West Shore & Buffalo Railroad led to the carrying of the mail for these inland towns by that road, and the business of the Nyack office was reduced.

The first fire company was organized in Nyack, October 4th, 1834, and " Orangetown, No. 1 " was purchased. This first machine was a " bucket " engine, worked by cranks. This engine was kept in service for a half century. It was in use at the burning of the Arrow, and at every large fire since, and for eighteen years was the only engine in the village. Cornelius T. Smith was the first captain or foreman. In 1884, No. 1 Company bought a Button steam fire engine, and have obtained a new house in South Nyack, near the railroad station. " Mazeppa " Fire Company, No. 2, was organized December 27th, 1852. The first officers were Wm. Perry, foreman; James Marks, assistant. In January, 1884, this Company bought a Silsby steam engine. A hose carriage was purchased in 1876. Mazeppa's old house was on Burd street, in the rear of the Commercial Building. Its present two-story brick building is on Main street, east of Broadway.

January 29th, 1863, " Empire " Hook and Ladder Company, No. 1

was organized, and a truck house built at Upper Nyack. Geo. W. Baker was the first foreman; Henry Palmer, the first assistant foreman. "Jackson" Engine Company, No. 3, was organized May 9th, 1867, with Charles G. Crawford, foreman, and James E. Smith, assistant. Re-organized May 2d, 1882; George Gurnee was elected foreman, and James H. Christie, assistant. The machine is a hand engine, and the engine house stands on Jackson avenue. In September, 1880, "Jackson" Hose Company was organized, with Frank Outwater, foreman, and Henry Strack, assistant. The carriage was purchased in 1883. The chief engineer and his assistants, of the Nyack Fire Department, are elected for two years, under an act of Legislature passed in 1859. George Dickey is chief engineer at this time, with John Foley, first assistant, and August Gross, second assistant.

The largest fires at Nyack have been, the burning of the Roman Catholic Seminary in 1838; the Arrow, at the Nyack landing, in 1840, and again later; the Storm's Wooden-ware Factory, in 1856: Sickle's mill, in 1865; Remsen's house, the barns of Isaac S. Lydecker and Garret Sarvent, and the factory corner of Railroad and De Pew avenues. Besides being at these fires, Nyack engines have been sent to Sing Sing, Tarrytown, Piermont, Rockland Lake and Tenafly to aid in fighting fires.

Since the introduction of the telephone to the village an alarm gong has been placed on the truck house at Upper Nyack and connected with the telephone office, as has the fire bell in Nyack. I think it proper here to relate a personal observation of the workings of the department. On November 21st, 1884, a barn was burned at Upper Nyack, two miles north of the Post office and a mile away from the nearest apparatus. The fire was discovered about eleven o'clock in the morning when every one was at work. The news of the fire was telephoned to Nyack by a neighbor, and, within twenty-five minutes from the discovery of the flames, an engine was on the spot, followed so rapidly by the rest of the department, that inside of forty-five minutes the whole apparatus was at the fire. Accustomed, as I am, to the paid and drilled Metropolitan departments, I must express my pleased surprise at this wonderful celerity in the volunteer department of a country village.

The first school at Nyack, built before 1800, stood near the present reservoir on Main street. It was built of unhewn logs, the spaces between them being filled with clay, which, when dry, was impervious to wind or weather. The seats were rough slabs, taken from the saw mill, and had no backs; the desks, also slabs, were raised but little higher than the seats. The name of the first teacher was Davenport. In 1806, a new school building, two stories in height, was erected on Broadway, a few feet south of the present post office. The school room of this building was down stairs, the second floor being used as a hall. In 1827, this building caught fire and was destroyed. It was rebuilt, but only one story high. In 1837, the school building was moved to its present situation. In 1851, a new building was erected on the same site, and Archibald Stewart became teacher. In 1867, a large addition was built to the school, and it remained sufficiently large to accommodate its pupils till, in 1884; then another addition became necessary and was built.

School No. IX., at Upper Nyack, was organized in 1844, with Jacob Voorhis, George Green and John T. Demarest, as Trustees. The first building was erected in 1845, on a lot donated by Wm. Palmer, on the south side of the mountain road, a little distance east of the present Midland avenue. N. G. Spencer was the first teacher, and his salary was $25 a quarter. In 1867, the school was repaired and an addition erected. Until 1884, this school was used; then a lot was bought, west of Broadway, in Upper Nyack, and a new frame building erected. This new house was first occupied in January, 1885; Garret Sarvent, J. P. Voris and Harvey Gilchrist, Trustees.

The records of the Rockland County Female Institute contain the following entries: "A meeting of sundry gentlemen was convened by the Rev. B. Van Zandt, pastor of the First Reformed, Protestant Reformed Dutch Church, of Nyack, at Union Hall, in the Village of Nyack, on Saturday evening, December 9th, 1854. The following persons were present: Simon V. Sickles, F. L. Nichols, John W. Ferdon, George Green, I. M. Dederer, Henry Oakes, D. D. Smith, Peter DePew, Thomas Burd, Tunis DePew, M. G. Leonard, D. D. Demarest, James Cooper, R. P. Eells, I. S. Lydecker and Rev. B. Van Zandt. Simon V. Sickles was called to the Chair, with B. Van Zandt, Secretary." Among the Rules and Regularions for a Female Institute at length adopted, were the following:

"The name of the institute shall be the Rockland County Female Institute; the same to be under the government of a board of trustees, representing the different religions of the county, one third of whom shall be elected annually by the shareholders."

"The object of the institute shall be to provide the best facilities for a practical, thorough and complete female education, on the same system of instruction as is adopted in the female seminary at Mount Holyoke." The following people subscribed for the stock at $50 a share:

	Shares.		Shares.		Shares.
S. V. Sickles,	160	Isaac Sloat,	2	M. S. Seymour,	5
Peter DePew,	4	C. T. Smith,	2	B. Van Zandt,	2
D. D. Smith,	5	Wm. B. Collins,	2	H. E. Storms,	10
M. G. Leonard,	10	J. W. Towt,	4	I. W. Canfield,	4
I. M. Dederer,	2	P. H. Taulman,	10	E. B. Johnson,	2
Henry Oakes,	2	Wm. Naugle,	5	James Coates,	2
Azariah Ross,	2	C. Winters,	2	Wm. Devoe,	2
T. Smith Tallman,	2	Jesse Blackfan,	2	James Westervelt,	10
L. F. Fitch,	10	S. V. Sickles,	40	J. V. B. Johnson,	2
Abram T. Bell,	2	Geo. Green,	4	C. J. Blauvelt,	10
Rev. Jared West,	2	F. L. Nichols,	10	Abram S. Crum,	2
Peter Voorhis,	5	J. W. Ferdon,	10	Edward Green,	10
S. M. Huyler & Sisters	10	Thos. Burd,	10	J. C. Demarest,	2
H. E. Storms,	5	D. D. Demarest,	2	Wm. H. Lee,	10
Wm. E. White,	2	James Cooper,	2		4
D. J. Blauvelt,	1	J. J. Ackerson,	2	R. De Cantillon,	2
Wm. Dickey,	2	E. E. Conklin,	10		
R. P. Eells,	2	Silas Seymour,	10		

The building now known as the Tappan Zee House, was erected and opened August 28th, 1856, under the charge of Rev. B. Van Zandt. Simon V. Sickles, who had conceived the idea, who placed $10,000 in the stock of the school, and who gave it other and valuable aid, never lived to see the result of his life's ambition; he died two days after the opening of the institution.

Had Sickles lived to watch over and guide the career of his work, the result might have been different: as it was, the Institute in no particular fulfilled its founder's wish. Mount Holyoke Seminary was the design he aimed to follow; but like many other grand designs, after the death of the artisan, who had planned and struggled, the current of this idea turned awry.

B. Van Zandt remained in charge of the Institute till January 27th, 1858, when he was superceded by L. Delos Mansfield, who received his appointment March 1st, 1858. For the first few years the finances of the institution were well managed, and every evidence of success was seen: then reverses and difficulties were encountered, which, when ended, left the Institute the private property of Mansfield. For many years the institution remained under Mansfield's management, but it never recovered from financial difficulties, and was finally closed.

In 1858, Christopher Rutherford, opened a private school at Nyack, and in 1859-60, through his efforts the Military Academy was built for him and opened under the trusteeship of Richard De Cantillon, Wm. Prall, J. W. Towt and Wm. Aspinwall. In the excitement of the Civil War, military tactics were introduced in many institutions of learning, and to the literary schedule of his academy, Rutherford added the manual of arms. A man of great scholarly attainments, urbane and of fine presence ; a conscientious man and teacher ; there are many sons of Rockland, who look back to him with respect. Mr. Rutherford continued his labors till 1870, the last year oppressed by the sufferings of Bright's disease, when he died, and the academy was closed.

In 1876, the institution was again opened by W. H. Bannister, A. M., under the name of the Rockland College. In 1878, the college was incorporated under the Regents of the University of this State, with the following trustees :

Hon. George M. Van Hoesen, *President*.

Merritt E. Sawyer,	D. D. Demarest,
R. De Cantillon,	I. W. Canfield,
Wm. H. Jersey,	M. W. De Baun,
Hagerman Onderdonk,	James D. Smith,
D. F. Ackerson,	J. H. Edwards,
Edmund Ehlers,	Andrew Fallon.

Under its present management Rockland College furnishes educational facilities for both sexes.

The number of private schools that have been established at different times in Nyack, is large and most of them have been well sustained. At present Willistine Hall, started 1881, by the Misses J. A. & J. Kempshall and since conducted by them, is situated at Upper Nyack. The Nyack Kindergarten, started in 1878, by Miss S. C. Robinson ; and the school kept by Imogene Bertholf, are the principle private schools.

The first public burial place at Nyack, was on the point north of the " Bight " in South Nyack. When the first interment in this ground took place, is not known. The last body was buried there in 1834, and in 1873, the remains of those lying on the point were removed to Oak Hill Cemetery. About 1730, a place of sepulcher was started on the Mountain Road, in Upper Nyack, west of Broadway. There lie many of the early settlers in the Nyack Valley, and the names of the Sarvents, Perrys, Snedekers, Palmers and Knapps, can still be deciphered. There were buried Major John L. Smith, who died August 22d, 1797, and his brother, Captain Auri Smith, officers in the War for Independence. The last body was interred at this spot about 1867. In 1800, the Presbyterian Cemetery was started, and used for a place of entombment till 1850, when the last body was deposited there. In 1869, the bodies were removed to Oak Hill Cemetery. In 1810, burial was permitted on a lot of the farm of John

Gesner, in the present South Nyack, and shortly after a negro burial ground was opened on the property of M. Cornelison, near the same spot, but little is known of the interments at these places. Another place of burial for negroes was on the south side of the Mountain Road in Upper Nyack, immediately west of the old school building and between it and Midland avenue. At the time the Roman Catholic College was being built at Upper Nyack, in 1832, on property now belonging to George Green, a chapel was opened in the rear of an old house, that stood north of and nearer the road than the present residence. In the yard attached to this chapel several of the laborers, who died while the college was being built, were interred. After the college was burned and the property abandoned; most of these bodies were removed.

The necessity of establishing a universal cemetery at Nyack was much discussed in 1847, and in February, 1848, a meeting of the citizens of Nyack was called, for a public consideration of the subject. The idea was approved, and the present site, then the property of D. D. Smith, selected.

On June 27th, 1848, Oak Hill Cemetery was dedicated in the presence of three thousand people, two-thirds of whom were from New York City. The exercises began at one o'clock, with a prayer by the Rev. Mr. Dowling, followed by an anthem sung by a choir under the direction of Mr. Baldwin, choirister of the Carmine street church. The Rev. Mr. Dunbar and the Rev. Dr. Adams then delivered eloquent addresses. The dedication service was then performed by Rev. Dr. Hardenberg. At the close of the dedicatory service, the Hon. Hugh Maxwell delivered an appropriate oration, which was followed by a second anthem; a prayer by the Rev. Mr. Hageman and the benediction by the Rev. Mr. Dewing. The Rev. Dr. Dewitt presided at the meeting.

Under its original organization, D. D. Smith was proprietor of Oak Hill Cemetery, and Thomas Burd, Isaac P. Smith and Jones F. Conklin the first Trustees, with John Mace of 75 Carmine street, Superintendent.

Up to March 17th, 1865, this place of burial remained the property of D. D. Smith, and such adjacent land as was purchased and added to the grounds was also vested in his name. Under this arrangement, D. D. Smith received four-fifths of the purchase money obtained from the sale of lots, while one-fifth was retained by the trustees for the improvement of the grounds. On the date in 1865, above mentioned, a special act was passed by the Legislature incorporating the cemetery. By the terms of this act, D. D. Smith transferred all of the unsold land in the cemetery to the trustees and with them fixed a price on the unsold lots. Of this price Smith was to receive seventy-five per cent.

In 1850, the number of lot owners in Oak Hill was one hundred and fifty, the price of a lot $25, and that of a grave from $4 to $6. In 1870, the number buried in this cemetery was 1,827, and by October 12th, 1885, the number had reached 4,415.

The Rockland County National Bank was opened for business June 23, 1860, on the south-east corner of Court street and Smith Place with the following Board of Directors.

Isaac P. Smith, *President.*
A. D. Morford, *Cashier.*

Isaiah Milburn,	D. D. Smith,
Tunis Smith	Wm. Voorhis,
C. A. Morford,	Wm. R. Knapp,
George Conklin,	A. J. Storms,
D. J. Blauvelt,	H. I. Haight,
Wm. Skelly,	I. M. Dederer,
John Peck,	C. A. Fellows,

E. V. Haughwart. .

After the passage of the National Bank Act of February, 1863, this institution became a National Bank with a capital of $100,000. In 1866, D. J. Blauvelt was elected President in place of Isaac P. Smith deceased. The bank continued on the corner before mentioned for some years, and was then removed to the corner of Broadway and Burd street, in the Commercial Building. Through bad management in its loans and the peculation of employees, the funds of the bank were exhausted, and while on Dec. 29th, 1877, the Bank statement showed a capital of $100,000 and a surplus of $40,000, on Dec. 28th, 1878 it suspended payment.

This action was hastened by the failure of the North River & New York Steamboat Co., which was indebted to the bank in the sum of $27,575.00, and of the firm of D. D. Smith, Jr. & Co. who had been loaned both as a firm and as individuals about $100,000. The failure, following closely on that of the Rockland Savings Bank, caused much feeling against the officers of the National Bank, who were generally believed to have been guilty of, to use the mildest term, gross carelessness. The stockholders finally decided that a voluntary liquidation was their best way out of the difficulty, and under the management of the late President the affairs of the bank were settled, paying to the stockholders in all four and one-quarter cents on the dollar. The Directors at the time of the bank's failure were :

D. J. Blauvelt, *President.*
A. D. Morford, *Cashier.*

John W. Towt,   Moses G. Leonard,
Isaac S. Lydecker,   I. M. Dederer,
Arnet Seaman,   Nicholas Blauvelt.

The Rockland Savings Bank was incorporated April 14th, 1871, and opened for business July 1st, 1871, with the following Board of Directors:

S. W. Canfield, *President.*
R. P. Eells, *Secretary* and *Treasurer.*

A. A. Demarest,   Isaac Pye,
John B. Gurnee,   Isaac Hart,
N. C. Blauvelt,   E. B. Weston,
John Wessel,   W. E. White,
S. B. Cole,   James C. Wool,
S. H. Doughty,   Wm. H. Whiton.
James Ketchel

The Bank continued in existence till July 1st, 1877, when a receiver was appointed and the affairs of the bank wound up with a loss of $38,000. The President and Treasurer of the bank were indicted by the Grand Jury on several counts and were acquitted. Civil suits were then brought against them and pressed for some time, but with no result.

The Directors of the bank at the time of its failure were:

S. W. Canfield, *President.*
R. P Eells, *Treasurer* and *Secretary.*

A. A. Demarest,   Isaac Pye,
Wm. B Collins,   J. W. Moison,
N. C. Blauvelt,   E. B. Weston,
John Wessel,   Wm. E. White,
S. B. Cole,   Jas. C. Wool,
S. H. Doughty,   Wm. H. Whiton,
Jno. I. Polhemus,   Abr. P. Smith.

The effect of these failures, while most disasterous to Nyack at first, seems to have been a blessing in disguise, inasmuch as it has banished from the leading places of that village men who had obtained public confidence without deserving it, and whose methods delayed the growth of the town.

The Nyack National Bank was incorporated in March, 1878, with a capital of $50,000, and began business in the building formerly occupied by the Rockland County National Bank, corner of Broadway and Burd street. The first Board of Directors were:

Wm. C. Moore, *President.*
C. A. Chapman, *Cashier.*

S. R. Bradley,   Quentin McAdams,
Rudolph Lexow,   William Voorhis,
J. Weddle,   George C. Stephens,
Peter K. Knapp.

During the year 1872, a number of the men at that time prominent in Nyack affairs, began the discussion of incorporating the village of Nyack, under a general act for the incorporation of villages passed by the Legislature April 20th, 1870. The original intention of those who led in this movement, was to include the present village of Upper Nyack, and to extend southerly beyond the present south bounds of South Nyack. Their design, as expressed among themselves, was to use the taxes obtained from the outlying sections of the incorporated village, in the immediate streets of the town, and to out vote the few tax-payers at a distance by those who were benefited. This design was early suspected by Garret Sarvent, of Upper Nyack, but for some time the suspicions were unconfirmed.

It came to pass, however, that positive proof of the intention of those who were at work in Nyack was put in the possession of a resident in the upper village, and the people of that place decided to incorporate the village of Upper Nyack. With this object in view, preparations were made as rapidly and secretly as possible, and on September 28th, 1872, the village of Upper Nyack was incorporated, only twenty-five days before Nyack. The bounds of this village are: The Hudson River on the east; the division line between Clarks and Orangetowns on the south; the mountain on the north, and on the west, by the middle of Highland avenue from the southern division line to the Mountain Road, and from thence by a line running north-east till it reaches the north boundary a few feet east of Midland avenue.

The first officers of the newly incorporated village, elected September 28th, 1872, were:

Garret Sarvent, *President.*

Trustees.

Charles A. Fellows,   William H. Jersey,
Peter Voorhis.
Wm. H. Kipp, *Collector.*   Isaac V. Smith, *Treasurer.*
D. M. Clark was appointed Clerk.

The term of office for the first officers lasted only till March 19th, 1873, when, at the annual election the same Board was returned. In the elections that have since occurred, Garret Sarvent has been returned to the office of President, a position he has thus held consecutively for over twelve years.

Under its new government the streets of Upper Nyack have been macadamized, and Broadway lighted by oil lamps. The low rate of taxes has drawn to it the main office of the Union Steamboat Company, and for a short time, the Pacific Mail Company. The post-office at Upper Nyack was established in August, 1885, with George C. Stephens, postmaster.

The vote on the question of incorporating Nyack was given on October 23d, 1872. The total number of ballots cast was 484, of which 292 were for, and 192 against incorporation. The first officers elected were D. D. Demarest, President—who had 341 votes to 186 for T. Blanch Smith—David L. Crane, Isaac Vervalen, Charles E. Hunter, Trustees; William B. Collins, Treasurer; Isaac W. Canfield, Collector; William T. B. Storms, Clerk. As in the case of Upper Nyack, these gentlemen only held office till the annual election, March 19th, 1873. At that time, D. D. Demarest was re-elected by 367 votes as against 38 for T. Blanch Smith, and 8 scattering; William H. H. Purdy was elected a Trustee in place of Charles E. Hunter; and J. De Baun, Collector, in place of Isaac W. Canfield.

Under the first administration, from October 23d, 1872, till March 19th, 1873, from fifty to seventy-five oil lamps were purchased and placed on the streets, and Smith Place and Burd street from the steamboat dock to Broadway, Broadway, from De Pew avenue to Main street; Main street to Franklin avenue, and Franklin to the old railroad station, were covered with crushed stone.

In the election held March 18th, 1874, T. Blanch Smith was elected President by a vote of 346 as against 215 votes cast for D. D. Demarest. James E. Smith, C. De Baun, J. I. Polhemus, Charles E. Hunter and George A. Cox were chosen Trustees; William B. Collins, Treasurer; Stephen De Clark, Collector; William T. B. Storms, Clerk; and Charles J. Crawford, Police Justice—Crawford declined to serve and Charles H. Meeker was appointed.

This year Broadway was macadamized with lime stone, from Upper Nyack to the bridge near Hudson avenue and graded at First avenue. De Pew and First avenues were graded from Franklin avenue to Broadway. The election in March, 1875, resulted in the choice of T. Blanch

Smith, President, with a few scattering votes against him; James E. Smith, C. Debaun, D. A. Ackerman, C. C. Powell, Abr. L. Smith, Trustees. Wm. B. Collins, Treasurer; Alonzo Johnson, Collector; Peter Stephens, Police Justice; Wm. T. B. Storms, Clerk. In April, T. Blanch Smith died and Wm. B. Collins was elected by the Board of Trustees to the position of President while George Collins was appointed Treasurer.

Meantime the fate which Upper Nyack had escaped, was falling heavily on the lower portion of the village. The heavy tax-payers claimed that they were the sufferers, while the non-taxpayers out-voted them, and at length they presented a petition to the Trustees asking that a meeting be called to determine whether the village should remain incorporated or not. This petition was denied. The petitioners then appealed to the law, and obtained a mandamus from the Supreme Court to compel the Trustees to call a meeting. On the day appointed, however, an injunction was served on the Trustees to prevent the election.

In March, 1876, Wm. B. Collins was chosen President by a vote of 357 as against 168 for D. D. Demarest ; Jno. A. Sickles and A. L. Smith, Trustees, in place of C. C. Powell and A. L. Smith; Orlando Humphrey, Treasurer; Peter Stephens, Police Justice; Wm. T. B. Storms, Clerk, and J. G. Perry, Collector. Perry refused to serve and J. C. R. Eckerson was appointed in his place. Little was done by the Board except to combat the anti-corporationists, who accused it of criminal extravagance and corrupt motives, while they constantly endeavored to force a vote on the question of annulling the incorporation. To the charge, the Board replied, that they were unjustly blamed for the acts of previous Boards, while in the Legislature they attempted to obtain a repeal of the law by which citizens were allowed to vote upon the question of a continuance of a corporation.

In the election held March, 1877, Tunis De Pew received 172 votes for President as against 169 for Wm. B. Collins; J. N. Perry, Garret Blauvelt, and George Dickey, were elected Trustees; Orlando Humphrey, Treasurer; Charles J. Crawford, Collector; Peter Stephens, Police Justice; Charles H. Meeker, Clerk. Tunis De Pew refused to serve, and Wm. B. Collins was declared President. Blauvelt and Dickey refused to serve, and C. C. Powell was elected in their places. The anti-corporationists had labored constantly, and, at length, compelled the Board of Trustees to call a meeting. at which the question should be settled. August 7th, 1877, was appointed ; and on counting the ballots there were found 71 for incorporation, 282 against. On February 7th, 1878, the first incorporated village of Nyack passed from existence, with Wm. B. Collins, President; and C. C. Powell, J. N. Perry, A. L. Smith, J. A. Sickles, Trustees. With the exception of some hydrants, the remains of a few street lamps, and a book-case, the village possessed nothing. The Treasurer reported that he had transferred $100, which was in the treasury, to the Supervisor; and the Collector reported the amount of unpaid taxes as $2,000.

Before the end of the incorporated village, two suits had been begun against it, one of which was settled by the Trustees; the other was that of John J. Blauvelt, for damage caused to his property by the grading of De Pew avenue.

On May 25th, 1878, the citizens of South Nyack decided to incorporate the district bounded on the north by Cedar Hill avenue; south, by the south line of the property of the late C. T. Smith; west, by the old Nyack patent line. At the first election held, June 22d, 1878, Garret Van Nostrand was elected President; John G. Perry, R. J. Lyeth, G. D. Wilson, Trustees; Wm. C. Moore, Treasurer; T. D. Seaman, Collector, and C. H. Meeker, Clerk. During the winter of 1882-3, an attempt was made to extend the limit of South Nyack as far north as De Pew avenue, and a petition was presented to the Board of Supervisors to that effect. But the people of Nyack regarded this as an attempt to obtain the school building and opposed the movement vigorously. The matter ended by the Supervisors denying the right of petition. On February 27th, 1883, the village of Nyack was re-incorporated, and at the first election Wm. De Groot was chosen President; John A. Burke, E. B. Sipple, George F. Morse, Trustees; Nicholas Blauvelt, Treasurer; G. W. Hart, Collector; and Edw. H. Cole, Clerk.

Gas was first introduced in the village by the Nyack and Warren Gas Light Company, which was incorporated November, 1859, I. W. Canfield, Manager.

The gas works were built in their present location, and the first mains laid in the same year. Later, Hon. William Voorhis bought out the works and became President. The Nyack Water Works Company was chartered March 28th, 1873, through the efforts of Hon. William Voorhis, its President. The first reservoir, standing east of Hillside avenue, proving insufficient to meet the demands, a second was built near the Prospect House, followed by a third on Main street, near the ice house. The supply being still insufficient, Mr. Voorhis tapped the Hackensack near the turnpike bridge in 1883, and by means of a powerful steam pump, forced the water up to his reservoir. By this procedure an unfailing supply is guaranteed.

On October 28th, 1883, the Westchester Telephone Company opened an office in the Commercial Building, Broadway and Burd street, with E. E. Blauvelt, Manager. The Nyack Cornet Band was organized in November, 1879, Frederick Noll being its first leader.

The first public hall in Nyack was on the second floor of the school, built in 1806. From the time of the destruction of this building by fire in 1827, till the building of Union Hall by R. P. Eells in 1853, no place of public resort existed. Such lectures, concerts or other amusements as were heard in the village took place in the Presbyterian church, or in a little building that stood on Main street, and the speeches of political campaigns or Independence Day were generally made in De Pew's Grove, which stood just south of De Pew avenue, and stretched from the present school to Franklin avenue. Within two score years celebrations have been held in that grove, of which now, but a few trees remain.

Union Hall, standing on the north side of Main street, just west of Broadway, was at once a success. There, were held the various forms of amusement, that appealed to the taste and pocket books of the villagers, for many years. There, were heard the first words of ominous import which betokened the approaching storm of civil war. There, during that war, met the Union men of the village, and that branch of the Loyal League established in Nyack; and there, when the Nyack Veterans returned at the close of the war, was a public reception given them.

In 1869, the Smith's closed the second floor of their store at the steamboat dock and turned it into a public hall, under the name of Smithsonian Hall. This resort remained open, until the failure of the firm in 1878 led to a transfer of the property. In 1873, Louis Hoffer, built a hall on DePew near Franklin avenues, 40 by 90 feet, and with seating capacity for 600 people, which he named the Nyack Opera House. In 1881, Hon. Wm. Voorhis opened a hall, corner of Main street and Broadway, 40 by 100 feet, and with seating room for 585 people, which he named Voorhis Hall. In 1868, the wigwam was opened by A. L. Christie, on the corner of Broadway and Church street, and used as a public hall for several years. In this building Horace Greeley spoke during the campaign of 1868.

The Rockland County *Journal* was established at Nyack by Wm. G. Haeselbarth, in 1850, the first copy appearing Saturday, August 3d, as a twenty-eight column 19 by 36 inch paper. The first three editions were printed in New York City. Up to 1861, the paper favored the Democratic Party, but on the first attempt at disunion, it entered upon the cause of the government. With fearless incision, Haeselbarth attacked the disloyal and drew upon himself and paper threats of vengeance. He was supported heartily in his course by the Republicans of Nyack, however, and the organization of the Loyal League, allayed the fierce desire for destruction that pervaded the more rampant members of the opposition.

In 1867, the *Journal* was bought by John Charlton, and the steam press was introduced by him in 1873. At a later period the paper was enlarged to eight pages and during 1882-83, a sixteen page paper was issued. In 1859, Robert Carpenter, foreman of the *Journal*, left that office and on May 19th, of that year brought out the first issue of the *People's Advocate*. The second issue bore the same title, but ere the third was issued, Carpenter had formed a partnership with Wm. Wirt Sikes, later an U. S. Consul, and the name of the paper was changed to *City and Country*. This business arrangement continued till Sikes left the concern and the paper remained in the hands of Carpenter. Until 1868, the paper was independent in politics. Then it took up the principles of the Democratic Party, and has adhered to them since.

In 1880, Carpenter died, and E. C. Fisk took the management of the paper. In 1881, Fisk and J. J. Hart, purchased the paper and it continued in their hands till September 20th, 1883, when Fisk became sole proprietor and editor. In November 1884, a stock company bought the paper and now controls it. In 1867, the *Monthly Gazette* was started by C. A. Morford, Jr., but had only a brief existence. On February 14th, 1879, the Rockland *Advertiser* was started by M. F. Onderdonk, with four pages, fourteen inch columns. In a short time H. G. Knapp, took charge, and conducted the paper under the name of the Rockland *Advertiser*, and *Chronicle* till September 1881 Then Lafayette Markle, obtained the paper and has since managed it under the name of the Nyack *Chronicle*.

The Tappan Zee Boat Club was organized in 1871, and obtained a barge, gig, six-oared shell, besides many private boats. The shed used as a boat house by this club stood at the foot of Spier street, on the north side of the present boat house, and the upper part was used by Chas. Haines, boat builder. The club passed from existence in 1879. The Nyack Rowing Association was organized in May 1881, with J. H. Blauvelt, President; Alex. Pollock, Vice President; Edw. Merritt, Treasurer. The boat house, on the remains of the old steamboat dock foot of Spier street, was built and opened June 15th, 1882.

Oneko Lodge, No. 346, I. O. O. F., was organized March 28th, 1848, with the following officers and charter members: J. N. Johnson, N. G.; S. Gesner, V. G.; Jno. Turnbull. Sec'y.; W. B. Collins, Treasurer; Henry

Gesner, A. A. Lydecker, P. Baker and W. Bedell. In August 1867, the number of the lodge was changed to 122. Rockland Encampment, No. 37, I. O. O. F. was instituted August 21st, 1867, with Thos. Lawrence, C. P.; W. B. Collins, H. P.; Nelson Puff, S. W.; John H. Blauvelt, Scribe; N. Blauvelt, Treasurer; George H. Cooke, O. H. Dutcher, L. W. Coates; C. D. Snedeker and T. Campbell. Ruth Rebekah Degree, No. 4, I. O. O. F. was organized December 30th, 1869, with Nelson Puff, N. G; Mrs. J. Perry, V. G.; Mrs. James Ketchell, Secretary; Patience E. Cook, Treasurer.

Rockland Lodge, No. 723, F. & A. M., held its first communication July 10th, 1872; the charter being granted June 4th, 1873. The first officers were: Charles H. Wessels, W. M.; Charles H. Meeker, S. W.; T. Blanch Smith, J. W.; J. H. Blauvelt, Treasurer; George H. Cook, Secretary; Stephen De Clark, Tyler. Nyack Division, No. 203, S. & D. of T, was organized June 12th, 1867, with Christopher Rutherford, Worthy Patriarch.

Waldron Post, No. 26, G. A. R., was organized May 24th, 1867, and named in honor of Towt J. Waldron; the first Commander was Jas. H. Christie. The charter of the Post was surrendered in 1875. On January 30th, 1879, the Post was re-organized as No. 82, with Robert Avery, Commander. John Hancock Post, No. 253, G. A. R., was organized in January, 1882, with George F. Morse, Commander, and thirty members. Post Silliman was organized July 21st, 1880, with twenty members. The first Commander was W. H. Myers. The Post had the honor of being the first composed of colored veterans in the State. The Jewish Society, of Nyack, was organized in March, 1870, with A. M. Brown, President; Isidore Senigaglia, Vice-President;. Robert Seigel, Secretary; N. M. Kosch, Treasurer.

Besides these societies, there are in Nyack: The Choral Society, organized January 12th, 1880; The National Provident Union, May 2d, 1883; Rockland County Branch, A. S. P. C. A., September 24th, 1875; Rockland County Society, Prevention of Cruelty to Children, 1884; The Orangetown Law and Order Society, organized February 19th, 1884, with Garret Van Nostrand, President; Seth B. Cole and William Best, Vice-Presidents; Howard Van Buren, Secretary; John H. Blauvelt, Treasurer.

The Nyack Helping Hand Association was organized October 2d, 1882, with George F. Morse, Superintendent; Mrs. J. G. Partridge and Wm. Lydecker, Assistant Superintendents; Charles Theis, Secretary; Mrs. J. M. Ackerman, Assistant Secretary; Mrs. Alexander Hudson, Treasurer; Mrs. C. F. Randolph, Assistant Treasurer. This association grew out of the charitable labor of the benevolent citizens of Nyack, and was intended to work still greater good by united effort. In the year ending November 1st, 1884, this association had received $414.04, and expended $307.76. It had helped 41 families and 137 individuals, and given relief to 123 individuals. Beside money, it received large donations of food supplies, clothing, coal and medicines.

PIERMONT.

The early settlers on the Orange Town patent made the creek or slote nowknown as Sparkill their outlet, and, in the progress of time, one of them built a mill upon it, in which, as necessity demanded, a mercantile business was carried on. The dam, belonging to the old mill, became the head of navigation on the slote, and, by the dam at the spot where Haddock's store now stands, was the Tappan Landing, the first port of entry in the County.

In this old mill a store was opened long before the Revolution, by Abraham Mabie, who kept it till the close of that war. About 1783, this store came into the possession of Major Abraham Taulman, who managed it till his death in 1835, when it passed into the possession of his sons.

During this period the name of Tappan as applied to the spot gradually ceased to be heard, and the place was either spoken of as the Landing or Taulman's Landing, the point outside of it being called Taulman's Point. This name continued till the building of the N. Y. & Erie Railroad in 1839, when Dr. Lord, combining the name of the long pier built for that corporation, with the mountainous nature of the surrounding country, called it Piermont. At the same time the Sparkill, which had theretofore been commonly spoken of as the slote or creek, received its present name.

The nature of the valley of the Sparkill is such, that but two main roads can exist and the opening of those from the south must have been contemporaneous with the settlement of the Landing. On the north, the road was probably opened as soon as settlement along the river bank occurred.

Major Taulman continued business in the old mill till 1805, when a new building was erected for a store. We have seen that at his death the store passed into the hands of his sons. They continued the business till 1856, when they sold out to John Myers who kept the store for a year. In 1857, Roger Haddock bought Myers out and began business. He remained in the old building till 1876, when he moved into a new store that he had had built the previous year. This new building is of brick, three stories in height and 40x88 feet in size. One of the floors of this building is used as a public hall and is known as Haddock's Hall.

Beside the store and grist mill at the landing proper, a saw and grist mill was erected further up the slote, early in this century, by John Moore, a negro, on property purchased from a Mrs. Graham. In 1810, Moore added to this business by starting a carding mill, which gave employment to three men. In 1815, William Ferdon bought Moore out, put improved machinery in the mill, and for many years ran it successfully as a woolen factory. In 1860, he rebuilt the structure, added still further improvements in machinery and let it to parties from Paterson, N. J. The mill changed hands once or twice in the next few years, and was finally destroyed by fire. At one time fifteen people found employment in this factory, spinning yarn and making blankets.

It may not be amiss to say a word further regarding John Moore. His trade was that of building mill wheels, and, among others constructed by him, was the wheel for De Pew's mill, which stood on the site now occupied by Grant's flock mill in Nyack. He was also a partner of Mr. De Pew for some time, and was regarded as an intelligent, upright man. His daughter, Mrs. Sisco, and grand-daughter, Mrs. James West, are now living on Piermont avenue in Nyack.

After the building of steamboats, a dock was run out at the mouth of the present Sparkill and it was there that the Orange landed, and that the Rockland was built. When the long pier was constructed, little further use was found for the old wharf and it gradually went to decay.

The post office at this place answered for both the Landing and Tappan and seemed to have been kept part of the time in one place and part in another. On March 25th, 1815, Philip Dubey, was appointed postmaster, and the name of the office was Orange. Dubey then owned the '76 House. On May 28th, 1830, Morris Bartow was made postmaster. April 9th, 1834, Peter H. Taulman became postmaster, and the name of the office was changed to Slote. This change lasted for only a few days, and on April 30th, 1834, we again find the name of the office, Tappan. Finally, June 26th, 1839, the name of the office became Piermont. After Taulman, David Clark became postmaster, April 28th, 1848, and he has been followed by S. A. Jessup, May 15th, 1867; John B. Wandle, May 17th, 1872; and Richard Wandle, January 13th, 1881. In 1872, May 13th, Sparkill, which up to 1870, bore the name of Upper Piermont, was given a separate office with Isaac A. Spencer, as postmaster. He was succeeded May 5th, 1880, by Lucretia Spencer.

The first schoolhouse at Piermont was built early in the century, and stood on the east side of the creek, on the road to Palisades. The lower part of the building was of stone, which was whitewashed, the upper part was wood, painted red. This building remained in use till 1845, when it was succeeded by a new frame house. In the course of time, the demands upon the facilities of the schoolhouse led to its enlargement. No further change was made till 1884, when the present school building was erected at an expense of $5,000.

The growth of Piermont depended entirely on the opening of the Erie Railroad, the location of its eastern terminus at this place, and the building of the locomotive and car works. On the withdrawal of this industry, the village began to decline. For an account of the building of the Erie Road, the reader is referred to Chapter XII. In due course of time, two round houses, a machine, car and paint shop, foundry, planing mills and the other structures needed at a railway terminus were constructed here, the total number of buildings covering at least four acres. This was the period of Piermont's greatest prosperity, and in 1860, her population reached 2,426. In 1852, the directors of the Erie Road, having had that clause in their charter, which prevented them from running in New Jersey repealed, made the eastern terminus of the road at Pavonia. After this, their works were gradually removed to that place, the large round house and other buildings were destroyed by fire, and at length, the few remaining structures were taken down, and disposed of in various ways. A newspaper item in January, 1862 tells us, that one-half of the inhabitants, and many buildings had already gone, and the remainder were to be moved before spring.

Until the opening of the Nyack spur of the road in 1870, Piermont remained the terminus for passengers and freight on the Northern Railroad, but since that time, it has gradually fallen into a condition of decrepitude, from which there appears to be no relief.

The village of Piermont was incorporated in 1850. The first officials consisted of Peter H. Taulman, President; J. G. Blauvelt, James A. Hopson, S. S Post and J. I. Walsh, Trustees; and Cornelius Hoffman, Clerk. Following P. H. Taulman, the Presidents of the village have been: James Westervelt, 1853; J. G. Blauvelt, 1854; John R. Baker, 1856; David Clark, 1857; Andrew Fallon, 1858; John W. Blauvelt, 1865; Andrew Fallon, 1866; Marcus Hoffman, 1867; John B. Wandle, 1868; Richard V. D. Wood, 1871; John Van Orden, 1873; Roger Haddock, 1882. The corporate limits cover an area two miles long and one and a half wide.

The Fire Department was organized in 1852, with James Westervelt as Chief. The first machine—Empire No. 1, and the engine house were the property of the Erie Railroad Company. Protection Company, No. 1, was organized in 1856, with David Cole as Chief. This company disbanded in 1878. Besides the destructive fires in the Erie Companies' buildings, the fire department has had an unusually large number of serious fires to combat. Perhaps the most disasterous conflagration was that which started at an early hour on the morning of November 20th, 1861. Flames were first discovered in Van Voorhis' meat market. The water supply gave out in a short time, and the following buildings were consumed: H. Cooper's two-story frame house; I. Van Voorhis' market drying house and barn, sheds, etc.; N. H. Lusk, two-story building and barn; A. L. Brown's clothing store; F. Bemhardy's drug store; Jacob Wagner's saloon; a building forty by thirty feet belonging to J. V. B. Johnson; a two-story building belonging to the Judge Blauvelt estate; the building used by Jacob Harrison as a clothing store, and the store and dwelling of Moses Oppenheimer.

Among the societies, social and secret, in Piermont, may be named: Piermont Lodge, No. 83, I. O. of O. F., which was organized February 1st, 1843, with William De Voe, N. G.; D. A. Mabie, V. G.; John J. Lawrence, Secretary; John B. Wandle, Treasurer.

Wawayanda Lodge, No. 315, F. & A. M., was organized in June, 1853, with D. B. Parsons, W. M.; R. H. Black, S. W.; E. G. Bennett, J. W.; John Randall, Treasurer; D. C. Noe, Secretary Levi F. Ward, S. D.; John R. Baker, J. D.

Rockland Chapter, No. 204, R, A. M., was organized in April, 1867, with John Van Orden, Jr., H. P.; W. L. Lawrence, K.; W. S. Van Houten, S.; Sumner Sturtevant, C. of H.; John W. Hutton, P. S.; D. Cranston, R. A. C.; A. Smith, M. 3d V.; J. W. VerValen, M. 2d V.; S. D. Clark, M. 1st V.; J. J. Lawrence, Secretary; A D. Onderdonk, Treasurer.

American Legion of Honor, Rockland Council, No. 491, was organized in April, 1881, with F. B. Wright, Commander; L. G. Clark, Vice-Commander; I. E. Gillies, Secretary; Geo. Pierson, Jr., Collector; George A. Knapp, Treasurer; Ward Phillips, Guide; G. V. A. Blauvelt, Warden; J. W. Adriance, Sentry; E. G. Tucker, Past Commander.

The Law and Order Association, of Piermont, was organized in February, 1884, with Hon. John W. Ferdon, President; I. M. Dederer and Cornelius Auryansen, Vice-Presidents; R. Haddock, Treasurer, and T. M. Peck, Secretary.

The Piermont Rowing Association was organized in October, 1879, with E. N. Whiton, President; L. G. Clark, Vice-President; F. B. Wright,

Secretary: G. A. Knapp, Treasurer; J. A. Styles, Captain; A. X. Fallon, Lieutenant. During the winter of 1879–80 a fine boat house was built.

In 1847, Eleazer Lord, LL. D., gave two hundred acres of land, at the point of the mountain near the present Sparkill, for the purpose of a cemetery, which he named Rockland Cemetery. At the time of this donation, the Erie Railway had its eastern terminus at Piermont: that place was an already populous and growing village, and the grant of land for public sepulture was not only a kind, but also a necessitous act. But another purpose was intended by Mr. Lord beside that of creating a merely local place for interment. The situation of his donation, on the main line of travel to and from a growing city, led him to expect this place for burial would be used by the inhabitants of New York. Greenwood had been incorporated barely nine years, and was far more difficult of access than Piermont; and the local church-yards in the metropolis were already over crowded.

The change of the Erie Railroad route, that caused the decline of Piermont, left Rockland Cemetery far from the line of travel. The ground became overgrown with weeds, and was a picture of desolation. In 1880, a change was worked through the efforts of William H. Whiton, Andros B. Stone, George S. Coe, Jose M. Munez, John W. Ferdon, and others, the cemetery was again placed in excellent order at a large cost. Most prominent among the spots of interest in this beautiful place for burial is Mount Nebo, upon which an observatory fifty feet in height has been erected, from which an extensive view can be had. The height above the sea on this observatory is 750 feet.

Among the many mad acts perpetrated in the southeastern part of our County, during the era of real estate speculation, from 1870 to 1876, was one incorporating the Sparkill Creek Canal Company. The redundancy of this name should have been sufficient to kill the project. This corporation was formed for the purpose of opening a canal from the New Jersey line, where the Sparkill crosses it, to the Hudson River. The capital was fixed at $100,000, and the incorporators were: John W. Ferdon, Hiram Slocum, Luciel Saniel, Ambrose Girandat, Isaac Smith Homans, Jr., H. G. Torrey, A. A. Demarest, J. V. B. Johnson, Walter Phelps, D. W. Kipp, C. Auryansen, Roger Haddock. Further than the passage of the act by the Legislature, on May 2d, 1871, the project never advanced.

Ere leaving the subject of Piermont it seems proper to speak of the road side cave or mine hole, a short distance from Haddock's store. This presents an excavation of two passage ways; the one extending in a west-outhwest course, a distance of five and seventy feet; the other extending west bearing rather north for a distance of between forty and fifty feet. These passage ways are cut through solid rock and range from four to six feet in width, and from three to nine feet in height. At the extremity of the longest passage is a beautiful spring of water about six feet in diameter, and eighteen feet deep. Nothing is known as to when or by whom this excavation was made.

PALISADES.

The first name by which this place was recognized, was that of the Westchester county ferryman, who gave the permanent appellation to his home landing of Dobb's Ferry. That the landing on this shore was oftentimes called Dobbs Ferry during the Revolution is undoubted. That name was never popular among our County people however, possibly because of its liability to be mistaken for the opposite hamlet, and shortly after the Revolution the name Sneden's Landing was generally used. That members of the Sneden family already conducted a ferry or were about to, in the early days of the War for Independence, is evinced by the order from the County Committee of Safety, forbidding them so to do. For years this spot was known as Sneden's Landing, and then the name was changed to Rockland. After existing for a number of years under that name, it was again abruptly re-christened and called Palisades. The hamlet contains many fine residences, and its streets and avenues are handsomely laid out. The old wharf, where for so many years, the produce of a large section of country was brought to be shipped by steamboat, has almost disappeared. All that remains of its old time customs, is a row boat ferry which still exists for the benefit of the casual traveller.

ORANGEVILLE.

This is a hamlet in the western part of the township on Narranshaw Creek. The first mill in the place was built in 1780 for Abram Cooper and John De Pew. The present building was erected for Rulef Van Houten, in 1862, and is at present conducted by Edw. C. Van Houten. A short distance southeast of Orangeville, on the Hackensack River, stand the Orangeburg Mills. The first mill on this spot was built in 1770, by a Mr. Mabie, a Huguenot settler who moved into Orangetown in early days. At a later period the large building known as the Atlantic Factory was built here for Peter C. Mabie, and about the same time, C. P. Mabie started a store in the hamlet. The nearest railroad station to this neighborhood is probably that on the "Branch" though the New Jersey and New York Railroad station at Pearl River, is but a short distance away.

ORANGEBURG STATION.

This is a country railway station and post-office, situated about half way between Sparkill and Blauveltville on the "Branch." A small chapel for Sunday school and church services, built by James E. Haring stands here. The post-office was started Feb. 27th, 1861, with Henry A Blauvelt as postmaster, and was discontinued Aug. 21st, 1867. It was re-established Jan. 12th, 1880, with James A. Haring postmaster. On Dec. 24th, 1883, he was followed by Rachel A. Blauvelt.

PEARL RIVER.

This is a local village in the extreme south west of Orangetown, and is a station on the New Jersey and New York Railroad. The place takes its name from the creek that passes near it, in which many pearl mussels have been found. Pearl River contains one store and a hotel. The post-office was organized Jan. 17th, 1872, with Julius E. Braunsdorf as postmaster. He was followed on Sept. 20th, 1880, by James Serven. In 1873, the Ætna Sewing Machine Works were erected by Mr. Braunsdorf and carried on till his death in 1880, giving employment to 100 men. Since that closing, until within a short period, the buildings have stood idle. An effort is now being made to use them for another branch of business.

THE NYACK AND NORTHERN RAILROAD.

For many years before the final construction of this railway spur, certain citizens in Nyack had endeavored to have the railroad from Piermont extended along shore to that village. Each and every one of these efforts were frustrated by property owners along the proposed route, placing so high a valuation on their lands, that the financial success of such an extension seemed impossible. At length in 1867-68, when the mad speculation that followed the Civil War was raging, these enterprising citizens, who had ever labored for the extension of the Erie Railroad, determined that longer waiting would be ruinous and that, if the road could not be brought along the shore, some other way of getting it extended must be found. Several informal meetings and interviews took place between those favoring the project and finally a delegation waited upon Messrs. Fisk, Gould, Sisson and Roorback, officers of the Erie & Northern Railroads in relation to the matter.

These men entered into the idea and promised, that if the people of Nyack would raise the sum of $60,000, they would add $40,000, making a sum sufficient to construct a road. The Nyack people at once began the endeavor to raise their amount, but only succeeded in obtaining $28,000. Upon learning this, the railroad men generously offered to accept that sum, and make good the balance themselves. Having obtained the Nyack subscription, the proposed road was immediately bonded for $100,000, a sum amply sufficient to cover all expense, and the bonds sold. By this arrangement the railroad men paid not one cent, and had $28,000 from Nyack.

The building of the road was begun in August, 1869, and it was opened in May, 1870. The occasion of the formal opening was a gala day for Nyack. The officers of the Erie and Northern Railroads visited the place on a special train, were received and welcomed by a display of flags, and the firing of cannon, and were given a dinner at the St. Nicholas Hotel on Main street. As soon as the road was completed, it was leased to the Northern Railroad Company, and has since been operated by it.

HIGHLAND AND MIDLAND AVENUES.

Though these roads pass for about an equal distance in the townships of Clarks and Orange, I have deemed it wise to speak of them in the chapter on Orangetown. The Tweed Ring had reached the summit of its power. It had prostituted legislatures, influenced the Executive, extended its corrupting presence to the Bench ; it had piled up a city debt in New York to an enormous figure, had so distorted public opinion and morality, that people began to think policy the best honesty, and money, however obtained, the sole criterion of social success ; and finally, it had defied with contempt, any attempt to overthrow it, and by reason of its immunity from punishment, had led to the formation of local rings in other places.

It was at this time, that the era of fantastic speculation in real estate reached Nyack. The opening of the Nyack and Northern Railroad had briskly advanced the price of real property ; the extravagance which followed the war led to the use of a credit system, at once impracticable and dangerous ; and people planned cities, erected buildings, and made fabulous wealth, in the maddest dreams that ever floated across the mental visions of an ordinarily common sense community.

Among the citizens of that section of the County between Rockland Lake and Sparkill, there were many who owned large farms, which the tremendous advance in value of land together with the rapid building of railroads throughout the country, permitting distant sections to enter into active competition with the Hudson River valley, had rendered unprofitable for agricultural purposes. These large land holders were seized with the mania for speculation, and determined to open their farms to purchasers. With this object in view, the Legislature, which was dominated by the Tweed Ring, was appealed to, and the Representative from Rockland—James Nelson—was found to be a willing tool for the work.

In the session of 1871, an act, authorizing the making and opening of two roads, was brought before the Legislature. One of these roads—now known as Highland avenue—was to extend, from the intersection of the highway running east of Rockland Lake, with the highway running from the lake to Rockland Lake landing, to the highway running from Upper Piermont to Orangeburg. This road was to be sixty feet in width, was to be opened, graded, macadamized, guttered and curbed, and the commissioners appointed to oversee the building of it were directed to "make and flag suitable walks along and upon either side of the same, and, also, to make all necessary culverts." The aggregate of expenses for all purposes was not to exceed $10,000 a mile. The cost of this work was to be met from taxes assessed on property lying within a quarter of a mile from the centre of the avenue, along its length and on "two strips of land lying immediately north and south of the termini of said avenue, within the limits of one-half mile north and south, respectively, by half a mile east and west." The commissioners were authorized to assess the pro rata tax upon each piece of property included within the taxable limits, and to appoint collectors to obtain the assessment; and they were further empowered "to sell the lands assessed, upon which the said assessment shall remain unpaid for the space of thirty days after the time for and the return of said warrant by said collector or collectors, * * * in the same manner as the Comptroller of the State is authorized to sell lands for the non-payment of assessments for taxes."

The commissioners named for appointment in this bill were: Peter Voorhis, David J. Blauvelt, William L. Lawrence, William A. Shepard, William Voorhis, W. C. Templeton, William H. Whiton, Henry Brinkerhoff, and Nelson Puff.

The other road now known as Midland avenue, was to be opened from Main street in the village of Nyack to the Hook Mountain. It was to be 70 feet in width, was to be graded, paved, curbed and guttered and the commissioners were empowered at their discretion, to cause side walks to be constructed and flagged. The cost of constructing this avenue was to be met by taxes assessed upon all property lying within nine hundred feet of the centre of the avenue.

In case the assessments were not paid in thirty days after the time for the return of the collector's warrant, the assessed property was to be disposed of in the same manner as in the case of Highland avenue. The commissioners named for appointment by this bill were: Peter Voorhis, Marcena M. Dickinson, Richard P. Eells and William C. Templeton.

The scheme for the passage of these bills was strongly backed, and for a time it appeared as though the project would be forced through. In view of the success of the measure the commissioners, named in the bill, began individual preparations for gain. One bought a tract of mountain land and erected a stone crusher for the purpose of furnishing gravel for the road: others purchased property contiguous to the proposed highway, and members of the Tweed Ring contemplated the erection of a large hotel on the top of the Hook Mountain.

Through the merest accident the citizens living along the proposed roads who were not in the ring, learned of this bill and after difficulty obtained a copy. At once opposition was started. Meetings were held, remonstrances were signed and a committee consisting of George H. Livermore, Hagaman Onderdonk, Daniel Clark, and Isaac Hart, was sent to Albany, to petition against the passage of the proposed act. It was then recognized how strong the influence in favor of the bill was and the committee, after combatting those who labored for the roads to the utmost, at length returned defeated.

By this time the full scope of the contemplated work was understood by those resident in the County and anger against the planners of the avenues, which were commonly called "boulevards" owing to Tweeds connection with the boulevard in New York city, was expressed on every side. Again the opponents of the proposed act petitioned against it, and a second committee, consisting of Isaac Hart, Garret Sarvent and George Green, visited Albany to appeal against the passage of the bill. This committee was joined by Francis Tillou, who bitterly objected to the measure. In spite of the earnest protestation of almost all the property holders, not named as commissioners, along the proposed route, it was found impossible to prevent the passage of the bill. But one course remained open, that of amending it so as to remove its dangers as far as possible. This was accomplished, and the act relating to Highland avenue was so amended as to abolish the clause for curbing, graveling, construction of culverts, and flagging of sidewalks; the expense of building was limited to five instead of ten thousand dollars a mile, and the time for the redemption of property was fixed at one year. The commissioners named in this amended act were: Peter Voorhis, John N. Perry, William L. Lawrence, William A. Shepard, William Voorhis, Richard DeCantillon, William H. Whiton, Henry Brinkerhoff and Cornelius T. Smith.

The amendments to the act relative to Midland avenue consisted of the exclusion of the clauses relative to grading, curbing, building culverts and flagging sidewalks, the reduction of the expense of construction from five to three thousand dollars per mile, an extension of the time for the redemption of property to one year, and an extension to three years for the time of building the road. The Commissioners appointed by the amended act were: Peter Voorhis, Marcena M. Dickinson, George Green, Garret Sarvent and Isaac Hart. The last named gentleman declined to serve and George H. Livermore was appointed in his place. Under this Board of Commissioners, the avenue was surveyed, opened and constructed for the sum stated in the amended bill, and the Commissioners discharged. In the case of Highland avenue, litigation was almost immediately begun because of unjust and illegal assessment. Work was stopped when the road was partially finished and all of the road bed, with the exception of the portion between Rockland Lake and the mountain road in Upper Nyack, has become overgrown with underbrush and weeds.

James Nelson, the Member of Assembly, who labored so hard for the passage of the bill, was overwhelmingly defeated in the elections of 1871, entirely through the efforts of Garret Sarvent, and because of his actions in the matter. Highland avenue still remains an open field for years of legal complications and legislative interference.

SUPERVISORS.

Rinear Kisarike, 1722.
Cornelius Haring, 1723–28.
Cornelius Smith, 1729–31.
Barent Nagle, 1732–33.
Gabriel Ludlow, Jr., 1734–39.
Henry Ludlow, 1740–46.
John Ferdon, 1747.
Adolph Lent, 1748–57.
David Blauvelt, 1758–59.
Daniel Haring, 1760–63.
Abraham Haring, 1764.
Johannes Blauvelt, 1765.
Thomas Outwater, 1766–74.
John M. Hogencamp, 1779–80, 1783–1796.

Jonathan Lawrence, 1782.
James Perry, 1797 – 1800–1804.
James Demarest, 1801.
Sam'l G. Verbryck, 1802-3-6-19-28-1829.
James Perry, 1804–5.
John Perry, 1820.
Richard Ellsworth, 1823.
William Sickles, 1824–27.
Isaac I. Blauvelt, 1830–34.
Benj. Blackledge, 1835–38.
John Haring, Jr., 1839–41.
John J. Haring, 1842.
John T. Blauvelt, 1843–45.
John S. Verbryck, 1846–47.

Simon D. Demarest, 1848–49.
Wm. E. Smith, 1850–51.
John C. Blauvelt, 1852–54.
J. J. Lawrence, 1855.
M. M. Dickinson, 1856 57.
James S. Haring, 1858–63–1865–71.
William Dickey, 1863–64.
Isaac M. Dederer, 1872–73.
D. D. Demarest, 1874–75
Henry A. Blauvelt, 1876–79.
Hagaman Onderdonk, 1882.
George Dickey. 1880–81, 1883–4.

TOWN CLERKS.

Henry Ludlow, 1744–45.
Robert Hallett, 1746–47.
John De Wint, 1748–52.

Richard Blauvelt, 1799–1817 1825–27.
Cornelius Sickles, 1818–20.

John S. Verbryck, 1848–49.
Henry A. Blauvelt, 1850–54 1869–72.

Thomas Outwater, 1754-55, 1761-73.	Richard Ellsworth, 1821-22.	Richard P. Eells, 1855-56.
Andries Onderdonk, Jr., 1758-60.	David Clark, 1823-24.	A. T. Blauvelt, 1857-58.
	C. I. Blauvelt, 1828-29.	John W. Blauvelt, 1859-67.
	J. J. Demarest, 1830-38.	James S. Haring, 1868.
Jan Myndert Hogenkamp, 1778-91.	J. B. Blauvelt, 1834-40.	John H. Blauvelt, 1873.
	Abram House, 1841-45.	John A. Haring, 1874-82.
James Demarest, 1792-97.	George Van Houten, 1846.	W. B. Slocum, 1883.
Tunis Smith, 1798.	J. Youmans, 1847.	Eugene C. Fisk, 1884.

Authorities referred to: Extracts from village papers; Lectures by William G. Haeselbarth; Session Laws; Papers and documents contributed by George R. Van Houten; "Notes on Nyack," published in 1878; Books and papers contributed by Garret E. Green.

CHAPTER XVIII.

THE TOWN OF HAVERSTRAW.

ORIGIN OF THE NAME—ERECTION INTO A TOWNSHIP—AREA—CENSUS—HISTORIES OF HAVERSTRAW VILLAGE—THIELL'S CORNERS—GURNEE'S CORNERS OR MOUNT IVY—GARNERVILLE—SAMSONDALE—JOHNSONTOWN—WEST HAVERSTRAW—MONROE AND HAVERSTRAW TURNPIKE—HAVERSTRAW COMMUNITY—TOWN OFFICERS.

It is claimed that the name of Haverstraw appears on a map found among the Dutch archives in Amsterdam, supposed to have been made about 1616. It may be so. We know that Hudson sailed up the river seven years before; that Adrian Block first built on the site of the present New York City two years before; and that the permanent settlement occurred ten years later, in 1626, and it may be somewhat of a tax on human credulity to believe, that at that date a map was made of a wilderness in which one place is located as "the Haverstroo" or "Haverstroo," still such a thing is not impossible.

The first mention I find of the name is in the map of New Netherland, by A. Vanderdonck, made in 1656, and it is there spoken of as Haverstroo." In June 1658, occurs the second mention of the name, that I have found, in *Stuyvesant's Journal* of his visit to Esopus ; " that the murder had not been committed by one of their tribe, but by a Newesink Savage, who was now living at Haverstroo, or about there ;" again in 1660 and 1664, the name occurs and after that is frequently used. It is doubtless true that this name was given to the place on account of the wild oats which grew along the river banks.

From 1686 till 1719, the present town of Haverstraw was included in the laws, taxes and militia duties of Orangetown. But that valley was increasing so rapidly in population, the distance was so great and the trail so poor between it and Tappan, that the inhabitants petitioned for separate existence and on June 24th, 1719, the following act was passed:

"An Act to enable the Precincts of Haverstraw in the County of Orange, to chuse a Supervisor, a Collector, two Assessors, one Constable, and two Overseers of Highways. * * *

WHEREAS, Several principall Freeholders and Inhabitants of Haverstraw, in the County of Orange, in Behalf of themselves and others, have by their Petitions to the General Assembly, prayed they may be enabled to elect one Supervisor, one Collector, two Assessors, one Constable and two Overseers of tbe Highways, by Reason of their great Distance from Tappan, in the said County.

Be it therefore enacted, by his Excellency the Governor, Council, and General Assembly, and by the authority of the same; That from and after the publication of this Act, it shall and may be lawful for the Inhabitants of the Districts and Precincts of Haverstraw, in the County of Orange, from the Northernmost bounds of Tappan, to the northernmost bounds of Haverstraw, and they are hereby required and impowered to assemble and meet together, at the most Convenient place in the said Districts, and Precincts, on the first Tuesday in April, annually, and then by a plurality of voices to elect and chuse among them one Supervisor, one Collector, two Assessors, one Constable, and two Overseers of the Highways, and the said Officers so chosen shall be of the Principall Inhabitants and freeholders, within the Districts above said, and also be invested with all the Powers, and be obliged to such Services and Duties as all other and like officers in the County of Orange, afore said, are impowered and obliged to do.

And the Assessors and Supervisor so chosen shall act in Conjunction with the rest of the like officers in the said County when and as often as occasion shall require, anything to the Contrary hereof in any wise notwithstanding."

In accordance with this Act the inhabitants of Haverstraw proceeded to hold their first town meeting and elect their town officers.

The Orangetown patent bounded the town within circumscribed limits, but the erection of the Haverstraw precinct gave a practically unlimited area to the jurisdiction of the new town's officers. The present townships of Clarks, Ramapo and Stony Point were all included under the name of Haverstraw, and the town possessed in 1790, 85,720 acres, about six times the area of Orangetown.

As in the case of Orangetown, no separate census existed for Haverstraw before 1738, when 654 people were resident within its limits. Between that date and 1790, the next census, the Pond patent, Kakiat, Scotland and Ramapo Clove had been largely settled and the population had increased to 4,826. The separation of the present towns of Clarks and Ramapo in 1791, brought the population of Haverstraw proper down to more moderate figures

In 1738, Haverstraw had 654 inhabitants.	In 1835, Haverstraw had 2865 inhabitants.
In 1790, " " 4826 "	In 1845, " " 4806 "
In 1800, " " 1229 "	In 1855, " " 6747 "
In 1810, " " 1866 "	In 1865, " " 4113 "
In 1820, " " 2700 "	In 1870, U. S. Census, 6412 "
In 1825, State Census, 2026 "	In 1880, " 7022 "

The same remark concerning the census of 1820, holds true in the case of Haverstraw as of the other towns. The change of the figures in 1865, is due to the separation of the town of Stony Point from her territory in the early part of that year.

HAVERSTRAW VILLAGE.

As we have seen in Chapter II, the earliest grant of land in the County was to Balthazar De Harte in 1666, and reads: "All that tract of land lying on the west side of Hudson's river called Haverstraw, being on the north side of the hills called Verdrietig Hook, on the south side of the Highlands, on the east side of the mountains, so as the same is bounded by Hudson's river and round about by high mountains." In Chapter III, I have spoken of the early transfers of land in the patent, and stated the names of the original owners of the property on which the village now stands.

The first road in Haverstraw was the continuation of the King's high way, which connected the early settlers with their neighbors in Tappantown. This was soon followed, as the influx of settlers from Long Island to Kakiat began, by a road from the river to the new Hempstead, a road which was later continued on to Sidman's Pass and down to Tappan and became the military road of the Revolution. Scarcely had these lines of communication been cut through, however, when the opening of Hassenclever mine and the erection of iron works along Florus Falls Creek, led to the construction of a road from the King's highway along the creek and Stony brook to the mine.

Already I have made mention of the dock where Andre is supposed to have landed in Haverstraw, and of that built by Edw. W. Kiers near the outlet of the Short Clove before the Revolution—this latter dock is now owned by Felix McCabe.

About 1812, John Allison ran out a dock in front of his property, a little north of the present steamboat landing; DeNoyelles built a dock on his land nearly opposite the end of South street, and Captain John Felter built still a third landing near the foot of Main street. For many years DeNoyelles' landing was the most public one, and from it the steamboats ran in early days, thus giving it the name, by which it is still known among the older people, of the lower steamboat landing.

As in the case of Tappan Landing and Nyack, Haverstraw had its early market sloops, which amply sufficed to carry to the city the settler's surplus products and bring back the few luxuries they wished. Until the advent of the steamboat, these sailing vessels were the only means of communication by water, and the few travellers of those early days found them both rapid and comfortable enough. The price of passage was a "York" shilling; the time made depended, in great measure, on the direction and force of the wind and tide, though some of the vessels were furnished with sweeps, and, if becalmed, both passengers and crew were expected to work their passage down. It is said that more than once vessels have been propelled the entire distance in this manner.

While the entrance of steamboats upon the route made terribly sad havoc with the sloop owners' profits, the market vessels were still continued.

The first steamboats, landing at Grassy Point, were too distant to be a serious injury, and even when the Rockland came, and, later, the Warren was built, these relics of an earlier age remained. I append an advertisement.

"Market Sloop. Haverstraw and New York. The subscribers will run for the season the new and fast sailing Sloop *Sarah Francis*, leaving the Dock of Abraham Jones, formerly J. Felter's, every Tuesday at 2 o'clock, P. M., and New York every Friday at 3 o'clock, P. M.

N. B.—All kinds of freight and produce taken on reasonable terms. The boat will run as soon as the ice will permit.

H. & W. R. KNAPP."

Haverstraw, February 22d, 1849.

Besides these market sloops, one, the J. G. Pierson, was built for the purpose of carrying the products of the Ramapo Iron Works to the city. From the factories, the goods were brought to the Haverstraw Landing in huge wagons, drawn by six mule teams. I have shown the causes which led to the withdrawal of this business from Haverstraw.

This village did not begin its growth as early as either Ramapo or Nyack, but for many years, until the discovery of James Wood revolutionized brick making, remained a country hamlet. In 1855, Jacob Wandell wrote in a letter to his sister Catherine Van Houten, the following description of the present village, at the close of the last century:

"My father removed from Tappan Sloat to Haverstraw in the year 1794. There was no village there then, only one house. Captain Shepherd bought the field where the village is built, of Joseph Allison, for £10 ($25), an acre. When he moved there, it was sown with rye. The river bank was the handsomest I ever saw. From Grassy Point down to where James Wood first set a brick yard, (this was on the river bank directly opposite the burying ground of the De Noyelles family), was a beautiful row of large chestnuts and oak trees, growing all along the banks. It was a beautiful walk."

Of that high river bank, the De Noyelles burying ground, still remaining on the top of a high hill, surrounded with clay pits, and viewed by brick makers with anxious eyes, is the only relic left. I have already spoken of the early transfers of land in the present Haverstraw village, until it became the property of Allison and De Noyelles. In 1792, Joseph Allison sold to Thomas Smith and John Shepherd the land bounded by the Present Broadway, West street, South street and Hudson River. In his will, Joseph Allison left to his wife, Elsie, the portion of his real estate lying between the present Broad and Main streets, and on the west side of Broadway, all the land between West Side avenue, (the road leading to the cemetery), and that part of Broad street which is west of Broadway.

Thomas Smith, who was the patriot brother of Joshua Hett Smith, previously mentioned, built a house where the United States Hotel now stands. This was the first house built on the lot, and was two stories in height, with a flight of stairs outside leading to the second story. It was burned early in this century. Smith died in November, 1795. In 1803, this lot was surveyed and divided into house-lots by Teunis Smith, of Nyack.

A street, now called Middle street, was run through the centre of the property from east to west, and numbered streets, beginning with First street, next the river front, were run across this. The price of a lot on the present Front street was $50. Before the beginning of the century, a lot on this property had been given for the Methodist church, and a house of worship was erected in 1800.

From a letter signed "Epsilon," written for the *Rockland County News*, November 10th, 1846, we get the following description of Haverstraw village in early days: "The farm of Thomas Smith covered the village before it was laid out in 1803. In 1804, there were only four houses in the place—Mrs. Green's, a short distance above Mr. Prall's; an old house on Martlin's corner, kept as a tavern and store; a small old house on the corner near Mrs. Martha De Noyelles, kept as a tavern; Judge De Noyelles' below J. S. Gurnee's. Only four buildings existed between the Hudson and the present Garner's factory." I may quote still further from "Epsilon," and give his description of the village in 1846, in this connection. "Now, there are three hundred dwellings in Haverstraw, including Samsondale and Garnerville, beside factories. There are five churches, two being built, one academy, twelve stores, one printing office, four clergymen, four physicians, one attorney. The amount of capital invested in Peck's iron and chemical works, Garner's calico, and Higgins' carpet factory, is $1,000,000. The annual product is $1,500,000. The number of hands employed is 1,000. There are 27 brick yards in operation, which employ 650 hands, and produce about 70,000,000 bricks a year."

By 1837, almost all the land between the present Main street and the neck of land known as the "Narrow Passage," was owned by George S. and Michael Allison. In that year, following the mania for real estate speculation then prevailing, these men had this tract surveyed and cut into building lots, and streets were run through and given the names, many of them still retain. The new village was called Warren, after the doctor General Joseph Warren, who was killed at Bunker Hill, and the development of the brick industry caused a rapid growth of the place.

The first store in Haverstraw was opened by George Smith, before 1815, and stood on the south corner of the present West Broad street and Broadway. Smith, it is said, charged so high a price for everything, that an opposition store was started by George S. Allison across Broadway. Liquor held a prominent place as a commodity at that time, New England rum seeming to be the favorite beverage. If we may judge from a remark I recently heard, that purchasers would produce a shilling and ask for "a penny-worth of tobacco, a penny-worth of sugar, and the rest in New England rum;" the business of those days was not in the nature of dry goods. The first hotel in Haverstraw was built on the spot where Thomas Smith's house had burned, and was kept by Samuel Johnson, as the Johnson Tavern. The present United States, built in 1852, stands on the same site. The American Hotel was preceded by the Temperance House, opened in 1848, by C. A. Rand and C. T. Mills. Where the saloon of Levi West stands on Main street, Abraham Van Tassel kept a tavern in 1819. It was here that the first meeting of the Free Masons was held in 1853. About 1820, De Noyelles and Gurnee opened a store at their dock, later, the steamboat dock. This was the principal store in the village at that time. Perhaps, although we have read "Epsilon's" letter, a view of the village, which has changed so radically and rapidly, as seen by Rev. A. S. Freeman, D. D., in 1846, may be of interest.

Where the Central Presbyterian Church now stands was an open field and fields of grain stood between it and Main street. From the village to Grassy Point stretched a bautiful grove of pine trees, and back of Grassy Point Landing was a sloping bank with gardens and shade trees. Front street, now filled with handsome residences, had then a few inferior buildings. On the corner of Main and Front streets, on the site of the present United States Hotel, stood a dilapidated wooden tavern kept by J. Marting, and from that corner, up Main street, to the National Bank building, stood a row of wooden buildings, which were swept away by fire in 1850. Almost all the village north of Main street, including Rockland, Broad, Division, Clinton, was a farm. Near the present residence of Ira M. Hedges, was a little school house kept by D. B. Loomis, after he left the Academy. Later this site was occupied by the Warren Hotel. Opposite Felter Bros. bakery, where L. D. West's restaurant stands, was the blacksmith shop of Amos Allison. The present steamboat landing was not used as such till 1865, when it was rebuilt by D. D. & T. Smith.

Among the store keepers of those days were: Wm. R. Lane, hardware; J. F. Mills, who opened a book store and restaurant, and whose rhyming advertisements, together with those of his rival in business " Uncle Benny" Smith, who was located on Main street, can be found in the files of the Rockland County *Messenger* of those days. Dr. Charles Whipple opened the first regular drug store in the village but drugs had previously been sold by Mr. Sherwood. In 1848, this store was bought by S. C. Blauvelt, who still carries on the business. In 1847, the store keepers of Haverstraw, announced in the *Messenger*, that thenceforth business should only be done on a cash basis.

The brick industry, which has made Haverstraw, we have already considered. Another manufacturing interest developed by the brick industry I am now to mention. In 1848, Myron Ward and R. A. VerValen, opened the Warren Foundry immediately south of the steamboat dock for the manufacture of stoves and ploughs. Upon the invention of the Automatic Brick Machine by VerValen, in 1852, their manufacture was begun in the foundry and has been continued till the present time. This industry employs from twenty to forty men. Myron Ward left the business in 1851.

The first school house in this village, built in 1810, stood opposite the site of the present M. E. Church. The first teacher was a young Irishman named Quinn. While Quinn was teaching the " young idea how to shoot," Cupid shot, and the pedagogue fell in love with and married one of his pupils, Eliza Wandell.

Whether such a startling, albeit romantic, termination to the course of education led the parents of that time to hesitate about sending their daughters to school or not, cannot now be answered; but certainly little further record of educational matters in Haverstraw exists till the year 1847.

In 1847, D. B. Loomis was principle of the public school. He resigned later and took charge of a school held in part of an old house, which stood near the present residence of I. M. Hedges. Loomis was followed at the Academy by I. I. Foot, Sheldon, Rev. S. W. St. John, George Secor, L. Wilson, Austin, W. P. Fisher. In 1847, Mr. Sanford opened a boarding and day school, and with his literary work combined dancing lessons.

In 1852, H. M. Peck, Amos Briggs and others invited Lewis B. Hardcastle, at that time teaching in Nyack, to open a school of advanced grade in Haverstraw. Accepting the invitation, Hardcastle purchased the property now known as the Mountain Institute from Geo. E. De Noyelles and erected beside the house a two story school building. The Institute was opened Oct. 31st, 1853. Among the corps of teachers at the beginning of the school were; C. M. Dodd, Mr. Jamieson, H. B. Millard, and Miss Mary Rutherford. Hardcastle continued the school till the fall of 1856, when he was succeeded by H. B. Millard, who kept it till the spring of 1857. L. H. Northrup assumed charge of the Institute May 4th, 1857, and continued till the fall of 1860. For some months the Institute remained closed. It at length was re-opened April 16th, 1861, under the present principle, Lavalette Wilson.

Up to 1854, Haverstraw was without fire apparatus of any sort; then the burning of Geo. De Noyelles' barn on the evening of Jan. 22d, roused the people to a recognition of their insecure condition. A meeting of the citizens was called at the ball-room of the American Hotel on the evening of Jan. 28th, 1854, and the necessary funds for a Hook and Ladder truck subscribed. Rescue Hook and Ladder Co. was organized with Asbury De Noyelles, Foreman, and James Creney, Assistant Foreman. The company remained in existence till April, 1859, when it was compelled by financial difficulties to transfer its apparatus to the village authorities who assumed the liabilities. In August 1881, a Holloway's fire extinguisher was obtained and attached to Rescue Hook and Ladder Company. The first truck house was situated in the M. E. Church shed yard.

Warren No. 1 Engine Company, was organized May 15th, 1854, with G. S. Myers as Foreman, and obtained its hand engine in September, of that year. In 1881, the company was disbanded by the Board of Trustees, because of personal ill will among its members. On December 13th, 1881, Warren Company was re-organized with Fred. Glassing, Jr., Foreman; John Braham, Assistant Foreman.

Lady Warren, Steam Fire Engine Company, was organized in July, 1869, with James H. Fleming, Foreman. It was re-organized February 20th, 1871, and a steamer obtained; this engine was rebuilt in 1876. The engine house of the company stands on Division street.

Triumph Hose Company was organized September 11th, 1878, with Daniel De Groot, Foreman; John Bernhart, Assistant Foreman. By the act of 1859, a Chief and two Assistant Engineers of the Fire Department are elected. The first chief was Samuel A. Ver Valen. Besides the great fire of 1850, there have been few destructive conflagrations in the village.

The distance between Haverstraw and the church grave yards at Tappan, Clarkesville, or Kakiat, rendered interments in local burial places a necessity. The Allison and DeNoyelles families located places of sepulture for the dead of their families on their farms. The earliest record in the DeNoyelles ground is that of John DeNoyelles, who died January

11th, 1775. The Waldron cemetery, situated by the side of the present "West Shore" Railroad, about half-way between Haverstraw station and Stony Point, was used as a general place of burial. The earliest record I have seen is that of Charlotte Ming, August 10th, 1792. On the north side of the road from Haverstraw to Ramapo, opposite the residence of the heirs of David Burns, and about midway between Mead's and Felter's corners is a burial place, donated by Colonel David Burns to the public. The oldest stone found there is that which marks the resting place of Phebe Smith, April 19th, 1803. Besides these places of interment, the church yard at the present Garnerville, was opened in 1790; and many bodies were laid at rest on private farms.

At length, John S. Gurnee, John D. Gardner, John R. McKenzie, Isaiah Milburn, Lewis R. Mackey, Walter S. Johnson, Silas D. Gardner, Leonard Gurnee, and Asbury DeNoyelles purchased thirteen acres of land of Asbury DeNoyelles for $1,200 as a cemetery for the Methodist Church. On Thursday, July 7th, 1853, this spot was dedicated as Mount Repose Cemetery, with appropriate ceremonies.

The ground was laid out in lots, and Isaiah Milburn and John S. Gurnee were authorized to give deeds for them. At a later period trouble arose, and a partition suit was begun. The land was sold at auction by order of the Court, and was bid in by Clarence Conger, who gave G. G. Allison power of attorney to sell the lots. Such is the present condition of the cemetery.

The first newspaper published in the old County of Orange was the "Goshen Repository," from which I have quoted in this work, issued at Goshen as early as August 14th, 1778. The first paper published in Rockland County was the *North River Palladium*, which was started in January, 1829, by Ezekiel Burroughs, in West at the head of North street. It had but a brief existence. The next paper was attempted in 1829. It was owned by J. T. Smith, and was called at first the *Rockland Register*. This sheet was brought out by Smith, who was then District Attorney, to aid him in his aspirations for a higher office, and was edited by Burroughs. After the election, in which Smith was defeated, the name of the paper was changed to the *Rockland Gazette*. In 1833, the *Rockland Advertiser* was started by John Douglass, and a year later, this paper and that of Smith's were combined under the name of the *Rockland Advertiser and Family Gazette*. Soon after the paper ceased to exist. In 1834, Alexander H. Wells began the publication of the *North River Times*. This paper also had an ephemeral life. During the existence of the two last-named rival papers, the public was kept interested by the spicy articles which appeared in one or the other, from the pens of contributors. One of the most incisive of the local writers was Dr. Mark Pratt.

In 1844, a paper called the *Rockland County News* was begun by John L. Burtis. Thirty-two numbers of this sheet were issued ere it died. The *Rockland County Messenger* was started by Robert Marshall, May 17th, 1846. Until 1852, the paper remained under Marshall's management. It was then taken by its present veteran editor and proprietor, Robert Smith, and for four and thirty years has been ably conducted by him. Since Mr. Smith has owned the paper a complete file has been preserved.

In 1879, the *Haverstraw Herald* was begun for political purposes. It lasted through a campaign. In April, 1883, the *Sentinel* was started by the efforts of Rev. R. Harcourt, as a temperance advocate. At first printed by the *Rockland County Journal* presses, in Nyack; it was at length moved to Haverstraw in April, 1884, and in the autumn of that year was bought by its present editor, B. A. Farr. It is still conducted in the interest of the temperance cause.

The post office at Haverstraw was established July 1st, 1815, with George Smith as first postmaster. On Jan. 1st, 1817, Smith was followed by Epenetus Wheeler and his successors have been: Samson Marks, May 18th, 1818; Abraham Marks, May 3d, 1819; Peter De Noyelles, April 9th, 1834; Lawrence De Noyelles, December 19th, 1840; Isaac Sherwood, June 24th, 1841; Sylvester Clark, January 23d, 1845; John S. Gurnee, January 19th, 1849; Isaac Sherwood, January 29th, 1850; Samuel C. Blauvelt, July 30th, 1853; Isaac Sherwood, May 7th, 1861; Richard A. Ver Valen, October 22d, 1877; Isaac M. Purdy, April 17th, 1882.

At the close of 1853, the residents of this village made preparations for incorporation. A petition was presented to the County Court by Henry P. Cropsey, Samuel C. Blauvelt, Abraham De Baun, Garret De Baun, Lewis R. Mackey, John C. Coe, James Creney, D. C. Springteen, John De Baun, Ezra Mead, A. E. Suffern and Samuel A. Ver Valen, praying for the incorporation of the village. A survey of the proposed limits was made February 6th, 1854, and the boundaries were as follows:

"Commencing on the bank of the Hudson River at a willow tree standing at the southwest corner of the brick yard of John Gardner, running thence south 61¾ degs. west 10 chains; thence north 24¼ degs. west 20 chains 38¼ links; thence north 51 degs. west 7 chains to a Hickory tree; thence north 38¼ degs. west 10 chains 23 links to a fence running east and west; thence north 48¼ degs. west 39 chains 50 links to a chestnut tree; thence north 28¼ degs. west 25 chains 18 links, to a large rock; thence north 7¼ degs. east 25 chains 53 links; thence north 74 degs. east 4 chains 50 links to Peck's railroad, and crossing of highway leading to Grassy Point; thence along said railroad north 88 degs. east 48 chains; thence south 51 degs. east, still along said railroad and the bank of the Hudson River, 18 chains 60 links to dock; then along the west shore of Hudson River, southerly 111 chains to the place of beginning."

The area embraced within the limits marked by this survey was 493 acres, and the number of inhabitants was 1,760.

Pursuant to an order of the Court, held February 14th, 1854, incorporating all that part of the township of Haverstraw, described in the order, as a village by the name of Warren, provided a majority of the electors of the proposed village should assent thereto; an election was held at the residence of John Begg, on March 11th, 1854. At this election 187 votes were cast of which 179 were for incorporation and 8 opposed to it.

An election for village officers was held at the house of John Begg, April 8th, 1854, and resulted in the following men being chosen:

Edward Pye, *President.*

Trustees.

H. P. Cropsey,	George De Noyelles,
H. G. Prall,	R. A. Ver Valen.
Samuel C. Blauvelt, *Clerk.*	Josiah Milburn, *Treasurer.*
George S. Myers, *Collector.*	Peter Titus, *Pound-Master.*

Assessors.

Isaac Sherwood,   Daniel G. Smith,   Andrew De Baun.

Following that first election, the Presidents of the village have been:

Edward Pye, 1855.
Cornelius P. Hoffman, 1856.
John I Cole, 1857.
John L. De Noyelles, 1858–70, 1877–78.
Richard A. Ver Valen, 1871–74, 1883–84.
James Osborn, 1875–76, 1879–82.

In 1855, the village charter was amended by an act of Legislature, so as to make it a road district, which included the Long and Short Clove roads. In 1859, gas was introduced by E. V. Haughwout, of New York. Trouble between the citizens and the gas company soon began, and continued till 1865, when a mass meeting was held to demand a reduction of rates, and some other radical changes. A conference between the citizens' representatives and Haughwout followed, and mutual concessions occurred.

Haverstraw has a complicated record of names. In another place, I have quoted an Act in which she is called Waynesburgh, and will take an extract from this Act, passed April 1st, 1814, again: "from thence, in a direct course as nearly as may be, to such a point in the village of Waynesburgh, late Warren, as the Commissioners, etc."

For what reason the name Waynesburgh was given to the hamlet, and the length of time it remained in force, have escaped my search. Warren, the hamlet had already been called, and to Warren it was changed again. But this name was never a popular one. People had long been accustomed to blend the name of the township and village in one, and call the latter, Haverstraw. At the establishment of the present Stony Point post office in 1847, it was named North Haverstraw. Commerce was carried on, not with Warren, but Haverstraw, and the name of the village post office was Haverstraw from its organization. Influenced by these and other less important reasons, the residents of the village appealed to the Legislature for relief, and, on April 14th, 1874, that body passed the following act :

"SECTION 1. The name of the Village of Warren in the County of Rockland, incorporated under the provisions of the Statute of the State of New York, authorizing the Incorporation of villages, is hereby changed to ' Haverstraw.' All proceedings now pending by or against the said Village of Warren shall be continued in the name of Haverstraw.

"SECTION 2. This act shall take effect immediately."

On June 1st, 1874, fire limits were established for the village which still govern the place. Under the rule of the village officials this place increased in population and material well-being. In 1865, the number of residents had increased to 2,150 and the proportion of increase still continues.

In 1854, the second floor of S. C. Blauvelt's drug store was enlarged and fitted up as a public hall, called Warren Hall. This was first used Oct. 26th, 1854, for a temperance meeting, at which Judge Allison presided and D. B Loomis was secretary. Addresses in the interest of temperance were made by Edward Pye and the clergymen of the village. The question of temperance had become one of vital interest in this section of our County before this meeting. As early as the Spring of 1851, H. G. Prall and some thirty others had issued a call for a mass meeting to take action on the illegal selling of liquor on the Sabbath. In response to that call a large gathering of citizens took place in the Academy and the meeting resulted in the formation of a vigilance committee and the swearing in of ten special constables for the purpose of detecting and bringing to justice such people as violated the law.

Since that time the fight against the traffic had continued and resulted in the year of which I speak, 1854, in the election of John I Suffern as Member of Assembly, on the Temperance Ticket. From that period till 1882, the subject of temperance was agitated time and again. In this latter year it broke out with renewed violence, and reached a vital stage in the "ballot-box outrage" of March 20th, 1883.

I may be permitted to give a brief account of this affair. In the election held for town officers at the time mentioned, two party tickets were in the field—one, the regular Democratic ticket, the other, a Citizen's ticket. Two ballots were cast by the voters of each party—one, the General Town Ticket, containing the names of all the town officers, except that for Excise Commissioners, this latter being on a separate ballot. The voting proceeded quietly, and at sunset at the close of the polls, the proper officers began counting the ballots. The General Town Ticket was counted first, and the result found to be in favor of the Citizens' Party.

The Excise Commissioner ballot was next prepared for canvassing. During the computation of the result of the Town Ticket, the room in which the election had been carried on was gradually filled with people who had entered by ones and twos. The canvass of the Excise Ticket had but just fairly started when the lights were extinguished, the stove overturned and dragged to the door, burning coals falling on the floor; the table holding the ballots was smashed and overset. Instantly there followed a rush for windows and door; missiles were thrown, chairs and stools broken; in fact, the room was wrecked so thoroughly by riot and fire, that the completion of the canvass was impossible.

Every attempt was made by the proper officials to bring those connected with this outrage to justice, but by one means or another all escaped punishment. It was from the feeling growing out of this affair, that the *Sentinel* newspaper was established.

To return again from a digression, which for the sake of sequence, it seemed wise to make; the next mention I find of Warren Hall, is on Saturday, November 18th, 1854, when Warren Lyceum was organized in it with A. E. Suffern, President; and Edward Pye, Secretary. Among those who lectured during the first season were: A. E. Suffern, Rev. A. S. Freeman, Rev. J. West, Edw. Pye, Wm. E. Haeselbarth, Rev. Van Zandt, Rev. J. Cory, R. J. Ianvooski, L. B. Hardcastle, Rev. P. J. H. Meyers, Rev. W. Van Doren, Prof. Schumacher and Samuel Osgood. Among those who took part in the debates were: R. A. VerValen, C. P. Hoffman, and Messrs. Brower, Lilienthal, Penfield, Coleman. Previous to the opening of this public hall, gatherings of the people for entertainment were usually held in some one of the churches. Business or political gatherings seem to have often been held in the Union Hotel. In 1860, the Wigwam was built on the common, south of the Central Presbyterian Church, and opened to the public on July 27th, of that year. This became the headquarters for public meetings, and, later, for volunteers, enlisted to save our Nation.

In 1871, the Haverstraw Bank was organized as a State institution, with a capital of $100,000. The first board of directors were:

Isaac Odell, *President.*
Ira M. Hedges, *Vice-President.*
George S. Smith, *Cashier.*

George S. Allison,	George S. Wood,
Richard A. Ver Valen,	John I. Cole,

John W. Gillies.

The bank opened its doors for business on Main street, April 15th, 1871. The institution continued a State bank till February 27th, 1875, when it was changed into a National Bank, with a capital of $50,000. The first board of directors under the change were:

Ira M. Hedges,	Theodore Fredericks,	George S. Wood,
Jacob Odell,	George S. Allison,	Richard Ver Valen,
R. Redfield,	John W. Gillies,	John I. Cole.

The institution has been well conducted, and, though two periods of great business depressions have occurred since its start and institutions of trust have been swept down around it, its reputation stands well for carefulness and wise management.

The Haverstraw Savings Bank opened its doors for business in 1871, with the following officers and trustees, who composed the various committees:

A. E. Suffern, *President.*
William Govan, *First Vice-President.*
Richard A. VerValen, *Second Vice-President.*
Garret O. House, *Secretary and Treasurer.*

G. G. Allison,	D. R. Lake,	Theo. Frederick,
E. W. Christie,	Geo. R. Weiant,	Peter E. Lee,
Jno. Turnbull,	Frederick Tomkins,	J. M. Nelson,
Wm. Call, Jr.,	Levi Knapp,	Louis Hohn,
Robert Smith,	Theo. Gardiner,	Wm. H. Wiles,
John Taylor,	Jno. Connley,	Jas. A. Barnes,
Chas. Kreuder,	Denton Fowler,	John Keenan,
Thos. Burke,	Amos Briggs,	Belding Barnes,
	Wm. E. King.	

The institution paid five per cent. interest on deposits and seemed in a prosperous condition till 1879, when it failed. The depositors in the defunct institution were paid 65 cents on the dollar.

Projecting well out in the river, with a bay on each side, is Pullen's Point, more generally known as "Peck's dock." The original name of this point is said to have been derived from one William Pullen, who was Sheriff of the County from 1730 to 1731, and who, it seems, by his liberal views on religious topics excited the ire of John Allison and Thomas Hughs, for in 1731, these men entered complaint against him for saying, "that the Pope of Rome was a good Christian." When Mr. Peck started the works at Samsondale, this point was the most convenient place on the river for the shipment of his productions. At it he built a dock and to it extended a railroad from his works. Here was built the only marine railway in Haverstraw, in 1851, by Henry Garner. It was at first carried on by Mr. Wiltsea, then by G. W. Snedeker, and at present by Henry Rodermond & Son. And here, owing to the depth of water and ease of access from the channel, the early Albany day boats, Armenia and Daniel Drew, landed for several years on their trips up and down the Hudson. The decadence of the industries at Samsondale, and the opening of railroads, changed the tide of travel. Pullen's Point is too difficult of access from the village to make it the regular landing, and now this once famous dock is relegated to the shipment of bricks, and to the ship yard artisans.

This village has been visited on several occasions by storms of extraordinary violence which have caused great damage. On July 9th, 1853, a storm of tornado character struck the place. During its continuance, an old frame building, formerly used as the weaving shop of Higgin's carpet factory, and after the cessation of that business, turned into a tenement house, was blown down. It was occupied by the families of brick yard laborers, who worked for Peck, Rutherford & Knapp. In this accident six people were killed and many wounded. Besides this house, many other buildings were damaged, and great injury was done to the brick yards along shore. In October, 1846, another storm visited Haverstraw, and among other injuries blew down the unfinished walls of the Central Presbyterian Church.

On March 27th, 1870, a terrible easterly gale swept along the Atlantic coast doing great injury. The exposed position of Haverstraw rendered the effects of the storm here exceedingly damaging. Seventeen vessels were either sunk at their anchorage or driven ashore, one at Grassy Point was driven up into the streets; five brick yards were washed away; two lumber yards were destroyed and a coal yard passed from existence. The total loss was estimated at $200,000.

We have seen that before the building of the Hudson River Railroad, the inhabitants of Haverstraw, who wished to reach New York City in winter, were compelled to ride to Piermont, and that to accommodate these travellers, Charles P. Snedeker, ran a stage between the two places. I have also mentioned the number of ferry charters which were granted after the Hudson River road was built.

While these ferry boats were of value in open weather, they were useless after ice had formed; and the residents of the village were then as distant from the Metropolis as ever, unless the river was solidly frozen. 1857, was one of the many severe winters that closed the Hudson River firmly, and during that season, Silas G. Mackey, ran a regular line of stages to Cruger's Landing on the ice.

Stony Point Lodge, No. 313, F. & A. M., was established in the village June 17th, 1853. The first meeting was held in the old tavern kept by A. Van Tassel. The first officers were: Henry Christie, W. M.; John Hunting, S. W.; Samson Marks, J. W.; A. H. Richmond, T.; Edward Payson, S.

Iona Lodge, No. 128, K. of P., was organized December 7th, 1874, with the following charter members: Alonzo Bedell, Louis Echstein, Edward Bedell, Cyrillus Myers, J. R. Smith, M. Washburn, John Gordon, George S. Myers, Charles Sears, M. Richmond and E. M. Newman.

The Ancient order of Hibernians, was established April 5th, 1882, with the following officers. Nicholas Murphy, County Delegate; Wm. P. Bannigan, President; Thos. Finnegan, Vice-President; Edw. Ryan, Recording Secretary; Thos. Sweeny, Financial Secretary; James McLaughlin, Treasurer.

THIELL'S CORNERS.

In the latter half of the past century, a Dane, named Jacob Thiell, arrived at Haverstraw, and following the Minisceongo till he reached the location which now bears his name, he bought some 3,000 acres of land and settled. In a short time, Thiell utilized the water power which the creek afforded, and started, in this secluded spot, a forge upon his property.

Little can be learned of this industry, except that it is reported to have been in operation during the Revolutionary War. Jacob Thiell died before the beginning of this century.

The spot on which he had settled slowly grew. In 1793, a grist mill was started further down the creek by Thiell, and carried on in conjunction with the forge. In 1862, a mill or factory, which stood some half mile east of Thiell's by the highway, was used by William McGeorge as a tannery and candle factory, and carried on till 1866. The increased population led, as we have seen, to the building of a Methodist church at this place, and further life was given to the hamlet by the advent of the N. J. and N. Y. Railroad, in 1874. It was made a post-office village in 1874, with Levi Knapp as first post-master; he was succeeded by Sylvester Knapp.

In 1850, Henry Essex, who eight years before had occupied part of the Samsondale works, leased the site of the old forge, and carried on the manufacture of needles. This occupation he abandoned in 1880, and the works are now dismantled. In his busiest years, Essex employed seven hands in this industry.

GURNEE'S CORNERS OR MOUNT IVY.

About four and three-quarter miles west of Haverstraw on the road to Ramapo, formerly stood the residence of W. F. Gurnee. At this place a road, known as the King's road, runs south to Hempstead and Spring Valley. Not far from the Corner is the house, formerly owned by John Hewitt and his wife—Anna Gurnee—in which Hon. A. S. Hewitt was born. Like many other places in the County called "Corners" with the prefix of the nearest resident property owner to designate the locality, this spot calls for no special mention. On the opening of the N. J. and N. Y. R. R., it was made a station and called Mount Ivy.

Not far west of Gurnee's Corners, John Anderson started a file factory and continued work for some years. The plant was then bought out by its present proprietor, John H. Secor, and is still continued, furnishing employment for four or five men.

GARNERVILLE.

As early as 1760, Cornelius Osborn erected a grist mill on the bank of the Minisceongo, where the Calico Works now stand. From the time of this mill till 1828, no further attempt seems to have been made to use the water power at that spot. Further up the creek, however, near the bridge, over which the road to Mead's Corner passes, a rolling mill and a nail factory were established early in the present century by John I. and George Suffern.

Previous to the building of these works, a grist mill occupied their site and at a later period the buildings were used in the manufacture of various products, their last use being that of a paper mill. This industry was carried on by John I. Suffern from 1850 to 1858, for the manufacture of coarse wrapping paper.

In 1828, John Glass, a Scot by birth, bought 45 acres of land on the south side of the Minisceongo, at the present village of Garnerville, and began the erection of buildings for calico printing, a business he had been engaged in in his native land. By the spring of 1831, the industry had obtained a firm start and gave every prospect of future success. On June 7th of that year, Glass took the first load of his goods to the dock at Grassy Point for shipment to the city. Violent opposition existed at this time between the owners of the steamboats Waterwitch and General Jackson. The first named boat had scarcely left the landing, and the goods were rapidly being loaded on the Jackson when her boiler exploded, killing fourteen people among whom was John Glass.

Until 1835, little was done at these works. Then they were purchased by William Cowdrey and held by him till May 1st 1838, when James Garner, Thomas Garner and Charles Wells bought the property. Under this new management, the print works rapidly grew. From time to time, as the business extended, additions were made to the buildings, and a village sprang up about the factory which was given the name of Garnerville. In 1853, the Rockland Print Works Company was incorporated, with a capital of $100,000, for the purpose of "Printing, and Dyeing Woolen, Cotton, or Linen goods."

The growth of calico printing led Resolve Waldron and Charles Benson to start a steam chemical factory on the south side of the Haverstraw and Monroe Turnpike, just east of the old toll gate, in 1840. The object of this factory was the manufacture of Pyroligneous acid, which was much used in calico printing. This industry was abandoned in 1843, but a year later it was re-begun by William Knight, in a factory near Cedar Pond.

The post office at Garnerville was established in June, 1875, with John D. Norris as post master, a position which he retains at the present time.

SAMSONDALE OR WEST HAVERSTRAW.

In 1830, Elisha Peck, head of the firm of Peck & Phelps, returned from England, where he had been in the interest of the firm's business for many years, bringing with him the machinery for a rolling mill. Land on the Minisceongo creek had already been purchased by Anson Phelps, and on this land the firm established a rolling mill, wire, and other works. To the village which sprang up around these works, and which was founded almost entirely by the necessities of the employees and their families, Peck gave the name of Samsondale, in honor of the ship *Samson*, on which he had returned from abroad.

At the time these works were erected, the road which is still known as the "Ramapo Road," ran as at present. From it, at the corner just southeast of the old factories, a road turned northwest, passed through the hollow by the works, and then turned to the north, to reach Grassy Point. The road, which now passes on by the Presbyterian church up to the West Shore Railroad depot, was not then in existence, and the traveller who desired to reach the section now known as Stony Point village, had to ride up to Mead's Corners, and then round through the present Garnerville to Benson's Corners, or else, drive down to Grassy Point, and from thence to his destination. The present road was opened by Mr. Peck, and beside it were erected a number of small houses for his employees. Some of these buildings, doorless, windowless, desolate-looking, still stand on the west of the highway on the level of its old grade.

The industry started at Samsondale was continued for some time, under Peck & Phelps. Then the latter partner left the business, which was carried on by Peck alone, till, in 1842, a change in the tariff laws rendered it unprofitable, and the works were closed. Previous to this, a chemical factory and screw works had been added to the industries of the hamlet.

Upon the withdrawal of Mr. Peck from business, the mill was hired by Henry Essex, who carried on the manufacture of needles in it till 1844, when it was leased by Higgins & Co. for a carpet factory. Under this firm one hundred looms were employed, and some 250 people obtained a livelihood. In 1850, Higgins & Co. closed the works here, and removed to West 43d street, New York City. The screw factory and wire works were at first leased by Day, Newell & Day, after Mr. Peck closed up, and turned into a lock factory. At a later period they were occupied by Hicks & Payson, who carried on the manufacture of percussion caps.

Since that time, the buildings have been leased by various parties, for different manufacturing purposes. On the morning of July 21st, 1885, one of the buildings, which was then used as a cracker factory and feed mill, caught fire and was entirely consumed.

While Elisha Peck was still engaged in business, he built a tramway from his factory to the dock at Pullen's Point, for the transportation of his material; this road is still in use, being now employed for the shipping of brick.

Previous to February 10th, 1883, a survey and census was taken of an area of 1, 24-100 miles, comprised in the present bounds of West Haverstraw. The resident population within this area was found to be 1,602. A call was then issued for an election to be held at George Taylor's hall, on March 29th, 1883, to determine the question whether or not the territory should be incorporated as a village by the name of West Haverstraw. The total vote cast at this election was 202, of which only 13 were in the negative.

The boundaries of the village are: South, by the village of Haverstraw, and the Ramapo road to its junction with a road that leads south to John Springsteen's; West, by a line running from this junction to the Stony Point line, near the N. J. and N. Y. Railroad; on the North, from the Stony Point boundary eastwardly to the road leading north from Benson's Corner, and by a line which continues the course of the said boundary to a point on the Minisceongo Creek, north of the Farley house, on the lands of the Haverstraw Clay and Brick Company; and on the East, by a line running southerly from the above point to the north line of Haverstraw. The first officers were:

Adam Lilburn, *President.*

Trustees.

| John Taylor, | Theodore G. Peck, | James G. Scott. |
| Henry M. Peck, *Treasurer.* | | Charles W. Gordon, *Clerk.* |

JOHNSONTOWN.

In the closing years of the last century, several brothers named Johnson, who were employed by a ship-building firm, came into this mountainous section to get out ship timber. At this time, the mountains were heavily wooded, and the supply apparently inexhaustible, and, with the prospect of a long residence before them, the Johnson brothers settled on the site of the present hamlet. At this spot, others, who were engaged in one way or another among the mountains, gradually settled. A store was started to supply the wants not only of these settlers, but also of those who were occupied as charcoal burners, or in the making of wooden ware, and who dwelt in the surrounding territory, and the settlement was called Johnsontown.

At the entrance of the Methodists into the County, this hamlet was visited by them and a mission established, which, in the course of time, grew strong enough to warrant the building of a church for that worship. The hamlet has gradually increased in population, and at present, three stores, that of John Secor, of Burton & Matthews, and of Johnson, are kept open. A sulphur spring of reputed medicinal value has been found in this neighborhood.

On March 10th, 1824, a Legislative Act was passed for the incorporation of the Monroe and Haverstraw Turnpike. In the petition praying for this Act it was set forth, that Roger Parmele and others had opened this road through the wilderness from the Orange Turnpike near Parmele's slitting mill to the creek landing at Haverstraw at their own expense. Few inhabitants resided upon it, and the burden of keeping it in order fell entirely upon the projectors. With an idea of making it partly, if not absolutely self-supporting, the following residents in both Orange and Rockland counties signed the petition: Roger Parmele, Joseph Blackwell, Hudson McFarlan, George Kyle, Robert Parkinson, Samson Marks, Abr. Gurnee, Abram Goetchius, George Weyant, Matthew Benson, Walter Brewster, Samuel Brewster, Samuel Goetchius, Samuel Smith, John Suffern, Edward De Noyelles, Lawrence De Noyelles, John F. Smith, Abram Dater, Jacob Marks, Elias Gurnee, John B. Secor, John Rose, Harman Felter and Jacob Odell.

The first Board of Directors were: Roger Parmele, Hudson McFarlan, Resolvert Waldron and George Kyle. A toll-gate was erected near the "Sand-field," and continued in operation till the repeal of the Act incorporating the Company. This occurred April 28th, 1870, and by the provisions of the Act for repeal Abram Weiant was appointed to settle up the affairs of the road.

Perhaps one of the most unlikely events in this township was the start of a communistic settlement within its boundaries. Utopian ideas have influenced a few people in every generation. A belief that the whole human race would live together in a common brotherhood, with a common interest from common toil, and thus avoid the competition, the successes, the failures of life as now presented to us; has been taught in theory since history has been recorded. Often too, the principle has been put in practice and has ended many times in failure and sorrow.

The Haverstraw community, like its predecessors began with every prospect of success. In 1826, a body of citizens, composed of artisans from almost every industry, to the estimated number of eighty, settled upon land previously purchased from John I. Suffern, at a spot now marked by the station of the N. J. & N. Y. Railroad west of Garnerville. The habits and characters of the members of this community are recorded as good. They were industrious. They are said to have displayed more than ordinary intelligence.

Upon the land which they had bought were dwelling houses, out buildings and a saw and rolling and slitting mill. A church was established in which lectures on ethical or industrial subjects were given. Everything seemed bright before the nascent colony. Then, at the expiration of a few months—five it is stated—the Haverstraw Community, like most of its predecessors, collapsed and disappeared from the face of the earth.

The founders of the experiment were Jacob Peterson, George Houston, Robert L. Jennings, and a Mr. Fay. The price asked for the land they bought, some 130 acres, was $18,000 and of this, one third was in cash, the remainder being left on mortgage. At the crash of the enterprise, the mortgage which was held by John I. Suffern, threw the property back into his possession.

SUPERVISORS.

Cornelius Haring, 1723-24.
Jacobus Swartwout, 1725-27-1730-34.
Cornelius Kuyper, 1728-29-1740.
Gabriel Ludlow, 1735-1738-39.
Garret Snedeker, 1736-37.
Adrian Onderdonk, 1741-43
Guisbert Kuyper, 1744-52-1780-81.
John Coe, 1753-63.
John De Noyelles, 1764-71.
Edward W. Kiers, 1772-79.
Tunis Kuyper, 1782-85.
David Pye, 1786-91.
Benjamin Coe, 1792-1801.
Samuel Smith, 1802-5.

Nathaniel Dubois, 1806-7.
Andrew Suffern, 1808-9.
Abraham DeCamp, 1810-11.
David DeBaun, 1812.
Samuel Goetchius, 1813-14-1821.
Halstead Gurnee. 1815-17.
James Taylor, 1818-20.
John I. Suffern, 1822-23.
Matthew Gurnee, 1824-25-1828-29.
Charles Smith, 1826-27.
Lawrence DeNoyelles, 1830-31-1834-1839-41.
James De La Montagne, 1832-33-1837-38.
Jacob Hauptman, 1835.
Henry Christie, 1836.

John W. Felter, Sr., 1842-46-1853-54.
George E. DeNoyelles, 1847-52.
Andrew Debaun, 1855-56.
Wesley J. Weyant, 1857.
Wm. R. Knapp, 1858-59.
John Lawrence DeNoyelles, 1860.
Prince W. Nickerson, 1861-64.
John I. Cole, 1865,-67.
Samuel C. Blauvelt, 1868-74
Henry Christie, 1875.
John W. Felter, 1876-79.
Josiah Felter, 1880.

Authorities referred to: Documents relating to Colonial History S. N. Y. U. S. and N. Y. State Census Reports. Magazine of American History, Vol. xiii. "History of Haverstraw" by A. S. Freeman, D. D., and W. S. Pelletreau. Lectures "Thirty Years in Haverstraw" and "Thirty Years in Rockland County," by A. S. Freeman, D. D. Files of the Rockland County *Messenger*. Session Laws, S. N. Y. I am indebted also to William Govan, M. D., John Lawrence De Noyelles an l Alonzo Wheeler, for information.

CHAPTER XIX.

NEW HEMPSTEAD, HAMPSTEAD OR RAMAPO.

DATE OF ERECTION—AREA—ORIGIN OF NAME - FIRST TOWN MEETING—CENSUS—HISTORY OF SUFFERNS—SLOATSBURGH—DATERS OR PLEASANT VALLEY—RAMAPO—STERLINGTON—HILLBURN—KAKIAT OR NEW HEMPSTEAD— SCOTLAND — SHERWOODVILLE — MECHANICSVILLE OR VIOLA—CASSADY'S CORNERS—LADENTOWN—POMONA—SPRING VALLEY —MONSEY—TALLMAN'S—MISCELLANEOUS—HISTORY OF THE OLD TAVERNS—NEW JERSEY AND NEW YORK RAILROAD STATIONS — THE ORANGE TURNPIKE—STAGES—TOWN OFFICERS.

In the history of this town I shall draw largely from the History of the Town of Ramapo, by Rev. Eben B. Cobb.

At the same time and for the same reasons, that led the people of the present Clarkstown to petition for a separate town existence, the residents of Ramapo asked the like privilege, and, in 1791, the town of New Hempstead was erected with an area of 34,545 acres.

Among the early settlers within the limits of the present town were a number of families from about Hempstead, in Queens county, and these immigrants gave to their new home the name of the one they had left, distinguishing it from the older settlement by calling it *New* Hempstead. The Indian name of this section was Hackyackawek, which soon became corrupted by the settlers to Kakiat, and for many years this portion of the County was indifferently called by either name. Upon the erection of the town, the name, that the settlers from Long Island had given their settlement, was adopted for the town. New Hempstead remained the appellation of the township till March 3d, 1797, when the Legislature passed an act from which the following extract is taken: "That the town of New Hempstead, in Orange County, shall hereafter be called, known, and distinguished by the name of Hempstead, any law, usage or custom, to the contrary notwithstanding."

Mr. Cobb, in his history of the town, regards this name as growing from an error in orthography, and thinks that *Hampstead* instead of Hempstead was intended. In proof of this view, he says: "We are led to this conclusion from the fact that in the town records and on deeds after this, the name is most frequently written Hampstead, and that Horatio Gates Spaffard, * * in a Gazetteer, published by him at Albany in the year 1813, states that from correspondence 'with old inhabitants of the Town, and some of its present officers,' he adopts the name of Hampstead." I would add to these reasons, that in the New York Civil List, under the caption of Obsolete Towns, the name is given as Hampstead.

Whatever the Legislature may have intended, however, Hempstead was the legal name given; and now followed "confusion worse confounded." If the prefix of *New*, had failed to distinguish this from the Long Island town, certainly matters were not bettered when that prefix was dropped. I, myself, recall hearing old people speak of the town, using the Indian or its other designations indifferently, and for some time found difficulty in recognizing that all the names applied to the same section; we may judge then how confusing such a multiplicity of names would be to a stranger. And, as if to add still further to the intricacy, the church at Clarksville, until 1840, was officially entitled: The First Reformed Dutch Church of New Hempstead.

Such a condition of affairs could not long be tolerated in a town so rapidly increasing in importance, and in the fall of 1828, a meeting of the residents was held at Cassady's Corners to petition the Legislature for a change. "The meeting is reported by those still living," says Mr. Cobb, "as 'quite stormy,' owing to the various names which were proposed. One was for calling the town Columbus, after the discoverer of America; another, Denton, in honor of Abraham Denton, the first man who settled in the town; another, Seamantown, after Jacomiah Seaman, the first white child born in the town; another, Ramapo, after the river and mountains of that name found in the town. Still another advocated New Antrim, after the place called New Antrim, founded by John Suffern near the point of the mountain, and still one more thought Mechanicstown should be the name, after a hamlet by that name just springing into life in the centre of the town.

At last, after much discussion, it was by a plurality of votes decided to petition the Legislature to make the name Mechanicstown." The Legislature did make it Ramapo, influenced, it is said, by a letter from Hon. J. H. Pierson, favoring that name. If posterity had no other cause to be grateful to Mr. Pierson, this act alone should make us revere his memory. Perhaps no greater wrong has been perpetrated in this country than the extinction not only of the Indian race, but also of their very names. The first mention of the name that Mr. Cobb has found is in a deed dated August 10th, 1700. It is there spelled Ramapough. In 1708, it is written Romopock; and later, becomes Romapuck or Ramapuck, Ramapaugh and Ramapo. Tradition gives its meaning as clear or sweet water.

The first town meeting in Ramapo, was held on the first Tuesday in April, 1791, at the house of Theunis Cooper, near the "Brick Church." The presiding Justices were Samuel Goetchius, Theunis Cuyper, and John Suffern; and the following officers were elected: Gilbert Cooper, Supervisor and Town Clerk; Abram Onderdonk, Garret Serven, Joseph Goetchius, Assessors; Henry Howser, Collector; Abram Onderdonk, Aury Blauvelt, Overseers of the Poor; Jacob Deronde, Peter Van Houten, Albert Cooper, Commissioners of Highways: Albert Cooper, Joseph Lyon, Constables; Stephen Gurnee, James Onderdonk, Henry Young, John S. Coe, John Myer, Thomas Onderdonk, Fence Viewers; Hendrick Wannamaker, Garret Eckerson and Johanes Smith, Pound Masters.

In spite of the difficulty in regard to the choice of a name, Ramapo pushed forward rapidly. From the erection of the town till 1835, it excelled any of the other towns in population. Then it lost in the race, and now ranks third.

In 1800, Ramapo had	- - - -	1,981 inhabitants.
" 1810, " "	- - - -	2,313 "
" 1820, " "	- - - -	2,072 "
" 1825, State Census,	- - - -	2,379 "
" 1835, " "	- - - -	2,576 "
" 1845, " "	- - - -	2,911 "
" 1855, " "	- - - -	3,414 "
" 1865, " "	- - - -	4,330 "
" 1870, U. S. Census,	- - - -	4,649 "
" 1880, " "	- - - -	4,952 "

NEW ANTRIM OR SUFFERN.

The first owner of land in the village, as we have seen, was Jacobus Van Buskirk, who, in 1762, obtained a mill site on the Mahwah River. In September, 1763, John Suffern, who was born near Antrim, Ireland, moved to the site of the present village, and secured an acre of land on the south side of the present Nyack Turnpike. Soon after, he removed diagonally opposite, and built upon the site now occupied by the house of George W. Suffern. Here he started a store at the division of the roads, one of which passed westward, through Sidman's and Smith's Passes, to reach the villages in the towns of Goshen and Minnisink, the other running north-easterly through Kakiat to Haverstraw and King's Ferry, which was the first in the present town.

As we have heretofore read, valid titles could not be obtained to real estate in this part of the town till after Jan. 18th, 1775. As soon as security in possession was assured, Suffern began the purchase of land, one of his first bargains being for the mill right of Van Buskirk. Here he ran a grist mill for many years. Shortly after, he started potash works, not far from his store, and about 1813, he built a forge on the west bank of the Mahwah, south of the Nyack Turnpike. Mr. Suffern also built and carried on a woolen factory on the Mahwah, about a quarter of a mile south of the Nyack Turnpike. These were the early industries of New Antrim.

Upon the opening of the Erie Railroad in 1841, the village took the name of Suffern in honor of its founder. At this time radical changes had taken place. The road to Haverstraw had been much shortened from those days when one had to pass through Kakiat to reach that place, and though, as we have seen, the attempt to build the Waynesburgh and New Antrim Turnpike had ended in failure, still the Haverstraw road had become of so much importance that it was kept in good order. The Nyack Turnpike had been long since cut through and had materially shortened the distance to the river, and both these roads joined the Orange Turnpike in the village. With these wagon routes was now combined the railroad.

The first post-office in Rockland County was established at New Antrim, Oct. 4th, 1797, and John Suffern became the first postmaster. The office at that time was in Suffern's store. In 1808, this office was discontinued. From 1844 till 1849, the office for the Ramapo works was kept by George W. and Jno. C. Suffern, in the store now occupied by Alanson Traphagen, but the Suffern office was not established till March 10th, 1858. At that time George W. Suffern was postmaster and held the office till 1861, when Alanson Traphagen received the appointment. He held the office till 1868, when Dwight D. Baker became postmaster. Baker was succeeded by James Wannamaker in 1882, and the office was moved to the postmaster's store. In August, 1885, Peter D. Johnson became postmaster.

The first store in the present village was built in 1842, by George W. Suffern. In 1884, the village contained 20 stores, 90 houses, 2 hotels, and a population of about 600 people.

Ramapo Lodge, No. 589, F. & A. M., was instituted June 1st, 1865, with Charles E. Suffern, W. M.; S. M. Hungerford, S. W.; George M. Crane, J. W.; R. F. Galloway, Treasurer; Daniel Sherwood, Secretary; W. D. Furman, S. D.; Stephen A. Ronk, J. D.; John W. Crum, S. M. C.; John H. Wannamaker, J. M. C.; Peter Sines, Tyler; A. R. Leport and W. T. Howard.

Ramapo Council, 436, A. L. of H. was instituted February 21st, 1880, with D. B. Baker, D. Cooper, C. F. Whitner, A. S. Bush, T. J. Yost, A. Zavistoskie, W. H. Hollister, W. D. Hall, J. L. Crane, E. Whitner, A. S. Zabriskie; A. C. Sherwood, and E. Roberts, charter members.

Industry Encampment, No. 103, I. O. O. F., was organized December 10th, 1883, with the following officers: H. R. Porter, C. P.; D. S. Wannamaker, H. P.; Harrison Bull, S. W.; John Finch, J. W.; W. G. Eaton, Scribe; E. S. Roberts, Financial Secretary; G. E. Remsen, Treasurer.; J. H. Wambough, Guide; J. L. Crane, J. Woods, J. Zabriskie and P. Slaven, first, second, third, and fourth watch; A. S. Bush and W. H. Sutherland, inside and outside sentinels; G. P. Miller and W. Blauvelt, guards of tent,

On November 23d, 1874, a violent storm passed over the village, during which the tower of the Episcopal Church was blown down and several buildings unroofed. No lives were lost. In February, 1875, the railroad station, erected in 1862, was destroyed by fire. Though the residents of the village had borne about two-thirds of the expense of this building, the railway company collected the insurance, and have, so far, done little toward restoring the citizens' money by erecting a respectable station house.

Among the great conceptions—still born—were the Ramapo Land and Water Company, incorporated April 23d, 1869, and the Suffern Dime Savings Bank, incorporated April 27th, 1869 Neither enterprise passed beyond the act incorporating it.

DATER'S WORKS OR PLEASANT VALLEY.

The early industries of this place have been considered in Chapter X. In 1854, the forges were finally abandoned. Upon a portion of their site a store was built, which is now occupied by Geo. W. Dater, grandson of the founder of the works; while upon another portion stands a large building, erected in 1882, by Hon. Charles Siedler, of Jersey City, for mill purposes, but, as yet, unoccupied. Since 1871, Edward Allen has used the building, formerly occupied by his father, Adna Allen, as a hoe factory, for a grist mill, to which he added saw and bark mills in 1878.

Half way between Pleasant Valley and Sloatsburg, formerly stood a grist mill used by the Sloatsburg Manufacturing Company. In 1874, this building was purchased by Mr. Knapp, and started as a shoddy mill. In 1878, it was burned by spontaneous combustion, but was immediately rebuilt, and now employs 21 hands, and turns out 18,000 pounds of shoddy in bulk, per month.

SLOATSBURG.

The first owner of land at this place was Wynant Van Gelder, who purchased the site of the present village from the Indians, March 7th, 1738. Isaac Van Duser, married Van Gelder's daughter, and obtained by gift from his father-in-law, the tract of land where Sloatsburg stands, on June 13th, 1747. Stephen Sloat in the course of time, won the hand of Van Duser's daughter, and received as dower the property which now bears his name, June 3d, 1763. The Indian name of this place was Pothat or Pothod. The original Sloat mansion is still standing, and is occupied by a decendant of Stephen Sloat. In days gone by this building served as a public house on the road from New York to Albany.

We have followed the early manufacturers of this place in Chapter X, and seen that the factories were closed in 1878. In 1882, the old mill was re-opened by Robert McCullough, and has since been used for the manufacture of spun silk thread.

The post-office at Sloatsburg was established March 27th, 1848, with Jonah Brooks, as first postmaster. He held the position till 1849, when Jacob received the appointment and retained the office till 1852. In that year Henry R. Sloat became postmaster. He was followed August 26th, 1885, by Theodore Haff.

This hamlet contained in 1884, six stores, and about fifty houses. It is the location where the only remaining gate on the Orange Turnpike is standing.

THE Y—PIERSON'S DEPOT—STERLING JUNCTION—STERLINGTON.

When the Erie Railroad was opened in 1841, the company built a Y at this spot, to turn their locomotives—a similar Y exists at Sparkill station, and was formerly much used. At a later period, the railroad company built a station-house at this point, and the place was called Pierson's Depot. In 1865, the Sterling Railroad was opened, and the place then began to be called Sterling Junction. In 1882, on the establishment of the post-office, the name was again changed to Sterlington.

The first post-office established at this place was opened as Pierson's Depot, April 1st, 1847, with George Mapes as post-master. The office was discontinued June 16th of the same year. On July 1st, 1882, an office was again opened as Sterlington, with John C. Messimer as postmaster. The Sterling Mountain Railroad, 7–6 miles in length, was built to carry ore from the Sterling iron mines and furnaces to the Erie Railroad. The company was organized May 18th, 1864, and the road opened

November 1st, 1865. The western terminus of this railway is at Lakeville, formerly Sterling Lake, another in the many instances of change in name without improvement. As originally built, the gauge of the road was six feet, but in 1882 it was altered to four feet, eight and one-half inches.

RAMAPO WORKS—RAMAPO.

For previous history of industries see Chapter X. In 1852, a new move in manufacturing interest was attempted here. A large building for a file factory was erected by Davis, Evans & Co. For some reason the enterprise fell through. In 1864, the manufacturing interests of this village were revived by C. T Pierson, who started the Ramapo Car Works in the building formerly occupied by Davis, Evans & Co., standing just west of the church.

In 1866, the Ramapo Wheel and Foundry Company was organized, with H. L. Pierson, President; George W. Church, Treasurer; C. T. Pierson, Secretary, and W. W. Snow, Superintendent. The company leased the old cotton mill, and is now manufacturing car-wheels and railroad castings. Beside those used in this country, many of the wheels from this shop are shipped to Cuba and South America.

The first store opened at this place was in the old Pierson homestead, shortly after the completion of the works. In 1805, the building at present occupied by William Van Wagenen, was built for a store. The post-office was established on November 11th, 1807, as the Ramapo Works, with J. H. Pierson, post-master. In 1821, Silas Sprague became post-master, and held the office while J. H. Pierson was a Member of Congress. In 1823, J. H. Pierson was again appointed, and held the office till 1844, when George W. Suffern was appointed. He was succeeded, in 1847, by John C Suffern, who remained post-master till 1849, and was followed by Edward V. Lord. In 1850, J. H. Pierson was again appointed, and was followed by John W. Ten Eyck in 1851, and he by Lucius D. Isham in 1853. In 1857, J. G. Pierson was appointed post-master, and remained in control of the office till 1862, when Abram Cornelius took charge. In 1863, Charles T. Pierson became post-master, and held that position till 1880, when he was succeeded by George B. Pierson. The name of the office was changed from Ramapo Works to Ramapo in 1879.

WOODBURN OR HILBURN.

In 1795, John Suffern erected a saw-mill on the Ramapo, about one mile south of the present Ramapo. This was followed in 1848, by a charcoal forge, for the manufacture of merchant-iron and to this, a rolling-mill was added in 1852. These works employed about 25 hands. The works were abandoned in 1872.

In August of that year, George Coffin, George Church and W. W. Snow purchased property at this place from James Suffern, and planned and began to lay out a village, to build houses, and to encourage and assist their employees to purchase lots, and erect homes. The place was first called Woodburn, but, when an application was made in 1882 for a post office, it was found that a place with a similar name already existed in the State, and the appellation of Hilburn was chosen instead.

The first school in this hamlet was erected in 1873, through the efforts of Rev. Peres B. Bonney and the generosity of the subscribers, on a plot of ground given by J. B. Suffern, and was used for both Sunday and day school, and also for church purposes. In 1884, it was found necessary to build a large addition to the edifice. In 1873, water was carried into the village, and every dwelling supplied. In 1876, a brass band was formed, under the leadership of Charles G. Hoar. The post office was established here on July 18th, 1882, with Wm. W. Snow as first post master.

On July 13th, 1881, the Ramapo Iron Works were started in buildings erected near the Erie Railroad. W. B. Wilkins was elected President, George Church, Treasurer, R. J. Davidson, Secretary, and F. W. Snow, Superintendent.

Turning now to that part of the town, which lies between Clarkstown and the mountain, we find an abrupt change from the mountain scenery of Ramapo Clove, to a fertile, agricultural country, well watered by the Mahwah, formerly Haverstraw, Saddle, and Pearl Rivers, formerly Pascack Brook, and the head streams of the Hackensack. And it can cause no wonder in our minds, that in the early days of our history, before man had touched the dark and rugged fastnesses, and wrested from this forbidding gorge, nature's aid, had toiled and moiled to win the fickle goddess, Fortune, and at last had succeeded in so combining art and nature, that the Clove has now become a spot as beautiful as any the world can show. It can cause no wonder, that when the pioneers appeared in our County, they shunned this repellant pass, and selected sites for homes in the open country to the east.

But the infelicity of the soil was not the only cause which led the first settlers to avoid the Clove. Uncertainty as to titles, as we have seen influenced them also. For these reasons the valley to the east of the mountains was first settled. Philip Vors, (English Fox), is supposed to have been the first white man to locate in this section and he, in 1700, built a log house about a hundred yards from the present dwelling of David Fox, near the 14th mile stone. In 1726, he built his third and permanent house, a stone building 20 feet square.

Fox was not long alone, for in 1712, arrived the band of immigrants from Long Island, who made Kakiat their home. On September 21st, 1739, when Charles Clinton, in surveying Cheesecocks patent, came to "the house of Edward Jeffers," from "Van Dusers, in ye Clove," situated about a half mile east of Sufferns, he notes in his journal: "Observed houses and settlements on every side." The first of the Kakiat settlers was Abram Denton, and his child, Jacomiah, is claimed to have been the first white child born in the town.

KAKIAT OR NEW HEMPSTEAD.

At the beginning of this chapter I have spoken of the origin of the name of this hamlet. Here was built before 1754, the first Presbyterian Church in the County and the first church in which divine service was conducted in English; here John D. Coe kept a store and tavern at which in 1769, the Board of Supervisors met and in 1780 John Andre, stopped to dine, with his guard on the way to Tappan.

The first post office established at this place was on September 11th, 1813, under the name of Kakiat. No business was ever transacted at this office. In 1829, the office was re-established under the name of West Hempstead, with Amasa Coe as post master.

SHERWOODVILLE.

Jacobus Van Buskirk, it is said, built a grist mill on a branch of the Mahwah, at this place, before the Revolution, and operated it for some years; the business was then changed and the building used as a bark mill until 1825. At that time J. Sherwood obtained the property and turned the old building into a factory for fulling cloth and carding wool, a business he continued till 1845. Since 1845, the mill has been used for the manufacture of cotton bats, by Jonathan and Elias Sherwood.

About 1800, a grist mill was erected, near the one above mentioned, by Gilbert Cooper and carried on for many years. It is now owned by Abram Cooper. The junction of the roads near this mill formerly was known as Cooper's Corners.

Less than a mile southwest of Sherwoodville, and one-eighth of a mile west of the Sufferns and Haverstraw road, stands Blauvelt's foundry. The first industry started here was a saw and grist mill, probably in the last century. About 1830, Richard Blauvelt, who had inherited the property, added to this mill a foundry for the manufacture of ploughs. In this foundry, it is claimed, was burned the first hard coal used in this section, by Richard Blauvelt. The works are now carried on by Edward Blauvelt, son of the originator.

LADENTOWN.

A generation passing away, only recognized this name as locating a section where ignorance, lawlessness, and Godlessness held full sway ; where every crime known in the calendar was committed, and where, if a stranger inadvertently entered, it behooved him well to "leave all hope behind." As usually happens, when a section obtains a bad name, the further removed the people were, who conversed on the topic, the worse grew the reputation of this locality, and none painted it so black as those who had never been near it. I speak entirely within the bounds of truth when stating, that so ill-favored did the name of Ladentown become to the inhabitants of this County, residing in other sections, that an unintentional stigma is cast upon people born there, and the expression "a Ladentowner" denoted and to a certain extent still denotes, a social pariah.

Situated midway between Suffern and Haverstraw on the highway, is a collection of some dozen houses and three stores. This hamlet is Ladentown. The name of the place is derived from Michael Laden, an Irishman, who at one time was employed as a nail cutter in the Ramapo works and who, in 1816, left that employment and opened a store and tavern near the present residence of Charles Hedges. Laden's old bu ild'n g still standing a short distance west of Hedge's dwelling.

Owing to his acquaintance with the teamsters of Pierson's works, to the fact that the liquor traffic in the Clove had been stopped, and because of its location midway on the road to and from the landing at Haverstraw, Laden's tavern at once became the stopping place on the road. Here the teamsters partook freely of the liquors they could not get at home, and, adding to their supply in Haverstraw, either disturbed that village with their riots or else returned to Laden's and created trouble there. With this unruly condition of affairs was added the fact, that not infrequently dances were held at the tavern to which the mountaineers came, and these usually ended in brutal fights and noisy confusion. Such seems to have been the only sins that the hamlet proper can be held responsible for.

But the name of Ladentown was applied to a far wider section. Throughout the mountains which stretched in almost primeval wildness from Laden's tavern north and west, dwelt a population so sunken in ignorance, so isolated from civilization that it seemed foreign to our century, and tales of this people, were attributed without regard to exactness to all the residents of this neighborhood. This population of the Ladentown mountains maintained an existence by burning charcoal, getting out hoop poles, or making *bockies*, baskets, and other wooden ware. Squatters in these wilds in early days had had children and grandchildren born to them, who had rarely if ever been outside of their mountain homes. Too few schools have ever been in the County, and those schools that did exist were near the thicker settlements. The good work of churches has ever been going on, but the wild and inaccessible mountains were far distant from the early houses of God.

So it had come to pass, that the little knowledge originally possessed by those who had first settled in the mountains, had been lost in their children till at last a population existed but little removed from barbarity. Of this population strange tales are told of promiscuous association of the sexes, of children born out of wedlock, of ignorance so dense, that on at least two occasions women over twenty one years of age confessed, when called to the witness stand, that they had never heard of and knew not the meaning of the name of God, and of moral perceptions so blunted, that the difference between mine and thine, when applied to the property of non-residents was not considered. As in every human population so here, there were gatherings of the residents at which too free a use of stimulants would be indulged in followed by the usual orgies which occur on such occasions. Serious as these social and moral defects were, they seem to have been the only sins committed. It must rest with the reader to judge whether these people were more sinning in their ignorance or more sinned against by a civilization, that for nearly a hundred years passed them by.

Large tracts of these mountain lands were owned as they still are by non-residents of the County, and these owners made constant complaint regarding and often employed men to prevent the cutting of their forests. This led to ingenious devices on the part of the mountaineers, and the watchers reported, that by tying his coat tightly about the trunk of the tree above the line of cutting, the woodman could so deaden the sound of his axe blows as to render it impossible to hear a sound a few hundred feet away. Tunis Smith, sometime Surrogate and a noted surveyor, from whom this information regarding the Ladentown mountains was obtained, related that on one occasion he accompanied Mr. Lorillard through a portion of his property. One night they lodged at one of the better houses and Lorillard, sitting before the fire after supper, complained bitterly of the way his wood was stolen to make baskets. The owner of the house and whilom host thereupon stated, that he had never made a basket in his life. Tunis Smith rose earlier than his companion next morning, and in walking about before breakfast came upon an out-house filled from floor to rafters with *bockies*. As he turned away his host came upon him and said: "Mr. Smith, I said I never made baskets. I didn't say anything about *bockies*. Don't bring Mr. Lorillard around this way."

The first missionary who entered these mountains probably and laid the foundation for the spread of civilization was, paradoxical as it may seem, Michael Laden. In the furtherance of business he began barter with the mountaineers, exchanging his groceries and dry goods for the wooden ware made by the residents in the woods. As the business grew, he had stated days of the week on which he would visit certain localities, and at last the exchange grew so great that more than one wagon had to be sent out. In 1836, Laden sold his property to John J. Secor, and removed to New York City, where he opened a wooden ware house.

Ere many years had elapsed, baskets and later wooden ware began to be made by machinery, the old charcoal forges passed from existence, and those sources of income were removed from the people dwelling in the mountains. Then came another important civilizing epoch for the mountaineers, one as paradoxical as Laden's influence, I refer to the Civil War. Volunteers from this wild territory were numerous. When the War ended or their term of enlistment expired, these volunteers returned to their mountain homes with new ideas and broader views of their mission in life and they leavened the whole section. In 1865, the Methodist denomination, which had been at work in this locality for half a century, built a house for worship at Ladentown, and met with success. In 1869, Rev. E. Gay had his attention drawn to those living further north, and started Sunday schools at the Sandfield, on the old Haverstraw and Monroe Turnpike, in the school house and at the bark mill in the woods. At the latter place a log cabin was fitted up for services and Sunday school. Margaret E. Zimmerman of New York becoming interested in this mission proposed the erection of a church and with her aid the corner-stone of the present church edifice at St. John's was laid June 23d, 1880, by Rev. E. Gay, Jr. In the fall of that year the building was opened with appropriate services. By the kindness of Mrs. Zimmerman a day school is maintained and regular services are held in the church. A post-office was established at St. Johns in 1882. The Ladentown post-office was established on Dec. 15th, 1871, with Charles A. Hedges as postmaster. The office was soon discontinued.

MECHANICSVILLE OR VIOLA.

About the year 1824, Luke Osborn started a blacksmith shop, Theunis and Henry Crum opened a silver plating factory, Henry Shuart erected a wheelwright shop, and Cornelius and Matthew Demarest began a tannery, on the road leading from the present Forshay's Corners to New Hempstead, and on account of these industries, the wife of Dominie Demarest suggested Mechanicsville as the name of the hamlet. The place grew with such rapidity, that at the town meeting called in 1828, to select a name for the township, a plurality of those present decided on Mechanicstown.

In 1866, John H. Goetchius built and opened the store still managed by him. On April 3d, 1882, a post office was established at this hamlet, by the name of Viola, a name selected by J. H. Hopper, the relevancy of which, it is difficult to discover. John H. Goetchius was appointed post master.

FORSHAY'S, FORSHAY'S CORNERS—ACKERMAN'S OR CASSADY'S CORNERS.

In 1851, W. S. Forshay built a small shop for the manufacture of segars, about a mile north of Viola. The business proved profitable, and in 1860, more room having become necessary, the present factory was erected. The industry now employs twelve hands and turns out 600,000 segars annually.

Two and a half miles from Sufferns, on the road to Haverstraw, a road leaves the Haverstraw highway and runs east, through Viola and New Hempstead to New City. This was the military road of the Revolution. From the long residence of members of the Forshay family at this spot, the junction has taken its name. During the early days of the century, Joseph Conklin conducted a distillery here. A short distance east of the Haverstraw road, on this road to New City, stands a grist and cider mill, which was built about 1808 by a man named Pullish. In 1814, Theunis Cooper bought this structure and used it as a grist and saw mill. It is now conducted by Abbot Cooper.

A mile east of Viola is Cassady's Corners. I have used the name of Ackerman's Corners also, because at one time the place was so called from D. D. Ackerman, who lived at the junction; priority, however, undoubtedly entitles Cassidy to the name. At this place Archibald Cassady dwelt before the beginning of this century, and at his house town meetings were held for seven and twenty years.

SPRING VALLEY.

In the year 1842, a meeting of the farmers of this neighborhood took place, to petition the Erie Railroad Company for a railway station. In reply, the company assented to stop their freight trains, if the residents would build a house. A plot of ground was obtained, the necessary money and material subscribed, and under the superintendence of Samuel C. Springsteel and Jacob Straut, a platform, with a wooden building 10 by 12 feet upon it, was erected. Henry Iserman at once occupied the station house, and established in it the first store in the village, an act which, as he had not thought it necessary to obtain the consent of the builders, caused no little annoyance.

At the meeting to decide upon a name for the nascent village, Samuel Coe Springsteel suggested that of Spring Valley, and after some discussion that name was adopted. Previous to the adoption of this name, the railroad people had called the place Pascack, while to another station, built a little further southeast, the name Laurel Hill was given; both of these names were eventually dropped.

Following Iserman, Jacob T. Eckerson opened a small store, and was succeeded by Isaac Conklin, who later built the brick store, now occupied by Smith & Burr. The Fairview House was begun in 1868 by Jacob A. Van Riper, and opened to the public in the following year. In 1884, Spring Valley contained 29 stores, 3 restaurants, 2 hotels, 2 livery stables, &c., and had a population of some 900 people. At the present time its inhabitants are discussing the advisability of becoming incorporated.

The post-office at Spring Valley was established June 5th, 1848, with Aaron Johnson as the first post-master. Previous to that year, Monsey had been the post-office village for that neighborhood, and Johnson the post-master at Monsey. He remained at the head of the Spring Valley office but eleven days, and was succeeded by Levi Carman, June 16th, 1848. In June, 1849, Richard W. Coe was appointed post-master, and held the office till December of that year, when he was succeeded by Gerrit DeBaun, who filled the position till 1851. At that time, Erastus Van Zandt became post-master till 1858; John A. Johnson, from March 10th till October 2d, 1858; Andrew Smith, from October 2d, 1858 till 1869; Stephen H. Burr, till 1873, Egbert B. Johnson, from 1873 till 1879, Jacob E. Haring, from 1879 till 1882; Stephen H. Burr, in 1882, and John D. Blauvelt in August, 1885.

Columbian Fire Engine Company, No. 1, was organized June 24th, 1861, with Andrew Smith, Foreman; John G. Cooper, Assistant Foreman. The company was named after Columbian Hook & Ladder Company, No. 14, of New York City. The first machine was paid for by subscription.

MONSEY.

This hamlet is five miles east of Suffern, on the railway between that place and Sparkill. In 1840, Eleazar Lord, then President of the Erie Railroad, bought 8½ acres of land at this place, upon which a station platform was built. Kakiat was cut upon this platform, as the name of the to-be village, but when the road began operations, the station, at the suggestion of Judge Sarven, was called Monsey, after an Indian chief by that name.

In a short time Angus McLaughlin built a twelve foot square shanty at this place, which he opened as a restaurant. The following year, 1843, Dr. Lord sold the property he had bought here to Aaron Johnson, who built and opened the first store in the village. The place has now six stores, two blacksmith shops, one carpenter shop, a lumber and coal yard, a steam feed mill, and a hotel.

The post-office was first established here February 13th, 1846, with Aaron Johnson first post-master. In June, 1848, as we have seen, it was moved to Spring Valley. On July 10th, 1848, the office was re-established at Monsey, with Aaron Johnson as post-master. In 1855, John H. Wigton was appointed to the office and held it till 1859, when he was succeeded by Levi Sherwood, who remained in charge till 1862, when Samuel G. Ellsworth became post-master. On September 10th, 1885, Levi Sherwood was again appointed.

Brewer Fire Engine Company, No. 1, was organized April 22d, 1879, with H. E. Sherwood, Foreman, S. H. Secor, Assistant Foreman. The first apparatus was a Babcock Chemical Engine, which was retained till the present Hook and Ladder Truck was obtained. A fire bell was presented to the firemen in 1885.

The Monsey Division of the Sons of Temperance was organized December 27th, 1883, with the following officers: Levi Sherwood, W. P.; Mrs. M. Brady, W. A.; E. C. Brady, R. S.; D. B. Smith, A. R. S.; W. Van Houten, F. S.; Rev. P. D. Day, Chaplain; Edwin Dicks, Conductor; Cassie Palmer, Assistant Conductor; Julia Rhinesmith, I. S.; Edward Ketchum, O. S.

TALLMANS.

This place, three miles east of Suffern, takes its name from Tunis I. Tallman, who settled here in 1836, and opened a store and tavern. The first station was built in 1844 by Tallman, but was soon after abandoned. In 1856, Henry T. Tallman built a second station at Tallmans, which stood till 1868, when the present house was erected by the neighbors. The first store in the village, built in 1860 by H. T. Tallman, is now occupied by T. R. Montrose. The first blacksmith shop was started in 1860 by Henry Van Orden, and the first wheelwright shop was opened in 1867 by Stephen Van Orden. The village now contains a church, three stores, two grist mills and twenty houses.

The post-office was established here June 1st, 1860, with Henry T. Tallman first post-master. He retained the office till 1878, when Garret Wortendyke was appointed. Thomas R. Montrose became post-master in 1879.

At the opening of the New Jersey and New York Railroad in 1875, six stations were located in the town—Spring Valley, Union, New Hempstead, Summit Park, Alexis, Pomona. Any one who is familiar with our County's history, will doubtless recognize the pertinence of these names at once. Only one station calls for notice—Pomona—where a post-office was established June 21st, 1876, with John Brockway as post-master. In 1880, Isaac L. Secor became post-master, and was followed, in 1883, by George E. Potts.

In the southeast corner of Ramapo township, a mile and a half south of Spring Valley, on the old post road, is the neighborhood known as Scotland, from the nationality of the first settlers. On Pascack Brook, south of Scotland, and on the stream, which runs parallel with and on the west side of the old road, many branches of industry were formerly conducted. On the latter brook there was a feed, a saw and a grist mill, and Carson & May's slitting mill. On the former, beside three saw and grist mills, George and Benjamin Hill had a foundry and machine shop.

A high hill in this neighborhood still bears the name of Scotland Hill, and here also is located the Scotland graveyard, long since abandoned.

On December 29th, 1827, a post-office was established at Scotland, with Peter D. Tallman as post-master. On June 5th, 1848, this office was discontinued.

About a mile southwest of Tallmans, is the hamlet called Masonicus— an Indian name. Here, from 1800 to 1820, Cornelius Wannamaker kept the Masonicus store and tavern, and here, in 1855, the Masonicus Church was built. Between Scotland and Masonicus is Saddle River, on which are located one grist and one saw mill, and a stream on the east side of Cherry Lane, on which are situated a grist and saw mill, and two mills which combine both these industries. At the junction of the Saddle River road with the Nyack turnpike, John Yeury formerly kept a tavern. This property later passed into the hands of Peter P. Jessey, who kept a store here for many years.

I have tried to tell in another part of this work how the early inhabitants found amusement. As new settlers arrived in the County, the old customs disappeared. The community of feeling, the tie of friendship brought about by long association in suffering and success, could not well have been extended to and would not have been appreciated by these new comers. Hence, the barn-dances and corn-huskings of an older time gradually gave way to the new order of things. But the axiom, that human nature is the same through all the world, was ever true. Young people desire relaxation and pleasure, and when these were no longer afforded at home, they sought them abroad. To meet this demand a new form of business was started—taverns.

A generation of people still living requires no explanation of what a tavern was, but there is a generation just entering the struggle of life, and there are generations yet to come to whom this name, as used in days gone by, might be an enigma. It seems wise, therefore, to pause a moment and look at these places. The old wayside inn of the Revolution, was a house where man and beast could obtain refreshment and comfort on their journey, and the focus for all the gossip from the city and country. The modern hotel is a place where the traveller can obtain board and lodging.

The tavern combined the uses of the ancient inn and the modern hotel, but to them added a third, a most important use, that of a public dancing hall. It was seldom that the taverns were used by casual travellers. At the most flourishing time of their existence, communication between business centres had found other channels beside the highways. They were used by the residents of this and neighboring counties, who found it necessary to pass by them, as a place for lunch and a spot where their horses could be fed.

The taverns were usually built upon the public highways, midway between two villages. Somewhere down stairs were a bar and dining room. On the first floor above was the ball room, running the length of the building. The remainder of the house was used for family purposes. This was the usual arrangement subject always to the changes necessitated by the architecture of the building. At a short distance from the house was a barn, and attached to it was a long shed fitted up with horse troughs for the accommodation of such travellers as carried the food for their animals with them.

These taverns were the resort for all the young people for miles around. In winter a dance would be held almost nightly in the ball room, the participants being couples, who had started out for a sleigh ride, and on stopping at the tavern and finding others present had organized a set. At times, generally the eve of some holiday, the proprietor would give a ball, but this in little wise differed from the usual dance save perhaps in the greater number of people present. These taverns were also the scenes of brawls. Any public resort where ugly dispositioned people meet and drink is liable to such disturbances—but the conflict, if it passed to blows, ended without serious injury to either party. The revolver was yet unknown.

The mention of the " Red Tavern," " 76 House," " Stephen's Tavern " in this County, of " The Jug," " Jim Bogert's " and " Nagle's " taverns, in northern New Jersey ; will call back to the older reader, recollections of many happy hours. But above all and far beyond all, in the memory of people three score years of age and upwards, natives of Rockland ; stands the tavern known as " Aunt Kate's." So widely popular was this hostelry of Mrs. Catherine Tallman's, that I have considered it more appropriate to speak of the customs of this era in social life, in the chapter devoted to the town in which she lived and reigned, than to place it elsewhere.

The days of inns passed away in this County upon the influx of strangers, and when the immigration had grown sufficiently large, taverns also ceased to be popular. The increase of population, the introduction of outside labor, the acquisition of wealth, led to the formation of classes in society and each now finds its amusement in its own way.

Between New Hempstead and the " Brick Church " is Summit Park Cemetery incorporated in 1882, with Andrew Johnson, President; Wm. H. Parsons, Secretary ; Aaron D. Johnson, Treasurer ; and John F. Hauptman, W. P. Hope, Peter S. Van Orden, John Haring, J. E. Jersey, and Wm. R. Pitt, Trustees, The grounds of this place of sepulcher consist of an acre and a half, principally deeded by Erastus Johnson. At the Brick Church graveyard, the oldest dates found are on the stones marking the resting places of William Smith, September 23d, 1794 and Hannes Smith, January 8th, 1794.

About three quarters of a mile northeast of Ladentown, on the road from Sufferns to Haverstraw, and on the extreme bounds of the township, is the place called Camp Hill, from the fact that during the Revolution, the American Army was in camp there.

Returning once more to the Ramapo Valley. From the Orange Turnpike west to the apex of the triangle in which our County ends, is a succession of mountains, still retaining much of their primeval solitude. In these hills, two and three-quarter miles from the store at Sloatsburg, is a sheet of water called by the Indians, Pothat or Potake, by early surveyors, Van Duser's Pond, known to residents of the County as Negro Pond, and found on old maps of Rockland under the spelling of Niggar Pond. West of this, and forming part of the boundary line between this State and New Jersey, is another pond, called Shepherd's.

In the field notes of a survey made October 27th, 1774, occurs the following: "Begun at the 17 miles end and continued our range N. 54 deg. 15 m. West; at 44 Chains, square Northward, about 12 or 15 Chains, a high, steep, rocky mountain, : at 60 Chains in a swamp; at 68 Chains, the West edge of said swamp; at 80 Chains, set up a chestnut stake with No. XVIII. in negro Guy's improvement, and put stones round it, Northeasterly of his house."

Tradition has it, that a " good Mr. Rutherford," who owned large tracts of land, allowed people to settle on it where they chose. Many of that unfortunate race, whose ancestors were torn from their native land, and survived the horrors of the " middle passage," to become the bondmen of a Christian people, seem to have settled in these mountain wilds at an early day; to have made homes among these forbidding rocks, and to have cultivated the sterile land, till even now, it is said, the cleared field and orchard of one of these fore-time negro settlers can be seen on the west of Negro Pond.

As has been said in speaking of Ladentown, the abandonment of manufactures and the development of machinery in the production of woodenware have withdrawn employment from many of the dwellers in these mountains, still, a large industry is carried on in getting out hoop-poles and cord-wood, and Sloatsburg, which is the depot for this business, has much of this material shipped yearly.

We must turn again to the general history of the township, and learn the history of the Orange Turnpike. Early in the settlement of the County, a road was forced through this Clove to permit the passage of settlers on their journeys to and from the settlements along the Delaware. As those settlements grew, as the section north of the mountains became populated, this, the only real pass between the Hudson and the Delaware into the interior of the State, came into constant use. The Revolution still further demonstrated the need of an excellent highway through the Clove, and finally the industries, which sprang up along the Ramapo River in the closing years of the last century, necessitated a better means of communication. To accomplish this, the Orange Turnpike Company was incorporated by an act of Legislature, April 4th, 1800, at the request of the following people:

Wm. Wickham,	David M. Westcott,
John Steward,	Antony Dobbin,
James Everitt,	Jonathan Sweezy,
James Carpenter,	John Wood,
Thomas Waters,	Solomon Smith,
James W. Wilkin,	John Gale, Jr.,

William Wickham, George D. Bradner, John Webb, Daniel Marvin, and Seth Strong Selah were appointed Commissioners. Two hundred and fifty shares of stock at $25 per share, were issued and taken up by 67 people among whom were Aaron Burr, Peter Townsend, Seth Marvin, J. G. Pierson & Brothers, John Suffern, &c.

At the time of the organization of this company, the old "Albany Road," bending to the north shortly after entering the State, ran in front of the present Episcopal Church at Suffern to what is now the Nyack Turnpike, where it turned to the left, following the course of the present Nyack Turnpike to a point between the Catholic and Methodist Churches, then striking directly across to the Eureka House, it proceeded westward along the Ramapo. The Turnpike Company opened the road parallel to the present railroad from the New Jersey line to the present Hilburn works and then lifted it from the valley to the side of the mountain. On May 3d, 1869, the Legislature authorized the Company to abandon the western half of the road. The Turnpike Company to-day own but ten miles of road, reaching from the New Jersey line, and on this there is only the toll-gate at Sloatsburg.

From Nyack and Haverstraw stages were run to Piermont during the winter season ere the railroads were extended to those villages; but at the best of times this means of communication was but temporary, only while the river was closed, and the vehicles used were the outgrowth of expediency. Already a generation has risen to whom these stage lines are unknown. If this be true of the eastern section of our County, with what interest must it be noted that, within the memory of men still living the Ramapo Valley was the passage way for stages running from New York via Paterson to Goshen, Newburgh, Albany and the West.

In 1798, the fare by the Goshen stages for a seat from Ramapo to New York was 11s. 4d., and 2s. for a trunk. In 1810, the time schedule can perhaps best be given by a copy of the mail arrivals at Ramapo.

DATE.	NORTH.	SOUTH.	DATE.	NORTH.	SOUTH.
Jan. 1st,	....	....	Jan. 17th,	....	7:15, A. M.
" 2d,	9:05, P. M.	....	" 18th,	9:00 P. M.	....
" 3d,	....	2:45, A. M.	" 19th,	....	9:50, A. M.
" 4th,	....	....	" 20th,	....	....
" 5th,	Midnight.	2:45, A. M.	" 21st,	....	2:45, P. M.
" 6th,	....	....	" 22d,	8:00, A. M.	....
" 7th,	....	6:50, A. M.	" 23d,	9:40, P. M.	....
" 8th,	11:50, A. M.	....	" 24th,	....	Noon.
" 9th,	9:10, A. M.	....	" 25th,	11:30, P. M.	....
" 10th,	....	10:34, A. M.	" 26th,	....	4:40, A. M.
" 11th,	10:41, P. M.	....	" 27th,	....	....
" 12th,	....	....	" 28th,	....	7:40, A. M.
" 13th,	....	8:30, A. M.	" 29th,	4:10, A. M.	....
" 14th,	10:50, P. M.	3:40, A. M.	" 30th,	10:50, P. M.	....
" 15th,	....	....	" 31st,	....	8:20, A. M.
" 16th,	10:30, P. M.				

In 1812-13, Henry I. Traphagen and William Southerland were running the stage with four horses. They were succeeded in 1814-16 by Levi and William Alger. In 1817, Joseph French ran an extra stage from Newburgh to New York four times a week with four horses. In 1819-20, Garret Bampa ran "through the Franklin Turnpike gate," and Abram Clearwater carried the stage on "through the Orange Turnpike gate." In 1821, Sturgis began running the stage. In 1823, Stephen Sloat had charge of it. In 1824-25, Dr. T. G. Evans. In 1826, Stephen Sloat & Co.; 1827-29, H. H. Zabriskie & Co. (daily) - 1830, Stephen Sloat & Co. (daily.) It was in those days that the Sloat mansion, at Sloatsburg, served as a tavern on the post road.

How strange this sounds in these days of lightning expresses, drawing room cars and electric appliances, which have annihilated space and time. It seems wise that we should review the period for a better realization of what our country and County were, and for a better appreciation of what those silent giants—inventors—have accomplished for this western continent.

SUPERVISORS.

Gilbert Cooper, 1791-1798.	Nicholas L. Haring, 1826.	Peter P. Jersey, 1857.
James Onderdonk, 1798-1801, 1802-4.	John Haring, 1839.	John Crum, 1858-9.
William Dusenbery, 1801.	James Yourey, 1840.	Henry R. Sloat, 1860.
Gilbert T. Cooper, 1805-6.	John A. Haring, 1837, 1843-1844.	John D. Christie, 1862.
Peter S. Van Orden, 1807-1811-1819.	John J. Coe, 1841.	Erastus Johnson, 1863-4.
David De Baun, 1811-1814.	Cornelius Demarest, 1842.	Andrew Smith, 1865.
Garret Sarven, 1814.	John Demarest, 1845-47.	James Suffern, 1866-70.
Abraham Gurnee, 1815-1818	William Forshee, 1848.	Dwight B. Baker, 1872-3.
James Taylor, 1818-1820.	John B. Gurnee, 1849-51, 1861.	Peter L. Van Orden, 1874-5
John J. Gurnee, 1821.	Frederick Van Orden, 1852-54.	Jacob Snider, 1876.
Peter R. Van Houten, 1822-1830-31.	Nicholas C. Blauvelt, 1855-6.	George W. Suffern, 1870-71, 1877-1883.
		Peter Tallman, 1883-84.
		A. D. Blauvelt,

TOWN CLERKS.

Gilbert Cooper, 1791-2, 1804-8.	Garret Sarven, 1809-1814, 1815-1818, 1820.	Tunis Cooper, 1845-6.
John Conklin, Jr., 1793-4.	John Knap, 1814.	John G. Serven, 1854-1859.
Arch. Cassady, 1795-7, 1799-1802, 1837-1843, 1847-1853.	Theunis Cooper, 1821.	D. D. Ackerman, 1859-61, 1863-71.
Gilbert T. Cooper, 1798.	James Taylor, 1822-26.	Thomas Reed, 1862.
Andrew Onderdonk, 1802-3	Isaac Finch, 1830-31.	William H. Gray, 1872.
	Theunis J. Cooper, 1844.	Wm. H. Parsons, 1873-79.
	Peter Tallman, 1880.	Esler Sherwood, 1881.

From 1791 till 1802, town meetings were held at the house of Theunis Cuyper, just southeast of the "Brick Church;" from 1802 till 1863, at Cassady's Corners; and from 1863 till the present time, at Monsey.

Authorities referred to: History of Ramapo, by Rev. Eben B. Cobb, assisted by E. Frank Pierson. New York State Session Laws. New York State Civil List. Archives of the Rockland County Historical Society.

CHAPTER XX.

CLARKSTOWN.

ORIGIN OF NAME—DATE OF ERECTION INTO A TOWNSHIP—AREA—FIRST TOWN MEETING—CENSUS—HISTORY OF CLARKESVILLE, NEW CITY—ROCKLAND LAKE—NANUET—DUTCH FACTORY—MACKIE'S AND STAGG'S CORNERS—WALDBERG, SNEDEKER'S OR WALDBERG LANDING—STRAWTOWN—BARDON'S STATION—PEAT BEDS—SILVER SPOON FACTORY—THE BREWERY—BURIAL PLACES—TOWN OFFICERS.

In the chapter relating to the transfer of land in early days, it was seen that the lower part of the Kakiat patent was sold to a party of five men, in 1716, among whom was Daniel De Clarke. De Clarke's property was divided, and parts of it sold. In one of these sales, bearing date July 16, 1764, the property is described as being at Clarke's Town. This is the first mention I find of the name. This town was separated from the town of Haverstraw, on March 18th, 1791, and was one of the four townships in existence at the time the County was erected. The boundaries of the town will be found with those of the County. The number of acres included in the new town was 24,091.

The same causes which had led the people of Haverstraw to petition for a separate town government nearly three quarters of a century before, influenced the inhabitants of the present Clarkstown and Ramapo, in 1791. Steadily had the population increased and with that increase had grown up serious objections to the distance necessary to be traveled to attend town meetings. Then too, the area of the old town of Haverstraw, was far larger than its officers could carefully attend to. The roads were bad, the demands on their time onerous and the temptation to shirk their duties, great. It was with mutual pleasure therefore that the people of the old and new towns separated.

The first minutes of a town meeting, that can now be found, read as follows: "At a Town meeting held on Thursday, the 4th day of April, 1809, by the inhabitants of Clarks Town, at the New City. Present, John I. Blauvelt, Peter D. Smith, Resolvert Stephens, Justices; Peter Stephens, moderator; John J. Wood, town clerk; Abram Snyder, supervisor; John Van Houten, Richard Blanch, Dowe Tenure, assessors; Martines J. Hogenkamp, collector; Abraham Polhamus, James Vanderbilt, poormasters; Dowe D. Tallman, Abraham Cole, Hendrick Stevens, constables; Hosman Perry, Jacob Vanderbilt, Peter D. Demarest, commissioners of highways; Abraham Storms, Isaac B. Van Houten, Samuel DeBaun, fence viewers; Abraham Storms, Isaac B. Van Houten, Samuel DeBaun, pound masters.

Road masters: Jacob Wood, John Jersey, Aurt Ramsen, Peter P. Demarest, Jr., Isaac I. Blauvelt, Henry A. Snyder, John C. Van Houten, Abraham Garrison, Thomas Ackerson, Jr., Daniel Thew, Garret Smith, Henry Stephens, Jacob Myers, Abraham D. Blauvelt, Charles Benson, Dowe Tallman, John E. Smith, William House, Adrian Onderdonk, Simon Post, John Felter, Solomon Waring, Jesse Beagle, Aury Demarest, Peter Benson, Garret T. Snedeker, Theodorus Ramsen.

To be raised for the poor $400.

Every dog that is bit by a mad dog is to be Killed Immediately; $5 fine for every 24 hours that they live afterward, the money to go for the use of the poor.

The Town Clerk is for to get a New Book for to enter the proceedings of the Town.

To be raised for Roads and Bridges $70.

The Law Respecting fishing in the Ponds with Seins Passed Last year is to stand.

Entered by JOHN J. WOOD,
Town Clerk."

The second largest town in area of the County with more tillable land than any of the others, Clarkstown, is devoted almost entirely to agriculture. No large villages are within its bounds. Until recently, all its communication with the Metropolis was by water, except in the extreme southwestern corner, and at no place on all its river front can the water be reached without crossing intervening mountains. Yet, despite these obstacles, the growth of the town has been steady though slow.

In 1800, Clarkstown had 1806 inhabitants.				In 1845, Clarkstown had 2797 inhabitants.			
In 1810,	"	"	1996	"	In 1855,	"	"	3572	"
In 1820,	"	"	1808	"	In 1865,	"	"	4023	"
In 1825, State Census,			2075	"	In 1870, U. S. Census,		4137	"
In 1835,	"	"	2176	"	In 1880,	"	4382	"

As in the case of the other towns suspicion must rest on the report of 1820.

NEW CITY.

In 1774, the court-house at Tappan was destroyed by fire. During the seven and forty years that Tappan had been the county-seat, the section of the County north of the mountains had become well populated, while Haverstraw exceeded Orangetown in its number of residents. Fairness demanded that in the building of a new court-house a more central location should be selected, and the site at New City was chosen.

The old settlers had a strong faith that at the spot where the County buildings stood, a city must of necessity spring up, so, when in 1774, it was decided to locate the court-house in Clarkstown, they named the new site New City. This new city has followed the old one of Tappan in the vigor of its growth. The first hotel at New City was opened by Jabez Wood, and this was followed by one opened by Abraham Hogenkamp.

The post-office at this place was established May 12th, 1815, under the name of Clarkstown, with Peter D. W. Smith as postmaster. He has been followed by: Abram Hogenkamp, December 28th, 1822; Jabez Wood, July 23d, 1839; William H. Melick, June 30th, 1849; John H. Stephens, February 13th, 1851; A. J. Van Houten, August 7th, 1855; Alcibiades Cornelison, June 8th, 1861, and Peter De Bevoise, July 19th, 1872. The name of the office was changed to New City, July 5th, 1876.

In 1844, the Rockland County Agricultural Society was organized, and its annual exhibitions or fairs held at New City till 1875. Even this addition to its income failed to give the hamlet stronger life. In 1875, the Nanuet and New City Railroad, now owned by the New Jersey and New York Railroad, was opened, and gave the place better communication with other parts of the County and State.

The first school built at New City stood on the common, near the site of the present County Clerk's office. From there, it was moved to where the hotel known as "Kossuth's" stands, and in 1853 to its present location. A new school building was erected in 1880. At the beginning of the century, Wood had a tannery a few feet east of the "street," which was discontinued about 1825, and at a later period, members of the same family carried on a distillery on the brook west of the "street."

A little east of the main road, near the Trotting Park in New City, is an old grave-yard, long disused and overgrown with brambles and ivy. Among the dates still legible are two, "1733, M. C.," and "1734, L. C.," and still a third, "1733, C. S.," bears the same early record.

CLARKSVILLE, NYACK TURNPIKE OR MONT MOOR.

When Daniel De Clarke advanced into the wilderness, which formerly occupied the soil of the present Clarkstown, and wrested from that wilderness a home, he may have felt that the spirit of justice in men in the coming years, would lead them to unhesitatingly acknowledge his courage and perseverance as the pioneer in this section, by retaining his cognomen as the name of the hamlet he settled. If such were his feelings we, his followers, fully realize that he was far from right. The township does indeed bear his name with the elision of the final letter, but the hamlet known as Clarkestown as long ago as 1764, has been re-named by the fastidious generations since and called Clarkesville, Nyack Turnpike, and now Mont Moor. The relevance of this last name, is, perhaps, known to the person who gave it.

The location of the church at this spot in 1752, gave the hamlet a definite existence, and its importance was further added to by the erection of grist and saw mills on the brook, which flows in front of the old church. Not till after the opening of the turnpike was there further business growth in the present village, and the hamlet more nearly resembled the present Orangeville than any other place. With the turnpike came a change of business centre and of life.

The first business enterprise was begun by William O'Blenis, who opened a store on the southeast corner of the pike and Sickletown road. In 1835, Samuel DeBaun was running a distillery on the opposite corner, where the hotel now stands. Five years later, the distillery was torn down to make room for the present hotel, which was built for Thomas Warner. The presence of store and tavern led to the establishment of a blacksmith at the corners, and then came the wheelwright shop.

While these changes were being made on the turnpike, a new enterprise was begun near the old church. In 1835, James Newsen utilized the water power of the brook by erecting a horse-blanket and woolen factory on the site now occupied by Abram Demarest's saw mill. Its existence was brief, and by 1838, it had been abandoned. About 1840, a cooper shop was built alongside the old road to Nyack, which ran north of the swamp, by Hiram Purdy, and added to the industries of the place.

The post-office was established under the name of Nyack Turnpike June 25th, 1834, with William O'Blenis as first post-master. He was succeeded October 16th, 1852, by Samuel G. Ellsworth. Since that time the post-masters have been : John R. Ten Eyck, October 24th, 1857; Samuel G. Ellsworth, October 1st, 1858 ; William J. Wilcox, May 23d, 1859; James I. Lydecker, May 10th, 1861 ; John T. Smith, April 15th, 1872 ; Benjamin Smith, December 15th, 1875 ; and Cornelius R. Martine, September 10th, 1885. On April 19th, 1880, the name of the office was changed to Mont Moor.

The district school of Clarksville, built on the site of the original edifice, which was erected toward the close of the last century, stands alongside the road from Pye's corner north to the brewery. It looks a relic of the idea, that such a building was good enough for the parents and must needs be for the children. It may be of interest to notice the long period that a school has existed at this place for a full appreciation of what I am now to relate.

This neighborhood has the doubtful honor of having been the scene of the last trial for witchcraft held in New York State, possibly the last among a so-called civilized people.

The supposititious victim of demoniac power in this Clarksville case, was the widow of a Scotch physician, named Jane Kanniff, who moved into the hamlet prior to 1816, took a small house situated a few rods west of the old church on the New City road, and devoted herself to the care of her only child, a son by a previous marriage, named Lowrie.

Jane, or as she was called in the vernacular of the Clarksville people, *Naut* Kanniff, seems to have been exceedingly eccentric, a person who would now be regarded by alienists as insane; but her vagaries at the worst took a harmless form. She was odd in dress, preferring parti-colors of wondrous diversity, queer in the fashion of arranging her hair. She was unsocial in a neighborhood where every one knew each other; and morose or erratic when forced to meet people. With these traits and habits, she combined one other. From her deceased husband she had gathered a smattering of medicine, and now, when placed where she could get at the herbs known in her Materia Medica, she made wondrous decoctions with which she treated such as came to her for aid, and I have been informed by those who knew her, with most excellent results.

In a spot where all others were connected by ties of blood or marriage, the advent of this stranger could but create comment, and the actions of Mrs. Kanniff formed an interesting topic of conversation. Inadvertently, perhaps, her name became associated with Satanic influence and her deeds, theretofore regarded as harmless, began to assume an appearance of diablery. The distrust of *Naut* soon spread from their elders to the children of the neighborhood, and, when compelled to pass her house on errands, the young ones of Clarksville would scurry by with palpitating hearts and starting eyes, looking askance for some manifestation of the evil one.

It did not take a long time for Jane Kanniff to learn the belief, concerning herself, that was gaining ground and the effect of that knowledge was to aggravate her oddities.

There seems to have been no one act of monstrous import that provoked the trial, but rather a culmination of suspected misdoings. The house wives of the locality found great difficulty in making their churnings "come off" well, and two or three averred that upon emptying their churns they had discovered the form of a horseshoe plainly ourned in the bottom. A worthy member of the church after passing a sleepless night, distracted by the lowing of his cattle, found, on visiting his farm yard in the morning, the best milker of the herd standing in a farm wagon. From that hour she is said to have yielded no milk.

Circumstances such as these, were of grave character in a God fearing peaceful community. It seems not to have occurred to these intelligent citizens that perhaps heat applied to the milk to aid the churning, and the known proclivity of the domestic dog to chase cattle; might have been factors in these events. They sought a preternatural cause, and fixed on the baleful influence of Naut Kanniff. It was determined that she should be tried for witchcraft.

A shrewd suspicion probably, that not only would no legally appointed judge listen for a moment to such a charge, but also that those who made it would become a public laughing stock; led the worthy people to take the law in their own hands; and from similar considerations they forbore mentioning their determination to their dominie. But the desire for justice was uppermost in their minds, and only reputable citizens were permitted to act in the matter. The choice for judge resulted in the selection of the resident physician and the jury was composed of the farmers in the neighborhood.

It may occur to the reader as it has to the writer, that the occupation of the practice of medicine might unfit a man from acting impartially as a judge in this case, the more especially because the accused interfered with that occupation by her treatment of disease. Such an idea however seems not to have entered the minds of her neighbors.

The place selected for the trial was an old mill, which stood on the site of the present mill, just south of Pye's Corner. The mode of trial was by balance. The suspected woman was brought to the mill, was seated in one dish of the big mill scale, and held till a board-covered, brass-bound Dutch Bible was placed in the opposite dish. If, in the test which was to follow, the Bible outweighed the woman, it would be conclusive evidence that she was in league with the evil one. If to the contrary, she raised the Bible, it was equally conclusive she was innocent. It is with regret I have to record that Mrs. Kanniff outweighed the Bible, sending it to the ceiling with a mighty bound; a regret which will be indulged by others, who, with a curiosity equal to my own, would much cared to have seen what the gentle men present would have done had the Holy Book sent the woman to the beam.

SLAUGHTER'S LANDING OR ROCKLAND LAKE.

In 1711, John Slaughter bought a tract of land in the Clove, at the present Rockland Lake, and built a landing which bore his name till changed by Barmore, Felter & Co., in 1835. Up to that time, the lake and the country about it was called the "Pond," Quaspeck having been lost or abandoned.

Until the genesis of the ice business, this spot was but an outlet for the back country, and held the same position, as a landing, as Snedeker's, Sneden's, Huyler's. The introduction of one form of business called for the establishment of others. A hotel became a necessity, as soon as the ice company had settled its plant, and that at the landing, now controlled by James Ackerson, was built by Barmore & Leonard in 1839. The first landlord was Captain Isaac Cook. In 1844, Thomas Ackerson took charge of this hostelry, and retained it till his death in 1883.

A year after the building of the hotel at the landing, in 1840, A. P. Stephens, later Member of Congress, built and opened the first store at Rockland Lake. At a later period this store passed into the possession of L. F. Fitch, and finally, in 1860, was turned into a hotel. It is now occupied by Walter Ackerson.

I have already spoken of the fierce competition for the control of the ice at Rockland Lake, which followed the organization of Barmore, Leonard & Co., in the chapter devoted to the business interests of the County; and then stated that this company purchased the landing. Prevented by their ownership from using the old dock, Cheeseman and Andrus built the lower dock, now used by Miranda's stone crusher, in 1841. Upon their removal from the Lake, this dock ceased to be of use for many years.

Influenced by the prospect of future growth, E. E. and J. L. Conklin started a wheelwright and blacksmith shop at the Lake in 1842. This firm at once took charge of the manufacture and repair of all the ice wagons and tools of Barmore, Leonard & Co., a business they retained till 1856, when the construction and repair shops of the Knickerbocker Company were erected in New York City. From that time, most of the work of the Knickerbocker Company was done in the city, but the Conklin brothers continued their business till the death of J. L. Conklin in 1864, when the shops were closed.

In 1850, Francis Powley built the marine railway at Rockland Lake for Barmore, Leonard & Co., who used it for the construction and repair of the vessels engaged in their business. At first, this ship yard was under the management of John G. and Henry Perry, who conducted it for a few years, when George Dickey took charge of it. He carried it on till his death. Since that time, nothing has been done, and the yard has disappeared.

In 1872, John Mansfield established a stone-crusher at the lower landing, and carried on the industry for a short time, when the plant was bought by M. M. Miranda. Under his charge, the business has increased till at present it ranks among the important industries of our County. Four crushers are worked from April till December in each year; an average of from 75 to 90 vessel loads of crushed stone are shipped annually, and employment is given to from 25 to 65 men, according to the season, and the demand for the product.

In 1873, James W. Smith obtained the grove now known, as Sylvan Grove, and fitted it up as a resort for pleasure parties.

The post-office at Rockland Lake was established March 10th, 1842, with Thomas J. Wilcox as first postmaster. In 1845, he was succeeded by A. P. Stephens, who held the office till Feb. 8th, 1850, when he was followed by Leonard F. Fitch. Sept. 16th, 1853, E. E. Conklin became postmaster and he has been succeeded by Austin T. Fitch, May 23d, 1859 and Thomas H. Woodcock, Feb. 16th, 1864.

The Knickerbocker Fire Engine Company of Rockland Lake was organized May 25th, 1861, with William Hoffman, Foreman; J. L. Conklin, Assistant Foreman. Several severe fires have occurred at the Lake. In 1841, the icehouse at "Stony Point" was burned; in 1863, another icehouse was destroyed by fire, and in 1879, still a third was consumed. After the Knickerbocker Co. was organized a shed was built over the dock at the Hudson on the river face of which was the painting of a gigantic man clad in Knickerbocker costume. This shed caught fire in 1870 and was utterly destroyed.

The first school in this village was held in a building belonging to John Smith, which stood on the lake side of the road opposite the property now owned by Sorrel. Tradition has it that the building had been used by Smith as quarters for his slaves and that he manumitted his bond people and gave their foretime home for the purpose of a school and meeting house. On March 19th, 1812, Hercules Ryder gave to Daniel Brady, George Myers and Samuel De Baun as trustees of the Union school house, a lot of land at the location of the present school house on the road near Valley Cottage. Among the teachers in this school was Moses G. Leonard, who wielded the ferule in 1828. The present school building was erected in 1861.

The first public school in the village was opened in a building erected on a site given by Mr. Wells for that purpose, in 1835. This building, now used as a dwelling, stands opposite the present school house. The present house was built in 1850, on land given by John D. Ascough. George M. Dennett, Thomas I. Wilcox, and E. E. Conklin being elected trustees for that year.

On October 13th, 1853, it was decided to make a free school district of the one at the Lake according to a Legislative Act for the establishment of Union Free Schools passed in 1852. This school continued free until January 1st, 1857, when, in accordance with a decision reached on Jan. 17th, 1856, the free school system was abolished in the district.

NANUET.

Until the opening of the Erie Railroad in 1841, this village had no existence, and not over a half dozen houses stood between the Turnpike and schoolhouse. The first name of the place was Clarkstown, a name it retained till 1856, when, at the suggestion of James De Clark, the present name, taken from that of an Indian chief, was given. This is one of the few, rare, instances in our County where, in christening a place, the old Indian names have been used.

The first store in the village, now owned by S. M. Drew, and used as a dwelling house, was built by David De Clark, in 1841. This was also the first railroad station. In 1849, D. P. Demarest built the house, a part of which was and still is, used as the station. In 1852, Dr. M. C. Hasbrouck built the brick store now occupied by William Hutton, Jr., and it was at once occupied by John W. and Henry O. Hutton, who, in combination with their other business, started the first lumber yard in the village. The Hutton Brothers also introduced a department devoted to agricultural implements, and kept on hand both mowing and raking machines. In 1869, the building now used by the firm was erected and opened in 1870.

The first hotel in the village was opened by Peter Demarest, Jr., and was conducted, after his death in 1839, by his son, D. P. Demarest. This hostelry, known as the "Old Red Tavern," stood just south of the present Nanuet schoolhouse, and before the Turnpike was opened, was on the main road from Suffern to Tappan Slote. In the early days of this tavern a grocery store was connected with it, which seems to have passed from existence when the railroad was opened.

In 1867, Abram D. Brower started a foundry in the buildings now used as a dwelling house, and standing south of Samuel Blauvelt's wheelwright shop. Brower continued the business but a short time, and then the place was closed. As early as 1794, Major Cornelius I. Blauvelt owned and conducted a saw-mill on Narranshaw, Naurashazink, or Naurashank Brook, a short distance southwest of the present village. About 1810, this property was sold to Abram C. Blauvelt, and since then has been owned by Aurt Van der Wall, Isaac Pye, David Benson, and the present owner, Gustav Boliz. As at present conducted, a considerable business is carried on in ship timber and kindling wood, and recently a turning lathe was added to the industry.

The Nanuet school " can without difficulty be traced back to 1812. At that time, Abram C. Blauvelt * * * was teacher, and was exempt from military duty on that account. The schoolhouse was an old red building, 14½ by 13½ feet on the outside, and it stood south of the Yeury barn, about where the road crosses the swamp, westward, This building is still standing on Henry E. Insley's place." In 1844, that part of the school at present occupied by the primary department, was erected on the lot where it now stands, and in 1869, the part used as the grammar school was built. The first mention of a school library was in 1839.

The Nanuet Fire Engine Company was organized in 1860, with William H. Snyder, Foreman, and J. W. Demarest, Assistant Foreman. In 1862, the company received a charter from the State Legislature. Until the erection of their engine house in 1868, the firemen used to meet in "Mechanics Hall." No severe fires have visited the hamlet.

The Nanuet Debating Society was formed by several of the residents of Nanuet, prominent among whom were C. A. Blauvelt, C. A. DeBaun, Andrew Hopper, A. J. Demarest, David Bogert and Nicholas C. Blauvelt, about 1845, for the purpose of combining with social intercourse a discussion of the important questions of the day. The old school house was purchased by the society and used as their place of meeting. Upon the disorganization of this society the Nanuet Temperance Society occupied the old school building for several years. "Mechanics Hall" was opened to the public by Samuel B. Blauvelt and C. L. Ackerson, in the spring of 1863.

The post-office was first established at Nanuet, March 6th, 1846, and David DeClark, was the first post master, the office being kept in his brick store. On February 13th, 1851, David P. Demarest, became post master, and he has been followed by William H. Snider, October 21st, 1862; Edward Hutton, August 3d, 1870; and William Hutton, August 1885.

The Nanuet Cemetery first came into general use at the time the church adjoining was built. The stone of Daniel DeClark however bears the date of a year earlier, September 22d, 1825.

DUTCH FACTORY.

In 1812, a cotton factory was built at this place, and was given the above name from the fact, that a majority of the stockholders were descendants of the original Dutch settlers of this section. This factory, which was used exclusively for the manufacture of cotton yarn, was burned in 1824. The property was then sold to John Gerow, who built and carried on a saw-mill on the spot. In a short time Gerow sold the mill to J. & L. Van Riper, who took down the saw-mill and erected another cotton factory in 1830. Under the Van Riper's management cotton yarn, coarse cotton blankets and candle wicking were manufactured, and the waste was used in making cotton bats. This factory, like the first, was burned in 1858. The Van Riper's then rebuilt on a larger scale, and began the manufacture of mosquito netting and hat buckram. In 1865, a stock company called the Spring Valley Manufacturing Company, was formed and the business was carried on more extensively than ever until the financial depression of 1873, fell disastrously upon the company, and the factory was closed.

From 1873 till 1882, the factory remained idle. Under a judgment against the company the property had been sold, and had been bought in by a Mrs. Ward, of New York City, who could neither use nor dispose of it. In the latter year the factory was bought by Wm. Hyenga, who began, and has since carried on in it, the manufacture of briarwood pipes.

A short distance above the Dutch factory. Cornelius Blauvelt owned and conducted a saw and grist mill in 1812. This property was later purchased by James Eckerson, who carried on the old business for a number of years. In 1853, the firm of A. & I. R. Blauvelt was formed, and this firm bought the mill and used it for the manufacture of stockings and yarn. This business was continued by the firm till 1858, when the term of partnership having expired, Abram sold out to I. R. Blauvelt, who carried on the business till 1865.

Just below the Dutch factory stands a charcoal mill, which is carried on by James Smith. This was originally built for a grist mill by Jacob Serven. Later it came into the possession of Lucas Eckerson, who sold it to Harman Westervelt; then it was purchased by John Stilwell, who in time sold it to John V. Smith. Under this last owner it was continued as a grist mill till 1857, when the business was changed to grinding charcoal. This industry was continued by John V. Smith till his death, and since then has been continued by the present proprietor, James Smith.

On the northwest corner of the junction of the turnpike with the road which passes the Dutch factory, J. Mackie formerly owned property, and to locate the neighborhood this place was called "Mackie's Corners. In the northeastern part of the township, at the junction of the Short Clove road with one which passes the residence of Cornelius De Pew, John Stagg erected a brick blacksmith shop in 1852, and this place took the name of "Stagg's Corner's." In recent years, a settlement of no inconsiderable size has sprung up here, and a church edifice of the M. E. Society has been built.

CEDAR GROVE CORNERS OR WALDBERG.

At the junction of the road running from Pye's saw-mill to Rockland Lake, with the road between Haverstraw and Nyack, a church was built in 1830, which bore the name among the people of the "Pond" or "Yellow Church." At a later period this junction was called Cedar Grove Corners, from a grove of cedar trees which stood on the opposite side of the road from the church. In 1835, the Central Hotel was built by Abram B. Snedeker just north of the corner. A few years later, by 1845, A. B. Conger began to purchase land in this section, and in the course of time, built a residence not far from the Long Clove, which he named Waldberg. This name gradually spread to the neighborhood, and prior to 1860 had been adopted by the residents of the school district as the name of the locality.

SNEDEKER'S LANDING OR WALDBERG LANDING.

The lack of sufficient depth of water at Haverstraw village led to the establishment at this place of a ship-yard and marine railway for the repair of vessels engaged in the brick business. In 1845, the railway was laid down, for Tunis M. and George W. Snedeker, by Joseph Walker, since largely known as the proprietor of Vinegar Bitters. For several years a prosperous business was carried on, and for one or two years the local steamboats made this a landing place. The building of marine railways at Tomkin's Cove and Rockland Lake in 1850, and at Peck's dock in 1851, drew business from this yard, and it was at length abandoned. The dock is rapidly being washed away, and an old house alone marks the site of a once important landing. In the general change of name for this section, the locality became known as Waldberg Landing, and it is so recorded on the charts of the U. S. Coast Survey.

While on the river front, I may perhaps speak of a project which was agitated between 1845-50. This was, the building of a carriage road from the end of Broadway at Upper Nyack, under the mountains along the river to Snedeker's Landing. The citizens of Haverstraw and Nyack joined in the movement, and a sufficient sum of money to build the road was subscribed. The enterprise was stopped by the extravagant price asked for his property by Isaac I. Blauvelt, who owned the river front at Calico Hook, south of Rockland Lake landing.

STRAWTOWN.

On the road, running south from Pye's saw mill toward Clarksville and next west of the Hackensack River, is a neighborhood, which has been known by the above name since a period beyond the memory of living men. Many reasons have been given for the appellation, among which the following seems as suitable as any. The increasing settlement of this section gradually led to an increase in the number of saw mills and a reduction in the price of shingles. Advantage was taken of this by the farmers of the County, and shingle roofs replaced the straw-thatched barns of an older time. In this neighborhood alone did the residents adhere to the old custom, and from their evident admiration for thatch, the remaining people called them "Strawtowners." In 1854, a store and shoe factory were kept in this locality by Nathaniel Burr.

BARDON'S STATION.

In 1861, a German, by name John Bardon, settled at this place and opened a distillery, gradually the neighborhood became settled by German immigrants and, when the railroad from Nanuet to New City was built, in 1875, this hamlet was made a station, taking for its name that of Bardon. The first and only store in the hamlet was then built by Bardon and has since been carried on by him and his family.

From the few villages of which I have spoken, it can be realized how thoroughly devoted to agriculture this township is. Shut in by the ridge of trap rock, which forms the Palisades and which has its origin but a short distance from the northwest boundary, on the north and east; and sheltered on the west by the high hills of eastern Ramapo; abundantly irrigated by the head waters of the Hackensack and the many streams which flow into that river, this section is well fitted for farming. The quarry business which at one time formed a profitable source of income, has long been abandoned for all practical purposes. The getting out of peat, which was found in large quantities in the township—one bog of 40 acres, 6 feet deep and estimated to contain 40,000 cords, south of the Long Clove, another near Walberg of 40,000 cords, and still another west of Nyack in the Valley of the Hackensack—while at one time in 1838, started as a business venture did not prove lucrative and was abandoned.

Among the industries of Rockland County in past days, mention must be made of the Silver Spoon Factory carried on by Joseph Blauvelt. This business was at first started in a small house south of New City in 1820 As the demand upon Blauvelt increased, more and more room had to be used, and finally he moved east of New City on the road to the brewery.

The material employed in the factory was sent to the County from New York stores, for which the manufactured articles were made. Beside supplying these metropolitan stores, however, Blauvelt did considerable local business and furnished many of the residents with silver ware. Horse power was employed in the business and some dozen people earned a living at the work. The industry was continued for many years and was not absolutely abandoned till 1865.

The building known as the "Rockland Brewery," which stands on the east side of the road from Clarksville to New City, about two miles north of Isaac Pye's corner, was built in 1855, by Huber & Aschenheimer. Previous to the erection of this building, a brewery had been carried on in a frame building, a short distance northeast of the Rockland Brewery. The business had not proved successful and had been discontinued, and the building was later used for the making of wine and vinegar.

When Huber & Aschenheimer first started the Rockland Brewery, the motive power was by horse and hand. After two years, the brewery was sold to Kiser & Maas, who failed, and the property fell into the hands of their creditors. In 1865, J. G. C. Schmersahl purchased it, remodeled the buildings, excavated a pond, put up ice houses, and introduced steam power. Under his management the business was carried on successfully for some time, and then came into the hands of the present proprietors, Schmersahl & Cross, the son and son-in-law of J. G. C. Schmersahl. Brewing was practically discontinued shortly after, and the place is now used as a hotel and pleasure ground.

The building of the New York, West Shore and Buffalo Railroad through the town in 1883, gave rise to three stations; Nyack Turnpike, Valley Cottage, two and three-quarter miles southeast of the Rockland Lake post-office, and Conger's, situated a short distance northeast of the Waldberg Church.

On March 20th, 1873, a post-office was established at Valley Cottage, with James A. Green, as post-master. It seems not to have been a success, and six years later, March 17th, 1879, it was discontinued.

I have already spoken of the burial grounds at New City, Nanuet and Clarksville, and in the history of Nyack have given the history of Oak

Hill, which extends into Clarkstown, and the old ground at Upper Nyack. More than in any other township, were interments in Clarks made in private ground. The isolation of the settlers from other settlements, the distance that existed between the early settlements and the few early churches, were greater than elsewhere Hence the number of family burial plots is very large. One of the oldest places of sepulture in the town is probably that which stands south of the road leading from New City to Hempstead. It is said that the date of either 1703 or 1708 has been found on one of the tombstones. On the Long Clove road, near Pye's saw mill, stands a local grave yard, and another about a mile further north, stands just east of the Hackensack. On the road from Waldberg church to Pye's saw mill, some six hundred yards west of the church, is a burial ground, and others are on the property of Onderdonk on both sides of the road from Rockland Lake to Valley Cottage; on the east side of the mountain road, formerly called the Lyon's Hill road, near its junction with the mountain road that leads from Upper Nyack to Valley Cottage; on the south side of the King's highway, between John Storms' old hotel and Valley Cottage; and a negro burial ground stands west of the Hackensack swamp, and north of the Turnpike.

SUPERVISORS.

David Pye, 1791-92.
Isaac Blanch, 1793-96, 1801-2.
Claus R. Van Houten, 1797-98-99, 1803-4.
Resolvert Stephens, 1805-7.
Abram Snyder, 1808-11-19.
Richard I. Blanch, 1812,15-20-24.
James Stephens, 1816-18.
Abram P. Stephens, 1825-32-37.

Abram Hogenkamp, 1826.
Albert Lydecker, 1831.
Jacob P. Demarest, 1833.
John O'Blenis, 1834.
A. J. Demarest, 1835.
Joseph P. Brower, 1842-48
John E. Hogenkamp, 1845-62-66.
Matthew D. Bogert, 1846.
Jacob J. Eckerson, 1851-52.
E. E. Conklin, 1853.
John T. Blanch, 1854.

Aaron T. Polhemus, 1856-57.
Isaac Tallman, 1858-59.
James L. Conklin, 1860-61.
Peter T. Stephens, 1867-68.
Tunis Blauvelt, 1869, 71-73.
Isaac Van Nostrand, 1872-77.
Nelson Stephens, 1874.
Barne Van Houten, 1879-80.
J. G. Demarest, 1881-82.
F. P. Demarest, 1883-84-85.

TOWN CLERKS.

John J. Wood, 1809-12.
Abram Cole, 1813.
Ebenezer Wood, 1814-20.
Abram Hogenkamp, 1815-19-26.
Jabez Wood, 1822-27-32.
Henry R. Stephens, 1823-25.
John E. Hogenkamp, 1833-35-42.

Peter T. Stephens, 1834.
Abram B. Hogenkamp, 1843-44.
John T. Cole, 1845.
Harman Blauvelt, 1846.
Isaac Blanch, 1847-50.
Abram A. Stagg, 1851-55-58, 59.
Abram J. DeBaun, 1856-57.

Martin Knapp, 1860.
Thomas L. De Noyelles, 1861-70-75.
Alfred Phillips, 1871-73.
Paul D. Spotte, 1874.
Joseph De Noyelles, 1876-84.

Authorities referred to: History of Clarkstown, by H. P. Fay. N. Y. S. Geological Report, by W. W. Mather. Archives of the Rockland County Historical Society.

CHAPTER XXI.

STONY POINT.

DATE OF ERECTION—ORIGIN OF NAME—AREA—FIRST TOWN MEETING—CENSUS—HISTORY OF GRASSY POINT—STONY POINT—TOMPKIN'S COVE—CALDWELL'S LANDING - DOODLETOWN—IONA ISLAND—STONY POINT PROMONTORY—BEAR HILL.—PINGYP HILL.—THE HOUSE OF THE GOOD SHEPHERD—LARGE TREES.

The people of Haverstraw township had seen two sections taken from their vast area and still their territory contained 27,084 acres. The development of the brick industry and the growth of the limestone business rapidly increased the population of the north end of this territory, and the inhabitants of the present town of Stony Point, felt that they should have a separate representative in the Board of Supervisors. With this cause was combined another. Haverstraw has long had the reputation of taking all political offices for her own people, and the inhabitants in the north end of the township found, that when they desired some of the public places, their wishes were unheeded as long as possible, and when refusal would no longer be tolerated, only the smallest crumbs that fell from the political table were allotted to them. These things bred ill-feeling, dissatisfaction grew by a constant interchange of grievances between the people who felt themselves injured, and at length the creation of a new township was advocated and secured.

On March 20th, 1865, the town of Stony Point was erected by Act of Legislature, with the following boundaries: "Beginning at a point on the Hudson River, the southeast corner of the land of Abraham B. Conger, about twenty-one chains southerly from the end of the steamboat wharf at Grassy Point, and running thence south about eighty-five and one-half degrees west eighteen chains to the 'Minisceongo Creek, and southwest corner of said A. B. Conger's land;' thence along said Minisceongo Creek, southerly, westerly and southerly, to the northeast corner of the land known as the 'Silas D. Gardner farm;' thence along said farm south eighty-eight and one-half degrees, west fifty-four chains to the public road leading from North Haverstraw to Benson's corner; thence along said public road, and west line of the said Silas D. Gardner's farm five chains and eighty-five links to southeast corner of the land of William C.

and James A. Houseman; thence along the line of said Houseman's land to the south line of William Call's land, the south line of Washington Waldron's land, the south line of Benjamin F. Valentine's land, and through other lands, north sixty-six and three-quarters degrees west, one hundred and thirty-five chains fifty links to an apple tree on the south side of the public road in front of Hiram Phillip's house; thence along said road, on the south side to the junction of the Monroe and Haverstraw Turnpike; thence along the south side of said turnpike westerly to the division line between 'Great Mountains lots,' three and four; thence following said division line north forty-five degrees, west to the division line between the Counties of Orange and Rockland; thence along said Orange County line northeasterly to the Hudson River; thence along the west shore of said Hudson River, southerly to the place of beginning." The new township, which was named from that bold, rocky promontory which Anthony Wayne made historical, contained 17,792 acres of land much of it rocky and unfertile in the extreme.

The first town meeting was held on April 11th, 1865, at the store of Robert Kerr; Frederick Tomkins, Abraham S. Vanderbilt, and George Knapp presiding, and Wesley J. Weiant was elected Supervisor, Benson Briggs, Town Clerk, and Alexander Waldron, Wesley J. Weiant, Alfred M. Wiles and Josiah M. Dalson, Justices. By the Legislative act which created the town, Henry M. Peck, Edwin Marks, Henry G. Knapp, William Benson, Abram Weyant, and Alexander Waldron were appointed Commissioners, to apportion the town debt on each town according to the valuation of the real estate on the last assessment-roll of the town of Haverstraw.

Owing to the nature of her land, Stony Point presents little inducement for agricultural immigrants, and her population, slowly increasing, is almost entirely located along the river banks. The census gives:

1865,	-	-	- 2,186.	1875,	-	-	- 3,272.
1870,	-	-	- 3,205.	1880,	-	-	- 3,308.

GRASSY POINT.

To the present observer, the dun-colored sand hills, crowned with a few tumble-down shanties, the ugly clay-pits, the long rows of roofs covering brick-kilns, and the clouds of smoke and dust that hang over this village in summer, must cause its name to appear satirical. But there have been other days for Grassy Point, when the beauty of its verdure, which grew down to the very river edge, and its charming location made it a delightful place for residence. It was in those days of pristine lovliness that the name it now bears was given it.

In tracing the early transfers of land in Haverstraw, we found that by purchase the property now embraced in the village came into the hands of John Allison. Allison died in 1754 and left the tract to his son Joseph, describing it in his will as " being a tract purchased of Albert Minnie and others, bounded North and East by Hudson River, South by the mountains, and running Westerly by Minisceongo Creek and the mountains."

Previous to his death, Joseph Allison gave to his sons Johh, William and Joseph, a deed for all the land between Minisceongo Creek and Hudson's River and the " Narrow Passage," described as "all that tract of land in Haverstraw called the further neck, bounded North and East by Hudson's River, West, by the marsh, or salt meadow, and South, by a fence, as it runs across the narrow passage, and stands nearly opposite the point of land and meadow of Mr. Thomas Hay's farm, on the west side of the creek, containing 103½ acres, more or less." This land they were to sell. If it brought £600, they were to retain that sum as their portion of their inheritance; if more, all over and above £600 was to be paid to him.

On April 9th, 1798, this land was sold to Jacob Sabriska, who, in a brief time, sold it to William Denning, Jr., and he, on July 4th, 1798, sold it to his father, William Denning. This William Denning, Sr., was a lawyer, who had accumulated sufficient wealth to permit of his passing his summer months in the country. Not far from the end of Grassy Point, he erected a handsome house, and remained a summer resident of our County till the time of his death.

At the time Denning built his house, the whole tract of land above described was heavily wooded with magnificent oak and chestnut trees. At the mouth of Minisceongo Creek, which, by reason of a long strip of meadow just southwest of the causeway that leads to Penny Bridge was narrower than to-day, was a high hill or bluff covered with trees and grass. At a later period, a small wharf was built which projected into the creek just opposite Crum Island. After several years, Denning sold ten acres at the south end of his purchase to William Smith, a nephew of Joshua Hett Smith, who built a large two-story house on his purchase, beautified the grounds, and gave to his place the name of Rosa Villa.

I have gone thus fully into detail to show that however much of a misnomer Grassy Point may seem now, there was a time when the name was appropriate. After the death of Denning, who was a brother-in-law of Joshua Hett Smith, his property passed through the hands of Philip Verplanck, Isaac L. Pratt, Dr. Lawrence Proudfoot, who bought it with the intention of cutting it up into lots. It was Proudfoot who built the double house still standing near the steamboat wharf. At this time, the tract was divided into three parts, of which the northernmost came into the possession of David Munn in 1834, the middle one, after some transfers, was purchased by A. B. Conger, and the third was bought by Thomas Murphy and E. Warner as a speculation. The latter also purchased the Crom farm, on the opposite side of the creek. In 1837, Murphy and Warner failed, and their property later became the cause of the case of Worall *vs.* Munn.

The first steamboat landing at Grassy Point was built by Dr Lawrence Proudfoot about 1830, and for many years, owing to the depth of water, it was the stopping place for steamers passing up and down the river. Till the Rockland extended her trips to Haverstraw, this landing was the shipping point for steam communication with the city for that section of our County north of the mountain. The first hotel at Grassy Point was kept by Dr. Proudfoot in his double house. On the north side of that house was a small addition in which Proudfoot kept a small store and bar, and in which the first post-office was opened. In 1845, O. C. Gerow opened a general country store in a building a few feet west of Proudfoot's house. In 1848, James Creney opened a hotel at the Point, on the property now occupied by Thomas Dinan, and kept it till 1850, when he purchased property at Haverstraw and moved to that place. The first lumber yard at the Point was started by W. F. B. & A. Gurnee and George H. Smith.

In speaking of the industries of the County, mention was made of the large iron works erected along Florus Falls Creek and of the brick yards stretching along the river shore. Another industry now demands note. In the spring of 1845, John I. Wiles moved from Orange county to Grassy Point with his family, and opened a shop for the purpose of doing business in the shape of blacksmith or wheelwright work. On the death of John I. Wiles, in 1851, the business, which even then had become profitable, was carried on till 1855 under the name of F. J. & A. M. Wiles, and from that time till 1861 under the name of F. J. Wiles & Co. Since 1861 the business has been managed by A. M. & W. H. Wiles. As business increased new works were added. In 1871, a foundry was built and started, and at the present time this branch of industry, which began in such a humble way, gives employment to many score men and is used in manufacturing machinery for flour and saw mills and brick-making.

The number of vessels engaged in the transportation of brick from the County made marine railways and ship yards near Haverstraw a vital necessity. Snedeker's Landing had become a thing of the past and at

Tomkin's Cove and Peck's old dock were the only ship yards north of the mountain. Regarding the opportunity as a good one, George L. Wicks started a yard at Grassy Point where the depth of water was favorable to the enterprise, and put down a marine railway in the autumn of 1883.

The first post-office at Grassy Point was opened on July 30th, 1834, with James De La Montanya as postmaster, On Aug. 21st, 1834, the name of the office was changed to North Haverstraw, and it retained this name till Sept. 10th, 1836, when it was changed back to Grassy Point. In 1838, Thomas Murphy became postmaster and held the position till 1844, when he was succeeded by Edward Strang and he in turn was followed by Oliver C. Gerow in 1845. On Sept. 5th, 1845, the office was discontinued. On April 14th, 1871, the post-office at Grassy Point was re-established with Alfred M. Wiles as postmaster.

NORTH HAVERSTRAW—FLORUS FALLS OR STONY POINT.

Eighteen years before the separation of the present township of Stony Point from that of Haverstraw, the population in the northern part of the territory had increased to such an extent as to warrant the establishment of a post-office in that section. Through the efforts of Dr. William Govan, an office was established in his house and named North Haverstraw.

The starting of this office made a change in the location of the business centre in this section. Theretofore the thickest population had been up the road toward Bulson's, and the few stores opened in the neighborhood were nearer the old tavern than Dr. Govan's corner. The only church edifice, that of the Methodist Society, which had been built in 1834, stood on the site of the present structure, and the prospect looked altogether in favor of the village, which could already be foreseen, starting in that location. The establishment of the post-office stopped this growth and created the present village.

This section bore the name of North Haverstraw till the separation of the territory, and the erection of Stony Point township, when it was changed to Flora Falls, the appellation of a pretty little cascade, which falls into the creek of the same name by the district school house in the present village of Stony Point. So evidently is this name a corruption of Florus, that I have so entitled it. The original owner of this property was Florus Crom. He, as well as others in the early days of settlement, was spoken of by his Christian name and this cascade, being a good guide to a locality and on Crom's property, was spoken of as Florus' Falls The name of Flora Falls was attached to the village till 1870, when it took that of Stony Point.

The post-office was established at this village on April 1st, 1847, with William Govan, M.D., postmaster. On May 11th, 1850, Wm. Knight was appointed postmaster and held the office till June 25th, 1853, when Dr. Govan was re-appointed. On Nov. 17th, 1856, Wm. Brewster became postmaster but held the office less than a month when he was superseded December 13th, 1856, by Dr. Govan. On November 16th, 1860, William Penny was appointed to the office, and he has been followed by: William Knight, from May 31st, 1861 to April 7th, 1870—during his term of office, on March 27th, 1865, the name of the office was changed from North Haverstraw to Flora Falls; Ezekiel O. Rose, from April 7th, 1870, till January 21st, 1885—during his term, on July 27th, 1870, the name was changed from Flora Falls to Stony Point; Mary A. Penny, from January 21st, 1885 till August 11th, 1885, and the present postmaster, Richard B. Stalter, August 11th, 1885.

The first drug store in this village was opened by E. O. Rose in 1865, and this was followed in 1883 by one opened by William Govan, M. D. The first public hall—Allison's Hall—was built in 1873 by B. J. Allison. Following the change produced by the establishment of the post-office, Theodore Smith built a store on the site now occupied by the store of E. O. Rose, which was occupied by William Knight, and in 1862 Richard Marks built a store on the site of that now occupied by Joseph Penny. This was destroyed by fire in March, 1865, being then occupied by Robert Kerr.

In 1844, William Knight bought the machinery which had been in use in the chemical works of Waldron & Benson, and started a chemical work for the manufacture of Pyroligneous Acid, not far from Cedar Pond. This industry, which furnished acid for the Garnerville Print Works, gave employment to three or four men, and was continued till 1868.

TOMKINS' COVE.

On another page will be found the early title to this land. As early as 1789, a small kiln had been started at the limestone cliffs by John Crom but, as in the case with brick making and stone quarrying, little was done before this century. From the time of Crom till 1838, nothing seems to have been accomplished with the quarries, and at the time of Daniel Tomkins' advent, the present scene of industry was a wilderness of bushes and rocks. In fact, Tomkins discovered the limestone only by searching carefully from Hoboken to the present Tomkins' Cove. During and after his search, he made several trips on foot between Haverstraw and Newark.

In the spring of 1838, having purchased twenty acres of land the year before for $100 an acre, Daniel Tomkins embarked at Newark, N. J., on board a sloop named *Contrivance*, with sixteen men, one woman, one horse, one cow, and a small quantity of lumber, and set sail for his new home. Upon arriving at the now thriving hamlet of Tomkins' Cove, the men and women were landed by small boat, while the animals were lowered into the water and allowed to find their own way to shore. A shanty for shelter was at once erected, and on the following day the work of quarrying out the limestone was begun.

This branch of business proved a success from the outset, and has steadily continued to increase in importance. Beside the manufacture of lime, the company owning the cliff has added to its business by crushing lime stone for macadamizing purposes.

When first begun, the business at Tomkins' Cove was carried on under the name of Tomkins, Hadden & Co. At a later period, the firm was changed to Calvin Tomkins & Co., and the members were Calvin and Daniel Tomkins and Walter Searing. In 1859, the Tomkins' Cove Lime Company was formed, and since that time the business has been conducted in its name.

The establishment of one industry soon led to a demand for another, and about 1842, a store was opened near the landing by Calvin Tomkins & Co. In 1850, the ship yard was started, and a marine railway laid down for the accommodation of vessel owners. It may not be uninteresting to know in this connection that the original vessel which brought the immigrants to the Cove, the *Contrivance*, is still in a good state of preservation, and makes regular trips to and from New York city.

Until 1874, the old district school house, a small wooden building which was open for only a brief period during each year, was the sole educational institution in this section. Then the present Union School edifice was erected, and presented to the public by Calvin Tomkins.

The post-office at this place was established March 15th, 1860, with Warren Searing as the first post-master. He held the office till January 25th, 1872, when he was succeeded by Walter T. Searing, who fills the position at the present time.

GIBRALTAR—CALDWELL'S LANDING.

At the point of the frowning Thunder Mountain, called by its Dutch name, Donderberg, Joshua Colwil, a descendant of John Cholwell, one of the original patentees of the Cheesecocks patent, had made a home before the beginning of this century, and on March 19th, 1800, was granted by

Legislative act, the right, in conjunction with Joseph Travis, of Peekskill, to run a ferry across the river from his landing to that of Travis. By what means Colwil's name became transferred to Caldwell is as unknown as the change from Chowell to Colwil, but it did become so altered, and the old name of Gibraltar gradually gave way to that of the first ferryman. A short time ago, one Charles H. Jones, a resident of Long Island, who owned some property at Caldwell's, exerted influence enough to get the railroad company and post-office authorities to give his name to the Point. Who this Jones is; what deeds he has performed that should entitle him, a stranger to our soil, to grace old Donderberg with his name, I have yet to learn. It is to be hoped that sooner or later the residents of Stony Point township will demand a change of the name back to Caldwell's.

At Caldwell's was carried on one of those visionary schemes that will be possible so long as people shall seek wealth without labor. On a preceding page I have said, that when the heavy ordnance was being moved from Stony to West Point, on its abandonment by the Americans, the flat boats engaged in the transportation were fired on by the Vulture and one of them sunk. In later days, a rumor was started to the effect that the famous pirate, Captain William Kidd, had lost his vessel at this point, and that untold treasure lay at the bottom of the river awaiting recovery. One story has it that a prospector for gold started the tale by his implicit confidence in his divining rod, which is reputed to have indicated the presence of gold at this spot; and, that on a superficial drag of the bottom a cannon was brought up. Another story is to the effect that a cannon fouled the anchor fluke of a sloop, and was hove up by the sailors.

Without pausing to learn how the cannon was discovered, enough to know that such an event did occur and was at once taken advantage of to obtain money. A stock company, named the *Kidd Salvage Company*, was formed June 20th, 1844, and a large amount of stock was put on the market in January 1845. A prospectus in pamphlet form, called "*Wonderful Mesmeric Revelations, giving an account of the discovery and a description of a sunken vessel near Caldwell's Landing, supposed to be that of the pirate, Kidd, including an account of his character and death at a distance of nearly 3,000 miles from the place,*" was published. Then a coffer dam was built at the extreme end of the Point, and a steam engine set at work pumping it clear. Some cannon were found, one of which was set in the curb at the corner of Wall and Broad streets, New York City, and one passed into the possession of William Blakely, of Verplanck's Point.

Work was continued at this folly till 1848, from one to three dozen men being constantly employed; stock was floated in England as well as in this country; a fortune was expended in keeping the dam intact against the tremendous pressure of water, and then—the engine stopped; the laborers disappeared, the stock company passed from existence, the Sheriff wound up the business, and the English cannon, captured by Anthony Wayne, and thought to have been destroyed by a shot from the Vulture, were returned to land to oxidize and become dust.

Abram V. Thompson and his son-in-law, Henry Sheldon, were active in the management of this transaction. Mr. Crane was the engineer in charge of the work. The property was bought by William Blakely, of Verplanck's Point.

The post office at Caldwell's was opened in October, 1885, with James A. De Groot as post master. Another event in the history of Caldwell's calls for mention. In the war of 1812, it was soon demonstrated that the hope of the United States lay in her fleet, and the Navy received every encouragement. A new yard was planned, less exposed to attack than that at Brooklyn, and Caldwell's Landing was talked of because of its safety, and the great depth of water at it. But, according to the tradition still preserved in this section, the legislators who decided on this spot, reckoned without their host. Colwil, or Caldwell was a Federalist of the most pronounced type. In his estimation, as in that of many of his confreres, the war with England was not only needless, but actually iniquitous, and he would lend no hand in the struggle. With this feeling, he placed so disproportionate a valuation on his property that the Government at once abandoned the project.

DOODLETOWN.

On the north side of Donderberg, and extending from that mountain north to Peploaps or Fort Montgomery Creek, and from the inlet west of Iona Island to the Orange county line, is a vast tract of inhospitable mountain and rock which bears the name of Doodletown. How this name was obtained is a matter for conjecture. At the time of the battle of Forts Clinton and Montgomery, the assaulting forces divided in this section and that division under Sir Henry Clinton, which formed the right wing, had a severe conflict with the American Militia at Highland Lake. That militia was composed of farmer lads, few of them over five and twenty years of age, and one of these boys may, in his enthusiasm, have shouted out "Give them Yankee Doodle!" a song that was even then popular. The shiboleth thus uttered clung to the spot and gave it its cognomen.

It is needless to say that this locality is sparsely settled, and that only by woodmen who are engaged in cutting and hauling wood to the landing northwest of Iona Island, for the brickyards, and their families. When Beveridge bought Iona Island, he attempted to civilize this section and erected a church edifice, of which I have already spoken, in 1851. Day school is held during nine months of the year in this building, which is called the Mountville Church. Mountville is populated, by one occupied house, and a family residing in the basement of the church. At the north end of Doodletown, is Highland Lake, and the Pell mansion on the site of Fort Clinton.

IONA ISLAND.

The original name of this place was "Waggons" a corruption of "Weyant's Island," being so called after the name of its owner. In 1847, it was purchased by John Beveridge, of Newburgh, and on it his son-in-law, Dr. E. W. Grant, began the cultivation of vines, and the propagation of the "Iona Grape" in 1858. At one time a vineyard of twenty acres, several thousand fruit trees, and eleven houses for the culture of grapes, were in operation. Dr. Grant carried on business till 1868. Then he failed in business, and his property was taken by De Graff, who obtained the mortgage against it from the Bowery Savings Bank. The Island was hired by Hasbrouck & Busnell, and fitted up as an excursion ground. It remained in the possession of these managers for some time, and then fell into other hands by whom it has since been carried on as a pleasure ground for excursion parties.

The territory of Iona Island consists of about 200 acres of marsh land, which is overflowed at high tide, 60 acres of rocky woodland and about 40 acres of soil cleared for tillage. The Island is at the northern limit of the sea breeze.

STONY POINT PROMONTORY.

We have already traced the ownership of the Point till it passed into the possession of the heirs of Rachel Lamb. On May 17th, 1802, James Lamb Armstrong sold one-eighth of the tract to Richard W. Brewster. Later, Abraham and wife sold one-eighth to Samuel Brewster, Catharine Waldron sold one-fourth to Wm. H. Brewster, and Cornelius Waldron and his wife sold one-eighth to the same purchaser.

In 1826, the National Government purchased a site on the Point for the erection of a lighthouse, and on March 23d, 1826, the State Legislature ceded the land to the United States. Difficulty in obtaining a title was found, owing to the existence of minor heirs and of heirs residing in other parts of the country. To obviate this difficulty, an act was passed appointing Commissioners to appraise the land and report its value. These

Commissioners valued the lot taken at $300, and the title was then declared vested in the United States, the money being deposited with the Court of Chancery, and the proceedings recorded in the County Clerk's office. The lot chosen includes the old fortifications within which the lighthouse stands. This house is 179 feet above the sea level and burns a "fixed white light." The fog signal is a bell struck by machinery at intervals of fifteen seconds.

On July 16th, 1850, a demonstration occurred at Stony Point in honor of the seventy-first anniversary of its capture by General Wayne. General Aaron Ward of Sing Sing presided and addresses were delivered by Hon. Hugh Maxwell, A. B. Conger, William Nelson of Peekskill and Edward Pye. It rained furiously all day. In 1857, the cornerstone of a monument to commemorate its capture by Wayne, was laid at Stony Point with imposing ceremony. Speeches were made by Hon. Amasa J. Parker, Hon. B. F. Butler, Erastus Brooks, A. B. Conger, Colonel Scrugham, and John Lawrence De Noyelles, and letters read from Franklin Pierce, Ex-President; Martin Van Buren, Ex-President; Hon. John A. King, Lewis Cass, Daniel S. Dickenson, Hamilton Fish, Washington Irving and others. At the centennial anniversary of the capture of the Point this corner stone was looked for and was found wanting.

On July 16th, 1879, occurred the 100th anniversary of the capture of the Point. A great celebration was planned, in which civic and military powers should take part and in which the National, State and County governments should be represented. On the part of the National government a detachment of artillery was sent to the Point by General Schofield commanding at West Point, and the vessels of war, Minnesota and Congress were anchored in the stream. On the part of the State, the 7th Brigade N. G. S., N. Y. was ordered to be present. The intense heat of the day—102 deg. in the shade—the limited space on the summit of the Point, the lack of sufficient preparation for the multitude that attended, all combined to render the demonstration less successful than was hoped for.

BEAR HILL AND PINGYP HILL.

The former mountain, situated on the west border of Highland Lake, rises to a height of more than 1,000 feet above the lake, and 1,123 feet above sea level. The latter mountain is situated in the western part of the town, on the Cedar Pond road, three and three-quarter miles from Stony Point village. In regard to the origin of the name, one story attributes it to the gorge, claiming that the name means a narrow passage. I incline to the opinion of Wm. Govan, M. D., that it is derived from the

Latin word *piniger*, meaning pine-bearing, as the mountains in this vicinity were formerly heavily wooded by that tree.

The charitable institution known as the House of the Good Shepherd, is situated in a beautiful location in the town, and is devoted to the noble work of caring for homeless orphans. This institution originated in the village of Haverstraw in 1865, when Rev. E. Gay, Jr., then rector of Trinity parish, was left, by the death of their parents, in charge of seven orphans. A house on the corner of Broad street and Broadway was taken in that village, and Mrs. Sarah A. Waters employed as a matron. On April 1st, 1866, the children were removed to Garnerville and remained there till 1872, when through appropriations of $17,000 by the State Legislature and donations of $12,000 from individuals, the managers were enabled to purchase the property and erect the buildings now owned by them.

For the first five years of its existence, the institution was regarded as a "parish home of Trinity" parish. In 1870, a board of managers was incorporated by act of Legislature under the title of "The House of the Good Shepherd, Rockland County, New York," and consisted of the following members: E. Gay, Jr., Hon. James M. Nelson, Wm. Govan, M. D., John Taylor, Francis Payson, Charles H. Dabney, A. G. Wood, S. Russell, Jr., Frederick Tomkins, S. G. Hitchcock, Rev. Franklin Babbitt, R. S. Mansfield, Walter Delafield, George W. Burr, and Wm. H. Tomlins. In this institution the children are taught the common branches of education and the various industries of farm, household and family life.

Two trees, standing within the township of Stony Point, deserve notice for their size, and in the case of one, for its historical association. On the road which passes the residence of John De Camp, and opposite that residence, is a magnificent walnut tree, which antedates tradition. At the height of a foot from the earth, the trunk of this veteran measures 17 feet, 6 inches in circumference. A short distance northeast of the Treason House, and in a field on the opposite side of the highway, stands another magnificent walnut tree, which measures 21 feet, 3 inches in circumference at a height of one foot from the earth.

Under this latter tree, it is said, that the Continental Army was paid while in this County. It may be a cause for rejoicing to learn that the Continental Army was ever paid anywhere. Originally there were two trees at this spot, and both were purchased by a keen speculator. One was cut down and made up into furniture, which was sold at exorbitant prices as relics. Ere the other could be cut down, a popular clamor against the desecration had arisen in the neighborhood, and the purchaser abandoned his project.

SUPERVISORS.

Wesley J. Weiant, 1865-66.
Daniel Tomkins, 1867.
George W. Weiant, 1870-75.

Hiram Osborn, 1876-77.
William E. King, 1878-79.

Frederick Tomkins, 1868-69-1880-84.
William K. Hammond, 1885.

TOWN CLERKS.

Benson Briggs, 1865.   Edward A. Thompson.

Authorities referred to: "Session Laws, S. N. Y.;" "U. S. and State Census Reports;" "History of Stony Point," by Rev. F. Gay, Jr.; "History of Haverstraw," and lectures; "Thirty Years in Rockland County," by Rev. A. S. Freeman, D. D.; "Nautical Almanac;" Lossing's "Hudson from its Source to the Sea."

APPENDIX A.

LIST OF VOLUNTEERS BESIDE THOSE ALREADY GIVEN.

In regard to the following list of volunteers from Rockland County, in the Civil War, I would state that I have taken the names from newspapers, muster rolls and the memories of veterans. I regard the list as most imperfect so far as completeness goes. Repeated efforts to have the friends of volunteers, or veterans themselves, send their names together with the arm of the service to which they belonged, and other data relative to their war life to me, have failed. To accept the rolls of the G. A. R. Posts would be incorrect because many veterans have moved from the County whose names do not appear and many names do appear of veterans who were not residents of Rockland, at the time of enlistment. I can only advise the people of the County once again, that it would be wise to send the names of relatives or friends who enlisted from this County to the Historical Society, before it be too late. The least claim a veteran can have upon us, is that his name should be recorded in history.

The following names are taken from the Rockland County *Messenger*, of 1861:

Jones, John C.	Herring, C. B.	Conklin, Eugene
Jones, Noble	Morrisy, John	Conner, John
Jones, Morton	Hutton, Fred.	Calhoun, J. W.
Jordon, Frank	Haight, Wm. H.	Seely, C. B.
Johnson, Alonzo	Felter, Chas. B.	Singler, Augustus*
Kunzle, Conrad*	Wallace, Wm. 1st N. Y. V.	Curtis, John
Kinch, Gilbert	Wallace, John	Dennis, J. W.
Osborn, Chas.	Weymouth, Wm.*	Domminick, L.
Palmer, John Sr.,	Wilkins, J. W.	Kenny, Jas.
Palmer, John Jr., 95th Regt.	Olmstead, F.	Miller, John
Pince, John	Goodrich, Chas. 17th N.Y.V.	Matthews, Orin
Holden, Dennis	Gernand, Philip 17th N.Y.V	Matthews, Wm. 17th N.Y.V
Hadler, Fred.	Acton, Joseph	Tompkins, S. B.
Hassler, Lewis	Brown, Geo. A.	Tremper, Daniel 17th N. Y. V.

The following are taken from different official sources:

From 95th Regt., N. Y. S., Vols., and other regiments.

Dikens, Wm.*	McClellan, Wm.	Barnes, Alexander
Blauvelt, Wm.*	Dyson, Wm.	Avery, Chas. A.
Kelly, James	Studley, Jno. H.	Beisinger, Edw.
Burns, Patrick	Herbert, Theo.	Stiners, George
Lupton, John	Brown, Geo. M.	Mott, Wm.
Gardenier, Geo. M. D.	McGovern, Chas.	Maroney, Geo.
Garrison, Jno. W.	Brooks, Wm. E.	Garrison, J. M.*
Lusk, Sidney* 87th N.Y.V.	Boyd, John	Collins, Austin,* 173d, N.Y.V.
Smith, Herman*66th N.Y.V	Fenton, Jas. L.* Engineers'	Miller, S. A.* 12th U. S. A.
Campbell, John D.*	& Mechanics' Regt.	Ulrich, M* 4th N. Y. Art.
Conklin, Peter A. 166th N. Y. V.	Matthews J. B. Navy.	Cisco, Francis* 26th U. S. Vols.
Dyson, John 61st, N. Y. V.	Brooks, John, Navy.	Lowe, Michael
Onderdonk, J. H.* 128th, N. Y. V.	Brockway, John H.*Navy.	Phillips, J. S.
Thompson, Uriah* 26th, U. S. Vols.	Brockway, Ezekiel* Navy.	Pitt, Sylvester
	Tremper, George* 146th, N. Y. V.	Phillips, Joe.
	McManus, John	Oldfield, George*
Rembon, Carl	Jordan, Patrick	Foster, Richard* Navy.
McGeorge, Wm.	Adams, Robt.	Miller, A.
Decker, John H.	Ferguson, Joe.	Brewer, Edw.

Tompkins, Fred. Quartermaster, 6th N. Y. Heavy Artillery.
Tompkins, Theodore F.* 6th N. Y. Heavy Artillery.

The following members of the 17th N. Y. S. M., held the rank opposite their names in the volunteer troops raised in New York State to serve in the Civil War:

Pye, Edw. Col. 95th Regt.
Creeney, James Lieut-Col. 95th Regt.
Jenkins, Jno. P. Adjutant 6th Art.
Keesler, 1st Lieut 95th Regt.

Gurnee, A. S. Captain 95th.
Burnes, B. B. Captain 95th.
Snediker, Abr. Captain 95th.
Brewster, D. 1st Lieut. 95th Regt.
Williard, J. Lieut-Col.

Cowdory, S. F. Captain 162d Regt.
Mackey, S. G. Captain 95th Regt.
Riggs, R. 1st Lieut. 95th Regt.

*Died in service.

APPENDIX B.

CIVIL LIST OF ROCKLAND COUNTY.

COUNTY JUDGES.

John Suffern, March 21st, 1798.
James Perry, March 26th, 1806.
Samuel Goetchius, March 1st, 1816.

Edward Suffern, June 1st, 1820.
William F. Fraser, June, 1847.
Edward Pye, November, 1855.

Andrew E. Suffern, 1859.
*Seth B. Cole, March 28th, 1881.
George W. Weiant, 1881.

SURROGATES.

Peter Taulman, 1798.
Tunis Smith, 1807.
Peter Taulman, 1808.
Garret Onderdonk, 1810.

Richard Blauvelt, 1811.
Bernard O'Blenis, 1820.
James Stephens, 1821.
John Van Houten, 1829.

John J. Wood, 1837
George Benson, 1841.
Horatio G. Prall, 1845.
County Judges since 1847.

DISTRICT ATTORNEYS. |

Edward Suffern, 1818.
John T. Smith, 1820.
William F. Fraser, 1833.
Horatio G. Prall, 1847.

Andrew E. Suffern, 1853.‡
Thomas Lawrence, 1859.
Marcena M. Dickinson, 1862.
L. V. E. Robinson, 1868.
Hiram B. Fenton, 1869.

Delos McCurdy, 1872.‡
Seth B. Cole, 1872.
Marcena M. Dickinson, 1875.
Alonzo Wheeler, 1878.

COUNTY TREASURERS.‖

John R. Coe, 1848.

Matthew D. Bogert, 1851.
John B. Gurnee, 1869.

Daniel D. Demarest, 1875.

COUNTY CLERKS.

David Pye, 1798.
Abraham Cornelison, 1805.
Thomas Howard, Jr., 1808, 1811.
John Cole, 1810.

David Pye, 1822.
James Stevens, 1828.
David Pye, 1831.
Abraham Hogencamp, 1834.
Isaac A. Blauvelt, 1846.
Cyrus M. Crum, 1868.

Abraham De Baun,§ 1850—June.
John E. Hogencamp, 1850 —November.
Abraham A. Demarest, 1856.

SHERIFFS.

Jacob Wood, 1798.
Peter Taulman, 1799.
Peter Stevens, 1800, 1808, 1811.

Richard Blauvelt, 1831.
Harmon Blauvelt, 1834.
John W. Felter, 1837.
John C. Blauvelt, 1840.

William Perry, 1858.
Daniel C. Springsteen, 1864, 1870.
William J. Penny, 1867.

Evert Hogencamp, 1804.
Isaac Blanch, 1810.
Thomas Hay, 1814.
John B. Haring, 1818, 1821, 1828.
Abraham Stephens, 1820.
A. P. Stephens, 1825.

Archibald Cassady, 1843.
Asbory DeNoyelles, 1846.
Hageman Onderdonk, 1849.
Henry L. Sherwood, 1852.
John H. Stephens, 1855, 1861.

Charles B. Benson, 1873.
William Hutton, 1876.
Henry Christie, 1879.
John A. Haring, 1882.
William A. Thompson, 1885.

SCHOOL COMMISSIONERS.¶

Edward Suffern, 1859.
Simeon D. Demarest, 1862.
Nicholas C. Blauvelt, 1865.

Leander V. E. Robinson, 1868.
Thos. W. Suffern, 1880, 1883.

Nelson Puff, 1871.
Spencer Wood, 1874.
William Van Wagenen, 1877.

---

* Seth B. Cole was appointed to fill unexpired term of A. E. Suffern, deceased.

† Previous to 1818, Rockland, with Delaware, Dutchess and Ulster Counties, formed the 9th District, in which this office was filled by appointment.

‡ Filled vacancy, caused by resignation of incumbent.

‖ Previous to the Constitution of 1846, this office was filled by appointment by the Supervisors.

§ Appointed, vice Blauvelt, deceased.

¶ The office of County Superintendent of Common Schools was held by Nicholas G. Blauvelt, appointed in 1843. Office abolished in 1847. Previous to 1857, School Commissioners were appointed by the Board of Supervisors.

www.ingramcontent.com/pod-product-compliance
Lightning Source LLC
Chambersburg PA
CBHW032007300426
44117CB00008B/933